TAX PLANNING

Anne Mathieson
with
Sue Short

Published by Certified Accountants Educational Projects Ltd

Subject consultants: Graham Holt, Andy Perkins, Suresh Tanna, David Haoorowven

Commissioning editor: Jane Elliot

Managing editor: Linda Auld

Copy editors: Linda Auld

Proofreader: James Griffin

Indexer: Indexing Specialists, Hove

Production: Frances Follin, Petra Green

Text design: Carla Turchini

Cover design: Fielding Rowinski

DTP layout: M Rules

Acknowledgement
Past exam questions are reproduced with the kind permission of the Chartered Association of Certified Accountants, the Institute of Chartered Accountants in England and Wales and the Chartered Institute of Management Accountants. The VAT return in Chapter 22 is Crown copyright, and is reproduced by courtesy of HMSO. All answers have been provided by the author.

First edition printed 1993

© Certified Accountants Educational Projects Limited 1993, 1994

Certified Accountants Educational Projects Limited
29 Lincoln's Inn Fields
London WC2A 3EE

ISBN 1 85908 067 7

All rights reserved. No part of this publication may be reproduced, stored in a retrieval system, or transmitted, in any form or by any means, electronic, mechanical, photocopying, recording or otherwise, without either the prior written permission of the copyright holder for which application should be addressed in the first instance to the publishers or a licence permitting restricted copying issued by the Copyright Licensing Agency Ltd, 90 Tottenham Court Road, London W1P 9HE.

Further information on Certified Accountants Educational Projects Limited products and services may be obtained from Certified Accountants Educational Projects Limited, 29 Lincoln's Inn Fields, London WC2A 3EE.

British Library Cataloguing in Publication data.
A catalogue record for this book is available from the British Library.

Printed in the UK by: Bell & Bain Ltd

Table of Contents

Overview	xi
Guide to Syllabus Coverage	xii
The Syllabus for Paper 11	xiii
Preface	xiv

Personal Taxation and Financial Planning

Chapter 1	**Establishing the Income Tax Liability and its Collection**	**1**
	The scope of income tax	1
	Definition of income	2
	Four main stages in establishing an individual's income tax liability for a fiscal year	5
	Inland Revenue method of computing the tax liability – a comparison	15
	Assessment of the tax liability	18
	Summary	20
	Self test questions	20
Chapter 2	**Husband, Wife, Children and Income Tax**	**23**
	Independent taxation of husband and wife	23
	Year of marriage (also year of reconciliation after period of separation)	26
	Year of separation or divorce or death	26
	Children	27
	Summary	28
	Self test questions	28
Chapter 3	**Income from Employment in the UK**	**32**
	The scope of Schedule E	32
	Fees, bonuses and commissions	36
	Benefits in kind	36
	Payments on termination of office	46
	Other payments and benefits	47
	Incentive schemes	48
	National Insurance contributions for employees	54
	Rewarding executives – planning	55
	Summary	56
	Self test questions	56
Chapter 4	**Taxation of Income from Property and Investments**	**59**
	Income from property	59
	Income from investments	69
	Life assurance	80
	Personal equity plans	81
	The Enterprise Investment Scheme (EIS)	82
	Summary	84
	Self test questions	85

Chapter 5	**Capital Gains Tax – General Principles**	**88**
	The scope of capital gains tax	88
	The charge to tax	91
	Collection of capital gains tax	95
	Format of the computation	96
	Part disposals	100
	Indexation allowance	102
	Disposals of assets held on 31 March 1982	104
	'No gain, no loss' disposals	106
	Hold-over relief	107
	Assets of negligible value	111
	Exceptions to general principles	112
	Summary	112
	Self test questions	113
Chapter 6	**Chattels, Wasting Assets, Land and Principal Private Residence**	**115**
	Chattels	115
	Wasting assets (not chattels)	118
	Leases of land	121
	Principal private residence	121
	Summary	123
	Self test questions	124
Chapter 7	**Shares and Securities**	**125**
	Matching rules	125
	Shares acquired after 5 April 1982 (Pool A)	127
	Shares acquired after 5 April 1965 and before 6 April 1982 (Pool B)	129
	Reorganisations	131
	Gilt-edged securities	136
	Qualifying corporate bonds	136
	Summary	136
	Self test questions	138
Chapter 8	**Inheritance Tax – General Principles**	**140**
	Background to inheritance tax	140
	The scope of inheritance tax	141
	The charge to tax	146
	Computing the tax liability on chargeable lifetime transfers	148
	Computing the tax liability on death	151
	Exemptions	156
	Computing the tax liability on death – further aspects	160
	Summary	161
	Self test questions	162
Chapter 9	**Inheritance Tax – Valuation Principles**	**164**
	Rules of valuation	164
	Valuation reliefs	168
	The estate at death	172
	Relief on death for fall in value of a chargeable transfer	175
	Adjustments for the sale of assets following death	176
	Summary	178
	Self test questions	178

Chapter 10	**Inheritance Tax – Additional Aspects**	**181**
	Gifts with reservation	181
	Associated operations	183
	Conditional exemptions	184
	Commorientes	185
	Variation of the provisions in a will	185
	Planning	186
	Accounts, returns and collection of tax	187
	Summary	188
	Self test questions	188
Chapter 11	**Personal Finance – Investment and Financing Alternatives Evaluated and Compared**	**190**
	Investment defined	190
	Types of investment	191
	Equities	194
	Investment trusts	194
	Unit trusts	195
	Life assurance	196
	Pensions	197
	Enterprise and Investment Scheme	198
	Land and property investments	198
	Cash investments	198
	Collectibles	200
	Finance – personal	200
	Finance – business	202
	Summary	203
	Self test questions	204
Chapter 12	**Personal Finance – The Investment Advisor**	**205**
	The Financial Services Act	205
	Investment business defined	207
	Conduct of investment business	208
	Summary	209
	Self test questions	209
Chapter 13	**Personal Finance – Determining the Appropriate Investments/Finance**	**211**
	Identifying the investor	211
	The elements of a portfolio	214
	Summary	218
	Self test questions	218
Chapter 14	**The Taxation of Trusts**	**219**
	The nature of a trust	219
	Income tax	219
	Capital gains tax	223
	Inheritance tax	225
	Tax planning	230
	Summary	230
	Self test questions	231

Question Bank: Personal Taxation and Financial Planning   **232**

Personal Business Taxation

Chapter 15 The Taxation of Profits from Trades, Professions and Vocations — 238
- Definition of trade — 238
- Is a trade carried on? — 238
- Annual profits or gains of trade — 240
- Allowable deductions — 241
- Adjusted profit computation — 246
- Examination of business accounts by Inspector of Taxes — 249
- Bases of assessment — 249
- Special relief – farmers — 255
- National Insurance contributions — 256
- Summary — 257
- Self test questions — 257

Chapter 16 Unincorporated Businesses – Capital Allowances — 260
- Capital expenditure — 260
- Plant and machinery — 263
- Industrial buildings — 272
- Agricultural buildings — 280
- Patents — 281
- Know-how — 282
- Scientific research — 282
- Mineral extraction — 283
- Summary — 283
- Self test questions — 283

Chapter 17 Partnerships — 286
- Tax status of a partnership — 286
- The partnership Schedule D Case I assessment — 287
- Capital allowances — 293
- Miscellaneous partnership matters — 295
- Summary — 296
- Self test questions — 297

Chapter 18 Trading Losses — 299
- Schedule D Case I adjusted losses — 299
- Established and ongoing businesses — 299
- New businesses – opening years — 309
- Cessation of trade – closing years — 311
- Miscellaneous trading losses — 313
- Partnership losses — 314
- Summary — 316
- Self test questions — 317

Chapter 19 Finance Act 1994 – The new current year basis of assessment — 319
- The new Schdule DI assessment rules — 319
- Capital allowances — 321
- Lossess — 321
- Partnerships — 322
- Summary — 322
- Self test questions — 323

Chapter 20	**The Disposal and Replacement of Business Assets**	**324**
	Business assets	324
	Interaction of capital gains tax and capital allowances	325
	Partnership disposals	326
	Replacement of business assets	328
	Gift of business assets	331
	Summary	332
	Self test questions	332
Chapter 21	**Disposal of All or Part of a Business; Retirement**	**334**
	Transactions between partners	334
	Disposal of a business	336
	Transfer of business to a limited company	337
	Retirement relief	339
	Gift of all or part of a business	343
	Re-investment relief	344
	Summary	346
	Self test questions	346
Chapter 22	**Value Added Tax**	**348**
	The scope of value added tax	348
	Administration	351
	The charge to tax	354
	The European Community – the Single Market	363
	Cash accounting	364
	Second-hand schemes	364
	Retail schemes	365
	Partial exemption	365
	Enforcement	366
	Partnerships	368
	Limited companies	369
	Interaction with other taxes	369
	Summary	370
	Self test questions	370
Chapter 23	**Tax Management**	**372**
	The organisation of the Inland Revenue	372
	Administration of income tax and capital gains tax	373
	Inland Revenue inquiry and investigation	381
	Administration of inheritance tax	384
	Organisation of Customs and Excise	386
	Administration of value added tax	387
	Summary	387
	Self test questions	388
Question Bank: Personal Business Taxation		**389**

Corporate Taxation

Chapter 24	**The Computation of Profits Liable to Corporation Tax**	**393**
	Background to corporate taxation	393
	Scope and general principles of corporation tax	394
	Sources of income	397

	Charges on income	401
	Trading losses	403
	Other losses	409
	Examination format	410
	Planning considerations	410
	Summary	412
	Self test questions	412

Chapter 25 Computation of the Corporation Tax Liability and its Collection 415

Liability to corporation tax	415
Payment of the corporation tax liability	419
Pay and file	419
Company distributions	422
Advance corporation tax (ACT)	423
Income tax	428
The computation of MCT	429
Examination format	436
Surplus franked investment income	437
Planning considerations	440
Summary	440
Self test questions	441

Chapter 26 Investment Companies and Close Companies 443

Clubs and associations	443
Investment companies	443
Close companies	444
Close investment-holding companies (CICs)	448
Summary	448
Self test questions	449

Chapter 27 Groups and Consortia 450

Overview	450
Associated companies	451
51% groups	451
Capital gains groups	456
75% groups	458
Consortiums	462
Groups and value added tax	465
Planning considerations	466
Summary	466
Self test questions	467

Chapter 28 Reorganisations 470

Background	470
A company joins or leaves a group	471
Share-for-share amalgamations	474
Capital reduction and purchase of own shares	475
Disincorporation	476
Liquidation	477
Summary	478
Self test questions	478

Chapter 29 Tax Planning and Tax Avoidance	479
Tax planning in general	479
Comparison of a limited company with an unincorporated business	479
Further aspects of tax planning	485
Anti-avoidance	486
Summary	488
Self test questions	489
Question Bank: Corporate Taxation	**490**

Overseas Activities

Chapter 30 Overseas Aspects of Personal Taxation	497
Residence, ordinary residence and domicile	496
Overseas income of UK residents	500
Overseas gains of UK residents	506
Inheritance tax and gift of non-UK property by UK residents	506
UK income of non-UK residents	507
UK gains of non-UK residents	508
Inheritance tax and non-UK residents	509
Summary	509
Self test questions	509

Chapter 31 Company Residence and Its Implications	511
Residence	511
The implications of UK residence	512
Becoming non-resident in the UK	512
Trading at artificial prices	513
Summary	515
Self test questionss	516

Chapter 32 Outward Investment by UK Companies	517
Overview	517
Operations overseas	517
Double tax relief	518
Controlled foreign companies	522
Branch or subsidiary?	524
Summary	525
Self test questions	525

Chapter 33 Inward Investment	527
UK-resident subsidiary	527
Direct investment in the UK	527
UK branch or subsidiary?	529
Summary	529
Self test questions	530

Question Bank: Overseas Activities	**531**

Chapter 34	**How to Tackle the Tax Planning Examination**	**534**
	General strategy	534
	Illustrations of key tax planning topics	535

Answers to End of Chapter Questions — **555**

Rates of Tax and Allowances 1994/95 — **646**

Glossary — **650**

Index — **654**

Overview

The book is organised so as to give maximum opportunity, at the earliest possible time, to practise the paper's multi-tax approach. This approach derives from considering situations and all the tax consequences of those situations. For this reason the book divides easily into four main sections (determined by likely circumstances):

- Personal Taxation and Financial Planning
- Personal Business Taxation
- Corporate Taxation
- Overseas Activities.

Within each section, each of the taxes which may apply are considered independently and from first principles. The end of chapter questions may build upon knowledge acquired in earlier chapters within that section (and possibly in earlier sections). At the end of each section, there is a question bank of representative exam-style questions which often cover the range of taxes for that section. It is essential that this type of question is practised as, on first encounter, they are quite daunting!

This layout has the added advantage that the new subject areas of Paper 11 (inheritance tax, groups and overseas) are dispersed one per section so that no section is too onerous.

Chapter 34 – How to Tackle the Tax Planning Examination – should be read very early in your studies and certainly before tackling any of the question banks. It should be re-read periodically during the course of your studies and again at the end, prior to starting revision.

At the end of the book, you will find a schedule of Tax Rates and Allowances. I suggest you remove the sheet from the book and put it in a protective transparent folder and keep it for ready reference (perhaps as a bookmark) as you work through the text. All this information will be given to you in the examination, if required.

Guide to Syllabus Coverage

CHAPTER TITLE		SYLLABUS SECTIONS	
1	Establishing the Income Tax Liability and its Collection	Paper 7	1d, e 2f, g, h, i
2	Husband, Wife, Children and Income Tax	Paper 7	1d, e 2f, g, h, i
3	Income from Employment in the UK	Paper 7	2a, b, c, d, e, i
4	Taxation of Income from Property and Investments	Paper 7 Paper 11	2n (i), (ii), i 9e
5	Capital Gains Tax – General Principles	Paper 7	4
6	Chattels, Wasting Assets, Land and Principal Private Residence	Paper 7	4
7	Shares and Securities	Paper 7 Paper 11	4 2
8	Inheritance Tax – General Principles	Paper 11	3a, b, c, d
9	Inheritance Tax – Valuation Principles	Paper 11	3a, b, c, d
10	Inheritance Tax – Additional Aspects	Paper 11	1b, 3a, b, c, d
11	Personal Finance – Investment and Financing Alternatives Evaluated and Compared	Paper 11	9d, e
12	Personal Finance – The Investment Advisor	Paper 11	9c
13	Personal Finance—Determining the Appropriate Investments/Finance	Paper 11	9a, b
14	The Taxation of Trusts	Paper 11	4
15	The Taxation of Profits from Trades, Professions and Vocations	Paper 7	2f, g, 5
16	Unincorporated Businesses – Capital Allowances	Paper 7 Paper 11	2f, g 1b
17	Partnerships	Paper 7	2f,g, i

Paper 11: Tax Planning

CHAPTER TITLE		SYLLABUS SECTIONS	
18	Trading Losses	Paper 7 Paper 11	2f, g, i 1b
19	Finance Act 1994 – The new current year basis of assessment	Paper 11	1a, b, 2
20	The Disposal and Replacement of Business Assets	Paper 11	1a, b, 2
21	The Disposal of All or Part of a Business; Retirement	Paper 11	5
22	Value Added Tax	Paper 11 Paper 7	8d 1
23	Tax Management	Paper 7	3a, b, d
24	The Computation of Profits Liable to Corporation Tax	Paper 11 Paper 7	1b 3c, e
25	Computation of the Corporation Tax Liability and its Collection	Paper 11	6c
26	Investment Companies and Close Companies	Paper 11	6a, 2
27	Groups and Consortia	Paper 11	6b
28	Reorganisations	Paper 11	1a, b
29	Tax Planning and Tax Avoidance		7a, b, c, d, e, g
30	Overseas Aspects of Personal Taxation		7a, f
31	Company Residence and Its Implications		6a, 7f
32	Outward Investment by UK Companies		7a, 6f
33	Inward Investment		Overview of paper

The Syllabus for Paper 11

The syllabus includes everything examinable in Paper 7, Tax Framework, but extends and deepens the coverage. It also includes some new areas. Topics will be examined so that emphasis is given to simple planning to minimise or defer tax; the application of the tax knowledge to problems encountered in practice; and the inter-relationship of taxes.

1 **Overview of personal business taxation**
   a Interactions between different taxes in a range of situations or transactions.
   b Tax planning: the application of tax planning measures appropriate to the particular situation.

2 **Capital Gains Tax**
   Application of Capital Gains Tax to individuals and corporate tax payers, with emphasis on business situations.

3 **Inheritance Tax**
   a Principles and scope.
   b Rules basis and application.
   c Calculating the tax due by clients.
   d Minimising/deferring tax liabilities by identifying/applying relevant exemptions, reliefs and allowances.

4 **Trusts**
   Application to trusts of Income Tax, Capital Gains Tax and Inheritance Tax.

5 **Value Added Tax**
   The application of Value Added Tax to transactions and other activities of corporate taxpayers.

6 **Corporate Taxation**
   a *Groups and consortia.*
   b The provisions covering liquidations and areas such as disincorporations, purchases of own shares, sales and acquisitions of subsidiaries, and share-for-share amalgamations.
   c Implications of a company being classed as an investment or close company.

7 **Overseas activities giving rise to taxation liabilities**
   a Definition of residence, ordinary residence and domicile.
   b The taxation of UK income and gains of non-domicile individuals.
   c Overseas income and gains: the UK tax treatment of overseas income and gains of UK resident individuals and companies, including relief for double taxation.
   d Overseas persons, the UK tax treatment of income and gains arising within the UK to non-resident individuals and companies.
   e The Inheritance Tax position regarding overseas assets of UK individuals and UK assets of non resident individuals.
   f Business structures, including a UK branch/subsidiary of a foreign company/group and a foreign branch/subsidiary of a UK company/group.
   g Anti-avoidance legislation relating to overseas activities, income or persons.

8 **General**
   a Interrelationship of taxes: the effect of any of the taxes in a given situation or on a particular transaction.
   b Anti-avoidance: appreciation of the main areas of anti-avoidance legislation and of the enquiry and investigation procedures of the Inland Revenue and Customs and Excise.

9 **Personal finance**
   a Assisting clients in the determination of personal financial objectives, taking into account such factors as individual circumstances, expectations and the economic environment.
   b Determining financial needs of clients (how much, when, for how long, and for what purpose?).
   c Regulations affecting investment advisers, and ethical considerations, including the definition of investment business.
   d Advising on sources and costs of different forms of finance and their applicability to different circumstances including
      i)   bank borrowing
      ii) finance houses
      iii) mortgages
      iv) money and capital markets.
   e Advising on investment of clients' personal funds
      i)   insurance policies
      ii)   pension funds
      iii) unit and investment trusts
      iv)   TESSAs
      v)   PEPs
      vi)   equity shares
      vii) gilt edged securities and other bonds
      viii) real property
      ix)   banks and building societies
      x)   national savings.

Preface

This book has been written specifically for those people who are preparing for the Tax Planning paper (Paper 11) of the Chartered Association of Certified Accountants (ACCA) and final taxation courses of other professional bodies. In writing it I have tried to provide a book that will enable the reader to meet the objectives of the syllabus as set out in the ACCA Teaching Guide so that they can:

- display an awareness of the impact of all the major taxes on the transactions of individuals, partnerships and companies
- apply that knowledge to practical situations involving computation, explanation, discussion and advice
- appreciate the importance of taxation in personal and corporate financial planning and decision making
- identify opportunities to minimise potential tax liabilities by making full use of available options, reliefs and exemptions
- demonstrate an understanding of the regulations associated with the provision of suitable investment advice to individuals
- demonstrate the skills expected at the Professional Stage.

I have sought to equip the reader to cope with an examination paper which aims to 'equip students with the ability to solve unstructured problems which draw on the interaction of taxes between income, profits and capital'. The book provides a solid technical framework around which options that may be available are used to illustrate opportunities to minimise or defer a tax liability.

I am aware that it may be some time since many readers sat and passed Paper 2.3/7, and that there continue to be fundamental changes in the application of taxation each year. In 1994/95 these involve particularly the changes to the basis of assessment for self-employed taxpayers, the introduction of the Enterprise Investment Scheme, reinvestment relief and the Foreign Income Dividend Scheme. Groups, overseas taxation and inheritance tax are new subject areas at Paper 11. Value added tax may, for some, also be a new subject. For these reasons, each topic is dealt with from first principles, ensuring sound technical knowledge as a basis for development.

While it is recognised that tax practice is a specialist activity, the impact of taxation on financial decision making underlines the need for a newly qualified accountant to have a sound understanding of the potential liabilities to income tax, corporation tax, capital gains tax, inheritance tax and value added tax, that can arise within the UK. It is the emphasis on potential liabilities rather than on actual liabilities that is most apparent when Papers 2.3/7 and 11 are compared: an emphasis that allows scope for an analysis of options, for careful timing of events, and for advice to be given.

I realise that many readers will have limited access to personal tutorial help; with this in mind, I have provided a glossary of technical expressions and a large number of worked examples within a carefully explained text. At the end of each chapter, there are a number of self-test questions. These are intended to reinforce and test the overall understanding of the contents of the chapter and to give the opportunity to practise answering questions on the relevant topic. Many past ACCA examination questions do not fall naturally within any chapter because of the paper's multi-tax approach. Some have been included in question banks at the end of each section; some have been subdivided into their component taxes and used as end-of-chapter exercises; others have been reserved for the Lecturer Resource Pack.

References are made in the text to cases that illustrate particular points of law. While the cases themselves are not examinable in detail they are useful background reading and provide a broader knowledge base. The cases can be referred to, as can other technical matters, in the following suggested reading:

- C. Whitehouse and E. Stuart-Buttle, *Butterworth Revenue Law* (Butterworth)
- A. Hamer and R. Burrows, *Tolleys Tax Guide* (Tolley)
- Arthur Anderson, *Personal Tax and Investment Planning* (Tolley)

It is also important that the ACCA *Students Newsletter* is read each month.

I should like to take this opportunity to thank my colleague Chris Baker, who gave me considerabe help in writing the chapters on personal financial planning, and to thank Sue Short who has done an admirable job updating the 2nd edition.

I believe that you will pass the examination if you conscientiously work through this book. Good luck!

Anne Mathieson
North Hampshire Business School

Establishing the Income Tax Liability and its Collection

CHAPTER 1

This chapter reviews the basic principles of the charge to income tax and recaps how income from all sources is aggregated in order to arrive at an individual's total income for a fiscal year. Table 1.1 will remind you of the main taxes and the legislative framework. The nature of charges on income is studied and the payments which so qualify are examined as are the circumstances in which personal allowances are available. The computation of the income tax liability in total and the manner in which it is sub-divided for collection are also illustrated.

The application of these rules in varying family circumstances and the scope for husband and wife to mitigate their joint liability are considered in the next chapter and the detailed rules relating to each individual source of income are considered in the following chapters.

The majority of these chapters on personal taxation should be revision of your previous studies.

Table 1.1 The main taxes and their base legislation

Direct taxation	Suffered by Individuals	Trusts	Companies	Base legislation
Income tax (IT)	x	x	n/a	Income and Corporation Taxes Act (ICTA) 1988 } plus Capital Allowances Act (CAA) 1990
Corporation tax (CT)	n/a	n/a	x	Income and Corporation Taxes Act (ICTA) 1988
Capital gains tax (CGT)	x	x	*n/a	Taxation of Chargeable Gains Act (TCGA) 1992
Inheritance tax (IHT)	x	x	n/a	Inheritance Tax Act (IHTA) 1984

*Companies pay corporation tax on capital gains

Indirect taxation
Value added tax (VAT) — Value Added Tax Act (VATA) 1983
National Insurance (NIC) — Social Security Contributions and Benefits Act (SSCBA) 1992
Customs duty, tobacco, petrol, stamp duty and other expenditure taxes — Sundry

Implemented by
Taxes Management Act (TMA) 1970
Customs & Excise Management Act (CEMA) 1979

Case Law (law of precedent)

Influential in the interpretation of statute

(Quasi-statutory)
Statutory Instruments
IR Statements of Practice
IR Press Releases
IR Extra-Statutory Concessions

The scope of income tax

This section provides a brief summary of the way in which the UK income tax net is cast. Income tax is suffered by individuals and trusts and is computed on the basis of a fiscal year.

Fiscal year

The fiscal year, otherwise referred to as the tax year or year of assessment, runs from 6 April in one year to 5 April the following year. For example, the fiscal year 1994/95 runs from 6 April 1994 to 5 April 1995.

The Chancellor in his Budget each year proposes changes which form part of the Finance Bill for that year. The Budget now takes place in November. It becomes law when it receives the Royal Assent, usually in the following April. The Finance Act 1994 contains provisions which mostly apply from 1994/95. This Act is examinable from December 1994.

Taxable persons

All individuals are taxable persons whatever their age unless they are specifically exempt.

The person who is resident in the UK in the fiscal year is in most cases liable to income tax on all his or her income irrespective of whether it is derived from inside or outside the UK, that is, worldwide income. However, other factors such as ordinary residence and domicile will also influence the liability to tax.

Persons who are not UK residents in the fiscal year, however, are normally liable only to the extent that they derive income from the UK.

The definition of residence, ordinary residence and domicile for income tax purposes is a complex area which is covered fully in the section on 'Overseas Activities'.

Exempt persons

The following persons are not normally liable to income tax:

- ambassadors, ministers and other representatives of foreign countries together with their staff
- visiting members and staff of foreign armed forces
- UK-registered charities
- friendly societies
- approved pension funds
- trade unions.

Definition of income

There is no concise or exact definition of income and the statutes refer to income, profits or gains at various times. This is because income is not easy to encompass in a single definition. The legislation gets round the problem by identifying sources of income liable to income tax. Sources of income which are omitted are not liable to income tax – they may, however, be liable to another tax.

The Schedules

The sources of income liable to income tax are detailed in the Income Tax Schedules. Each of the Schedules, A to F, outlined in Table 1.2 establishes a set of rules governing the manner in which that source of income is charged to tax as well as being a convenient system for gathering statistical information.

The rules established by the Schedules determine:

- the basis of assessment
- the deductions available as expenses if any
- the eligibility for capital allowances and pensions
- the relief available for losses

- the method of tax collection
- the due date for payment of tax.

Table 1.2 The Schedules

Schedule	Source of income	Deductions	Normal basis of assessment
A	Income from land and buildings in UK [except furnished lettings]	Rent, rates, insurance, maintenance, services etc. Capital allowances	Rent receivable in fiscal year, less expenses paid
B*	Abolished by Finance Act 1988		
C*#	Interest from public revenue (UK) and interest from public revenue (foreign) paid through UK agent	None	Assessed on UK agent
D Case I	Profits of trade in UK	Expenses wholly and exclusively for purpose of trade, profession etc. Capital allowances Personal pension premiums	Adjusted profits of accounts for year ending in preceding fiscal year
D Case II	Profits of profession or vocation in UK		
D Case III	Interest and other annual income received gross	None	Income arising in the preceding fiscal year
D Case IV	Interest from foreign securities (such as debentures)	None	Income arising in the preceding fiscal year
D Case V	Income from foreign possessions (such as shares, property, business)	Depends on income – compare similar UK income	Income arising in the preceding fiscal year
D Case VI	Any income not taxable elsewhere plus furnished letting income and other specified profits	Depends on income	Income arising in the current fiscal year
E	Emoluments from offices and employments Pensions Taxable social security benefits	Expenses incurred wholly, exclusively and necessarily in performance of duties of employment Superannuation contributions Personal pension premiums Charitable donations – GAYE	Income arising in the fiscal year – collected by PAYE system
F #	Dividends from UK companies	None	Received in the fiscal year + imputed tax credit

*No examination relevance
#These sources of income appear under 'Income taxed at source' in the individual's tax computation. Tax under Schedule C and Schedule F is not levied on the recipient but on the payer. Individuals receive such income 'tax paid'.
Note that the preceding year basis of assessment is in the process of being phased out. The new rules, introduced by the Finance Act 1994, are considered in chapter 19.

Income taxed at source

Certain types of income, not covered by the Schedules, suffer basic rate income tax at source (that is, only 75% of the gross entitlement is received by the taxpayer). Dividend income is accompanied by a tax credit equal to 20/80 of the dividend received (that is, 80 per cent of the gross entitlement is received by the taxpayer).

In all cases, the amount to be included in the taxpayer's total income is the gross amount: the amount received plus the amount of income tax deducted at source. However, the amount of income deducted at source is set off against the taxpayer's income tax liability.

The following are examples of income taxed at source:

- debenture and loan stock interest from UK companies
- patent royalties
- income received under deed of covenant

- interest on UK government securities (except 3 1/2% War Loan) unless purchased at a post office through the National Stock Register
- income portion of a purchased annuity
- income from trusts and settlements. (**Note:** Income from discretionary trusts, which include accumulation and maintenance trusts, will have suffered tax at the rate of 35% at source.)
- building society interest and bank interest unless a claim has been made for the interest to be paid gross.

The basis of assessment for income taxed at source is the gross amount arising in the current fiscal year. No deductions are allowed.

Earned income and investment income

The distinction between earned income and investment income is largely historic. Up to and including 1983/84, investment income was subject to an additional tax called investment income surcharge. The legislation still makes the distinction.

Generally earned income derives from employment or from a trade, profession, or vocation. Pensions from past employments or self-employments are earned income. In addition all taxable social security benefits and income from furnished holiday lets are deemed to be earned income.

Sources of income exempt from income tax

Certain items, though they may be classified as income, do not come within the scope of income tax. It is at least as important to know which items of income are exempt from tax as to know what is taxable.

Tax-free investments have been used to great advantage in tax planning in the past although the recent reductions in the marginal rates of income tax have reduced the benefits since these investments usually bear a comparatively low rate of interest.

Certain incomes originating from the government

Interest:

- interest on National Savings Certificates*
- interest and bonuses on Save As You Earn contracts*
- prizes from premium bonds
- interest on certain government securities held by persons not resident or ordinarily resident in the UK
- first £70 of interest on ordinary account National Savings Bank* (to each of husband and wife; £140 on a joint account).

*indicates that there is a limit on the maximum that can be invested.

Social security benefits
Some examples would be:

- invalidity benefit
- attendance allowance
- maternity allowance
- child benefit
- family income supplement
- Christmas bonus for pensioners
- war disablement and war widow's pensions.

Certain payments for service in the armed forces

Certain payments in relation to employment:
- payments under youth training opportunities schemes
- statutory redundancy pay
- profit-related pay.

Other miscellaneous payments:
- scholarships and educational grants
- prizes from competitions, gambling and lottery wins
- voluntary allowances from friends and relatives
- capital portion of purchased life annuity
- lump sums under approved superannuation schemes, retirement annuity contracts and so forth
- interest on tax exempt special savings accounts (TESSAs)
- income withdrawn from a personal equity plan (PEP)
- maintenance payments.

Four main stages in establishing an individual's income tax liability for a fiscal year

In its general outline, the computation of the income tax liability is straightforward. The process can be broken down into four main stages, illustrated in the pro forma income tax computation (Table 1.3). Each stage is considered in detail below.

Table 1.3 Pro forma income tax computation

Four stages		Unearned and earned	Tax deducted at source if any
		£	£
1)	Schedular Income	X	X
	list in detail - split between earned and unearned if wish		
	Gross income from which BR Income tax deducted at source	X	X
	list in detail		
	TOTAL INCOME	X	X(B)
			Tax retained
	Less amount of charges paid	(X)	X
	Less: 50% Class IV NIC re year	(X)	
	Less: private medical insurance – gross	(X)	X
	Less: qualifying donations to charities – gross	(X)	X
		(X)	X(A)
2)	STATUTORY TOTAL INCOME	X	
	Less: relief for losses on shares subscribed for in unquoted trading companies	(X)	
	Less: Personal Allowances	(X)	
3)	TAXABLE INCOME	X	
		£	
	Taxable income at appropriate tax rates	X	
	Less: tax credits on certain allowances	(X)	
	Less: tax credits on mortgage interest paid gross	(X)	
	TAX BORNE	X	
	Add: tax retained on charges (A above)	X	
	TAX LIABILITY	X	
	Less: tax deducted at source (B above)	(X)	
4)	TAX PAYABLE / (REPAYABLE)	X	

Total income

The first stage in establishing the liability is to bring together all the separate sources of an individual's income, net of those deductions specific to particular sources of income. This establishes total income.

The amounts of the separate sources of income are not necessarily the amounts received in the fiscal year but will be the amounts assessable according to the basis of assessment applicable to each individual source of income. The normal bases of assessment for each schedule were set out in Table 1.2. The situations where the normal basis does not apply will be considered in later chapters. Income taxed at source is always assessed as to the gross amount arising in the fiscal year.

There are detailed rules (and much case law) to determine the extent to which expenses are deductible from particular sources of income. The general rules were set out in Table 1.2. The detailed rules and case law, where appropriate, will be considered in later chapters.

EXAMPLE 1.1

Mr X wishes to calculate his total income for income tax purposes for 1994/95. He has received the following amounts and paid the following expenses:

a) Rent on an unfurnished property was due quarterly in advance. The following amounts were received:

1 January 1994 (the due date)	£500
10 April 1994 (due 1 April)	£500
1 July 1994 (due date, rent increased)	£600
1 October 1994 (due date)	£600
11 January 1995 (due 1 January)	£600
15 April 1995 (due 1 April)	£600

Rates were paid on 1 April and 1 October 1994 (£450 each) and again on 1 April 1995 (£500); property insurance amounted to £300 for the year 1 October 1994 to 30 September 1995 – this was paid on the due date and was a 10% increase on the previous year.

b) He had been in business for many years. His adjusted trading profits were as follows:

Year ended 31 May 1993	£25,000
Year ended 31 May 1994	£20,000
Year ended 31 May 1995	£21,000

c) Interest on bank accounts (opened in 1979) was credited on 31 December each year as follows:

	Ordinary account NSB £	Deposit account Barclays £
1993	200	146
1994	240	168
1995	180	120

d) Building society interest was also received as follows:

30 June 1993	£390
31 December 1993	£330
30 June 1994	£420
31 December 1994	£360
30 June 1995	£390

e) Dividends from XYZ plc were received as follows:

12 May 1993 (final dividend y/e 31 December 1992)	£1,020
14 November 1993 (interim dividend)	£840

15 May 1994 (final dividend y/e 31 December 1993)		£1,180
2 December 1994 (interim dividend)		£900
9 May 1995 (final dividend y/e 31 December 1994)		£1,110

f) He also received interest on £3,000 10% Treasury Stock at half-yearly intervals (June and December)

Computation of total income 1994/95

	£
Income per Schedules	
Schedule A (see note 1)	1,150
Schedule D Case I (y/e 31 May 1993)	25,000
Schedule D Case III (see note 2)	130
	26,280
Gross amount of income taxed at source	
Bank deposit interest (168 x 100/75)	224
Building society interest (420 + 360 x 100/75)	1,040
Interest on government securities (3,000 x 10%)	300
Dividends received (1,180 + 900 x 100/80)	2,600
TOTAL INCOME 1994/95	30,444

Notes

1 Rent receivable means the date on which it is due to be received whether received or not, whether accrued due or not. The first date in 1994/95 on which rent of £600 is due is 1 July 1994 and the same amount is due quarterly thereafter.

			£	£
Rent receivable:		4 x 600		2,400
Expenses paid:	Rates	1 October 1994	450	
		1 April 1995	500	
	Insurance	1 October 1994	300	(1,250)
				1,150

2 National Savings Bank interest is not taxed at source like other bank deposits. It is taxed under Schedule D Case III on the amount arising in the preceding fiscal year. In this case, the amount arising in 1993/94 is £200. As it is an ordinary account the first £70 is exempt from tax.

Statutory total income

The second stage in establishing the individual's tax liability is the deduction of the gross amount of charges on income (also known as annual payments) and other specified payments to arrive at statutory total income.

Charges on income

A charge on income is a legal transfer of income from one taxpayer to another recognised by the Inland Revenue. It is deducted from the payer's total income and included in the recipient's total income – hence the term 'statutory total income' (for example, any statistics based on total income would double count charges on income; this does not happen when statutory total income is used).

Charges on income are deductible from any source of income; there are still some circumstances when it can be desirable to preserve earned income. Charges fall into two categories.

▶ Non-retainable charges – amounts paid gross to the recipient; in the hands of the recipient this is Schedule D Case III income.
▶ Retainable charges – amounts paid net of income tax (at the lower or basic rate) to the recipient; in the hands of the recipient, this is income taxed at source.

In both cases, it is the gross amount paid in the fiscal year which is deducted from total income but in the case of retainable charges the payer is only so far out of pocket by the net amount. How does the basic or lower rate tax 'retained' or 'deducted at source' reach the Inland Revenue? It is added to the tax borne at stage four of the computation.

It is important always to establish statutory total income as it is required in future studies.

The Finance Act 1994 has changed the treatment of mortgage interest. This is no longer deductible as a charge in computing statutory total income. Instead, if the interest is paid gross, relief is given by means of a tax credit in computing the taxpayer's income tax liability. Interest paid under the MIRAS scheme can be completely ignored as relief is given at source.

Table 1.4 The principal charges on income

Non-retainable charges	Retainable charges
▶ eligible interest paid to UK residents (except interest specified as retainable charge) ▶ copyright royalties	▶ interest on certain loans to purchase an annuity ▶ patent royalties ▶ charitable deeds of covenant ▶ annuities (for which consideration is given) ▶ eligible interest paid to non-UK residents

Deeds of covenant

A deed of covenant is a legally binding agreement whereby the payer agrees to make payments without receiving consideration.

A deed of covenant is eligible to be treated as a charge on income if it is:

▶ to a charity
▶ irrevocable
▶ entered into for a period capable of exceeding three years
▶ given freely out of income and not as satisfaction of a debt.

Mortgage interest

Interest paid on qualifying loans to purchase the borrower's main residence in the UK or Eire qualifies for tax relief. If it is paid to a 'qualifying lender' (recognised financial institutions such as banks and building societies) it will fall within the MIRAS arrangements.

MIRAS stands for 'mortgage interest relief at source'. The interest is paid net of lower rate income tax.

To qualify, the loan must be for the purchase of land and buildings for use as the borrower's only or main residence. This includes large caravans and houseboats. There are exceptions to this rule whereby a taxpayer may be absent from the residence and it will still be treated as his or her only or main residence:

▶ up to one year, for any reason
▶ up to four years at any one time, for reasons of his or her employment (minimum of three months' residence required between successive absences)
▶ where he or she currently occupies job-related accommodation and the loan is for the purchase of an intended main residence (see Chapter 3 for meaning of job-related accommodation).

Relief for mortgage interest also extends to:

▶ loans where the borrower's new home is substituted as security for a loan on the borrower's previous home

▶ loans where the borrower moves out of his or her home and puts it up for sale but does not purchase a new home.

For loans granted before 5 April 1988, relief is also available if they were home improvement loans or were to purchase or improve the main residence of a divorced or separated spouse or a dependent relative of the borrower. This relief will be lost if the loan is replaced for any reason or if the dependent relative is not the same dependent relative.

The maximum qualifying loan is £30,000 in total (if the loan exceeds £30,000 only the first £30,000 qualifies) but, where the borrower is moving house the relief is more generous; a loan of £30,000 on each property for a period up to 12 months (or more, at the inspector's discretion) will be allowed.

For loans granted from 1 August 1988, relief is not only limited to £30,000 per borrower but also to £30,000 per residence irrespective of the number of borrowers. Residence is defined as a building designed for use as a single residence whether divided or not. There are detailed rules (ICTA 1988, s. 356) for the allocation of the maximum between borrowers particularly where they have borrowed more than this.

▶ Unmarried borrowers – Briefly the residence basis applies and the £30,000 limit is shared equally between the borrowers. The unused share of any borrower may be split between the other borrowers in proportion to their unrelieved loans. For loans granted before 1 August 1988, existing arrangements will continue unless the borrowers change or they elect for the above basis.
▶ Married couples – Generally, if the loan is in both names, the interest on the loan is divided equally between them. (See Chapter 2.)
▶ Married couple and other borrowers – This is a combination of the above. The £30,000 limit is shared between the borrowers (treating the married couple as two borrowers). The tax relief on the married couple's share is divided equally between them.

Note: The relief available on mortgage interest is restricted to the lower rate of 20% for 1994/95. As the correct amount of tax relief is given through the MIRAS scheme, you must omit such payments when computing a taxpayer's income tax liability.

Interest on other loans

Interest on other loans is eligible interest and is treated as a charge on income when the loan is used for a qualifying purpose. It is only allowable at a 'commercial rate'. Note that the borrowing must be in the form of a loan; overdraft interest is never eligible, whatever the purpose of the overdraft. Interest on loans for the following qualifying purposes is a non-retainable charge (that is, paid gross) unless indicated otherwise.

▶ *For the purchase or improvement of land and buildings let commercially.* The property must be in the UK or Eire and must be let commercially for more than 26 weeks out of any 52-week period and must have been available for letting throughout that period. There is no limit to the amount of the qualifying loan but the maximum deductible in any year is limited to the net letting income from that or any other property. Unrelieved interest can be carried forward and deducted from future letting income.
▶ *For the purchase of a life annuity by a person aged 65 or over.* A loan, secured on the borrower's only or main residence (in the UK or Eire), of which 90% of the funds borrowed are used for the purchase of a life annuity. The maximum loan eligible for relief is £30,000. MIRAS will usually apply. Relief is restricted to the basic rate of 25%. As the correct amount of tax relief is given through the MIRAS scheme, you must omit such payments when computing a taxpayer's income tax liability.
▶ *For the purchase of an interest in a partnership, or further investment in a partnership by an existing partner.* The funds must be used for the purpose of the

trade, profession or vocation of the partnership throughout the period of the loan. A loan to a limited partner is not eligible for relief.
- *For the purchase of ordinary shares in, or lending to, a close company.* The borrower must, together with his or her associates, control more than 5% of the ordinary share capital or hold some ordinary shares and be a full-time manager or director.
- *For the purchase of shares in an employee-controlled company.* The company must be a UK unquoted trading company. More than 50% of the ordinary shares and votes must be held by employees of the company and their spouses. The borrower must be a full-time employee of the company throughout the duration of the loan.
- *For the purchase of a share in, or lending to, a co-operative.* A co-operative is an enterprise within the meaning of the Industrial Common Ownership Act 1976. The borrower must work for the co-operative for the greater part of his or her time throughout the duration of the loan.
- *For the purchase of plant and machinery for use by the borrower in his or her employment or in a partnership business.* The interest is not eligible for relief if paid more than three years after the end of the year of assessment in which the loan was acquired. The borrower must be eligible for capital allowances and the relief is reduced proportionately for any private use.
- *For the payment of inheritance tax* by the personal representatives. Inheritance tax must be paid before the grant of probate is obtained. Interest is only allowable for 12 months from the date of the loan.

Business interest

Any interest paid wholly and exclusively for the purpose of the trade is deductible in the Schedule D Case I computation (see Chapter 15). This includes interest on overdrafts and credit card interest. This is not a charge on income.

Other payments

- A self-employed person (sole trader or partner) may claim a deduction of 50% of his or her Class 4 National Insurance contributions for the fiscal year as a deduction from total income. This is considered in more detail in Chapter 15.
- A taxpayer making qualifying maintenance payments under the new rules may receive relief for the lesser of the aggregate qualifying maintenance payments falling due in the fiscal year and the amount of the married couple's allowance (£1,720 in 1994/95). These arrangements are considered in more detail in Chapter 2. Relief is restricted to the lower rate of 20% and is given by means of a tax credit.
- There is relief for premiums on eligible private medical insurance contracts providing cover for people aged 60 and over, whether paid by the insured or by a third party. The taxpayer is entitled to deduct basic rate tax at source from the premium. Relief is restricted to the basic rate of 25% and is given by means of a tax credit.
- Relief is available for 'qualifying donations' to charity individually in 1994/95 of £250 (net) or more. This relief will also be deducted in arriving at statutory total income. The gifts must be made net of basic rate tax (as with deeds of covenant) and relief is available at both basic rate and higher rate.

Insufficient income

A charge on income should be paid out of income and relief is only available to the extent that it is paid out of income.

If the charge is a retainable charge, the basic rate income tax deducted at source is still due to the Inland Revenue and an assessment will be raised for the outstanding amount under ICTA 1988, s. 350.

TAX PLANNING

The manner in which this is done in practice is illustrated in Example 1.5 below.

As illustrated below, no assessment is raised in similar circumstances where the retainable charge is mortgage interest under MIRAS. The intention of this is that taxpayers who are below the income tax threshold also receive assistance towards the payment of mortgage interest (previously this would have been given through the Special Mortgage Option Scheme).

Taxable income

The third stage in establishing tax liability is the deduction of personal and other allowances to give taxable income.

Personal allowances

Most personal allowances are deductible from statutory total income and if they exceed statutory total income in any fiscal year they are wasted. They cannot be carried forward to another year nor can they be transferred from one taxpayer to another (except between husband and wife in certain circumstances – see Chapter 2).

They are generally only available to UK residents (see Overseas activities). The major personal allowances are usually subject to a minimum annual indexation in line with the increase in the retail price index (note that this provision was overruled in the Finance Act 1993 and again in the Finance Act 1994). From 1994/95 the increase in the retail price index over the 12 months to September will be used.

The Finance Act 1994 changed the treatment of certain personal allowances. For 1994/1995 onwards, relief for the married couple's allowance, additional personal allowance and widow's bereavement allowance is given by means of a tax credit rather than by a deduction in computing taxable income.

PA – personal allowance

The basic personal allowance (1994/95 £3,445) is available to all taxable individuals. It is the person's minimum entitlement to personal allowances provided they are resident in the UK.

It is available to single or married persons, children, widows, widowers, divorced or separated spouses.

MCA – married couple's allowance

A married man, who lives with his wife for any part of the tax year, may claim a married couple's allowance (1994/95 £1,720) in addition to his personal allowance. A husband is treated as living with his wife unless they are separated under a court order or a written deed or are separated in such circumstances that the separation is likely to be permanent. Relief is restricted to the lower rate of 20%. The MCA should be completely omitted from the computation of taxable income. Relief can then be given by means of a tax credit.

EXAMPLE 1.2

G is a married man with statutory total income of £25,000 for 1994–95. G's income tax liability is as follows:

	£
Statutory Total Income	25,000
Personal allowance	(3,445)
Taxable income	21,555

	£
Tax due:	
£3,000 × 20% =	600
£18,555 × 25% =	4,639
	5,239
MCA relief: £1,720 × 20% =	(344)
Income tax liability	4,895

Chapter 2 deals with the allowance available in the year of marriage, separation, divorce and death, and circumstances in which it may be claimed by a wife or transferred from husband to wife.

APA – additional personal allowance

The additional personal allowance (1994/95 £1,720) is available to a person who has a 'qualifying child' living with him or her for all or part of the fiscal year. It is equivalent to the married couple's allowance and is also restricted to the lower rate of tax. Relief is given by means of a tax credit.

It is available to a claimant who is:

- a woman who is either unmarried, or living apart from her husband for all or part of the fiscal year
- a man who is not entitled to the married couple's allowance
- a married man, entitled to the married couple's allowance, whose wife is totally incapacitated (physically or mentally) throughout the fiscal year.

A qualifying child is:

- any child of the taxpayer under 16 at the beginning of the fiscal year
- any child of the taxpayer over 16 at the beginning of the fiscal year and receiving full-time instruction at any university, college, school or other educational establishment or receiving full-time training (minimum two years) with an employer for any trade, profession or vocation
- any child, not the taxpayer's own child, under 18 at the beginning of the fiscal year and maintained for the whole or part of the fiscal year by the taxpayer at his or her own expense who, if over 16, satisfies the second condition above.

In the year of marriage, a married man may elect to claim additional personal allowance, instead of the married couple's allowance.

A taxpayer is entitled to only one allowance irrespective of the number of qualifying children he or she has. If more than one person is entitled to an allowance in respect of the same qualifying child, the allowance will be apportioned between them as agreed by them or, failing agreement, in proportion to the amount of time during which the child was resident with each during the fiscal year.

Where an unmarried couple have more than one qualifying child living with them, and each would be entitled to an additional personal allowance, they are only entitled to an allowance for the youngest child.

WBA – widow's bereavement allowance

This allowance (1994/95 £1,720) is given to a widow for the fiscal year in which her husband dies and for the following fiscal year provided that he was entitled to the married couple's allowance in the year of his death. The allowance is not available in the fiscal year following her husband's death if she re-marries before it commences. Relief is restricted to the lower rate of 20% and is given by means of a tax credit.

AA – age allowance

Age allowance as appropriate can be claimed instead of the basic personal allowance where the taxpayer is 65 years of age before the end of the fiscal year. For 1994/95 the allowance is as follows:

	£
Age allowance (65–74)	4,200
Age allowance (75+)	4,370

An allowance is available in full if statutory total income does not exceed (in 1994/95) £14,200. It is reduced by £1 for every £2 that statutory total income exceeds £14,200. It is of benefit therefore to taxpayers whose statutory total income is less than or only marginally in excess of £14,200.

There is also a married couple's age allowance if either the husband or wife are above the relevant age:

	£
Married couple's age allowance (65–74)	2,665
Married couple's age allowance (75+)	2,705

This allowance, given initially to the husband, will also be reduced by half of the excess over the income limit less any deduction already made to his personal age allowance. For this purpose, only the husband's income is relevant. Once again relief is restricted to the lower rate of 20% and is given by means of a tax credit.

Chapter 2 deals with the allowance available in the year of marriage, separation, divorce and death.

EXAMPLE 1.3

Mr and Mrs Y were married and lived together throughout 1994/95. Mr Y is 73 and his statutory total income is £16,500. Mrs Y is 72 and her statutory total income is £12,000.

Mr Y	£	£
Personal allowance (65–74)	4,200	
Less: 1/2 x (16,500 – 14,200) = 1,150 restricted to	(755)	
Minimum personal allowance		3,445
Married couple's allowance (65–74)	2,665	
Less: 1/2 x (16,500 – 14,200) – 755 = 395 unrestricted	(395)	
Married couple's allowance > basic (1,720)		2,270
Allowances available to Mr Y 1994/95		5,715

Mrs Y	£	£
Personal allowance (65–74)	4,200	
Less: income restriction	Nil	
Allowances available to Mrs Y 1994/95		4,200

As you can see, the order in which the allowances are reduced is not beneficial to the taxpayer because the personal allowance (which is eligible for relief at the taxpayer's highest marginal rate) is reduced prior to the married couple's allowance (which is only eligible for relief at 20%).

Blind person's allowance

A person who is registered on the local authority's blind person's register is entitled to an allowance (1994/95 £1,200). If both husband and wife are registered blind, two allowances are given.

Other allowances

Relief for losses on investments in unquoted companies is given by deduction from statutory total income as if it were a trading loss. Full details of the relief available are given in Chapter 18.

Computation of income tax liability

The fourth and final stage in establishing tax liability is the computation of the tax. Taxable income is subjected to tax at graduated rates to give tax borne. Tax borne is the total incidence of income tax on that individual's income for that fiscal year (the income tax suffered).

The rates of tax for 1994/95 are:

	Rate of tax
First £3,000	20%
£3,001 – £23,700	25%
£23,701 +	40%

Credit is then given for the relief due on:

- certain personal allowances (MCA, APA, WBA),
- maintenance payments
- mortgage interest paid gross.

The tax retained on retainable charges is added as a separate liability at basic rate (see below for Inland Revenue alternative presentation) to give the total income tax for which the taxpayer must account to the Inland Revenue.

As we have already seen, some of the income has already been subjected to tax either in full, to basic rate or to lower rate only. Where this is the case, these amounts must be deducted to give the net amount payable or, in some cases, repayable. The principal payments to be credited are as follows.

- PAYE collected on Schedule E income
- Imputed tax credit on dividend income (see below)
- Basic rate tax deducted at source.

Care should be taken in the examination to read the question carefully and give the answer required – whether tax borne, tax liability or tax payable.

Tax liability on dividends

For 1993/94 *et seq.*, the value of the tax credit falls to 20% of the dividend plus the tax credits. The credit on a dividend of £75, for example, is £18.75 (20/80 of £75 or 20% of £75 plus £18.75). This matches the lower rate of income tax on the grossed up dividend.

The effect on the tax liability of an individual shareholder depends on the marginal rate of income tax of that shareholder:

- Not liable to tax or exempt from tax on dividends — repayment of the tax credit at the lower rate of 20%. This also applies to tax credits paid to holders of Personal Equity Plans (see Chapter 4).

- Liable to tax at 20% — the tax credit matches the liability to tax on the dividend income. There is no repayment nor is there any further tax to pay.

- Liable to tax at 25% — the grossed up dividend is deemed to be the tax payer's top slice of income, but will be liable to tax at 20% only (the effect is to extend the lower rate band by the amount of the grossed up dividend; that is, £3,000 plus the grossed up dividend at 20%, the balance of taxable income at 25%). There is therefore no further tax to pay on the dividend.

▶ Liable to tax at 40% the grossed up dividend is deemed to be the top slice of income and to the extent that the higher rate threshold (£23,700) is exceeded, an additional 20% tax will be payable.

The Finance Act 1994 introduced the new Foreign Income Dividend (FID) which will be considered in chapter 24. A shareholder receiving a FID will be treated as receiving income net of 20% tax and, as for normal dividends, there will be no further liability for lower and basic rate taxpayers. However, non-taxpayers will not be able to reclaim any tax as the FID does not carry a tax credit.

EXAMPLE 1.4 (Example 1.1 continued)

Mr X paid mortgage interest of £1,920: it was paid under MIRAS. He was only entitled to the basic personal allowance.

Answer to example 1.4

			£
Total income as above			30,444
Less personal allowance			(3,445)
Taxable income:	Dividends	2,600	
	Other income	24,399	26,999
Tax borne			
On non-dividend income	£3,000 × 20%		600.00
	£20,700 × 25%		5,175.00
	£699 × 40%		279.60
On dividend income	£2,600 × 40%		1,040.00
Gross income tax liability			7,094.60
Less tax credits on dividends £2,600 × 20%			(520.00)
Less tax deducted at source £1,564 × 25%			(391.00)
Tax payable			6,183.60

The mortgage interest has been omitted from the calculation as it receives tax relief through the MIRAS scheme.

Inland Revenue method of computing the tax liability – a comparison

The Inland Revenue does its income tax computations in respect of charges on income and other payments from which income tax is retained in a different way from that used above. This can make life confusing. The purpose of this section is to explain the Revenue method and, through a series of examples, to illustrate both methods of computation side by side to facilitate comparison. The opportunity is also taken to compare the taxpayer's total outlay (in terms of the cost of the charge and his or her total tax liability) when charges are non-retainable and when charges are retainable.

The Revenue method is concerned with three types of payment rather than the two outlined above.

▶ paid gross and tax relief given at both basic and higher rate (for example, eligible loan interest other than mortgage interest) – Type 1

- paid net and tax relief given at both basic and higher rate (for example, patent royalties and charitable deeds of covenant) – Type 2
- paid gross and tax relief given at lower rate only (for example, eligible loan interest not paid through MIRAS – Type 3.

The Revenue method varies according to the type of payment.

For type 1, the method is the same as the one set out above, see Example 1.5(A).

For type 2, the payment is ignored completely in arriving at taxable income and when the tax liability is calculated the basic rate band is extended by the gross amount of the charge. See Example 1.5(B).

For type 3, the payment is ignored completely in arriving at taxable income. Relief is given by means of a tax credit. See Example 1.5(C).

You may have noticed that our list of charges has not mentioned interest paid through the MIRAS scheme. This is because such payments should now be completely ignored when computing a taxpayer's income tax liability, because the correct amount of relief is given at source.

EXAMPLE 1.5

A is a single person and has income and charges in 1994/95 as follows:

	£
Total income (no dividends)	32,000
Gross charges on income	4,000

A) Type 1 – paid gross, basic and higher rate relief given:
The two methods are the same in this case.

Income tax computation 1994/95

	£
Total income	32,000
Less: gross charges on income	(4,000)
Statutory total income	28,000
Less: basic personal allowance	(3,445)
Taxable income	24,555

Tax borne

3,000	@ 20%		600.00
20,700	@ 25%		5,175.00
855	@ 40%		342.00
24,555			

Gross tax liability	6,117.00

Taxpayer's total outlay	£
Cost of charge	4,000
Tax liability	6,117
	10,117

B) Type 2 – paid net, basic and higher rate relief given

Income tax computation 1994/95

i) Correct method

	£
Total income	32,000
Less: gross charges on income	(4,000)
Statutory total income	28,000
Less: basic personal allowance	(3,445)
Taxable income	24,555

Tax borne		
3,000 @ 20%		600.00
20,700 @ 25%		5175.00
855 @ 40%		342.00
24,555		6,117.00
Add: tax retained 4,000 @ 25%		1,000.00
Gross tax liability		7,117.00

ii) Revenue method

	£
Total income	32,000
Less: basic personal allowance	(3,445)
Taxable income	28,555

3,000 lower rate band 20%		600.00
20,700 basic rate band		
4,000 basic rate band extended		
27,700 @ 25%		6,175.00
855 @ 40%		342.00
28,555		
Gross tax liability		7,117.00

Taxpayer's total outlay (both cases)

	£
Cost of charge	3,000
Tax liability	7,117
	10,117

C) Type 3 – paid gross, lower rate relief only given. The two methods are the same in this case.

Income tax computation 1994/95

	£
Total income	32,000
Less: basic personal allowance	(3,445)
Taxable income	28,555

Tax borne	
3,000 @ 20%	600.00
20,700 @ 25%	5,175.00
4,855 @ 40%	1,942.00
	7,717.00
Less: tax credit	
4,000 @ 20%	(800.00)
Tax liability	6,917.00

Taxpayer's total outlay	
Cost of charge	4,000
Tax liability	6,917
	10,917

Note that the overall cost to the taxpayer is £800 more in case C than in either case A or B. This is the higher rate tax relief which is not available (£4,000 @ 40 – 20%).

You will note that the method originally outlined in the text is referred to as the correct method while the Revenue method gives the same answer and is obviously simpler. Why is the Revenue method not used? The reason is that it does not show statutory total income (a figure that is required for more complex computations like age allowance) and that it does not distinguish between tax borne by the taxpayer and the overall tax liability. Your examiners have stated that a student will not be penalised for using the Revenue method (or any short cut) provided the answer is correct, but penalties may result if the answer is incorrect.

The following example illustrates how the two methods deal with charges where there is insufficient income. To arrive at the correct ICTA 1988 s. 350 assessment, it is necessary to use the Inland Revenue method.

EXAMPLE 1.6

A is a single taxpayer and has income and charges in 1994/95 as follows:

	£
Total income	5,000
Gross charges on income	2,000

Charge is type 2 payment such as a deed of covenant.

Income tax computation 1994/95

i) Correct method

	£
Total income	5,000
Less: charge	(2,000)
Statutory total income	3,000
Less: personal allowance	(3,445)
Taxable income	Nil
Tax borne	–
Add: tax retained 2,000 @ 25%	500.00
Gross tax liability	500.00

ii) Revenue method

		£
Total income		5,000
Less: personal allowance		(3,445)
Taxable income		1,555
Gross tax liability		
1,555 @ 20%		311.00
s350 assessment		
1,555 @ 5%		77.75
455 (2,000 – 1,555) @ 25%		111.25
		500.00

Taxpayer's total outlay (both cases)

	£
Cost of charge (net of basic rate tax)	1,500
Tax liability	500
	2,000

The Inland Revenue will not recover the tax retained by an individual if the payment to which it relates is:

▶ interest paid under the MIRAS scheme
▶ private medical insurance premiums for persons aged 60 or over.

These exceptions ensure that individuals on low incomes receive some relief.

Assessment of the tax liability

At present, the Inland Revenue assesses the tax due on each source of income separately (a fragmented approach is taken). A computation of the total income tax liability of an individual applies in practice only when it is necessary to consider the application of higher rates or to effect a repayment claim.

From the taxpayer's point of view, the computation of the total income tax liability serves as a total check on the Inland Revenue assessments. It makes him or her aware of the total incidence of taxation on his or her income.

Notwithstanding the above, the taxpayer will often wish to anticipate, for budgeting purposes, the amount and the possible timing of the assessments by the Inland Revenue and the professional adviser must be able to do this. The normal due date for tax is 1 January in the fiscal year of assessment – except for Schedule D Case I and II when half is due on 1 January in the fiscal year and half is due on 1 July following the end of the fiscal year. Any additional income tax due on income that has been taxed at source (excluding Schedule E) has a normal due date of 1 December following the end of the fiscal year.

Using as an illustration Examples 1.1 and 1.4, the Inland Revenue method is illustrated in Table 1.5. The following notes should help you to follow the computation.

▶ The total income column is extended into analysis columns for each separately assessed type of income: Schedule A, Schedule D Case I, Schedule D Case III, and taxed investment income.
▶ The approach to charges on income and similar payments is as described above.
▶ Type 1 payments and personal allowances are always allocated in priority to the taxpayer's main source of earned income – in this case, Schedule D Case I.
▶ The lower rate and basic rate tax band are also usually allocated in priority to the taxpayer's main source of earned income – the balance being allocated to the other income not taxed at source and finally to taxed investment income.
▶ Any remaining income not taxed at source is assessed to higher-rate tax. The balance of any taxed income being assessed at the excess over lower or basic rate 15/20%.

Table 1.5 An example of the fragmented approach to the collection of income tax

	Total income	Total tax	A	Tax	D Case 1	Tax	D Case 3	Tax	Taxed inv income	HR tax
	£	£	£	£	£	£	£	£	£	£
A	1,150		1,150							
D Case 1	25,000				25,000					
D Case 3	130						130			
F	2,600								2,600	
Bank int.	224								224	
BSI	1,040								1,040	
Govt sec.	300								300	
	30,444		1,150		25,000		130		4,164	
SA	(3,445)				(3,445)					
Taxable	26,999		1,150		21,555		130		4,164	
Lower	(3,000)	600.00			(3,000)	600.00				
Basic rate	(20,700)	5,175.00	1,150	287.50	18,555	4,638.75	130	32.50	(865)	
Higher	3,299	1,319.60							3,299	
									2,600 @ 20%	520.00
									699 @ 15%	104.85
		7,094.60								
Tax paid		520.00								
		391.00								
		£6,183.60		£287.50		£5,238.75		£32.50		£624.85

When the taxpayer's main source of income is from employment, the Inland Revenue has more scope to merge some of its assessments. Untaxed income and even income taxed at source, when small in comparison, may be adjusted for in the PAYE code number.

From 1996/97 all of a taxpayer's income regardless of the source will be included on a single tax statement and the taxpayer will face a single tax bill.

Summary

- Income tax is assessed on a fiscal year basis.
- Income is not defined; instead the legislation identifies sources of income (the Schedules) which are taxable.
- Each Schedule sets out rules for charging that source of income to income tax.
- Income which is taxed at source or deemed to be taxed at source, must be included in total income as a gross figure.
- Total income of the fiscal year for tax purposes may not be the actual income of the fiscal year; it will be the aggregate of income from each source established according to the relevant rules.
- Certain income is specifically exempted from income tax. The income tax computation falls into four main stages; total income, statutory total income, taxable income and the computation of the tax liability.
- Total income aggregates income from all sources established according to the individual rules for each type of income. So far, these rules have only been considered very generally and the next chapters will deal with them in more detail.
- The provisions for charges on income are very detailed and must be studied carefully. It is essential that you have a good grasp of the principles and the payments which qualify to be treated as charges.
- Personal allowances should be familiar to you but take care that you understand how they are applied.
- The adjustments for charges complicate the computation of the tax liability and you should be familiar with both the correct method and the Inland Revenue method.
- You should be familiar with the manner in which the tax liability is assessed, in particular, with the manner in which the liability on dividends is calculated.

Self test questions

1. Describe the income tax year from 6 April to 5 April in two other ways.
2. What is the general definition of deductions allowed under Schedule E?
3. What is the normal basis of assessment under Schedule A?
4. An old age pensioner receives an allowance from her daughter of £15 per week. Is it taxable?
5. A has a mortgage of £40,000 on which he pays interest at 10% gross. The mortgage is not under the MIRAS scheme. How much interest is eligible for income tax relief in 1994/95 and how will that relief be given?
6. What covenants are tax effective?
7. Are copyright royalties paid over gross or net?
8. Compute the allowances available to a married taxpayer aged 70, whose wife turns 75 during the fiscal year and whose statutory total income is £15,000.
9. A's wife died in the fiscal year. Can he claim WBA?
10. B is ten years old. Is he entitled to any personal allowances?
11. C. Dickens, a solicitor, submitted the following income tax returns:

	1994/95	1995/96
Income for the year ended	5 April 1994	5 April 1995
	£	£
Fee income for year ended 31 December 1993 (1994)	20,000	23,000
Net rental income – furnished	586	640
Net rental income – unfurnished	2,312	2,246
Net rental income – holiday lets	1,634	1,816
Dividends received	1,200	1,600
Building society interest received	600	720
Income from discretionary trust (gross)	1,000	1,400
National Savings Bank Investment Account interest	100	150

He is single. You are required to compute the income for tax purposes for 1994/95, showing the basis of assessment used in each case. Calculate the income tax payable.

12 John and his wife, Mary, have asked for your advice on the following.

Mary's mother is widowed and is aged 79. Her only income is a state retirement pension of £2,704 per annum. Mary wishes to give her further financial assistance but is not sure of the best method. Two alternatives are being explored:

a) the payment of a monthly allowance
b) the gift of a lump sum which could be invested by her mother in a building society account, with interest paid monthly.

Mary is liable to pay higher rate tax. You are required to write to John and Mary advising them on the taxation implications of the above. (Limit your answer to the income tax aspects only.)

13 Oliver has been advised that it is likely that the business currently being run by Kwik Sell Ltd will be offered to the management and employees of the company as a 'management or employee buy-out'.

Oliver wishes to participate fully, partly using some of the money from his father's estate and partly using money he plans to borrow from the bank.

You are required to advise Oliver:

a) what is meant by a management or employee buy-out;
b) what conditions must be satisfied before tax relief will be available on interest paid on the money borrowed.

14 Grant took up a position as marketing manager with GB Ltd on 1 June 1994. He and his wife had difficulty in selling their house in Scotland on which they had a mortgage of £30,000 from a qualifying lender but finally succeeded on 31 August 1994 when the loan was repaid. The interest paid for the period from 6 April to 31 August amounted to £1,200.

They had purchased property in Surrey on 1 July 1994, negotiating a mortgage of £50,000 with a local bank. They opted not to join the MIRAS scheme. The interest paid for the period to 5 April 1995 amounted to £6,000.

Grant also owns a house in London which is divided into bedsits. The rents received during 1994/95 amounted to £28,695 and expenses paid totalled £9,675. Rents receivable at 5 April 1995 amounted to £450 and expenses accrued totalled £700. He had borrowed £120,000 to finance the purchase of the house and interest paid during the year on this amounted to £19,000.

They also paid school fees of £4,000 in respect of their son who attends a private school and Grant paid £3,000 to the British Heart Foundation, a registered charity, by deed of covenant.

Grant earned £40,000 (inclusive of benefits) in the year ended 5 April 1995. Their only other income is bank interest of £1,750 credited to their account during the year and child benefit income of £7 per week for each of their two children paid directly to his wife.

You are required to compute Grant's income tax liability for 1994/95 giving clear but concise explanations of your treatment of his income and payments. They have elected for the mortgage interest paid to be allocated to Grant.

Answers on pages 555–557

Husband, Wife, Children and Income Tax

This chapter outlines the main features of the system of independent taxation for married couples as it takes effect from the year of marriage through until the year the marriage terminates as a result of separation, divorce or death. The treatment of maintenance payments following the Finance Act 1988 is described and the income tax system as it affects children is outlined.

Independent taxation of husband and wife

The Finance Act 1988 introduced provisions for a new system of independent taxation to apply to married couples from 6 April 1990. The rules for aggregation of husband and wife's income ceased to apply and each has a personal allowance equivalent to the previous single person's allowance, a married couple's allowance is available (see below) and each has a lower rate and basic rate tax band.

As a result a married couple are now better off from a tax point of view than they were prior to their marriage (Table 2.1 illustrates this).

Table 2.1 Tax computation of couple before and after marriage

	Unmarried		Married	
	A	B	Husband	Wife
	£	£	£	£
Income	28,000	28,000	28,000	28,000
Allowances	(3,445)	(3,445)	(3,445)	(3,445)
Taxable	24,555	24,555	24,555	24,555
Tax borne:				
£3,000 at 20%	600	600	600	600
£20,700 at 25%	5,175	5,175	5,175	5,175
£855 at 40%	342	342	342	342
	6,117	6,117	6,117	6,117
MCA relief				
£1,720 at 20%	–	–	(344)	–
	6,117	6,117	5,773	6,117
Total tax	£12,234		£11,890	

Property owned jointly

Income arising from property held jointly in the names of husband and wife who are living together will normally be regarded as belonging to them in equal shares. If, however, they are entitled to the income in unequal shares, or one of them is not beneficially entitled to any of the income, they may make a formal declaration to that effect, and will then be taxed accordingly. This does not apply to earned income, to any income of a partnership or to any income from joint bank or building society accounts.

A declaration of unequal entitlement to joint income must be made by them jointly and is irrevocable. It must give details of their beneficial interests in both the income and the underlying property. If these interests do not coincide no declaration can have effect. Notice of the declaration must reach the Inland Revenue within 60 days of being made and will apply to income arising on or after the date of the election.

If their interests in the jointly held property change, a fresh declaration must be made. Note that this will result in a transfer of all or part of a source of income between husband and wife, causing the cessation or commencement rules to be applied if applicable (see below).

Gifts between husband and wife

Income from a gift of an asset between husband and wife will be treated as the recipient's for tax purposes, only if it is an unconditional gift of the asset and the related income. Otherwise the income will be treated as the donor's.

Similarly, if the asset is put into a trust to give income to the spouse while control of the asset is retained or transferred to a third party, the income will be treated as the donor's.

Where an asset is transferred during the year and the income therefrom is taxable on a current year basis, the income will be divided between husband and wife according to their respective rights on an actual basis. If the income from the asset is taxable on a preceding year basis, the normal cessation and commencement rules apply to the proportion of the asset (and therefore the income) which has changed hands.

Mortgage interest relief

A husband and wife is each entitled to his or her own share of the £30,000 limit in respect of interest which he or she actually pays (the rules for reallocating unused amounts of the £30,000 limit will apply as described in Chapter 1). Usually, however, if the loan is in joint names, the interest will be divided between them.

If husband and wife do not wish these rules to apply, they can jointly choose to share both the limit and the tax relief in any way they wish by making an 'allocation of interest' election. For instance, a wife can have all the tax relief even though the loan is in her husband's name.

The election must be made on a special form (Form 15 (1990)), signed by both husband and wife no later than 12 months after the end of the fiscal year to which it applies. The election will remain in force until changed or withdrawn.

In most cases, the election will be of no benefit as relief is restricted to the lower rate of tax. Thus the election cannot be used to reduce higher rate liability. However, the election will be relevant where the interest is not paid under the MIRAS scheme and one spouse has insufficient tax liability to offset the tax credit.

Transfer of allowances

The married couple have the right to allocate the whole of the married couple's allowance to the wife, or split it equally between them by joint election. If no preference is expressed, the allowance will go to the husband. Alternatively, the wife has the right to claim half the allowance. Claims/elections should be made before the commencement of the tax year and once made, will remain in force until revoked. This election is now of little benefit as relief is restricted to the lower rate of tax. It will, however, be relevant if one spouse has insufficient liability to offset the tax credit.

Where either the husband's or the wife's income tax liability is insufficient to offset the full tax credit, the excess married couple's allowance may be transferred. Liability for this purpose is before taking account of any tax retained on the payment of charges.

The election to transfer the surplus allowance must be made within six years of the end of the tax year concerned. The election is irrevocable.

Any excess blind person's allowance is also transferable if the husband's or wife's income is insufficient to absorb it.

EXAMPLE 2.1

Percy is married and is entitled to the basic married couple's allowance. In 1994/95 he has income of £5,000 before the deduction of any charges. Assume that he makes the following separate payments during 1994/95:

(a) A deed of covenant of £3,000 (gross).
(b) A deed of covenant of £500 (gross).
(c) Mortgage interest of £3,000 (gross) paid under the MIRAS scheme.

The amount of married couple's allowance that Percy will be able to transfer to his wife is computed as follows:

	(a) £	(b) £	(c) £
Income	5,000	5,000	5,000
Less charges	(3,000)	(500)	–
STI	2,000	4,500	5,000
Personal allowance	(2,000)	(3,445)	(3,445)
Taxable	–	1,055	1,555
Tax due at 20%	–	211	311
MCA relief	–	(211)	(311)

(a) As Percy has no liability, the full MCA of £1,720 can be transferred to his wife.
(b) The full MCA relief is £344 (£1,720 x 20%). Percy has utilised relief of £211, this leaves relief of £133 (£344 – £211) to be transferred to his wife. This equates to an allowance of £665 (£665 x 20% = £133).
(c) Mortgage interest under MIRAS is no longer deductible as a charge. Percy has utilised relief of £311, this leaves relief of £33 (£344 – £311) to be transferred to his wife. This equates to an allowance of £165 (£165 x 20% = £33).

Note that Percy and his wife could have jointly elected, before the commencement of 1994/95, for the whole of the married couple's allowance to be transferred to the wife.

Age related married couple's allowance

Where an election/claim is made above to share the married couple's allowance (or transfer it wholly to the wife), it is only applicable to the basic allowance and not to the age-related increase, which always remains with the husband.

Where a transfer of the married couple's allowance is made, due to insufficient liability to offset the tax credit as illustrated above, this may include the age related increase.

Year of marriage (also year of reconciliation after period of separation)

Husband

The married couple's allowance in the year of marriage is reduced by 1/12 for every complete tax month before the date of the marriage.

A tax month runs from the 6th of one month to the 5th of the next month.

EXAMPLE 2.2

Y gets married on 3 October 1994. What married couple's allowance will he be entitled to?

There are five complete tax months before 3 October 1994.

$$(1{,}720 - 5/12) \times 1{,}720 = £1{,}003$$

A similar calculation applies if a couple, entitled to age allowance, marry during the year.

If the couple elect to allocate some or all of the above allowance to the wife in the fiscal year of marriage, the election may be made during the fiscal year.

A married man who divorces and remarries in the same year will be entitled to only one married couple's allowance. The amount of this is determined by the age in that year of the oldest of the man and the two wives.

If the husband was single and had a qualifying child or children living with him in the fiscal year prior to the marriage he would have been entitled to the APA which would be more than a proportion of the married couple's allowance. In this case he has the right to claim APA instead of a proportion of MCA.

If a married couple separate in one year but are reconciled in a later year, and were not divorced meanwhile, the husband gets the full married couple's allowance in the year of reconciliation. It is not reduced as in the year of marriage.

Wife

The wife can continue to claim the allowances appropriate to her in the year of marriage including the additional personal allowance (if she had/has a qualifying child or children living with her prior to the date of the marriage), and widow's bereavement allowance.

Year of separation or divorce or death

A married couple are deemed to have split up from the earlier of the following dates:

- the date of the court order or deed of legal separation
- the date on which they become separated in circumstances likely to be permanent.

The husband is entitled to the full married couple's allowance in the year of separation or death of either husband or wife. Any surplus married couple's allowance may be transferred to the wife.

The wife is entitled to the full personal allowance and can claim the additional personal allowance if she has qualifying children living with her, and, if her husband dies, the widow's bereavement allowance.

If the couple reconcile in the year of separation, the separation is ignored for tax purposes.

Maintenance payments

This section considers maintenance payments made under court order or written agreement. Voluntary maintenance payments are not allowable for tax purposes to the payer nor are they taxable on the recipient.

The Finance Act 1988, introduced a new system for the tax treatment of maintenance payments made under court orders and maintenance agreements entered into on or after 15 March 1988. Payments under existing arrangements at that date were subjected to transitional arrangements or an opportunity was given for the payer to elect to switch to the 'new rules'.

Payments under new rules

The payments are no longer within the scope of the legislation as charges on income and they are paid gross.

The payer may obtain relief for income tax purposes for qualifying maintenance payments, up to an amount equivalent to the married couple's allowance (1994/95 £1,720). Relief is now restricted to the lower rate of tax in the same manner as the married couple's allowance, and is given by means of a tax credit.

Qualifying maintenance payments are those made under a court order in a member state, or under a written agreement to which EEC law applies, to a former spouse for his or her maintenance or for the maintenance of a child of the family under the age of 21. No deduction is available for payments made direct to a child, nor for payments made at a time when the former spouse has remarried.

The recipient is not taxable on maintenance payments received.

The Child Support Agency has now taken over much of the work of the courts on child maintenance. Maintenance is collected by the Agency and passed to the person entitled, or may be paid directly to the Department of Social Security in respect of a person in receipt of income support. In both cases, where the person entitled to maintenance is the divorced or separated spouse of the payer, tax relief will be available as if the payment had been made direct.

Children

A child is a taxable person and, to the extent that the child has income in his or her own right (except in the circumstances outlined below), will be taxed on that income in the same way as any other taxpayer. A child is entitled to the basic personal allowance.

The majority of income which a child has in his or her own right is likely to be investment income taxed at source. When the income tax computation is done and the personal allowance is deducted, a repayment will usually result. It should be remembered that income received from a discretionary settlement (which includes an accumulation and maintenance trust) will have suffered tax at source at the rate of 35%.
Scholarships and educational grants are not income of the child for tax purposes.

Parental dispositions

Any income derived by a minor child from a parental disposition is treated as income of the parent providing the property unless the aggregate amount per child in any tax year does not exceed £100. A child is a minor if unmarried and under the age of 18.

The purpose of the legislation is anti-avoidance: to prevent the parent of a minor child transferring income to the child to use his or her personal allowance (and perhaps basic rate tax band) while remaining in control of the funds as the child's guardian.

A parental disposition includes trusts set up by a parent in favour of a child of his or her (otherwise than on death of the parent); assets transferred by the parent to the child or purchased by the parent for the child; covenanted payments by a parent to a child.

If the child is employed by the parents in their trade, wages will be payable provided they are reasonable for the work done and employment legislation is not infringed.

Summary

- Independent taxation of husband and wife applied from 6 April 1990.
- The married couple may jointly elect to transfer the married couple's allowance to the wife or share it between them. Alternatively, the wife may claim one half of the allowance without reference to her husband.
- For 1994/95, relief for the married couple's allowance is restricted to the lower rate of tax, and is given by means of a tax credit.
- Unabsorbed married couple's allowance may be transferred to the wife. This applies in any year in which it is available including years of marriage, separation and death.
- Similarly, unabsorbed blind person's allowance is transferrable.
- Care should be taken over the allocation of joint income between husband and wife and any transfers of property between them.
- The rules relating to maintenance payments were radically altered by the Finance Act 1988. You are only required to be familiar with the new rules. Relief is now restricted to the lower rate of tax and is given by means of a tax credit.
- A married couple planning to minimise their joint tax liabilities should aim to use each spouse's personal allowances, lower rate and basic rate tax band before either incurs a higher rate liability. This should be done by making the appropriate declarations of beneficial interest in jointly held assets, and allocation of interest paid or possibly by transferring property or the married couple's allowance from one spouse to the other.

Self test questions

1   What is a tax month?

2   State the time limits for making a declaration of unequal entitlement to joint income.

3   Who must make the declaration referred to in 2 above?

4   Compute the married couple's allowance to a taxpayer who marries on 10 December 1994.

5   Under independent taxation, to what extent is unrelieved eligible interest transferable:
    a) from husband to wife
    b) from wife to husband?

6   Who must make an allocation of interest election and what are the time limits?

7   Mr D (age 30) marries Miss A (age 75) on 30 June 1994. What allowances will Mr D be entitled to for 1994/95?

8   Where a maintenance payment under a post 15 March 1988 agreement is made direct to a child, how is it taxed?

9   Mr and Mrs Mott separate on 1 August 1994. What allowances will Mr Mott be entitled to for 1994/95?

10 David Knight is a widower, his wife, Elizabeth, having died on 15 August 1987 after being incapacitated for the two years preceding her death.

He has one son aged nine living with him and he employs Mr and Mrs Dean as gardener and housekeeper respectively. They live in a flat which is part of the house David and his son live in.

David is a partner in a firm of computer consultants, entitled to a one-third share of the profit. Recent results of the firm, adjusted for taxation have been:

Year ended 31 March 1993: £54,000 profit
Year ended 31 March 1994: £72,000 profit

David and Carol Harris, a single woman, plan to marry on 3 January 1995.

David's other income and outgoings are (estimated where necessary) as follows.

Income

He receives child benefit of £7 per week for his son, plus the additional benefit for single parents of £4 per week. The additional benefit will be received for 39 weeks during 1994/95.

He has had an ordinary account with the National Savings Bank for a number of years. In the year to 5 April 1994, interest credited was £100, and in the year to 5 April 1995, interest credited will be £150.

Outgoings	1993/94	1994/95
	£	£
Gardener's salary to Mr Dean	5,000	6,000
Housekeeper's salary to Mrs Dean	3,000	4,000
Personal pension premium	1,500	1,800
Payment under deed of covenant to Cancer Research, a national charity	1,000	1,000

Carol is a manager in an electronics company. Her salary for the year ended 5 April 1995 will be £15,000. The company provided no benefits in kind.

She has some savings which have been invested and which gave the following returns:

	1993/94	1994/95
	£	£
Abbeyford Building Society, interest credited to account	120	180
Dividends received from Electrics Ltd	480	512

Her father died three years ago, and she pays £500 per annum to support her mother aged 51, whose only income is a widow's pension (which is less than the basic single retirement pension).

You are required to prepare an estimate of David and Carol's income tax borne for 1994/95, including concise explanations of your treatment of their income and outgoings.

11 Edward, aged 42, is a sales executive with Hightech plc. On 4 January 1995, while at work, Edward died following a heart attack. In his will Edward left his shares to his 12-year-old daughter Geraldine and the remainder of his estate to his wife. The estate was administered and all necessary transfers made by early March 1995.

You are required, from the following information, to prepare income tax computations for 1994/95 for Edward, his wife Frances and their daughter Geraldine, showing tax payable or repayable (if any).

Edward's salary was £1,500 per month plus a bonus calculated on quarterly sales and paid a month later as follows:

January to March 1994	£1,400 paid 30 April 1994
April to June 1994	£1,700 paid 31 July 1994
July to September 1994	£1,500 paid 31 October 1994
October to December 1994	£1,800 paid 31 January 1995

Edward had the use of a 1600 cc car from January 1994. The car was bought new for £11,000 by Hightech at that date. Edward paid for all his private petrol. He covered 1,000 miles on company business during 1994/95.

On Edward's death, Hightech made an ex gratia payment of £5,000 to Frances. She also received a lump sum of £24,000 from the company's pension scheme and a pension of £400 per month gross, commencing on 31 January 1995.

Dividends received on shares owned by Edward were as follows:

4 February 1994	£2,100
12 June 1994	£1,800
19 August 1994	£2,900
7 October 1994	£1,100
2 January 1995	£1,500
28 March 1995	£730
15 April 1995	£1,700

Frances has carried on her own business as an insurance consultant for a number of years, her recent adjusted profits being:

Year ended 29 February 1993	£12,000
Year ended 28 February 1994	£13,500
Year ended 28 February 1995	£12,800

The only capital asset used in the business was a 1600 cc motor car with a tax written down value at 6 April 1994 of £4,800. On 1 February 1994 Frances bought a new 1600 cc car costing £12,200 receiving a part exchange allowance of £4,000 for the existing car. Her annual mileage was 9,000, 70% of which was on business.

Frances received interest on a building society account and a National Savings Bank ordinary account as follows:

Building society account – interest credited

30 September 1993	£450
31 March 1994	£500
30 September 1994	£550
31 March 1995	£600
30 September 1995 (est)	£650

National Savings Bank ordinary account – interest credited

31 December 1993	£150
31 December 1994	£160
31 December 1995 (est)	£170

Geraldine receives interest from a National Savings Bank investment account on money left to her some years ago on her grandfather's death. Gross interest credited was as follows:

31 December 1993	£500
31 December 1994	£560
31 December 1995 (est)	£600

During 1994/95, Frances pays mortgage interest of £146 per month on a £20,000 mortgage taken out in 1975 on the purchase of their home. Edward pays interest of £150 per month on a £15,000 loan taken out in 1978 to finance the building of an extension. Both loans are under the MIRAS scheme. Edward's loan was covered by a life assurance policy, which discharged the loan shortly after his death. Frances also pays household bills of, on average £600 per annum for her widowed mother whose only income is the state retirement pension.

Answers on pages 557–560

CHAPTER 3

Income from Employment in the UK

The purpose of this chapter is to examine the scope of Schedule E including the rules for assessing benefits in kind and the rules governing the deduction of expenses. Employee incentive schemes are outlined, as are the provisions for taxing payments on termination of employment.

The scope of schedule E

Schedule E is divided into three Cases. This chapter covers the taxation of all emoluments of a person resident and ordinarily resident in the UK in respect of duties performed in the UK which is principally Case I. The taxation of emoluments of UK residents for duties performed outside the UK and the taxation of persons who are not UK resident (or who are resident but not ordinarily resident) for duties performed in the UK are covered in the section on Overseas Activities.

Income chargeable

Schedule E assesses emoluments from an office or employment. Emoluments include all salaries, wages, bonuses, fees, commissions and 'profits whatsoever'. These mostly take the form of payments in money but the definition also covers any payments which are convertible into money (this principle stems from the case of *Tennant* v. *Smith*). They need not necessarily be made by the employer provided they arise from the office or employment (for example, gifts from third parties, tips). In *Cooper* v. *Blakiston* a collection made by parishioners and others and given to a vicar in response to an appeal by the bishop was held to be assessable under Schedule E.

If it can be shown that the payments do not derive from the office or employment, they will not be assessable. This principle has been established in a number of cases. In *Ball* v. *Johnson* a bank insisted on its employees sitting the examinations of the Institute of Bankers although continued employment was not conditional on them being passed. Cash awards were made to successful candidates. It was held that the awards were not remuneration for services and were not assessable.

In *Hochstrasser* v. *Mayes* employees, transferred from one part of the country to another, were compensated through a housing scheme operated by the employer for losses on the sale of their houses. It was held that the compensation was not remuneration for services.

In addition to the above cases, subsequent legislation has made further benefits specifically assessable under Schedule E on all or certain categories of employee.

Also taxable under Schedule E are any pensions or annuities resulting from employment paid in the UK (including the state pension and pensions from approved superannuation funds and personal pension plans). Also certain social security benefits are taxable, of which the principal ones are:

- unemployment benefit
- statutory sick pay, statutory maternity pay, invalid care allowance and invalidity allowance to supplement the retirement pension
- retirement pension, old person's pension, widow's pension, widowed mother's allowance and widow's allowance.

All emoluments under Schedule E are aggregated to give the employee's gross emoluments from employment.

Expenses deductible

The following expenses are deductible from an employee's gross emoluments from employment to give his or her net emoluments:

- contributions to approved occupational pension schemes (maximum 15% of remuneration)
- premiums for approved retirement annuity contracts or personal pension plans
- donations to charity through an approved payroll giving scheme (GAYE £900 per annum maximum from 6 April 1993)
- subscriptions to professional bodies on a list approved by the Inland Revenue, if relevant to the employment
- travelling expenses necessarily incurred by the holder of an employment 'in the performance of the duties of the office or employment' (ICTA 1988, s. 198);
- other expenses incurred 'wholly, exclusively and necessarily in the performance of the said duties' (ICTA 1988, s. 198)
- capital allowances on plant and machinery necessarily provided for use in the performance of the duties and interest incurred on loans to purchase such items.

The last three are general categories of expenses but the provisions are very strictly applied. The words 'holder of an employment' have been interpreted as allowing relief only for those expenses which every holder of an employment would incur, and not for expenses which are incurred as a result of the personal circumstances of a particular employee.

Relief for contributions to approved occupational pension schemes and donations to charity through an approved payroll giving scheme is given automatically through the PAYE system under the net pay arrangements but relief for the other items must be claimed by the taxpayer in his or her end-of-year tax return (see Chapter 22).

Travelling expenses

Generally speaking the costs of travelling from home to work (or from a self-employed person's place of business to work) are not allowable since the duties of the employment do not commence until arrival at work *(Ricketts v. Colquhoun)*.

By contrast, in *Pook v. Owen,* it was held that travel expenses from one place of work to another were deductible even although one of the places of work may be the taxpayer's home.

Additional car expenses incurred in excess of those reimbursed, based on public transport costs, are generally not allowable since the excess expenses are not necessary if public transport could have been used (*Marsden v. CIR*).

Many employers reimburse their employees for motoring costs incurred while performing the duties of employment by giving a fixed rate per business mile. In many cases, the rate per mile is greater than the motoring costs for which tax relief is due and the profit element is a taxable emolument under Schedule E. The fixed profit car scheme (FPCS) assesses any excess in the rate paid by the employer over a tax-free mileage rate (based on engine capacity and the number of business miles) (see Table 3.1) – called 'chargeable mileage profit'.

The statutory basis remains available to any employee who so wishes, provided that adequate records are kept, that is, a claim under s. 198 for the costs incurred in running a car for travelling in the performance of the duties of employment (including petrol, oil and a proportion of road tax, insurance and repairs), and capital allowances. Transitional arrangements also exist for members of previously approved schemes. Interest paid on a loan taken out for the purchase of a car used for business purposes may qualify for tax relief – it is not included in the FPCS rates.

Table 3.1 Fixed profit car scheme rates 1994/95

Cars with a cylinder capacity of	Up to 4,000 miles	Over 4,000 miles
Up to 1,000 cc	27p	15p
1,001 to 1,500 cc	33p	19p
1,501 to 2,000 cc	41p	23p
Over 2,000 cc	56p	31p

Other expenses

There are many cases where it has been shown that expenses were incurred necessarily for the employment but were not necessary for the performance of the duties of the employment. For example, in *Humbles* v. *Brooks*, the expenses of a history teacher in attending weekend lectures to improve his knowledge of history were held not to be incurred in the performance of his duties as a teacher. In *Brown* v. *Bullock*, a bank manager in London was obliged to join a London club upon his appointment, one half of the subscription being paid by the bank (assessable under Schedule E). The bank manager claimed the whole subscription as an expense. It was held to be not allowable, the test being not whether the employer imposes the expense but whether the duties do

On the other hand, in a similar case (*Elwood* v. *Utitz*) a company bore the cost of two subscriptions to London clubs for its managing director on the grounds that it was cheaper for him to stay in the clubs when visiting London than in hotels. He claimed a deduction for the subscriptions. The expense was allowed on the grounds that it was cheaper overall to the employer.

Expenses may also be necessary in the performance of the duties without being exclusively referable to those duties or may be necessarily and exclusively incurred without being wholly incurred for the performance of the duties. A number of cases in regard to clothing have established the principle that the cost of ordinary clothing is not allowable as the expenditure has a personal element (warmth and decency); the cost of protective or special clothing is, however, allowable (*Hillyer* v. *Leeke*).

In many cases, clothing, food and tools allowances are negotiated by trade unions on behalf of their members. These are usually flat-rate allowances claimable by members irrespective of the amount spent by them in any year.

An employee or director who provides business entertainment from his salary will not be entitled to any deduction for expenses incurred. On the other hand, if an employee is paid an entertainment allowance or is reimbursed for entertainment expenses incurred, these will be assessed as emoluments on him, but he will be entitled to deduct from his emoluments any entertainment expenses incurred – provided he can show that they satisfy the general rule of being wholly, exclusively and necessarily incurred in the performance of his duties. (In this case the entertainment allowance will not have been allowed as a deduction in computing the Schedule D Case I profits of the employer.)

Capital allowances and interest

Examples of plant and machinery necessarily provided by the employee for use in the performance of the duties of the employment might be the word processor of a journalist, or the tools of a craftsman. The Finance Act 1990 withdrew the term 'necessarily' for cars provided by an employee for use in the performance of the duties of the employment. Any car so used is deemed to have been acquired at open market value on 6 April 1990 or the date of first such use, if later. Where the car is used partly for the purpose of the office or employment and partly for other purposes, the allowances will be reduced proportionately (see Chapter 16).

Employed or self-employed?

There can be a very fine dividing line between whether a person is employed or self-employed.

Employment has been said to exist where there is a **contract of service**, whether written or verbal (*Fall* v. *Hitchen*). Employees perform their duties in the manner prescribed by the employer. In contrast, a **contract for services** can be said to exist between a self-employed individual and a customer; it is up to the individual how the work is done and, to some extent, when, provided that the finished product comes up to a certain standard.

In the vast majority of cases it is readily apparent whether an individual works for himself or for someone else but there are situations where it is not clear cut and the question might be asked whether a person is freelance or has several part-time employments. There are several factors which may be considered in determining whether the person is in business on his or her own account. The case, *Market Investigations Ltd* v. *Minister of Social Security* (1969), concerned whether or not market researchers who were recruited on an ad hoc basis as and when assignments arose and who went out with clipboards and questionnaires, were employed. The judge in his summing up outlined factors which had to be considered: financial risk undertaken; whether he or she is an employer; level of investment in equipment, stock and so on; the number of customers; the extent to which he or she makes his or her own business decisions re pricing, financial management and so on and has the opportunity to profit from them. The Inland Revenue leaflet *Employed or Self-Employed* provides a useful list of questions to be answered in reaching a conclusion.

The most important recent case on this topic is *Hall* v. *Lorimer*. This concerned a vision mixer who undertook short term engagements for various production companies. The Court of Appeal held that he was self-employed despite the fact that he provided personal services and used equipment provided by the companies engaging him. The deciding factor in this case was the number of engagements; the taxpayer had 574 in four years, mostly for one day.

Persons working at home almost exclusively for one 'customer' and using equipment provided by that 'customer' have been held to be employees fulfilling a contract of service.

Taxpayers generally given a choice would prefer to be self-employed rather than employed. This is partly because the expenses deductible under Schedule D Case I are less restricted but also because the basis of assessment and therefore the due date for payment of tax is not so immediate. The cost of National Insurance contributions is also significantly less.

On the other hand, self-employed persons are more difficult for the Inland Revenue to keep track of and more difficult for them to collect the tax from. The PAYE regulations have, therefore, become stricter over the years and the casual worker is required to be treated as an employee (even if only employed for a week) unless the worker can show that he or she is self-employed (by, for example, producing a tax exemption card).

Agency workers, (with the exception of actors, entertainers and models), are specifically brought within Schedule E with the tax being accounted for under PAYE either by the client or the agency.

Fees, bonuses and commissions

The basis of assessment of income chargeable under Schedule E is the amount received in the fiscal year (the receipts basis).

Directors and other employees may receive pay some time after the end of the period for which it is earned by virtue of fees, bonuses and/or commissions. These earnings now form part of the emoluments of the fiscal year in which they are received.

For employees other than directors, earnings are treated as received on the earlier of:

- the time when payment is made
- the time when entitlement to payment occurs.

Also, where the emoluments are in respect of an office or employment with a company the holder of which is a director of the company, receipt is the earlier of the rules above and those set out below:

- the time when sums on account of the emoluments are credited in the company's accounts or records
- the end of the accounting period to which the sums relate, if they are determined before the end of the period
- the date when the sums are determined, if they relate to an accounting period and are determined after the end of the period.

Remember that a director is defined as being not only those persons who bear the office of director but any person on whose directions or instructions, given other than in a professional capacity, the directors (by title) are accustomed to act.

Emoluments received in a year of assessment before an office or employment is commenced are treated as emoluments of the year of assessment in which employment commenced.

Similarly, emoluments received in a year of assessment in which the office or employment is no longer held are treated as emoluments of the year of assessment in which the employment terminated.

For PAYE and NI purposes, the definition of when remuneration is received corresponds with the above.

Benefits in kind

Emoluments, as defined, include non-cash payments which are convertible into money, that is, benefits in kind. Subsequent legislation has also brought into charge to tax under Schedule E for certain employees, benefits in kind which are not convertible into money.

Employees fall into two categories for the assessment of benefits in kind:

- Employees whose gross emoluments are less than £8,500 a year. This includes directors whose emoluments are less than £8,500 a year if they are also full-time working directors (or the company is non-profit-making or a charity) and they have no material interest in the company. This group is commonly referred to as P9D employees.
- Employees whose emoluments are £8,500 or more per annum and all directors other than those above. This group is commonly referred to as P11D employees.

A full-time working director is one who is required to devote substantially the whole of his or her time to the service of the company.

A material interest in a company is one where that person together with his or her associates is able to control more than 5% of the ordinary share capital of the company.

In determining whether a person's emoluments are £8,500 or more per annum, emoluments include all cash remuneration, all expenses payments and allowances, and the value of all benefits in kind (calculated as if for a P11D employee). These are calculated before the deduction of any allowable expenses other than contributions to an approved superannuation fund in respect of which the individual is entitled to tax relief, and donations to an approved payroll giving scheme as follows:

	£
Salary, fees, bonuses, commissions and so on	X
Expenses, payments and allowances (including those reimbursing out-of-pocket expenses of the employee)	X
Benefits in kind (calculated as if for a higher-paid employee)	X
	X
Less contributions to an approved superannuation fund	(X)
	X ? >= £8,500
Less other allowable deductions	(X)
Net Schedule E Emoluments	X

Where a person is employed by more than one employer, each employment is taken separately to determine whether the employee is higher paid in that employment. However, if there are two or more employments with the same employer (including employments with more than one company within the same group) they are all treated as higher paid if the total emoluments exceed £8,500 or if one of the employments is as a director.

Some benefits in kind are assessable on all employees while the manner in which others are assessable depends on the category of employee to whom it is given.

Returns by employer

The employer is required to make returns to the Inland Revenue on forms P11D (for directors and employees whose emoluments are £8,500 or more per annum) and P9D (for employees whose emoluments are less than £8,500 per annum) not later than 6 June following the end of the fiscal year – giving details of any chargeable benefits in kind given to individual employees during the year.

For P11D employees only, details of reimbursed expenses must be included on the P11D if not covered by a dispensation. For P9D employees, employers must include on the P9D only those expenses paid to the employee which were not incurred in the performance of duties.

Dispensation

Details of expenses payments covered by a dispensation need not be shown on form P11D.

The employer may apply for and be granted a dispensation if the system of reimbursing out-of-pocket expenses of employees is such that only those expenses are reimbursed which, when claimed by the employee, would be allowable under ICTA 1988, s. 198 (see above).

EXAMPLE 3.1

An employee, whose emoluments amounted to £12,000 in 1994/95, was reimbursed during the year for out-of-pocket travelling expenses incurred in the performance of her duties amounting to £1,000. The employer did not have a dispensation.

	£
Remuneration in cash	12,000
Expenses reimbursed per P11D	1,000
Gross emoluments	13,000
Expenses claimed under s. 198 by taxpayer	(1,000)
Net Schedule E Emoluments	12,000

Where the expenses payments are covered by a dispensation the Schedule E emoluments still amount to £12,000. Nevertheless, the employer's time in keeping records and completing the P11D is saved, the employees' time in keeping records and completing their tax returns is saved and the Inland Revenue time in checking both is saved.

Benefits assessable on all employees

Non-cash vouchers

The cost of providing vouchers which can be exchanged for goods or services, to an employee or his or her family, is taxable on that employee less any contribution made by the employee.

Examples of non-cash vouchers include transport vouchers and cheque vouchers. Transport vouchers are documents which can be used to obtain passenger transport (excluding those held by employees of transport organisations which are assessed on a different basis). Cheque vouchers are vouchers given to employees which they are expected to use in exchange for specific goods or services.

Luncheon vouchers fall into this category but are exempt from tax provided that they are non-transferable, used only for meals, are available to lower-paid staff and are limited to 15 pence per working day. If the face value exceeds 15 pence, only the excess over 15 pence is taxable.

Vouchers to obtain a car-parking space at or near the place of work are non-taxable.

Vouchers enabling an employee or his or her family to obtain entertainment or hospitality are non-taxable if not provided by (or procured directly or indirectly by) the employer or a person connected with the employer and if they are not in recognition or in anticipation of services rendered in the course of his or her employment. The entertainment and hospitality intended to be covered by these provisions is that provided to the employees of business contacts and clients as a means of generating goodwill. It covers the provision of seats at sporting and cultural events. Any tax charge on non-cash vouchers arises in the fiscal year in which the expense is incurred by the employer or, if later, the year in which the voucher is exchanged for goods or services.

Cash vouchers

In some holiday pay schemes, the employer stamps a card on a weekly basis which can be 'cashed' by the employee whenever he or she takes a holiday. The tax charge arises whenever the employer incurs the cost, that is, when the card is stamped.

Credit cards

Where an employer provides a credit card for employees, the employee will be taxable on the cost to the employer of settling any liabilities incurred by the employee less any contribution made by the employee towards that cost.

The benefit arises when the employee takes possession of the goods or services rather than when the employer pays. The cost of provision of the card and any interest charges arising on late payment are not assessable.

The cost of fuel and vehicle running expenses paid by credit card is specifically excluded as these benefits are separately assessed. The cost of car-parking, entertainment and hospitality paid by credit-token in circumstances similar to those above is also specifically excluded as these benefits are exempt from tax.

Payment of liabilities on behalf of employees

Where the employer pays for an item which is the legal liability of the employee, the cost to the employer is a taxable benefit.

Living accommodation – the basic charge

Where an employer provides living accommodation for an employee, the basic charge for that provision is the annual value of the property (the gross rateable value) or if greater, the rent paid by the employer for the property. This benefit is reduced by any contribution made by the employee and by any expenses deductible under ICTA 1988, s. 198.

This charge is simply for the use of the accommodation. Further benefits may be assessable under the general rules for higher- and lower-paid employees for ancillary benefits provided in connection with the accommodation (for instance the provision of services, furniture and so on).

If the accommodation is provided by the employer for any of the following three reasons, the accommodation is 'job-related' or 'representative' and no taxable benefit will arise.

- If it is necessary for the proper performance of the duties of the employment (for instance, a caretaker)
- If it is provided for the better performance of the duties of the employment and it is customary (for instance, hotel staff, clergy)
- If it is provided as part of special security arrangements as a result of a special threat to the employee's security.

Note that only the last reason above applies to directors. Directors cannot have job-related accommodation under the first or second.

Living accommodation – expensive

If the cost of providing the accommodation (the cost of acquisition plus improvement expenditure incurred before the year of assessment, less any capital contribution by the employee) exceeds £75,000 an additional benefit is levied on the employee or director as follows:

$$(\text{Cost} - £75{,}000) \times \text{official rate of interest}$$
$$\text{(as per beneficial loans)}$$
$$\text{at start of fiscal year}$$

Market value at date of first occupation by the employee may be substituted for cost of acquisition and improvements to that date if the employer acquired the property more than six years before employee moved in.

If it is job-related accommodation as defined above there will also be no benefit under this heading.

If the contribution made by the employee exceeds the taxable benefit arising from the basic charge, the excess contribution may be deducted from the additional benefit.

EXAMPLE 3.2

Albert had the use of a company house throughout 1993/94 and 1994/95. The rateable value of the house was £1,000. It had cost the company £150,000 in August 1980. Since then the company had carried out improvements as follows:

| March 1990 | cost | £10,000 |
| September 1993 | cost | £15,000 |

The market value of the house at 6 April 1993 (date of first occupation) was £200,000. Albert paid £2,000 per annum for the use of the house. Assume that the official interest rate at 6 April 1994 was 10% per annum.

	£
Annual value	1,000
Additional charge	
$(215,000 - 75,000) \times 10\%$	14,000
	15,000
Less contribution	(2,000)
Assessable benefit 1994/95	13,000

P9D employees

General rule

P9D employees are only assessed on further benefits if the benefits are convertible into money or money's worth. They are assessed at their 'cash equivalent' or 'second-hand value' (the amount they would fetch if disposed of by the employee to a third party) less any contribution by the employee. This rule can be illustrated by a number of examples.

▶ An employer gives an employee a suit of clothes, retail value £100. The assessable benefit is the estimated resale value of the suit which is likely to be very much less than £100.
▶ An employer provides a television set valued at £400 for the use of the employee throughout the fiscal year. The employee is not free to dispose of the television set and it therefore has no 'cash equivalent' value. No benefit is assessable.
▶ An employer provides free board and lodging to hotel staff. The benefit is non-transferrable and has no 'cash equivalent' value. No benefit is assessable.

Ancillary benefits to the provision of living accommodation follow this general rule and are only assessable on a lower-paid employee if they are convertible into cash (or under the previous section, if the employer discharges a liability of the employee). If the accommodation is job-related, no taxable benefit normally arises.

Directors and P11D employees

General principles

Directors and P11D employees are generally assessed on the cost of providing additional benefits for themselves or their families – less any contribution they make, unless the benefit comes within one of the classes to which special rules apply.

Where a gift is made outright of a new asset, the cost to the employer is self-evident. In other cases, the cost of providing the benefit is not so easily ascertained and certain rules must be followed:

- The gift of an asset that is not new, is the market value of the asset at the date of the gift.
- If the asset is made available for the use of the employee or his or her family or household throughout the fiscal year without ownership passing, the cost to the employer is taken to be the annual value of the asset plus any ancillary expenses incurred.
- The annual value of an asset for the above purposes is 20% of the market value of the asset when first made available for the use of the employee or, if the asset is rented or hired, the rental or hire charge if greater.
- The gift of an asset which has previously been available for the use of that or another taxpayer (and charged) is the greater of:
  - its market value at the date of the gift; and
  - its market value when first given less the aggregate benefits assessed.

Note that this rule discourages the practice of delaying the gift of an appreciating asset so that the taxable benefit can be spread over a number of years.

The application of these general principles can be illustrated by a number of examples.

- An employer gives an employee a suit of clothes, retail value £100 but the employer obtained a trade discount of 10%. The value of the benefit is the cost to the employer, £90. Note that a cash discount would not normally be passed on to the employee nor would any interest charged on a late payment.
- An employer provides a television set valued at £400 for the use of the employee throughout the fiscal year. The benefit would be £80 (20% of £400).
- An employer rents, at a cost of £10 per month, a television set valued at £400 for the use of the employee throughout the fiscal year. The benefit would be the greater of £80 (20% of £400) or £120 (12 × £10), that is, £120.
- An employer provides free board and lodging to hotel staff. The benefit is the cost to the employer. A recent House of Lords ruling (in the case of *Pepper* v. *Hart*) has clarified the meaning of 'cost to the employer' when applied to in-house benefits in kind as marginal cost (and not an average cost basis as was previously applied). Although the marginal cost depends on the individual circumstances, the following principles have been set out:
  - rail or bus travel by employees such that fare-paying passengers are not displaced involves no or negligible additional cost.
  - goods sold at a discount such that employees pay at least the wholesale price involves no or negligible net benefit.
  - teachers paying 15% or more of a school's normal fees involves no or negligible net benefit.
  - professional services not requiring additional employees or partners incur no or negligible cost to the employer provided that the employee meets the cost of any disbursements.
- An oil painting costing £1,000 was made available to X throughout 1991/92, 1992/93, and 1993/94 and was finally transferred to X for £400 on 6 April 1994 when it had a market value of £3,000. The benefit would be the greater of:

i)

	£
Market value at disposal	3,000
Less price paid	(400)
	£2,600

ii)

		£
Original market value		1,000
Less: Assessed	1991/92	(200)
	1992/93	(200)
	1993/94	(200)
		400
Less price paid		(400)
		Nil
Assessable benefit 1994/95		2,600

▶ The cost of a scholarship provided to an employee's child will be assessable as a benefit on the employee if it is deemed to have been given by reason of his employment.

Ancillary benefits connected with living accommodation

Ancillary benefits to the provision of living accommodation follow these general principles.

If the accommodation is job-related, the amount assessable in respect of ancillary benefits is restricted to ten per cent of the employee's net emoluments (excluding the ancillary benefits) less any contribution by the employee.

EXAMPLE 3.3

A receives a salary of £15,000 together with a company car (benefit £1,460). He pays 10% of his salary into an approved superannuation scheme. He occupies a company house which it is agreed is job-related. The following expenses are paid by his employers:

	£	
Lighting and heating	600	
Redecoration	800	
Gardener's wages	250	

Benefits assessable:		
	Lighting and heating	600
	Redecoration	800
	Gardener's wages	250
		1,650

	£
Net emoluments:	
Salary	15,000
Car benefit	1,460
	16,460
Less pension contributions	(1,500)
	14,960

Plus ancillary accommodation benefit restricted to 10% of £14,960	1,496
	16,456

Company cars available for private use

This section refers to motor vehicles of a 'private type'.

The value of the benefit for the use of a company car is established by reference to the manufacturer's list price of the car at the time the car was first registered. This price includes VAT, delivery charges and the list price of any 'extras' added to the car when it was first made available. Accessories added after the car was first made available will also be added to the list price if their cost exceeds £100. The list price may be reduced by up to £5,000 in respect of capital contributions made by the employee towards the cost of the car.

In the case of classic cars which are at least 15 years old by the end of the year of assessment, the market value will be substituted for the list price where the market value exceeds £15,000 and is greater than the list price.

A ceiling of £80,000 has been imposed on the figure on which the benefit will be calculated.

The full value of the benefit is 35% of the list price of the car. This benefit is then discounted by one-third where the employee travels at least 2,500 business miles per annum, and by two-thirds where the business travel exceeds 18,000 business miles per annum. Business miles are those which a person is necessarily obliged to do in the performance of the duties of his employment.

If the car is four years old or more by the end of the year of assessment, the benefit is then reduced by one-third.

Second cars are also taxed on their list price. However, there is no reduction for business mileage unless it exceeds 18,000 miles per annum, in which case the benefit is reduced by one-third.

Once the benefit has been determined it may be adjusted by the following factors:

- If the car is not available for the whole of the year of assessment, the benefit is reduced proportionately.
- If the car is incapable of being used for any continuous period of at least 30 days (for example, if it is being repaired), a proportionate reduction is also made.
- Payments by the employee for the private use of the car will reduce the benefit on a pound for pound basis.

The benefit covers all other expenses in respect of the car (for instance, road tax, insurance, repairs) with the exception of fuel for private motoring, mobile telephones and the provision of a chauffeur. This is the case whether these expenses are paid directly by the employer, a third party providing the car, or reimbursed to the employee.

A charge does not apply to 'pooled cars' which are treated as not having been available for the private use of any of the employees. A pooled car is one that satisfies all the following conditions:

- it is used by more than one employee, being available by reason in each case of their employment, and is used by none to the exclusion of the others
- the private use of each employee is incidental to the business use
- it is not normally kept overnight at or near the home of any of the employees.

Fuel provided for private motoring

In addition to the charge for the car itself, there will be an additional benefit if any fuel is provided for the employee's private use and is not paid for in full by the employee. This benefit is established by reference to a table (reproduced at the back of the book).

The fuel benefit as determined by the table (according to the cylinder capacity and the type of fuel on which it runs) is the benefit for a full fiscal year. This scale figure is adjusted to take into account if the car is not available for the full fiscal year. There is no adjustment with respect to the level of business mileage. There is no reduction if the employee pays for only part of his private fuel costs. Journeys between home and place of work are regarded as private motoring.

EXAMPLE 3.4

A was provided with company cars in 1994/95 as follows:

	6 April 1994 to 5 December 1994	6 December 1994 5 April 1995
Engine size	1800 cc	2300 cc
List price	£9,000	£14,500
First licensed	October 1991	December 1994
Running costs (inc private petrol)	£1,300	£1,500
Business mileage	8,500	9,000

Computations were as follows:

	£		£
Car benefit:			
6 April 1994–5 December 1994			
£9,000 × 35%	3,150		
Less one-third discount	(1,050)		
	2,100	× 8/12 =	1,400
6 December 1994–5 April 1995			
£14,500 × 35%	5,075		
Less two-thirds discount			
9,000 business miles in four months equates			
to 27,000 business miles per annum.	(3,383)		
	1,692	× 4/12 =	564
			1,964
Fuel benefit (petrol):			
6 April 1994–5 December 1994	810	× 8/12 =	540
6 December 1994–5 April 1995	1,200	× 4/12 =	400
			2,904

Chauffeur

Any costs of providing a chauffeur will always be an additional benefit assessable on the employee. To the extent that the chauffeur is used on journeys necessarily made in the performance of the employee's duties, the employee may claim a deduction under ICTA 1988, s. 198.

Company vans

Any employee with available private use of a van (3.5 tonnes or less) will be assessed in 1994/95 on a standard benefit of £500. (Vans more than four years old on 5 April 1995 – £350) This applies for a full fiscal year per van. It will be reduced if the van is available for less than a full fiscal year, in the same way that the car scale benefit is reduced: if private use of the van is shared between a number of employees, the standard charge will be apportioned between them; and any contribution made by the employees towards private use will be deducted. An employee can also claim for his benefit to be computed using the alternative figure of £5 per day of use.

The standard benefit includes fuel provided for private use. There is no benefit assessable on pooled vans. (These are defined as for pooled cars.)

Mobile telephones

Where an employee has a mobile telephone whether or not installed in a car, the taxable benefit is £200 if there is any private use not paid for in full by the employee. The standard charge is proportionately reduced where the telephone is not available for the full fiscal year, in the same way as for the car benefit.

Beneficial loans

Where an employee or a member of his or her family has a loan by reason of his or her employment at a beneficial rate of interest, the difference between the interest charged and that calculated by using an official rate is a taxable benefit. Loans made to employees on commercial terms by employers who lend to the general public will be exempt from charge. In addition, there is an exemption for small loans up to a total of £5,000 per employee. For the purpose of calculating the charge, all loans by the employer to the employee in the fiscal year will be aggregated and treated as one loan. The official rate of interest is amended as necessary to ensure that it remains broadly in line with mortgage rates. An average official rate of interest to be used for a fiscal year is also published. (Ten per cent will always be used for examination purposes.)

There are two methods of calculating the amount of the benefit:

▶ Simple average method – which will be applied unless an election is made by the taxpayer or notice is given by the inspector of taxes for the alternative method of calculation. In this case, the average loan is calculated by taking the loan outstanding at the beginning and end of the fiscal year (or on the dates on which it was made and discharged, if not in existence for the whole of the fiscal year).

The official rate of interest or, if the rate changed, the average rate is then applied to the average loan for the number of complete tax months for which it was in existence and from this, any interest paid is deducted.

▶ Precise method – by which the interest is calculated by applying the official rate to the loan outstanding on a day-to-day basis and then deducting any interest paid. This method is likely to be used where the balance of the loan has fluctuated widely during the fiscal year.

EXAMPLE 3.5

A had a balance on his loan account of £10,000 at 6 April 1994. He increased the loan by £7,500 on 20 January 1995. The loan agreement provides for interest to be charged at 3% per annum on the balance at the beginning of the fiscal year.

Method 1

Average loan $\dfrac{10{,}000 + 17{,}500}{2} = £13{,}750$

	£
13,750 × 10%	1,375
Less interest charged (10,000 × 3%)	(300)
Benefit	£1,075

INCOME FROM EMPLOYMENT IN THE UK

Method 2

$$10,000 \times \frac{289}{365} \times 10\% \qquad 792$$

$$17,500 \times \frac{76}{365} \times 10\% \qquad \underline{364}$$

$$1,156$$

Less interest charged (as above) (300)

Benefit 856

A would elect for the precise method.

If the loan is for a qualifying purpose (see Chapter 1) the assessable benefit is computed as normal and included as part of the taxpayer's emoluments. The taxpayer is then treated as having paid loan interest of the same amount as the assessable benefit. Relief for this notional interest is given as a tax credit.

Where any loan is wholly or partly written off, the amount written off is a taxable benefit in the fiscal year in which it is written off or waived (whether or not the taxpayer is still an employee). There are two exceptions to this rule:

- a loan written off on an employee's death
- a loan to an employee's relative from which the employee can show that he derived no benefit.

Payments on termination of office

This section applies only to payments which are income and excludes those payments which are of a capital nature (a question of fact). There are three categories of income payments, for income tax purposes, on termination of an office or employment:

- If the payment is taxable under the normal rules of Schedule E (by way of reward for services, past, present or future including any amount payable under the terms of a contract), it is taxable in full under PAYE at the time of payment.
- Some payments are specifically exempted from tax under ICTA 1988, s. 188:
  - payments made on termination of employment as a result of the employee's injury, disability or death
  - lump sum payments made under approved superannuation, retirement annuity schemes or personal pension plans
  - terminal grants and annuity payments to retiring members of the armed forces.
- Subject to the above, ICTA 1988, s. 148 brings into charge to tax under Schedule E any other payment made, whether under legal obligation or not, to any person (or person connected with that person) which is directly or indirectly connected with his or her termination of office or change in the function of that office or employment unless it can be shown to be capital in nature.

Payments brought into charge to tax as a result of this latter section are partially exempt. The first £30,000 is non-taxable, and any further amounts are taxable in full.

The cost of outplacement counselling provided to redundant employees, previously included in s. 148, is now exempt.

For this purpose, statutory redundancy payments and any payments made under the Employment Protection (Consolidation) Act 1978, which are exempt from tax under the normal rules of Schedule E are potentially taxable under s. 148, that is, they count as part of the non-taxable £30,000.

Wages paid in lieu of notice are normally within this category unless the facts indicate that the payment includes remuneration for work done.

The taxation treatment of termination payments has become more complex following a change of Inland Revenue practice for pension purposes: an ex gratia payment made in connection with an employee's retirement will be regarded as providing a relevant benefit under an approved pension arrangement and therefore will be taxable or not in the same way as other relevant benefits. Further guidance is awaited from the Inland Revenue who have so far only confirmed that genuine payments for compensation for loss of office are not relevant benefits.

Other payments and benefits

Lump sum payments made to a person taking up employment ('golden hellos') may either be inducements (non-taxable) or emoluments (taxable). The distinction is a question of fact. In *Shilton* v. *Wilmshurst* (1991) a transfer fee paid by his old club to a professional footballer was taxable as an emolument of his new employment.

Suggestion scheme awards are not taxable by Inland Revenue concession provided there is a formally run scheme open to all employees.

Long-service awards to employees and directors with 20 or more years of service, of tangible articles or shares in the company, will not be taxed by concession provided the cost does not exceed £20 per year of service and it is at least ten years since a previous such award.

Gifts (other than cash) from a third party up to £100 in value per fiscal year are also not taxable by concession provided that they are provided in circumstances similar to entertainment and hospitality vouchers (see above, pp 37–8) and are not part of a reciprocal arrangement.

Payments made to employees or their families under sick-pay arrangements entered into by the employer are taxable, whether actually paid by the employer or by some other person, for example, a trustee or insurance company. To avoid a 'double charge' to tax on the higher-paid employee, the cost to the employer of providing such sick-pay cover for these employees is not taxed as a benefit in kind. (This arrangement is only concerned with employer-financed schemes and does not apply to permanent health insurance policies entered into and financed by the individual, the benefits from which are paid to the employee during absence through sickness or disability and are assessable under Schedule D Case III. By concession, no assessment is raised unless the benefit continues for more than 12 months.)

No taxable benefit will arise where in-house sports and recreational facilities are provided by employers for use by staff generally and used wholly or mainly by them. The exemption will also cover facilities provided by an employer's association and facilities run or managed externally. A similar relief is available for child care facilities provided by the employer.

Where additional expenditure is incurred as a consequence of a change of residence necessitated by employment, the employer may pay the relocation expenses on the employee's behalf. No assessment will be raised on the benefit up to a ceiling of £8,000 whether the amount paid is for new employees or for employees transferring to another location within the organisation. Employees will no longer be required to sell their original home to qualify and any payment by an employer to compensate for loss on sale will not qualify. Tax relief on beneficial bridging loans will still be given and the existing statutory reliefs for international travel remain available.

Contributions by employers to extra ongoing costs incurred by employees moved to higher-cost housing areas have in the past been non-taxable by extra-statutory concession. The concession was withdrawn with effect from 6 April 1993.

Incentive schemes

Profit-related pay

Profit-related pay (PRP) was introduced in 1987. The concept was not new but the introduction of tax privileges was an innovation. The purpose was to encourage employees through the tax system to accept profit-related remuneration as a substitute for increases in basic pay.

Subject to certain limits, and provided it is paid under a scheme which has been registered with the Inland Revenue, an employee's profit-related pay can be exempt from income tax. An employee can only receive tax free PRP from one scheme.

Benefits to the employee

Profit-related pay up to a limit of the lower of £4,000 or 20% of total pay per profit-making year (that is, non profit related pay for PAYE purposes, excluding benefits, plus the profit related pay itself) qualifies for full tax relief.

For example, for an employee earning £20,500 per annum, plus £4,500 profit related pay, (for the profit period ending in 1994/95) and paying £1,000 into a superannuation scheme the PRP qualifying for relief, for the employer's year ending 31 March 1995, will be the lowest of:

- £4,000
- £4,800 being 20% (20,500 − 1,000 + 4,500)
- £4,500 the profit related pay itself.

The relief amounts to £4,000 tax free, a tax saving to a higher-rate taxpayer of £1,600.

How does a PRP scheme work?

The employer makes a contribution to the scheme based on a percentage of the profits of a 12-month profit period of an employment unit. The contribution goes into a PRP 'pool' to be distributed to eligible employees.

The scheme must have written rules setting out the way in which an employer's contribution to the scheme will be ascertained and the way in which the pool will be distributed to employees. The contribution is a legal commitment by the employer, who may not retain any discretion over the amount paid into the pool or the manner in which sums are distributed to employees.

The whole of the PRP pool must be distributed each year (either on an annual, quarterly, monthly or even weekly basis) and eligible employees must participate on similar terms. The pool may be divided by reference to basic pay, total pay, length of service or any similar basis or combination of bases.

PAYE need not be applied to the amount of PRP which is anticipated to be exempt, but any under-deduction of PAYE resulting from a miscalculation of the amount of tax free PRP to which an employee is entitled for the year, will be recoverable from the employer and not the employee. The whole amount of PRP is liable to National Insurance.

Employer's contributions

The profits of the employment unit are determined according to normal accounting principles and must be audited. The following adjustments (provided consistently applied) may or may not be included:

- interest receivable and similar income
- interest payable and similar charges
- goodwill

- tax on profit or loss on ordinary activities
- research and development costs
- extraordinary items.

The contribution must be calculated under either Method A (a fixed percentage of the defined profit) or Method B (a percentage of the pool for the previous profit period).

The scheme rules may provide for a nil contribution if profits are lower than a specified amount or for a maximum contribution by the employer (say 160% of the amount that would have been payable in the base year or preceding profit period).

Employment unit

An 'employment unit' may be either the whole or a part of a business provided that the 'unit' can be identified and that it is conducted with a view to making a profit (for instance, a particular department or division of the company).

An employer registering one or more schemes as above will also be able to register a separate scheme or schemes for general or central units (for instance, a Head Office or Research and Development Division) – with PRP based on the profits of the whole undertaking rather than on that particular unit. The number of employees covered in this case will be restricted to 33% of the number of employees covered by the other conventional schemes.

Eligible employees

At least 80% of the eligible employees in the employment unit must be included in the scheme (part-time employees and employees with less than three years' service may be excluded).

Eligible employees are those that do not have a material interest (that is, control, together with associates, of more than 25% of the company's ordinary share capital) in the company. The remuneration of ineligible employees is non-deductible in determining the profits for purposes of the employer's contribution.

Profit-sharing schemes

Companies may set up schemes which, satisfying specified conditions, receive Inland Revenue approval and allow shares to be transferred to the ownership of employees without any or with only partial liability to income tax.

The reliefs available with respect to the transfer of the shares do not extend to any income tax liability arising on dividends from the date the shares are appropriated to the participant or to any capital gains tax liability arising on disposals for more than their original value.

Benefits to the employee

The initial market value of shares which may be appropriated to any one employee in a year of assessment is the greater of £3,000 or 10% of his or her taxable salary of the current or previous year, subject to an overall maximum of £8,000. Taxable salary is salary for PAYE purposes, that is after deductions under the net pay arrangement (see above) and exclusive of benefits. All eligible members must be able to participate on similar terms except that the number of shares appropriated may vary with respect to remuneration, length of service, or similar factors.

The shares must be part of the ordinary share capital and either quoted or of a company not under the control of another, unless the controlling company is a quoted 'open' company (not a close company, see Chapter 25). They must be fully paid, irredeemable shares and not subject to restrictions unless the restrictions apply to the whole class of shares.

Eligible employees

At the time the shares are appropriated to them, eligible employees must be resident and ordinarily resident in the UK, and must have been directors or employees for at least five years. They must not belong to another such scheme in a company under the same control and must not at any time within the previous 12 months have had a material interest (25% + holding) in a close company whose shares are involved.

How does a profit-sharing scheme operate?

The money allocated to the trustees by the company is treated as a trading expense, and therefore deductible from the Schedule D Case I profits of the company for tax purposes. It is used to purchase shares for appropriation to participants in accordance with a pre-determined formula but the shares must be held in trust for them for a period of retention. The period of retention ends on the earliest of the following:

- the second anniversary of the date on which they were appropriated
- the date of the participant's death
- the date on which the participant reaches pensionable age
- the date on which the participant ceases to be an employee of the company by reason of injury, disability or redundancy.

The release date is the fifth anniversary of the date on which the shares were appropriated to the participant. After the release date, there will be no income tax liability on the realisation of the shares and the shares need no longer be retained by the trustees beyond this date.

The trustees may be instructed to dispose of the participant's shares after the period of retention but before the release date. In this case there will be a charge to tax under Schedule E on the 'appropriate percentage' of the lower of the initial market value or the market value (sale proceeds) at the time of the disposal.

The appropriate percentages are as follows:

Period after appropriation date	Death of participant	Injury, disability, redundancy, retirement	Other
Up to 4 years	Nil	50%	100%
4–5 years	Nil	50%	75%
More than 5 years	Nil	Nil	Nil

Shares are deemed to be disposed of on a FIFO basis.

EXAMPLE 3.6

A Ltd had set up an approved profit-sharing scheme for its employees. The market value of the shares when acquired by the trustees and appropriated to the participants on 6 April 1990 was £1.10 and this had risen to £1.20 on 6 April 1991. The price has continued to rise. X, an employee, was eligible to receive £500 worth of shares per annum and on 15 August 1994, he decided to sell 750 shares at the current market value of £3.00.

The shares are disposed of on a FIFO basis and therefore 750 of the shares which had been appropriated to him as follows were disposed of:

a) 1990/91 500/1.10, thus, 455 shares appropriated

These shares had been held for between 4 and 5 years.

Lower of:	1) Sale proceeds (455 @ £3)	£1,365
	2) Original value	£500

Appropriate percentage 75%
Assessable under Schedule E (75% of £500)   £375

(b) 1991/92 500/1.20, thus, 417 shares appropriated

These shares had been held for less than 4 years.

Lower of	1) Sale proceeds (750–455 @ £3)	£885
	2) Original value (750–455 @ £1.20)	£354

Appropriate percentage 100%
Assessable under Schedule E (100% of £354)   £354
Total assessable 1994/95   £729

In addition, a charge to capital gains tax may arise on the excess of the disposal proceeds over the acquisition value (£1.10 and £1.20)

Share options

A share option is a right to buy a certain number of shares in a company at a fixed price at a future date. Depending on the option price and the value of the shares at various times, there are a number of potential charges to income tax under Schedule E; these are as follows:

- on the difference between the market value of the shares at the date the option is granted and the option price
- on the difference between the market value of the shares at the date the option is exercised and the option price less any amount assessed under the point above
- on the growth in value of the shares from the date of acquisition until the earlier of:
  - the expiry of seven years
  - the date of disposal
  - the date when all restrictions/conditions attaching to the shares are removed.

Finally, there would be a liability to capital gains tax on the eventual disposal of the shares (the option price plus any amounts assessed under Schedule E above being allowable costs).

In addition, if the purchase price of the shares is lent or unpaid there will be a deemed loan of that amount with a corresponding benefit in kind under the beneficial loan provisions.

However, despite the tax penalties above, there is general recognition that wider share ownership should be encouraged. One way of doing this is through the profit-sharing schemes listed above.

There are also two forms of approved share option scheme which receive more favourable tax treatment, which we shall now deal with.

SAYE (Save As You Earn) share option scheme

Directors and employees of companies may be granted options to acquire shares under schemes linked to a building society or government Save As You Earn scheme and there will be no income tax liability on the grant or on the exercise of the option.

This type of share option scheme operates as follows:

- The money to purchase the shares under the option must arise from the proceeds of a certified contractual savings scheme and the rights cannot normally be exercised before the bonus date (that is usually five or seven years after commencement) or more than six months after the bonus date. Exceptions to this rule are made for the death of the employee or, under certain circumstances, if the employee leaves the office or employment.
- Employees' contributions to the SAYE scheme cannot be more than £250 per month. The minimum contribution that the scheme may impose cannot be more than £10 per month.
- The price at which the shares can be acquired must not be less than 80% of the market value of the shares of the same class at the time the option is granted. Also, the total purchase price must not exceed the proceeds of the SAYE contract.
- Conditions as to the type of shares and the eligibility of employees participating are as for profit-sharing schemes above.

FA 1984 share option scheme

Options granted after 5 April 1984 are eligible to come within these schemes. The rules relating to this type of option scheme are more liberal. There will usually be no income tax liability on the grant nor on the exercise of the option (provided the scheme is still approved), nor on any increase in value of the shares between the date of the grant and the exercise of the option.

It need not be linked to a Save As You Earn scheme and there is no requirement for the scheme to be made available to all employees on equal terms. The employees may be granted options to acquire shares in their own company, its controlling company or a consortium member. It can be operated in conjunction with a SAYE related scheme or a profit-sharing scheme or both. Also, the individual employee may participate in more than one type of scheme.

This type of scheme operates as follows:

- The option price of the shares at the date the option is granted should not be 'significantly less' than the market value of shares of the same class (the Inland Revenue will agree values in advance), unless the scheme is operated in conjunction with an approved 'all-employee' share scheme when the option price in the approved discretionary scheme may be at a discount of up to 15%.
- The aggregate value of shares for which the employee may at any time hold unexercised options (under this or any other approved scheme) may not exceed the greatest of:
  - £100,000
  - four times relevant emoluments of the current year
  - four times relevant emoluments of the preceding year.

  Relevant emoluments are pay for PAYE purposes (that, is after deductions under net pay arrangements and excluding benefits) as defined in the schemes above.
- Participation is limited to full-time directors (25 hours plus per week) and qualifying employees (20 hours per week) but the scheme need not be open to all such employees. Within limits the personal representatives of a deceased employee and employees who have left the employment may exercise options.
- The shares over which options may be granted must meet similar conditions as for SAYE related option schemes and profit-sharing schemes.
- Options may not be exercised before three, or after ten, years from the granting of the option, nor may options be exercised more frequently than at three-yearly intervals (although two or more options may be exercised on the same day) except on death.

The purpose of the last condition is to restrict benefits to those employees with a long-term commitment to the company and to avoid the scheme being used as a means of remuneration. It is possible to limit the scheme to a selected group of employees and extend it to any companies it controls.

Employee share ownership plans (ESOPs)

ESOPs, also referred to as ESOTs, are designed to encourage further UK-resident companies to promote employee share ownership through trusts set up for the purpose. Trusts are already used in profit-sharing schemes, but ESOP trusts will operate differently in some fundamental respects:

- Shares may be acquired by the trust from a fresh issue or more usually on the open market. The trustees' functions must include receiving sums of money from the founding company and other monies (by loans or otherwise) in order to acquire and distribute shares (LIFO applies).
- The trusts will be permitted to borrow to acquire shares rather than relying entirely on funds provided by the company. The Companies Act 1989 permits companies (including public companies) to guarantee external borrowing.
- The trusts will be able to hold on to the shares for up to seven years, for example, to accumulate funds to repay borrowings.
- The trusts may, in the case of unquoted companies, provide a market-place in which employees can dispose of their shares.

A company may buy its own shares lawfully using an ESOP. The dilution of earnings per share associated with the previous schemes is avoided.

This type of trust already existed but until now has not benefited from specific tax reliefs. Now, payments by companies to an ESOP trust set up to acquire and distribute shares to its employees will qualify for corporation tax relief, provided certain conditions are met. The key conditions relate to the trust benefiting all employees on similar terms, to a majority of the trustees being independent of the company and of those who have or have had a material interest in the company and to the trust being administered in the proper manner.

There are provisions to impose a tax charge equivalent to the corporation tax relief given if a trust breaks the conditions for approval.

'Administered in the proper manner' means that monies received by the trustees must be used, within nine months of the company's year end, for one or more of the following purposes:

- acquisition of shares in the founding company
- payment of interest/capital on borrowings
- payment of expenses
- distribution of monies to beneficiaries.

The trust itself will not benefit from any tax reliefs and will be liable to income tax and capital gains tax in the normal way. Employees receiving shares will also be liable to income tax if they pay less than the market value for them. However, it is envisaged that the trust will operate in conjunction with profit-sharing schemes and approved share option schemes set up under previous legislation referred to above and that shares will be distributed to employees in this way (no income tax liability will then arise).

Provided certain conditions are satisfied, capital gains tax hold-over relief is available to encourage owners of shares in unquoted companies to sell shares to qualifying ESOPs.

National Insurance contributions for employees

National insurance contributions are traditionally not regarded as a tax but have a serious impact both on an employee's net pay and on the employer's payroll cost.

Class 1 contributions affect employees and their employers and are charged on gross earnings. In principle, earnings should be the same whether the NIC rules, tax rules, statutory sick pay rules or state benefit rules are being applied. However, case law decisions in one area are not binding in other areas and indeed the legislation in each area differs. Earnings for NIC purposes (for an employed person) is remuneration. Social security case law defines remuneration as:

- any sum paid as a wage or salary
- excluding the value of any benefit in kind and sums paid in cash by someone other than the employer
- including the following to the extent that it represents a profit or surplus in the hands of the employee: 'a sum which is agreed to be paid by way of reimbursement or on account of expenditure incurred by the employee'.

The Finance Act 1994 introduced new anti-avoidance legislation in response to the increasing use of payments in kind to avoid national insurance contributions.

The new regulations make liable to NIC any payment in the form of a beneficial interest in an asset capable of being sold on a recognised investment exchange or the London Bullion Market. This catches payments in the form of gold bullion, other traded commodities, or any vouchers for such commodities.

Such payments were previously taxed as a benefit in kind. The PAYE regulations are also being amended to treat such payments as pay, thus preventing the use of this method to delay the payment of income tax.

The rate of contributions for 1994/95 is as follows.

Table 3.2 National Insurance contributions 1994/95

Weekly earnings	Employee % of all earnings	Employer % of all earnings
£0–£56.99	0	0
£57–£99.99		3.6
£100–£144.99	2% on first £56.99	5.6
£145–£199.99	10% on balance up to	7.6
£200 and over	£430 maximum	10.2

These weekly limits are increased pro rata for four-weekly and other pay intervals.

If the employer has 'contracted out' because it operates an occupational pension scheme, the above rates are reduced by 1.8% (employee) between the upper and lower limit and 3% (employer)

Employees

These rates are per employment. Where an employee pays NIC in more than one employment such that he or she exceeds the maximum limit, he or she may apply to defer the liability in some of the posts or alternatively apply for a refund at the end of the fiscal year.

The liability to NIC is calculated for non-directors based on the normal payment interval and therefore an NIC advantage can be obtained for employees normally earning below the weekly maximum by staggering the payment interval of bonuses, commissions and so on. The effect is for the maximum to be exceeded on these occasions and the incidence of NIC to be reduced.

EXAMPLE 3.7

Compute the NIC liability for August 1994 for Mary (an employee) who is paid the following

- Four-weekly salary of £1,500
- Bonus for year ended 30/6/94 paid August 1994 of £500.

August 1994			
Gross pay £2,000	NIC	$4 \times 57 \times 2\% =$	£4.56
(other months gross pay £1,500)		$4 \times (420 - 57) \times 10\% =$	£145.20
Class I NIC liability			£149.76

This does not apply to directors. A director cannot pay himself a small weekly wage for 51 weeks and then a large director's bonus (in excess of the maximum) in week 52 and only pay maximum NIC in that one week. His NIC will be based on a weekly or monthly equivalent of his total remuneration (that is, total remuneration including director's bonus divided by 52 or 12). From a practical point of view this is done by calculating the NIC on a cumulative basis over the fiscal year.

National Insurance contributions are collected via the PAYE scheme and remitted by the employer at the same time as the PAYE. They are not a deductible expense for Schedule E purposes.

Employers

The incidence of NIC contributions on the employer's cost is significant and warrants careful attention. As an employee's weekly earnings move from one band to the next, there is a disproportionate increase in NIC as the increased rate is charged on the whole of the weekly earnings and not just on the increase. Job splitting can therefore save NIC. Once weekly earnings exceed £200, the NIC cost is 10.2% of payroll cost.

Employers are required to pay Class 1A NIC at 10.2% on the benefit of company cars and private fuel provided to employees (no charge is made on employees). Any increase in the benefits also therefore has an inpact on the employer's NIC liability. The employer's contributions represent a staff cost and are a deductible expense under Schedule D Cases I and II (see Chapter 15).

Rewarding executives – planning

A company will usually wish to reward its executives with a remuneration package which is tax efficient for the company and which provides an incentive to the employees to perform well. In some cases there may also be an attempt to make the package such that the employee can only receive maximum benefits by staying with the company (for instance, FA84 Share Option Scheme) – referred to as 'golden handcuffs'. Most benefits provided to employees by virtue of their employment are liable to income tax but some forms of remuneration provide a tax advantage either to the employer or the employee.

Changes in income tax rates and the capital gains tax structure may affect the way remuneration packages are structured. National Insurance must also be taken into account.

Cash is now a more attractive form of remuneration than in the past due to reductions in the top rates of income tax while, by way of contrast, the changes to the capital gains tax structure have made schemes to provide remuneration in forms subject to capital gains tax relatively less attractive.

The most appropriate method of rewarding executives in a tax-efficient manner will vary from company to company and may depend on the position of the executive within the company. Profit-sharing schemes, approved share option schemes and ESOPs are all incentive schemes with tax savings. The judicious planning of benefits-in-kind packages can minimise exposure to income tax and NIC: in-house benefits; small loans up to £5,000; private use contributions for cars allocated to car use not fuel (making sure the paperwork is correct!).

Unlike the benefit of shares issued under the above schemes or any assessable benefit in kind other than cars and fuel for private use, payments of salary and bonuses (and profit-related pay) are subject to National Insurance contributions (NIC). The use of 'bonuses in kind' should be considered. A bonus in the form of a holiday, a case of wine or even a house extension would not atract NIC provided that the employer was not discharging a contractual liability of the employee.

Although National Insurance is not a tax, the abolition of the upper earnings limit for employer's contributions virtually makes it a payroll tax on the employer equivalent to 10.2% on the employees' total earnings. It is, therefore, a sizeable expense. It must be considered whether part of an employee's overall remuneration can be provided in a form which is disregarded for National Insurance purposes – perhaps, dividends or non-car benefits in kind.

There is, however, a disadvantage to this approach depending on the age of the executive. For those executives thinking about pensions, dividends and often benefits in kind do not count as final remuneration for determining pension benefits.

Summary

▶ Emoluments deriving from an office or employment include all salaries, wages, bonuses, fees, commissions and 'profits whatsoever' irrespective of who pays them. The definition is very wide and it is necessary to study some of the cases to appreciate this.
▶ Expenses deductible, on the other hand, are very narrowly defined. Again it is necessary to study some of the cases to appreciate exactly how strict the rules can be.
▶ The basis of assessment under Schedule E is the amount received in the fiscal year.
▶ The assessment of benefits in kind varies depending on whether the employee is described as a director or P11D employee or as a P9D employee. The test to establish into which category an employee falls should be understood as should the alternative assessments.
▶ Means of rewarding employees tax efficiently and at the same time, providing incentives for them to perform well are becoming increasingly important with tax savings being made available for government-approved schemes.
▶ National Insurance contributions are a sizeable expense and must therefore be a major consideration when evaluating means of rewarding employees.

Self test questions

1   Is it true that only directors and employees earning £8,500 per annum or more are assessable on the additional benefit arising from the provision of living accommodation with a cost greater than £75,000?

2   Robert, who had a salary of £12,000 per annum, was given a dishwasher by his employer. It cost the employer £400. The retail price was £450. Is a benefit assessable and if so, how much?

3   John has had a company car throughout the fiscal year (1950 cc and less than 4 years old). The car has a list price of £12,000. He did 20,000 business miles in the year and 5,000 private miles. His employer paid for all the petrol but he paid £300 towards the cost. Calculate the assessable benefits for the fiscal year 1994/95.

4   The employer reimbursed John's car parking costs incurred while he was at work. Is this an assessable benefit?

5   When Alan received a new company car, his old company car was sold to him for £1,000. It had a market value of £1,500. Does a taxable benefit arise and if so how?

6   On being made redundant, Anne received a non-contractual terminal payment of £35,000 and statutory redundancy pay of £4,000. How much is taxable?

7   Under an approved profit-related pay scheme, what is the maximum profit-related pay on which tax relief is available?

8   Under an approved profit-sharing scheme, what is the maximum value of shares which can be appropriated to an employee in 1994/95?

9   Mr J. King, a UK resident aged 31 years, is production manager of a manufacturing company in the north of England at a salary of £32,000 per annum. After several successful years, Mr King is made the following offers of employment by two companies in another part of the UK, which will require him to move his home with effect from 1 April 1994.

   a) Delta plc proposes an annual salary of £40,000, medical health insurance of £1,250 per annum for himself and his family and 1,000 ordinary £1 shares valued at £3.50 each from a profit-sharing scheme approved by the Revenue under ICTA 1988, s. 185. It will also lend him £80,000 at 5% per annum to assist in purchasing a house outside London. His removal expenses, estimated at £3,500, will be reimbursed in full by Delta plc. He will also be given an annual allowance of £1,000 for the next five years to compensate for the higher costs of living in London as compared to the north of England.

   His duties will generally include a two months' continuous period visiting company locations in Europe and USA. Expenses for such a trip paid by the company are expected to be: travel and hotel, £4,600; medical insurance, £250; expenses of visit by his wife and 17-year-old daughter – travel £1,100, hotels, £950.

   He will have the sole use of a company-owned car, 3,500 cc, costing £30,000 in 1992: its annual running expenses met by the company will include fuel (diesel) £1,150; insurance £490, chauffeur's wages £6,500 per annum; estimated business mileage is 20,000 for the year.

   b) Kappa Ltd would contract to pay him £37,500 per annum. He will have the sole use, rent free, of a company owned flat, gross annual value £25,000 in London recently purchased for £150,000 and furnished at a cost of £20,000. He will also have use of a car, 3,000 cc, costing £25,000 in 1993, mileage for which will be 15,000 a year for business and 5,000 private. All running expenses including petrol will be paid by the company. Education fees for his daughter will be paid by the company up to £6,750 per annum.

   He will have an option under a scheme approved in terms of ICTA 1988, s. 185 to purchase 2,500 ordinary shares in Kappa Ltd for £5 each between 6 April 1997 and 6 April 2000: at April 1994, the date the option will be granted, the company's shares will be worth at least £6 and the managing director hopes their value will increase to £9.50 at least by 1999. Kappa Ltd will also agree to pay him £50,000 if it terminates his contract before 6 April 2000.

Mr King will pay £100 to the employment agency who found him the position in consideration of special advice and assistance given by the agency and annual subscriptions of £145 to a recognised professional body and £385 to a golf club where he expects to meet business acquaintances. He will also pay £1,000 for new clothing of a standard considered necessary for either of the new positions.

You are required to prepare brief notes for an interview with Mr King on the tax consequences of each of these proposals. Assume that the official rate of interest is 10%.

Answers on pages 560–562

Taxation of Income from Property and Investments

CHAPTER 4

The purpose of this chapter is to consider the taxation treatment of income from property and a variety of financial investments; to describe the income chargeable under Schedule A, Schedule D Case III and Schedule D Case VI and the basis of assessment under each. Tax legislation designed to encourage saving and investment through tax incentives is considered as it refers to pensions, life assurance policies, personal equity plans, and the Enterprise Investment Scheme.

Income from property

The Schedules and Cases apply to income from land and buildings as follows:

Schedule A	Income from the letting of land and unfurnished property in the UK (including ground rents and sporting rights) plus premiums received on the granting of short leases
Schedule D Case VI	Income from furnished lettings in the UK
Schedule D Case V	Income from any of the above sources arising outwith the UK, that is, income from foreign possessions (see Overseas activities).

Income from the occupation of commercial woodlands has not been taxable since 1988. On the same basis, losses arising are not trading losses and no relief is available for such losses.

Schedule A

Income assessable

This covers not only rents, but also certain incidental receipts from land such as feu duties, payments for sporting rights, easements, ground rents and wayleaves. Premiums received on the grant of a short lease are also assessable.

It does not, however, cover loan and mortgage interest, mineral rents and royalties, or the occupation of commercial woodland.

Basis of assessment

The landlord is assessable on the income which becomes due and payable in the year of assessment whether or not he receives it (prepayments and accruals are ignored).

Rental agreements usually specify how the rent is to be paid. This may be at any specified interval (for instance, annually, quarterly, monthly or weekly) either in advance or in arrears. If the agreement specifies payment by reference to the usual quarter days, this would mean 25 March, 24 June, 29 September and 25 December.

EXAMPLE 4.1

A lets a property at an annual rent of £12,000 per annum payable quarterly in advance on the usual quarter days. As from 29 September 1993, the rent is increased to £16,000 per annum.

Compute the income assessable under Schedule A for 1994/95.

		£
Rent due and payable in 1994/95:	24 June 1994	3,000
	29 September 1994	4,000
	25 December 1994	4,000
	25 March 1995	4,000
		15,000

Relief is not available for arrears of rent unless it is proven to be irrecoverable (after any reasonable steps have been taken to enforce payment) or that it was waived to avoid causing hardship to the tenant. If the rent is subsequently received after relief has been given, the Inland Revenue must be notified within six months in order that the assessment can be amended.

The normal due date for tax under Schedule A is 1 January in the year of assessment. This is before the income for the year can be ascertained (tenants may leave, the property may be unoccupied for some or all of the time). It is usual for the Inland Revenue to estimate the amount assessable on the basis of the previous year's net Schedule A income and to adjust the amount assessed after the end of the year of assessment when the final income is known.

Permitted deductions

Under the general rules, expenses, in order to be deductible, must relate to the property comprised in the lease during the currency of the lease while in the ownership of the landlord. They should not be separately reimbursed to the landlord by any other consideration.

The main categories of deductions are:

- maintenance, repairs, insurance and property management costs
- any other services which the landlord is obliged to provide under the terms of the lease
- water rates and rates/council tax to which the occupier is liable if paid and not recovered by the landlord (other than from rent received)
- rents and ground rents payable to a superior landlord.

Any interest paid is not a 'permitted deduction' but may be deductible as a charge on income if it is eligible interest paid on a loan for a qualifying purpose (that is for the purchase or improvement of land and buildings let commercially – see Chapter 1 for the detailed rules). There is no limit to the amount of the qualifying loan but the maximum interest deductible in any year is limited to the net letting income from that or any other property. Unrelieved interest can be carried forward and deducted from letting income in future years up to the amount of the letting income in these years.

Expenses are deductible from the income arising from a particular property and a particular lease on that property and computations are usually laid out on that basis. (However, see below where pooling arrangements are possible provided there is no owner-occupation). They are normally deductible in the fiscal year in which payment is made but if relief cannot be given in that year (because there is insufficient income), deduction will be allowed in the year in which the payment became due.

Rates is a topical issue and may cause problems. Business rates still exist and if levied on let property are a deductible expense. Rates on domestic property have been superseded by the community charge (poll tax) and, now (1993), the council tax. The council tax is primarily a liability of the occupier and, if paid by a landlord of let property, will be deductible.

In addition, capital allowances may be available on plant used for the maintenance, repair or management of the property. Also, industrial buildings allowance may be available on qualifying industrial buildings let for industrial use (see Chapter 16).

Expenditure incurred in void periods

Under the general rules above, only that expenditure which was incurred during the currency of the lease of the premises to which the payment relates is deductible.

A void period is one during which the property is neither occupied by the landlord nor let. Expenditure incurred during a void period may be deducted provided that the void period either:

- immediately follows and is followed by a period of letting at full rent
- begins with the acquisition of the property and is followed by a period of letting at full rent.

Occupation by the landlord in the void period or immediately preceding a void period may therefore prevent expenses in the void period being deducted. Similarly, the existence of a lease at less than a full rent may also prevent expenses in the void period being deducted.

The purpose of these restrictions is to ensure that, for example, the cost of repairs making good dilapidation resulting from a period of owner occupation cannot be relieved.

Relief for losses

Schedule A losses may only be relieved against Schedule A profits. There is no facility to deduct them from the taxpayer's other income.

The manner in which relief is available depends on the nature of the lease. There are two main types of leases: leases at full rent; and leases not at full rent (or at nominal rent). They are now outlined.

Leases at full rent

Leases at full rent can be defined as leases from which the landlord, taking one year with another, expects to recover his or her costs under the lease. It does not necessarily mean an open market rent or a commercial rent.

There are two types of lease at full rent:

- **Landlord repairing lease (LRL)** – This is a lease under which the landlord is required to maintain the property both inside and out.

  Profits and losses under landlord repairing leases may be pooled. Any net loss may be carried forward to the following fiscal year and deducted from the pool of profits and losses in that year provided that the property on which the loss arose is still owned and is not in owner-occupation
- **Tenant's repairing lease (TRL)** – This is a lease under which the tenant is responsible for all or substantially all repairs other than structural repairs to the property.

  Profits and losses under tenant's repairing leases may not be pooled. All profits on such leases are taxable but relief may be obtained for losses as follows:
  - a loss on a tenant's repairing lease may be deducted from the 'pool' of net profit (if any) on landlord repairing leases of current year or, if none, of future years; and/or
  - it may be carried forward and deducted from future profits arising on leases of the same property (not necessarily to the same tenant).

Leases not at full rent (or leases at nominal rent)
These leases can be defined as leases at rents which are not sufficient, taking one year with another, to meet the landlord's costs under the lease.

Profits under leases not at a full rent are taxable but losses arising under such leases may only be carried forward and deducted from future profits on the same lease.

EXAMPLE 4.2

Fred has several properties in the UK which he lets:

Shop 1
A butcher's shop on a tenant's repairing lease. The annual rental is £1,660 expiring on 29 September 1994 and the lease was renewed on that date at £2,360 per annum for seven years.

Shop 2
A shop selling textiles also on a tenant's repairing lease. The annual rental is £1,500 under a seven year lease expiring on 25 March 1996. The quarter's rent due on 25 March 1995 was not paid until 30 April 1995.

Shop 3
A shop selling light fittings. This was let to a relative of Fred at an annual rental of £100 when a commercial rent would have been £1,200. Fred's relative is responsible for all outgoings, with the exception of insurance.

Shop 4
This shop has been let on a tenant's repairing lease at an annual rental of £3,500 until 24 June 1994, when the tenant, who had been selling clothing, informed Fred that he could not afford to pay the rent and vacated the premises forthwith. Fred agreed through his agent to re-let the premises to a new tenant from 25 March 1995, who would be selling pottery imported from Scandinavia. The new rental was £4,000 per annum for ten years.

The rents are due in advance on the normal English quarter days. Details of expenditure in the year ended 5 April 1995 were:

	Shop 1 £	Shop 2 £	Shop 3 £	Shop 4 £
Insurance	97	123	95	210
Ground rent	20	10	–	100
Repairs, decorating	–	–	–	1,527
Accountancy	25	25	25	25
Bank charges	10	10	10	10

Fred employs agents to collect the rents of shops 1, 2 and 4. He pays them 10% when they collect the rent.

(Note on repairs: Included in the figure of £1,527 is £725 which was spent on decorating the premises in July and August 1994)

Calculate the Schedule A assessment for 1994/95.

Leases at full rent – tenant's repairing leases

	Shop 1 TRL £	Shop 2 TRL £	Shop 4 TRL £
Rent receivable	415	375	
	590	375	
	590	375	
	590	375	1,000
	2,185	1,500	1,000
Less Agent's commission	(218)	(112)	(100)
Less Insurance	(97)	(123)	(210)
Less Accountancy	(25)	(25)	(25)
Less Repairs			(1,527)
Less Ground rent	(20)	(10)	(100)
	1,825	1,230	(962)

Bank charges do not fall within any of the categories of deductions.

Decorating costs (£725) are assumed to be the cost of making good dilapidations during the previous lease. July/August was part of a void period.

Lease not at full rent (assuming £100 is not sufficient, taking one year with another, to cover the landlord's outgoings under the lease, the fact that it is not the commercial rent is irrelevant).

	NR Shop 3 £
Rent receivable	100
Less Accountancy	(25)
Less Insurance	(95)
	(20)

Schedule A assessment 1994/95

		£
Tenant repairing leases	Shop 1	1,825
	Shop 2	1,230
		3,055

There are no profits on landlord repairing leases against which the loss (£962) on shop 4 can be set off. Therefore, it will be carried forward and deducted from future profits on the same property. The loss (£20) on the lease not at full rent must be carried forward to set off against future profits under the same lease.

Premiums on short leases

Where a landlord grants a lease he or she may receive a premium (an initial lump sum for the granting of the lease). If the lease is a short lease (one for a period not exceeding 50 years) this premium is treated as additional rent and is taxable in the fiscal year in which it is received.

This was originally an anti-avoidance measure to counteract Schedule A income being replaced by a capital gain (subject, at the time, to lower rates of tax) through a large premium being received in exchange for a low annual rental under the lease.

The amount taxable is reduced by 2% of the premium for each year of the life of the lease other than the first (only complete years are taken into account).

EXAMPLE 4.3 (continuing Example 4.2)

Fred received a premium of £1,000 on shop 4 from the incoming tenant on 25 March 1995. The lease was granted for ten years.

	£
Premium	1,000
Less 2% (10 – 1) × 1,000	(180)
Schedule A assessment	820

This would be included in the above computation reducing the loss on shop 4 to £142 (962–820).

Payments for the variation of the terms of a lease are treated as premiums. The value of any capital work carried out by the tenant on the property (which would be improvements if carried out by the landlord) is also deemed to be a premium received by the landlord.

Duration of the lease

In the vast majority of cases there is no doubt about the duration of the lease. However, there is an anti-avoidance measure which provides that leases end on the date they are most likely to terminate. This is usually the date on which the landlord has the power to terminate the lease or substantially increase the rent.

In the case of a premium for the variation of the lease, the number of years will be the period for which the variation is effective.

Premiums received in instalments

If a premium is to be received in instalments, and the landlord can satisfy the Inland Revenue that to pay all the tax on the premium at once would cause undue hardship, the tax may be paid in instalments over the shorter of either:

▶ eight years
▶ the period over which the premium is to be received.

Premiums paid – deduction from premiums and rent received

If the landlord does not own the property but leases it from a superior landlord under a short-lease, he or she may actually have paid a premium for the grant of that lease (called the 'head-lease'). The landlord is entitled to relief for the premium paid as a deduction from any Schedule A assessment in respect of the premium and rent received from any sub-lease, calculated as follows:

$$\text{Premium assessed on superior landlord} \times \frac{\text{Duration of sub-lease}}{\text{Duration of head-lease}}$$

EXAMPLE 4.4

Colin acquired a 30-year lease on 31 August 1982 for a premium of £15,000. On 1 May 1994 he granted a ten-year sub-lease for £10,000.

Compute the Schedule A assessment in respect of the premium on the sub-lease.

	£	£
Premium received	10,000	
Less 2%(10 – 1) × 10,000	(1,800)	
Taxable		8,200

Less relief for premium paid under head-lease:		
Premium paid	15,000	
Less 2%(30 – 1) × 15,000	(8,700)	
Premium assessed on superior landlord	6,300	
Relief available 6,300 × $\frac{10}{30}$		(2,100)
Net Schedule A assessment		6,100

If the deduction for the premium paid is greater than the amount assessable for the premium received the excess may be divided by the number of years of the sub-lease and that amount deducted from the rent received from the sub-lease each year.

Premiums paid by person assessed under schedule D case I/II

Where a premium is paid on the grant of a short-lease by a Schedule D Case I or II taxpayer in respect of property occupied for the purpose of his or her trade, the taxpayer may deduct a part of it from his or her taxable profits in each year of the lease. The amount deductible is calculated as follows:

$$\frac{\text{Premium assessed on superior landlord}}{\text{Duration of the lease}}$$

An example of the computation will be found in the questions at the end of Chapter 15.

Schedule D Case VI – furnished letting income

Income from furnished lettings is normally assessable under Schedule D Case VI. However, on certain occasions, depending on the nature of the lettings, their duration and frequency, and the extent to which services are provided by the landlord (cleaning, laundry, caretakers, for instance) they may amount to a Schedule D Case I trade.

The line is fine between a trade and a furnished letting. The activities must be over and above the exploitation of rights through the ownership of property and sufficiently significant to be regarded as principal rather than secondary (*Griffiths* v. *Jackson*). Otherwise, the provision of the services themselves may be separated from the provision of accommodation (the income being appropriately apportioned) and that part treated as a trade. Similarly, the letting of caravans with the provision of associated services (say shops) may amount to a Schedule D Case I trade.

The basis of assessment is strictly on the profits arising (that is, accruals basis) but in practice, the Inland Revenue accept a 'Schedule A basis' or, if the income is of a recurrent nature, the assessment may be on a preceding year basis along Schedule D Case I lines. Losses may be set off against other profit or gains charged under Case VI, if any, or may only be carried forward and deducted from future Schedule D Case VI income.

The general structure of the computation is the same as for Schedule A, with additional relief for further out-of-pocket expenses such as insurance and repair of contents. An additional allowance is available for wear and tear of furniture, calculated as 10% of the net rents (capital allowances are not normally available). Net rents are rent less rates.

In any fiscal year the taxpayer may claim to be assessed under Schedule A on that part of the rent attributable to the premises, leaving the rent attributable to the contents to be assessed under Schedule D Case VI. The expenses must also be apportioned appropriately. This is advantageous if, in the fiscal year, there are losses under Schedule A which may be relieved against a Schedule A profit arising on furnished property. An election must be made within two years of the end of the year of assessment for which the claim is made.

If a furnished property is occupied at some time during the year by the owner, the deductions for rates, light, heat, repairs and so on are restricted to the proportion:

$$\frac{\text{Weeks property available to let}}{\text{Weeks property available to let} + \text{period of owner-occupation}}$$

EXAMPLE 4.5 (continuing Examples 4.2 and 4.3)

Fred also let the following properties:

House 1
A furnished house let on weekly tenancies. During 1994/95 the property was let for 37 weeks. The all-inclusive weekly rental was £115. An election has been made for the rent in respect of the property (agreed with the Inland Revenue at £95 per week) to be assessed under Schedule A instead of Schedule D Case VI.

House 2
A furnished house also let on weekly tenancies. During 1994/95 the property was let for 43 weeks. The all-inclusive weekly rental was £120. An election has been made for the rent in respect of the property (agreed with the Inland Revenue at £105 per week) to be assessed under Schedule A instead of Schedule D Case VI.

Details of expenditure in the year ended 5 April 1995 were:

	House 1 £	House 2 £
Insurance – buildings	135	117
Insurance – contents	34	25
Ground rent	5	6
Repairs, decorating	1,296	1,935
	(Note 1)	(Note 2)
Accountancy – Schedule A	25	25
Accountancy – Schedule D Case VI	10	10
Newspaper adverts	117	134
Gardener's wages	120	132

The expenditure on the houses has been agreed with the Inland Revenue as that being applicable to the rent of the property (as opposed to the rent of the furniture). In addition, all necessary apportionments to the expenditure on a time basis have already been made in arriving at the figures shown.

Notes on repairs

1. This figure of £1,296 includes £1,050 spent on dry rot remedial treatment prior to letting. The dry rot was present in the house when Fred purchased it in November 1993. None related to the furniture or contents.
2. Included in the figure of £1,935 is an amount of £1,428 spent on retiling the house roof. The old tiles were re-used whenever possible to comply with local planning regulations. None related to the furniture or contents.

Calculate the additional amount assessable under Schedule A in respect of the houses and the Schedule D Case VI assessment for 1994/95.

Leases at full rent (landlord repairing)	House 1 £	House 2 £
Rent receivable (exclusive of furniture)		
(£95 × 37)	3,515	
(£105 × 43)		4,515

Less Expenses		
Insurance	(135)	(117)
Ground rent	(5)	(6)
Repairs, decorating	(246)	(1,935)
Accountancy	(25)	(25)
Newspaper adverts	(117)	(134)
Gardener's wages	(120)	(132)
	2,867	2,166

The cost of dry rot remedial treatment represents capital expenditure (compare *Law Shipping* case discussed in Chapter 15).

The full cost of retiling is allowed as there is no improvement value – the life of a roof is linked to the age of the tiles principally.

Newspaper advertisements and accountancy could have been split between Schedule A and D VI but have been ignored as immaterial.

As these are landlord repairing leases, all profits and losses on them will be pooled and any losses on his other tenant repairing leases may be set off against any net profit on the pool.

Schedule A assessment 1994/95

	£
Landlord repairing leases (LRL Pool)	2,867
	2,166
Less loss on TRL (per Examples 4.2 and 4.3)	(142)
	4,891
Profits on TRLs (no pool) (per Example 4.2)	3,055
	7,946

Schedule D Case VI Assessment 1994/95

	House 1 £	House 2 £
Rent receivable (exclusive of furniture)		
(£20 x 37)	740	
(£15 x 43)		645
Less Insurance - contents	(34)	(25)
Accountancy	(10)	(10)
Wear and tear 10% (3,515 + 740)	(425)	
Wear and tear 10% (4,515 + 645)		(516)
	271	94 = 365

Rent a room income

This gives tax relief to people who let out furnished rooms in their own homes. Income from this source, up to £3,250 per fiscal year, is exempt. (A taxpayer with more than one source of rent a room income will get £3,250 divided by the number of sources, per source of rent a room income). If the rent is more than the exempt amount, the taxpayer may choose either to:

▶ pay tax on the total profit (rent less expenses) under Schedule D VI as above
▶ pay tax on the amount by which the rent exceeds the exempt amount.

If the latter alternative is chosen, an election should be made within 12 months after the end of the fiscal year in which the income arose.

Furnished holiday lettings

Income from furnished holiday accommodation is assessable under Schedule D Case VI but is treated as trading income provided certain conditions are satisfied.

Conditions

To qualify to be treated as trading income, the lettings must be on a commercial basis with a view to the realisation of profit and:

1. the property must both:
   a) be available for letting for at least 140 days in the fiscal year (or 12 month accounting period)
   b) actually be let for at least 70 days
2. for a period of at least seven months (not necessarily continuous), including the 70 days in 1 above, it must not normally be in the same occupation for a period exceeding 31 days.

Where there is more than one letting property, it is possible to average the letting periods of any or all of the properties. Provided the average letting period is 70 days per property or unit, condition 1(b) will be satisfied. A claim to average must be made within two years of the end of the fiscal year or accounting period to which the claim relates.

Consequences

Although the income is assessed under Schedule D Case VI, for all other purposes (except the preceding year basis of assessment), the Schedule D Case I rules apply.

▶ Capital allowances are available for plant and machinery (see Chapter 16).
▶ Relief is available for pre-trading expenditure (see Chapter 18).
▶ Relief is available for losses as if they are trading losses (see Chapter 18).
▶ The income is classified as earned income.
▶ The income tax liability is payable in two equal instalments on 1 January in the fiscal year and 1 July following the end of the fiscal year.
▶ Retirement annuity premium and personal pension contribution relief is available (see later in this chapter).
▶ Retirement relief, roll-over relief for the replacement of business assets and relief for gifts of business assets is available under capital gains tax (see Chapters 19 and 20).

EXAMPLE 4.6

Robert owns a number of properties which he lets as holiday cottages. The following information is available for 1994/95.

	Days available	Days let
Cottage 1	145	45
Cottage 2	160	85
Cottage 3	150	80
Cottage 4	120	100

None of the cottages was let for more than 31 days to any one person.

Which of the cottages qualify as 'furnished holiday accommodation'?

Cottages 2 and 3 satisfy both conditions and qualify.
Cottage 4 does not satisfy condition 1a) and cannot qualify.
Cottage 1 satisfies condition 1a) but not condition 1b) and therefore can only qualify if it can be averaged with either or both cottages 2 and 3:

$$\frac{45 + 85 + 80}{3} = 70 \text{ days so it qualifies provided a claim is made before 5 April 1997.}$$

TAX PLANNING

Income from investments

Income from investments is treated in a number of different ways for tax purposes.

The income from a few investments is tax free but the extent to which an individual can benefit is usually restricted in some way (for example, by a maximum permitted investment). As only the government has the ability to grant tax-free status to income, the majority of the investment opportunities in this category are government sponsored.

Income from some investments has had basic rate income tax deducted at source while dividends are deemed to have had 20% income tax deducted at source. The investor is liable to income tax on the 'grossed up' amount of income but the tax liability arising is satisfied by the tax deducted or deemed to be deducted at source (as illustrated in Chapter 1). In this case the investor is only concerned with the tax implications of the income to the extent that either:

▶ the investor has personal allowances which he or she is able to set against the income and therefore possibly obtain a tax repayment; or
▶ the investor is liable to higher-rate tax (he or she will have a further liability to tax of 15% (40-25% already paid) on the gross amount of the income) 20% (40-20% deemed to be paid) on the gross amount of dividend income).

Income from other investments is paid to the investor in full (gross) and subjected to tax in the investor's hands under Schedule D Case III as appropriate (to both basic rate income tax and higher-rate tax if necessary).

Tax-free investments

National Savings Bank ordinary account

The first £70 of interest per fiscal year from a National Savings Bank Ordinary Account is tax free. A husband and wife are each allowed £70 (if the account is a joint account £140 will be allowed) tax free. The interest on this type of account is relatively low. The return on capital, although tax free, must be compared with the after-tax return on alternative investments.

These accounts are of greatest benefit to higher-rate taxpayers but since the reduction in the high marginal rates of income tax (up to 60%) of 1987/88 and earlier they have become less attractive.

Interest in excess of £70 is taxed under Schedule D Case III (see below).

National Savings Certificates

These are certificates which can be purchased at post offices in small units (minimum £100). They increase in value at a pre-defined rate (which may be index-linked) and if held for a specified period of time (usually five years) an additional bonus is added to the value of the certificates. When cashed in, the proceeds are free of both income tax and capital gains tax. There is a maximum permitted holding of each issue of certificates (£10,000 for the 41st issue with a re-investment limit of £20,000).

Save As You Earn (SAYE) or Yearly Plan

These are schemes to encourage regular saving by offering a tax-free return at the end of a fixed period (usually five years). The investor contracts to save a regular sum per month (minimum £20 – maximum £400) for one year which must then be allowed to mature for a specified number of years (usually four years). A guaranteed return, tax free, is paid on maturity (if cashed in before the maturity date, a lower guaranteed tax-free return is paid).

These schemes are available through National Savings at post offices or through building societies. The Finance Act 1990 allowed banks also to offer SAYE contracts.

Premium bonds

Premium bonds can be purchased in units of £100 at post offices and may be redeemed at any time for their face value. No interest is paid but while in issue the serial numbers are entered in a monthly draw for cash prizes. These winnings are tax free. The maximum permitted holding is £20,000.

Tax Exempt Special Savings Account (TESSA)

Anyone over 18 is able to open one of these accounts with a bank or a building society. It is a five year contract and provided the savings are left in the account any interest is tax free. The maximum investment over the five years will be £9,000: £3,000 in the first year (12 months), £1,800 in the second, third and fourth years and £600 – £1,800 in the final year depending on the amount invested in years 1–4; or £150 per month. Investors will be able to withdraw an amount equivalent to the net interest earned to date at any time during the contract.

National Savings Pensioners' Guaranteed Income Bond

This was introduced by the Finance Act 1994 with the aim of giving pensioners some certainty regarding the amount of income their capital would produce. Interest is fixed for the bond's full five-year term. The interest is paid gross on a monthly basis. but is taxable. Early withdrawal loses 60 days interest. The minimum investment is £500 and the maximum is £20,000.

Investments – income taxed at source

Government securities (gilt-edged securities or 'gilts')

These are fixed-interest securities issued by the government as a means of raising finance. The interest rates vary considerably from issue to issue and may be linked to the retail price index. The redemption date is usually fixed on issue and on that date the nominal value of the security will be paid to the holder. They are quoted on the Stock Exchange and the market price fluctuates, among other factors, to reflect how the interest rate compares with other interest rates obtainable at that time.

The interest is paid 'net' to UK residents (except on 3.5% War Loan) unless the securities are acquired through the National Savings Stock Register (at post offices) when it is always paid gross.

The securities are exempt from capital gains tax on disposal. Inevitably, at the date of disposal there will be some accrued interest reflected in the purchase price which without adjustment would escape income tax. This loophole was exploited and the accrued income scheme was introduced in 1986 to charge this income to income tax (see later this chapter – Schedule D Case VI and Chapter 28).

Local authority bonds (yearling bonds)

These are lump sum investments for a period between one and five years (minimum £1,000). They are, however, readily transferable. They are issued by local authorities to finance short-term borrowing requirements and the rates of interest are usually very competitive. Interest is payable half-yearly. These bonds are also subject to the accrued income scheme.

Purchased life annuities

Where a lump sum is invested to purchase a life annuity, the annuity is split into two parts: a capital element representing a return to the individual of the purchase price; and an income element representing a return on the capital sum invested. The capital element is then treated as being entirely free of tax and the income element is taxable and is subject to deduction of basic rate income tax at source.

The capital element is determined by the ratio that the actuarial value of the annuity bears to the total cost and once determined is constantly applied. If the annuity is only terminable by reference to the actual duration of life, as in most cases, this can confer attractive benefits. The higher the age at which the annuity is purchased and the longer-lived the individual, the greater are the tax-free benefits likely to be received. On the other hand, if the individual is only short-lived, no capital is recoverable. Purchased life annuities are often linked to life assurance policies.

In terms of a tax efficient investment, this is likely only to attract the pensioner and, if combined with the higher tax threshold conferred by the age allowance, it can produce substantial tax-free income.

The purchase of a life annuity can also be effected by a pensioner with a loan secured against his or her only or main residence, and this can produce a tax-efficient means of supplementing income. It combines the tax advantages of the purchased life annuity with the eligibility for tax relief of the interest payable on the loan (see Chapter 1).

The above rules do not apply to retirement annuities, pension annuities or to annuities purchased by a trust fund or under the terms of a will.

Bank and building society interest

Building society and bank deposit interest (other than interest from National Savings Bank accounts) paid to individuals has basic rate income tax deducted at source. Individuals not liable to tax may receive their interest gross if the appropriate declarations are completed.

Investments – income deemed to be taxed at source

Dividends from UK companies

When a UK company pays a dividend, it must account for advance corporation tax (ACT). This is an amount which when added to the dividend is equivalent to lower rate income tax on the total.

Although this ACT is not income tax it is 'imputed' to the dividend so that the investor is liable to income tax on the gross amount. Dividend income is treated as the top slice of the taxpayer's income, as explained in Chapter 1. The low income investor is able to obtain a tax repayment of the imputed tax credit (20%) while a basic rate investor will have no further liability A higher rate investor will pay a further 20% (40–20%).

Unit and investment trusts

The purpose of both the unit trust and the investment trust is to enable the investor to take advantage of risk-spreading, since with limited resources he or she cannot hope to obtain such a wide spread of investments as by purchasing units or shares in a trust. In addition, both have professional investment management as well as the ability to specialise in different markets (for instance, commodities, industries or countries) or with different aims (for instance, high income or capital growth).

Unit trusts are bound by a trust deed, the holders of the units not being owners of the company or entitled to vote, and the funds are invested under the guidance of managers. The units depend for their value on the market value of the portfolio of investments in which the trust places its money. The income arising to the trustees from the portfolio of investments, which is made available to unit-holders, is treated as dividends from a UK company in the hands of unit-holders.

Investment trusts, on the other hand, are ordinary limited companies with shares traded on the Stock Exchange in the normal way. The individuals investing in an investment trust become shareholders in the limited company, their dividends dependent upon the performance of the portfolio of their investments.

Schedule D Case III

Income assessable

Under Schedule D Case III, there is assessed any interest not taxed at source including:

- interest on National Savings Bank accounts (but the first £70 of interest on an ordinary account to each of husband and wife is tax free)
- interest on certain government stocks (in particular 3.5% War Loan, but also any purchased through the National Savings Stock register)
- interest on certificates of tax deposit (see Chapter 22)
- interest on loans between individuals
- interest on quoted Eurobonds
- discounts on Treasury Bills
- sickness and disablement benefits received from insurance companies and friendly societies for periods in excess of one year (see Chapter 3)
- income from deep-discount securities (see below).
- interest on National Savings Pensioners' Guaranteed Income Bonds.

Basis of assessment

The fiscal year in which income is assessed under Schedule D Case III is determined by when it arises. Where there is an established source of income, the income assessed in any fiscal year is that arising in the preceding fiscal year.

Interest 'arises' when it is available to the recipient or due and payable (for example, when it is credited to a bank deposit account). Accrued interest is ignored and no deductions are allowed.

Each individual investment is treated as a separate source of income.

Acquisition of a new source of interest

First year – In the first fiscal year in which income arises, the actual income arising in that fiscal year is assessed.

Second year – In the second fiscal year, the actual income arising is again assessed (unless the income first arose on 6 April in the first year, when the assessment is on the income of the previous (first) year).

Third and subsequent years – The income arising in the preceding fiscal year.

The taxpayer may elect in the third year of assessment (or the second year if it would be assessed on a preceding year basis), to have the assessment for that year based on the actual income arising in that year. The claim must be made within six years of the end of the relevant year of assessment.

EXAMPLE 4.7

A National Savings Bank Investment Account was opened on 15 April 1990, and interest was credited as follows:

	30 June	31 December
	£	£
1990	30	45
1991	60	70
1992	75	65

The assessments will be as follows:

1990/91 Actual		75
1991/92 Actual		130
1992/93 Preceding year	130	130
Actual at taxpayer's option	140	
1993/94 Preceding year		140

Disposal of a source of interest

Final year – In the fiscal year in which a source of income is disposed of, the actual income arising in that year is assessed.

Penultimate year – The income assessed in the first instance will be that arising in the preceding fiscal year but the Inland Revenue may increase the assessment to the actual income arising in the penultimate year if it is greater.

The disposal of the source of income is the critical factor rather than the fact that it may temporarily cease to produce income.

If no income arises from a source for six consecutive years, a claim may be made, within two years after the end of the six years, to be assessed as if the source had ceased immediately before the end of the six years. Any income arising subsequently is treated as a new source.

Additions to/reductions in a source of income

A major addition to or reduction in an existing source of income may be treated by the Inland Revenue as an acquisition or disposal of a source of income following the rule in *Hart* v. *Sangster*. In practice no adjustment is made unless the fluctuations in income are considerable.

The Finance Act 1994 introduced a new basis of assessment for Schedule D Case III income. New sources commencing after 5 April 1994 will now be assessable on a current year basis. The opening and closing rules referred to above will therefore not apply. Sources commencing prior to 6 April 1994 will continue to be assessed as outlined above for the time being.

Deep-discount securities and deep-gain securities

Deep-discount securities are redeemable securities which are issued at a discount greater than 15% of the amount payable on redemption (or 0.5% per annum until the earliest redemption date). They were a means of converting income into capital for tax purposes until provisions were introduced to counteract them. The definition of securities covers securities issued by the UK and overseas non-corporate sector and also situations where the issue is not at a fixed discount or has other variable features.

Certain securities issued on or after 9 June 1989 may be excluded as 'qualifying convertible securities' or 'qualifying indexed securities'. These are bonds which are convertible into ordinary share capital of the issuing company and which meet certain conditions, and indexed bonds which meet the qualifying conditions.

The entire redemption or sale surplus of deep discount securities other than those which are qualifying securities, is charged to income tax under Schedule D Case III rather than to capital gains tax in the year in which the disposal takes place (that is, not the normal preceding year basis for Schedule D Case III).

The redemption proceeds are payable gross without deduction of tax at source.

Coupon stripping

Where a company issues deep-discount securities which are 'chargeable securities', the person acquiring the chargeable security is chargeable on the accrued interest, as calculated below. This is under Schedule D Case III on a current year basis at the end of each income period falling wholly or partly within the period of ownership.

Discount

The discount is treated as interest accruing over the life of the security on a compound basis. The 'income element' is the proportion of the discount accruing in each 'income period'.

The income element for a fiscal year is calculated according to the formula:

$$\frac{A \times B}{100} - C$$

where: A = issue price (plus all accrued income in earlier income periods)
B = percentage yield to maturity
C = the amount of any annual interest, if any, payable.

The accrued income attributable to each accounting period is treated as a charge on income of the issuing company and is therefore deductible in arriving at the profits chargeable to corporation tax.

Schedule D Case VI

Annual profits or gains not falling under any other Schedule or case of Schedule D are charged to tax under Schedule D Case VI. 'Annual', in this context, does not necessarily imply that the profits occur from year to year – simply that they represent income. In addition, the legislation provides specifically for assessment under Case VI of a variety of sources of income and deemed income associated with the anti-avoidance provisions.

One of the most common forms of income assessed under Schedule D Case VI is income from furnished letting including holiday lets, both of which were considered earlier in this chapter.

Other income assessed under Schedule D Case VI includes:

- profits on the sale of patent rights
- profits of a casual or speculative nature
- balancing charges on a lessor of industrial buildings (see Chapter 16)
- post-cessation receipts (say, where accounts are compiled on a receipts basis with no WIP and the tax charge has been similarly based – WIP at the date of cessation becomes a cash receipt, for example of the retired partner, a tax liability also arises)
- sums received for the sale of future earnings
- insurance commissions except when part of a trade
- income assessable under the accrued income scheme (see below)
- Enterprise Allowance, that is, allowances paid to assist people setting up their own businesses. Previously taxable as trading receipts (Schedule D I/II), liability under Schedule D VI avoids the onerous double tax of opening year assessment (see Chapter 15). Schedule D I implications are retained re pension contributions and liability to class 4 NIC
- chargeable event gains on life assurance policies (see below).

The basis of assessment is the actual profits or gains arising in the fiscal year, less any expenses incurred in earning that income. Capital allowances for plant and machinery cannot be claimed but relief may be available under the renewals basis.

Losses under Schedule D Case VI may be set against other Schedule D Case VI.

Also any unrelieved amount may be carried forward and set off against any future Schedule D Case VI assessments not necessarily on the same source of income.

Accrued income scheme (bondwashing)

This scheme counteracts the practice of disposing of fixed-interest securities when the price obtained reflected a significant element of interest (income was converted into capital gains).

Under the scheme, the gross interest is treated as accruing on a day-to-day basis, and on disposal, the disposal proceeds (and the acquisition cost of the purchaser) are apportioned between the interest element and the capital element:

- If the securities are disposed of 'cum interest' the interest for the whole of the interest period will be received by the transferee who will also be entitled to relief for the interest accrued to the date of acquisition, while a charge to interest will arise on the transferor.
- If the securities are disposed of 'ex interest' the interest for the whole interest period will actually be received by the transferor. The transferor will then be entitled to relief for the interest accrued from the date of disposal to the end of the interest period, while a charge to interest will arise on the transferee.

The various charges and reliefs to which a person is entitled to on securities of the same kind for a fiscal year are aggregated. If the overall result is a sum chargeable to tax, it is taxed under Schedule D Case VI (as if it was income received at the end of the interest period). If the overall result shows entitlement to relief, the relief is given as a deduction from the interest received at the end of the interest period.

The scheme does not apply to individuals where the nominal value of fixed interest securities held does not exceed £5,000 at any time during the fiscal year or the previous year.

Securities

The term 'securities' includes any loan stock or securities, whether issued by a UK body or not. For example, it includes company debentures and loan stock, government securities, and local authority or other public authority bonds.

EXAMPLE 4.8

John purchased £3,000 10% Exchequer Stock on 1 June 1994 cum interest for £2,600. Show the amount chargeable to income tax if the stock is sold to Robert as follows: 'ex interest' on 15 September 1994 for £2,640 – settlement date 24 September 1994. Interest is payable on 30 September and 31 March.

Assume that John owned chargeable securities with a nominal value in excess of £5,000 during the year. John sold the securities ex interest, so he will receive the full six months' interest on 30 September, that is, £150.

Accrued income scheme
John: Relief for interest accrued to date of acquisition
(included in purchase price) 1 April–31 May

$$\frac{61}{183} \times 150 = £50.00 \quad \text{(Capital element of purchase price £2,550)}$$

Relief for interest accrued from date of disposal (forfeited in price) 24 September–30 September

$$\frac{7}{183} \times 150 = £5.74 \qquad \text{(Capital element of sale price £2,645.74)}$$

Income assessable £94.26   Income accrued over period 1 June–24 Sept or six monthly interest £150 less £50.00 and £5.74 calculated above.

Pensions

On retirement, any individuals who have paid National Insurance contributions are entitled to the basic state retirement pension. During their working life, they may make further provision for a pension of their own on retirement, or may have a pension provided for them by an employer. The tax system encourages individuals and employers, through tax incentives, to make provision for retirement.

Excluding the State Earnings Related Pension Scheme which is considered further below, there are three principal means of providing a retirement pension:

- occupational pension schemes
- retirement annuity policies
- personal pension schemes.

Each of these receives beneficial tax treatment provided certain conditions are met.

Occupational pension schemes (or superannuation funds)

Introduction

All employers are obliged to make pension arrangements for their employees either through the state scheme mentioned earlier or through a separate scheme.

Where provision is made through the state scheme, the employer and the employee both pay the 'contracted-in' rate of National Insurance contributions (see Chapter 3) which contributes to the State Earnings Related Pension Scheme (SERPS). The SERPS will provide an extra pension from state retirement age on top of the basic state pension. No tax relief is available to the individual for his or her National Insurance contributions but the employer may deduct National Insurance costs from his or her trading profits.

Where a separate scheme is set up, there are safeguards via the Occupational Pensions Board (OPB) to ensure that no employee would receive a smaller pension than under the state scheme. If these minimum requirements are met and the employer so wishes, he or she may 'contract-out' of SERPS, which means that both the employer's and the employee's National Insurance contributions are reduced (see Chapter 3). If they are not met, a separate scheme may still be set up but the employer may not 'contract-out' of SERPS.

Employers may set up a separate scheme themselves (a 'self-administered' scheme) or via an insurance company (an 'insured' scheme). The scheme may be 'contributory' or 'non-contributory' (that is, it may or may not require the employees to pay into the scheme). Beneficial tax treatment is given to schemes approved by the Inland Revenue making them the most tax efficient way of saving for retirement.

Approved schemes

The potential benefits of approval are considerable:

- Employee's/member's contributions obtain Schedule E expense relief (see below for limit).
- Employer's contributions are deductible as an expense from Schedule D Case I trading profits and are not assessed on employees as benefits in kind.
- The pension fund has tax free status, both its investment income and capital gains being free of income tax and capital gains tax.
- The pensions paid are treated as earned income and generally taxed under PAYE.
- Lump sums in cash on retirement are tax free.
- Lump sums on death in service are generally free of income tax and inheritance tax.
- Leaver's refunds and surplus AVC benefits refunded (that is, where an employee leaves the employment or has become entitled, as a result of making additional voluntary contributions, to a greater pension than may legally be paid to him or her) are taxed at a reduced rate.

However, to earn these advantages, schemes must be approved. They must therefore meet certain requirements particularly in relation to the maximum benefits which can be derived from the scheme and the amount which can be contributed to the scheme.

Different types of approval are available to different schemes. The Pension Schemes Office (PSO) of the Inland Revenue is responsible for approving schemes. It issues practice notes in conjunction with the Occupational Pensions Board referred to above, to help employers to set up schemes.

For schemes set up after 14 March 1989 and for new entrants to existing schemes after 1 June 1989, the principal conditions are as follows:

- The employee's contributions (including AVCs – see below) are restricted to 15% of a maximum of £76,800 (1994/95) gross emoluments.
- The maximum pension is restricted to two-thirds of a maximum final salary of £76,800 (1994/95) at a specified retirement age, between 60 and 75 (subject to completion of 20 years' service).
- If part of the pension is commuted to give a lump sum on retirement, the maximum lump sum is restricted to the higher of 3/80 of a maximum final salary of £76,800 (1994/95) for each year of service up to 40 or 2.25 times the amount of the pension before commutation. (This effectively limits the cash sum to £115,200.)

These rules govern the maximum that can be done to provide retirement benefits and as such do not necessarily affect the retirement benefits payable to the majority of employees. Employees (that is, members of an occupational pension scheme) may increase their pension entitlement on retirement – within the maximum limits indicated above – by making additional voluntary contributions. They can do this either through the occupational pension scheme (AVCs – tax relief through the net pay arrangement) or make contributions to an approved free standing additional voluntary contribution scheme (FSAVC). Tax relief is given by reducing the premium payable by basic rate income tax. Employees suffering tax at higher rates must therefore claim higher-rate relief through their tax return.

The introduction of restrictions on the size of retirement benefits does, however, limit the use of approved schemes in tax planning for smaller companies. In their case maximising pension contributions for director/shareholders was a tax effective means of reducing the company's taxable profits while, if the scheme was self-administered, leaving the funds available to the company in the form of loan capital.

Employers can set up top-up pension schemes under unapproved arrangements without jeopardising the approval of the above schemes. These will not have the tax advantages, but may be used to provide more generous benefits than the tax rules allow.

Unapproved schemes

Contributions by an employer on behalf of an employee to a funded scheme will be taxed as the employee's income.

Benefits from an unfunded scheme will be taxed when paid.

Retirement annuity policies

The system of retirement annuities was replaced by a new system of personal pensions with effect from 1 July 1988. However, existing contracts at that date continue under the original legislation unless transferred to a personal pension scheme. Retirement annuities were used by:

- self-employed individuals
- individuals in non-pensionable employment (including those who chose not to join their employer's occupational pension scheme).

They were encouraged by tax reliefs to build up a fund with which they could purchase an annuity on retirement. Premiums were limited to 17.5% of net relevant earnings, the limit being increased for individuals over the age of 50.

Personal pension schemes

Personal pensions like retirement annuities are a tax efficient means for individuals (whether employed or self-employed) to provide pensions for themselves on retirement. The purpose of introducing personal pension schemes (introduced with effect from 1 July 1988) was to extend choice and flexibility.

Transfers can be made into a personal pension scheme from an employer's scheme, from retirement annuity contracts, and from other personal pension plans. Transfers may also be made from a personal pension plan into an employer's scheme.

Retirement benefits may be taken at any time from the age of 50 up to 75. Unlike occupational pension schemes, there are no guarantees as to the size of the pension that will be received, but no limits either. It will depend on the amount of the contributions paid in which are subject to the earnings cap (see below) and how well they have been invested. (The individual, subject to Inland Revenue guidance, will have a choice as to how contributions are invested.) The pension can be paid at a fixed rate or cost of living increases can be built into it. Up to 25% of the fund can be taken as a lump sum on retirement.

The fund built up as a result of the contributions paid in is tax exempt and therefore free of both income tax and capital gains tax.

Personal pension schemes approved by the Inland Revenue may be offered by a wide variety of financial institutions including life assurance companies, friendly societies, banks, building societies, and unit trusts.

Contributions

The maximum amount of contributions for which relief is available in any fiscal year is 17.5% of 'net relevant earnings' (up to £76,800 maximum 1994/95) unless the individual is over 35 when the limit is increased as follows:

	%
36 to 45	20
46 to 50	25
51 to 55	30
56 to 60	35
61 and over	40

A part of this amount (maximum 5% of net relevant earnings) may be used to provide a lump sum for a widow or dependants if death occurs before retirement age.

Employees

Employees cannot normally be in an employer's scheme and pay into a personal pension scheme, but from April 1988 they have been able to choose. It is no longer possible for an employer operating an occupational pension scheme to require employees to join it. Employers may nevertheless contribute to employees' personal pension schemes if they wish.

However, if the employer's scheme is 'contracted-in' to the State Earnings Related Pension Scheme (SERPS), a personal pension can be used to 'contract-out' – as long as the rules of the personal pension scheme provide for DSS minimum contributions to be paid into the scheme. DSS minimum contributions are the difference between the contracted-in rate and the contracted-out rate of National Insurance contributions. The employee and employer pay the full contracted-in rate to the DSS but the DSS pays minimum contributions into the scheme.

The contribution limits listed above apply to the aggregate of both the employee's and the employer's contributions. Any DSS contributions are additional.

The net relevant earnings of an employee are defined as his or her Schedule E emoluments (provided that the employment is non-pensionable employment or that the employee has chosen not to join the occupational pension scheme) less Schedule E allowable deductions. Earnings of controlling directors of investment companies do not qualify.

Relief is given to employees by reducing the amount payable under the scheme by basic rate income tax. The pension provider is able to claim back basic rate income tax from the Inland Revenue and add it to the scheme. (For example, if the total contribution is £100 then the amount payable by the employee will be £75, and £25 will be claimed back from the Inland Revenue.) Higher-rate employees must claim higher-rate relief through their tax return (when the PAYE code will normally be adjusted).

Self-employed

Self-employed individuals do not contribute to SERPS and cannot therefore contract out.

Net relevant earnings in this case are defined as earnings taxable under Schedule D Cases I and II (and including income from qualifying furnished holiday letting) less the amount by which trade charges exceed other income, capital allowances, and relief claimed for trading losses (to the extent that this relief is deducted from non-trading income, net relevant earnings of the following year must be reduced and so on).

Relief is given by adjustment of the Schedule D Case I assessment or, if later, a repayment will be made.

Carry back of contributions

An election may be made for all or part of the contribution in a fiscal year to be treated as if paid in the previous fiscal year (or if net relevant earnings in that year were nil, as if paid in the year before that). The election must be made within three months of the end of the fiscal year in which the premium was paid.

Unused relief carried forward

In any fiscal year, where the contributions paid fall short of the limit for that year, the unused relief may be carried forward for use in a future year. Up to six years' unused relief can be carried forward and must be used in order starting with the earliest year. It may only be used to increase the maximum allowable contribution.

EXAMPLE 4.9

John, who is 42, has kept a record of net relevant earnings and contributions as follows:

Tax Year	Net relevant earnings £	20% limit £	Contribution paid £	Unused relief £	Carried forward £
1	8,000	1,600	1,000	600	600
2	8,500	1,700	1,000	700	1,300
3	9,000	1,800	2,000	–	1,100
4	9,500	1,900	2,000	–	1,000
5	10,000	2,000	2,000	–	1,000
6	10,500	2,100	2,000	100	1,100
7	11,000	2,200			

In year 7, John is left some money and decides to contribute £2,400. He automatically gets relief on £2,200. The unused relief brought forward is sufficient to allow him to pay a further £200.

Only £800 unused relief is available for carry forward made up as follows:

	Unused relief £	Unused relief utilised			Unused cf £	Year 8 £
		Year 3 £	Year 4 £	Year 7 £		
Year 1	600	200	100	200		100 wasted
Year 2	700				700	
Year 6	100				100	
					800	

In year 8, John paid a contribution of £100 and elected for it to be treated as if paid in year 7 and therefore prevented the unused relief from year 1 from being wasted.

Life assurance

Qualifying policies

The rules surrounding the granting of tax relief for life assurance policies are carefully drawn to give relief only to 'qualifying policies'. Policies qualify only if they satisfy certain conditions. The significant features are as follows:

▶ They are issued by an insurance company or branch legally established in the UK or by a registered friendly society.
▶ The contract is made by the individual or his or her spouse on the life of the individual or his or her spouse.
▶ They follow certain conditions as to the length of the policy, the spread of the

premiums paid and the degree to which the policy is a genuine life assurance policy paying a capital sum on death. Briefly these are:
- premiums must at least be payable annually
- the premiums payable in any 12 months must not be more than twice those payable in any other 12 months
- the policy term must be at least ten years
- the capital sum payable on death (or for a whole life policy at age 75) must be at least 75% of the total premiums payable over the life of the policy (if taken out before the age of 55).

The interpretation of these rules is relaxed to include family income protection policies (where a series of capital sums are payable on death within a specified term) and mortgage protection policies (where the capital sum reduces over the life of the policy to nothing).

Tax reliefs

Originally there were two advantages to the holder of a qualifying policy but the second of these has been abolished for all new policies issued:

▶ Provided the benefits are paid out on maturity or after the expiry of at least ten years, the gain (the excess of the proceeds over the total premiums paid) is free of both income tax and capital gains tax.
▶ Life assurance premium relief was available (LAPR). This was abolished for policies issued after 13 March 1984 but relief continues for policies in issue at that date unless varied or extended.

Non-qualifying policies and policies surrendered within ten years

If a policy does not qualify, or qualifies but is surrendered within the ten year period, there is no capital gains tax liability (except where it has been assigned for money or money's worth). There may, however, be an income tax penalty.

If the proceeds exceed the total premiums paid, the gain is regarded as a 'chargeable event' and there is a charge to income tax at the excess of higher rate over basic rate (15%) on the gain to the extent that the taxpayers' marginal rate of tax is at higher rate.

Top-slicing relief is available to mitigate the effect of the lump sum being taxed wholly in the year of receipt. As the lump sum has accrued over a number of years, only the annual equivalent gain (the amount of the gain divided by the number of years the policy was held) is subjected to income tax as the top-slice of the taxpayer's income for the year. The resultant tax is then multiplied by the number of years to find the overall liability.

Special rules exist where a non-qualifying policy is surrendered in stages.

Personal equity plans

Personal equity plans (PEPs) encourage investment in shares in UK companies by offering tax incentives.

The plan

Individuals aged 18 and over who are resident and ordinarily resident in the UK can invest up to £3,000 in a single-company PEP as well as up to £6,000 per fiscal year in a general PEP. Note that the scheme is not open to children, trusts and companies.

An individual can only invest in one of each plan per year regardless of how little is invested. Usually investment can be made by lump sums or in instalments.

The individual transfers cash to a 'plan manager' (approved by the Inland Revenue) who purchases the shares and holds them on the investor's behalf. An investor's existing shareholdings cannot be passed over to the plan. Nevertheless, investors who subscribe for new issue shares (including privatisation issues) can normally transfer all or part of their allocation (within 42 days) into their plan so that they can benefit from the tax reliefs. The value of the shares at offer price will count towards the annual investment limit. In addition, shares acquired under approved all-employee share schemes can be transferred into a single-company PEP.

The general PEP investment may be wholly or partly in either unit or investment trusts or in ordinary shares of UK companies quoted on the Stock Exchange or the USM. The range of investments also extends to shares quoted in other EC member states and to unit and investment trusts investing mostly in EC equities. The investor retains beneficial ownership of the investments at all times and all shareholder's rights. The plan manager has custody of the investments and manages them on a day-to-day basis.

Since the introduction of PEPs, the rules have been considerably relaxed. There is now no minimum period for investments to be held in a plan and no necessity for the dividends to be re-invested in the plan.

Withdrawals may be made from the plan of cash or of the investments themselves. For capital gains tax purposes, if the investments are withdrawn from the plan the investor's base cost is the market value at the date of withdrawal.

Tax reliefs

Dividends arising on shares and units held in a plan are entirely free of income tax, whether or not the dividends are reinvested or paid in cash to the investor. The plan manager is able to claim back the tax credits on all dividends for reinvestment.

There is no capital gains tax charge on disposals or withdrawals from the plan.

The value of the capital gains tax exemption to the small investor is debatable, because the annual exemption of £5,800 would probably exempt the gains in any case. However, the facility to roll up the dividends together with the tax credit should enable a greater investment to be built up than could otherwise be done out of taxed income.

The Enterprise Investment Scheme (EIS)

The Enterprise Investment Scheme was introduced on 1 January 1994 to replace the old Business Expansion Scheme. It is intended to provide new equity finance to unquoted trading companies.

Qualifying investors

A qualifying investor is an individual who is liable to UK income tax, whether or not actually resident in the UK. In addition, the individual must not be connected with the company. An individual is connected if he is an employee of the company, or a shareholder who, together with associates, owns over 30% of the company's ordinary share capital.

After the issue of the shares, an individual can become a paid director of the company without affecting entitlement to EIS relief.

Qualifying companies

The company in which the EIS investment is made must be an unquoted company which trades in the UK. It is not necessary for the company to actually be incorporated in the UK.

The scheme excludes the property sector and so prevents investors from securing a safe return by investing in bricks and mortar.

Under the scheme, a company can raise up to £1 million during a specified period. This specified period is the longer of the period of six months ending with the date of the issue of the shares or the period beginning with the preceding 6 April and ending with the date of the issue. Relief is not available in respect of shares exceeding £1,000,000.

The relief

Under the scheme an individual may invest a minimum of £500 and a maximum of £100,000 per fiscal year in new equity shares of qualifying unquoted trading companies. Income tax relief at the lower rate of 20% will be given in respect of the sum invested. The relief is given by means of a tax credit.

Relief on half the amount an individual invests between 6 April and 5 October can be carried back to the previous tax year, subject to a maximum carry back of £15,000.

EXAMPLE 4.10

Howard decides to invest in two companies qualifying under the Enterprise Investment Scheme. He subscribed £10,000 for shares in Aba Ltd on 1 September 1994 and £40,000 for shares in Decka Ltd on 1 November 1994.

Howard is single. His statutory total income was £10,000 in 1993/94 and £36,000 in 1994/95.

As Howard has insufficient tax liability in 1994/95 to be able to utilise the full relief of £10,000 (£50,000 × 20%), he should carry back some relief to 1993/94. The maximum amount he can carry back is £5,000 as this is half of the amount subscribed prior to 5 October 1994. His tax liability after giving EIS relief will be as follows:

	1993/94	1994/95
	£	£
Statutory total income	10,000	36,000
Less: Personal allowance	(3,445)	(3,445)
Taxable income	6,555	32,555
Tax due:		
£3,000 at 20%	600	600
£3,555/£20,700 at 25%	889	5,175
£8,855 at 40%	–	3,542
	1,489	9,317
EIS relief:		
£5,000/£45,000 at 20%	(1,000)	(9,000)
	489	317

Any gain arising on the first disposal of shares acquired under the scheme will be exempt from capital gains tax, provided that relief has not been withdrawn. In order to qualify for exemption from CGT the shares must be held for a minimum of five years. If the investor realises a loss, he will be able to claim relief against either income or capital gains.

The withdrawal of relief

Relief will be withdrawn if the investor disposes of the shares within five years. This withdrawal is by means of a Schedule D VI assessment for the year of assessment for which the relief was given.

If the disposal is not at arm's length, the full relief is withdrawn. If the disposal is at arm's length the relief withdrawn is the lower of:

- the full relief, and
- an amount equivalent to the consideration received multiplied by the lower rate of income tax for the year of assessment for which relief was given.

If only some of the shares acquired qualified for relief, these are deemed to be disposed of in priority to any shares not qualifying for relief.

EXAMPLE 4.11

Continuing with example 4.10, assume that Howard disposes of all of his shares in Aba Ltd in August 1995 for £7,000.

The Schedule D VI assessments will be based on the consideration received as this is less than the relief given.

The tax due will be:

	1993/94 £	1994/95 £
Schedule DVI	3,500	3,500
Tax due at 20%	700	700

Relief will be withdrawn in the same manner if, within three years of the date on which the shares were issued, the company ceases to be a qualifying company, or if the investor receives value from the company. An investor receives value if the company:
- redeems or purchases his share capital
- makes a loan to him, other than an ordinary trade debt
- waives any liability of his to the company
- provides any benefits to him.

Relief is not withdrawn if the investor dies or the company is wound up for bona fide commercial reasons.

Summary

- All income from land and buildings in the UK (except from furnished lettings) is assessed under Schedule A.
- The profits and losses per property are calculated on a rent receivable, less expenses paid, basis.
- Only revenue expenses incurred during the currency of the lease while the property is in the ownership of the taxpayer may be deducted. Special provisions cover expenses incurred (say, for repairs) while the property is empty upon acquisition or following the termination of a lease.
- The availability of relief for expenses in excess of the rent receivable depends on the type of lease: landlord repairing lease (full rent); tenant repairing lease (full rent); lease not at full rent.

- Lump sums received on the grant of a short lease (a lease of 50 years or less) are in part treated as Schedule A income.
- Income from furnished letting is assessed under Schedule D Case VI.
- Rent-a-room income up to £3,250 per fiscal year is exempt.
- Furnished holiday letting income receives special status being taxed under Schedule D Case VI but being treated for all other purposes as if it were trading income. It is important to appreciate the advantages that this brings.
- It is important to appreciate how different types of investment are brought into charge to tax and how individual taxpayers will be affected. It is as important to recognise investments which are tax free as it is to know which are taxed at source and which are paid gross.
- The commencement and cessation rules for interest received gross under Schedule D Case III should be learned.
- You should be familiar with the various types of income normally taxed under Schedule D Case VI.
- The taxation of deep-discount securities and the accrued income scheme are areas of anti-avoidance legislation which have become applicable to normal transactions.
- A broad knowledge is required of pensions, life assurance, personal equity plans and the Enterprise Investment Scheme. You should ensure that you are familiar with the way in which each operates and the tax benefits which accrue.

Self test questions

1. What will be the assessable income for 1994/95 in the following circumstances? Rent of £6,000 per annum to 30 June 1994 and subsequently increased to £8,000 per annum, receivable quarterly in advance on 1 January, 1 April, 1 July and 1 October.

2. What is a lease at full rent?

3. What is the due date for payment of tax under Schedule A?

4. How are losses on a landlord's repairing lease at a full rent relieved?

5. What will the duration of the lease be for purposes of calculating the assessable premium in the following circumstances?
   X grants a 21-year lease which either party has the right to terminate after seven or 14 years.

6. If Robert grants a lease to Alan for 30 years, at a premium of £15,000, how much will be assessable under Schedule A?

7. What is the time limit for claiming that the rent in respect of a furnished let property be apportioned and assessed under Schedule A?

8. If a property is to qualify as furnished holiday lettings, for how many days must it be let in the fiscal year and for how many days must it be available for letting?

9. How is income from a unit trust taxed?

10. Is Schedule D Case VI income taxed on an actual or preceding year basis?

11. Under the new Schedule D Case III commencement rules, what is the basis of assessment?

12. Briefly define deep-discount securities.

13. Briefly describe the accrued interest scheme.

14. How is the carry forward of unused relief arising from the payment of personal pension premiums restricted?

15 John Brown owns or rents several properties in Greaton which he lets on various types of lease.

The properties let by him during the year to 5 April 1995 were:

Property	Type	Annual rent £	Type of lease	Interval of rent payments (in advance)
1	House	3,600	Full rent	Monthly
2	Flat	500	No formal lease	Annually
3	Warehouse	16,000	Full rent (TR)	Quarterly
4	Retail shop	6,400	Full rent	Quarterly
5	House	100	Nominal rent	Monthly
6	House	4,800	Full rent	Monthly

The expenses incurred by John during the year in respect of the various properties were:

Property	Agent's fees £	Rent £	Maintenance and repairs £	Water and insurance £
1	360	–	600	900
2	–	–	800	480
3	2,400	–	8,000	2,920
4	640	1,800	2,000	1,600
5	–	–	–	800
6	480	–	2,200	800

Property 2 is let to John Brown's nanny whom he feels obliged to support.

Property 3 was unlet at 6 April 1994 but a new tenant was found to occupy the premises from 5 October 1994 on a 30-year lease. To secure the tenancy, the new tenant agreed to pay the cost of a small extension to the warehouse. As a result of this work it has been estimated that the value of the property to John Brown was increased by £18,000.

The rent from property 4 due on 1 February 1995 was not paid until May 1995.

Property 5 is occupied by John Brown's widowed sister.

You are required to calculate the amount of John Brown's Schedule A income for the year to 5 April 1995.

16 R owns a seaside cottage, which is retained for family use for eight weeks each year, but is available for letting the rest of the year.

During 1994/95, the cottage was let for a total of 34 weeks at rents totalling £2,450. Expenditure during the year was:

	£
Council Tax	592
Insurance	150
Repairs to structure	268
Repairs to contents	110
Advertising for tenants	98
Cleaning (excluding any amounts applicable to period of occupation by family)	340

You are required to show the assessment on R for 1994/95.

17 Oliver, aged 42, has recently been left a large sum of money following the death of his father. Among other plans, he is considering making a lump sum payment

of £15,000 in July 1994 to top up his existing personal pension plan. He provides you with the following information.

He is employed by Kwik Sell Ltd, receiving a non-pensionable salary. He has paid a premium of £1,500 on 15 February each year since 1978 under a retirement annuity policy, which he recently transferred into his personal pension plan.

His employment, as sales manager of Kwik Sell Ltd commenced on 1 April 1982 with a three-year contract at an annual salary of £10,000. His salary has increased as follows:

> £12,000 pa from 1 April 1985
> £15,000 pa from 1 April 1988
> £18,000 pa from 1 April 1991
> £20,000 pa from 1 April 1994

You are required to advise Oliver on the tax consequences of paying the lump sum.

Answers on pages 562–565

CHAPTER 5

Capital Gains Tax – General Principles

This chapter begins by looking at the way capital gains tax legislation has developed over the years and outlines the basic principles of the charge to capital gains tax and its administration. The general principles for computing chargeable gains and allowable losses are covered in full. The manner in which these principles are modified in respect of specific assets is considered in the next two chapters and business aspects of capital gains tax are studied in Chapters 19 and 20. The examiner has stated that a detailed knowledge of the rules applying to the disposal of assets held on 6 April 1965 is not required for examination purposes. The rules applying to these assets have therefore been omitted.

The majority of these chapters on capital gains tax should be revision of your previous studies.

The scope of capital gains tax

Legislation

Capital gains tax was introduced by the Finance Act 1965 to charge to tax gains arising after 6 April 1965. The Finance Act 1982 introduced the indexation allowance in order to give some relief for inflation – its calculation was significantly amended by the Finance Act 1985 and again in the Finance Act 1994.

The Finance Act 1988 introduced a fundamental alteration to the computation of chargeable gains and for disposals after 5 April 1988; *only gains accruing after 31 March 1982* will be chargeable. Since the indexation allowance is also based generally on the 31 March 1982 value, the whole of the inflation element is removed, leaving only the real gains to be taxed.

All this legislation was consolidated into the Taxation of Chargeable Gains Act 1992.

Terminology

A chargeable gain or allowable loss may arise where there is a chargeable disposal of a chargeable asset by a chargeable person. Before proceeding it is necessary to define these terms.

Chargeable gains

The words 'chargeable gains' are used rather than simply 'gains' because only that part of a gain computed as accruing since 31 March 1982 is considered to be taxable or chargeable. If the computation produces a loss instead of a gain this is called an 'allowable loss'.

Disposal

A disposal takes place where there is a sale, a part sale, a gift, a receipt of a capital sum in compensation or in exchange for rights to an asset, or the entire loss or destruction of an asset. A disposal may be deemed to take place in situations where an asset is reduced to a negligible value.

The date a disposal takes place is the date of the contract, that is, the date of acquisition by the new owner – not necessarily the date of the actual transfer of the asset.

Unless a disposal is an exempt disposal it will be chargeable. The following disposals are absolutely exempt:

- assets transferred on death
- assets transferred as security (for a mortgage, for instance)
- gifts of 'eligible property' for the public benefit to suitable non-profit-making organisations (the Board of the Inland Revenue must approve the gift as being exempt).

Some disposals are partly exempt while others are treated in such a way that 'no gain, no loss' arises. Examples of these latter disposals are transfers between spouses, transfers between group companies, gifts to charities and (after the Finance Act 1989) gifts of land to housing associations.

Value shifting

In addition to the disposals considered in the previous section, it should be noted that the following transactions give rise to a chargeable disposal:

- Where property is subject to rights and restrictions, and the person entitled to exercise or enforce the rights or restrictions gives up that entitlement, the surrender, in whole or part, of such rights is treated as a disposal.
- Where, following a sale and leaseback type of arrangement, the terms of the lease are adjusted in such a way that the lessee (the original owner) gives up further rights to the property, the adjustment of the lessee's rights under the lease is treated as a disposal.
- Where a person has control of a company and that control is exercised in such a way that value
  - passes out of the shares in the company owned by him or her (or persons connected to him or her) or rights in the company to which he or she (or persons connected to him or her) is entitled
  - passes into other shares or rights in the company not owned by him or her

a disposal is deemed to have been made out of those shares or rights. No allowable loss can arise from such a disposal. Two or more persons may also exercise control in this way. An omission to act may be treated as an exercise of control *(Floor* v. *Davis)*.

If these disposals are made for no consideration or at an undervalue, the disposal value is taken as that which would be obtained from a bargain at 'arm's length'.

Chargeable assets

Any capital asset wherever situated and whatever its form (tangible or intangible) is potentially chargeable to capital gains tax unless it is specifically stated to be exempt. Revenue assets of a business (for instance, trading stock) are not liable to capital gains tax, as the gain arising on their disposal in the course of a trade is a trading profit and is assessed to income tax.

In computing gains for capital gains tax, any part chargeable to income tax or corporation tax is excluded from the charge to capital gains tax. (Any expenditure allowed as a deduction for those taxes will also not be allowed as a deduction for capital gains tax.) The order of priority is therefore income tax before capital gains tax.

The list of assets which are exempt, wholly or partially, is fairly extensive. The main absolute exemptions are:

- private motor cars (mechanically propelled road vehicles constructed or adapted for the carriage of passengers), unless of a type not commonly used as a private vehicle and unsuitable to be so used
- British Government securities (see Chapter 7)
- qualifying corporate bonds (see Chapter 7)
- investments in personal equity plans (see Chapter 4)
- savings certificates and other non-marketable securities
- life assurance policies (unless purchased)
- currency for a person's own use
- betting and lottery winnings
- decorations for valour if awarded or inherited
- compensation for personal injury
- wasting chattels not used for business purposes (see Chapter 6)
- the taxpayer's principal private residence throughout the period of ownership (see Chapter 6)
- the first disposal of shares purchased under the Enterprise Investment Scheme.

Assets not covered above may bear some form of partial exemption.

Situation of assets

In some circumstances the situation of the assets is critical and there are specific rules to determine the situation of specific kinds of assets:

- immoveable property is situated where it is physically located
- tangible moveable property is situated at its location at the time of disposal
- shares and so forth, along with patents, are situated in the country in which they are registered
- debts are situated in the country in which the creditor is resident
- government securities are situated in the country of issue
- goodwill is situated where the business is carried on.

Chargeable person

Individuals

The liability of individuals to capital gains tax depends primarily on their country of residence.

A UK-domiciled and resident individual is liable to capital gains tax on chargeable gains arising on disposals of assets situated anywhere in the world. Equally, a non-UK-domiciled but UK-resident individual is liable to capital gains tax on chargeable gains arising from the disposal of UK situated assets (and foreign assets if the gain is remitted to the UK).

An individual who is not UK resident or ordinarily resident but who carries on a trade in the UK through a branch or an agency is chargeable to capital gains tax on chargeable gains arising on the disposal of business assets situated in the UK. Also, there is a deemed disposal of such assets if the UK branch or agency ceases or the asset is removed from the UK.

There are anti-avoidance provisions which enable UK shareholders in certain foreign companies and UK beneficiaries in certain foreign trusts to be assessed on a proportion of any chargeable gains accruing to the company or the trust. (See 'Overseas Activities'.)

Partnerships
A partnership is not a legal entity in England and Wales separate and distinct from its members. All assets of a partnership belong to the individual partners in their agreed shares. The sale proceeds are therefore split between the partners in this ratio allowing each partner to be charged individually to capital gains tax (see Chapter 19).

Companies
Companies pay corporation tax on their chargeable gains (see section on 'Corporate Taxation').

Trustees and personal representatives
Trustees and personal representatives are liable to capital gains tax in that representative capacity.

Exempted persons
The list of persons exempt from capital gains tax includes superannuation and pension funds, friendly societies, local authorities, scientific research establishments and charities (provided the gains are used for charitable purposes).

The charge to tax

Basis of assessment

Capital gains tax is assessed on a fiscal year basis on the net chargeable gains accruing to a chargeable person in that year. (Companies pay corporation tax on the net chargeable gains accruing in the accounting period.)

It should be noted that the net chargeable gains of an individual who incurs a trading loss in any fiscal year from 1991/92 onwards may be reduced by the amount of the available trading loss (see Chapter 18). Individuals have an exemption for each fiscal year as follows:

	£
1994/95	5,800
1993/94	5,800
1992/93	5,800
1991/92	5,500
1990/91	5,000

Where this amount is unused in any fiscal year it is wasted and cannot be carried forward or otherwise utilised. This exemption is also available to personal representatives of a deceased taxpayer in the year of death and the two following years. One half of the full annual exemption is available to trustees of settlements except where the trust is for a mentally handicapped person or a person receiving the attendance allowance, when the full exemption is available.

Rates of tax

The basic rate of capital gains tax is equivalent to the basic rate of income tax (25% in 1994/95). However, for individuals, if their marginal rate of income tax is lower or higher, capital gains tax will be levied at that lower or higher rate – as if the gains were the top slice of taxable income.

It must be stressed that although this calculation is made by reference to income tax rates the tax, when computed, is paid as capital gains tax and not income tax.

Unused personal allowances may not be deducted from net chargeable gains for the year nor is the computation of the age allowance for income tax purposes affected by any chargeable gains in the year.

If an individual's income includes dividends, and his other taxable income (after deducting allowances) is less than the lower rate band, the balance of the lower rate band is available to set against gains. The basic rate band, however, is set against dividend income in priority to chargeable gains.

EXAMPLE 5.1

Adam is single. In 1994/95 he received a salary of £4,500 and dividends of 16,000. He realised chargeable gains of £11,000.

Income Tax	£	Capital Gains Tax	£
Salary	4,500	Gains	11,000
Dividends	20,000	Exemption	(5,800)
	24,500		5,200
PA	(3,445)		
Taxable income	21,055		
Tax due:		Tax due:	
On non-dividends		£1,945 × 20% =	389
£1,055 × 20% =	211	(3,000 – 1,055)	
On dividends		£700 × 25% =	175
£20,000 × 20% =	4,000	(20,700 – 20,000)	
		£2,555 × 40% =	1,022
	4,211		1,586

Returns

Information about chargeable gains must be included in the annual tax return of a chargeable person.

Where the chargeable gains of individuals do not exceed the exempt amount for the year (£5,800 for 1994/95) and the total consideration for the disposal of chargeable assets does not exceed twice the exempt amount (£11,600 for 1994/95) a statement to this effect is all that is required on the return.

The worth of this concesssion is dubious as it is still necessary to do the computations for the year in case there are net allowable losses which will be available for carry forward for relief in future years.

Losses

Allowable losses

To the extent that allowable losses exceed the chargeable gains in any year, the excess losses may be carried forward and deducted from chargeable gains of the following and subsequent years.

Indexation losses (individuals and trustees of settlements made before 30 November 1993 only)

To the extent that an indexation loss arises in 1993/94, it may be deducted from the relevant gain for that year (i.e. the net chargeable gains – total chargeable gains less allowable losses of the fiscal year) up to the lower of:

1. £10,000, or
2. the amount by which the relevant gain for 1993/94 exceeds the exempt amount for that year.

In 1994/95, an indexation loss arising in 1994/95 or an indexation loss brought forward from 1993/94 may be deducted from the relevant gain for that year up to the lower of:

1. £10,000 less any indexation loss deducted in 1993/94, or
2. the amount by which the relevant gain for 1994/95 exceeds the exempt amount for that year.

Losses brought forward by individuals

In any fiscal year in which an allowable loss or an indexation loss is brought forward by an individual, it need only be used to the extent that the relevant gain of that year exceeds the exempt amount for that year. The indexation loss (maximum £10,000 over 1993/94 and 1994/95) is used in priority to any allowable losses carried forward from any previous year. Where the net chargeable gains of the year do not exceed the exempt amount for that year then none of the losses brought forward need be used, and any allowable losses will be carried forward to the next fiscal year. Indexation losses, unused at the end of 1994/95, will *not* be available to carry forward to 1995/96 or later years.

EXAMPLE 5.2

In 1994/95, John has a chargeable gain of £8,000 and allowable losses of £5,000. He also has losses brought forward of £3,000.

His net chargeable gains for 1994/95 are £3,000 (£8,000 – £5,000).

The annual exemption for 1994/95 is £5,800 and therefore John will not have a liability to capital gains tax in 1994/95. The losses brought forward of £3,000 are also unused and may be carried forward to 1995/96.

EXAMPLE 5.3

In 1994/95, Mary has chargeable gains amounting to £9,000 and allowable losses of £3,000. She also has losses brought forward of £2,000.

Her net chargeable gains for 1994/95 are £6,000 (£9,000 – £3,000). Only part of the losses brought forward (£200) will be set off against this, leaving an amount equal to the annual exemption of £5,800. There will be £Nil liable to capital gains tax in 1994/95 and unused losses for carry forward to 1995/96 of £1,800.

EXAMPLE 5.4

Harold has the following net chargeable gains, indexation losses and allowable losses brought forward in 1993/94 and 1994/95:

	1993/94 £	1994/95 £
Relevant gain (i.e. net chargeable gains of the year)	10,000	20,000
Indexation losses	5,000	2,000

There were allowable losses brought forward from 1992/93 of £4,000.

	1993/94 £
Relevant gain	10,000
less lower of 1) £10,000 2) Relevant gain less annual exemption (10,000 – 5,800) = £4,200 3) Indexation loss £5,000	(4,200)
less allowable loss brought forward	(–)
less annual exemption	(5,800)
Taxable	NIL

Indexation loss to carry forward (5,000 – 4,200) = £800

	1994/95 £
Relevant gain	20,000
less lower of 1) £10,000 less £4,200 = £5,800 2) Relevant gain less annual exemption (20,000 – 5,800) = £14,200 3) Indexation loss £2,000 plus £800 brought forward = £2,800	(2,800)
less allowable loss brought forward	(4,000)
less annual exemption	(5,800)
	7,400

Losses on transactions with connected persons

A loss incurred on a disposal to a connected person is only deductible from future gains on disposals to the same connected person (see below).

Net losses in the year of death

In the fiscal year of death, if net losses are incurred prior to the date of death these may be carried back and be deducted from the amounts chargeable to capital gains tax in the three years prior to the year of death – taking a later year in priority to an earlier one. Any losses then remaining will be unrelieved.

EXAMPLE 5.5

Alan died on 10 January 1995. He had incurred net allowable losses in 1994/95 to the date of death of £4,500. His capital gains position (before annual exemptions) for the previous three years was as follows:

	1993/94	gains	£2,000	
	1992/93	gains	£7,000	
	1991/92	gains	£8,000	

	1991/92 £	1992/93 £	1993/94 £
Gains	8,000	7,000	2,000
Less loss c/b year death	(2,500)	(1,200)	–
Revised taxable amount	5,500	5,800	2,000
Annual exemption	(5,500)	(5,800)	(5,800)
Liable to capital gains tax	–	–	–

		Loss memo
Year of death	1994/95	4,500
	1993/94	–
	1992/93	(1,200)
	1991/92	(2,500)
Loss unrelieved		800

Married persons

Under independent taxation the chargeable gains and allowable losses of each spouse are computed and aggregated separately and are assessed independently on each spouse at the appropriate marginal rate of income tax. Each has an annual exemption. The losses of one spouse cannot be set against the gains of the other. Unused losses of a married couple at 5 April 1990 were allocated to each spouse according to the manner in which they arose.

Transfers of assets between spouses continue to be treated as giving rise to neither a gain nor a loss.

Collection of capital gains tax

The normal due date for payment of capital gains tax is 1 December following the end of the fiscal year while the Table date is six months later. (That is, 1 June following the 1 December following the end of the fiscal year.) The provisions for appeals, postponement of tax charged, actual due dates for payment of the tax and the computation of interest on overdue tax (and repayment supplements) are identical to income tax (see Chapter 22).

Payment by instalments

Where all or part of the consideration for a disposal is payable over a period of more than 18 months from the date of disposal, the resulting tax liability may be paid by instalments if the taxpayer can show that to pay it in one sum would cause undue hardship. The period over which the instalments may be spread must be negotiated with the Inland Revenue. However, the maximum period over which instalments may be spread is generally eight years or, if less, the period until the last of the consideration is due to be received.

Following amendments made by the Finance Act 1989 to the availability of hold-over relief (see below), further provisions have been made for the payment of capital gains tax by annual instalments over ten years. These apply to gifts of either:

- land
- a controlling shareholding in a company
- minority holdings of shares or securities in a company not quoted or dealt in on the USM

where hold-over relief would previously have been available. The first instalment will be due on the normal due date.

Format of the computation

In its general outline, the computation of chargeable gains (or allowable losses) is comparatively straightforward:

	£
Disposal value	X
Less allowable deductions	(X)
Unindexed gain / (loss)	X
Less indexation allowance	(X)
Chargeable gain / (allowable loss)	X

Disposal value

The disposal value is the actual consideration as agreed by the parties (the sale price or other capital sum received). This is provided that the transaction is a bargain 'at arm's length' and that the consideration can be expressed in monetary terms. (An example is a capital distribution by a company of assets *in specie.*)

However, if the transaction is either:

- between 'connected persons', or
- a bargain not 'at arm's length' (for example, disposal wholly or partly by way of gift)

the disposal value of the vendor and the acquisition value of the purchaser will be deemed to be market value.

Market value

Market value is the price which an individual asset could reasonably be expected to fetch on the open market. No allowance is made for a quantity of items being placed on the market at one time.

There are special rules for arriving at the market value of specific assets.

Quoted shares and securities
Prices for these are quoted on the Stock Exchange Daily Official List. The market value is the lower of:

- the buying price (the lower of the two prices) quoted on the day of disposal, plus a quarter of the difference between the higher and lower prices (the 'quarter up' rule)

- the average of the highest and the lowest marked bargains recorded on the day of disposal, if any.

Where the Stock Exchange is closed on the day in question, the prices to be taken are those from the latest previous date or those from the earliest subsequent date, whichever gives the lower value.

EXAMPLE 5.6

Shares in X plc were disposed of when they were quoted at 210–218p, the high and low recorded bargains of the day being 208p and 220p.
The market value will be the lower of:

a) $$210 + \frac{218-210}{4} = 212p$$

b) $$\frac{208 + 220}{2} = 214p \qquad \text{i.e. } 212p$$

Securities dealt with on the USM are not regarded as listed or quoted for this purpose. Evidence of recent bargains at open market value may be used as a basis for valuation but other factors may also need to be considered. The Share Valuation Division of the Capital Taxes Office deals with these matters.

Unquoted shares
The market value of unquoted shares is arrived at on the assumption that 'all information which a prudent prospective purchaser might reasonably require before entering into an arrangement to purchase at arm's length from a willing vendor', is available. The Share Valuation Division of the Capital Taxes Office deals with such valuations.

Connected persons

Bargains made with close relatives and others who are called connected persons are always regarded as not being made at 'arm's length' and are therefore deemed to be made at market value.
There are four categories of connected persons for this purpose:

An individual is connected with his or her relatives
An individual is connected with his or her husband or wife, or with their relatives, or with the husband or wife of such a relative. Relatives are defined as brother, sister, ancestor or lineal descendant (that is, a person in direct ascent or descent). A widow or widower is no longer a spouse nor are divorced spouses, although descendants will include children from a previous marriage.

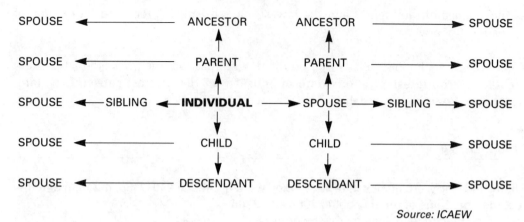

Figure 5.1 The individual in this chart is connected with all the persons shown.

A trustee of a settlement

Such a trustee is connected with the settlor and with any person who is connected with the settlor (see above). This means that any capital gains tax transaction between a trust and the person who set up the trust or someone closely related to that person will be deemed to take place at market value.

Partners in a partnership

These are connected with each other and, in addition, with the spouse and relatives of their partners. The market value rule does not, however, apply to the acquisition or disposal of partnership assets as a result of bona fide commercial arrangements. Therefore most transactions concerning a partnership's business assets and the interests of the partners are outside the rule.

Companies

These are connected to another person (company or individual) if that person controls the company, or that person and persons connected to him or her have control of the company.

Companies may be connected to each other in the following circumstances:

- where the same person has control of both
- where a person has control of one company and persons connected to him or her have control of the other
- where a person has control of one company and he or she and connected persons have control of the other
- where the same group of persons control both companies
- where a group of persons control one company and a group of persons connected to them have control of the other.

Any losses that arise on transactions with connected persons may only be set off against chargeable gains arising subsequently on a disposal to the same connected person (while he or she is still connected).

There is further anti avoidance legislation surrounding transactions between connected persons (see Chapter 28).

Allowable deductions

Allowable deductions fall into two categories:

- those relating to the cost of the asset being disposed of
- those arising at the time of disposal.

Capital cost of asset

The capital cost of the asset being disposed of generally reflects the standard accounting definition of capital expenditure and may be subdivided into two parts:

▶ Amounts wholly and exclusively incurred in the acquisition of the asset plus any incidental costs so incurred (see below for examples of incidental costs). Where the asset has been created, the costs of its creation may be substituted.
▶ Amounts wholly and exclusively incurred for the purpose of enhancing the value of the asset and reflected in the state of the asset at the date of disposal. Also included is expenditure incurred in establishing or defending the title to or a right over an asset.

Expenditure specifically excluded from the above is that which is deductible in computing profits or losses for income tax purposes, or that would be deductible if the asset were held for the purpose of a trade. Also excluded is any expenditure recoverable as a result of government or local authority grants.

Where the asset is inherited, the acquisition value will be the probate value in the deceased estate. Equally, where the asset is received as a gift, the acquisition value will be the deemed disposal value (usually market value) of the donee.

Each of the items of expenditure should be shown separately in the computation along with the dates relating to each. This will not necessarily be the date of payment but should be the date the expenditure is reflected in the value of the asset.

Incidental costs of disposal

These include:

▶ professional fees for the services of a surveyor, auctioneer, accountant, solicitor, valuer and so on
▶ legal charges associated with the transfer or conveyance of property (including stamp duty)
▶ advertising for a buyer
▶ costs of ascertaining market values and so forth, where these are required for purposes of the computation of the chargeable gain/allowable loss and any other costs reasonably incurred.

The accountant's fees referred to cover fees for the valuation of unquoted shares and similar matters but do not cover fees for agreeing computations.

EXAMPLE 5.7

The following is an example of the computation of the unindexed gain accruing to a taxpayer who bought a house for letting, later improved it and finally sold it:

			£
Disposal value – gross sale proceeds 25 January 1995			150,000
Less	Incidental costs of disposal		
	Advertising for sale	300	
	Legal expenses	400	
	Estate agent's commission on sale	4,000	
			(4,700)
			145,300
Less	Cost of acquisition 25 August 1982	40,000	
	Survey fee	50	
	Legal fees, including stamp duty	650	
			(40,700)

		£	£
Less	Enhancement cost 15 June 1984		
	Architect's fee	250	
	Building costs	9,750	
			(10,000)
Less	Enhancement cost 20 September 1985		
	Architect's fee	250	
	Building costs	5,000	
			(5,250)
Unindexed gain			89,350

Part disposals

Where only a part of an asset is disposed of, this is also a chargeable disposal for capital gains tax purposes and may give rise to a chargeable gain or allowable loss. The difficulty in this case is finding the relevant allowable deductions for the part of the asset disposed of to match with the disposal value in order to calculate the gain.

Those allowable deductions which do not relate specifically to the part disposed of or the part retained are regarded as relating to the asset as a whole. The formula for apportioning the allowable deductions relating to the asset as a whole between the part disposed of and the part retained is as follows:

If the disposal value of the part is A and the market value of the part which remains is B then the allowable deductions pertaining to the whole are each apportioned to the part disposed of by the formula:

$$\frac{A}{A+B}$$

The balance of the allowable deductions relates to the part of the asset retained. Any allowable deductions which relate specifically to the part disposed of (rather than to the whole) will be deducted in full from the disposal value of the part.

EXAMPLE 5.8

A acquired an asset at a cost of £10,000 and subsequently enhanced it at a cost of £5,000. Two years later he disposed of a part of it for £10,000. The incidental costs of disposal were £500 and the market value of the part not disposed of at the same date was £15,000.

The acquisition cost of the part disposed of is calculated proportionately as being:

$$\frac{10,000}{10,000 + 15,000} \times £10,000 = £4,000$$

The enhancement cost of the part disposed of is calculated proportionately as being:

$$\frac{10,000}{10,000 + 15,000} \times £5,000 = £2,000$$

The unindexed gain is therefore 10,000 − (£4,000 + £2,000 + £500) = £3,500. The allowable deductions on a disposal of the remainder of the asset will be acquisition cost of £6,000 (£10,000 − £4,000) and enhancement cost of £3,000 (£5,000 − £2,000).

Part disposals of land

Special provisions apply to small part disposals of land. A part disposal of land is regarded as small where A (as defined above) does not exceed one-fifth of A+B (as defined above).

In certain circumstances the transferor may claim that the transfer is not treated as a chargeable disposal. The disposal value which would have been used in the computation of the chargeable gain/allowable loss is instead deducted from the allowable expenditure for purposes of any future disposal of the remainder of the land.

The circumstances referred to are that the disposal value of the part must not exceed £20,000 and, if there were other disposals of land in the fiscal year, then the total disposal value of land in the fiscal year must not exceed £20,000.

The above circumstances do not apply if the disposal of the land is as a result of a compulsory purchase order.

EXAMPLE 5.9

B acquired some land at a total cost £50,000. Some years later, he sold a small section of it to a neighbour for £10,000. The market value of the remainder was £90,000.

The disposal value of £10,000 is less than £20,000 and less than 20% of the value of the land immediately before the disposal [20% × (10,000 + 90,000) = 20,000] and therefore B may claim that the transfer is not treated as a chargeable disposal but that the sale proceeds are deducted from the cost for future disposals. In this case the cost of the remaining land carried forward will be £40,000 (£50,000 − £10,000).

Piecemeal disposals of property to connected persons

As previously stated, all transactions with connected persons are deemed to take place at market value. However, if a group of assets is subdivided, the sum of the market values of the individual parts is usually less than the market value of the group. Taxpayers might be tempted therefore to avoid tax by making piecemeal disposals if it were not for this section. This legislation affects disposals after 20 March 1985.

This section applies to 'linked' disposals to one or more connected persons (other than between husband and wife and certain intra-group transfers) if the sum of the market values of the component assets (original market values) is less than the market value of all the 'linked' transactions (aggregate market value) (that is, considering all the assets together as if disposed of at the time of the latest disposal). Two or more transactions are linked if they take place within a period of six years.

For this purpose the value of the latest disposal is computed as 'the appropriate portion of the aggregate market value of the assets'. The appropriate portion is that fraction which is reasonable in describing the relationship of the asset disposed of with the others in the series of transactions.

The classic example of a situation to which this section might apply would be a set of antique chairs which is split up between members of the family. (This may perhaps be with the intention that they could be brought back together again as a set sometime in the future.) It could also be applied to the splitting of a substantial shareholding in an unquoted company.

EXAMPLE 5.10

Assets A, B, and C are identical parts of a set.

A is disposed of first (to a connected person) when its market value is £5,000. This is the first in the series and as yet is not a 'linked' transaction. The disposal value would be £5,000.

B is disposed of next (also to a connected person) when its market value is £6,000. It is linked to the disposal of A (provided less than six years have elapsed) and the £6,000 is described as original market value.

If A and B had been disposed of together, their market value (aggregate market value) would have been £14,000. This is more than the sum of the market values of A and B individually, £11,000 (£5,000 + £6,000). As A and B are identical, the appropriate portion of the aggregate market value applicable to B is one half (£7,000). The disposal value of B would be taken as £7,000.

C is finally disposed of (also within the six-year period and to a connected person) when its market value is £7,000. The aggregate market value of A, B, and C is £24,000 while the sum of their original market values is £18,000 (£5,000 + £6,000 + £7,000). They are linked transactions and the disposal value of C will be taken as one-third of £24,000 (£8,000). The computation of the gains arising on each of the assets A and B would also be revised to show a disposal value in each case of £8,000.

Indexation allowance

The indexation allowance was introduced in the Finance Act 1982 as a relief for inflation included in gains arising after that date.

The allowance is given whenever there is a disposal after 5 April 1982 (or 31 March 1982 in the case of a company). For disposals made on or after 30 November 1993, indexation may reduce a gain, but cannot increase or create an allowable loss. Instead, the unused indexation will (up to 5 April 1995) create an indexation loss (maximum £10,000) which can be used to reduce CGT liabilities for 1993–94 and 1994–95 (see above).

Calculation of indexation allowance (for disposals post 5 April 1985)

The indexation allowance is the sum of the indexed rises for each item of relevant allowable expenditure. Relevant allowable expenditure is the acquisition cost plus any enhancement expenditure. No indexation allowance is available on the incidental costs of disposal. The indexed rise for each item of expenditure is calculated by multiplying the cost of each item by the increase (correct to three decimal places) in the retail price index between the month in which the disposal occurred and the month in which the expenditure was incurred, or March 1982, if later. If the retail price index has not risen between these two dates, there is no indexed rise for that item of expenditure.

A table of retail price indices can be found at the back of this book.

EXAMPLE 5.11

Using the information in Example 5.7, the indexation allowance would be calculated as follows (disposal date January 1995):

	Indexation allowance £
Cost of acquisition 25 August 1982	
$\dfrac{144.7 - 81.9}{81.9} = 0.767$	
40,700 × 0.767	31,217
Enhancement cost 15 June 1984	
$\dfrac{144.7 - 89.2}{89.2} = 0.622$	
10,000 × 0.622	6,220
	37,437
Enhancement cost 20 September 1985	
$\dfrac{144.7 - 95.4}{95.4} = 0.517$	
5,250 × 0.517	2,714
Incidental costs of disposal	Nil
Indexation allowance	40,151
Unindexed gain from Example 5.7	89,350
Chargeable gain	£49,199

Assets held on 31 March 1982

For disposals after 5 April 1988, the indexation allowance is automatically based on the higher of the actual cost and the 31 March 1982 value of the asset.

EXAMPLE 5.12

An asset was sold on 4 January 1995 for £30,000 which had been purchased on 31 December 1980 for £8,000 and which had improvements made in April 1981 at a cost of £2,000 and in April 1983 at a cost of £3,000. Its value at 31 March 1982 was £12,000.

Acquisition cost December 1980	£8,000
Enhancement cost April 1981	£2,000
Actual cost at 31 March 1982	£10,000
Market value at 31 March 1982	£12,000

For disposals after 5 April 1988, the higher of these two figures would be used automatically to calculate the indexation allowance. (Prior to this date an election would have been required to use the market value at 31 March 1982.)

The indexation allowance would be calculated as follows:

	Indexation allowance £
Market value at 31 March 1982	
$\dfrac{144.7 - 79.4}{79.4} = 0.822$	
12,000 × 0.822	9,864
Enhancement cost April 1983	
$\dfrac{144.7 - 84.3}{84.3} = 0.716$	
3,000 × 0.716	2,148
Indexation allowance	12,012

Part disposals

The apportionment of the relevant allowable deductions will already have taken place before the indexation allowance is calculated. The indexation allowance is then given on the allowable deductions attributable to the part of the asset disposed of.

Reductions of allowable expenditure

Where account must be taken of receipts or other adjustments which affect the allowable deductions for capital gains purposes these will affect the computation of the indexation allowance. Occasions when account must be taken of such items are called 'relevant events'.

It has already been shown after a small part disposal of land that on a subsequent disposal of the remainder of the land, the proceeds of disposal of the small part would be deducted from the allowable cost of the remainder. This would be a relevant event in the computation of the indexation allowance.

A further example of a relevant event is the sale by a shareholder of rights not being taken up. In these circumstances the indexed rise is calculated for all the allowable deductions without regard to the reduction. The indexed rise is also calculated for the reduction (from the date of the small disposal) and deducted from the other indexed rises to give a net indexation allowance.

An illustration of this computation will be found in Example 5.19 towards the end of this chapter.

Disposals of assets held on 31 March 1982

The Finance Act 1988 introduced a fundamental alteration to the way in which chargeable gains/allowable losses are measured. Prior to this gains and losses arising post 5 April 1965 were relevant to the computation of capital gains tax. The effect of the Act was to restrict chargeable gains and losses to a maximum of those arising post 31 March 1982. This is called 're-basing at 31 March 1982'.

General rule

For all disposals after 5 April 1988, the computation will, except in limited cases, be based on the 31 March 1982 value of any assets held by the transferor at that date. Such assets are deemed to have been sold and immediately reacquired by him or her at market value on 31 March 1982. However, unless a special election is made to apply the 31 March 1982 value in every case (see below), the use of the 31 March 1982 value cannot increase a gain or a loss compared with that which would have arisen under the old rules. The following guidelines therefore apply:

▶ The gain based on the 31 March 1982 value is chargeable unless a smaller gain can be established under the old rules.
▶ A loss based on the 31 March 1982 value is only allowable if a larger loss can be established under the old rules.
▶ If a gain arises on the 31 March 1982 value but a loss would have arisen under the old rules, the gain is not chargeable.
▶ If a loss arises on the 31 March 1982 value but a gain would have arisen under the old rules, the loss is not allowable.
▶ If the restriction of indexation results in one of the computations producing a nil position and the other producing a gain, there will be no gain and no loss. (See Example 5.13)

It is therefore always necessary to compute the gain or loss which would have arisen pre-Finance Act 1988. Thus, a two column computation is required (as illustrated below in Example 5.13).

Old rules

Under the rules which existed prior to the Finance Act 1988, the chargeable gain was the difference between the disposal value and the allowable deductions plus the indexation allowance in all cases except where the asset was owned on 6 April 1965 (when capital gains tax was introduced).

EXAMPLE 5.13

X acquired an asset in 1970 for £10,000. Enhancement expenditure was incurred in November 1978 of £4,000 and in April 1985 of £8,000. The asset was sold in January 1995 for £60,000. The market value of the asset at 31 March 1982 was £40,000.

	31 March 1982 value £	Old rules £
Disposal value	60,000	60,000
Less: acquisition cost 1970		(10,000)
Less: Enhancement cost 1978		(4,000)
Less: 31 March 1982 value	(40,000)	
Less: Enhancement cost 1985	(8,000)	(8,000)
Unindexed gain/(loss)	12,000	38,000
Less: indexation allowance:		
on 31 March 82 value		
$\dfrac{144.7 - 79.4}{79.4} = 0.822 \times 40,000$	(12,000)	(32,880)
On enhancement cost		
$\dfrac{144.7 - 94.8}{94.8} = 0.526 \times 8,000$	–	(4,208)
	–	912

Note that the indexation due has been restricted in the March 1982 column as it is no longer possible for indexation to create a loss.
There is therefore no gain and no loss.

Election for universal 31 March 1982 valuation

The taxpayer has the right to elect for all disposals after 5 April 1988 to be based on the 31 March 1982 valuation. The election is irrevocable. It had to be made in writing to the Inspector of Taxes at any time before 6 April 1990 or, if later, within two years after the end of the fiscal year in which the first disposal of such an asset is made.

Husband and wife each have the right to make an election in respect of his or her own property.

Consequences of the election

If the election is made by the taxpayer it applies to all disposals after 5 April 1988 (including any made before the election) of assets held by him or her on 31 March 1982. The exceptions and restrictions referred to in previous paragraphs are then disregarded. In some cases the election may be beneficial but in others it may be to the taxpayer's disadvantage. A taxpayer should therefore calculate the potential effect on any significant assets before making the election.

The indexation allowance, where an election has been made for universal 31 March 1982 re-basing, is automatically based upon the 31 March 1982 value.

The requirement to do two or more capital gains tax computations in every case and the necessity to keep records of earlier acquisition dates and costs is obviated.

'No gain, no loss' disposals

Disposals on this basis apply principally to transfers between husband and wife, gifts to charities, and to intra-group transfers (see Corporate Taxation).

The transferor's disposal value is deemed to be such that when the chargeable gain is computed neither a gain nor a loss results. The disposal value is therefore equal to the allowable deductions plus the indexation allowance calculated in the normal way to the date of the transfer.

EXAMPLE 5.14

A gives his wife an asset with a market value of £20,000 on 1 August 1986. The asset was bought in March 1983 for £10,000. The deemed disposal value is calculated as follows:

	£
Cost of the asset	10,000
Indexation allowance:	
$\dfrac{97.8 - 83.1}{83.1} = 0.177$	
10,000 × 0.177	1,770
Deemed disposal value	11,770

This disposal value is also deemed to be the transferee's acquisition value such that on a subsequent disposal by the transferee it would be an allowable deduction in addition to any subsequent enhancement expenditure carried out and any incidental costs of disposal. An indexation allowance would on this occasion be calculated from the date of transfer to the date of disposal.

EXAMPLE 5.15

Continuing the previous example, A's wife subsequently sold the asset for £30,000 on 31 January 1995.

	£
Disposal value	30,000
Less: deemed acquisition value	(11,770)
Unindexed gain	18,230
Less: indexation allowance	
$\dfrac{144.7 - 97.8}{97.8} = 0.480$	
11,770 × 0.480	(5,650)
Chargeable gain	12,580

Finance Act 1988: re-basing provisions

A number of alternative combinations may arise, of which the main ones are:

- The transferor held the asset being transferred on 31 March 1982 and transferred it on a no gain, no loss basis to the transferee before 6 April 1988. The transferee disposes of the asset post 5 April 1988.

  The transferee is treated as having held the asset at 31 March 1982 (that is, he or she takes over the transferor's allowable deductions). Under the provisions of the Finance Act 1988, the 31 March 1982 value will be used in the computation subject to the normal restrictions and the *right of the transferee to make an election for universal re-basing* at 31 March 1982.

- The transferor held the asset on 31 March 1982 and transferred it on a no gain, no loss basis to the transferee after 5 April 1988. The transferee subsequently disposes of the asset.

  An election for universal 31 March 1982 value made by the transferee does not apply to his or her subsequent disposal of that asset but if the transferor makes such an election (either before or after the transfer) it will apply to any disposal of that asset by the transferee.

EXAMPLE 5.16

William purchased a holiday cottage in May 1980 for £20,000. On 31 March 1982, its agreed value was £25,000. On 31 August 1987, William gave the cottage to his wife Mary. On 19 January 1995, Mary sold the cottage for £80,000.

The disposal from William to Mary is a no gain, no loss disposal.

On the disposal in January 1995, Mary is treated as if she had held the asset on 31 March 1982:

	31 March 1982	Cost
	£	£
Sale proceeds	80,000	80,000
Deemed cost	(25,000)	(20,000)
Unindexed gain	55,000	60,000
Less: indexation allowance		
$\dfrac{144.7-79.4}{79.4} = 0.822 \times £25,000$	(20,550)	(20,550)
Chargeable gain	34,450	39,450

The lower gain of £34,450 will be assessable on Mary for 1994/95.

Hold-over relief

The tax assessment on certain types of disposals may in some cases be deferred. This is called hold-over relief. Hold-over relief is given as detailed in the following sections.

Gifts

A gift, whether or not to a connected person, is not a bargain at arm's length and the disposal value must therefore be market value. The availability of hold-over relief on gifts was restricted in the FA 1989 and is now given for the following categories of gifts:

- Gifts of property which result in an immediate charge to inheritance tax (principally gifts to discretionary trusts and companies). This includes gifts which are non-taxable only because they fall within the annual exemption or nil rate band. (PETs are not regarded as bearing an immediate charge to IHT – see Chapter 8.)
- Gifts of heritage property and gifts to funds for the maintenance of heritage property where exemption from inheritance tax is available (see Chapter 8).
- Gifts to political parties and trusts for political parties where exemption from inheritance tax is available (see Chapter 8).
- Gifts of agricultural property on which agricultural property relief (inheritance tax) is available (see Chapter 9).
- Gifts of business assets and shares in unquoted or family trading companies (see Chapter 19).

Gains may also be deferred by reinvestment relief. This will be considered in Chapter 20.

Holdover relief is given as nil consideration and part consideration.

Nil consideration

The gain which would otherwise be chargeable and the donee's acquisition value are each reduced by the 'held-over gain'. So the chargeable gain is reduced to nil and the donee's acquisition value becomes market value at the date of the transfer less the held-over gain.

EXAMPLE 5.17

A made a gift to a discretionary trust on 25 January 1995 of an asset with a market value of £10,000. The asset was bought for £5,000 on 30 September 1984.

	£
Disposal value	10,000
Less: cost	(5,000)
Unindexed gain	5,000
Less: indexation allowance	
$\dfrac{144.7 - 90.1}{90.1} = 0.606$	
Less 5,000 × 0.606	(3,030)
Chargeable gain to be held over	1,970

	£
Market value at date of gift to trust	10,000
Less: gain held-over	(1,970)
Acquisition value of trust	8,030

Part consideration

As above, the gain which would otherwise be chargeable and the donee's acquisition value are each reduced by the 'held-over gain'. In this case the held-over gain is the chargeable gain reduced by the amount the actual consideration exceeds the total allowable deductions (before indexation).

EXAMPLE 5.18

Using Example 5.17, assume that the trust paid £6,000 for the asset.

	£
Disposal value	10,000
Less: cost	(5,000)
Unindexed gain	5,000
Less indexation allowance	

$$\frac{144.7 - 90.1}{90.1} = 0.606$$

		£
5,000 × 0.606		(3030)
Chargeable gain		1,970
Less: Gain remaining chargeable:		
Consideration	6,000	
Allowable deductions	(5,000)	
(assessable)		(1,000) (assessable 1994/95)
Amount to be held-over		970

	£
Market value at date of gift to trust	10,000
Less: gain held over	(970)
Acquisition value of discretionary trust	9,030

In both cases the effect is to defer the assessment of the gain until future disposal of the asset by the donee.

On a subsequent disposal by the donee (the trust in the above examples), a deduction would be allowed in the computation of the chargeable gain. This would be of an amount equal to the inheritance tax attributable to the value of the asset when transferred to the donee. (Note that this deduction cannot give rise to an allowable loss.) A further indexation allowance would also be available, calculated from the date of the gift to the date of disposal and applied to the acquisition value as calculated above.

The above provisions do not apply if the transferee is not UK resident and ordinarily resident or would not otherwise be liable to capital gains tax on a subsequent disposal of the asset concerned.

If the donee becomes neither resident nor ordinarily resident in the United Kingdom within six years of the end of the year of assessment for which hold-over relief is claimed, while still in possession of the asset, then a chargeable gain is deemed to arise at that time, equal to the held-over gain.

Prior to 14 March 1989, hold-over relief on gifts was more generally available and gains held over before that date will still be adjusted against acquisition values of the assets concerned.

Compensation and insurance receipts

If an asset is destroyed, compensation or insurance receipts will usually be treated as the disposal value in a capital gains computation. However, if it was used wholly or in part to replace the asset within 12 months of its receipt, a claim may be made to hold over the gain against the cost of the replacement asset.

EXAMPLE 5.19

A holiday cottage, bought in April 1984 for £10,000, was destroyed by fire in January 1995. Insurance proceeds of £25,000 were received two months later and were used to purchase another cottage costing £20,000 in October 1995.

		£
Insurance proceeds		25,000
Less: cost of destroyed asset		(10,000)
Unindexed gain		15,000
Less indexation allowance		
$\dfrac{144.7 - 88.6}{88.6} = 0.633$		
10,000 × 0.633		(6,330)
		8,670
Less: gain remaining chargeable:		
Compensation	25,000	
reinvested	(20,000)	
		(5,000) (assessable 1994/95)
Gain held over		3,670

The allowable deductions on the new cottage are reduced as follows:

	£
Cost	20,000
Less: gain held over	(3,670)
Allowable deductions	16,330

If an asset is damaged as opposed to being destroyed and the greater part of the compensation or insurance monies are employed (at least 95%) in restoring the asset or are incidental (less than 5% of the asset value) then a claim may be made to deduct the monies from the cost of the asset. This avoids a part disposal computation. (Note the effect on the computation of the negative indexation allowance as described earlier.)

EXAMPLE 5.20

An asset which cost £20,000 in May 1982 is damaged by flood in January 1993. Compensation of £8,000 was received in March 1993 of which £7,950 was used in restoring the asset in July 1993. The asset was subsequently disposed of in January 1995 for £50,000.

A claim can be made to deduct the compensation from the cost of the asset as follows:

	£
Original cost of asset May 1982	20,000
Cost of restoration July 1993	7,950
	27,950
Less: compensation March 1993	(8,000)
Revised allowable deductions	19,950
Sale proceeds	50,000
Allowable deductions (as above)	(19,950)
Less: indexation allowance	30,050

$\dfrac{144.7 - 81.6}{81.6} = 0.773 \times 20,000$ 15,460

$\dfrac{144.7 - 140.7}{140.7} = 0.028 \times 7,950$ 223

$\dfrac{144.7 - 139.3}{139.3} = 0.039 \times 8,000$ (312)

	(15,371)
Chargeable gain	14,679

Finance Act 1988: re-basing provisions

Where an asset, acquired after 31 March 1982 but the subject of a hold-over claim, is disposed of after 5 April 1988 the held-over gain is halved if it is wholly or partly attributable to a gain arising before 31 March 1982. This relief must be claimed within two years of either the end of the year of assessment in which the asset is disposed of or the deferred gain accrues

EXAMPLE 5.21

A received an asset as a gift in October 1984 when its market value was £20,000 (it was owned by the donor at 31 March 1982). Hold-over relief was claimed of £5,500. A disposed of the asset in January 1995 for £30,000.

	£
Disposal value	30,000
Less: acquisition value $(20,000 - \dfrac{5,500}{2})$	(17,250)
Claim on or before 5 April 1996	
Unindexed gain	12,750
Less: indexation allowance	

$\dfrac{144.7 - 90.7}{90.7} = 0.595$

17,250 × 0.595	(10,264)
Chargeable gain	2,486

Assets of negligible value

If the value of an asset has become negligible, the owner may make a claim to that effect to the Inspector of Taxes. If the inspector is satisfied that the claim is a valid one, the asset will be treated as sold and immediately reacquired at the value at that date. Where appropriate a loss claim may then be made. Note that the value at the date of the claim becomes the taxpayer's base cost.

Exceptions to general principles

The general principles of computation outlined above are modified when applied to certain types of assets:

- chattels
- wasting assets (not chattels)
- leases of land
- principal private residence
- shares and securities.

These are dealt with in the next two chapters.

Summary

- Chargeable gains and allowable losses arise from chargeable disposals of chargeable assets by chargeable persons. The definitions of these terms should be known.
- Chargeable gains and allowable losses arising in a fiscal year are aggregated and the net chargeable gain for the year is charged to capital gains tax after deducting the annual exemption.
- The rate of CGT for 1994/95 is 25% unless the chargeable person is an individual, in which case 20% or 40% will be payable. This is to the extent that his or her marginal rate of income tax is 20% or 40%, or would be 20% or 40%, on all or part of an amount of additional income equal to the net chargeable gains in the fiscal year.
- Net allowable losses in a fiscal year may be carried forward and deducted from net chargeable gains of the next following fiscal year, to the extent that they exceed the annual exemption for that year.
- Under independent taxation, husband and wife are separate chargeable persons. Each is assessed on his/her own net gains. Losses are not transferable one to the other and each has a separate entitlement to an annual exemption. Each suffers capital gains tax at his/her marginal rate of income tax.
- The Finance Act 1988 re-basing provisions mean that for disposals after 5 April 1988, only gains and losses arising after 31 March 1982 are brought into charge for capital gains tax.
- In general, this means that market value at 31 March 1982 will be used in the computation instead of earlier costs. However, if this gives gains and losses greater than those which would have been given under the old rules, the old rules will apply.
- The taxpayer may elect for universal re-basing to 31 March 1982 – that is, the 31 March 1982 value should be applied to all his or her assets.
- Although the basic computation may therefore be very much simpler as a result of the re-basing provisions, from an examination point of view the legislation and the options available to the taxpayer have been increased.
- Care must be taken where exemptions and reliefs were claimed in the period between 31 March 1982 and 5 April 1988 (no gain, no loss disposals; hold-over relief) as there are special provisions in each case to apply FA 1988 re-basing.
- The connected person rules are widely defined with many anti-avoidance clauses.
- For disposals made on or after 30 November 1993, indexation will only be able to reduce a gain. It cannot increase or create an allowable loss. Instead for 1993/94 and 1994/95, unused indexation will create an indexation loss (maximum £10,000) which will be available to reduce the CGT liability in these years.

Self test questions

1. In 1994/95, an individual has the following chargeable gains/(allowable losses): £1,000, £4,000, £(500), £200, £(800); he or she has indexation losses for the year of £1,000 and has allowable losses brought forward of £1,000. Compute the net chargeable gains for 1994/95 and the losses, if any, available for carry forward.

2. What is the normal due date for payment of capital gains tax?

3. Outline the circumstances when a capital gains tax liability may be paid in instalments.

4. On 31 May 1994, shares in A plc were quoted at 197p–205p, the high and low recorded bargains of the day being 195p and 205p. What was the market value for capital gains tax purposes?

5. List the four main categories of connected persons.

6. How is the use of losses, arising in transactions with connected persons, restricted?

7. To how many decimal places must the increase in the retail price index between the month of disposal and the month the expenditure was incurred be calculated?

8. Without an election for universal 31 March 1982 re-basing, when will the 31 March 1982 value not be applied for purposes of computing any chargeable gain/allowable loss?

9. State the time limit in which an election for universal 31 March 1982 re-basing must be made.

10. State the time limit for claiming relief on a held-over gain relating to an asset held at 31 March 1982.

11. In 1994/95, Mr Herriot made a chargeable gain of £8,700 on the disposal of an interest in some land, an allowable loss of £500 and an indexation loss of £1,200 on the disposal of some shares to his sister-in-law. In the same year, Mrs Herriot sold a painting making a chargeable gain of £800. They have allowable losses brought forward from 1993/94 created as follows:

	Mr Herriot	Mrs Herriot
	£	£
Losses of	Nil	9,000

    Their taxable incomes for 1994/95 are £23,500 and £14,500 respectively. Calculate their capital gains tax liabilities for 1994/95.

12. Richard, who is single and 79 years of age, disposed of a substantial number of his shareholdings on 1 May 1994 making net chargeable gains of £10,500. He made no other disposals in 1994/95.

    His only income during the year was the basic state retirement pension of £2,704 and investment income of £550. Compute both his income tax and his capital gains tax liabilities for 1994/95.

13. Reginald, aged 75, has suffered from ill health for a number of years. Some time ago he began reviewing his assets with a view to simplifying his estate.

    a) In August 1994 he decided to sell the freehold holiday cottage left to him by his mother on her death on 1 October 1974. His mother bought the cottage on 28 March 1968 for £1,500. Its value in 1974 was £2,500. In June 1976 when the cottage was valued at £4,000, Reginald added an extension costing £1,000. The cottage was valued at £15,000 in March 1982.

On 1 September 1994 Reginald accepted an offer for the cottage of £26,500. Contracts were exchanged on 31 January 1995 and completion was on 30 March 1995. Costs of sale amounted to £610 including the estate agent's commission of £400.

b) In December 1994 he decided to gift to his wife Joan a plot of building land he had bought in June 1984 for £12,000. The deed of gift was executed on 20 December 1994 when the land was valued at £20,000.

c) On 20 January 1995 Reginald and Joan left the UK on a round-the-world cruise, having spent £4,500 on foreign currency to spend on the cruise. They returned to the UK on 2 April 1995 having spent two-thirds of the currency. Due to exchange differences, the remaining one-third was exchanged for £1,900 sterling.

Compute the chargeable gains/allowable losses arising on the above transactions.

Answers on pages 564–565

Chattels, Wasting Assets, Land and Principal Private Residence

CHAPTER 6

This chapter outlines the way in which the general principles of computation are modified when a disposal of a chattel, wasting asset, lease of land or principal private residence is made.

Chattels

Chattels are tangible moveable property and can be conveniently split into two categories:

- wasting chattels
- non-wasting chattels.

Wasting chattels

A wasting chattel is one with a useful life of 50 years or less. It is exempt from capital gains tax unless it is used for business purposes and of a type where capital allowances are available (whether claimed or not – see Chapter 19).

Non-wasting chattels

A non-wasting chattel is one with a life expectancy of more than 50 years and would include antiques, works of art, jewellery and so forth (legal tender currency of any description is excluded). These are chargeable assets for capital gains tax but there are a number of special provisions which apply (see below).

Chattels exemptions

These apply to non-wasting chattels and to wasting chattels not exempted above.
The purpose of the special provisions is to take the lower-value items out of the charge to tax. Four situations may arise:

- Wholly exempt if both the disposal value and the allowable deductions (and 31 March 1982 value if applicable) are £6,000 or less. Neither a gain nor a loss will arise.
- Fully taxable if both the disposal value and the allowable deductions (or 31 March 1982 value if applicable) are greater than £6,000.
- Marginal relief for gains may be available if the disposal value is greater than £6,000 and the allowable deductions (or 31 March 1982 value if applicable) are £6,000 or less.
- Restriction of losses if the disposal value is less than £6,000 but the allowable deductions (or 31 March 1982 value if applicable) are greater than £6,000.

The first two situations are self-explanatory. The third and fourth are described below.

Marginal relief for gains

Marginal relief may reduce a chargeable gain. If the disposal value is greater than £6,000, the chargeable gain is the lower of the gain calculated under the normal rules or five-thirds of the amount by which the disposal value exceeds £6,000:

thus, (disposal value – 6,000) × 5/3

EXAMPLE 6.1

An antique vase, purchased in 1975 for £1,000, was sold in March 1995 for £6,500. It had a market value at 31 March 1982 of £2,500.

	31 March 1982 value £	Old rules £
Disposal value	£6,500	£6,500
Less: allowable deductions:		
Cost 1975		(1,000)
31 March 1982 value	(2,500)	
Unindexed gain	4,000	5,500
Less: indexation allowance:		
$\frac{145.0 - 79.4}{79.4} = 0.826$		
31 March 1982 value > cost		
2,500 × 0.826	(2,065)	(2,065)
	1,935	3,435
Marginal relief restricts gain to a maximum of:		
(6,500 – 6,000) × 5/3	833	

In conclusion, applying the FA 1988 re-basing provisions the gain would be £1,935 restricted to £833. The chargeable gain would therefore be £833.

Restriction of losses

If the disposal value is less than £6,000, the allowable loss would be restricted by substituting £6,000 for the disposal value in the computation.

EXAMPLE 6.2

A painting was purchased in May 1984 for £7,000 and was sold at auction in January 1995 for £2,500. The auctioneer's commission was £250.

	£
Deemed disposal value	6,000
Less: incidental costs of disposal	(250)
	5,750
Less: cost	(7,000)
Allowable loss	(1,250)

An indexation loss will also arise.

Part disposals

Where a right or a part share in tangible moveable property is disposed of (for instance a one-third share in a work of art) the $A/(A+B)$ formula, where A is the disposal value and B is the value of the remainder, is retained and where $(A+B)$ is greater than £6,000 the gain is restricted to:

$$[(A+B) - 6{,}000] \times \frac{A}{A+B} \times \frac{5}{3}$$

If a loss arises, the disposal value of the part is deemed to be:

$$6{,}000 \times \frac{A}{A+B}$$

Fragmentation of sets

Abuse of chattel relief led to anti-avoidance legislation in 1985. Parts of a set, disposed of on different occasions to the same person (or persons connected with that person or persons acting in concert with that person) are treated as a single disposal for the purpose of chattel relief.

EXAMPLE 6.3

On 31 January 1990, X disposed of one of a pair of silver jugs, purchased in May 1983 at a cost of £1,500, to Y for £3,500 (when the value of the remaining jug was also £3,500). Five years later he sold the second jug to Y for £4,500.

In the first instance, in 1989/90, the gain on this disposal would be restricted to £833 as follows:

$$[(3{,}500+3{,}500) - 6{,}000] \times \frac{3{,}500}{3{,}500+3{,}500} \times \frac{5}{3}$$

After the second disposal to the same or a connected person, the first disposal would be reviewed and computations done as follows:

1

	£
Disposal value 31 January 1990	3,500
Less: cost $\frac{3{,}500}{3{,}500 + 3{,}500} \times 1{,}500$	(750)
Unindexed gain	2,750
Less: indexation allowance	
$\frac{119.5 - 84.6}{84.6} = 0.413$	
750 × 0.413	(310)
Gain	2,440

2

	£
Disposal value January 1995	4,500
Less: cost (1,500 – 750)	(750)
Unindexed gain	3,750
Less: indexation allowance	
$\frac{144.7 - 84.6}{84.6} = 0.710$	
750 × 0.710	(533)
Gain	3,217
Total gain	5,657
Restricted to $[(3{,}500 + 4{,}500) - 6{,}000] \times \frac{5}{3}$	3,333

In this case, marginal relief restricts the total gain of £5,657 and the gain after marginal relief (£3,333) will be assessed, less £833 assessed in 1989/90, that is £2,500 will be assessed in 1994/95.

Wasting assets (not chattels)

These are assets with a predictable life of 50 years or less. Tangible moveable property which is a wasting asset has been dealt with above. Freehold land, whatever the circumstances, can never be a wasting asset. Leases of land which are wasting assets are covered in this and the next section.

General rule

Where an asset disposed of is a wasting asset, it erodes over time. It is therefore necessary to adjust the allowable costs on disposal of the asset to take account of that part of them which has been eroded during ownership.

If the asset had a 15 year life on acquisition and was disposed of after five years, the disposal value would reflect that the asset had a remaining life of ten years. The allowable deductions would be those that related to the remaining ten years.

Each of the allowable deductions are treated as diminishing evenly over time (i.e. on a straight line basis – see Figure 6.1) having first taken into account the expected residual value of the asset. The following formula applies:

$$(\text{Original cost} - \text{residual value}) \times \frac{\text{Remaining life}}{\text{Life at acquisition}}$$

Where a wasting asset was held at 31 March 1982 and disposed of after 5 April 1988, the 31 March 1982 re-basing provisions cause the 31 March 1982 value to be substituted for original cost in the above formula and the life remaining at 31 March 1982 to be substituted for life at acquisition.

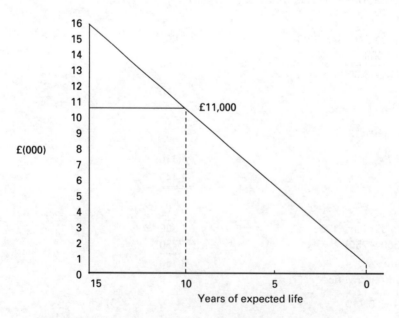

Figure 6.1

The allowable deduction on sale, after five years, of a wasting asset purchased for £16,000 with a 15 year life and a residual value of £1,000 will have diminished as shown.

The indexation allowance is calculated on the reduced cost or, in the case of a wasting asset held at 31 March 1982, on the reduced 31 March 1982 value.

Examples of the type of property to which the general rule applies are copyrights, trademarks, options other than those mentioned below, life interests and leases of property other than land. (Note that patents are not included, any profit on disposal being assessable as income under Schedule D Case VI.)

Exceptions to the general rule

Options (traded and financial) and futures (commodity and financial)

These are options and futures quoted on a recognised stock exchange or a recognised futures exchange. They are not wasting assets.

An option may be granted to buy or sell within a specified time period. The granting of an option for consideration is treated as a chargeable disposal of an asset for which there is no allowable deduction. Thus, the apportionment of cost using the part disposal rules do not apply.

If the option is exercised, the grant of the option and the consequent purchase or sale are treated as one transaction. Any consideration received by the grantor for granting the option is therefore either added to the sale proceeds or deducted from the cost of purchase. The person to whom the option is granted may, depending on whether it is an option to buy or sell, add the cost of the option to the cost of the asset acquired or deduct it from the proceeds of sale of the asset as an incidental cost of disposal.

If the option is not exercised, it is either abandoned (that is, it lapses) or it may be sold on a recognised exchange (if one of the types listed above). An abandoned option constitutes a chargeable disposal for nil consideration and will give rise to an allowable loss if it is a type listed above which is not a wasting asset.

Since 5 April 1985, gains and losses arising from dealing in these options on a recognised exchange have been chargeable to capital gains tax (previously they were subject to income tax). The terminology used in the option markets should be explained:

▶ A 'call' option is a contract between the grantor of the option and a prospective purchaser. It means that the prospective purchaser pays a sum of money to acquire the right to purchase shares from the grantor at a fixed price on or before a certain date. The grantor of the option undertakes to sell the shares to the grantee or his or her agent at the agreed price if called upon to do so at any time during the life of the option contract.
▶ A 'put' option is the opposite and gives the holder the right to sell shares to the grantor of the option at a fixed price on or before a certain date. The grantor of the option undertakes to buy the shares from the grantee or his or her agent at the agreed price if called upon to do so at any time during the life of the option contract.

Options and futures on gilt-edged securities and qualifying corporate bonds are exempt.

Short leases of land

A lease of land becomes a wasting asset when it has 50 years or less to run. From that point its value diminishes on a curved line rather than on a straight line basis, according to the table in TCGA 1992, Schedule 8. The table is reproduced at the back of this book and illustrated diagrammatically in Figure 6.2 (see over).

On the sale or assignment of a short lease, the cost must be diminished according to the formula:

$$\text{Original cost} \times \frac{\text{\% re: remaining life at date of assignment}}{\text{\% re: life on acquisition}}$$

If the time periods are not exact numbers of years, the percentages given in the table must be interpolated to the nearest month.

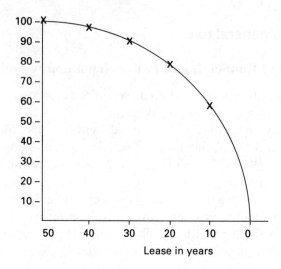

Figure 6.2 Diminishing value of a short lease of land.

EXAMPLE 6.4

A lease with 40 years to run was acquired for £25,000 on 1 April 1981 and disposed of on 1 April 1994 for £30,000. Its 31 March 1982 value was £27,500.

		31 March 1982 value	Old rules	Gain/(Loss)
		£	£	
Disposal value		30,000	30,000	
Less: cost	$25,000 \times \dfrac{83.816}{95.457}$		(21,951)	
	$27,500 \times \dfrac{83.816}{94.842}$	(24,303)		
Unindexed gain		5,697	8,049	
Less: indexation allowance:				
on 31 March 1982 value				
$\dfrac{142.6 - 79.4}{79.4} = 0.796$				
$24,303 \times 0.796 = 19,345$		(5,697)	(8,049)	
		–	–	
Allowable loss				Nil

Where: 83.816 is the lease per cent for 27 years (lease @ 1/04/94)
95.457 is the lease per cent for 40 years (lease @ 1/04/81)
94.842 is the lease per cent for 39 years (lease @ 31/03/82)

Note: All allowable deductions diminish in value in this way, that is not merely the cost of the lease but any enhancement costs and also the 31 March 1982 value.

The old rules would have given the lower loss and there is, therefore, an indexation loss of £11,296 (19,345 – 8,049), which is restricted to the maximum of £10,000.

Leases of land

The granting of a lease of land, whether out of a freehold or an existing leasehold interest, is a chargeable part disposal. However, complications in the computation of gains or losses may arise as a result of two factors:

- Leases of 50 years or less (short leases) are wasting assets.
- A premium received for granting a short lease (the disposal value in the computation of chargeable gains) is chargeable in part to income tax (see Chapter 4) and care must be taken not to charge any of it to tax twice.

The examiner has stated that the granting of a lease or sub-lease out of either a freehold, long lease or short lease is not examinable.

Principal private residence

The disposal of a dwelling-house which has been an individual's only or main residence throughout his or her ownership is exempt from capital gains tax. If only a part of the property is the main residence – for example the remainder is used for business purposes – only a part of the gain on disposal is exempt. The exemption also applies to a part disposal of the dwelling-house or grounds.

The definition of a dwelling-house includes residential caravans and houseboats. Grounds up to 0.5 of a hectare inclusive of the house are generally permitted, although a larger area may be permitted by the Commissioners having regard to the size and character of the house, if sold with the house.

Dwelling-house not only or main residence throughout ownership

Where the house has been occupied solely as the taxpayer's only or main residence for a part of the period, only a proportion of the gain is exempt:

$$\text{Gain} \times \frac{\text{Period of occupation as main residence}}{\text{Total period of ownership}}$$

For disposals after 5 April 1988, occupation and ownership prior to 1 April 1982 must be ignored in the above calculation.

In calculating the period of occupation as a main residence, there are periods of non-residence which are deemed to be periods of occupation as main residence – provided that the taxpayer had no other main residence eligible for relief at the time.

Deemed occupation

The first 12 months of ownership qualifies provided there is good reason why occupation has not been taken up. (For example, this could be while the house is being altered or extended or while the previous house is being sold.)

The last 36 months of ownership is always exempt if the dwelling-house was, at some time during ownership, the taxpayer's main residence.

Certain other periods of absence are also deemed to be periods of occupation provided that the taxpayer had no other dwelling-house qualifying for exemption during that period and that at some time, both before and after the period of absence, the taxpayer actually occupied the property as his or her main residence. Whether or not the dwelling-house was let during this period is immaterial. The periods of absence that qualify for this purpose are:

- any period of absence for whatever reason up to three years (or periods totalling not more than three years)
- any periods of absence of whatever length when the taxpayer was required by his employment to work outside the UK
- any period of absence up to four years (or periods totalling not more than four years) when the taxpayer was required by his employment to live elsewhere in the UK.

In the first and third situation above, current Inland Revenue practice allows three or four years out of any longer total period of absence to qualify. Current practice also allows periods of absence under the second and third situation above to follow each other without any intervening period of actual occupation if this is required by the terms of his or her employment.

EXAMPLE 6.5

A musician purchased an estate in Scotland in 1970 for £15,000. From 1970 until 1975 he occupied the estate but after 1975 he lived in London until June 1978 when he was required to travel as an international star. He made the estate his home again in April 1981 and resided there until April 1986 when he again took up residence in London. The estate was subsequently sold in January 1995 for £150,000. The value at 31 March 1982 was £60,000.

	31 March 1982 value	Old rules	Gain/(Loss)
The gain on sale is:	£	£	£
Disposal value	150,000	150,000	
Less: 31 March 1982/cost	(60,000)	(15,000)	
Unindexed gain	90,000	135,000	
Less indexation allowance			

Less: $\dfrac{144.7 - 79.4}{79.4} = 0.822$

60,000 × 0.822	(49,320)	(49,320)	
Gain	40,680	85,680	40,680

Private residence exemption on smaller gain:

	Ownership	Occupation
from 1 April 1982		
till April 1986	4 years	4 years (actual)
till January 1995	8.75 years	3 years (last 36 mths)
	12.75 years	7 years

Exemption 7/12.75	(22,334)
Chargeable gain	18,346

Note: May 1986–Dec 1991 would not qualify since he did not occupy the house again.

Job-related accommodation

Where an individual resides in job-related accommodation, he or she may acquire a dwelling-house for occupation, in due course, as his or her sole or main residence and obtain private residence relief.

Accommodation is job-related if it is provided for the taxpayer by reason of his or her employment or if it is provided under tenancy and so forth by reason of a trade, profession or vocation, carried on as follows, either:

- where it is for the proper performance of the duties of the employment; or
- where it is necessary for the better performance of the duties of the employment and it is customary; or
- where it is part of special security arrangements necessary as a result of the taxpayer's employment.

The first two do not apply to accommodation provided for a director.

More than one main residence

An individual or a married couple living together may only have one main residence. If more than one residence is used, an election may be made, within two years of acquiring the second residence, which is to be the main residence. If no such election is made, the main residence may be determined by the inspector.

Sole residence of a dependent relative

The disposal of a dwelling-house before 6 April 1988 that was the sole residence of a dependent relative of the taxpayer or his or her spouse and which was provided to the dependent relative rent free, was also exempt from capital gains tax.

For disposals after 5 April 1988, gains attributable to a period of occupation by a dependent relative before 6 April 1988 will also be exempt. A taxpayer (and spouse) may only have one house qualifying for relief in this way at any one time.

Let as residential accommodation

Where a gain accrues to a taxpayer on a dwelling-house under the above rules, and the house or part of it has been let at any time during his ownership as residential accommodation, the part of the gain resulting from the period of letting is exempt to the lower of:

- £40,000 (£20,000 pre 19 March 1991)
- the amount of the gain otherwise exempt under the rules above.

Note that no allowable loss can be created. (This effectively further limits the letting exemption to the gain accrued during the letting period.)

Summary

- A wasting asset is one with a life of 50 years or less.
- Chattels (or tangible moveable property) may be wasting assets or non-wasting assets. Wasting chattels are exempt from CGT on disposal provided they were not used for business purposes such that capital allowances were available.
- Chattels not exempt under the circumstances above are fully taxable on disposal subject to a small disposals exemption and a marginal relief for gains (or restriction of losses) under certain circumstances.
- Anti-avoidance legislation counteracts the fragmentation of sets in order to take advantage of chattel relief.
- Wasting assets, other than chattels, diminish over their life, and this is reflected in the CGT computation by proportionately reducing the allowable deductions. The diminution in value is on a straight line basis over the assets' life except for short leases which diminish according to a table contained in TCGA 1992, Schedule 8.

▶ The disposal of a principal private residence occupied throughout ownership is exempt. Where it is not so occupied throughout ownership, certain periods of absence are deemed to be periods of occupation and the proportion of the gain attributable to periods of actual or deemed occupation is exempt.

Self test questions

1   What is a wasting asset?

2   Under what circumstances is the disposal of a non-wasting chattel exempt from capital gains tax?

3   What is the formula for marginal relief of a gain on the disposal of a non-wasting chattel?

4   How does the restriction of the loss on a disposal of a non-wasting chattel operate?

5   Give three examples of a wasting asset (not chattels) which diminish in value on a straight line basis.

6   Elizabeth sold her house on 6 January 1995 for £69,000. She had lived there since purchasing the house for £2,000 on 6 April 1969 and had always sub-let one half of the house for residential purposes.
    The value at 31 March 1982 had been agreed with the Inland Revenue as £35,000:
    On 30 January 1995 she sold by auction a clock which had been left to her by her grandfather. The probate value on her grandfather's death on 1 July 1970 was £300. The clock was sold for £6,600 and the auction expenses were £360.
    She had acquired a 55-year lease on a retail shop for £32,000 on 31 March 1973. On 20 August 1983 she extended the premises at a cost of £20,000. On 31 March 1995 she sold the lease for £75,000. The value of the lease on 31 March 1982 was £50,000.

You are required to calculate, before the annual exemption, the capital gains for 1994/95.

Answers on pages 565–566

Shares and Securities

CHAPTER 7

This chapter considers the special problems which arise in matching disposals of shares and securities to particular acquisitions. It also outlines the way in which the general principles of computation are modified when applied to shares and securities.

Disposals of shares and securities held at 6 April 1965 are not examinable. Reorganisations of share capital are covered as are gilt-edged securities and qualifying corporate bonds.

Matching rules

Where a taxpayer has an investment in any company which has been built up as a result of acquisitions on two or more separate occasions, and then disposes of a part of his or her investment, it is necessary to identify which shares have been disposed of. This is not possible by an examination of the shares themselves, since these are fungible assets (one share is identical to another). Nevertheless, the allowable deductions in the capital gains computation (and therefore any chargeable gain which results) may be materially affected by such a decision.

EXAMPLE 7.1

A taxpayer made the following purchases of shares in A plc:

		£
1 January 1987	500 shares	1,500
1 July 1987	500 shares	2,000
1 December 1987	500 shares	625

If 500 shares were disposed of on 1 January 1995, which were they?

In the absence of specific rules to identify the shares disposed of, the taxpayer would be able to choose the acquisition which was to his or her best advantage dependent upon the disposal value and his or her net chargeable gains to date in the fiscal year.

Needless to say to avoid this potential loss of revenue, there are specific rules to identify which shares have been disposed of. These are called 'matching rules'.

Over recent years, a new set of matching rules has been drawn up almost every time there has been a major change in the capital gains tax legislation. The principal reason for this is to cater for the changes in the computation of the indexation allowance. Different sets of matching rules apply to:

- disposals before 6 April 1982 (companies – 1 April 1982)
- disposals after 5 April 1982 (companies – 31 March 1982)
- disposals after 5 April 1985 (companies – 31 March 1985).

For examination purposes, a knowledge of the matching rules for disposals prior to 6 April 1985 will not be required. This means that where shareholdings existed and disposals took place before 6 April 1985, any examination question will identify the shares remaining after such disposals have been dealt with.

Identification rules for disposals after 5 April 1985

Disposals of shares and securities after 5 April 1985 are identified with acquisitions of shares and securities of the same class, in the same company, and held by the same person in the same capacity in the following order:

1. shares acquired on the same day or subsequently (see below)
2. shares acquired within the previous nine days
3. shares acquired after 5 April 1982 and ten or more days before disposal
4. shares acquired after 5 April 1965 and before 6 April 1982
5. shares acquired before 6 April 1965.

The computation of chargeable gains and allowable losses within each of the groups 3 to 5 is unique and care must be taken. Groups 3 and 4 are dealt with in turn below. (Group 5 is not examinable.)

Securities within the accrued income provisions are excepted from the above rules (see Chapter 4).

EXAMPLE 7.2

At 5 April 1985, A held shares in X plc acquired as follows:

			£
1 April 1955	800	shares	800
4 June 1960	500	shares	600
1 April 1978	500	shares	550
1 October 1978	500	shares	800
1 January 1983	500	shares	1,000
1 September 1984	1,000	shares	1,500
31 March 1985	500	shares	1,500

A disposal of 3,000 shares on 1 January 1995 would be identified with the above acquisitions in the following way.

Assuming no further transactions had taken place within the nine days prior to 1 January 1995:

i) shares acquired after 5 April 1982 and ten or more days before disposal:

			£
1 January 1983	500	shares	1,000
1 September 1984	1,000	shares	1,500
31 March 1985	500	shares	1,500
	2,000	shares	
Disposal 1 January 1995	(2,000)	shares	

ii) shares acquired after 5 April 1965 and before 6 April 1982;

1 April 1978	500	shares	550
1 October 1978	500	shares	800
	1,000	shares	
Disposal 1 January 1995	(1,000)	shares	

Leaving A with the following shareholdings in X plc:
1 April 1955   800 shares   800
4 June 1960   500 shares   600

Shares acquired on the same day

Shares disposed of are matched with acquisitions by the same person on the same day. No pooling arrangements apply. If more shares are disposed of than are acquired, and there are no earlier acquisitions, the disposal will be matched with the first subsequent acquisition.

Shares acquired within the previous nine days

Shares disposed of are matched with acquisitions within a ten-day period. Where more than one acquisition takes place within the period, they are deemed to be disposed of on a FIFO basis. No indexation allowance is available.

Shares acquired after 5 April 1982 (Pool A)

These are shares acquired:

- after 5 April 1982 and still held on 5 April 1985
- after 5 April 1985.

These shares were separated from other holdings of shares in the same companies following the amendments to the calculation of the indexation allowance in the Finance Act 1985, which allowed pooling arrangements to be introduced.

All shares of the same class in the same company in this group are pooled and treated as a single asset. A disposal of some, but not all, of the shares in the pool is treated as a part disposal.

This pool will be referred to hereinafter as Pool A.

Setting up and operating Pool A

Setting up

Pool A operates as an indexed pool of expenditure. To set up the pool at 6 April 1985, the shares held have to be valued. This is done as follows:

1 The acquisition cost of the shares held at this date (all acquired after 5 April 1982) and
2 An indexation allowance from the date of purchase to 6 April 1985 for each separate acquisition of shares of the same class in the same company

are added together to form an indexed pool of expenditure as at 6 April 1985.

The pool balance is then carried forward until the first 'operative event'.

EXAMPLE 7.3

A had acquired shares in X plc as follows:

			£
31 January 1983	500	shares	1,000
1 September 1984	1,000	shares	1,500
31 March 1985	500	shares	1,500

Compute the value of Pool A at 6 April 1985:

Pool A – X plc	Number of shares	Pool value £
a) 31 January 1983	500	1,000
b) 1 September 1984	1,000	1,500
c) 31 March 1985	500	1,500
	2,000	4,000
Indexation allowance:		
a) $\dfrac{94.8 - 82.6}{82.6} \times 1{,}000$		148
b) $\dfrac{94.8 - 90.1}{90.1} \times 1{,}500$		78
c) $\dfrac{94.8 - 92.8}{92.8} \times 1{,}500$		32
Value of pool at 6 April 1985 cf	2,000	4,258

Operative events

An operative event is either an acquisition or a disposal of shares of the same class in the same company.

Whenever there is an operative event, the following procedures must be observed.

▶ The pool must be re-indexed to the date of the operative event. Re-indexation is achieved by calculating the indexed rise which has taken place over the period from the last operative event (or 6 April 1985 if none) to the current operative event as follows:

$$\text{Pool value} \times \frac{RE - RL}{RL}$$

where RE is the retail price index for this operative event and RL is the retail price index for the last operative event.

Note that for Pool A there is no requirement to restrict the indexed rise for purposes of the indexation allowance to three decimal places. This is then added to the pool value brought forward.

▶ As appropriate, the cost of shares acquired is added to the pool or the indexed cost attributable to shares disposed of is deducted from the pool. The value attributable to disposals is calculated by applying the number of shares disposed of as a proportion of the total number of shares in the pool, to the pool value.

▶ The balance remaining in the pool is the pool value for carry forward to the next operative event.

- Where the operative event is a disposal the value attributable to the shares disposed of is the allowable cost for purposes of the capital gains computation. No further indexation allowance is appropriate.

EXAMPLE 7.4 (Example 7.3 continued)

A disposed of 1,000 shares in X plc on 31 January 1995 for £3,600. The remaining shares were disposed of on 15 February 1995 for £3,700.

Calculate any chargeable gains/allowable losses arising on the disposals and the value of the pool after each operative event.

Pool A – X plc	Number of shares	Pool value £
Value of pool at 6 April 1985 bf	2,000	4,258
Indexed rise from 6 April 1985 to 31 January 1995: $\dfrac{144.7 - 94.8}{94.8} \times 4,258$		2,241
	2,000	6,499
Disposal $\dfrac{1,000}{2,000} \times 6,499$	(1,000)	(3,250)
Value of pool at 31 January 1995 cf	1,000	3,249
Indexed rise from 31 Jan 1995 to 15 Feb 1995: $\dfrac{144.9 - 144.7}{144.7} \times 3,249$		4
		3,253
Disposal 15 February 1995	(1,000)	(3,253)
Value of pool at 15 February 1995 cf	Nil	Nil

Computation of the gain/(loss) on disposal 31 January 1995
Disposal value	3,600
Less: allowable cost (indexed)	(3,250)
Gain	350

Computation of the gain/(loss) on disposal 15 February 1995
Disposal value	3,700
Less: allowable cost (indexed)	(3,253)
Gain	447

Shares acquired after 5 April 1965 and before 6 April 1982 (Pool B)

These are shares acquired between 6 April 1965 and 5 April 1982 which were still held on 5 April 1985.

The shares are separated from other holdings of shares in the same companies following the introduction of the indexation allowance. All of these shares are eligible for indexation allowance from 31 March 1982.

The costs of all shares of the same class in the same company in this group are pooled. A disposal of some, but not all, the shares in the pool is treated as a part disposal. The indexation allowance on disposal is calculated from 31 March 1982 to the date of disposal.

The indexed rise for purposes of the indexation allowance is again calculated to three decimal places only. This pool will be referred to hereinafter as Pool B.

Setting up and operating Pool B

Setting up

Pool B operates simply as a pool of expenditure on shares of the same class in the same company. To set up the pool at 6 April 1985, the acquisition costs of the shares held at this date (acquired between 6 April 1965 and 5 April 1982) are aggregated.

The pool balance is then carried forward until any of these shares are disposed of when the part disposal rules are followed.

EXAMPLE 7.5

On 6 April 1985, A held shares in X plc acquired as follows:

		£
April 1978	500 shares	550
1 October 1978	500 shares	800

Compute the value of Pool B at 6 April 1985:

Pool B – X plc	Number of shares	Pool value
a) 1 April 1978	500	550
b) 1 October 1978	500	800
Value of pool at 6 April 1985 cf	1,000	1,350

Operating Pool B

Pool B is often referred to as the frozen pool as there can be no further additions to it (but see below) and therefore the rules for operating the pool only deal with disposals.

On disposal, shares are removed from the pool at average cost. The general principles of computation for assets held on 31 March 1982 are then applied. Thus, gains/(losses) are computed by reference to the value at 31 March 1982 unless this gives a higher gain or a higher loss than would otherwise have been the case under the rules prior to the Finance Act 1988. The indexation allowance is calculated on the higher of the 31 March 1982 value or the cost from 31 March 1982 to the date of disposal.

EXAMPLE 7.6 (Example 7.5 continued)

A disposed of 800 shares in X plc on 25 February 1995 for £2,600. Having already disposed of his Pool A shares, this disposal was identified with his Pool B shares. The market value of a share at 31 March 1982 was £1.75.

Calculate any chargeable gains/allowable losses arising on the disposal and the value of the pool to be carried forward:

	Number of shares	Pool value
Pool B – X plc		
		£
Value of pool at 6 April 1985 bf	1,000	1,350
Disposal 25 Feb 1995 $\frac{800}{1,000} \times 1,350$	(800)	(1,080)
Value of pool at 25 February 1995	200	270

Computation of the gain/(loss) on disposal 25 February 1995

	31 March 1982 value	Old rules	Gain/(Loss)
	£	£	
Disposal value	2,600	2,600	
Less: 31 March 1982 value/cost	(1,400)	(1,080)	
Unindexed gain	1,200	1,520	
Less: indexation allowance on 31 March 1982 value $\frac{144.9 - 79.4}{79.4} = 0.825$			
$0.825 \times 1,400$	(1,155)	(1,155)	
	45	365	
Chargeable gain			45

Reorganisations

This section considers the effect on a shareholding for capital gains tax purposes of certain transactions which may be undertaken by the company.

Reorganisations for this purpose include the making of bonus issues and rights issues of either shares or debentures pro rata to the original holdings, reductions and reorganisations of share capital, and 'paper for paper' takeovers.

Such reorganisations are not normally regarded as disposals. The additional or replacement shareholding is treated as acquired at the same date as the original shareholding. Any additional consideration given by the shareholder (for example, on a rights issue) is added to the cost of the original shareholding in much the same way as enhancement expenditure on other types of assets.

Bonus issues

Bonus issues or scrip issues of quoted or unquoted shares or securities are deemed to be acquired at each of the dates of acquisition of the original holdings. No change in the total cost of each holding arises, but that cost relates to a greater number of shares (the cost per share is diluted). This must, of course, be taken into account when a subsequent disposal takes place and the matching rules are applied.

EXAMPLE 7.7

B had made the following acquisitions of shares in Y Ltd when Y Ltd made a bonus issue of 1 for 4 on 31 July 1994.

12 August 1970	800 shares	£1,000
25 September 1978	1,000 shares	£2,000
31 December 1987	1,000 shares	£1,500

700 bonus shares would have been received. Show the balances in each of Pool A and Pool B as at 31 July 1994.

Pool A – Y Ltd	Number of shares	Pool value £
Acquisition – 31 December 1987	1,000	1,500
Indexed rise from 31 December 1987 to 31 July 1994:		
$\dfrac{143.3 - 103.3}{103.3} \times 1,500$		581
		2,081
Bonus 1 for 4 – 31 July 1994	250	Nil
Value of pool at 31 July 1994	1,250	2,081

Pool B – Y Ltd	Number of shares	Pool value £
12 August 1970	800	1,000
25 September 1978	1,000	2,000
Value of pool brought forward	1,800	3,000
Bonus 1 for 4 31 July 1994	450	Nil
Value of pool at 31 July 1994	2,250	3,000

A bonus issue need not be of shares of the same class as the original holding and in this case it is necessary to apportion part of the cost of the original holding to the bonus shares issued. This is done in proportion to the value of the shareholdings immediately after the bonus issue. Note that such values are readily available for quoted shares but not for unquoted shares.

EXAMPLE 7.8

A holds 800 £1 ordinary shares in Z plc which were acquired on 24 June 1981 for £2,400.

On 1 April 1995 Z plc made a bonus issue of one preference share for every ten ordinary shares. On the first day of trading after the issue, the value of a preference share was £1 and the value of an ordinary share was £2.50.

Show how the cost of the original holding would be apportioned between the two shareholdings after 1 April 1995.

Value of shareholdings 1 April 1995:

	£
80 preference shares @ £1	80
800 ordinary shares @ £2.50	2,000
Total	2,080

Cost attributable to 80 preference shares $\dfrac{80}{2,080} \times £2,400 = £92$

Cost attributable to 800 ordinary shares $\dfrac{2,000}{2,080} \times £2,400 = £2,308$

On 1 April 1995, the preference shares will be deemed to have been acquired on 24 June 1981 for £92 and the ordinary shares will be deemed to have been acquired on 24 June 1981 for £2,308. These two holdings are not of shares of the same class and must each go into a Pool B for shares of that class in that company.

Rights issues

Rights issues offer an opportunity (usually advantageous) to existing shareholders to purchase further shares or securities of the same or a different class.

The price paid for shares and securities acquired in this way is added to the cost of the original holding if of the same class as that holding. If of a different class, an apportionment is made of the total cost (including the cost of the rights) between the two, on the basis of the market value of the shares on the first day of trading after the issue. (Such an apportionment would also apply to the 31 March 1982 value where the original shares were held at this date and the rights issue took place some time later.)

For purposes of calculating the indexation allowance, the expenditure on the acquisition of the rights is taken as occurring on the date of issue of the rights and not on the date of acquisition of the original holding.

EXAMPLE 7.9

On 6 April 1985, A had the following ordinary shareholdings in S plc:

16 August 1978	750 shares	£900
10 June 1980	400 shares	£600
15 June 1982	800 shares	£1,000
14 August 1984	600 shares	£1,200

On 15 February 1995, S plc made a rights issue of 1 for 5 at £2.50 per share. A took up the rights.

Show the balances in each of Pool A and Pool B as at 15 February 1995.

Pool A – S plc	Number of shares	Pool value £
a) 15 June 1982	800	1,000
b) 14 August 1984	600	1,200
	1,400	2,200
Indexation allowance to 6 April 1985:		
a) $\dfrac{94.8 - 81.9}{81.9} \times 1,000$		158
b) $\dfrac{94.8 - 89.9}{89.9} \times 1,200$		65
Value of pool at 6 April 1985	1,400	2,423
Indexed rise from 6 April 1985 to 15 February 1995:		
$\dfrac{144.9 - 94.8}{94.8} \times 2,423$		1,281
		3,704
Rights 1 for 5 @ £2.50 (15 February 1995)	280	700
Value of pool at 15 February 1995	1,680	4,404

Pool B – S plc	Number of shares	Pool value £
16 August 1978	750	900
10 June 1980	400	600
Value of pool brought forward	1,150	1,500
Rights 1 for 5 @ £2.50 (15 February 1995)	230	575
Value of pool at 15 February 1995	1,380	2,075

It is important to note on Pool B that, on a subsequent disposal of some of the shares (say 500), the cost deductible will be an appropriate proportion (500/1,380) of the £1,500 plus the same proportion of the £575. Indexation allowance will be available on the higher of the 31 March 1982 value of the shares disposed of or the appropriate proportion of £1,500 from 31 March 1982 and on the appropriate proportion of £575 from 15 February 1995.

The layout of Pool B can be adapted as follows to accommodate subsequent disposals and make the calculations very much simpler:

Pool B – S plc	Number of shares	Pool value £	Rights 15/02/95 £
16 August 1978	750	900	
10 June 1980	400	600	
Value of pool brought forward	1,150	1,500	
Rights 1 for 5 @ £2.50 (15 February 1995)	230		575
Value of pool at 15 February 1995	1,380	1,500	575

It is also useful to add a 31 March 1982 value column if this value is known. A disposal of 500 shares from Pool B would be achieved by deducting 500/1,380 from *each* column to leave the values attributable to 880 shares in the pool. The figures deducted would be used in the capital gains computation for cost as at 31/3/82 value and costs subsequent to 31/3/82 respectively.

Sale of rights

If the shareholder does not take up the rights, but sells them to a third party for a consideration, the proceeds are treated as a capital distribution (see below).

Sale of fractions

Similarly, it is normal when a bonus issue or a rights issue is made and the offer would not give individual shareholders an exact number of shares for the company to give the next lowest whole number of shares. The remaining fractions are then collected together and sold off by the company. The proceeds from the sale of fractions are then split and paid to the shareholders entitled to the fractions. These also are capital distributions (see below).

Capital distributions

A capital distribution is any distribution by a company to its shareholders in money or money's worth which is not taxed as income. For capital gains tax purposes it is deemed to result from a disposal of an interest in shares and is therefore treated as a part disposal.

Capital distributions may occur on a repayment of cash as a result of a capital reduction scheme, on liquidation, on a sale of rights or sale of fractions.

If the capital distribution is small (per Inland Revenue, 5% or less of the value of the shares at that date), it may not be treated as a part disposal. However, the proceeds would be deducted from the acquisition cost of the shares. (Note the adjustment in the calculation of the indexation allowance – as described in Chapter 5.)

If the capital distribution is not small, the normal part disposal rules apply.

Distributions taxed as income

Where a repayment of capital is followed by a bonus issue, for example, the bonus issue will be taxed as income. The shareholder however will have acquired a new holding of shares, the cost of which is deemed to be the income (net of basic rate tax).

Capital reductions and reorganisations

Where the company reorganises its share capital in such a way that a shareholder receives new shares or a mixture of shares and debentures in place of his or her original holding, no disposal takes place for capital gains tax purposes. The new shares stand in place of the original shares. The original cost must be apportioned between the new holdings in the manner outlined for bonus issues (or for rights issues, if additional cash is paid over).

'Paper for paper' takeovers and amalgamations

Where companies amalgamate (or there is a takeover) and a shareholder receives new shares and securities in exchange for his or her original holding, no disposal takes place for capital gains tax purposes provided that certain conditions are met. The new holdings are deemed to have been acquired at the same date and for the same cost as the original holding. If more than one class of shares and securities is acquired in exchange, the original cost must be apportioned between the new holdings in the manner outlined above for bonus issues.

The principal condition which must be met is that the acquiring company acquires, as a consequence of the exchange, more than 25% of the equity share capital of the company in which the shareholder has shares.

In a takeover situation, this treatment applies if the exchange results from a general offer to all shareholders (or all of one class of shareholders) such that, if successful, it would acquire control of the company. (The condition is therefore satisfied whether or not the takeover is successful.)

Cash forming part of the consideration

If cash forms part of the exchange then a part disposal computation will be required.

EXAMPLE 7.10

A holds 1,000 shares in P plc which were acquired on 15 March 1986 for £4,000. P plc is taken over in June 1994 by Q plc and the shareholders receive four shares in Q plc and £3.00 cash for every five shares held in P plc.

On the first day of trading following the takeover, Q plc shares are quoted at £7 each.

Compute the chargeable gain, if any, arising.

Value due to A following takeover:

		£
Shares	$\frac{4}{5} \times 1{,}000 \; @ \; £7$	5,600
Cash	$\frac{1}{5} \times 1{,}000 \; @ \; £3.00$	600
		6,200

The cash (£600) is more than five per cent of the total value and therefore the small part disposal rules do not apply. There is a part disposal.

Value of Pool A – P plc June 1994	Number of shares	Pool value £
Cost 15 March 1986	1,000	4,000
OE – June 1994 $\dfrac{143.0 - 96.7}{96.7} \times 4,000$		1,915
Value @ June 1994		5,915
Attributable to cash consideration $\dfrac{600}{600 + 5,600} \times 5,915$		(572)
Transfer Pool A – Q plc June 1994	1,000	5,343

	£
Disposal proceeds	600
Cost (as calculated above)	(572)
Chargeable gain 1994/95	28

Gilt-edged securities

No capital gains tax is chargeable on disposals of gilt-edged securities.

Gilt-edged securities are British Government and public corporation securities which are specified from time to time by the Treasury. The list includes Treasury Stocks, Exchequer Stocks, War Loan, Treasury Loan, Exchequer Loan and so on. Similarly, no allowable losses can arise.

Qualifying corporate bonds

No capital gains tax is chargeable on disposals of qualifying corporate bonds..

Qualifying corporate bonds are fixed interest securities of companies, Governments, public and local authorities wherever situated, issued or acquired after 13 March 1984. They should be normal commercial loans (not convertible into shares and not at an excessively high interest rate) in sterling.

From 14 March 1989 deep-gain securities also qualify (see Chapter 4). An allowable loss can arise where all or part of the loan is irrecoverable after the redemption date.

Summary

Figure 7.1 summarises diagrammatically the procedures which apply on a disposal of shares post 5 April 1985.

▶ Disposals of shares must be identified with specific acquisitions of shares of the same class in the same company.
▶ You are required to know the rules for identification of disposals with acquisitions which apply to disposals after 5 April 1985. The matching rules for these disposals are as follows:

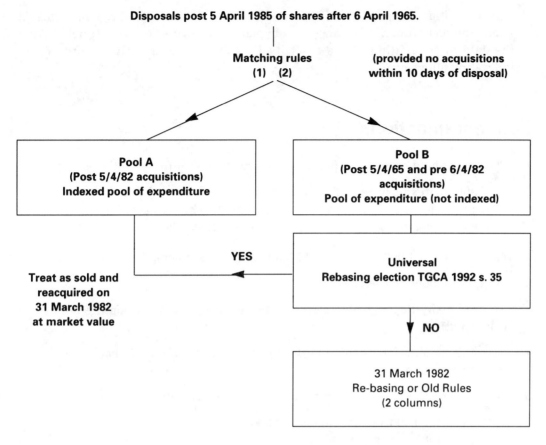

Figure 7.1 Summary of procedures for dealing with disposals of shares and securities

a) post 31 March 1982 acquisitions (6 April 1982 for individuals, 1 April 1982 for companies)
b) acquisitions between 5 April 1965 and 6 April 1982 (1 April 1982 for companies)

▶ The acquisitions in sub-sections a) and b) above are grouped into pools of expenditure, Pool A and Pool B respectively. Acquisitions pre 6 April 1965 are matched with disposals on a LIFO basis and are not examinable.

▶ Pool A is an indexed pool of expenditure. Each time an 'operative event' takes place (an acquisition or disposal of shares of the same class in the same company) the pool balance must be indexed forward, from the date of the previous operative event to the date of the current operative event, before the cost of the new shares can be added or the cost of the shares disposed of can be deducted.

▶ Pool B simply collects the costs of all shares acquired of that class in that company during the period. On disposal, the average cost is deducted from the pool. As all of these shares were held on 31 March 1982 the gain/loss is calculated using the 31 March 1982 re-basing unless the old rules give a lower gain or a lower loss.

▶ If an election is made for universal 31 March 1982 re-basing (TCGA 1992 s. 35), it will not be necessary to keep records of acquisitions prior to 31 March 1982 nor will any computations be required under the old rules.

▶ When bonus issues, rights issues, or any other form of reorganisation (including paper for paper takeovers) takes place, the new holding is treated as acquired at the same time as the original holding and for the same cost. Where the new holding is of a different class from the original holding, the cost of the original holding will need to be apportioned between the relevant holdings.

Any additional expenditure (for example, on the acquisition of rights) is treated in an identical fashion to enhancement expenditure (an additional cost not altering the date of acquisition of the asset itself). Care is required in computing the indexation allowance.

Self test questions

1. A taxpayer held shares in A plc on 1 January 1995, acquired as follows:

    1,000 shares acquired 25 August 1986. 800 shares inherited on the death of his grandfather (on 12 August 1987) who had acquired them on 15 September 1970. 500 shares acquired 1 December 1988.

    He disposed of 1,000 shares on 13 March 1995, which were they?

2. What is an 'operative event'?

3. To how many decimal places should the indexed rise for updating Pool A be calculated?

4. Give the formula for calculating the indexed rise for updating Pool A when an operative event occurs.

5. A taxpayer holds shares in Q plc on 1 January 1995, acquired as follows:

    | May | 1970 500 shares purchased £500 |
    | Aug | 1982 Bonus issue 1 for 1 |
    | Nov | 1985 800 shares purchased £1,000 |
    | Oct | 1990 Rights issue 1 for 4 @ £1.10 (taken up) |

    Calculate the number and value of shares in each of Pool A and Pool B at 10 October 1990.

6. A taxpayer holds 1,000 shares in B plc (cost £1,500 on 15 January 1995) when it is acquired by X plc. On a paper for paper exchange, he is entitled to one preference and four ordinary shares in X plc for every five shares held in B plc.

    Calculate the cost of each of the new holdings (the value of the shares in X plc on the first day of trading following the takeover were: preference shares £2.00 and; ordinary shares £3.00.)

7. a) Suzanne acquired 2,500 shares in J. Ryan Ltd an unquoted company, on 6 October 1965 for £3,500. She sold the shares on 6 January 1995 for £15,000. The agreed value at 31 March 1982 was £4,000.
    You are required to calculate the capital gain arising to Suzanne in 1994/95.

    b) Frances sold 11,000 ordinary shares in The Hastings Hardening Company plc, a quoted company, on 17 February 1995 for £30,000. She had bought ordinary shares in the company on the following dates:

	No of shares	Cost £
3 November 1967	2,000	1,000
16 March 1968	2,000	1,000
29 June 1980	2,000	1,300
19 September 1982	2,000	1,700
17 January 1985	2,000	6,000
12 December 1985	2,000	5,500

The value of each of the shares on 31 March 1982 was 75p.

You are required to calculate, before the annual exemption, the capital gain for 1994/95.

8 Paul made the following disposals:

a) On 30 March 1995, he sold for £2,600, 1,000 ordinary shares out of a holding of 1,500 shares in XY Ltd. The holding of shares had been built up as follows:

Date acquired	No of shares	Cost £
May 1985	2,000	3,500
March 1986 – Bonus issue	500	
	2,500	
Less sold May 1988	(1,000)	
	1,500	

b) On 2 April 1995, he sold 1,500 preference shares in CD Ltd for £2,100.

These shares had been acquired as a result of a reorganisation of CD Ltd's share capital on 31 March 1987. Paul had originally purchased 3,000 ordinary shares in CD Ltd in March 1986 for £4,500. As a result of the reorganisation Paul received the following shares and debentures:

	Market value on day following reorganisation
2,500 ordinary shares of 50p	80p per share
2,000 10% preference shares of £1	90p per share
£1,000 12% Debentures	£90 per £100 of stock

c) On 4 April 1995, he sold a racehorse for £70,000. The horse was acquired in January 1985 for £32,000.

You are required to compute the total capital gains to be included in Paul's tax return on 5 April 1995, giving full explanations where appropriate.

adapted from CIMA 3 Nov 1988

Answers on pages 566–569

CHAPTER 8

Inheritance Tax – General Principles

This chapter looks at the development of inheritance tax legislation. It outlines the scope of inheritance tax and illustrates the general principles for computing the inheritance tax liability for both lifetime transfers and on death. The detailed application of the exemptions are discussed and illustrated.

Many of the terms used in the legislation will be unfamiliar to you and this chapter attempts to give an overview of the way they fit together; definitions and explanations which are brief are given where possible.

This is a totally new subject and is very different from the other taxes you have studied.

Background to inheritance tax

A knowledge of this background helps to explain the development of inheritance tax over recent years.

Estate duty

Prior to 1974 estate duty was the main tax on capital. It was designed to be levied on the wealth of an individual at the point where it was passed to his descendants on his death. The rates at which the tax was levied were steeply progressive and this provided the incentive to avoid the tax wherever possible.

This was relatively easily accomplished initially by making gifts prior to death. Latterly, however, legislation was introduced to counter this, by deeming gifts made in a specified period prior to death as being made on the date of death so as to bring them into the estate.

By 1974, the specified period had been extended from the original one month to seven years. The rich, however, succeeded in making lifetime transfers into discretionary trusts which were not subject to estate duty and thus ensured that their wealth was not taxable on death.

A major criticism of the tax was that it was only paid by the unfortunate or the unprepared.

Capital transfer tax (1975–1986)

Capital transfer tax was introduced by the Finance Act 1975. It came into force immediately in relation to transfers of value made by individuals after 26 March 1974. It was designed to remedy the shortcomings of estate duty by:

▶ taxing all gifts on a cumulative basis over the complete life span of an individual, including those passing on his or her death
▶ levying a periodic charge (every ten years) on the property in discretionary settlements.

The tax was moderated by exemption for transfers between spouses and the introduction of a lower rate of tax for *inter vivos* (that is, lifetime) transfers made more than three years before death. There was also an extended range of conditional exemptions for works of art and national heritage property.

Administrative problems of recording transfers over such a long period plus the relatively low yield of the tax led to major changes in capital transfer tax in 1981. The cumulation period for lifetime gifts was reduced to ten years and gifts in the ten years before death were included in the estate at death.

Introduction of inheritance tax – 1986

The Finance Act 1986 made various changes to capital transfer tax and renamed it as inheritance tax. The Capital Transfer Tax Act 1984 which consolidated all previous legislation on capital transfer tax, became the Inheritance Tax Act 1984 (IHTA 1984) although it must be noted that inheritance tax was not introduced until 1986.

The main purpose of the changes to capital transfer tax by the FA 1986 was to remove *inter vivos* gifts between individuals from the charge to tax, provided that the donor survived seven years. Not all lifetime transfers have been removed from the charge to tax however, and *inter vivos* transfers to some trusts remain chargeable. These are cumulated over a seven-year period. (Any transfers cumulated for capital transfer tax within the seven-year period are counted to determine the starting point on the inheritance tax scale.)

Since 1986, rates of inheritance tax have been vastly reduced and the threshold where tax begins to be levied has increased.

The scope of inheritance tax

Inheritance tax is charged on two principal occasions:

- on the value transferred by a chargeable transfer of value on or after 18 March 1986
- on property held in discretionary settlements at each ten year anniversary (covered in Chapter 14) and on certain other occasions (covered in Chapter 10).

This chapter and the next two chapters are concerned with the first of those occasions.

Figure 8.1 attempts to illustrate what a chargeable transfer of value is. There is a great deal of unfamiliar terminology involved and the diagram cannot be fully understood without an understanding of these terms. The next few sections therefore attempt to define and explain the terms.

Chargeable transfer of value

This is a **transfer of value** of **chargeable property** made by a **chargeable person**, which is not an exempt transfer and which has been allowed all available exemptions and reliefs.

Transfer of value

A transfer of value is any disposition made by a person (the transferor) as a result of which the value of his or her estate immediately after the disposition is less than it would be but for the disposition; and the amount by which it is less is the value transferred by the transfer (irrespective of the value gained by the transferee). This definition is fundamental to inheritance tax.

Following the definition to its conclusion, the value of any transfer of value resulting in payment by the transferor of inheritance tax will be the total diminution in value of the estate. (That is, the value of the property plus the amount of the inheritance tax.) No other taxes or expenses of transfer are included.

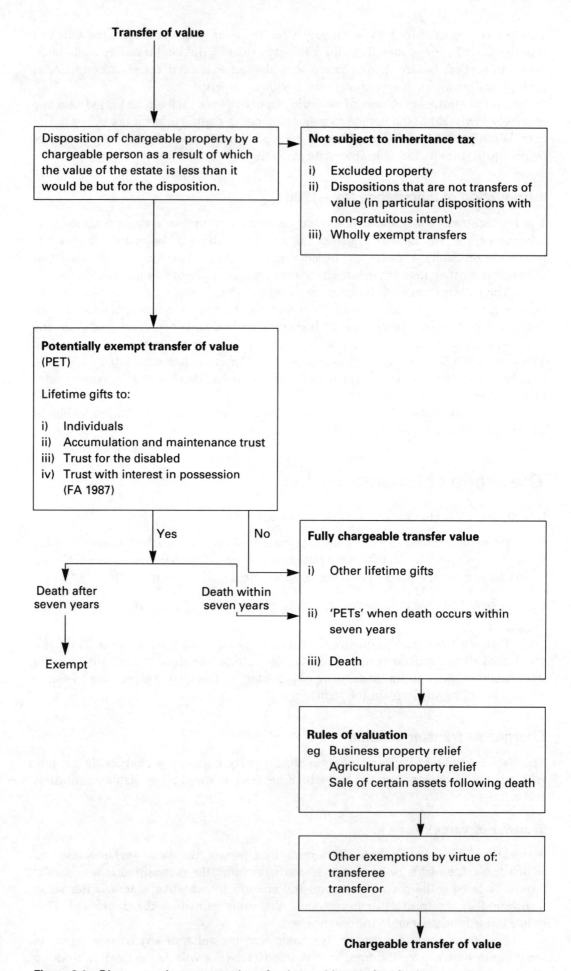

Figure 8.1 Diagrammatic representation of a chargeable transfer of value

Disposition

A disposition is not defined in the legislation and is simply the disposal of the beneficial ownership of property or an interest therein. It includes the following:

- Any disposal carried out by means of associated operations (see Chapter 10).
- The omission to exercise a right if as a result the estate is diminished and another person's estate is increased (unless the omission was not deliberate). The latest date on which the right could have been exercised is taken as the date of the disposition.

The following dispositions are specifically exempted from being transfers of value.

- A non-gratuitous disposition – if there is no gratuitous intent, and it is a transaction genuinely made at arm's length between unconnected persons or could have been so made, it constitutes a non-gratuitous disposition. Therefore any commercial bargain is precluded from being a transfer of value, albeit that the transferor suffers a loss and therefore his or her estate is diminished.
- Dispositions for family maintenance – this covers spouses, including provision on divorce, children up to the finish of their education, and dependent relatives.
- Dispositions allowable as expenditure for income and corporation tax – these are not gratuitous in most cases but specifically cover employer contributions to approved pension schemes. These include personal pension arrangements entered into by an employee, and comparable amounts to unapproved schemes provided they are not in respect of connected persons.
- Dispositions to certain trusts by close companies for the benefit of employees of the company.
- Waivers of remuneration – the remuneration waived must have been liable to income tax under Schedule E and should be formally waived (by deed); the employer's taxable profits should be increased by a corresponding amount.
- Waivers of dividend – the right to the dividend must be waived within 12 months before the dividend was declared.

Chargeable property

Chargeable property is all property wherever situated other than excluded property.

Excluded property

The following is excluded property and is outside the scope of inheritance tax.

- Property (not part of a settlement) situated outside the UK and belonging to a person not domiciled in the UK. (Property that is part of a settlement and is situated outside the UK is excluded property if the settlor was domiciled outside the UK when the settlement was made.) The extended definition of domicile (see below) applies.
- Reversionary interests (see below) unless acquired at any time for monetary consideration, or linked to the determination of a lease (upon a person's death, for instance), or in a settlement to which either the settlor or spouse is, or has been, beneficially entitled.
- Certain other specified property including: overseas pensions; government securities issued as exempt from UK taxation to persons not domiciled nor ordinarily resident in the UK; certain savings of persons domiciled in the Channel Islands or Isle of Man (National Savings Bank and Trustee Savings Bank accounts, National Savings Certificates, premium savings bonds, SAYE schemes). The extended definition of domicile (see below) does not apply.

Situation of assets

The inheritance tax legislation contains no specific rules for determining the situation of property and therefore the general law rules apply.

- Immovable property is situated where it is physically located.
- Tangible movable property is situated at its location at the time of disposal.
- Shares and so forth and patents are situated in the country in which they are registered or in which they would normally be dealt with in the ordinary course of business. Bearer shares and securities are situated in the country in which the certificate of title is kept.
- Debts are situated in the country in which the debtor is resident; judgement debts are situated where the judgement is recorded.
- A bank account is situated at the branch at which it is kept.
- A business is situated where the business is carried on.

The general law rules above also apply to trust property. A double tax agreement may override any of the above rules of law.

Chargeable persons

Individuals

An individual domiciled in the UK is liable to inheritance tax on a disposition of any chargeable asset wherever situated. A non-UK domiciled individual is only liable to inheritance tax on assets situated in the UK.

Domicile for inheritance tax purposes follows the common law rules except on certain occasions when it has a special definition.

The general principle is that a person may only have one country of domicile at any time. This is normally the country where he or she has his or her permanent home. A person acquires a domicile of origin at birth and subsequently a domicile of dependency (usually from the father or person on whom he or she is legally dependent). Later, however, when majority has been attained, that person may change it to a domicile of choice, provided this is established by conduct (the acquisition of a burial plot, for instance).

If any later action demonstrates that this domicile of choice has been abandoned, domicile of origin will automatically be reacquired. From 1 January 1974, a married woman may have a domicile independent from that of her husband.

Inheritance tax extends the boundaries of UK domicile to include any person who 'at the relevant time' (being the date of the transfer/death) was either:

- domiciled in the UK at any time within the immediately preceding three years
- resident (for income tax purposes) in the UK for at least 17 of the 20 fiscal years ending with the fiscal year in which the 'relevant time' falls.

The United Kingdom, for this purpose, is made up of England, Scotland, Wales and Northern Ireland. The Channel Islands and the Isle of Man are not included.

Husbands and wives are taxed independently for purposes of inheritance tax. The estate of each includes that property (or share of property) that actually belongs to him or her.

Partnerships

A partnership is not a legal entity in England and Wales separate and distinct from its members. All assets of a partnership belong to the individual partners in their agreed shares. The inheritance tax legislation applies to each individual partner and to his or her interest in the partnership assets (see Chapter 17).

Companies

Although by definition there is nothing to prevent a company making a transfer of value, a company is not a chargeable person and cannot make a chargeable transfer of value. Where, however, a close company makes a transfer of value, the close company may be 'looked through'. The transfer of value may then be apportioned between the participators (see Chapter 26).

Settlements

A settlement or trust exists whenever a disposition is made in such a way that property is held:

- for the benefit of a succession of persons
- for any person upon the occurrence of a specified contingency
- for trustees to accumulate or make payment out of income or capital at their discretion.

There are two principal categories of trust; trusts with an interest in possession, and discretionary trusts.

Trusts with an interest in possession

These are trusts where one or more persons are entitled to the income arising from the trust property, or to the use of trust property (for example, a house), generally for life.

A reversionary interest is an interest in a trust or settlement that will take effect at a future date upon the happening of a future event.

For example, a trust may be set up so that X receives all the income from the trust during his or her lifetime and upon his death, the capital in the trust will be paid to Y. X is known as the life tenant of the trust or is said to have an interest in possession. Y is known as the 'remainderman' and is said to have a reversionary interest in the settlement.

These trusts are regarded as forming part of the estate of the life tenant(s). Thus the underlying capital value of the trust property is treated as being owned by the life tenants in proportion to their interests in the income. These trusts are therefore not chargeable persons in the sense that tax is assessed independently on them. They do, however, bear the tax attributable to that part of the capital value of the trust property which is deemed to pass on the death of the life tenant.

Discretionary trusts

These are trusts with no interest in possession. Discretionary trusts take many forms – accumulation and maintenance trusts and trusts for the disabled are examples.

Because discretionary trusts are not linked to the life of any person, the charge to inheritance tax cannot be triggered by the death of a chargeable person. Therefore, separate provisions exist in inheritance tax to charge to tax property held in a settlement in which there is no qualifying interest in possession. The manner in which the charge to tax is made is considered in Chapter 14.

Accumulation and maintenance trust

This is a trust where the trustees have power to accumulate income and capitalise it for one or more minors. Alternatively income may be paid out for the maintenance, education or benefit of a beneficiary at the discretion of the trustees. Property in the trust *must* vest in the beneficiaries on or before each of them attain the age of 25 (that is, each beneficiary must become absolutely entitled or, at least, entitled to an interest in possession). It is a privileged form of discretionary trust often set up for the settlor's children or grandchildren.

Potentially exempt transfers (PETs)

A potentially exempt transfer (PET) is a lifetime transfer of value (of property or of an interest in possession in settled property) made by an individual on or after 18 March 1986 to either:

- another individual
- an accumulation and maintenance trust (see above)
- a trust for the disabled (a privileged form of discretionary trust)
- a trust with an interest in possession (after 16 March 1987).

These transfers are exempt unless the transferor dies within seven years, and are therefore not subjected to tax at the time of the transfer. If the transferor dies within seven years, the gift becomes taxable, being treated as if made at the date of the original transfer but using the rates of tax applicable at the date of death. The following transfers cannot be PETs:

- Any transfer which would otherwise be exempt (see below).
- A transfer to be charged to tax as if a transfer of value had been made, that is, a deemed transfer. (An example is the apportionment to participators of a transfer of value by a close company; see Chapter 26.)

Exempt transfers

Certain transfers are wholly exempt irrespective of their size while other transfers are exempted only to a limited extent. The exemption may be given by reason of:

- the rules of valuation – in some cases a percentage of the value, such as business property relief
- the transferee – wholly exempt or exempt up to a fixed monetary limit
- being within exemptions available to the transferor – monetary limits.

If a transfer is wholly exempt for any reason, there is no need to proceed with it further but some transfers of value may be subject to limited exemptions under each of the above. The order in which the reliefs are given is critical in arriving at the value of the chargeable transfer and should be as listed above. (Full details of exemptions are given later in this chapter.)

The charge to tax

The fiscal year has no relevance for inheritance tax other than for the regulation of certain exemptions (see below).

Inheritance tax is calculated on each transfer chronologically. Each later chargeable transfer is added to the total of previous chargeable transfers. As the cumulative total reaches a higher point on the appropriate scale (the one applicable at the date of the current transfer) the current transfer is taxed at each level at the appropriate rate.

The cumulation period is seven years, earlier transfers gradually dropping out of the cumulative total – transfers on 1 January 1988 will drop out on 1 January 1995 and so on.

Any transfers cumulated for capital transfer tax are counted towards the starting total on the inheritance tax scale, if they fall within a seven year period prior to the transfer under review.

The charge to inheritance tax is illustrated diagrammatically in Figure 8.2.

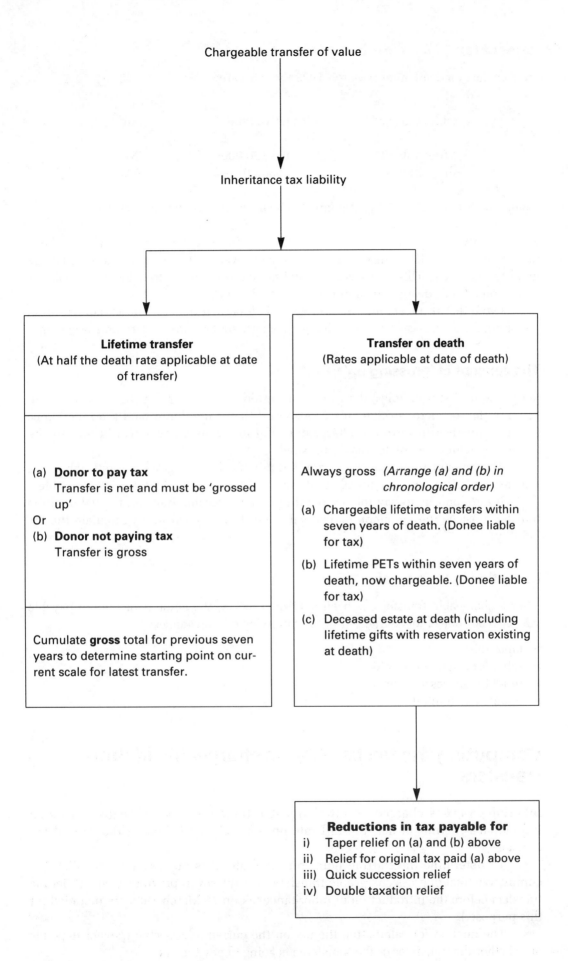

Figure 8.2 The charge to inheritance tax

Rates of tax

For transfers on death after 9 March 1992 the rates are:

Gross taxable transfers £	Cumulative totals £	Gross rate
First 150,000	0 – 150,000	Nil
Above 150,000	150,001 +	40%

(**Note**: The Finance Act 1994 made no change to the inheritance tax scale.)

Where lifetime gifts are chargeable, the tax payable is calculated as half the above (death scale) rate. If death occurs within seven years, however, an additional tax liability may arise. This increases the total tax payable on the transfer to the liability arising on the full death scale applicable at the date of death.

(Note that if the amount due on death is less than the amount actually paid on the original transfer – as a result of budget changes to the scale – no refund is made.)

The concept of 'grossing up'

Returning to first principles, the value transferred was measured as the diminution in value in the transferor's estate. It was also said that if the donor paid the inheritance tax liability resulting from a chargeable lifetime transfer, this would add to the amount by which the estate was diminished.

The amount by which the estate is diminished is the gross amount, while the transferee receives the net equivalent of the gross amount on which tax is chargeable.

If the donor is to pay the tax liability on a chargeable transfer, the value of the transfer must be the net amount. The value must be grossed up to calculate the tax liability.

Reduction in tax payable

After a chargeable transfer has been subjected to tax, the amount of the tax payable may also be subject to a reduction in the following circumstances:

- taper relief
- relief for original tax paid
- relief for successive charges
- double taxation relief.

Computing the tax liability on chargeable lifetime transfers

Inheritance tax is charged on all chargeable transfers of value made during an individual's lifetime at half the full rate on the scale applicable at the date of the transfer.

To determine the starting point on the scale, it is necessary to establish the cumulative total of gross chargeable transfers over the seven previous years. (Lifetime transfers before the introduction of inheritance tax on 18 March 1986 are included for this purpose.)

The method for calculating the tax on the current chargeable transfer depends on whether the transferor or the transferee is going to pay the tax.

Transferee to pay tax

When the transferee is going to pay the tax, the value of the chargeable transfer is the amount of the gift. The tax is simply the percentage appropriate to the band, or bands, into which the transfer falls.

EXAMPLE 8.1

A, who had made no previous chargeable transfers, made a chargeable transfer (after all exemptions and reliefs) of £160,000 to a discretionary trust on 15 August 1994. The trustees agreed to pay the tax liability arising.

£160,000 is the gross transfer.

	Gross gift £	Tax £	Net gift £
Brought forward at 15 August 1994	Nil		
15 August 1994 discretionary trust	160,000	2,000	158,000
(150,000 @ 0% = Nil			
10,000 @ 20% = 2,000)			
Carried forward at 15 August 1994	160,000		

Thus, A diminished estate by £160,000 (the gross gift) but the trust property was increased by £158,000 (the net gift).

EXAMPLE 8.2

F had previously made the following chargeable transfers:

£100,000   1 August 1983
£50,000   1 July 1988

F then gave £160,000 (after all exemptions and reliefs) to a discretionary trust on 15 August 1994. The trustees agreed to pay the tax liability arising.

The starting point will be the cumulative total over the seven-year period from 16 August 1987 to 14 August 1994, that is, £50,000.

	Gross gift £	Tax £	Net gift £
Brought forward at 15 August 1994	50,000		
15 August 1994 discretionary trust	160,000	12,000	148,000
(100,000 @ 0% = Nil			
60,000 @ 20% = 12,000)			
Carried forward at 15 August 1994	210,000		

Thus, F diminished his estate by £160,000 (the gross gift), but the trust property was increased by £148,000 (£160,000 less tax, £12,000), the net gift.

Transferor to pay tax

When the transferor pays the tax, the value of the chargeable transfer represents the net amount of the gift. The amount of the tax must be calculated by working back from this (in other words, 'grossing up' the gift).

The first step is to extend the scale of rates given as follows.

	Gross taxable transfers £	Lifetime rate	Tax on band	Cumulative net transfer £	Grossing up fraction
First	150,000	Nil	Nil	150,000	Nil
Above	150,000	20%			20/(100–20)

This must usually be done in the examination as only the basic death scale rates are given. Since 15 March 1988, there have only been the two bands (the threshold has increased over the period from £110,000 to £150,000). This exercise does not cause a problem but for earlier years there were a larger number of bands and the exercise was more complicated.

The second step is to calculate the tax at the current rate on the gross cumulative total (from the previous seven years) to arrive at the net cumulative total brought forward. This determines the starting point on the net gift scale.

The previous examples have been adapted to allow comparison.

EXAMPLE 8.3 (8.1 Modified)

A, who had made no previous chargeable transfers, made a chargeable transfer (after all exemptions and reliefs) of £160,000 to a discretionary trust on 15 August 1994. He agreed to pay the tax liability arising. £160,000 is the net transfer.

	Gross gift £	Tax £	Net gift £
Brought forward at 15 August 1994	Nil		
Tax/Net restated @ 1994/95 rates		Nil	Nil
15 August 1994 discretionary trust	162,500	2,500	160,000
(150,000 @ 0% = Nil			
10,000 @ 20/(100 – 20) = 2,500)			
Carried forward at 15 August 1994	162,500		

Thus, A diminished his estate by £162,500 (the amount of the gift £160,000 plus the amount of the tax £2,500) while the trust property was increased by £160,000, the net gift.

EXAMPLE 8.4 (8.2 Modified)

F had previously made the following chargeable transfers:

        £100,000   1 August 1983
        £50,000   1 July 1988

He gave £160,000 (after all exemptions and reliefs) to a discretionary trust on 15 August 1994. He agreed to pay the tax liability arising.

	Gross gift £	Tax £	Net gift £
Brought forward at 15 August 1994	50,000		
Tax/Net restated @ 1994/95 rates		Nil	50,000
15 August 1994 discretionary trust	175,000	15,000	160,000
(100,000 @ 0% = Nil			
60,000 @ 20/(100 – 20) = 15,000)			
Carried forward at 15 August 1994	225,000		

Computing the tax liability on death

Inheritance tax is charged on death on the following:

- on the chargeable lifetime transfers over the previous seven years (additional liability arising on death)
- on the lifetime transfers which were PETs made within the previous seven years
- on the deceased's estate at the date of death.

The tax on the first two above is arrived at by reworking the lifetime computation after slotting the PETs now chargeable into their chronological order. The scale of rates applicable at the date of death is then used. Taper relief is given and the tax paid at the date of the original transfer, if any, is credited to give the additional tax liability on death. Note that although the cumulation period is the seven years prior to death, chargeable lifetime transfers in the seven years prior to these seven years will affect the cumulation at any given date.

The additional tax liabilities arising are the responsibility of each of the transferees – irrespective of who agreed to pay the tax at the date of the original gift. It may, however, be reduced by taper relief. (This is outlined in more detail below).

Estate at date of death

The deceased's estate at the date of death is made up of the following:

- the deceased's 'free estate'
- lifetime gifts with reservation, not removed at the date of death (this topic is covered in Chapter 10)
- the value of any property to which the deceased is beneficially entitled (for example, an interest in possession in settled property).

The transfer on death is the final transfer made by the deceased and is always gross. It will suffer tax by adding it to the cumulative total (from the previous seven years) brought forward above (including all PETs now chargeable) and charging tax at the percentage appropriate to the band, or bands, into which the transfer falls.

The total tax on the deceased's estate at date of death is calculated as a percentage of the estate to give the **estate rate**. The estate rate is the average rate of tax suffered by the estate.

The personal representatives or executors are responsible for paying the inheritance tax on the free estate (out of the free estate). This is calculated as:

Free estate × Estate rate = Tax suffered by free estate

The trustees of the settled property are responsible for paying the inheritance tax on this part of the estate (out of trust property) and this is calculated as:

Settled property × Estate rate = Tax suffered by settled estate

Relief is available for successive charges to tax where a person dies within five years of a transfer to him or her which increased the value of his or her estate (see below).

Relief is also available where tax of the same type is payable on the same property in the UK and another country. This relief will be governed by the terms of the double tax agreement between the countries. Alternatively, if there is none, or if it is more beneficial, relief will be governed under the unilateral double tax relief arrangements which exist in the UK (see Chapter 30).

Note that for examination purposes you are not expected to be familiar with the terms of individual double tax treaties – unilateral relief is appropriate for examinations.

Free estate

This is the property that the deceased actually owns and is free to dispose of at the date of death.

EXAMPLE 8.5

A died on 1 December 1994. He left an estate of £200,000. This included an interest in possession in settled property valued at £50,000. A had made no chargeable transfers and no PETs in the previous seven years.

	£
Chargeable transfers brought forward	Nil
PETs now chargeable	Nil
Estate on death	200,000
	200,000
IHT on death – estate only	
150,000 @ Nil%	Nil
50,000 @ 40%	20,000
	20,000
Estate rate $\dfrac{20,000}{200,000}$ =	10%

The estate rate is used to apportion the tax payable on the estate between the various parties responsible for it. In this case, the trustees of the settled property are responsible for the tax attributable to the interest in possession while the personal representatives of the deceased are responsible for the tax on the remainder.

Tax attributable to the interest in possession payable by the trustees:		
	£50,000 @ 10%	£5,000
Tax attributable to the free estate payable by personal representatives:		
	£150,000 @ 10%	£15,000

Taper relief

Taper relief is given on the tax calculated for PETS and chargeable lifetime transfers. The tax is calculated on the scale applicable at the date of death, and taper relief is given before any tax paid at the time the transfer was made is deducted. It is calculated according to the number of years between the gift and death, as follows.

Years between gift and death	% reduction in tax payable
0–3	0
3–4	20
4–5	40
5–6	60
6–7	80

If the gift was made more than seven years before death, there is no liability on death. This means that some tax could still, theoretically, be payable on PETs made less than seven years before death. In reality, however, it is unlikely that any additional tax will actually become payable on chargeable transfers made more than five years before death once the tax originally paid is deducted.

It is important to note that there can be no repayment of tax where the tax originally paid is more than the liability on death after taper relief.

EXAMPLE 8.6

B died on 5 March 1995. He left an estate valued at £200,000 and had given his son £160,000 (after all exemptions and reliefs) on 10 October 1990. He had made no chargeable transfers.

	£
Chargeable transfers brought forward	Nil
PETs now chargeable	160,000
Estate on death	200,000
	360,000

IHT on death – estate only

200,000 @ 40%	80,000
	80,000

Estate rate	$\dfrac{80,000}{200,000}$ =	40%

IHT on death – lifetime transfers

Chargeable transfers brought forward @ 10 October 1990 (11/10/83 to 9/10/90)	Nil
10 October 1990	160,000
Carried forward	160,000
Tax @ rate applicable at date of death	
150,000 @ Nil%	Nil
10,000 @ 40%	4,000
	4,000
Taper relief 4–5 years 40%	(1,600)
	2,400
Less: tax paid originally	—
Payable by transferee	2,400

Where there are several lifetime transfers, this layout becomes a little tedious. A more compact layout is illustrated below. This will be used in future examples.

IHT on death – lifetime transfers

	Gross	Tax on death £	Taper relief £	Tax paid £	Tax payable £
£					
b/f @ 10 October 1990	Nil				
10 October 1990	160,000				
(150,000 @ Nil%					
10,000 @ 40%) Taper 4–5yr		4,000	(1,600)	Nil	2,400
c/f	160,000				

EXAMPLE 8.7

C died on 15 December 1994. He left an estate valued at £200,000 and had given his son £160,000 (after all exemptions and reliefs) on 10 October 1990. He had made a chargeable transfer of £130,000 (after all exemptions and reliefs) to a discretionary trust on 1 December 1990 on which he had paid the tax. No previous chargeable transfers had been made.

Calculate the inheritance tax liabilities arising.

Lifetime	Gross gift £	Tax £	Net gift £
Brought forward at 10 October 1990	Nil		
10 Oct 1990 PET	160,000		
Brought forward at 1 December 1990	Nil		
Tax/Net restated @ 1990/91 rates		Nil	Nil
1 Dec 1990 discretionary trust	130,500	500	130,000
(128,000 @ 0% = Nil			
2,000 @ 20/(100–20) = 500)			
Carried forward at 1 Dec 1990	130,500		

Death 15 December 1994

	£
Chargeable transfers brought forward	130,500
PETs now chargeable	160,000
Estate on death	200,000
	490,500

IHT on death – estate only

200,000 @ 40%		80,000
Estate rate: 80,000/200,000 =		40%

IHT on death – lifetime transfers

	Gross £	Tax on death £	Taper relief £	Tax paid £	Tax payable £
b/f @ 10 October 1990	Nil				
10 October 1990 PET	160,000				
(150,000 @ Nil%					
10,000 @ 40%) Taper 4–5yr		4,000	(1,600)	(Nil)	2,400
c/f 1 Dec 1990	160,000				
1 December 1990	130,500				
(130,500 @ 40%) Taper 4–5yr		52,200	(20,880)	(500)	30,820
	290,500				

EXAMPLE 8.8

D died on 4 September 1994. He left an estate valued at £200,000 and had made the following lifetime gifts (after all exemptions and reliefs):

1 December 1985	A gross chargeable transfer for CTT purposes of £91,000, tax being paid of £3,300.
5 May 1991	A gift to his daughter of £60,000.

Calculate the inheritance tax liabilities arising.

Lifetime

	Gross gift £	Tax £	Net gift £
Brought forward at 5 May 1991	91,000		
5 May 1991 PET	60,000		Nil
Brought forward at 1 December 1992	151,000		
Less treansfer at 1 December 1985	(91,000)		
Brought forard at 4 September 1994	60,000		

		£
Chargeable transfers brought forward (over 7 years)		Nil
PETs now chargeable		60,000
Estate on death		200,000
		260,000

IHT on death – estate only

90,000 @ 0%		Nil
110,000 @ 40%		44,000
Estate rate: 44,000/200,000 =		22%

IHT on death – lifetime transfers

£	Gross £	Tax on death £	Taper relief £	Tax paid £	Tax payable
b/f @ 5 May 1991	91,000				
5 May 1991 PET	60,000				
(59,000 @ Nil%					
1,000 @ 40%) Taper 3–4yr		400	(80)	(Nil)	320
b/f 1 Dec 1992	151,000				
Less: 1 December 1985	(91,000)				
Cumulative total @ death	60,000				

Quick succession relief

The purpose of this relief is to reduce current IHT arising on property, if that same property has been the subject of an earlier IHT charge within 5 years. The current IHT charge, for non-settled property, must arise on death.

Where death occurs within five years of an earlier transfer which increased the deceased's estate, the tax payable on death is reduced as follows:

$$\text{Original tax} \times \frac{\text{Net transfer}}{\text{Gross transfer}} \times \text{\% QSR}$$

The % QSR is on a sliding scale as follows:

Years between transfer and death	% QSR
0–1	100
1–2	80
2–3	60
3–4	40
4–5	20

EXAMPLE 8.9

A died on 14 January 1995 leaving free estate of £200,000 (estate rate 22%). Included in his estate was property which A had received in May 1990 on which IHT of £6,000 had been paid (gross chargeable transfer £30,000).

IHT on free estate 200,000 @ 22%	44,000
Less: Quick succession relief	
$6,000 \times \dfrac{24,000}{30,000} \times 20\%$	(960)
IHT payable by personal representatives	43,040

INHERITANCE TAX – GENERAL PRINCIPLES

Exemptions

As we have seen, there are a number of exemptions available which either wholly exempt or reduce the value transferred. Some exemptions apply to both lifetime transfers and transfers on death while other exemptions only apply to lifetime transfers. The exemption may be given via any of the following:

- the rules of valuation – in some cases a percentage of the value (for instance, business property relief)
- the transferee – wholly exempt or exempt up to a fixed monetary limit
- being within exemptions available to the transferor – monetary limits.

A transfer which is wholly exempt, for any reason, may be disregarded henceforth. Care must be taken, however, with transfers of value which are subject to limited exemptions under any of the above. The order in which the reliefs are given is critical in arriving at the value of the chargeable transfer and should be as listed above.

Valuation reliefs (listed in Figure 8.1)

Valuation reliefs take priority. They may wholly exempt the transfer, reduce it by a percentage or reduce it by a nominal amount – they are considered in full in the next chapter.

Exemptions by virtue of the transferee

These exemptions mostly result in the transfers being wholly exempt.

- Transfers between spouses – limited to a cumulative total of £55,000 if the spouse is non-UK domiciled.
- Gifts to UK charities – both lifetime and on death.
- Gifts to qualifying political parties – both lifetime and on death. A qualifying political party is one which gained at least two seats in the House of Commons at the preceding general election or one seat and at least 150,000 votes.
- Gifts for the public benefit of eligible property to non-profit making bodies – both lifetime and on death. Board approval must be obtained and undertakings may be required concerning the use, disposal, preservation and public access of the property. Eligible property includes land or buildings of scenic, historic or scientific interest. Also, a gift of property to provide for the upkeep of the above, and objects and collections of national, scientific, historic or artistic interest.
- Gifts for national purposes to certain national bodies – both lifetime and on death – whether of national heritage property or not. The approved bodies include museums, art galleries, the National Trust, libraries, educational institutions, and government departments.
- Gifts to employee trusts of shares in a company provided certain conditions are satisfied principally:
  - that the beneficiaries of the trust include all or most of the employees of the company
  - at or within one year of the transfer, the trustees must have control of the company (that is, more than 50% of ordinary shares and votes)
  - no part of the trust property may be applied for the benefit of a participator – excluding participators who are not entitled to 5% or more of the shares or assets on the winding up of the company.

Exemptions available to the transferor

These exemptions are dealt with in two sections:

a) those that result in the gifts being wholly exempt
b) those that may or may not result in the transfer being wholly exempt.

Small gift exemption (a)

A transferor may make lifetime transfers up to £250 per fiscal year per person. Any number of such gifts may be made but it cannot exempt part of a larger gift.

Normal expenditure out of income (a)

Any transfer made by a transferor in his or her lifetime can be exempt if the transferor can show that it is normal expenditure out of income taking one year with another. After all such transfers, the transferor must be able to show that sufficient income remained for him to maintain his usual standard of living.

Examples of such gifts are birthday and Christmas presents, deeds of covenant, and the payment of life assurance premiums on a policy for the benefit of another person.

Death on active service (a)

Gifts in consideration of marriage (b)

An exemption is available to the transferor making lifetime gifts in consideration of marriage as follows:

- £5,000 by a parent of either party to the marriage
- £2,500 by one party to the marriage to the other; or by a grandparent or remoter ancestor
- £1,000 in any other case.

As husband and wife are totally independent of each other for inheritance tax purposes, each of them may make exempt gifts as above in consideration of marriage. These amounts may exempt part of a larger gift.

The gifts must be made outright to a party to the marriage or settled for the benefit of a party to the marriage, its offspring or the spouse of the offspring.

Annual exemption (b)

The first £3,000 of lifetime transfers per fiscal year is exempt from inheritance tax. It may be used to exempt part of a larger transfer or several smaller transfers not otherwise exempted. It must, however, be set off against such transfers in chronological order as they arise in the fiscal year. (That is, the transferor cannot choose to use the exemption to reduce one gift as against another.)

In any fiscal year where the annual exemption is not used or is not used in full, the balance may be carried forward to the following fiscal year. It can then be offset against transfers of that year not otherwise exempted, after the allowance for that year has been used.

There is some doubt about the way in which the annual exemption interacts with potentially exempt transfers, which we will now look at further.

The original Inland Revenue view

This was that potentially exempt transfers should be ignored for purposes of the annual exemption unless they later became chargeable. In this case each PET was deemed to take place in the actual fiscal year of the transfer, but after all non-exempt transfers. The allocation of the annual exemption within the fiscal year could not therefore be upset by a PET becoming chargeable.

If a PET subsequently became chargeable in an earlier year, to the extent that the annual exemption of that year was unused in that year and had been carried forward, it would be reallocated to the PET now chargeable. This would thus disturb the exemptions allocated in the later year.

The view published by the Inland Revenue (Booklet IHT 1)
This suggests that if a transfer of value (otherwise a PET) is entitled to the annual exemption it will be an exempt transfer and not a potentially exempt transfer.

Although the rights and wrongs of the current Revenue view are unclear, it is this latter interpretation which will be used in subsequent examples. From a planning point of view, this treatment means that PETs should be timed after chargeable transfers in the fiscal year, lest the transferor survives seven years and the annual exemption is wasted.

The amount of the exemptions are deducted from the value transferred, irrespective of whether the transferor or the transferee is to pay the tax. After all exemptions have been deducted, the balance of the transfer is the gross transfer if the transferee is to pay the tax and the net transfer if the transferor is to pay the tax.

Exemptions on death are deducted from the value of the free estate to give the chargeable estate on death.

Summary of wholly exempt transfers

These are available for both lifetime and death transfers unless otherwise stated.

- transfers between spouses (both UK domiciled)
- gifts to UK charities
- gifts to qualifying political parties
- gifts for the public benefit of eligible property to non-profit making bodies
- gifts for national purposes to certain national bodies, whether of national heritage property or not
- gifts to employee trusts of shares in a company
- small gift exemption (lifetime) up to £250 per fiscal year per person
- normal expenditure out of income (lifetime)
- death on active service.

Conditional exemptions

There is an opportunity to defer tax on the transfer of heritage property and woodlands, provided certain conditions continue to be fulfilled. (These are considered further in Chapter 10.)

EXAMPLE 8.10

A, who had made no previous transfers, made the following lifetime transfers:

10 September 1987	£100,000 to a discretionary trust, the trustees to pay the tax.
21 December 1989	£150,000 to his son on the occasion of his son's marriage.
5 February 1990	£30,000 to the discretionary trust, he agreed to pay the tax.

A died on 1 August 1994 leaving a free estate of £400,000 of which £100,000 was bequeathed to charity.

Lifetime

	Gross gift £	Tax £	Net gift £
Brought forward at 10 Sept 1987	Nil		

10 Sept 1987 gross   100,000
Less: AE 1987/88   (3,000)
      AE 1986/87   (3,000)

	94,000	600	93,400

(90,000 @ 0% = Nil
(4,000 @ 15%= 600)

Brought forward at 21 Dec 1989   94,000
21 Dec 89   150,000
                    ME   (5,000)
            AE 1989/90   (3,000)
               1988/89   (3,000)
                   PET   139,000

	–		

Brought forward at 5 Feb 1990   94,000
Tax/Net restated @ 1989/90 rates   Nil   94,000
5 Feb 1990 net   30,000
Less: AE   Nil

Net (24,000 @ 0%   =   Nil   31,500   1,500   30,000
     6,000 @ 20/(100-20) = 1,500)
Brought forward at date of death   125,500

Death 1 August 1994

	£
Chargeable transfers brought forward	125,500
PETs now chargeable	139,000
Estate on death (£400,000 less £100,000 exempt)	300,000
	564,500

IHT on death – estate only
    300,000 @ 40%   120,000

    Estate rate: 120,000/300,000 =   40%

IHT on death – lifetime transfers

	Gross £	Tax on death £	Taper relief £	Tax paid £	Tax payable £
b/f @ 10 Sept 87	Nil				
10 Sept 87	94,000				
(94,000) @ Nil%		Nil	Nil	600	Nil
c/f 21 Dec 89	94,000				
21 Dec 89 PET	139,000				
(56,000 @ Nil = Nil					
83,000 @ 40% = 33,200) 4–5yr		33,200	(13,280)	Nil	19,920
c/f 5 Feb 90	233,000				
5 Feb 90	31,500				
(31,500 @ 40% = 12,600) 4–5yr		12,600	(5,040)	(1,500)	6,060
Cumulative total @ death	264,500				

IHT on gift to son (£19,920) will be payable by son.
Additional IHT on gift to discretionary trust (£6,060) will be payable by trustees.

INHERITANCE TAX – GENERAL PRINCIPLES

Computing the tax liability on death – further aspects

The deceased may make one or more specific gifts in his or her will requiring specified property to be given to specified persons. Specific gifts do not normally bear their own tax unless the deceased indicates that this is his or her intention. They may therefore be described as 'tax free' and the tax is borne by the residue of the estate.

EXAMPLE 8.11

A died on 1 March 1995 leaving an estate valued at £300,000. He had made no previous chargeable transfers but, in his will, he bequeathed £50,000 to his nephew and the residue to his son.

Death 1 March 1995

	£
Chargeable transfers brought forward	Nil
PETs now chargeable	Nil
Estate on death	300,000
	300,000

IHT on death – estate

	£
150,000 @ Nil	Nil
150,000 @ 40%	60,000
	60,000

$$\text{Estate rate} = \frac{60,000}{300,000} = 20\%$$

Distribution of estate:

	£
Inheritance tax	60,000
Nephew – tax-free legacy	50,000
Residue to son	190,000
	300,000

In general the grossing up principle only applies to lifetime transfers where the donor is paying the tax. However, there is one situation where the principle applies on death.

If the residue of the estate is exempt (for example, if it is left to the spouse), then the legacy is the only chargeable part of the estate. It must be grossed up by the amount of the tax related to that property in order to determine the value of the exempt remainder.

If the tax-free legacy is the only chargeable transfer, the IHT on death is relatively straightforward to calculate.

EXAMPLE 8.12

A died on 1 March 1995 leaving an estate valued at £320,000. He had made no previous chargeable transfers but, in his will, he bequeathed £160,000 to his son and the residue to his wife.

	£
Death 1 March 1995	
Tax-free legacy	160,000
Tax thereon:	
Net	
(150,000 @ Nil	
10,000 @ 40/(100 − 40)	6,667
Grossed up legacy	166,667
IHT on death	6,667

It is now possible to determine the value of the property left to the widow which is exempt:

	£	
Value of estate	320,000	
Chargeable as above	(166,667)	
Residue – exempt	153,333	(i.e. £160,000 less £6,667)

This type of calculation can become very complicated where the residue is divided so that part of it is chargeable and part of it is exempt. An example is where the residue of the estate is to be shared equally between the wife and the son.

The residue is what is left after the tax and all legacies have been paid but the tax on the chargeable estate cannot be calculated until the residue is ascertained. In turn, the residue cannot be ascertained until the tax is calculated. The argument is circular.

The legislation sets out the detailed procedures to be followed in these circumstances. It involves calculating an assumed rate of tax on a hypothetical chargeable estate in order to determine the value of the exempt estate. This type of computation would *not* be required in your examination.

Summary

▶ Inheritance tax arises on a chargeable transfer of value on or after 18 March 1986.
▶ A chargeable transfer of value is a transfer of value of chargeable property by a chargeable person, which is not an exempt transfer and which has been allowed all available exemptions.
▶ It is important that the definitions of these terms are known and understood for an overall understanding of the tax to be obtained. You should be able to follow any transfer through Figure 8.1 and arrive at the correct conclusion for inheritance tax purposes.
▶ Husband and wife are treated independently for inheritance tax purposes.
▶ Where a transfer is subject to a number of limited exemptions the order in which the reliefs are given is critical.
▶ A potentially exempt transfer (PET) is a lifetime transfer of value reduced by all available exemptions, to an individual or certain types of trusts which will only become chargeable if death occurs within seven years.
▶ The fiscal year has no relevance to the charge to inheritance tax. Its only function is as a reference point for the allocation of the annual exemption, and renewal of the small gift exemption.
▶ There are now only two rate bands for inheritance tax – a nil rate band and a 40% band (reduced to 20% for chargeable lifetime transfers with an additional charge arising if death occurs within seven years).
▶ If the tax on a lifetime transfer is to be paid by the transferor, his or her estate is diminished by the value of the transfer and the amount of the tax. The value of the

transfer must be 'grossed up' to arrive at the gross amount by which his or her estate is diminished.
- ▶ The starting point on the scale is determined by the cumulative gross total for the previous seven years.
- ▶ Whether a lifetime transfer is gross or net is determined by who pays the inheritance tax arising. If the transferor is to pay the tax the transfer itself is the net amount and must be 'grossed up'.
- ▶ On death, there are three areas of liability to inheritance tax.
  - Additional liability on chargeable lifetime transfers within seven years of death. The lifetime computations in this case are reworked using the full rates of inheritance tax according to the scale at the date of death.
  - Liability on PETs within seven years of death, which become fully chargeable. These are slotted chronologically into the lifetime computation being reworked above.
  - Liability on the estate of the deceased at the date of death. This is a gross transfer and is treated as the final transfer of value made by the deceased. It is added to the cumulative gross total in the previous seven years.
- ▶ The liability to pay the tax arising on death falls to the transferee in the first and second instance above but on the personal representatives or trustees of settled property in the case of the third.
- ▶ Once the liability has been calculated a number of reliefs are given to reduce the tax actually payable.
- ▶ Where the deceased has made specific bequests out of his or her estate, the tax on these gifts is normally borne by the residue of the estate. If the residue of the estate is wholly or partly exempt, there are special procedures for determining the tax liability.

Self test questions

1. Define a transfer of value.
2. List the principal dispositions which are specifically exempted from being transfers of value.
3. What is excluded property?
4. How is the definition of domicile extended for purposes of inheritance tax?
5. What is the small gifts exemption?
6. What is normal expenditure out of income?
7. What is the estate rate?
8. Why is it necessary to calculate the estate rate?
9. Where tax paid on a chargeable lifetime transfer exceeds the tax liability arising as a result of death within seven years, can this be repaid?
10. Where a transfer of value is subject to a number of limited exemptions, state the order in which the exemptions should be given.
11. Should exemptions be set against a PET?
12. Describe the principal rules surrounding the annual exemption.
13. You are to assume that Mr and Mrs Alderson, who are both in their late sixties, have recently attended an interview at the office of the firm of certified

accountants you work for. At the interview they asked for advice and assistance regarding their inheritance tax position.

They read, some time ago in a newspaper article that the Chancellor of the Exchequer had 'abolished tax on lifetime gifts'.

Mr Alderson estimates the value of his estate to be £300,000, and that of his wife to be £40,000.

They have made no previous lifetime transfers, but Mr Alderson is now considering making substantial transfers to:

- a granddaughter to set up in business
- an accumulation and maintenance trust for two infant grandsons
- a charity
- a discretionary trust, one of the beneficiaries of which will be their daughter.

You are required to prepare for the Aldersons:

a) A concise summary of the inheritance tax position on
   i) the making of lifetime gifts, including potentially exempt transfers
   ii) death.
b) A statement explaining how the above proposed gifts will be treated both when made, and on the eventual death of Mr Alderson.

14 Norman has supplied you with the following information regarding transfers of capital he has made.

In February 1988 he gave a freehold house to a discretionary trust. After deducting available exemptions the chargeable transfer amounted to £80,000. The trust paid the inheritance tax on the due date. In December 1994, he made further gifts as follows:

3 December	£10,000 cash to his son Peter on his 25th birthday to expand the business Peter set up in 1987.
5 December	£80,000 cash into a discretionary trust for his four grandchildren.
18 December	A new £9,000 car to his wife Margo on her birthday.
21 December	A watch valued at £200 to his godson.
23 December	A £35,000 flat into a trust, his sister being the life tenant.
30 December	£2,000 cash to his goddaughter on her marriage.

Inheritance tax, if any, on the above transfers is to be paid by the donees/trustees, except for any tax on the transfer made on 5 December which Norman will pay himself.

a) Compute the inheritance tax, if any, payable on each of the above transfers.
b) Compute the inheritance tax which would become payable if Norman were to die in March 1998, leaving an estate valued at £180,000, having made no further lifetime transfers since 30 December 1994.
In each case you should state who will be liable to pay the tax. (Assume 1994/95 tax rates apply.)

c) Briefly advise Norman of any inheritance tax advantages of making further lifetime transfers out of his estate rather than allowing such assets to pass on his death.

Answers on pages 569–572

CHAPTER 9

Inheritance Tax – Valuation Principles

This chapter examines the basic computation of the value transferred by a transfer of value which is not an exempt transfer, including the valuation of the estate on death. Subsequent adjustments to that value and the reliefs available are then considered.

Rules of valuation

The following general principles of valuation apply to both lifetime transfers and the valuation of the free estate on death unless otherwise stated. They are also generally applicable in valuing an interest in settled property.

General principles of valuation

The value of any property at any time for purposes of inheritance tax is 'the price which the property might reasonably be expected to fetch if sold in the open market. The price is not to be reduced to take account of the whole property being placed on the market at any one time.

In most cases, this will also be the amount by which the transferor's estate is diminished in value, as discussed in the previous chapter.

The notable exception, where the two definitions appear to be irreconcilable, is the valuation of a transfer of shares which causes a majority holding to become a minority holding. In fact they are not irreconcilable. The estate is valued according to the price the transferor's holding would fetch on the open market both before the transfer (the majority holding) and immediately after the transfer (the minority holding). The difference (the diminution in value) is the value transferred.

Unless otherwise available, the open market value will normally be ascertained by professional valuation: valuer, estate agent, auctioneer or (for unquoted shares) an accountant. The Inland Revenue has its own experts in these fields: District Valuer, Capital Taxes Office, Share Valuation Division.

Any exclusions or restrictions on the transferability of any property that may have been set up since its acquisition by the transferor will affect the market value of that property. These will only be taken into account for inheritance tax purposes in determining the value of the property at the date of transfer to the extent that consideration in money or money's worth was received in exchange or the contract itself was a chargeable transfer.

Quoted securities

The Stock Exchange Daily Official List (closing prices) is used to establish the market value. As for capital gains tax, this is taken as the lower of either:

▶ the lower of the two prices quoted for the day plus one-quarter of the difference between the prices; or
▶ the average of the high/low marked bargains of the day, if any.

If no prices are available on the date, the price must be taken as the lower of the price on the immediately preceding day of trading and the price on the next following day of trading.

On death, share prices should be 'cum div'. Prices quoted are normally cum div unless stated to be 'ex div'. For valuations on death if the price is quoted ex div the whole of the next dividend (net of tax) should be added to obtain the value. However, for purposes of valuing an interest in possession in settled property, it should be remembered that any interest accrued (included in a cum div value) is due to the estate of the deceased life tenant. It must be deducted from the value of the settled property and added to the 'free estate' of the deceased.

Shares in companies listed on the Unlisted Securities Market (USM) are treated as quoted shares for inheritance tax purposes.

Unit trusts

These are normally valued at the managers' buying price for the day (that is, the lower of the two prices quoted) or, if none published on that day, the last published price.

Unquoted shares and securities

Unquoted shares and securities can be difficult to value since there is usually not an easily identifiable market value.

Statute states that in determining the open market price,

...it shall be assumed that in that market there is available to any prospective purchaser of the shares or securities all the information which a prudent prospective purchaser might reasonably require if he were proposing to purchase them from a willing vendor by private treaty and at arm's length.

This direction resulted from a case (*re Lynall deceased* 1972) where it was held that unpublished information confidential to the directors should not be taken into account.

The valuation of unquoted shares is a subject in its own right. In addition to the above (the extent of which may depend upon the size of the holding), any restrictions in the articles of association on the future transfer of shares may be reflected in the price. Reference may be made to recent arm's length transactions that have taken place. The size of the holding and the degree of control will usually have some bearing on whether an assets-based, earnings-based or dividend-based valuation is appropriate.

Land and buildings

In the first instance, a professional valuer's opinion will normally be taken by the taxpayer. The Capital Taxes Office may ask for the district valuer's opinion and if this is different there may be some negotiation between the two experts. There is provision for appeal to the Land Tribunal and from there to the courts.

Where land is owned by tenants in common, the value of a half share of the land is half the vacant possession value less a discount (possibly 15%) to reflect the limited market for the property.

Life assurance policies

Where a life assurance policy matures on the death of the person who took it out (and who was at that time the beneficial owner), the maturity value is included in the estate and is chargeable to inheritance tax.

If the terms of the policy are such that it is, under the Married Woman's Property Act, for the benefit of the spouse and/or children, the proceeds are effectively in trust for them. The deceased, whose life was assured, does not, then, have an interest in the proceeds. The proceeds in this case will not form part of the deceased's estate.

A similar situation arises if the policy is assigned to a third party or put into a trust for the benefit of a third party. Its value at the date of transfer is the greater of the premiums paid at that date and the 'cash in' value of the policy. This will be a PET unless otherwise exempt.

If the deceased continued to pay the premiums, payments would be lifetime transfers of value and would be PETs unless they could be exempted as normal expenditure out of income or under the small gifts exemption (value less than £250 per annum) or annual exemption.

Pension rights

Where a person is entitled to an interest under an approved superannuation scheme or fund (including retirement annuity contracts and, after 22 July 1987, personal pension arrangements), the interest is not part of his estate for purposes of inheritance tax if:

- it is a right to a pension or annuity
- it does not result from the proceeds of any benefit provided by the scheme other than a pension or annuity.

If, however, a person is entitled to other benefits, such as the right to a repayment of contributions, or has the power to dispose of the benefits as he sees fit, the value of the interest will form part of the person's estate. (It is usual, therefore, for the trustees to retain discretion when paying lump sums payable on death in service.)

Property outside the UK

Overseas property is valued on the same basis as would be used for the equivalent UK property but it should be converted into sterling at the exchange rate ruling at the transfer date which gives the lowest sterling equivalent.

Overseas taxes (excluding the overseas equivalent of inheritance tax for which double tax relief may be available) and other liabilities are deductible. On death any additional costs of administering and realising the overseas assets are also deductible subject to a maximum of 5% of the gross value of the assets.

Related property

In arriving at the value of any property in a person's estate, any related property must be taken into account, if this would give a higher value than that otherwise obtained. Property is related either if:

- it forms part of the estate of the spouse or is settled property in which the spouse has an interest in possession; or
- it is, or was at any time during the preceding five years, owned by a charity, qualifying political party or national body (as listed under exempt transfers) as a result of an exempt transfer made by that person or his or her spouse.

The purpose of the provisions is to counteract a material reduction in the value of property occurring as a result of the fragmentation of property using the inter-spouse and other exempt transfers.

The related property provisions ensure that estate property and related property are valued as a whole. A part of the whole is then apportioned to the estate property in the proportion that its unrelated value bears to the sum of the unrelated values.

EXAMPLE 9.1

A owns some land worth on its own £30,000. It adjoins land which his wife inherited the previous year and which is worth on its own £60,000. Together the two properties are worth £150,000. A wishes to give his land to his son.

The value transferred will be the greater of:
a) the value of the land on its own (£30,000) or
b) the value of the land as part of related property, calculated as follows:

$$\frac{30,000}{30,000 + 60,000} \times 150,000 = £50,000$$

The value of the transfer will be £50,000

The related property provisions may be applied to any property which when combined with any property of the spouse, has a higher combined value than the sum of the parts.

Such a situation is likely to apply to a leasehold interest and the freehold reversion. It is particularly important when applied to shareholdings of the same class in an unquoted company. Note that in this case, the value of the combined shareholding is allocated to the parts *in proportion to the number of shares* not their value.

EXAMPLE 9.2

Shares in B Ltd are valued as follows:

%	Value of £1 share
1–9	£1.25
10–25	£1.50
26–49	£2.00
50	£2.50
51–74	£3.00
75–89	£3.25
90–100	£4.00

A and his wife each own 45,000 shares (45%). A's wife wishes to give half her shareholding to their son.
Calculate the value of the transfer.

	Before transfer		After transfer	
	No shares	Value £	No shares	Value £
A	45,000 @ £2.00	90,000	45,000 @ £2.00	90,000
A's wife	45,000 @ £2.00	90,000	22,500 @ £1.50	33,750
Combined	90,000 @ £4.00	360,000	67,500 @ £3.00	202,500

The value transferred will be the greater of:
a) the diminution in value of his wife's unrelated shareholding (£90,000 − £33,750) £56,250; and
b) the diminution in value of his wife's share of the related shareholding of £112,500, calculated as follows:

		£
Before	$\frac{45,000}{45,000 + 45,000} \times 360,000$	180,000
After	$\frac{22,500}{45,000 + 22,500} \times 202,500$	67,500
Diminution in value (wife's share) of combined shareholding		112,500

The value of the transfer will therefore be £112,500.

Valuation reliefs

Once the value of the transfer has been arrived at according to the above principles, the availability of reliefs to reduce this value must be considered.

Business property relief

Business property relief (BPR) is available in respect of both lifetime and death transfers provided that:

- the business is a qualifying business
- the property transferred is relevant business property
- conditions as to a minimum period of ownership are satisfied
- further conditions are satisfied at the date of death in respect of lifetime transfers which take place within the seven years prior to death.

The relief is a percentage reduction in the value of the relevant business property transferred *before* effect is given to any exemptions. It is available on property situated both within and outside the UK and is given automatically without being claimed.

Qualifying business

A business is a qualifying business unless it is within the range of businesses designated as **non-qualifying business**. Businesses do not qualify if they are not carried on with a view to making profits, or if they consist wholly or mainly of dealing in or the holding of shares, securities, land and/or buildings. (Businesses carried on by 'market makers' and discount houses are excepted, as are those of holding companies of qualifying trading companies. A 'market maker' is a person recognised by the Stock Exchange as being willing to buy and sell securities at a price specified by him or her.)

Relevant business property

Business property relief is given at different rates depending on the category of business property being transferred.

		% Relief
1	The whole or part of a business or interest in a business (for instance, sole trader or partnership interest)	100
2	Unquoted and USM shares (including related property)	
	– more than 25% holding	100
	– holding of 25% or less	50
3	Quoted shares in, or securities of, a company controlled by the transferor (including related proprty).	50
4	Land, buildings, plant and machinery used for the purpose of a business carried on by a company of which the transferor had control or by a partnership or which the transferor was a partner.	50
5	Land, buildings, plant and machinery owned by a trust and used by a life tenant of the trust in his or her own business/partnership in which he or she is a partner/company of which he or she has control.	50

If a binding contract for sale has been entered into by the transferor at the time of the transfer, the property will not qualify as relevant business property – unless the sale is merely the transfer of the business to a company wholly or mainly in exchange for shares, or is part of a scheme of reconstruction and amalgamation.

The type of situation envisaged where business property relief would not be available is if there is an agreement between partners or fellow shareholders that on the death of one, before retirement, the interest of that person would be sold by the personal representatives to the others.

The value of the relevant business property excludes value attributable to **excepted assets**. These are assets which are both: not used wholly or mainly for the purposes of the business throughout the two years preceding the transfer (or since acquisition if later); and not required for future use in the business at the time of the transfer. This provision may be applied to investments, large cash balances, and assets with private use.

Minimum period of ownership

To qualify for relief, the relevant business property must either:

- have been owned by the transferor throughout a two-year period prior to the transfer; or
- have replaced other relevant business property with the combined period of ownership being at least two years out of the five years preceding the date of transfer (BPR is available on the lower of the two property values).

The transferor is deemed to satisfy the above conditions if the property was eligible for business property relief when he or his spouse acquired it and either the acquisition or the current transfer was/is on death. The conditions are also satisfied where the property is a minority shareholding acquired as part of a scheme of reconstruction and the original shareholding qualified as above.

Further conditions at date of death re lifetime transfers

Two more conditions must be satisfied where the lifetime transfer was a PET and is now chargeable or where a chargeable lifetime transfer becomes subject to additional tax as a result of the death of the transferor within seven years.

- The same property must be owned by the transferee throughout the period from the transfer to the date of the transferor's death or transferee's death, if earlier.
- The property must still be relevant business property at the date of the transferor's death or transferee's death, if earlier.

If these conditions are not satisfied, the tax liability on death will be calculated without business property relief.

EXAMPLE 9.3

A gave his son a half share in his business on the occasion of the son's marriage on 4 September 1994. A had operated the business as a sole trader since 1980. The assets of the business at the date of transfer totalled £300,000. They included a residential flat (valued at £30,000) above the business premises which since acquisition had been occupied by A's widowed mother, and an investment in government securities (value £10,000) held pending a major outlay on fixed assets. A had made no previous transfers of value.
  Calculate the value of the transfer.

		£
Transfer of value – half share of business assets		150,000
Less: business property relief		
business property	300,000	
Less: asset not used for businesss	(30,000)	
Relevant business property	270,000	
Half share – 100% BPR	135,000	(135,000)
		15,000
Less: marriage exemption		(5,000)
AE 1994/95		(3,000)
1993/94		(3,000)
PET		4,000

Note: the government securities are assumed to be required for future business requirements.

Agricultural property relief

Agricultural property relief (APR) is available in respect of both lifetime and death transfers provided that:

- the property transferred is agricultural property
- the conditions as to a minimum period of occupation and ownership are satisfied
- further conditions are satisfied at the date of death in respect of lifetime transfers which take place within the seven years prior to death.

The relief is a percentage reduction in the agricultural value of the agricultural property transferred before effect is given to any exemptions. It is given automatically without being claimed.

The agricultural property is often part of an agricultural business and therefore business property relief may also be available. Agricultural property relief is given in priority to business property relief on the agricultural property. Business property relief may nevertheless be available on the non-agricultural property (for instance, sundry business assets) if the relevant conditions are satisfied.

There are two rates of relief:

	% Relief
a) with vacant possession (or the right to obtain vacant possession within the next 12 months)	100
b) tenanted	50

Agricultural property

Agricultural property is defined as:

- agricultural land or pasture situated in the UK, Channel Islands or Isle of Man
- cottages, farm buildings, and farm houses, of a character appropriate to the property together with the land they occupy
- woodlands occupied with agricultural land or pasture
- buildings used in connection with the intensive rearing of livestock, fish or the breeding of horses on a stud farm.

Relief has been given on growing crops, although not included in the definition. The following are not included (but may qualify for business property relief):

- livestock
- deadstock
- harvested crops
- farm plant or machinery.

If a binding contract for sale has been entered into by the transferor at the time of the transfer, the property will not qualify for agricultural property relief – unless the sale is merely the transfer of the business to a company wholly or mainly in exchange for shares, or is part of a scheme of reconstruction and amalgamation.

Agricultural value

This is the value of agricultural property as if it were subject to a perpetual covenant limiting its use to agricultural purposes. Values attaching to planning permissions, mineral deposits and so on for non-agricultural purposes are ignored.

EXAMPLE 9.4

A transfer of agricultural land and buildings (value £1,000,000) includes agricultural property satisfying the relevant conditions and having an open market value of £800,000 and an agricultural value of £500,000.

	£
Transfer of value	1,000,000
Less: APR 100% of 500,000	(500,000)
	500,000

Business property relief may be available on the open market value of the non-qualifying agricultural property (£200,000 (1,000,000 – 800,000)) and on the value of the agricultural property in excess of its agricultural value.

Minimum period of occupation or ownership

To be eligible for relief, the transferor must have either:

▶ occupied the property for the purpose of agriculture throughout the two years before the transfer, or
▶ owned the property for at least seven years before the transfer while it was occupied for the purpose of agriculture by the transferor or somebody else.

Where the current property replaced other agricultural property the conditions will be deemed to be satisfied if, overall, the transferor occupied the properties for two out of the last five years. Equally, if the transferor owned the properties (and somebody had occupied them for the purpose of agriculture) for at least seven out of the preceding ten years the conditions will be deemed to be satisfied. APR will be available on the lower of the two agricultural property values.

Periods of occupation or ownership by a deceased spouse can count towards satisfaction of the above conditions by the surviving spouse. Where the transferor inherited the property on another's death, he or she is deemed to have owned it from the date of that death. If the transferor subsequently occupies the inherited property, he or she will be deemed to have occupied it from the date of that death.

Further conditions re lifetime transfers

As for BPR, two more conditions must be satisfied where the lifetime transfer was a PET and is now chargeable or where a chargeable lifetime transfer becomes subject to additional tax as a result of the death of the transferor within seven years.

- The same property must be owned by the transferee throughout the period from the transfer to the date of the transferor's death or transferee's death, if earlier. If only part of the agricultural property is still held, only a proportionate amount of relief will be given.
- The property must still be agricultural property at the date of the transferor's death or transferee's death, if earlier.

Shares and securities in companies owning agricultural property

Where a company owns agricultural property and satisfies the above conditions, APR is available to an individual (who controls the company) in respect of the agricultural value that can be attributable to the shares transferred. The shares must have been held by the transferor for the relevant period (either two years or seven years).

The estate at death

The value of the estate transferred on death is the total value of all property in the deceased's estate (arrived at according to the above rules) less liabilities. It includes all property owned immediately prior to death plus anything which happens to the estate by reason of death (for example, life assurance monies receivable). It also includes any property to which the deceased was beneficially entitled at the date of death (for example, property subject to a reservation and an interest in possession in settled property).

The following points should be noted.

- *Surviving spouse exemption.* Where a spouse has had an interest in possession under the terms of the will of the deceased spouse (who died before 13 November 1974), the settled property will not form part of the estate for inheritance tax purposes as it will already have suffered estate duty on the death of the first spouse.
- *Survivorship clauses.* If a will specifies that property is to be held for a person provided that he or she survives the deceased for a specified period up to six months in length, the dispositions that finally take place are to be treated as having had effect from the date of death.
- *Non-resident's bank accounts.* A qualifying foreign currency account held on his or her death by a person not UK domiciled, resident or ordinarily resident in UK is not included in his or her estate for inheritance tax purposes.
- *Reversion to settlor.* No liability to inheritance tax arises if, or to the extent that, on the termination of a life interest the trust property reverts to the settlor or the settlor's UK-domiciled spouse during the settlor's lifetime or within two years of the settlor's death. This is provided that neither of them acquired the reversionary interest by purchase.
- *Accrued interest to a deceased life tenant.* The interest (after tax) accrued to the date of death included in the value of the settled property must be deducted from the value of the settled property and added to the free estate of the deceased. This is illustrated in the pro forma computation of the estate at death (Figure 9.1).

Liabilities

Liabilities, unless imposed by law (for example, taxes due to the date of death), may only be taken into account if incurred for full and valuable consideration. Payments outstanding under deeds of covenant and gambling debts, for example, are not allowed. Liabilities are brought into account as follows.

1. Any liability which is an incumbrance on any property must be deducted, as far as possible, from the value of that property.

2   A liability due outside the UK should be deducted, as far as possible, from property outside the UK.
3   The amount of the liability should be reduced to the extent that a reimbursement of all or part of it is due, unless the reimbursement cannot reasonably be obtained.
4   The amount of the liability should be reduced to the extent that it is not due and payable immediately (that is, discounted).

In addition, the following can be deducted: reasonable funeral expenses (mourning for family and friends and a gravestone); inheritance tax and capital transfer tax liabilities outstanding from a previous transfer; expenses of administering and realising property overseas (up to 5% of property value).

Exemptions

Exemptions available on death are deducted from the value of the free estate to give the chargeable estate on death.

Computation of estate at death

The layout of the computation to value the chargeable estate at death generally takes the following form.

```
FREE ESTATE
Personality (listed in detail)
All property, other than freehold property,                              X
    both in the UK and overseas including personal
    chattels and debts due to the deceased
Cash and bank (including net interest accrued to                         X
    date of death)
Net accrued income to life tenant of settled                             X
    property
                                                                         ___
                                                                         X
Less: liabilities of deceased                          (X)
      funeral expenses                                 (X)     (X)
                                                               ___

Realty
Freehold property – UK                                  X
Less: mortgage and accrued interest                    (X)      X

Total freehold property – overseas                      X
Less: mortgage and accrued interest                    (X)      X
                                                               ___
Total free estate                                               X
Less: exempt transfers (listed in detail)                      (X)
                                                               ___
                                                                X
SETTLED PROPERTY
Value of interest in possession                         X
Less: accrued income of life tenant                    (X)      X

GIFTS WITH RESERVATION                                          X
                                                               ___
CHARGEABLE ESTATE AT DEATH                                      X
                                                               ___
```

Figure 9.1 Proforma illustration of the computation of the estate at death.

EXAMPLE 9.5

A, a widower, had made full use of all his available exemptions during his lifetime and had no cumulative chargeable transfers at death and no PETs. His estate at death on 30 September 1994 consisted of:

1. a freehold property valued at £170,000
2. a life assurance policy with a maturity value of £20,000
3. 20,000 £1 ordinary shares in ABC plc quoted at 220–228p, with recorded bargains of 218p, 222p, 220p and 221p
4. 30,000 25p ordinary shares in XY plc quoted at 157–165p, with recorded bargains at 156p, 159p, 162p and 164p
5. bank balances of £25,000 including interest accrued to date
6. furniture and personal chattels valued at £40,000
7. a painting by a British artist valued at £120,000 which qualifies as heritage property.
8. debts which were: income tax £12,000; sundry liabilities £3,500; funeral expenses £1,000, including £400 for the gravestone, and a mortgage on the freehold property of £15,000.

A legacy was left to the RSPCA of £10,000 and the painting was left to the National Gallery.

He was life tenant of a trust set up in July 1988. The property in the trust at the date of death was made up as follows:

1. 30,000 shares in Night plc, quoted at 325–329p
2. A property in London (let) valued at £150,000
3. Bank balance of £9,000
4. Amount owed to life tenant £1,500.

Calculate the value of the estate at date of death.

FREE ESTATE – UK	£	£
Personalty		
Life assurance policy		20,000
Shares in ABC plc 20,000 @ 220p		44,000
Shares in XY plc 30,000 @ 159p		47,700
Bank balances		25,000
Furniture and chattels		40,000
Painting		120,000
Amount due from trust		1,500
		298,200
Less: income tax	12,000	
sundry liabilities	3,500	
funeral expenses	1,000	
		(16,500)
		281,700
Realty		
Property	170,000	
Less: mortgage	(15,000)	155,000
		436,700
Less: exempt transfers – national body		(120,000)
Less: exempt transfers – charity		(10,000)
		306,700
SETTLED PROPERTY		
Shares in Night plc 30,000 @ 326p	97,800	
Property	150,000	
Bank	9,000	
	256,800	
Amount due to life tenant	(1,500)	255,300
Chargeable estate at date of death		562,000

TAX PLANNING

Relief on death for fall in value of a chargeable transfer

Relief may be available where assets have been transferred within the seven years prior to death if the value of the asset has fallen since that date. The property must still be owned by the transferee or have been sold prior to the date of death at arm's length to an unconnected person.

There are restrictions on the relief where the property transferred is a wasting asset or has changed in a fundamental manner. In particular, no relief is available on tangible movable property which is a wasting asset (plant and machinery, for instance).

The relief reduces the transfer value to the value at date of death (or to the amount of the sale proceeds) for that particular transfer only, the cumulative total for carry forward is unchanged.

EXAMPLE 9.6

A, who had made no previous chargeable transfers, made a transfer of shares to his son on July 1988. The shares were valued at £130,000 in July 1988. His son sold the shares on the open market in October 1990 for £80,000. A died on 13 July 1994, leaving an estate of £200,000.

The transfer of the shares would have been a PET in July 1988 but on his death the transfer would have become fully chargeable. Annual exemptions were not otherwise used.

		£	£
IHT on death – lifetime transfers			
Chargeable transfers brought forward @ July 1988			Nil
July 1988 PET now chargeable			
	Value of shares	130,000	
	Less: AE 1988/89	(3,000)	
	Less: AE 1987/88	(3,000)	
		124,000	124,000
	Relief for fall in value		
	(cumulative total unaffected)	(50,000)	
		74,000	
Tax @ rate applicable at date of death			
	74,000 @ Nil	Nil	
	Taper relief 5–6 years 60%	—	
		Nil	
	Less tax paid originally	n/a	
	Payable by transferee	Nil	
Carried forward to date of death			124,000
Chargeable transfers brought forward			Nil
PETs now chargeable			124,000
Estate on death			200,000
			324,000
IHT on death – estate			
	26,000 @ Nil	—	
	174,000 @ 40%	69,600	
			69,600

Adjustments for the sale of assets following death

Quoted investments sold within 12 months of death

Where quoted securities, units in authorised unit trusts, and shares in approved investment funds are sold within the 12 months following death and are sold at a loss by the person liable to the tax on death (for example, the executor), that person *may claim* to have the estate value reduced by the amount of any loss on sale. The purpose is to give relief where assets are sold to raise funds to meet tax liabilities.

The loss on sale is calculated as the aggregate estate value of all securities disposed of less the aggregate sale proceeds of those same assets (no allowance is made for costs of sale and so on). *The loss is restricted* to the extent that any of the proceeds are re-invested preceding, or within the two months following, the last qualifying sale by the formula:

$$\text{Loss on sale} - \left(\text{Loss on sale} \times \frac{\text{Proceeds re-invested}}{\text{Sale proceeds}} \right)$$

EXAMPLE 9.7

An estate included quoted shares to the value of £80,000. All these shares were sold eight months after death for £55,500 after deducting commissions of £500. After paying the inheritance tax due of £30,000 the balance was reinvested a month later in quoted shares. What relief is available for the loss on sale?

	£
Probate value	80,000
Less gross sale proceeds	(56,000)
Loss on sale	24,000
Reduced by:	
£24,000 × 25,500/56,000 =	(10,929)
Reduction in estate value	13,071

No claim can be made unless the difference between the sale proceeds amnd the probate is at least £1,000 or 5% of the probate value, if less.

Quoted investments suspended within one year of death

When trading in shares is suspended within one year of the date of death, and the shares have not been sold, they may be valued for inheritance tax purposes at their value 12 months after the date of death.

Sale of land within four years of death

Where an interest in land is sold within four years following death, by the person liable to the tax on death (such as the executor), that person *may claim* to have the sale value substituted for the estate value. If a claim is made, the same value will be applied for capital gains purposes. *All* interests in land owned by the deceased and sold by that person within the four years following death must be considered provided certain conditions are satisfied:

- the difference between the estate value and the sale value should be more than the lower of £1,000 or 5% of the estate value in each case
- the sale must be to a person unconnected with the property over the period from

date of death to sale and must be an outright sale with no right to re-acquire the interest or any other connected interest.

A claim may be made whether the sale value is greater or smaller than the estate value and is also effective for capital gains tax.

The adjustment in value is *restricted* if the property is a short leasehold, by reference to the amortisation table, or if any purchases of land are made by that person between death and a date four months after the last disposal (within the four years following death). The restriction in the latter case is calculated as follows:

$$\text{Loss on sale} - \left(\text{Loss on sale} \times \frac{\text{Proceeds re-invested}}{\text{Sale proceeds}}\right)$$

Expenses of purchase and sale are ignored for this purpose and arm's length values should be substituted for both purchase and sale prices if appropriate.

If the property is eligible for business property relief or agricultural property relief at 100%, there would be little to be gained from making a claim under this section. The estate at date of death would be unchanged and the only consequence would be, for chargeable gains/allowable losses (capital gains tax) to no longer arise to the deceased's estate. The principal relevance of this section is therefore to assets not eligible to BPR or APR in full and to non-business assets.

Sale of 'related property' within three years of death

If property valued on death by reference to the related property provisions is sold within the next three years at less than the valuation (allowing for changes in circumstances up to the time of the sale), a claim may be made to reduce the value to that of the property on its own without reference to the related property.

Certain conditions must be fulfilled. These generally provide that the sale should be at arm's length and independent of any sale of the related property (no person connected with the sale should be connected with any person connected to the purchase).

Note that there can be some interaction with the business property rules and it may not always be worthwhile claiming this relief.

EXAMPLE 9.8

X had a 20% shareholding in an unquoted company Y Ltd which, when taken together with his wife's shares gave him a 30% shareholding. The shareholdings at the date of his death were valued as follows:

30% holding	£54,000
20% holding	£30,000
10% holding	£10,000

Fifteen months after his death, his executors sell his shares for £32,000.

Value of shares on death using related property rules:

	£
$\dfrac{20\%}{20\% + 10\%} \times £54,000$	36,000
Less: Business property relief –100%	
(minority holding unquoted shares > 25%)	(36,000)
	Nil

Value of shares if a claim for relief is made:

20% shareholding (ignore related property)	30,000
Less: Business property relief – 50%	
(minority holding unquoted shares < 25%)	(15,000)
	15,000

It would not be worthwhile to make a claim in this case because the business property relief is reduced to 50% as a result of related property being ignored. A claim would not reduce the value of the estate for inheritance tax purposes.

Summary

- Property should initially be valued according to the established principles for each type of property.
- To the extent that there is related property, a further valuation should be carried out taking the related property rules into account. If this value is greater, it should be used in the computation.
- There is relief on death for a fall in value of a chargeable lifetime transfer. It is important to remember that the cumulative total for carry forward is unchanged in this case.
- Where quoted shares are disposed of within 12 months of death at a loss, a claim may be made for the reduced value to be substituted. A similar claim may be made where land is sold within four years of death.
- A claim may be made to substitute the unrelated property value of property valued according to the related property rules which is sold within three years of death.
- Business property relief is a very important and wide-reaching relief. It is given on the value remaining after all the above adjustments. Careful consideration must be given to a claim to substitute the unrelated property value (see above) where it interacts with BPR.
- Agricultural property relief is given in priority to BPR where property could qualify for both reliefs.

Self test questions

1. £10,000 3.5% War Loan was quoted at 30–32p ex int at the date of death. What is the inheritance tax valuation?

2. Shares were quoted at 164–168p with marked bargains of 162p, 166p, 163p and 165p at the date of death. What is the inheritance tax valuation?

3. How is the related property fraction in relation to shares computed?

4. What is the restriction on claims for losses on the sale of land within four years of death?

5. A gave 51% of his shares in his unquoted family company to his daughter on 14 January 1995. Their value was agreed at £200,000. He had owned the shares for the previous ten years and the company had owned agricultural property for all that time – let to a tenant for agricultural purposes. The open market value of the agricultural property represents 50% of the asset value of the company, the agricultural value is 30% of this. What reliefs are available?

6. The personal notes of Robert Denton record that his cumulative chargeable transfers at 5 April 1984 amount to £173,000 gross, and that all annual

exemptions available to him at 5 April 1990 have been claimed. Subsequently he made the following transfers of value:

a) On 23 April 1990 he gave his son Tom £82,000 in cash.

b) On 1 July 1990 he sold shares in Oldfarm Engineering Co. Ltd for £50,000 to his son Bob when their value was agreed to be £120,000. Mr Denton retains shares in the company worth £160,000 which still give him control. Mr Denton, who was born on 3 April 1924, purchased all his holding in Oldfarm Engineering Ltd for £84,000 on 5 July 1981. He continues as chairman of the company. Both Mr Denton and Bob elected for hold-over relief for capital gains tax under FA 1980, s. 79.

c) On 10 April 1992 Mr Denton transferred to his son Jack 20,000 £1 ordinary shares, his entire holding, in Midas Ltd, the family trading company (incorporated in 1950), of which he and his two brothers are each equal shareholders and working directors. Share values are now agreed by the Capital Taxes Office – 60,000 shares £360,000; 40,000 shares £220,000; 20,000 shares £100,000.

d) He gave his daughter Anne £25,000 as a wedding gift on 25 May 1992.

e) He died on 31 May 1994. His estate was then valued at £160,000, including investments worth £42,000, which he inherited on his late uncle's death in September 1991, when they were worth £30,000; his late uncle's executors had paid inheritance tax of £16,500 attributable to these investments.

You are required to calculate the inheritance tax due on death . (Note that the nil rate band for inheritance tax purposes between 6 April 1990 and 5 April 1991 was £128,000.)

7 a) i) Explain the term 'related property'.
    ii) State the conditions necessary for business property relief to apply.

b) The shares of Cornworthy Ltd, an unquoted trading company with an issued share capital of 15,000 ordinary shares, were held as follows on 1 January 1994:

	No of shares
Alan Cornworthy	6,000
Brenda Cornworthy (Alan's wife)	3,000
Michael Cornworthy (Alan's son)	750
Henry Cornworthy (Alan's brother)	2,250
Estate of George Elstow deceased (in which Brenda Cornworthy has a life interest)	2,250
The Flaxley Settlement (a discretionary settlement in which both Alan and Henry Cornworthy have an interest)	750
	15,000

During the twelve months to 31 December 1994 the following occurred:

May   Brenda Cornworthy transferred 2,250 shares to trustees to be held on discretionary trusts.

July   Henry Cornworthy died leaving his entire holding by will to his son Robert.

November   Alan Cornworthy died, leaving his entire holding by will to his son, Michael.

Values for shareholdings in the company, in respect of all three transactions were agreed as follows:

% of share capital	£
100	340,000
90	304,000
80	267,000
75	252,000
65	195,000
60	172,800
35	70,500
25	50,000
20	38,000
15	34,500
10	22,000
5	9,000

Calculate the value transferred in respect of each of the three transactions in Cornworthy's shares in 1994.

Answers on pages 572–574

Inheritance Tax – Additional Aspects

CHAPTER 10

This chapter examines some additional and more complex aspects of inheritance tax which must be considered. These include gifts with reservation, associated operations, conditional exemptions, and deeds of arrangement. Some of the administrative requirements of inheritance tax are also considered.

Gifts with reservation

A gift with reservation is one made in such a way that the possession and enjoyment of the property is not passed to the donee to the virtually entire exclusion of the donor. (The donor retains some of the enjoyment or derives some benefit from the property disposed of.)

Special rules surround this type of gift as, otherwise, lifetime gifts could be made as PETs many years before death and totally escape charge to tax, while possession and enjoyment of the property are not forfeited. The special rules do not apply to gifts with reservations which are covered by any of the specific inheritance tax exemptions other than the annual exemption and normal gifts out of income.

The gift of a house would be a gift with reservation if the donor continued to live there rent-free. It would not be a gift with reservation, however, if the benefit was small and, for example, the donor enjoyed the house while making a short visit to the donee.

If full consideration in money or money's worth is given for any right of possession, occupation or enjoyment retained, then the gift is not treated as being subject to reservation.

Similarly, if subsequent enjoyment of an interest in land is as a result of a change in circumstances of the donor and is no more than reasonable provision for the care and maintenance of a dependent relative, and not as a result of a reservation at the time of the original gift, no reservation will be treated as existing.

In Chapter 8, the use of trusts was cited as an example of the way in which the charge to estate duty was escaped. Under that legislation (and CTT legislation also) it was possible to create a discretionary trust where the settlor was a potential beneficiary. This was prudent as the settlor had access to the trust funds if this became necessary.

For inheritance tax, if the settlor is a potential beneficiary, the creation of the trust is a gift with reservation. It is, however, possible for the settlor to be a trustee of the fund without the creation of the trust being a gift with reservation. This is useful, for example, when a parent wants to dispose of shares in a family company but does not want to relinquish control.

Special rules

At the date of the gift, a gift with reservation is treated in the normal way – that is, as a PET or as a chargeable transfer (a gift to a discretionary trust, for example).

Reservation removed

At the date the reservation is removed, there is deemed also to be a PET, or a chargeable transfer, of the value of the whole of the property at that date. (The amount of the benefit or enjoyment which had been retained is not important.) This provision is especially important where an asset has increased in value. If death occurs within seven years of that date then it will become fully chargeable.

Reservation exists at date of death

Any property which is property subject to a reservation at the date of death, which would not otherwise form part of the estate of the deceased, is treated as property to which the deceased was beneficially entitled at the date of death. The value of the whole of the property is added to his or her estate at death (see Chapter 9). As above, this is of significance particularly where the asset has increased in value.

Double charge to tax

A double charge to tax may therefore arise if the original disposition was, or becomes, a chargeable transfer. Provisions exist to avoid this provided certain conditions are met.

On death, the inheritance tax must be calculated as the higher of:

1. *if the reservation exists at the date of death*; the property subject to reservation will be treated as part of the estate on death. This will be according to its value at that date and ignoring the original disposition subject to reservation. (Any inheritance tax paid on the original disposition will nevertheless be deducted, subject to a maximum of the tax on death attributable to that property)
2. *if the reservation has been removed within the seven years prior to the date of death*; there will be a chargeable transfer at the date the reservation was removed and the original disposition will be ignored
3. *charging the original disposition subject to reservation and omitting the property from the estate on death*; or omitting the transfer at the date the reservation was removed, if applicable (giving credit for inheritance tax paid on the original disposition, if any, subject to a maximum of the tax chargeable on death).

EXAMPLE 10.1

A made a PET in September 1986 of £120,000. In October 1989 he made a gift to his son of a house valued at £160,000, in which he continued to live. This was treated as a PET at that time.

A died in January 1995, while still living in the house. His estate at death is valued at £300,000 including the house currently worth £200,000

1. **Include the house as part of the estate at death and ignore the gift with reservation.**

		£
September 1986	PET now exempt	
October 1989	PET = gift with reservation, ignored	
January 1995	Death estate	300,000
	Tax (150,000 @ Nil = Nil	
	(150,000 @ 40% = 64,000)	60,000
	Credit for tax paid on original gift with reservation, nil as none paid originally	

   Maximum credit would be $\frac{200,000}{300,000} \times 60,000$

   Total tax due as a result of A's death   60,000

2 Charge the gift with reservation and ignore the house in the estate at death

			£
September 1986	PET now exempt		
	Cumulative total at October 1989		Nil
October 1989	PET = gift with reservation, now fully chargeable £160,000		
	Tax (150,000 @ Nil = Nil		
	(10,000 @ 40% = 4,000)	4,000	
	Taper relief 5–6 years 60%	(2,400)	
	Credit nil as none paid originally		
	Maximum credit (4,000 – 2,400)		1,600
January 1995	Death estate £100,000 excluding gift with reservation		
	Tax 100,000 @ 40% = 40,000)40,000	40,000	40,000
Total tax due as a result of A's death			41,600

The first calculation gives the higher amount of tax and this is the one that would apply

Associated operations

This is an anti-avoidance section aimed at preventing transactions being subdivided into several parts, the sum of which would be less than the total value actually transferred.

The effect of this section is that the separate transactions are treated as associated operations and are deemed to comprise one transfer of value.

Associated operations are defined as two or more operations of any kind, whether or not carried out by the same persons and whether or not carried out at the same time, such that:

- they affect the same property, or if not the same property, property which is directly or indirectly related to the other property
- one operation is carried out with reference to the other or in order to enable the other to be carried out, and any further operations carried out in a similar way.

Where the operations are carried out at different times, they are treated as taking place at the date of the last of them. The final transfer of value is reduced by the amount of previous transfers by the same transferor, except to the extent that the previous transfers were covered by the inter-spouse exemption if that exemption would not apply to the operation as a whole.

This section is a carry-over from the original capital transfer tax legislation. It was thought originally that a gift by a husband to a wife who then 'chose' to use the money to make other gifts might be caught by these provisions. It has, however, been stated that the associated operations provisions would not be applied in such cases unless the gift by the husband was blatantly 'on condition that' it be used for such further gifts.

Specific exceptions to transactions which may be regarded as part of an associated operation exist in the following cases:

- An operation carried out after 26 March 1974 cannot be associated with an operation carried out before that date.
- A lease granted for full consideration cannot be associated with an operation which takes place more than three years later.

The greater the time between the various transactions, the easier it is to defend against an associated operations attack, as it can be claimed that there was 'no intention' at the date of the first gift.

Conditional exemptions

Conditional exemptions may be claimed on two types of property provided certain specified conditions are met in each case.

Heritage property

Property designated by the Board as eligible national heritage property is exempt from inheritance tax if certain conditions are met and undertakings given. A chargeable event occurs if an undertaking is not observed or if the person beneficially entitled to the property dies or disposes of the property. Tax will then be chargeable.

Property within the meaning of national heritage property includes:

- items of national, scientific, historic or artistic interest such as pictures, books, works of art and collections of scientific or other interest
- land of outstanding scenic, historic or scientific interest
- buildings to be preserved for their historic or architectural interest, associated land for its protection and related objects.

The Board will designate property when a claim by the taxpayer is submitted.

The effect of the conditional exemption is that property may continue to be privately owned but may pass from generation to generation without any charge to tax – providing the undertakings are not broken.

Conditions to be met

The exemption applies to either transfers on death or lifetime transfers. For lifetime transfers to be eligible, however, the transferor or his or her spouse must either have been beneficially entitled to the property throughout the previous six years or have acquired the property on death as a conditionally exempt transfer.

Undertakings

This must be given by a person regarded by the Board as appropriate. It must continue until the person beneficially entitled to the property dies or disposes of the property. An undertaking generally ensures that the property in question will not be removed from the UK, will be preserved and that there will be reasonable access for the public.

Chargeable event

Where a chargeable event takes place the sale proceeds (or the market value if appropriate) net of capital gains tax and expenses of sale are treated as the top slice of the estate of the 'relevant person'. This is treated as a gross figure and the rates of inheritance tax at the date of the chargeable event are used.

Lifetime rates are used if the relevant person was alive when the asset was originally transferred; death rates are used if the relevant person bequested the asset on death. The person liable for the tax is the person for whose benefit the property was disposed of.

The relevant person is the last person who transferred the asset subject to the conditional exemption. Alternatively, if there has been more than one conditionally exempt transfer within the previous 30 years, the Inland Revenue can select the relevant person. (This is usually the one which generates the highest tax liability.)

Death, or a disposal otherwise than by sale, is not a chargeable event if the transfer itself is conditionally exempt, or the undertakings previously given are replaced by corresponding undertakings by another person regarded as appropriate by the Board.

Since March 1986, a gift of this type of asset is a PET. The Inland Revenue do not consider conditional exemption at the time of the PET. If the donor does not survive seven years, the Inland Revenue will consider a retrospective claim for conditional exemption at that time – provided the donee has not breached what would have been the undertakings in the meantime.

Note that although the Inland Revenue may ignore the gift while it is a PET for inheritance tax purposes, it may not be ignored for capital gains tax.

Woodland relief

On death, an election may be made for the value of growing trees or underwood on land in the UK to be omitted from the estate for purposes of inheritance tax (the value of the land is not excluded). Certain conditions must, however, be satisfied.

The election must be made within two years of death (or longer if the Board allows) by the person liable for all or part of the tax. Also the property must not be agricultural property eligible for agricultural property relief. The charge to tax is effectively deferred until it becomes chargeable on a subsequent disposal.

Conditions

Before the election can be made, certain conditions must have been satisfied by the deceased. He or she must have been beneficially entitled to the land throughout the five years preceding death. Either that or he or she must have acquired the property other than for valuable consideration.

Tax charge

Tax becomes chargeable on any subsequent disposal (excluding inter-spouse transfers). This could be of the land and trees or the timber on its own, unless the subsequent disposal takes place on death (before the trees are sold) when the exemption may be continued.

If the timber is sold the charge to tax is based on the sale proceeds, less any of the following expenses not otherwise allowed for income tax: selling expenses and the costs of replanting (within three years) to replace the trees disposed of. If the trees would have been eligible for business property relief in the deceased's estate, the net proceeds are reduced by 50 or 100%.

The rate of tax to be charged is calculated as the top slice of the estate of the deceased, using the rates of tax which apply at the date of sale. The person liable for the tax is the person for whose benefit the property was disposed of.

Commorientes

Under the law of property, where two persons die at virtually the same time and it cannot be shown which of them died first, the elder is deemed to have died first. For inheritance tax purposes, however, this does not apply and they are treated as having died in the same instant.

For example, where father and son die in the same accident, the law of property dictates that the father is deemed to have died first. As a result, property bequeathed by him to his son passes to his son's estate and is taxed accordingly. The son's estate is then distributed according to the son's will. For inheritance tax purposes, however, there will be no further inheritance tax on the property bequeathed by father to son.

Variation of the provisions in a will

The provisions in a will may be varied in certain circumstances by application to the courts where the family and dependants of the deceased feel that they have not been adequately provided for in the will. Under some circumstances the court can also review dispositions made by the deceased within the six years before his or her death – if it can be shown that these were made with the intention of defeating such an application to the court.

Alternatively, a voluntary variation or disclaimer to the terms of a will (or under the provisions for intestacy) may be made by the persons who would benefit under the will. This is often called a deed of family arrangement. It must be done without consideration by an instrument in writing within two years of death and it may be done for any purpose (for instance, to make the distribution of the estate fairer or to reduce the tax).

To be effective for tax purposes, an instrument of variation must be submitted to the Capital Taxes Office. It must also be accompanied by an election under IHTA 1984, s. 142, within six months of the date of the instrument.

In both these cases, the variation is not treated as a transfer of value and is deemed to have been an amendment to the original will effected by the deceased.

Gifts with reservation and settled property cannot be affected by the above provisions.

Planning

It is important that a detailed knowledge of inheritance tax is not seen simply as the ability to calculate a liability, if any, when it falls due. The role of accountants in regard to inheritance tax is most frequently that of giving advice to clients about how their affairs should be structured, so as to minimise exposure to inheritance tax in the future. Examination questions therefore often take this form.

A structured approach is important. The starting place is very often the calculation of inheritance tax liabilities if nothing is done. This serves two purposes: it focuses your attention on the areas where there is currently a tax liability and where planning may be appropriate; and it allows the improvement resulting from your planning to be measured. The finishing point, needless to say, is to calculate inheritance tax liabilities on the assumption that your advice is taken.

The following paragraphs summarise some of the strategies that may be considered.

Lifetime

Exemptions

The exemptions available to the transferor are relatively small. Although they are not, therefore, a major consideration in estate planning, they are worth bearing in mind as over the years they can amount to a sizeable figure.

PETs

Potentially exempt transfers, and the reduction of the accumulation period to seven years, has virtually made inheritance tax voluntary – unless planning is left too late or death strikes unexpectedly. If the taxpayer survives seven years after the date of the gift, there is no inheritance tax. If he/she survives three years, taper relief reduces the tax liability. In all cases the value of the gift is fixed at the date of the transfer. If the asset appreciates in value, the appreciation from the date of the gift to the date of death escapes inheritance tax.

It should, however, be remembered that the transferor must retain an income commensurate with his or her standard of living. Note also that although lifetime gifts may escape inheritance tax, a liability to capital gains tax may result. The choice of the asset to be gifted is therefore significant.

Where business property relief and/or agricultural property relief apply, it is important to ensure that the relevant conditions will be satisfied at the date of death to retain the relief.

The rules surrounding gifts with reservation ensure that the individual makes outright gifts.

A married couple may be advised to make lifetime transfers between themselves so that each has an estate at least equal to the nil rate band. If they should die together or if they can afford to will asset values equivalent to the nil rate band away from each other, the combined estate will then enjoy the full benefit of two nil rate bands. A married couple may avoid inheritance tax only in the short term if each spouse has a will leaving most of his/her property to the other spouse.

Trusts can be used extensively in inheritance tax planning in conjunction particularly with PETs.

Death

It is important that individuals make wills so that their estates may be distributed in a tax efficient manner and the rules of intestacy do not come into play. A will should be regularly reviewed to ensure it is still appropriate.

Where business property relief and/or agricultural property relief may apply, it is important that the taxpayer takes steps to ensure that the relevant conditions are complied with.

Deeds of family arrangement are an important planning tool in reducing tax.

It is possible to provide for future inheritance tax liabilities by insuring the transferor's life under a policy written in trust to provide the tax, or to take out temporary insurance to cover the risk of death before PETs fall out of account.

Accounts, returns and collection of tax

Accounts and returns

Information about chargeable transfers must be delivered to the Board (usually the Capital Taxes Office for lifetime transfers and the Probate Registry on death) within twelve months of the end of the month of the transfer. Similarly, any person who may be liable for tax on the death of the transferor (that is, from a PET now chargeable or simply additional tax) must notify the Board.

An account is the name given to a document completed by the transferor or other taxable person. He or she is required to 'deliver an account' to the Board.

A return is a document required from a third party about transactions affecting others.

There is no requirement to deliver an account for lifetime transfers if the transfer is a PET at the time it is made, or if it is an exempt transfer. There is also no requirement to deliver an account if the value of the latest chargeable transfer, together with all previous chargeable transfers of the individual in the fiscal year, does not exceed £10,000 and the total of such chargeable transfers over the previous ten years does not exceed £40,000.

There is no requirement to deliver an account on death where the total gross value of the estate on death does not exceed £125,000, of which not more than £15,000 is situated outside the UK, if the deceased was domiciled in the UK and had made no chargeable lifetime gifts (including PETs within the seven years before death and gifts with reservation). A grant of representation for probate is still required, but it is only necessary to swear on oath as to the above particulars.

Collection of inheritance tax

The normal due date for payment of inheritance tax on chargeable lifetime transfers is six months after the end of the month of the transfer or, if made between 6 April and 30 September, by 30 April following. On death, the tax is due six months after the end of the month of death and probate cannot be obtained until it is paid. Note that, in both these instances, the due date is before the date for delivery of the account.

There is provision for assessments, appeals, payment by instalments and interest on overdue tax (see Chapter 23).

Summary

- The rules surrounding gifts with reservation are an important aspect of inheritance tax since it is always tempting both to avoid a charge to tax and to retain an interest in the property. You should make sure that the rules are thoroughly understood.
- The associated operations provisions are an anti-avoidance section. They are widely defined and potentially far-reaching.
- The conditional exemption for heritage property allows that property to continue to be privately owned and to be passed from generation to generation without any charge to tax arising, providing the undertakings are not broken. If broken, a retrospective charge to tax arises to the person who made the conditionally exempt transfer.
- A claim for woodland relief results in the value of growing timber being left out of the estate on death. It will be deferred until subsequently disposed of, at which time it is taxed as the top slice of the estate.
- The main planning points stem from full use of all exemptions and reliefs, providing the taxpayer can afford to do so. Equalisation of the estates of husband and wife can allow both parties to use their exemptions.

Self test questions

1. Give two circumstances when the donor may have an interest in property transferred but which will not be treated as a gift subject to reservation.

2. Do the rules for gifts with reservation apply if the gift was an exempt transfer?

3. Conditional exemption is available for designated heritage property. How does the property become so designated?

4. When will a chargeable event occur if conditional exemption for heritage property has been claimed?

5. What is the time limit for claiming woodlands relief?

6. a) Edward owns two Georgian silver candelabra, each of which would have a market value of £8,000 but which, as a pair, he has been told could be worth £20,000. Edward proposes to sell one of the candelabra to his daughter Mary, immediately, for £8,000 cash, then in two years' time to make her a gift of the remaining candelabrum.

    Advise Edward of the inheritance tax effects of his proposals.

    b) John is considering gifting the house in which he and his wife live, and in which they will continue to live, to their son.

Advise John how the proposed gift will be treated both when made, and on his eventual death.

c) State two sets of circumstances in which the following would *not* result in a charge to inheritance tax under the gift with reservation provisions.

James makes a gift of a cottage by the sea to his daughter and son-in-law following the birth of their first child. Several years later James, who is then sixty-two years of age and a widower, sells his house in town and takes up residence in the cottage.

7 a) In January 1995, Grant gave away two paintings both of which were designated as being National Heritage property. They were purchased by Grant at auction in 1989. One, valued at £40,000, was given to the National Gallery, and the other, valued at £30,000, was given to his daughter.

Advise Grant how these gifts would be treated for inheritance tax purposes.

b) William died in July 1994 leaving a free estate of £400,000 made up as follows:

Land used commercially for forestry which he had inherited from his father ten years earlier:

The value of the freehold land is	£100,000
The value of the trees is	£60,000
Other property	£240,000

The estate is left to his children equally except for £50,000 left to charity.

Calculate the value of his estate on William's death.

Answers on page 574

CHAPTER 11

Personal Finance – Investment and Financing Alternatives Evaluated and Compared

The purpose of this chapter is to consider the types of investments that are available and to evaluate them from the investor's point of view. Aspects such as risk, liquidity, income production (including income tax implications) and capital growth (capital gains tax implications) will be compared. This chapter will draw on the contents of Chapters 4 to 7 and will help to build an all-round picture of the strengths and weaknesses of each type of investment.

Investment defined

Investment means different things to different people.

The process of investment to an economist is the allocation of corporate funds to the purchase of land, buildings, machinery and training of personnel – the factors of production. This is 'real' investment. Individuals also make real investments, the most common example being home ownership, but also including the purchase of gold, paintings, antiques and other 'collectibles'.

Another form of investment is 'financial' investment and this is the area of primary concern. Money held now is given over to others to use in return for an anticipated future gain. There are four main categories of this and it is important to distinguish between them:

- savings
- investment
- speculation
- gambling.

Savings

Savings are usually monies accumulated out of income. The saver may be looking for return on capital, capital security or a combination of both. Saving is often done with an objective in mind – for example, a holiday, a car or new furniture or to invest – and although the returns on savings are frequently poor, this may be less important than capital security.

The Government encourages savings and to this end certain investments have been given advantageous tax treatment or exemption from taxation (see below and Chapter 4). Savings are encouraged because they defer consumer spending and this helps to keep down the rate of inflation.

Financial advisers have a duty to indicate the 'true rate' of return on a savings medium (see Chapter 12). True interest is the amount received after allowing for inflation (retail price index) and often indicates a minus return.

Investment

Investment is usually money found out of capital but originating from savings. It may give income, capital growth or a combination of both. While the provision of income may satisfy short-term objectives, capital growth is likely to be medium (5 years) or long term (providing for a 'rainy day' or retirement). Returns are rarely certain and investment often involves an element of risk, with short-term fluctuations in value being smoothed over by long-term trends.

In practice, investors nowadays often do not invest directly in investment products but more often invest indirectly via institutions such as pension funds, insurance funds, unit trusts and investment trusts which are marketed to suit a range of needs.

Speculation

Speculation is essentially short term. It involves activities which offer the possibility of quick profits. Speculating on the International Stock Exchange, for example, involves 'bulls', 'bears' and 'stags': bulls hope to make a gain on a rising market; bears hope to make a gain on a falling market and stags subscribe for newly issued shares and dispose of them as the new share makes its impact on the market. Most of the privatisation issues in the UK in recent years have involved large stagging operations by members of the public speculating on an immediate profit.

The distinction between investment and speculation is often blurred. The higher or the quicker the return, the greater the risk. The speculator looking for high returns may well lose capital, while an investor would not expect to see his or her capital eroded.

Gambling

Football pools promoters and betting shops may elevate their enterprises by the use of the term investing. The majority of such 'investors' will, however, be lucky not to lose their entire stakes most of the time. The potential gains can be enormous but the chances of this occurring are remote.

The exception to this is the premium bond (see Chapter 4) which pays big prizes from a pool while keeping the stake intact. Portfolio managers may recommend the acquisition of a small holding of premium bonds for the private investor as this encourages continuous interest in the portfolio.

Types of investment

Investments are available in such large numbers today that the establishment of general descriptive categories is essential. Various permutations of features exist and some products do not fit easily into a specific category.

Quoted and unquoted

Quoted investments are those in which dealing is permitted on the Stock Exchange. Unquoted investments include savings with banks and buildings societies but also include shares, loan stocks and warrants in limited companies (where dealing is not permitted on the Stock Exchange).

All quoted investments (also referred to as 'listed' securities) can be found in the Stock Exchange Daily Official List (SEDOL). These investments are subject to market forces and will have fluctuating values. Direct investments on behalf of clients in such a potentially dangerous area should be avoided.

Fixed income, variable income and nil income

The taxation categories of income from property and investments have been fully considered in Chapter 4 and should be referred to if you are in doubt – only a brief reference to the category is given below. Similarly, where there is capital appreciation, there is likely to be a liability to capital gains tax – the circumstances in which this would occur have been considered in Chapters 5 to 7 and should be referred to if you are in doubt.

Fixed income

Fixed income securities include: government securities ('gilts') and local authority bonds (see Chapter 4); company loan stock (or debentures) and preference shares (see Example 11.2 for a comparison of the returns).

Each of these is issued with a fixed coupon (interest rate). They may, however, be traded and in this case the value of the coupon will depend on the price paid on the market for each unit of stock.

EXAMPLE 11.1

On 1 August 1994, 10% Treasury stock were quoted at 116. The fixed income (amount received plus basic rate tax deducted at source) is £10 per £100 of stock but the return on an investment made on 1 August 1994 would be £10 per £116 invested (that is, 8.62 %).

EXAMPLE 11.2

A taxpayer holds 100 10% debentures of £1 each and 100 10% preference shares of £1 each.
Calculate the gross taxable income in each case for 1994/95.

	Debentures	Preference shares
	£	£
Cash received	7.50	10.00
Basic rate income tax deducted at source (25/75)	2.50	
Tax credit (20/80)		2.50
Gross income	10.00	12.50

The return on investment in each case would depend on the price paid. In the above example, one would expect to pay more for the preference shares than for the debentures.

Variable income

Typical examples of variable income investments are ordinary shares ('equities') including investment trusts; Enterprise Investment Scheme shares; unit trusts; rented real estate; building societies; and National Savings (although for certain products, including National Savings certificates, the income is declared at the outset).

Nil income

Investments in this category, with the possible exception of owner-occupied real estate, tend to be acquired for capital appreciation. Examples are premium bonds, owner-occupied real estate, warrants (low-cost traded securities giving rights to acquire shares at some future date); and chattels (collectibles such as *objets d'art*, rare stamps). Note that the latter are not only nil income but involve relatively high maintenance outlays in the form of security costs, insurance premiums and climate control which are non-deductible from the capital gain arising. They are also at risk from counterfeiting and fashion trends.

Direct and indirect investment

Financial advisers can deal, on behalf of clients, directly with banks, building societies and so on, but may also invest indirectly, on behalf of clients, using the services of a unit trust, life assurance company or pension fund. These organisations exist as intermediaries receiving funds from investors and re-investing the funds in a range of other investments – they are professional fund managers and are 'investing in investments'.

During the last 50 years, the private investor using the direct method has declined considerably; a notable exception is the government privatisation issues such as British Telecom. At the same time, the rise of the institutional investor has been spectacular. Under the Financial Services Act, the institutions are regulated by special regulatory bodies (see Chapter 12) set up for the purpose of ensuring that good standards are maintained. Theoretically, therefore, financial advisers can feel confident when investing clients' money in this way. Table 11.1 below compares the principal features of unit trusts, investment trusts and insurance policies.

Table 11.1 Unit trusts, investment trusts and insurance bonds – some comparisons

	Unit trusts	Investment trusts	Insurance bonds
Legal status	Trust	Limited Company	Regulated insurance policy
Value	SIB Formulae	Market (ISE)	Insurance company
Early encashment	Loss on Bid/offer prices	Loss on Buy/Sell turn	Substantial loss possible
Advertised	Yes	No	Yes
Liquidity	Good	Good	Poor
Available	From trust managers and application forms in periodicals and newspapers	Stockbroker	Insurance company

Indirect investment has two principal advantages:

▶ professional fund management skills
▶ diversification.

Diversification

The association of good returns from investment with risk to capital has already been mentioned. By investing in a large number of different investments, all promising good returns, the risk of capital loss is spread more widely and therefore lessened. Only a very large private fund could establish a sufficient spread of different shareholdings in each of several market sectors; in this case dealing costs would be prohibitively high.

Personal equity plans (PEPs)

These are a range of products which result from indirect investment and therefore benefit from the acquisition of management skills and often, if investment is then made in unit trusts, from diversification. This is a government-sponsored product in that tax incentives are offered to the investor – the purpose being to extend ownership of shares to the smaller investor (see Chapter 4 for investment restrictions and taxation advantages).

Equities

Direct investment in the equity capital of UK companies has been discussed above in terms of risk and returns. Returns on investment are mostly in the form of dividends (twice yearly) which are decided by the directors on the basis of the company's profits; some companies offer 'perks' to shareholders. The dividend received is grossed-up by lower rate income tax on the grossed up equivalent (the fraction for 1994/95 is 100/80; see Chapter 1). Shareholder perks are not normally taxable unless the company is a close company (see Chapter 26). Capital appreciation is subject to capital gains tax on realisation after an allowance for indexation and the annual exemption (see Chapter 7). Investment is normally made for capital growth rather than high income and attention is drawn to the warning that investment values can go down as well as up. The need for diversification together with stamp duty on purchase and other dealing costs means that relatively large sums are needed.

Investment trusts

(For more information, see also Chapter 4.)

These are limited companies which differ from ordinary trading companies in the type of business they conduct. They are investment companies (see Chapter 26) and hold a portfolio of shares in other companies as a fixed asset. As the portfolio appreciates in value and good returns on investment are achieved, the value of the investment trust's own shares and its dividends increase (see above for taxation).

Investment trusts are not as popular with the private investor as perhaps they should be – they have performed very well against unit trusts over recent years. This may be attributable to the fact that they are not permitted to advertise individually – the trade association invites potential investors to send for information about the 'industry'.

As an investment product, they are described as 'closed ended', since the share portfolio is limited to the value of the trust's issued share capital, reserves and borrowing.

An approved investment trust has the following advantages:

▶ The investment trust is not assessable on the chargeable gains arising from the buying and selling of shares in the invested portfolio.
▶ The investment trust is not permitted to distribute capital gains as dividend and it must not invest more than 10% of its assets in a single company – there are also further regulations on the way the funds are invested so that diversification is ensured.

Unit trusts

(See also Chapter 4)

Unit trusts are trusts and not limited companies, the trustees normally being the trustee company of a bank. They are similar to investment trusts in that investors benefit from low dealing costs, diversification, exemption from tax on chargeable gains and the services of investment managers.

Unit trusts are 'open ended', meaning that one expands or contracts in relation to the numbers of units purchased and sold respectively. The more units that are purchased the larger is the fund available to acquire shares for the portfolio – as the portfolio appreciates in value, the value of a unit increases. The income from the portfolio is passed to the unit holders as dividends. Income tax and capital gains tax applies in the same way as for equities.

Unit trusts are permitted to advertise if they have been given the status of 'authorised' by the Securities and Investment Board. The Securities and Investment Board (SIB) is a regulatory body under the Financial Services Act (see Chapter 12) and as such it imposes regulations as to the securities which are approved for investment purposes and the spread of the portfolio. Many unit trusts invest some of the fund overseas (for increased diversification) while others specifically target a country or trading area such as the Far East or Europe, allowing investors to gain comfort from national economies performing better than the UK and from movements in exchange rates. The performance of such unit trusts is affected by international economic and political problems such as the debate over membership of the ERM.

Unit trusts derive income from UK dividends on which tax has been paid (franked investment income – see Chapter 24); from other taxable sources (from which income tax may have been deducted at source); and the balance from gains on disposal of investments on which the trust, if approved, is exempt from capital gains tax. The proportion of income derived from the various sources will also therefore have an impact on the performance of the trust.

An advantage of many unit trusts is that they offer the opportunity to invest small sums regularly. Most accept sums of £20 to £50 per month. Over a period, investing in this way produces a demonstrably better result than that achieved by a lump sum investment. This is attributed to the theory of 'pound cost averaging'

Pound cost averaging

By accepting regular monthly amounts, the difficulty of timing a lump sum investment is levelled out. Regular saving ignores market fluctuations and ensures that more units are purchased when units are priced at their lowest. The average cost per unit will always be lower than the average price over the period. Over a long period it will be substantially less giving enhanced capital benefits.

Classification

The majority of the unit trust invested market is placed in the following areas:

- UK Growth – funds are in low-yielding portfolios (paying low dividends to unit holders) and are chosen for their capital growth. They are particularly suited to the wealthier client paying higher rate income tax
- UK Income – these unit trusts will invest in steady company shares where the profits generate dividends which are better than average. They are chosen by investors requiring income.
- UK General Fund – this provides both income and capital growth.

All the other funds – international and sector (such as energy, property, mining) – exist under the same basic categories of growth, income and general. Unit trusts should always be seen as true investments and never as short term or speculative.

Life assurance

This type of investment should be seen primarily as protection. Life assurance will, up to retirement age, provide a useful part of an investor's portfolio. The life companies have always been permitted to advertise and have traditionally linked with the unit trust business. Unit trusts have not always had this freedom and have found the association with assurance useful in marketing. Proceeds of qualifying life assurance policies are mostly tax free (see Chapter 4).

Types of policy

Whole life

The proceeds of this type of policy are payable only on death and should not therefore be regarded as investment products.

Term assurance

These policies pay out in the event of death within a specified period – they are therefore similar to whole life policies above and should not be regarded as investment products. They are, however, usefully included within the portfolio of an investor with dependants where there are substantial commitments over a specified period, such as a repayment mortgage or school fees.

Endowment assurance

There is a wide variety of policies within this category. The matured policy pays out a fixed sum at the end of a specified period or prior death. They are often used in conjunction with a mortgage loan and indeed the two are often sold as a package – these are popular with banks and building societies because of the generous commissions paid by the insurance companies to the banks or sales people. Moreover, many purveyors of endowment policies are associated with financial businesses.

Policies can be taken out 'with profits' by paying a higher premium. This means that the eventual maturity proceeds will be enhanced by bonuses:

- **Interim or reversionary bonuses** are declared at regular intervals during the life of the policy; the amount depends on the life company's results since the last bonus – once declared, an interim bonus cannot be removed.
- **Terminal bonuses** are only declared at maturity.

Many policies carry an entitlement to both types of bonus but individual life assurance companies vary considerably in their performance and in the balance between interim and terminal bonuses (terminal bonuses give the company greater flexibility but give the policyholder less security – they are often larger in order to compensate).

The maturity proceeds of policies are always based on historical performance and some companies perform better than others.

Nowadays companies are not permitted to make extravagant claims for the future based on past performance. Each company is limited to giving potential investors two quotes based on each of 7% and 10.5% growth on achieved value. The performance of individual companies is so diverse that this could be misleading but LAUTRO (the regulatory body for life assurance – see Chapter 12) have established this norm for good reason. As a result of this, the financial press publishes 'league tables' which allow comparison of companies and individual policies based on past performance.

Unit linked policies

Traditionally life assurance companies invested in equities, fixed income securites such as gilts, and real estate. These policies are linked to units in a fund operating in the same way as a unit trust. The sum paid on maturity or encashment is the value of the units in the fund at the relevant date which in turn is dictated by the value of the underlying fund assets. The spread of the underlying assets is governed by the same regulations as apply to unit trusts and, in the same way, the investor is able to choose a preferred orientation of fund. For example, if a property trust were chosen the premiums would be invested in a variety of real estate company shares.

It is important to remember that these are primarily an insurance product and whereas for the younger investor the insurance element of the premium may account for only 5%, older investors will find that the insurance element is considerably larger leaving less to be invested in units. As a consequence, older investors with more expensive life cover will ultimately receive less proceeds. Statements are sent to investors on a regular basis showing how many units have been purchased on their behalf as well as the unit prices.

Single premium policies

As the name suggests, these involve the investment of a single lump sum and also have the following features:

- The insurance is usually small and reducing over the period.
- Withdrawals (5% of premium) may be made annually as income without incurring tax liability.
- Such withdrawals, if not taken annually, may be rolled up during the period, becoming payable when the investor loses income (such as on retirement).
- These are non-qualifying policies (as referred to in Chapter 4). On final encashment only income tax at 15% (40–25) is payable and this only on annualised gains set against the taxpayer's total liability to the extent that it causes it to fall into the higher rate tax band (top-slicing relief). These policies are usefully acquired in middle age and encashed after retirement when perhaps liability for higher rate of tax may have ceased. They are also useful for the investor with fluctuating income.

Other single premium policy investments include managed and property bonds.

Managed bonds (or 'three way' bonds)
These involve the fund managers switching funds between the traditional life assurance investments of equities, fixed interest securities and real estate according to the economic conditions prevailing.

Property bonds
In this case the funds are invested totally in different classes of real estate. This type of investment has traditionally provided a hedge against inflation and may be appropriate to balancing a portfolio. The fund suffers from the need to maintain liquidity in an area where liquidation of assets can be very slow.

Pensions

Provided that planning for a pension is started early, a pension is a long-term investment with a range of tax advantages. The various types of pension opportunities were set out in detail in Chapter 4 and should be referred to in the context of financial planning.

Enterprise Investment Scheme

This is a fairly risky type of investment as the companies involved will probably be young trading companies with only a short history. The investment must be held for five years otherwise the relief given on the initial investment will be withdrawn. In addition, any disposal within that five year period will be chargeable to capital gains tax. The details of the scheme were considered in Chapter 4.

Land and property investments

Home ownership – main residence

This is probably the first and largest investment undertaken by most individuals. It yields no income in the main although there is tax relief for those letting a furnished room in their main residence (see Chapter 4) and any capital appreciation realised on disposal is tax free (see Chapter 6). Interest relief is available on loans up to £30,000 taken out to purchase a main residence (see below and Chapter 1).

Home ownership – other

This is the acquisition of a second house for weekend/holiday occupation. It is assumed that the property is not let (see below).

It yields no income and capital appreciation on disposal is subject to capital gains tax after indexation allowance and annual exemption. The size of the investment required varies considerably and is illiquid. The main potential is current enjoyment – running expenses may be high and there may be security problems.

Property for letting

This type of property falls into two categories:

- residential
- business.

The returns on investing in residential property for letting depend on the location of the property, whether seasonal or not, whether the lets are long term or not. The taxation aspects of letting income are set out in Chapter 4 and the capital gains implications are as above (additional reliefs are available if the property can be classified as furnished holiday accommodation which make the exercise tax effective).

The returns on investing in business property are also variable. In addition to the normal rules for taxation of letting income, the investor may be able to claim industrial buildings allowances which can be deducted from rental income (see Chapter 16). Capital growth may also be achieved.

Cash investments

The majority of savers insist on investing in products that will return their original cash value at a pre-arranged future date or within a few days. Amongst the range of institutions offering such facilities are the National Savings Bank, the high street banks, and the building societies.

National Savings Bank (NSB)

The National Savings Bank is part of the Department for National Savings, a government department. The Post Office acts as its agent. The range of products tends to give good returns and have been designed to suit all needs. Financial advisers may register to receive regular updating information. A list of the principal products is given below with comments where applicable as to the main features:

- *NSB ordinary account* (considered in Chapter 4) Interest paid gross – first £70 interest tax free, balance taxable Schedule D Case III
- *NSB investment account* – interest paid gross and taxable under Schedule D Case III (see Chapter 4). The interest rate is higher than on the ordinary account but one month's notice of withdrawal is required
- *National Savings Certificates* – a tax-free investment considered in detail in Chapter 4
- *National Savings Income Bonds* – interest paid gross on a monthly basis at a competitive rate taxable under Schedule D Case III. They are designed to provide a regular income to persons living off the income from capital. The minimum investment is £2,000, further deposits can be made in multiples of £1,000 up to a maximum of £50,000 – three months notice of withdrawal is required
- *National Savings Capital Bonds* – interest paid gross annually on the anniversary of purchase but added to the value of the bond; taxable under Schedule D Case III. The bonds are for a five-year period and there is a very competitive fixed return. However, the interest rate increases over each of the five years to encourage investors to retain the bond for the whole five years (there is no formal notice period for withdrawals). The minimum investment is £100 and further deposits must be in multiples of £100, maximum £100,000.
- *National Savings Pensioners' Guaranteed Income Bonds* – interest paid gross on a monthly basis at a fixed 7% p.a. taxable under Schedule D Case III (see Chapter 4).
- *National Savings First Option Bonds* – these bonds are for a period of 12 months. The rate of interest is fixed at the outset. At the anniversary of purchase, the holder has the option to receive repayment of the sum invested, plus interest, or to reinvest the bond for a further twelve months at a new guaranteed rate. The interest is paid net of basic rate tax. The minimum investment is £1,000 and the maximum is £250,000. A higher rate of interest is available if the sum invested is £20,000 or more.

Banks and building societies

Both of these institutions offer a variety of deposit accounts to savers. Although various in-house names are given to these accounts the basic conditions are the same; namely that the greater the amount of funds invested and the longer the period it is invested for, the higher the rate of interest paid.

It is possible to earn higher rates of interest in the money markets. Banks and building societies have access themselves to the money markets and may offer schemes whereby the private investor can place substantial funds on deposit. Once again larger funds attract bigger returns. The basis of the return is the current market rate and this fluctuates with the London Interbank Offered Rate (LIBOR). Rates for longer periods will depend on the money futures situation and will not necessarily be as good as the short-term rate.

The interest paid is normally net, having had basic rate income tax deducted at source. The tax position was considered in detail in Chapter 4.

Interest rates

Interest rates are influenced by two basic factors:

- time – the investor is being compensated for loss of liquidity
- risk – the investor depositing a large sum of money for a fixed period, or agreeing to give a long period of notice for withdrawals, is taking a risk. The risk is not that he or she will lose the money but that general interest rates will rise over the period of the deposit when the investor is committed to a lower one.

Tax exempt special savings accounts (TESSAs)

These accounts offer tax-free savings in return for savings committed for a five-year period. They were considered in detail in Chapter 4. They are an example of the use of tax incentives in the private sector to achieve a reduction in consumer spending by government. The same principles as those above apply to the interest rates offered on these accounts and, of course, the level of savings is restricted to government-set limits.

Collectibles

A wide range of investments is possible in this area. It is unlikely that they will produce income but often give personal enjoyment and capital growth. As mentioned earlier, maintenance costs can be high. On disposal, gains will be chargeable to capital gains tax (unless the Inland Revenue claims that the transactions amount to a trade) but may be eligible for chattels exemptions or marginal relief (see Chapter 6).

Finance – personal

Individuals and families may make real investments. The acquisition of the family home is perhaps the most significant real investment made by the majority of families, but other examples are acquisitions of 'collectibles' (stamps, antiques or vintage cars) or for the improvement of their well-being (washing machine, family car or a course of education). Savings may be used to meet such needs but often are not available or sufficient and the funds must therefore be borrowed.

The personal borrower is protected from exploitation by the Consumer Credit Act 1974 (CCA 1974). The Act is designed to promote 'truth in lending' and includes the following provisions:

- Agreements for credit of £15,000 or less must be 'regulated agreements'.
- Advertised credit must conform to certain standards:
  - the full cost of borrowing must be shown
  - the true interest rate must be quoted that is, the annual percentage rate (APR)
  - written details must be available on request
  - the APR must be shown more prominently than any other interest rate.
- Lenders must not canvas the borrower.
- The right to cancel must be given – the level of cancellation penalties is controlled.

The purpose of the Act is to ensure a 'fair deal' and lenders must be licensed under the Act.

Annual percentage rate (APR)

The traditional loan is not generally offered to the personal customer but the calculation of the APR is based on this concept. The APR is the interest rate which if applied to a traditional loan would give the same interest charge.

The traditional loan over two to five years involves regular monthly repayments from a current account and a quarterly payment of interest charges from the same current account on the outstanding balance at the beginning of each quarter.

Types of personal finance

There are four main types of personal lending product:

- bank loan
- bank overdraft
- finance house loan
- house mortgage loan.

Each is considered individually below.

Bank loans

A bank loan for a personal customer falls into one of two broad categories:

- personal loan
- secured home improvement loan or revolving credit.

Profitability governs the range of loans available and although these differ from bank to bank they share one factor – a relatively high APR.

Personal loans

These are referred to as consumer loans and have developed over the last 25 years: at the outset the interest over the full period of the loan is added to the principal and this total is divided by the number of repayments. The interest rate is generally fixed; the loans are instantly available and are usually unsecured.

EXAMPLE 11.3

At a time when the bank base rate is 6% (retail price index 4%), it would be normal for interest on a personal loan to be quoted at a flat rate of 9.75%. This translates into an APR of 19.9%!

Secured home improvement loan or revolving credit

Banks do not like unsecured lending and the personal loan rates referred to above reflect the risk they are taking. Theoretically the banks will take security in the form of real estate, endowment assurance or stocks and shares. In practice the majority of secured loans are secured to real estate; this reflects the traditional reliability of bricks and mortar in relation to average earnings and the inflation rate.

At a time when bank base rate is 6%, home improvement and revolving credit facilities might cost 10% APR; this rate would be variable, fluctuating with base rate. The bank's risk is less and this is reflected in the lower interest rates; however, the borrower is now at risk – changes in base rate in the past have caused repayments to double.

Secured home improvement loans are conventional loans for a period of five to ten years secured by a first or second mortgage over the borrower's house. Monthly repayments have a capital and interest element. The name suggests that the purpose for which these loans are given is restricted but since tax relief on this type of loan ceased, the purpose for which the funds are used is irrelevant.

Revolving credit involves the opening of a separate account with its own cheque book to which a fixed monthly transfer is made from a current account. The size of the monthly transfer determines the credit limit on the account. Interest is added to the account based on the credit taken up. When interest rates are low only a small proportion of the monthly repayment goes towards the interest but when interest rates suddenly become high, a much larger proportion of the monthly repayment goes towards the interest and the borrowing is reduced more slowly than was planned – the loan is therefore extended over a longer period than was anticipated.

Bank overdraft

This is the facility to overdraw a current account to an agreed limit and is ideal for overcoming the irregularities in expenditure and income. It is often assumed that a current account customer is entitled to overdraw the account but this is not the case and should only happen by prior arrangement.

Overdrawing the account is cost effective because interest is charged on a daily basis on the overdrawn balance. While the interest rate on an arranged facility reflects the convenience and flexibility of the system, interest charged on an unarranged overdraft is penal.

Finance house loans

Finance houses provide similar facilities for the personal customer to those provided by the banks, but they tend to be more expensive (the interest on a personal loan for instance could be between 2 and 4% higher). In addition, they offer hire purchase, generally available at the point of sale. The purchased item is security for the finance since it remains the property of the finance company until a final, nominal payment is concluded (the Consumer Credit Act offers protection to the consumer as regards the right of the finance company to repossess). Hire purchase is expensive reflecting the risk to the finance house.

House mortgage loans

A mortgage is not a loan. The mortgage is a legal document which ensures that a loan is secured against real estate. The mortgagee (lender) has legal right to sell the house, for example, in the event of default. It is the house equity which is given as security as follows:

	£
House value	100,000
1st mortgage Grand Bank	(35,000)
Equity	65,000
2nd mortgage Dogger Bank	(20,000)
New equity	45,000

The equity is always at risk from a fall in property prices. Both mortgagees have legal power of sale and default on either loan can lead to loss of the family home.

By contrast, the cost of this type of borrowing is comparatively low. Unfortunately, the setting up costs are high due to the need for a solicitor and the payment of registration charges.

Finance – business

Finance available to the smaller business (that is sole traders, small partnerships and limited companies with perhaps one or two members) is very similar to that available to the personal borrower. Any finance given to the smaller business is likely to be secured by the borrower's private assets, and failure of the business may mean surrender of the security.

In addition to conventional finance, sources of finance available from the public sector should also be considered.

Enterprise Allowance Scheme

This scheme is operated through local Training and Enterprise Councils. Startup payments from £20 to £90 per week are available to people becoming self-employed over periods ranging from 6 months to 15 months depending on the potential the business is considered to have. The usual sum is £40 per week for 52 weeks (£2,080).

The allowance is taxable in the hands of the recipient under Schedule D Case VI (if it were treated as income of the trade it would be taxed more than once under the commencement rules – see Chapter 15) but is treated as trading income for purposes of Class IV National Insurance contributions and personal pension premiums.

Local authority schemes

A variety of local schemes exist which involve rent-free accommodation for the business and/or grants.

Loan guarantee scheme

Loans of up to £250,000 (pre-FA 1993, £100,000) are available for periods between one and seven years – the government will guarantee up to 85% (previously 70%) of the loan. This means that small businesses can raise finance even though there are insufficient personal assets for security.

A premium is charged of between 0.5% and 1.5% on the loan for the guarantee (previously 2.5%).

Enterprise Investment Scheme

Unquoted trading companies can raise funds through the Enterprise Investment Scheme. To do so they must issue new equity finance to individuals who are not connected with the company. Up to £1 million a year can be raised under the scheme.

Summary

- ▶ Money or financial investment differs from real investment.
- ▶ Investment is a respectable activity usually involving the institutions and aimed at long- or medium-term gain.
- ▶ Speculation is riskier than investment and is short term – higher returns are therefore expected.
- ▶ Savings come from income and are normally placed on terms giving guaranteed encashment – returns are correspondingly less.
- ▶ Investment trusts are companies which have shares in other companies as their asset base.
- ▶ Unit trusts are not companies. Through the sale of units they purchase a large, diversified portfolio of shares.
- ▶ Both unit trusts and investment trusts achieve diversification for the investor.
- ▶ Endowment assurance combines a savings medium with life assurance – diversified investment with life cover.
- ▶ Single-premium policies provide growth in return for a lump sum, together with life assurance – a withdrawal facility without tax liability enables the provision of income.
- ▶ Lending to the personal borrower is regulated by the Consumer Credit Act 1974.
- ▶ Banks lend in two basic categories:
  - – personal loans – unsecured but high interest
  - – security linked loans – lower interest

- Overdrafts are for current accounts that occasionally dip into the red – interest is charged on a daily basis.
- House mortgage loans cost less (even on a second mortgage) but the house is at risk in the event of default.
- Small business lending is much the same as for the private individual. Government schemes should be chosen where practicable – they may be slightly more expensive but do not require security.

Self test questions

1. What is the difference between investment, speculation and savings?
2. Does investment in a unit trust suit all investors?
3. Which type of assurance is appropriate for the regular investor?
4. What is the advantage of the single premium bond?
5. List the advantages and disadvantages of a personal loan.
6. Can a current account at the bank be overdrawn?

Answers on page 575

Personal Finance – the Investment Advisor

CHAPTER 12

This chapter considers the regulations, under the Financial Services Act (1986), which affect accountants and tax advisers who are involved in investment business. The term investment business is defined.

The Financial Services Act

Practising accountants will from time to time become involved in investment business on behalf of clients or be asked to introduce clients to financial institutions or be asked for advice about investment products. All such tasks are now subject to the provisions of the Financial Services Act 1986 (FSA 1986) and the Act requires those offering sevices in these areas to be authorised by either:

- a recognised professional body
- a self regulating organisation, or
- the Securities and Investment Board

In practice, most firms of Certified Accountants requiring authorisation will apply to the Chartered Association of Certified Accountants which is a recognised professional body. If, for any reason, they fail to meet the criteria laid down by ACCA, they can apply to a self regulating organisation such as FIMBRA (Financial Intermediaries, Managers and Brokers Regulatory Association) or directly to the Securities and Investment Board (SIB). Figure 12.1 illustrates the regulatory structure.

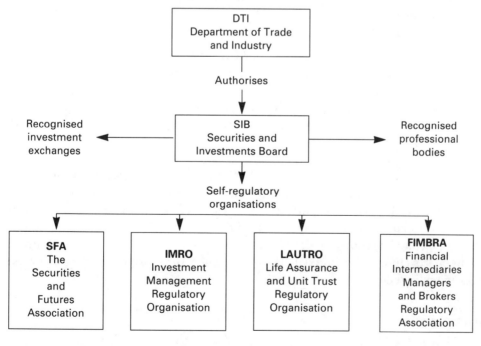

Figure 12.1 The regulatory structure

Registration and authorisation

The Securities and Investment Board is the designated agency authorised by the Department of Trade and Industry to regulate the conduct of the investment business in the United Kingdom. Regulatory powers and responsibilities have in turn been delegated by the Securities and Investment Board to the various self regulating bodies, recognised investment exchanges and recognised professional bodies (which include ACCA).

The self regulating organisations

There are four main self regulating organisations (SROs) each of which has a particular area of specialism as follows:

- *FIMBRA* (Financial Intermediaries, Managers and Brokers Regulatory Association) has the largest membership. A member will usually be involved in giving investment advice, arranging deals in investments (particularly life assurance and pensions) and may manage and hold client investments. FIMBRA members are independent – they give advice based on all the investment products on the market.
- *IMRO* (Investment Managers Regulatory Organisation). Firms which advise on or manage large investment portfolios are members.
- *SFA* (Securities and Futures Authority) members deal with the purchase and sales of securities including equities, gilts, local authority bonds, options, futures and contracts for interest rate swaps.
- *LAUTRO* (Life Assurance and Unit Trust Regulatory Organisation) regulates the marketing of life assurance and unit trust products. Members of LAUTRO are 'tied agents', only selling the products of the firm they represent – they will often sell to investors via FIMBRA members or IMRO members.

Banks are regulated by the Bank of England as regards banking business but in so far as they provide financial services to individuals, they would belong to one of the regulatory organisations above.

Authorisation by ACCA

The ACCA in its capacity as a RPB authorises firms satisfying certain criteria to carry on investment business.

Firms applying for authorisation must be either:

- a sole practitioner who is a member of ACCA, or
- a partnership where each of the partners is a member of an RPB and at least one of which is a member of ACCA; and
- the main business of the sole practitioner or partnership must be the practice of accountancy. (This will exclude any firm whose income from investment business exceeds 20% of its total income.)

Individuals within firms cannot be authorised. Firms with several offices (trading under the same name) need only register once. A partnership where a partner is not a member of an RPB may be authorised if that partner holds an equivalent qualification (such as from the Institute of Taxation). Where a partner does not hold an equivalent qualification or does not practice accountancy, the firm, in order to be authorised, will need to change its constitution to ensure that such partners exercise no management and control.

Regulation

From the investor's point of view, there is now considerable protection.

All authorised individuals have been vetted and approved by a regulatory organisation or by a professional body and are subject to continuous monitoring in the conduct of investment business.

A central compensation fund has also been created under the Act to compensate investors who lose money as the result of the fraud, negligence or bankruptcy of an authorised person.

Ombudsman schemes have been set up in a number of financial sectors to deal with grievances against financial institutions in those sectors. The financial sectors involved are banking, building societies, insurance, pensions and investment. The Ombudsman in each case is independent – if a complaint is justified, he has power to make an award against the member.

Penalties

It is a criminal offence for any person to carry on investment business without authorisation.

Investment business defined

It is important to understand the scope of the legislation, not least to find out whether authorisation to carry on investment business is appropriate.

The definition is subdivided into two broad categories:

- investments
- investment activities.

Investments

Investments are considered to be:

- shares
- debentures
- government and public securities
- instruments entitling the holder to shares or securities such as warrants
- certificates representing securities such as deposit receipts (ADRs)
- options – over shares, currency, bullion
- futures – including all LIFFE contracts, commodity futures and currency futures
- contracts for differences such as interest rate swaps
- long-term insurance contracts such as endowment policies, whole life policies, insurance-based pensions and those linked to unit trusts.

The following are not to be included in the list of investments:
- real property
- works of art
- gold
- building society deposits
- savings accounts
- repayment mortgages.

Investment activities

Investment activities fall into the four principal categories listed below.

Dealing in investments

Dealing in investments includes buying, selling, subscribing for or underwriting investments. This covers the acquisition of shares or unit trusts (or other investments listed above) in a client's name.

Arranging deals in investments

This category can be summarised as covering: an introduction to any person who deals in investments as principal or agent and with whom arrangements exist, unless the introduction is 'independent'.

It excludes, however, any such introductions to a broker who does not act as principal or agent and excludes introductions where no arrangements exist.

Managing investments

Any person who manages, or offers to manage or agrees to manage investments for a third party is carrying on investment business.

Giving investment advice

It is safest to assume that the giving of any advice in a professional capacity may be caught whether or not for consideration.

Other investment activities exist which have not been mentioned (examples include employee share schemes, sale/purchase of business, trustee and personal representative functions).

Conduct of investment business

The ACCA acknowledges that authorised members will be involved in investment business to a greater or lesser extent. For the purposes of its investment rules, therefore, it divides investment business into two types: discrete, and non discrete.

Discrete business

Any investment business which is not covered by the categories noted below is likely to be considered as discrete. Examples are the selling of life assurance and pension products. Separate rules have been established for these activities (not included).

Non-discrete business

This covers four main types of activity:

- The business is undertaken in the capacity as personal representative for a deceased's estate.
- The business is transacted through or in conjunction with a permitted third party.
- The business is incidental to the provision of professional accounting services.
- The business relates to a deal for an 'execution only' client.

The compliance requirements

The following are a summarised version of the ACCA rules which apply to non-discrete investment business. They conform generally with those implemented by all other regulatory organisations and professional bodies authorised by the Securities and Investment Board.

- *General.* Firms dealing with potential clients must not make misleading or untrue statements and should not accept clients where it is believed they are involved in insider dealing or a criminal offence. (Note the EC Directive on Money Laundering, which is far reaching in its scope and requires accountants, among others, to report suspicions of dubious activity to authorities without the client being aware of the disclosure. This is in contrast with the traditional view of confidentiality between accountant and client)
- *Independence.* Any association which may interfere with a firm's dealings must be disclosed. Firms are not permitted to give or receive gifts and any commissions receivable must be notified to the client. Introduction fees may not be paid
- *Sophisticated clients.* A client who displays a good knowledge of the risks and conditions prevailing in the investment field may be treated as a sophisticated client
- *Documentation.* Firms must exercise reasonable care when holding documents of title (for example share certificates) on behalf of clients. Records of such transactions must be kept and must be available for inspection for three years.
- *Advertising.* Any advertisement must conform to the Advertising Standards Authority tests for legality, honesty and truthfulness. There are specific rules for advertising in respect of investment business, particularly in the area of insurance where claims about past performance are restricted. Care must be taken when comparisons are made to compare like with like
- *Records of transactions.* Whenever transactions are undertaken on behalf of a client, they must be recorded as soon as possible (nature, date and time); similarly whenever a third party is instructed; if a transaction is carried out on behalf of more than one client, the apportionment and the time should be recorded. Clients have the right to inspect the records and complaints must be referred to the Association without delay
- *Charges and commissions.* Rewards must not be paid to third parties for introductions and business should not be conducted where there may be a conflict of interest (it may be permissable where the firm's interest is declared and agreed by the client)
- *The firm.* Responsibility for the investment business lies with the firm – any person within the firm whose main business is investment may not be the firm's representative. Any change to the status or constitution of the firm must be notified to the Association. Annual reviews of records and compliance must be made.

Summary

- The conduct of investment business is governed by the provisions of the Financial Services Act 1986.
- The Securities and Investment Board is authorised to regulate the conduct of investment business.
- The Association of Certified Accountants is delegated to regulate its conduct and the conduct of its authorised members as a Recognised Professional Body.
- A practising member of the ACCA will normally apply for investment business authorisation to the ACCA.
- Investment business requiring authorisation is clearly defined by the ACCA.
- Authorised members must conform to the compliance requirements of the Association.

Self test questions

1   Accountants may be authorised to conduct investment business by their own professional body. How else may they be authorised?

2   Can an individual accountant be authorised by the ACCA to conduct investment business?

3   Should the accountant treat all clients the same when dealing in investment business?

4   Your client, a local barber, produces £10,000 cash and asks you to invest it. Would this transaction incur special consideration?

Answers on page 575

Personal Finance – Determining the Appropriate Investments/Finance

CHAPTER 13

The purpose of this chapter is to look at the methodology involved in determining the appropriate investment or finance for a particular individual taking into account his or her personal circumstances.

Identifying the investor

Every investor is different. There is no investment strategy which is appropriate to every investor. Portfolio selection depends on the individual investor's profile and a questionnaire should be completed at the outset by either the investor or the accountant. This is not just good practice but a requirement of the Financial Services Act 1986. Completed questionnaires, after use, should be kept on file for a minimum of three years for the following reasons:

- compliance with the Financial Services Act – best advice/execution
- availability for amendment after changed circumstances
- marketing potential should further professional involvement be appropriate.

In drawing up the investor/client profile, the following factors should be considered:

- the individual and dependants
- earned income after tax
- existing commitments
- accumulated wealth
- personal feelings.

Each of these is considered in more detail below.

The individual and dependants

Age

As a general rule, the young person requires income in order to manage on a low salary, and save for a home. The middle-aged person is expected to no longer have these burdens and would be expected to be looking to pension provision and growth. At retirement age, the emphasis again changes to income provision – which should be considered in conjunction with pension arrangements. The objective should be to generate sufficient net income from investments throughout retirement and care must be taken to achieve a suitable balance between current income and capital growth.

Married

A spouse may affect investment decisions. While both partners are young and without children, this should be a period of high income but expenditure will also be high as a home and furniture are acquired. A period of saving should follow to provide financial stability for the future. Life assurance arrangements should be considered for a surviving spouse and because such arrangements are cheaper if made while young. Health insurance and pension provision are also appropriate for the same reasons. If there is a disparity in their respective ages, this would influence the portfolio.

As spouses are now taxed separately, the tax-saving opportunities outlined in Chapter 2 should be considered throughout their lives together.

Children

Children are a burden on the younger investor and should be considered in the portfolio – the emphasis is likely to be on income again. There may have been a loss of one salary, a move to a larger home may be necessary and outgoings will have increased. School fees may need to be provided for; security becomes increasingly important and both life assurance (to provide for a surviving spouse and children) and pension provision should be reviewed.

State of health

This may affect the chance of acquiring life assurance at reasonable premiums; the possibility of working until retirement age will be affected. The portfolio should be reviewed and plans adjusted accordingly. The advisor should not assume that an investor intends to provide for dependants.

Earned income after tax

While the disposable income is being established, other earnings-related enquiries should also be made as follows:

- Are there any additional earnings?
- Is the main income secure?
- Will the income steadily improve?
- What is the marginal rate of tax – 25 or 40%?
- What are the gross and net earnings?
- Does sickness cover exist?
- Is there a contributory or non-contributory pension scheme?

These questions are much the same as those included in credit card and loan applications and the answers will help to build up the investor's profile.

Existing commitments

From the enquiries above, various disbursements, or lack of them, will be in evidence, including commitments to life assurance and pension schemes. They should be reviewed as to their appropriateness and adequacy.

Pension contributions

The client may well have a good occupational scheme but, if not, a private one may be appropriate. Opting out of SERPS (see Chapter 4) may be considered, depending on the client's age.

Mortgage

It may be possible to reduce outgoings by switching schemes. In view of the tax relief (lower rate only) on mortgages up to £30,000, should a smaller mortgage than this exist, it may well be worth taking out a mortgage of £30,000 if a house move is being considered. Note that tax relief on a second mortgage is unlikely to be available as although such a loan is secured on the property it is not taken out to purchase the property.

Life assurance

As stated above, this should be closely examined in view of current and foreseeable circumstances.

Accumulated wealth

Few clients have a true picture of their immediate worth and should a well-thought-out portfolio already exist, the capital gains position will be important, ensuring that allowable losses are brought forward and utilisation of annual exemption is practised.

Personal feelings

Investors are increasingly being influenced by factors other than the obvious financial ones affecting investment choice. These can be examined under the following headings:

- attitude to risk
- ethical considerations
- sentiment.

Attitude to risk

Some investors will consider the safety of their capital as the most important consideration. Both for those seeking income and others for whom capital appreciation is paramount, various risks exist.

Market risks affect all investments while specific risks are associated with a specific business or sector.

Market risks
- *Inflation* erodes both interest received and the purchasing power of the invested capital. Interest rates are occasionally lower than the retail price index and may therefore produce negative returns
- *Interest rates,* if high, produce good returns for the investor but unfortunately cause low real investment in industry, erode profits and tend to be detrimental to share prices
- *Financial risk.* Highly geared companies (those with a high debt-to-equity ratio) must service their loans. An increase in interest rates has an immediate and dramatic effect on shareholders when the rate of interest on loan capital becomes higher than the rate of return on capital employed in the company
- *Currency risk.* Fluctuations in rates can erode or destroy profits for companies with overseas interests. Fixed or narrow banded rates are preferable as exemplified in the disciplines imposed with the European exchange rate mechanism.
- *Liquidity* is the ability to convert an investment into cash. The higher the liquidity, the lower the profits must be.

Specific risks
- *Internal risks* relate to all the factors within a company which make for success. This would include management, marketing, and labour relations
- *Industry risk.* This includes factors which may affect a whole sector such as the imposition of barriers in an overseas market.

All of the above-mentioned risks are likely to have an immediate or anticipated effect on traded securities. They may come as a surprise to the average investor and enhance or detract from expectations. However, within the investment industry, or the markets, there may be little noticeable effect – it will have been anticipated, prices will have adjusted and the effects will be 'in the market'. Few private investors possess the skills or the information to anticipate potential losses in the way that professionals are able to.

The portfolio of an investor who is risk averse may be confined to cash investments. Short-dated gilts (that is, those moving towards maturity) should be considered as should investment bonds in the longer term. These steadier investments, whilst liable to some fluctuation, will avoid those wild swings which upset a nervous investor.

Ethical considerations

Many investors have strong feelings about companies which trade or have connections with products, areas or political systems to which they object. The obvious products which may offend are alcohol, nuclear power, tobacco, fur clothing and armaments. The actual extent to which a particular company may be involved with the offending product is less obvious. Occasionally, members of pressure groups acquire shares in offending companies in order to cause trouble at company meetings.

Ethical funds are becoming more prominent in the UK and Europe following the lead from the USA. Such funds avoid the areas previously listed, but are also concentrating broadly or specifically on care for the environment. Forthcoming European legislation will require companies to carry out environmental audits and impact assessments – financial penalties may be imposed for non-compliance.

Sentiment

Sentiment may override logic in investment decisions. Statements such as 'I wish to invest in Midshire County Council Bonds because I lived there as a child' are not uncommon.

Shareholders' 'perks' may also be included in this area. Benefits such as the right to discounts in dry cleaning costs, handout hampers at AGMs and cheap cross-channel ferry fares are well known.

The elements of a portfolio

In seeking a balanced portfolio, three elements will always appear:

- liquidity
- short- or medium-term flexibility
- growth.

It is only the proportion of each which will vary.

Liquidity

As the most liquid investments give the poorest returns, this element should be kept to a minimum. The actual amount will depend on the security and regularity of the investor's income and perhaps the physical ability to get to a bank and so on. Liquid funds may generally be an expensive luxury, but there are times when rates paid by the National Savings Bank, for example, are better than the returns from equities, banks, building societies and so on. On these occasions, the private investor can fare better than institutions which do not have this option. (The term liquid can reasonably be applied to investments encashable within 10 days.)

Short- and medium-term flexibility

Investments in this category should be realisable within a reasonable time without the risk of serious loss. A long-dated gilt might be an example of an unsuitable investment – it is subject to fluctuations in value – while the short-dated gilt might suit.

Fixed interest securities are all at risk from being marked down when interest rates rise but the short-dated ones suffer less and are more suitable to the forced sale situation. Gilts have become more popular since they became exempt from capital gains tax, despite the bondwashing provisions. An investor seeking income could produce a regular monthly income from six short- or medium-term gilts – provided they were chosen to pay their coupon on different months (January/July, February/August and so on).

Growth

This element can be long term. The equity market is appropriate and diversification is important. To achieve this, at least 20 different equities should be selected across several sectors on the International Stock Exchange. Alternatively, the diversification and sector spread could be achieved from four to five unit trusts. The concentration on equities is not without reason – equities have outgrown most other investments over recent years.

Determining the proportions

Due to the variation in investors, there are no hard and fast rules. The basic rate taxpayer with limited funds (approximately £20,000) will require liquidity and flexibility. Thereafter, and for investors paying higher rate tax, growth becomes the main consideration (equities and unit trusts considered above but acquired through personal equity plans to avoid higher rate tax and capital gains liabilities are ideal). Table 13.1 sets out figures which may serve as a guide.

Table 13.1

Available to investor	£5,000	£20,000	£20,000 plus
	No tax liability %	25% taxpayer %	40% taxpayer %
Liquid	5–100	10	5
Short and medium-term	0–50	20–50	20
Growth	–	40–60	60–80

There would be no advantage for a non-taxpayer acquiring a PEP, because the tax reliefs are of no value. Other factors which may be considered are shown below:

Income or capital growth may depend on an investor's existing portfolio, if any, and individual preference.

The investor's age will influence the balance – an elderly investor should not be involved with a long-term growth product, regardless of existing wealth. Some of the portfolio should, however, seek to prevent erosion by inflation.

Economic conditions will affect the performance of investments and if liquid investments are faring best then even the wealthier investor should choose these. Inflation has already been mentioned as the most insidious of the economic conditions.

However, personal preferences of the investor may defeat any investment logic of the advisor.

Table 13.2 sets out two alternative selections of investments for the higher-rate taxpayer, one for low risk and one for high risk. There is an emphasis on those investments which are free of income tax or capital gains tax or both, and on those which provide no income but concentrate instead on capital growth. Table 13.3 sets out a selection for the basic rate taxpayer.

Table 13.2 Some investments for the higher rate taxpayer

Low risk	High risk
Short-term	
Low coupon short-date gilts NSB ordinary account (to tax-free interest limit) NSB First Option Bonds	Options (no income)
Medium-term	
National Savings Certificates ordinary and index-linked (tax free)	Warrants (no income)
Personal equity plans (tax free)	Premium Bonds (tax free) Offshore commodity funds
Tax-exempt special savings (TESSA) accounts (tax free)	Chattels – gold, silver
	Enterprise Investment Scheme
Longer-term	
Friendly society bonds (tax free)	Unit and investment trusts
Pension schemes	
Index-linked gilts	
Owner-occupied property and further real estate (no income)	

Table 13.3 Some Investments for the basic rate taxpayer

Short-term

High-interest bank accounts (for example, one year notice)

High-interest building society accounts (similar notice)

Money market funds (bank)

NSB Ordinary Account (small amount for convenience)

Medium-term

National Savings Certificates – ordinary and index-linked (small amount)

Investment and unit trusts – regular savings (pound cost averaging advantage)

Tax Exempt Special Savings Scheme (TESSA)

Personal Equity Plans

NSB Investment Account – taxable but good return

Longer-term

Owner-occupied property

Pension scheme

Single Premium Insurance Policies

Unlike the higher-rate taxpayer, the basic-rate payer is unlikely to invest in anything of a high-risk nature. Most of this investor's investments will be of a liquid or semi-liquid nature.

TAX PLANNING

EXAMPLE 13.1

Fred Jones, aged 40, is a qualified ex-army chef in charge of the kitchen at Le Moulin d'Argent. His salary is £31,000. He is a single parent and receives an army pension of £4,200. His present position is not pensionable and he has made no provision for his children. His estranged wife has recently died and he has received the proceeds of a life policy amounting to £60,000. He has an outstanding mortgage of £16,000 (MIRAS).

a) Suggest suitable investments for Mr Jones
b) Indicate other provisions Mr Jones may consider.

a) Mr Jones's income tax position must be evaluated

	£
Basic income	31,000
Army pension	4,200
Total income	35,200
Personal Allowance	(3,445)
	31,755
Tax borne	
3,000 @ 20%	600
20,700 @ 25%	5,175
8,055 @ 40%	3,222
	8,997
Less APA relief (1,720 × 20%)	(344)
	8,653

An increase in income is certain to increase the 40% tax liability. It is assumed that Mr Jones would not need much liquid investment (due to his income level) and his portfolio would therefore be designed to protect his position in both the medium and long-term. An appropriate division of the £60,000 would perhaps be as follows:

	£
Liquid	5,000
Medium term	15,000
Long term	40,000
	60,000

Mr Jones is not likely to require a large increase in income and therefore concentration on long-term investment is appropriate. His portfolio may look like this:

Liquid
NSB Ordinary Account	£1,000
Bank/building society (short-notice accounts)	£4,000

Medium term
National Savings Certificates	£5,000
PEPs	£3,000
TESSAs	£3,000
First Option Bonds (to review)	£4,000

Long term
Single premium bonds	£20,000
Investment or unit trusts – growth	£20,000

b) Mr Jones must make pension provision. Whilst his army pension may be adequate as an index-linked item it will need supplementing. Mr Jones should not opt out of SERPS. The mortgage is relatively small but there is little point in increasing it when he will still remain liable for higher-rate tax. He should ensure that his children are financially provided for, should he meet an untimely death. This can be achieved while he is reasonably young by taking up appropriate life assurance, either whole life or a long-term large endowment.

Mr Jones could also consider investing part of his lump sum in the Enterprise Investment Scheme. This involves purchasing equity shares of unquoted trading companies. Lower rate tax relief is given on the sum invested. If the shares are held for five years they are free of CGT on the first disposal. However, this is a very risky investment and should only be considered if Mr Jones can afford to lose the capital sum invested.

Summary

- Accountants must complete a questionnaire for each client seeking investment advice.
- Young clients are normally considered to require income as they may be on low incomes and in the process of acquiring homes, furnishings and children.
- Middle-aged clients should, in contrast to the young, seek growth. They are assumed to be established, having the house and most of the consumables they require. They may be looking towards the provision of capital to produce an income on retirement.
- The first step in finding an investment strategy is to establish earned income after tax (including the marginal tax rate).
- The second step is to review the existing portfolio/contributions.
- Personal feelings – attitude to risk, ethical considerations, and sentiment – must be considered.
- Portfolios should contain elements of liquidity, medium-term availability and growth.

Self test questions

1. Why is it necessary to establish the tax position of the investor?
2. The investor's accumulated wealth should be established and reviewed. Why is this important?
3. What are medium investments?
4. Explain the importance of diversification.

Answers on page 575

The Taxation of Trusts

CHAPTER 14

Earlier chapters have looked at the taxation consequences to the individual of transferring property into trusts. The purpose of this chapter is to show the taxation implications on the trust of income arising from trust property and of disposals of trust property. The application of inheritance tax to trusts is also considered. Note that you are only required to have a broad knowledge of this area of the syllabus.

The nature of a trust

A trust is created when someone, known as the settlor, transfers assets to trustees to hold for the benefit of one or more persons who will receive income and/or capital from the trust, currently or at some future date. It can be created during the settlor's lifetime or on death (by will or under the intestacy rules). As has been seen in Chapters 8 to 10 the transfer of assets into a trust is a transfer of value for inheritance tax purposes – either a chargeable transfer or a PET depending on the type of trust.

The two principal categories of trust (trusts with an interest in possession and discretionary trusts) were described in Chapter 8 as well as some of the related terminology. You should ensure that you are familiar with these terms before continuing.

Income tax

Trusts receive income from a variety of sources as do individuals. One of the principal sources of income to a trust is dividends. Dividends received in 1994/95 are deemed to be net of income tax at 20% (see Chapter 1). This causes a number of complications – you should study this section slowly and carefully to ensure you understand it.

Trusts with an interest in possession

In an interest in possession trust, one or more beneficiaries has a right to the trust income (subject to the trustees claim for expenses and other outgoings payable from trust income). The trustees have no power to accumulate income. Note that it is possible for an interest in possession trust not to generate any income (for example, the trust property may be a house, and the beneficiary has the right of occupation).

The trustees are responsible for paying basic rate income tax on all of the trust income other than dividends which are only liable to tax at 20% (there is no higher rate tax). This is computed for a fiscal year. The definition of income and the bases of assessment are the same as that for an individual. Expenses which are specifically allowable under a particular Schedule are deductible for tax purposes but administration expenses of the trust are not allowable, and no personal allowances are given.

The income after tax and after expenses must be shared out between the annuitants and the 'life tenants' according to their respective interests in the trust.

Administration expenses are deemed to have been paid out of dividend income in priority to other income (FA93). Sums paid to annuitants are retainable charges (basic rate income tax must be deducted at source). It is therefore convenient to deduct the annuity from other income. To the extent that payments to life tenants are attributable to dividend income (net of trust management expenses) of the trust they are deemed to have had 20% deducted at source; payments attributable to income from other sources are net of basic rate tax; all such payments must be grossed for inclusion in their personal tax computations. A form R185 should accompany the payment showing the net payment, the tax and the gross equivalent.

The sums due to annuitants are normally expressed as gross amounts while the expenses must be paid out of taxed income. The formal method commonly used to compute the amount due to the life tenant can be effectively checked through a trust income and expenditive account as in the example below:.

EXAMPLE 14.1

An interest in possession trust received the following income in 1994/95:

Schedule A	£4,000
Dividends received	£1,600

Trust expenses amount to £150. There are two life tenants, B and C, who share equally in the remaining income of the trust after an annuity of £2,000 per annum has been paid to A.

Calculate the tax payable by the trustees and the amounts due to each of the beneficiaries.

	Dividend income £	Other income £	Total income £	Tax paid £
Schedule A		4,000	4,000	–
Dividends (1,600 × 100/80)	2,000		2,000	400
Total income	2,000	4,000	6,000	400

				Tax due £
Tax due by trustees:				
on dividends @ 20%	(400)		(400)	
on other income @ 25%		(1,000)	(1,000)	1,400
Income after tax	1,600	3,000	4,600	
Less: trust expenses	(150)	—	(150)	
	1,450	3,000	4,450	
Less: annuity net (75% of 2,000)		(1,500)	(1,500)	
Distributable to life tenants	1,450	1,500	2,950	
B	725	750	1,475	
C	725	750	1,475	
Tax payable				1,000

The life tenants will each receive cash of £1,475.
The gross income to be entered on each of their tax returns will be:

	£
725 × 100/80 =	906.25
750 × 100/75 =	1,000.00
	1,906.25

This type of analysis is straightforward and should be used to check the answer produced by the more formal presentation below:

	Dividend	Other	Total
	£	£	£
Gross income	2,000	4,000	6,000
Annuity – gross to A	–	(2,000)	(2,000)
	2,000	2,000	4,000
Tax @ 20%/25%	(400)	(500)	(900)
Net income of trust	1,600	1,500	3,100
Expenses	(150)	–	(150)
Shared equally between B and C	1,450	1,500	2,950

B	gross £1,906 (as above)	net £1,475
C	gross £1,906 (as above)	net £1,475

As all the income of the trust must be appropriated to the beneficiaries each year, and therefore included in their personal tax computations each year, there is no scope for income tax avoidance. A higher rate liability cannot be avoided by a beneficiary.

Discretionary trusts

Discretionary trusts include accumulation and maintenance trusts. In a discretionary trust, the trustees have a discretionary power as to the distribution of income and no-one is entitled to it by right. The same principles apply to discretionary trusts as to trusts with an interest in possession but with these modifications:

- The income of a discretionary trust need not be appropriated to beneficiaries in full each year – instead the trustees make such payments from the trust as they see fit. Without rules to the contrary, therefore, it would be possible to accumulate income in the trust and for beneficiaries to avoid a higher-rate liability. To counteract this, a discretionary trust is liable to tax at a single rate of 35%.
- Payments to beneficiaries are therefore regarded as net of tax at 35% and must be grossed up in their personal tax computations by the fraction 100/65.
- Income used to meet administration expenses of the trust, is not liable to tax at 35% but at 20% if it is dividend income and 25% if it is other income. Expenses are deemed to have been paid out of dividend income in priority to other income.

EXAMPLE 14.2

The Alpha Trust, a discretionary trust, received the following income in 1994/95:

Schedule A	£8,000
Dividends received (net)	£3,000
Interest taxed at source (net)	£1,500

The trust administration expenses for the year amounted to £300 and cash of £4,000 was paid to a beneficiary.
Calculate the tax payable by the trustees and the amount assessable on the beneficiary.

	Dividend income £	Other income £	Total income £	Tax paid £
Trust income (gross)				
Schedule A		8,000	8,000	–
Dividends (3,200 × 100/80)	4,000		4,000	800
Taxed interest		2,000	2,000	500
Total income	4,000	10,000	14,000	1,300
Less expenses (300 × 100/80)	(375)		(375)	
	3,625	10,000	13,625	

	Tax due £
Less: tax due by Trustees:	
On dividends 375 @ 20%	(75)
3,625 @ 35%	(1,269)
On other income 10,000 @ 35%	(3,500)
	4,844
Distributable income (net)	8,781
Paid	(4,000)
Carried forward	4,781
Tax payable	3,544

The beneficiary would be treated as receiving gross income of £6,154 (£4,000 × 100/65).

Residence

The liability to UK tax of trusts is determined largely by the concepts of residence, ordinary residence and domicile – as it is for other chargeable persons. However, residence, ordinary residence and domicile in relation to trusts are relevant as they affect settlors, beneficiaries or trustees.

Trustees are assessable to UK income tax in respect of worldwide trust income where at least one of the trustees is UK resident and the settlor, at the relevant time, was resident, ordinarily resident or domiciled in the UK. The relevant time is the date or dates on which funds were provided to the trust.

Settlement of parent in favour of own child

In general, income arising from dispositions by parents in favour of an unmarried minor child is deemed to be that of the parent (see Chapter 2).

An exception to this rule is a transfer to an irrevocable accumulation and maintenance settlement. The income is subject to tax at 35% (an accumulation and maintenance settlement is a form of discretionary settlement) in the hands of the trustees and is not deemed to be that of the parent. However, any amounts paid to or applied for the education or maintenance of the child by the trustees will be deemed to be the income of the parent in the year of payment.

Where 35% is less than the parent's marginal rate of tax there may be some benefit to the parents in creating a trust of this type and allowing the income to accumulate. When the accumulated income is transferred (when the child reaches the appropriate age), it is transferred as capital and therefore does not attract tax.

Tax avoidance legislation

Income from settlements, where the settlor or the settlor's spouse retains an interest in the settled property (they are beneficiaries under the trust), should be treated as income of the settlor.

Capital gains tax

When property is transferred into a trust, a chargeable disposal arises for capital gains tax purposes (unless the transfer took place on the death of the settlor).

The trustees are connected to the settlor of a settlement so that the disposal/acquisition will be deemed to have taken place at market value.

The holdover rules under gift relief apply where an inheritance tax liability arises (for example, on a gift to a discretionary trust) or on a transfer of qualifying assets (for example, business assets or shares in an unquoted personal trading company). Note that gift relief was more widely available before the Finance Act 1989. In some cases therefore, the settlor may not have paid any capital gains tax on his disposal. In these cases the 'held over' gain will be deducted from the market value (the deemed acquisition cost of the trustees) at the date of the gift. In this case, the provisions for re-basing to 31 March 1982 must be remembered and in particular the possible claim for the held-over gain to be halved when the asset is subsequently disposed of.

Disposal of trust assets

In both interest in possession trusts and discretionary trusts, a disposal of trust assets may occur or be deemed to occur in a number of circumstances:

- A change of investment – the disposal of one asset and the purchase of another.
- Whenever a beneficiary becomes absolutely entitled, the appropriate proportion of the trust assets becomes the property of the beneficiary. Absolute entitlement arises, for example, when a beneficiary of a discretionary trust reaches a pre-determined age, when a life interest in an interest in possession trust comes to an end without there being another life tenant, and when a contingent interest vests.
- The transfer is deemed to take place at market value at the date the beneficiary becomes entitled (not the eventual date of transfer). It will be a chargeable disposal giving rise to a capital gains tax liability (gift relief may apply), except if the occasion is the death of the life tenant in an interest in possession trust when it is treated as a transfer on death at market value at the date of death (no capital gains tax liability arises, except to the extent that a held-over gain may crystallise).
- On the termination of a life interest in an interest in possession trust, the assets remaining settled property (that is, the remainderman does not become entitled). For example, the trust assets settled on A for life (or specified period, for example, for such a period as a widow remains unmarried) then on B for life (or specified period) then to C absolutely.
  - On death of A the property is treated as disposed of and immediately re-acquired by the trustees at market value. No capital gains tax liability arises as the transfer is treated as taking place on death. If gift relief was claimed on the transfer of the property into the settlement the held-over gain will crystallise. It may be possible to hold over the gain a second time.
  - Other than on the death of A (for example, if widow remarries), this is not a disposal for capital gains tax purposes.
- On the migration of a trust after the trustees are treated as having disposed of, and immediately re-acquired at market value, all of the assets which would fall out of charge to UK tax on the change of residence status. (It does not therefore apply to UK assets used in a trade carried on in the UK by the trustees.) Roll-over relief is not available.
- The trustees may claim to hold over any gains by reinvestment relief. To qualify for relief, the gains (on the disposal of any asset) must be reinvested in an unquoted trading company. This relief is covered in Chapter 21.

Rate of capital gains tax

Interest in possession trusts pay capital gains tax at a flat rate (after annual exemption) of 25%, irrespective of the beneficiary's marginal rate of income tax.

Discretionary trusts pay capital gains tax at a flat rate (after annual exemption) of 35%.

In both cases, capital gains tax will be at a rate lower than the top rate for individuals (unless the settlor or the settlor's spouse have an interest in the trust) giving considerable scope for planning.

The rules for the annual exemption, indexation losses and losses brought forward and carried forward are identical to those for individuals. However, if a trust has accumulated capital losses when a beneficiary becomes absolutely entitled, then the losses, or a proportion of them, may be transferred to the beneficiary.

If the settlor or the settlor's spouse have an interest in the trust (present or future) any gains made by the trustees are taxed as if they were the settlor's personal gains.

Annual exemption

An annual exemption of £2,900 (one-half of the annual exemption of an individual) is given to trustees of settlements. If several trusts are set up by the same settlor, the exemption is divided between them subject to a minimum of one-tenth of the annual individual exemption (that is £580).

The full exemption (£5,800) applies to personal representatives for gains accruing to an estate in the year of death and in the two following years of assessment. A full exemption also applies for trustees of a trust for a mentally handicapped person or for a person receiving the attendance allowance.

EXAMPLE 14.3

X settled shares (cost £10,000 in July 1980) into an interest in possession trust on 30 July 1985 when their value was £100,000. The trust was for the benefit of John and Anne for the duration of Anne's life (50% each) and thereafter to Dorothy. Anne died in March 1995 when the value of trust property was £300,000.

RPI factor	Mar 82 – Jul 85	0.200
	Jul 85 – Mar 95	0.523

Compute the gains arising, assuming all possible claims to mitigate and defer tax are made.

		£
Creation of trust – 30 July 1985		
Market value		100,000
Base cost to X		(10,000)
		90,000
Indexation allowance 10,000 × 0.200		(2,000)
Gain held-over (gift relief)		88,000
Death of Anne – March 1995		
Market value		300,000
Base cost to trustees	100,000	
Held-over gain (50% claim)	(44,000)	(56,000)
		244,000
Indexation allowance 56,000 × 0.523		(29,288)
Gain arising		214,712

		John	Anne
John's share (termination not on death)		107,356	£
Anne's share (termination on death)			107,356
chargeable 1994/95			
lower of a) 107,356			
b) 50% 44,000 gain held over			22,000
Total gain (subject gift relief – provided qualifying assets)	129,356	107,356	22,000
Dorothy market value @ date of absolute entitlement			300,000
Gain held-over			(129,356)
Dorothy base cost			170,644

EXAMPLE 14.4

A grandparent set up an accumulation and maintenance trust for four grandchildren. The trustees must accumulate income for each beneficiary until they reach the age of 25 and thereafter each beneficiary is absolutely entitled to an appropriate share of the trust fund.

The value of the trust property (all chargeable) when the trust was set up was £50,000 and on 31 January 1995 when the eldest grandchild attained the age of 25, the trust property had a market value of £200,000. One quarter of the property was transferred finally on 30 June 1995.

The date of disposal for capital gains purposes would be 31 January 1995. The computation would take one quarter of £200,000 as the disposal value and one quarter of £50,000 as the base cost. The capital gains liability at 35% (after indexation and after annual exemption £2,900) would be deducted from the beneficiary's share of the property prior to transfer.

Residence

The trustees, for purposes of capital gains tax, are treated as a single body separate and distinct from the persons who from time to time may be trustees. This body is treated as resident and ordinarily resident in the UK unless the administration of the trust is normally carried on outside the UK and the trustees, or a majority of them were not resident and ordinarily resident in the UK.

Until FA 1991, there was no penalty if the residence of the trustees and thus the trust subsequently changed. The Finance Act 1991 introduced a capital gains tax charge where the trustees of a settlement cease to be resident in the UK (see above).

Note that a general understanding of the concept of residence for trusts is important, but residence of trusts is not examinable.

Inheritance tax

Trusts with an interest in possession

The life tenants of these trusts are regarded as being entitled to the underlying capital value of the trust property in proportion to their interests in the income.

On the death of a life tenant, there is a chargeable transfer of the underlying capital value. (See Chapter 9 for the principles of valuation to be applied.) This is included in the life tenant's estate on death to determine the 'estate rate' (see also Chapter 9). However, the inheritance tax liability on that part of the tenant's estate is payable by the trustees out of the trust assets. An annuitant's interest in the underlying trust assets is taken as equivalent to settled property which would produce income equal to the amount of the annuity – usually this would be the same proportion of trust assets as the annuity is of trust income. There may be circumstances in which this is capable of manipulation to the detriment of one or other of the parties involved (for example, where there is more than one interest in an interest in possession trust and they do not terminate simultaneously). The legislation therefore sets parameters for the determination of acceptable rates of return.

- Minimum – the gross dividend yield of the All-Share Index.
- Maximum – the irredeemables yield of Fixed Interest Securities.

EXAMPLE 14.5

An interest in possession trust provides for an annuity of £4,000 to be paid to Joan and the balance to be paid to Bob.

i) If the trust income over the past year was £12,000 and the fund was valued at £120,000 and both Joan and Bob's interest terminated simultaneously the trust would be split –   Joan 1/3 (4,000/12,000)
   Bob 2/3 (8,000/12,000)
   There is no need for special rules as the whole fund is changing hands.

ii) Only Joan's interest terminated.
   Assume   Minimum – 8%
              Maximum – 12%
   Trust fund – actual yield 10% (12,000/120,000 × 100%)

   If the trustees wished to minimise the value of Joan's annuity, they would have invested in high yield assets to reduce her proportion of the total trust income: it is therefore the 'maximum' which should be used.
   Joan's share will therefore be the greater of:

   a) $\frac{4,000}{12,000} \times 120,000$, that is £40,000 as above

   b) The annuity £4,000 capitalised at the maximum, that is $\frac{4,000}{12\%} = 33,333$

iii) Only Bob's interest terminated.
   If the trustees wish to minimise Bob's share, they would invest in low yield assets, increasing Joan's share of the total trust income: it is therefore the 'minimum' which should be used.
   Bob's share will be the greater of:

   a) $\frac{8,000}{12,000} \times 120,000$, that is £80,000 as above

   b) The fund (£120,000) less annuity (£4,000) capitalised at the minimum, that is
   $£120,000 - \frac{4,000}{8\%} = £70,000$

If the life tenant ceases to be entitled to the income in his or her lifetime, and either it:

- passes to another person for life
- passes to another person absolutely
- is transferred into an accumulation and maintenance trust or a trust for the disabled

then the transfer will be potentially exempt (a PET). Tax will only become chargeable if the life tenant dies within seven years. Again, the tax will be calculated according to the life tenant's cumulative position but the liability will be payable by the trustees out of the trust assets. Quick succession relief is available to the trustees where there are successive charges on the trust property within five years (see Chapter 9).

Discretionary trusts

For purposes of inheritance tax, accumulation and maintenance trusts and trusts for the disabled are distinguished from other discretionary trusts and receive favoured treatment (see below).

Because discretionary trusts are not linked to the life of any person, the charge to inheritance tax cannot be triggered by the death of a chargeable person. Therefore, separate provisions exist in inheritance tax to charge to tax 'relevant property' in order to prevent inheritance tax avoidance.

A transfer of property into a settlement with no interest in possession generally gives rise to a chargeable transfer of value and therefore to a charge to inheritance tax on the settlor.

Thereafter, there is: a) a **principal charge** at ten-yearly intervals on property still held in the settlement: and b) a charge for a proportionate part of the ten years since the previous charge, whenever property leaves the settlement or on termination of the trust – an **exit charge**.

Principal charge

Tax is charged at 30% of the 'effective rate'. Where any of the property in the trust has not been relevant property for the whole ten year period, the tax is reduced by 1/40 for each complete quarter (three months) which expired before the property became relevant property.

The effective rate is determined by expressing the tax chargeable using lifetime rates (half the death scale) on an assumed chargeable transfer of the whole of the trust property at each tenth anniversary as a percentage of the assumed chargeable transfer. This will be a maximum of 20% (1994/95) and therefore the maximum charge on a ten-year anniversary cannot exceed 6% (30% of 20%).

The starting point for the trust is the aggregate of:

- the cumulative gross transfers of the settlor in the seven years prior to the creation of the trust
- the amounts on which any exit charges have been made in the ten years to the current anniversary.

To this is added an assumed chargeable transfer approximately equal to the value of the relevant property at the tenth anniversary.

Inheritance tax is calculated on the assumed chargeable transfer at the appropriate point on the scale, based on rates applicable to lifetime transfers at the date of the tenth anniversary.

EXAMPLE 14.6

A settlor created a discretionary trust on 15 September 1984, transferring assets valued at £100,000. His gross transfers of value in the seven years immediately prior to the transfer amounted to £80,000 and he had used all his available exemptions to date. The trustees paid the capital transfer tax arising of £12,000.

At 15 September 1994, the value of the trust assets was £200,000. Calculate the principal charge.

	Gross £	Tax £
At 15 September 1984 brought forward	80,000	
At 15 September 1994 assumed transfer	200,000	26,000
(70,000 @ Nil = Nil		
130,000 @ 20% = 26,000)		
		26,000

Effective rate $\dfrac{26,000}{200,000} \times 100 = 13\%$

Rate of principal charge $30\% \times 13\% = 3.9\%$

Principal charge £200,000 × 3.9% — 7,800

Exit charge

An exit charge arises where property ceases to be relevant property or where the trustees make a disposition out of relevant property.

Tax is charged on the amount by which the value of the relevant property is reduced (the grossing up principle applies where the trust pays the tax).

The rate of tax is the rate which is applied to the principal charge at the latest tenth anniversary (or which would have been calculated on commencement of the trust if the disposition takes place before the first tenth anniversary), adjusted to treat property added to the trust since that date as if held in the trust at the tenth anniversary and recomputed where there has been a change in rates since the tenth anniversary. The rate is then multiplied by 1/40 for each complete quarter (three months) from the date of the most recent principal charge to the date of the disposition.

EXAMPLE 14.7 (Example 14.6 continued)

On 15 March 1995, the trustees make a distribution of £15,000 to one of the beneficiaries, the trustees to pay the tax.

Calculate the inheritance tax liability arising.

Rate of latest principal charge	3.9%	
Rate applying to distribution: 3.9% × 2/40	0.195%	
Exit charge £15,000 × $\dfrac{0.195}{100 - 0.195}$		£29.31

As the trustees are to pay the tax, this is effectively the 'grossing-up' calculation.

EXAMPLE 14.8

A settlor, with cumulative transfers to date of £120,000, settled £100,000 into a discretionary trust on 25 December 1993. The settlor paid the inheritance tax due. On 30 September 1994, £20,000 of trust funds left the trust (an exit charge became due).

	Gross £	Tax £	Net £
Settlors cumulative total b/f	120,000		
Funds settled	117,500	17,500	100,000
Total c/f	237,500	17,500	100,000

(30,000 @ Nil
70,000 @ 20/80 = 17,500)

Rate of tax for exit charges within the next 10 years

$$\frac{17,500}{117,500} \times 100 \times 30\% = 4.47\%$$

Number of complete quarters till funds left trust = 3

Exit charge: $\frac{3}{40} \times 4.47 \times 20,000 = £67$ payable out of trust funds

---

Relevant property

Relevant property is property other than excluded property held in all trusts in which there is no qualifying interest in possession other than certain special trusts, the principal examples of which are accumulation and maintenance trusts, and charitable trusts.

Qualifying interest in possession

A qualifying interest in possession is an interest in possession to which an individual is beneficially entitled or to which a company is beneficially entitled. (This is provided that the business of the company is principally the acquisition of interests in settled property and that it acquired the interest for full consideration from an individual beneficially entitled to it.)

Accumulation and maintenance trusts

Transfers into these trusts are PETs, and there is no subsequent charge to inheritance tax on the trust assets either on a capital distribution or when the beneficiary becomes absolutely entitled or gets an interest in possession. There are a number of conditions to be satisfied:

▶ The beneficiary must become absolutely entitled or get an interest in possession before attaining the age of 25.
▶ No interest in possession must currently exist in the property.
▶ *Either* not more than 25 years must have elapsed since the trust was created *or* all the beneficiaries must have a common grandparent.

Tax planning

The planning opportunities for interest in possession trusts exist where there is a need to transfer wealth without transferring control. The settlor can be the first-named trustee (retaining voting control) but can effectively pass on his or her wealth.

There is no real scope for tax planning with an interest in possession trust as all the income is appropriated to the life tenants on an annual basis. Where the beneficiary has unused personal reliefs, it is more efficient to arrange for income to be paid direct to the beneficiary, since trust income is depleted by trust expenses (paid out of net income). This should probably be compared with a marginal rate of 40% if the settlement had not been made. A capital gains tax charge arises to the trust whenever a chargeable disposal is regarded as having been made – albeit at a flat rate of 25%. (If the settlor settles property on him or herself in an interest in possession trust, the capital gains like the income are deemed to be the settlor's own personal gains.) For inheritance tax purposes the underlying capital of the trust is regarded as part of the life tenant's estates, and suffers tax accordingly.

A discretionary trust is not in theory a device for mitigating tax liabilities – its purpose is to allow a person to set aside property such that the income and capital beneficiaries can be determined as appropriate in the light of future events. However, in the past, such substantial tax savings resulted from their use that they became associated with the term 'tax avoidance'. The tax regime has since been tightened up in respect of discretionary trusts and only special categories retain favourable tax treatment. The income tax rate and capital gains tax rate are marginally lower than the individual's top rates.

The inheritance tax position is unattractive since the cumulative transfers of the settlor when the trust is created are never lost throughout the life of the settlement and will directly or indirectly affect the calculation of the tax liability whenever an inheritance tax charge arises. On the other hand, a transfer into a discretionary trust by a settlor who had made no previous chargeable transfers up to £150,000 (the nil band), would not attract inheritance tax. Also, provided both the property and nil band increase in line with inflation, it would not subsequently attract inheritance tax.

An accumulation and maintenance trust is an example of a trust which still receives favourable treatment as regards inheritance tax. It is ideally suited to grandparents and parents. At the time of settlement it is a PET and will escape inheritance tax if the settlor survives seven years. If the settlor does not survive seven years, the value of the transfer will be the value at the date of the original gift and taper relief will be available.

Summary

- There are two principal categories of trust – trusts with an interest in possession and discretionary trusts.
- Interest in possession trusts:
  - Income tax – the trustees are charged to basic rate tax on all trust income (except dividends charged at 20%) with no allowance for expenses and no personal reliefs. All income is allocated to beneficiaries each fiscal year and is treated as having suffered 20/25% tax at source.
  - Capital gains tax – a flat rate of 25% is payable on a chargeable disposal of trust assets (after annual exemption of £2,900). Note that the termination of a life interest will be treated as a disposal of trust assets.
  - Inheritance tax – the underlying capital is regarded as part of the estate of the life tenant. A lifetime transfer of the life interest will be a PET while a chargeable transfer will arise on the death of the life tenant.

▶ Discretionary trusts:
  - Income tax – the trustees are charged to tax at 35% on all trust income remaining after expenses. There are no personal reliefs but trust expenses are deductible firstly from dividend income which has been taxed at 20% at source and secondly from other income (taxed at 25% at source). Any income paid to beneficiaries is treated as having suffered tax at 35% at source.
  - Capital gains tax – a flat rate of 35% is payable on a chargeable disposal of trust assets (after annual exemption of £2,900). A capital distribution of trust assets will be a chargeable disposal.
  - Inheritance tax (except accumulation and maintenance trusts) – this is complex and depends upon the position of the settlor. Charges arise at ten-yearly intervals and whenever funds leave the trust; the rate is 30% of the lifetime scale (that is a maximum of 6%).
▶ Accumulation and maintenance trusts (inheritance tax) – there is no ten-yearly charge and no charge when a distribution is made to a beneficiary.

Self test questions

1 What rate of income tax applies to the trustees of a discretionary trust?

2 Explain what expenses, if any, are deductible in a discretionary trust?

3 What conditions must an accumulation and maintenance trust satisfy to qualify for favourable treatment for inheritance tax?

4 What charges to inheritance tax apply to discretionary trusts?

5 What anti-avoidance provisions exist for income tax purposes as regards income from trusts?

6 In 1984, A created a discretionary trust for his children, Alan and Alison. He transferred a portfolio of shares to the trustees to a total value of £200,000.

   In 1988, the trustees allocated half of the share portfolio (worth £150,000) to Alan for life – on his death the remainder was to be shared between his three children provided they reached the age of 25.

   In 1989, the remaining half of the share portfolio was transferred to Alison (worth £200,000).

   Alan died in 1994. Advise the trustees as to the tax consequences of the above events.

Answers on pages 575–576

Question Bank – Personal Taxation and Financial Planning

1   Deborah, an acquaintance of yours, living in the north of England, is studying to qualify as a quantity surveyor. She will sit her final examination in nine months' time. She has recently applied for a job in London, and has received the following letter inviting her for interview:

5th December 1993

Dear Ms Taylor,

I refer to your recent letter and would like to invite you for an interview on 3 January 1994 at 2.00pm.

For your information, the salary payable to persons studying for their final examinations is in the region of £13,000 per annum. In addition the firm:
- operates an approved superannuation contributory pension scheme;
- supplies a company car, part of the cost of which you would be expected to meet;
- has a canteen open to all staff supplying meals free of charge;
- operates a suggestion scheme under which payments can be made to employees;
- reimburses expenditure incurred on business entertaining.

Should we make you an offer of employment, we would be prepared to meet your removal expenses, and allow you to occupy a furnished flat, owned by the firm for the first two years of your employment. At the end of that period we would offer you a loan, not exceeding £40,000 at a low rate of interest, to assist in purchasing a property, plus a further £5,000 on the same terms towards the costs of furnishing it.

Yours sincerely
Abbott & Co

a) Prepare for Deborah, prior to her interview, notes explaining concisely the taxation position on each part of the above employment package.

Subsequent to her interview, Deborah receives the following letter from Abbott & Co:

9 January 1994

Dear Ms Taylor,

Further to your recent interview, we are pleased to offer you a position with our firm at a salary of £13,750 per annum. You will be required to contribute six per cent of your salary into the firm's superannuation fund, the firm contributing a further four per cent of your salary on your behalf.

Lunchtime meals will be available free of charge in the firm's canteen – at a cost to the firm of £800 per annum per employee – and your annual membership of the BUPA private medical scheme of £260 will also be met by the firm.

You will have sole use of a 1600cc Maestro car, acquired new on 1 January 1990, for a junior manager at a cost of £7,200. Its current value is £4,000. As your mileage in carrying out your employment duties is not expected to exceed 1,500 miles per annum you will be required to pay for your private petrol in full. However, your business petrol, estimated at £80 per annum, and servicing and other running expenses estimated at £1,200 per annum will be met by the firm, although you will contribute £20 per month for the private use of the car.

For the first two years of employment you can live rent-free in a flat owned by the firm which cost £40,000, two years ago, and has a current value of £70,000 (gross rateable value £500). The firm also pays the cleaning costs of £320 per annum but heating bills estimated at £650 per annum will be paid by you.

The flat was furnished two years ago at a cost of £4,800, the furniture having a current value of £3,000. A new video, TV and music system has recently been installed at a cost of £700.

You will be expected to pay your own professional body subscriptions of £70 per annum together with membership costs of £120 per annum at the City Club, at which you are likely to make a number of useful business contacts. In addition, you are likely to have to spend £200 on professional clothing suited to your position, though the firm will pay for your evening course fees of £120 and examination fees of £80 for your final examination.

The cost of selling your house etc, and moving your possessions to London, estimated at £1,500, will be reimbursed by the firm, though the monthly travel costs of £60 to visit your family you will bear.

TAX PLANNING

During July and August you will be required to spend six weeks in Spain surveying a number of holiday complexes. Your travel costs of £250, together with your weekly hotel bills of £140 per week and a special BUPA private medical premium of £60 to cover you whilst overseas, will all be met by the firm. I understand that at the end of the six weeks you wish to stay in Spain for two weeks holiday, in which case, the additional hotel bills of £280 will be payable by you.

We look forward to hearing from you.

b) Assuming that Deborah accepts the above offer of employment, and commences on 1 April 1994, estimate her income assessable under Schedule E for 1994/95, stating clearly your treatment of each item, whether taxable or not.

2 Your client, Charles, a wealthy widower, is a director and majority shareholder in a large unquoted trading company.

His wife had died suddenly and unexpectedly six months ago, leaving her estate comprising shares in quoted companies, life assurance policies, cash, jewellery and personal possessions valued in total at £95,000, to Charles.

Though aged only 62 Charles is considering retiring within the next year or so. He is also considering disposing of some of his assets, either by sale or possibly by gift, but is undecided whether to dispose of them during his lifetime or by will on his death.

Taxation will be a major factor influencing his decisions regarding the disposition of his assets, and he has clearly stated that he wishes to minimise any tax liability arising.

He has estimated his total estate to have a value of approximately £540,000, including the £95,000 left to him by his deceased wife.

Included in his estate is:

a) His 70% shareholding, in the unquoted family trading company, valued at £140,000.
b) His 28% shareholding in an unquoted company, which supplies the family company, valued at £60,000.
c) Quoted shares valued at £108,000.
d) His private residence valued at £95,000.
e) A plot of land on which he and his wife had planned to build a bungalow for their retirement, valued at £20,000.
f) A life assurance policy on his life with a market value of £40,000 and a surrender value of £36,000.
g) Furniture, jewellery and other chattels with a total value of £25,000, the highest value item being valued at £2,500.
h) Cash at bank, building society and at home – total value £24,000. Private motor car valued at £9,000.

He has one daughter and two grandsons, one of whom joined him last year in the family company. He has also developed a considerable interest in Heartbeat (UK), a registered charity.

He appreciates that capital gains taxes could arise on the disposal of his assets but is confused about the difference between capital gains tax and inheritance tax.

You are required to prepare a concise report for Charles:

a) summarising, for both taxes:
   i) the events giving rise to a charge
   ii) the amount chargeable
   iii) the rates of tax
   iv) some common exemptions and reliefs
   v) whether phasing of disposals is advantageous
   vi) the advantages/disadvantages of lifetime disposals as compared to a transfer on death
   vii) the benefits, if any, of Charles emigrating.
b) suggesting action he might take and disposals he might make during his lifetime which would result in a nil or small tax liability, and which would reduce the tax payable on his eventual death.

3 You are the tax adviser to Ms Needle, who is single and aged 66, who is in uncertain health (you should assume that she will die at some time within the next ten years). She owns 80% of the ordinary share capital of Mildew Ltd, a private trading company which is currently undergoing a rapid increase in profitability. Ms Needle is a full-time director of the company. The current market value of her shares is estimated at £370,000

The summarised balance sheet of Mildew Ltd at today's date (which you should assume is 1 January 1995) is as follows:

	£	£
Buildings	160,000	
Plant and machinery	30,000	
		190,000
Investments (quoted shares)		80,000
		270,000
Working capital		30,000
		300,000
Financed by: Ordinary shares		1,000
Reserves		299,000
		300,000

All the assets are shown at their current valuations, except for goodwill which is valued at £100,000. Plant and machinery consists of various items, none of which cost in excess of £5,000 or is currently valued in excess of £2,000.

The rebased cost of Ms Needle's shares in Mildew Ltd for CGT purposes, including any indexation allowance due, is £14,000. Ms Needle subscribed for her shares on 1 June 1975, at which time she took up her directorship. Ms Needle has incurred capital losses in previous years of £50,000.

Ms Needle made a cash gift of £107,000 to her grandson, Mr Simper, on the occasion of his marriage on 1 February 1994. Ms Needle had made no previous transfers of assets, and owns several valuable assets apart from her shares in Mildew Ltd. She wishes to transfer her shares in Mildew Ltd to Mr Simper, but she is uncertain whether to gift them to him or to bequeath them to him in her will. Mr Simper would be responsible for IHT (if any) on a gift.

Mr Simper, who is aged 30, intends to retain the shares in Mildew Ltd as an investment but would probably sell them once he had reached the age of 65. Mr Simper is currently earning £48,000 per annum as an executive. He intends to leave his present job and to become involved in the management of Mildew Ltd once he acquires the shares in the company.

a) Describe the CGT and IHT implications arising if:
  i) Ms Needle were to make an outright gift of the shares immediately to Mr Simper. Include a discussion of what would happen if she were to die in the next ten years.
  ii) Ms Needle were to bequeath the shares to Mr Simper and she died on 31 March 1996. Assume that all available reliefs will be claimed. You should take into account Mr Simper's long-term tax position following his acquisition of the shares.
b) State whether you consider from a tax viewpoint that Ms Needle should i) make an outright gift, or ii) bequeath the share to Mr Simper. Give reasons for your conclusions. You should again take into account Mr Simper's long-term tax position.

4 Mr Gog, who was born in Ruritania in 1932, came to live and work in Scotland in May 1979. Mr Gog, whose wife has died, hopes to return to Ruritania when he is 70. Mr Gog is in good health.

Details of Mr Gog's assets and liabilities at today's date (which you should assume is 5 April 1995), together with their current market values, are as follows:

	£
Deposit account with National Bank of Ruritania (held with branch in Glob, the capital of Ruritania)	60,000
Current account with UK bank held in Glasgow	23,000
Private residence (located in Scotland)	127,000
10,000 shares in Bah plc, an investment company quoted on the UK Stock Exchange with a total issued share capital of 5,000,000 shares	150,000
3.5% War Loan Government Stock, Nominal value £80,000	27,000
Ruritanian antique kept in private residence	6,000
Scottish farm acquired in January 1980 and occupied since that date by farming tenants. Mr Gog has the right to obtain vacant position with six months if he so wishes	116,000
	509,000
Less: Building society mortgage loan on private residence (12% fixed rate – paid under MIRAS)	(40,000)
	469,000

Further information is available as follows:

i) On 1 June 1994 Mr Gog disposed of an investment property located in Ruritania. The disposal gave rise to a 'no gain, no loss' position for CGT purposes.

ii) Mr Gog had let out the property continuously for many years at a rent of £300 per month (gross) payable at the end of each month. The rents were subject to Ruritanian tax at a rate of 20%. Ruritania does not have a double tax treaty with the UK. Mr Gog transferred £200 of his rental income each month to Scotland, any balance remaining being lodged to his Ruritanian bank account.

iii) Mr Gog acquired his shares in Bah plc for £20,000 in August 1985. Mr Gog has not received any dividends from Bah plc since he acquired the shares.

iv) Mr Gog acquired the 3.5% War Loan Stock for £25,400 in January 1993.

v) Mr Gog acquired the antique for £5,000 in April 1990.

vi) Due to the availability of previous years' losses, no taxable income has arisen from the farmland for several years. The farmland was acquired in January 1980 at a cost of £95,000 and had a market value of £40,000 at 31 March 1982. Mr Gog has decided not to make an election to treat all of his assets held prior to 31 March 1982 as having been sold and re-acquired on that date.

vii) Interest credited to the Ruritanian bank deposit account has been as follows:
  Year ended 5/4/94: £2,000
  Year ended 5/4/95: £1,500
  These amounts are net of Ruritanian tax of 10%. No amounts of this interest were brought back into the UK.

viii) Mr Gog's gross salary for the year ended 5 April 1995 was £29,350, which was subject to PAYE of £7,500.
ix) Mr Gog is anxious to transfer some assets, other than his private residence, to his son Enrico. Enrico, who is 23, was born in Scotland and intends to remain there for the rest of his life. Enrico is keen to manage the farm in Scotland. Mr Gog would like to transfer assets to Enrico as quickly as possible. Mr Gog is, however, not prepared to make transfers which could give rise to IHT liabilities if he were to die within the next seven years. He understands that he may be able to avoid such liabilities by making transfers of 'excluded property' as well as using his 'nil rate band'. Mr Gog is also not prepared to make transfers of assets which would give rise to CGT liabilities. He intends to leave the balance of assets retained by him to a charity under his will.
x) Mr Gog has made no previous transfers of assets.

a) Compute Mr Gog's income tax liability for 1994/95.
b) Explain to Mr Gog his likely present domicile status for IHT purposes, and why this may alter in future years.
c) Advise Mr Gog as to which of his assets he should transfer on 5 April 1995. Show all supporting calculations. You should assume that Mr Gog is non-UK domiciled for IHT purposes at 5 April 1995.
d) Assuming that Mr Gog follows your advice under (c), describe the IHT consequences of his dying before 6 April 2002.

5 You have been asked to provide tax advice at today's date (which you should assume to be 1 February 1995) to the personal representatives of Richard. Richard was aged 65 and died on 2 November 1994, leaving the following assets:

	Probate value £	Current value £
1,000 shares in Bluechip plc (a quoted company with a share capital of 2,000,000 shares)	22,000	17,000
2,500 shares in Giltedge plc (a quoted company with a share capital of 3,000,000 shares)	15,000	20,000
6,000 shares in Nobody Ltd (a private investment company with a share capital of 100,000 shares)	39,000	30,000
Private residence	190,000	230,000
Holiday home	55,000	40,000
	321,000	337,000

Potential selling costs are estimated at 2% of sale price in respect of each asset.
Richard had made the following transfers prior to his death:

i) Annual gifts of £3,000 made out of capital to his nephew, Oscar on 6 April of each year.
ii) A gift of £90,000 cash to a discretionary trust on 3 September 1985. All taxes on the gift were borne by the trustees.
iii) A gift of £111,000 cash to his son Boris on his marriage on 1 September 1991.
iv) A gift of 4 hectares of farmland to his son, Christian on 1 July 1992. The land was valued at £150,000 and was subject to a mortgage of £55,000. Richard had occupied the land and farmed it since January 1985. Christian sold the land to an unconnected third party on 11 October 1994 for £120,000. He used the proceeds to pay off the mortgage and also to buy himself a yacht.

In his will Richard left all his assets to his sons Boris and Christian. He appointed his brother Nigel as his executor. He was confident that his sons would look after his widow, Maria, who is aged 73 and owns no assets in her own right. Maria is in very poor health and is not expected to live much longer.

a) Calculate the IHT arising as a result of Richard's death.
b) Explain whether the IHT arising could be reduced by disposing of all or any of Richard's assets before winding up his estate. Indicate any possible disadvantage in such a course of action.
c) Explain whether it would be advisable from an IHT viewpoint to alter the terms of Richard's will. Outline the conditions which must be satisfied for such an alteration to be valid for IHT purposes.
d) Describe briefly Nigel's responsibilities as executor for making returns in respect of IHT on his brother's estate. State when any IHT due should be paid in order to avoid interest charges, bearing in mind the availability of instalment relief. Explain who becomes liable if Nigel fails to account for the IHT due to the Inland Revenue.

6 Hubert Bright, who is aged 44 and for whom you act as tax adviser, had over the years acquired 3,000 £1 ordinary shares in Bod Limited, an unquoted trading company with an issued share capital of 5,000 ordinary shares. All the assets of Bod Limited are in use for the purpose of its trade. Mr Bright is a full-time working director of the company. His wife, Rose, also owns 1,000 ordinary shares in the company.
Hubert had acquired his shares as follows:

	No	£
6/9/76	1,200	1,000
1/11/83	1,200	1,800
18/8/85	600	3,000

The value of a holding of 1,200 shares at 31 March 1982 was £4,000.

The current market value attributable to various percentage shareholdings in Bod Limited is estimated as follows:

% Shareholding	Value of £1 ordinary share
100	40.50
80	36.67
60	25.00
40	18.00
Below 40	16.00

On 5 April 1995 Mr Bright sold 2,000 of his shares in Bod Limited for £10,000 to his daughter Maxine who intends to retain them for the foreseeable future.

He had made no previous transfer of assets other than an assignment of a lease to a discretionary trust (which was not an accumulation and maintenance trust and did not include Mr Bright as a beneficiary) on 1 May 1994. The lease had cost him £100,000 on 31 March 1981, at which time it had exactly 48 years left to run. The value of the lease on 31 March 1982 was £120,000 and on 1 May 1994 was £210,000. Mr Bright had agreed to bear any costs or taxes in respect of the assignment of the lease. Apart from his shares in Bod Limited Mr Bright currently has no other assets apart from cash of £40,000. He has left everything in his will to his son Roger. You should assume that today's date is 6 April 1995.

a) Advise Mr Bright of his potential inheritance tax and capital gains tax liabilities for 1994/95.
b) Describe to him any claims for relief which he could make to reduce these liabilities, based on the facts stated above.
c) Advise Mr Bright on the inheritance tax implications which would arise if he were to die on 20 April 1995. Assume that the rates and bands of inheritance tax remain at 1994/95 levels throughout.
d) Set out the dates for any inheritance tax payable if Mr Bright were to die on 20 April 1995 and indicate where such tax may be payable by instalments.

7   At today's date (which you should assume is 1 July 1994), George Rowe, a single man aged 42, is expected to earn £65.000 from his employment as an oil company executive for the year ended 5 April 1995 (subject to PAYE of £19,708). Of this amount £5,000 will represent profit-related pay under a scheme approved by the Inland Revenue. During the year George expects to receive net dividends of £24,000 from his shareholdings.

On 6 April 1994, George had sold quoted shares in a multinational company Gong plc, which realised a capital gain of £90,000. He also intends to transfer further shares in Gong plc, with a value of £160,000, into a trust for his brother Bob, on 5 April 1995. This transfer will realise a further capital gain of £35,000. Bob is aged 12 and lives with George who has maintained him since the death of their parents in 1987. George is unsure whether the trust for Bob should be an accumulation and maintenance trust or a discretionary trust (of which George would not be a beneficiary). George has made no previous transfers of any assets. He will pay any taxes or costs associated with setting up the trust. George is in excellent health.

George had acquired a house in Derby, together with grounds of 0.3 hectare on 1 August 1981 for £280,000. The house is subject to a mortgage from a building society of £100,000, bearing a fixed rate of interest of 10% per annum. The interest is payable under the MIRAS scheme. There was no change in the value of the house up to 31 March 1982. The house is currently worth £550,000. George's history of occupation of the house is as follows:

1/8/81 – 30/6/82	Occupied
1/7/82 – 31/12/84	Sent by employer to Saudi Arabia
1/1/85 – 30/9/87	Occupied
1/10/87 – present	Working in various parts of the UK on an extended three-year tour of duty.

George intends to sell the house on 31 December 1994 but is unsure whether or not he should reoccupy the house between 1 October 1994 (when his UK tour of duty ends) and 31 December 1994. He will rent a flat in Brighton from 1 January 1995 at a rent of £400 per month, payable in advance, from a friend of his who lives in the USA.

a) Discuss the current *and* potential CGT and IHT implications for George of setting up (i) an accumulation and maintenance trust for Bob; (ii) a discretionary trust for Bob.
b) Compute George's income tax liabilities for 1994/95.
c) Discuss whether George should occupy the house in Derby between 1 October 1994 and 31 December 1994. Show all supporting calculations.

8   Andrew and Betty Cloud, aged 53 and 50 respectively, are the principal shareholders and are full-time working directors of ABC Ltd, an unquoted trading company. The share capital of ABC Ltd consists of 50,000 issued £1 ordinary shares, of which Andrew owns 20,000 and Betty 10,000. Their daughter Debbie has recently been made a director of ABC Ltd, and the couple have decided to make her a gift of

10,000 of their shares on 31 January 1995. The value of ABC Ltd's shares agreed by the Inland Revenue is as follows:

Shareholding	Value per share
	£
20%	7
40%	10
60%	21
80%	24

Andrew originally acquired 6,000 shares at par on 1 January 1980, the date of ABC Ltd's incorporation, and purchased a further 4,000 shares on 15 April 1987 for £12,000. On 1 January 1989 ABC Ltd had a 1 for 1 rights issue at the market value at that date of £4 per share which Andrew took up in full. The market value of ABC Ltd's shares at 31 March 1982 was £2 per share.

Betty's shares had originally been acquired by her father upon ABC Ltd's incorporation. She inherited them when she died on 30 June 1988, the shares being included in his estate at a value of £35,000. Betty did not take up her entitlement in the rights issue, but sold her rights to another director for £1,000.

Andrew and Betty had not made any previous transfers of value for inheritance tax purposes.

a) i) Calculate the chargeable gain if Andrew makes the gift of 10,000 ABC Ltd shares to Debbie.
   ii) Calculate the chargeable gain if Betty makes the gift of 10,000 ABC Ltd shares to Debbie.
b) i) Calculate the inheritance tax liability in respect of the ABC Ltd shares if Andew makes the gift to Debbie, and was then to die within the following three years.
   ii) Calculate the inheritance tax liability in respect of the ABC Ltd shares if Betty makes the gift to Debbie, and was then to die within the following three years.

You should assume that the present inheritance tax rates and reliefs apply into the future.

(ACCA December 1992)

Answers on pages 576–589

CHAPTER 15

The Taxation of Profits from Trades, Professions and Vocations

This chapter looks at the criteria used to establish whether a business is being carried on and if so, how the profits for that business are computed and assessed to income tax. The greater part of the subject matter has already been covered by you in your Paper 7 syllabus, the aim here is to provide some revision and to develop a more in-depth understanding of the taxation of business profits.

Definition of trade

The annual profits or gains arising from any trade, profession or vocation are charged to tax under ICTA 1988, s. 18(3). Schedule D Case I applies to profits arising from a trade and Schedule D Case II applies to the profits arising from the exercise of any profession or vocation. The rules set out under Schedule D Cases I and II are identical and therefore from most points of view the distinctions between a trade, profession and vocation are relatively unimportant and will be treated as such hereafter.

It is first of all necessary to consider the definition of a trade in order to establish if one is being carried on, and then to consider if there are annual profits or gains from that trade to be charged to tax. It should be noted that annual profits or gains arising other than from a trade, profession or vocation (and not falling to be taxed under any other Schedule or Case) will be taxed under Schedule D Case VI. Similarly, profits or gains whether made by a trade or not, not being annual profits or gains, may be charged to tax elsewhere (to capital gains tax, for example).

The distinction between these various forms of profits or gains needs to be clearly understood. Incorrect classification could be costly in terms of the eventual tax liability, since the rules set out for the computation of profits under Schedule D Case VI and capital gains tax are substantially different from Schedule D Cases I and II.

Trade

The word 'trade' is defined as including 'every trade, manufacture, adventure or concern in the nature of trade'.

The definition is very broad and includes transactions which are not part of a trading operation but which may themselves be regarded as an adventure 'in the nature of trade'.

Is a trade carried on?

There is a substantial body of case law on the subject of whether or not a trade exists. The major considerations established by the courts, to identify whether a trade was being carried on, were summarised as long ago as 1955 by the Royal Commission on the Taxation of Profits and Income into what are now known as the 'badges of trade'.

The badges of trade

The subject matter of the realisation

Any asset may be the subject of trading, but certain types of asset (shares, jewellery, works of art) are more frequently purchased for reasons other than sale at a profit. Assets which do not yield income or personal enjoyment by virtue of ownership are more likely to have been acquired for resale. For example, the purchase and resale of a large quantity of toilet rolls was ruled adventure in the nature of trade (*Rutledge* v. *CIR*, 1929) since they were not for 'own use' or an investment.

The length of the period of ownership

In general, assets which are the subject of trading are realised within a short time of acquisition.

The frequency or number of similar transactions

If transactions in similar types of assets occur in succession over a period of years or several such transactions take place at or about one time, there is a presumption that a trade is being carried on. This does not mean that an isolated transaction cannot be the subject of trading, merely that the probability of a trade being carried on is greater, the more acquisitions/realisations of similar assets there are. An example would be the profit from a series of purchases and sales of cotton mills in *Pickford* v. *Quirke*, 1927.

Supplementary work on or in connection with the property realised

If the asset is modified or in any way made more marketable during ownership (processing, renovation or packaging, for example), there is some evidence of trading. Similarly, the efforts made to market the asset can be relevant – large-scale advertising, the opening of an office or the employment of salesmen. The purchase of a quantity of South African brandy for shipping to the UK where it was subsequently blended and re-casked for resale was held to amount to a trade (*Cape Brandy Syndicate* v. *CIR*, 1921).

The circumstances that were responsible for the realisation

There may be an explanation for the transactions which negates all other evidence of trading, for example an opportunity or an emergency which required ready cash.

Motive

A profit-seeking motive is enough to establish that a trade is being carried on. However, where this is not admitted (for example, the taxpayer is claiming that the asset was acquired for personal enjoyment) the motive may be inferred from the surrounding circumstances – unless direct evidence of the purpose behind the acquisition and disposal can be established.

Acquisition by gift or inheritance would normally be sufficient to infer that there was no trading motive. The acquisition of a large quantity of silver bullion, on the other hand, was held to be an adventure in the nature of trade (*Wisdom* v. *Chamberlain*, 1969).

Other factors

In addition to these badges of trade there are other factors to be taken into account:

- The way in which the asset was acquired. The subsequent disposal of an asset inherited or acquired by gift is very unlikely to be regarded as trading.

- The trade, profession or vocation of the taxpayer. Transactions in a similar field could lead to a profit-seeking motive being inferred in these transactions.
- The method of finance. Where a loan is arranged to purchase an asset and its repayment is beyond the normal means of the taxpayer, it is likely that the asset will be sold to repay the loan or the loan will be repaid out of the sale proceeds. There is clearly a trading intent.

There is a large body of case law on this subject which may be referred to, to gain a wider perspective. The following leading cases will be found in the sources quoted in the Preface.

Martin v. *Lowry*
Pickford v. *Quirke*
Wisdom v. *Chamberlain*

Annual profits or gains of trade

Receipts that, by definition, are taxable under another Schedule or Case cannot be trading profits. Even when it has been established that a trade exists, not all receipts will be profits or gains of the trade. Accounts prepared for a trader will not necessarily correspond with the profits assessable under Schedule D Case I or II.

Gambling and illegal activities

The profits of gambling and illegal activities have been the subject of a number of cases and the general principles decided are as follows:

- The profits of the 'punter' are not assessable.
- The profits of the bookmaker are assessable.
- The profits of illegal activities are assessable although the Inland Revenue have not made a habit in the past of assessing such profits to tax.

More than one trade

A single taxpayer may have more than one trade, and therefore an isolated transaction which is not part of the existing trading operation may itself be a separate adventure in the nature of a trade.

Non-recurrent receipts

It may be argued that particular receipts being of an unusual nature are not profits or gains of the trade and should also be excluded. An example of this is profits or gains of a capital nature. The question, whether an item is a capital or revenue receipt, is one which has given rise to a large number of tax cases. The following examples illustrate the general principles:

- Compensation received for the loss of a capital asset is deemed to be a capital receipt.
- Compensation received for the loss of trading stock, on the other hand, is a trading receipt.
- Compensation for the loss of an agency contract depends on the significance of the contract to the business. If it was fundamental to the conduct of the business the compensation monies for its loss would be treated as a capital receipt. If it is not fundamental to the business, or only one of many agency contracts, any receipt would be treated as a trading receipt.

Receipts related to prior years

Receipts related to prior year trading losses are treated as trading receipts of the current period. However, in some cases the Inland Revenue has insisted that the prior year accounts have been re-opened.

Grants

Regional development grants (grants under Part II of the Industrial Development Act 1982) are not to be treated as trading receipts. However, most other grants made under the Industrial Development Act 1982 or under the Industry Act 1972 must be treated as taxable trading receipts.

Stock for own use

Any stock taken by a trader for use by that trader or his or her family has to be treated for tax purposes as a sale at full market value (not merely wholesale cost). This is an example of income often not shown in the accounts, which is taxable.

The following tax cases can be referred to in the sources quoted in the Preface:

Van Den Berghs Ltd v. Clark
McGowan v. Brown & Cousins
Sharkey v. Wernher

Allowable deductions

Once the profits or gains of the trade have been established, all admissable expenditure must be deducted to arrive at a balance of taxable profits – the adjusted Schedule D Case I or II profits.

In the first instance, deductible expenditure is determined by applying the ordinary rules of bookkeeping and accountancy (including the accruals concept). The legislation lists specific items that are not deductible – most of these are consistent with the above rules of accountancy, the remainder will be dealt with below. The overriding principle is that expenses will only be deductible if they are incurred *wholly and exclusively for the purpose of the trade*.

Non-deductible expenditure

Expenses and losses which are *not* deductible fall into the following groups.

Expenses or losses of a capital nature

The legislation specifically disallows capital expenditure but does not define it. There can therefore be considerable difficulties in determining what is capital and what is revenue. The usual accounting definition of capital expenditure is a useful starting point – the cost of additions or improvements to assets acquired for long-term use in the trade and not for re-sale, plus the incidental costs thereof.

▶ Any expenditure in connection with fixed capital must be disallowed unless it is an ordinary repair and maintenance expense with no element of improvement. There have been a number of tax cases brought on this point, the most famous of which is *Law Shipping Co. Ltd v. CIR* (the decision here indicated that repairs to an asset acquired in a defective condition were of a capital nature).

More recently in *Odeon Associated Theatres v. Jones*, this view has been modified (The decision here allowed that the rectification of defects in an asset

which was usable immediately following acquisition, was revenue although the defects resulted from the previous owner's wear and tear.)
- Replacement of an entire asset is capital, while replacement of a part of an asset is revenue. A factory chimney for a colliery company became unsafe after several years and was demolished. Another improved chimney was built near the original site. The whole cost was held to be capital (*O'Grady* v. *Bullcroft Main Collieries* 1932).
- Expenditure which is incurred with the intention that it will lead to the acquisition of a capital item is itself of a capital nature whether or not the acquisition succeeds – for example, legal costs preliminary to the purchase of property which is subsequently not acquired.
- Lump sums paid to secure rights, although intangible, have been held to be capital – for instance payments to an employee on his removal from office in order to prevent him from competing with the company; purchase of additional pension rights for employees in order to secure their loyalty.
- Depreciation through the operation of the accruals concept is a loss of a capital nature. (The alternative view is that depreciation is a general provision against the current year's profits – either way it is not allowable, see below.) Similarly, losses on sale of fixed assets are capital as are goodwill and preliminary expenses written off.
- Expenses in raising, and repaying, long-term loan finance are of a capital nature. However, since 1980 they have been specifically allowable provided that the interest on the loan is deductible for Schedule D Case I purposes – fees, commissions, advertising and the like but not stamp duty, discount on issue or premium on redemption.

Appropriations of profit

Only those expenses incurred in earning the profits of the trade are deductible. This automatically excludes any items which come within the definition of drawings:

- salary drawn by a proprietor
- any expenditure for domestic or private purposes
- any stock removed for personal or family consumption (but see above – the computation of the annual profits or gains of the trade).

Other expenses, when examined in detail, are found to be an appropriation of profit:

- Tax due or paid on the profits of the trade together with Class II and IV National Insurance contributions of the trader.
- Partnership salaries and interest on capital.
- Transfers to general provisions and reserves. (The Inland Revenue may accept transfers to specific provisions as an expense incurred in earning the profits of the trade – for example, a provision against specific trade debts being irrecoverable. It does not, however, accept the accounting distinction between general provision and reserve.)
- The provision for depreciation may be regarded as a specific provision against a specific capital loss or as a general provision or reserve for the replacement of assets – either way it is not deductible.

Specific expenses disallowed by statute

Even if an item of expenditure is revenue expenditure, it may be disallowed by law. In addition to those that are consistent with the normal rules of accountancy, ICTA 1988 lists the following:

- Annual charges from which income tax has been deducted at source – the amount to be disallowed should be the amount debited in the accounts.

- Any expense or loss which is recoverable, for example under insurance or other indemnity contract.
- The cost of business entertainment, with certain specified exemptions, is not deductible and the disallowance will be made either in the Schedule D Case I or II computation of the trader, or, if applicable, in computing the tax liability of the employee (see Schedule E). From the trader's point of view there are two exemptions:
  - staff entertaining
  - gifts, being articles bearing a conspicuous advertisement, provided that they do not exceed £10 in any one year to any one person and are not food, alcohol, tobacco or vouchers exchangeable for goods – these restrictions on allowable gifts do not apply to gifts to charities.
- Any payment which itself constitutes a criminal offence by the payer. An example might be the payment of a bribe.
- Any payment which is induced by a blackmail demand.

Expenses not wholly and exclusively for the purpose of the trade

Although this rule is not as restrictive as the one which applies to those being taxed under Schedule E (wholly, exclusively and necessarily) – it does prevent expenses being deducted which have nothing to do with the trade and also those which are for a dual purpose (for example, part business and part private). In practice, Inspectors of Inland Revenue do allow the apportionment of expenses between business and private (for example, motor expenses, home telephone, costs of accommodation if the trader 'lives in' – usually two-thirds is the maximum for business use). However, the taxpayer cannot expect support in the courts in the event of disagreement with an Inspector regarding this question.

There is a great deal of case law on the interpretation of 'wholly and exclusively'. A few of the resulting principles are listed below:

- Fines and penalties are not for the purpose of the trade. They are regarded as being incurred because the person conducting the trade infringed the law. The payment of fines incurred by employees has been allowed, being regarded as additional remuneration and taxable under Schedule E on the employee.
- A loss resulting from the writing off of a loan to an ex-employee who absconded, where the trade was not that of lending money, was not for the purpose of the trade.
- Subscriptions and donations to political parties not securing a specific trade advantage are not for the purpose of the trade. Although charitable donations are no longer caught by the restrictions on business gifts (see above), they may still be restricted by this section, that is, gifts to national charities (for example Red Cross) are not allowable. To avoid being caught some business advantage should be shown. This may be through benefit to employees – local charities – or through public relations. Deductions from the taxpayer's total income are allowed for gifts and donations and deeds of covenant to charity – see Chapter 1.
- The cost of audit work and tax compliance work is generally allowable but the cost of tax appeals, interest on overdue tax, and special investigations is not.

A synopsis of the following tax cases can be found in material referred to in the Preface:

Samuel Jones & Co. (Devondale) Ltd v. *CIR*
Copeman v. *Flood*
Smiths Potato Estates Ltd v. *Bolland*

Deductible expenses

It is useful to look now at expenses from a positive point of view and consider what is allowable.

Allowable by statute

The following are the main deductible expenses specifically allowable by statute:

- Costs of registering patents and trade marks, obtaining grants or extensions of patents or in connection with rejected or abandoned applications.
- Premiums paid for a short lease of business premises by the formula:

$$\frac{\text{Premium} - 2\% \, (n - 1) \, \text{premium}}{n} \text{ per annum}$$

  where n is the number of years of the lease.

- Voluntary redundancy/compensation payments for loss of office to staff *on cessation of trading*, up to three times the statutory redundancy pay.
- The salary and other costs of employment of an employee seconded to charity (or educational establishment after 26 November 1986 and before 1 April 1997).
- Payments for technical education related to the trade made to an approved educational establishment.
- Incidental costs of obtaining or repaying qualifying loan finance (see above).
- Contributions to scientific research associations relating to the trade and/or to a university, college or research institute for scientific research related to the trade.
- Ordinary annual contributions to approved pension funds. (Contributions to unapproved pension schemes may be allowable as 'wholly and exclusively for the purpose of the trade'.) Special contributions may need to be spread forward.
- Contributions to approved profit-sharing schemes.
- Hire charges for cars under a lease rental arrangement, restricted in the case of expensive cars (costing >£12,000) to an amount given by the following formula:

$$\frac{12,000 + \dfrac{P - 12,000}{2}}{P} \times R$$

where P is the cash price of the car being leased; and R is the annual rent.

Where the hire agreement splits the annual rent between a rental cost and a maintenance cost (in the case of an operating lease) the restriction is applied only to the rental element.

Other allowable items

The following list covers the main items of difficulty which you are likely to come across. It is not intended to be comprehensive.

Interest

Annual interest is allowable as a business expense provided it is incurred wholly and exclusively for the purpose of the trade – overdraft interest, hire purchase interest, credit card interest and bank interest are examples. Difficulty often arises as to the treatment of interest on a loan for a qualifying purpose (see annual charges).

The basic rule is that interest which fits this definition should be treated as such, and therefore disallowed in the Schedule D Case I computation. Any other interest is deductible in the computation provided it fits the relevant criteria.

Legal expenses

Where these are incurred in the normal course of trading, they will be allowable. Examples are costs of debt collection, normal taxation work, rating valuation appeals, renewal expenses of short leases (but not expenses associated with the grant of a lease), the cost of defending title to assets or maintaining existing trading rights and costs connected with breach of trading contracts.

Losses

Exchange losses incurred in trading are allowable. The Finance Act 1993 introduced measures which begin to bring the tax treatment of foreign exchange gains and losses into line with the accounts treatment, that is, recognising differences on monetary assets and liabilities as they accrue. The reform will be effective for accounting periods which begin after a date yet to be announced. Losses through defalcation of an employee are generally allowable but not if made by a person who has control (for example, a partner or director).

Remuneration and pensions

All pensions, including voluntary pensions to former employees, are allowable. Remuneration based on profits is allowable as are payments to remove employees from office and lump sum payments on retirement, provided they can be justified as a trade expense.

Repairs and renewals

A deduction is allowed for the cost of renewal of plant and equipment (original cost is capital) on which capital allowances are not received (for instance, replacement of a shop front). The need to distinguish between repairs and improvements has already been discussed.

Bad and doubtful debts

Only bad debts incurred in the course of the trade are allowable. This generally means that loans to employees written off are disallowed – unless it can be shown that it was in the course of the trade or that it was remuneration and taxable under Schedule E on the employee. Movements in general bad debt provisions are also disallowed. An analysis of the account is often necessary to divide the charge to profit and loss account into its component parts and label each as allowable or disallowable. (Note that taxable and non-taxable respectively are the opposites.)

EXAMPLE 15.1

Bad and doubtful debts account

	£		£
Trade debts w/o	450	Specific provision b/f	429
		General provision b/f	250
Loan to ex-employee written off	160	Trade debt of previous year – recovered	85
Specific provision c/f	484		
General provision c/f	200	Profit and loss account	530
	1,294		1,294

	Allowable/ (Taxable)	Disallowed/ (Non-taxable)	Total
	£	£	£
Trade debts written off	450		450
Trade debts recovered	(85)		(85)
Employee loan written off		160	160
Increase in specific provision	55		55
Decrease in general provision		(50)	(50)
	420	110	530

Stock valuation

A primary requirement is that a consistent method of valuation should be applied from year to year. The normal basis of valuation for tax purposes is the lower of cost or market value, with a reasonable addition for processing costs being made to work-in-progress (compare SSAP 9). Where there has been a change in the basis of valuation of stock during the year, an adjustment must be made for tax purposes. This is a complex subject and is not developed further in this text.

Value added tax

A registered trader may suffer non-recoverable VAT on items such as entertaining. This VAT would normally be included with the expense in the accounts. If the expense itself is deductible, then the associated VAT will also be deductible.

The VAT on bad debts is often not recoverable from the Customs and Excise, and in this case the whole debt including VAT is deductible (provided that the debt itself is deductible).

A non-registered trader does not analyse out his or her VAT and it is therefore deductible if the expense itself is deductible.

A partially exempt trader falls between the above categories – being able to deduct any VAT on allowable expenses which has not been recovered against output tax.

Adjusted profit computation

The taxable profits and gains and the allowable deductions have now been considered at length. It is evident that the normal accounts prepared by, or on behalf of, a trader do not suffice for tax purposes.

Although it is always possible to compute the adjusted Schedule D Case I or II profits from scratch as described, the more practical and preferred approach is to start with the profit in the accounts and convert it to the taxable profit for the same period.

All of the points considered above fall into one of the following categories – it is normal in practice for each individual item to be listed and very important that this is done in examinations. (All workings should be shown and often also the reasons why a particular item is thought to be allowable or disallowable.)

Suggested layout

	£
Net profit (before tax) per accounts for period	X
Add expenses per accounts not deductible Schedule D I	X
Add income omitted accounts but taxable Schedule D I	X
	X
Less income per accounts not taxable Schedule D I	(X)
Less expenses not in accounts deductible Schedule D I	(X)
Schedule D Case I adjusted profit/(loss) for period	X

When you are satisfied that you understand how all the detailed adjustments considered so far fit into the suggested layout you should work through the following example.

EXAMPLE 15.2

Dougal and Henry have been in business as booksellers for many years. They make up accounts to 30 April each year and the profit and loss account for the year ended 30 April 1994 shows the following:

		£	£
Sales			156,782
Less:	Cost of goods sold:		
	Opening stock	14,604	
	Purchases	98,358	
		112,962	
	Less: closing stock	(11,650)	(101,312)
Gross profit			55,470
Interest on loans to staff (Note 6)			200
			55,670
Less: expenses:			
	Staff wages (Note 1)	20,280	
	Rent and rates	2,620	
	Heat and light	3,615	
	HP interest	896	
	Repairs	1,024	
	Travelling and entertaining (Note 2)	4,232	
	Professional expenses (Note 3)	1,429	
	Miscellaneous expenses (Note 4)	1,877	
	Bad debts (Note 5)	912	
	Depreciation	3,520	
	Loss on sale of fixed assets	262	
	Partners salaries	7,000	(47,667)
Net profit			8,003

Notes

1. Staff wages includes £30 per week paid to each of Dougal's and Henry's wives, for secretarial duties.
2. Travelling and entertaining expenses are:

	£
Motor expenses (1/3 private use agreed)	1,062
Travel and hotel	580
Entertaining: UK customers	940
Overseas customers	568
London agent of overseas customer	72
Christmas gifts: Whisky to 50 UK customers	368
Calendars to 200 UK customers	350
Staff Christmas party	292
	4,232

3. Professional charges are:

Accountancy	960
Surveyor's fees re premises not subsequently acquired	324
Debt collection	145
	1,429

4. Miscellaneous expenses include:

Donations to local charities	150
Chamber of commerce subscription	100

5. Bad debts:

Trade debts written off	602
Loans to staff written off	60
Increase to general provision for doubtful debts	250
	912

6. Interest at 10% on a loan of £2,000 to a shop manager is received annually on 30 April. The loan is repayable in 1996.

You are required to compute the adjusted Schedule D Case I profits.

Dougal and Henry
Schedule D Case I Computation
for the year ended 30 April 1994

	£	£	Notes
Net profit per accounts		8,003	
Add Expenses not allowed			
Motor expenses (1062 x 1/3)	354		(private use)
Entertaining UK customers	940		(by statute)
Overseas customers	568		(by statute)
London agent	72		(by statute)
Christmas gifts: whisky	368		(gift alcohol)
Surveyor's fees	324		(capital)
Loans to staff	60		(not trade)
Increase in provision	250		(appropriation)
Depreciation	3,520		(capital)
Loss on sale of fixed asset	262		(capital)
Partners' salaries	7,000		(appropriation)
		13,718	
		21,721	
Less: Income not taxable D I			
Interest on loan		(200)	(assessable D III)
Schedule D I adjusted profit		21,521	

It is often wise in an examination to explain why you have not found it necessary to disallow certain expenses. Few expenses are so clear-cut that there cannot be room for an alternative view:

1. The salaries paid to the wives are assumed to be reasonable reward for the duties performed.
2. The staff Christmas party costs are assumed to be reasonable (less than £50 per head is considered reasonable).
3. Donations to local charities have been assumed to be for the purpose of the trade, in that staff and families potentially benefit from community services.

Miscellaneous notes

Income taxable under another Schedule

Income included in a trader's accounts that is not taxable under Schedule D Case I or II is likely to be taxable under another Schedule or Case. As the basis of assessment for each Schedule and Case is different, care must be taken to include the correct figure in the appropriate Schedule or Case.

For example, rent receivable included in accounts to 30 September 1994 amounted to £3,500 made up of four payments paid, according to the lease, quarterly in arrears (31 December, 31 March, 30 June and 30 September). The amount due under the lease had been increased on 1 April 1994 from £3,000 per annum to £4,000 per annum.

The amount per the accounts, not taxable in the Schedule D I computation for the year ended 30 September 1994 is £3,500 but the amount taxable under Schedule A for 1994/95 is £4,000 (the amount receivable in the fiscal year).

Pre-trading expenditure

Expenses of a revenue nature, incurred prior to the commencement of trading, are not deductible in arriving at the Schedule D Case I profits of the first accounting period of a sole trader or partnership (see Chapter 18 re pre-trading losses).

Annual payments not deductible

A situation similar to the one for income taxable under another Schedule arises for annual payments disallowed in the Schedule D Case I computation. The amounts disallowed will have been included in the accounts on an accruals basis for the accounting period. Annual charges are deducted from total income of the fiscal year on a payments basis.

Examination of business accounts by Inspector of Taxes

Owing to the growth in the number of unincorporated businesses over recent years, and the consequent pressure on Revenue resources, the Inland Revenue have become more selective in their examination of accounts submitted to them. Selection is not at random, but based upon the District Inspectors' experience and knowledge of local conditions. Notes are also made available to Inspectors to provide them with general guidance on the financial and business background to particular trades. (These are now available to the businesses themselves in a series called 'Business Economic Notes').

Accounts selected for inspection are examined in detail to ensure that the basic records of the taxpayer are correct and complete. In the case of accounts not selected for detailed examination – the majority, in fact – the accounts, as submitted, are generally accepted as the basis for assessment.

Bases of assessment

The 1993 Budget proposed a major reform of the system of assessing personal tax to be implemented in 1996/97. The 'preceding year basis' outlined below will be abolished and 'self-assessment' will be introduced. The new provisions are considered in Chapter 19. In the meantime, the existing system is summarised below.

Income tax is charged for a fiscal year of assessment but as we have seen above the Schedule D Case I adjusted profits are computed for an accounting period. The normal rule is that the Schedule D Case I assessment is made by reference to the Schedule D Case I adjusted profits of the accounting period ending in the preceding fiscal year of assessment, provided this is a valid accounting period. This is known as the 'preceding year basis of assessment'.

Where the adjusted profit computation for any accounting period shows a loss, the related Schedule D Case I assessment will be £Nil.

A valid accounting period is defined as:

▶ one which is 12 months in length
▶ the only accounting period ending in that fiscal year
▶ one which commences the day after the previous valid accounting period ended or which commenced at the commencement of trade.

Where there is no such valid accounting period, the Inland Revenue can decide on the basis period for the year of assessment and also revise the basis period for the previous year of assessment to correspond if they see fit. (This latter action may be appealed against but not the former.)

EXAMPLE 15.3

A business has made up accounts for many years to 30 April. The adjusted Schedule D Case I profits for the year ended 30 April 1993 will be assessed to tax in the fiscal year 1994/95 provided that the accounting period to 30 April 1993 was a valid one.

There are therefore difficulties in applying this normal basis in three circumstances:

- on the commencement of a business
- on the cessation of a business
- when there is a change in the normal accounting date or accounts are not regularly made up to a particular date.

Commencement of a business

Only a brief summary is given here for revision purposes, as you should already be familiar with these procedures.

First year of assessment

A business is first assessable under Schedule D Case I in the fiscal year in which trading commences and the amount assessable is the actual Schedule D Case I adjusted profit from the first day of trading to the following 5 April. It is not necessary that accounts are prepared for this period – a proportionate part of the accounts of the business will be assessed. Note that in practice, the proportion is calculated by reference to the number of days. For examination purposes, the odd five days should be ignored and the proportion calculated in months.

EXAMPLE 15.4

X commences business on 1 October 1992 and decides to make up the accounts of the business to 30 June in each year. The first accounts are therefore prepared for the period from 1 October 1992 to 30 June 1993. The first year of assessment will be 1992/93 – the fiscal year in which the first day of trading falls – and the amount assessed will be 6/9 of the Schedule D Case I adjusted profit for the period.

Second year of assessment

The amount assessable in the following year is the Schedule D Case I adjusted profit of the first 12 months of trading. Once again, proportions of adjusted profits for accounting periods may have to be used to arrive at a figure of profit for the 12 month period.

EXAMPLE 15.5

Continuing the previous example, the second year of assessment will be 1993/94, and the amount assessed will be the whole of the adjusted profit for the nine months to 30 June 1993 plus 3/12 of the adjusted profit for the year to 30 June 1994.

Third year of assessment

The assessment in this year will be based on the Schedule D Case I adjusted profit of the accounting period ending in the preceding fiscal year if this is a valid accounting period (that is, the normal basis). Otherwise, the Inland Revenue will normally select the adjusted profits of the first 12 months' trading – repeating the second year's assessment.

EXAMPLE 15.6

Continuing the previous example, the third year of assessment will be 1994/95. There is no valid accounting period ending in 1993/94 (the period ending 30 June 1993 is only nine months long) so the adjusted profit of the first 12 months' trading would normally be assessed (as in the second year's assessment).

One point of difficulty occasionally arises in the third year of assessment where the first set of accounts is made up for a period greater than 12 months.

EXAMPLE 15.7

W commences a business on 1 October 1991 but makes up his first accounts to 31 December 1992, a 15 month period. All subsequent accounts are prepared to 31 December each year.

First year of assessment	1991/92	Adjusted profits for the period 1 October 1991 to 5 April 1992. (6/15 of adjusted profit of the accounting period)
Second year of assessment	1992/93	Adjusted profits of the first 12 months' trading (12/15 of adjusted profit of the accounting period)
Third year of assessment	1993/94	No valid accounting period ending in 1992/93. Assess adjusted profits of 12 months ending on proper accounting date that is, 12 months to 31 December 1992. (12/15 of adjusted profit of the accounting period)
Fourth year of assessment	1994/95	Year ended 31 December 1993 is assessable as it is a valid accounting period ending in 1993/94

Although it makes no difference to the amount of profit assessable, the dates identifying the basis period become very important when looking at capital allowances.

Taxpayer's option to elect under ICTA 1988, s. 62

The taxpayer may elect for the assessments in the second and the third years to be based on the adjusted profits of those years of assessment (the actual basis). Once again it may be necessary to take a proportion of the adjusted profits of the relevant accounting periods, to arrive at an amount of profit for the fiscal year. If the total assessable is less on this basis than it is on the statutory basis, it is worth while making the election.

The election must be made within seven years of the end of the second year of assessment (it may be revoked within six years of the end of the third year of assessment).

EXAMPLE 15.8

T commenced business on 1 July 1991 and his Schedule D Case I adjusted profits have been agreed as follows:

		£
Period ended	30 April 1992	4,000
Year ended	30 April 1993	2,400
Year ended	30 April 1994	3,600

		Assessed £
Statutory basis:	1991/92 1 July 1991–5 April 1992 (9/10 × £4,000)	3,600
	1992/93 1 July 1991–30 June 1992 (£4,000 + 2/12 × £2,400)	4,400
	1993/94 1 July 1991 30 June 1992 (as for second year)	4,400
	1994/95 Year ended 30 April 1993	2,400

If the taxpayer elected for the actual basis, then the second and third years would be altered as follows:

	£
1992/93 6 April 1992 – 5 April 1993 (1/10 × £4,000 + 11/12 × £2,400)	2,600
1993/94 6 April 1993 – 5 April 1994 (1/12 × £2,400 + 11/12 × £3,600)	3,500

It can be seen in the example that by making the election, the taxpayer reduces the assessable profits of these two years by £2,700 (£6,100 as against £8,800).

There is a consequential effect on the capital allowances computation (see Chapter 16) of making the election. In practice this would therefore be considered by the taxpayer before a decision to elect was made.

Note that it is a feature of the commencement rules that some profits are assessed more than once; making the election merely postpones this event. It is therefore unlikely to be worthwhile making the election if the trend of profits is rising.

Examination questions at this level usually require the candidate to advise a taxpayer about a possible future tax situation – this may require you to state the statutory situation and details of the election and time limits. Using the information available (remembering that in practice future results must often be estimated), computations may be required and a conclusion drawn – in the light of the figures used – as to whether an election should be made. Alternatively, you may be required to advise the taxpayer as to the possible advantages of preparing accounts to, say, 30 April as against 31 March.

Cessation of a business

Only a brief summary is given here for revision purposes, as you should already be familiar with these procedures.

Final year of assessment

The fiscal year in which the last day of trading falls is the final year of assessment and the Schedule D Case I adjusted profit from 6 April to that date is assessable. Once again a proportion of the adjusted profits for the accounting period may need to be taken.

EXAMPLE 15.9

S ceased trading on 31 December 1994, having prepared accounts to 30 September for a number of years. The final year of assessment will be 1994/95 (the fiscal year in which he ceased trading) and he will be assessed on the adjusted profit for the period 6 April 1994 to 31 December 1994. (That is 6/12 of the adjusted profits of the year to 30 September 1994 and the whole of the adjusted profits for the three months to 31 December 1994).

No further adjustments need be made under statute. All previous years, including the penultimate year of assessment, continue to be assessed on the normal basis (preceding year).

Inland Revenue option to elect under ICTA 1988, s. 63

Although the earlier years of assessment may continue to be assessed on the normal basis, the Inland Revenue will exercise the option to amend the assessment of the two years prior to the final year (known as the penultimate and the ante-penultimate years) to the actual Schedule D Case I adjusted profits of those fiscal years if this is beneficial.

They will normally exercise this option if the aggregate profits assessable in this way exceed the profits assessable under the normal basis.

EXAMPLE 15.10

A business ceased trading on 30 June 1994 and the adjusted profits for the relevant accounting periods have been agreed as follows:

		£
Year ended	31 December 1991	4,000
Year ended	31 December 1992	5,000
Year ended	31 December 1993	2,000
Period ended	30 June 1994	500

		Assessed £
Statutory basis	1994/95 6 April 1994 – 30 June 1994 (3/6 × £500)	250
	1993/94 year ended 31 December 1992	5,000
	1992/93 year ended 31 December 1991	4,000

If the Inland Revenue elected for the actual basis of assessment for the penultimate and ante-penultimate years, then the assessments would be amended as follows:

	£
1993/94 6 April 1993 – 5 April 1994 (9/12 × £2000 + 3/6 × £500)	1,750
1992/93 6 April 1992 – 5 April 1993 (9/12 × £5000 + 3/12 × £2,000)	4,250

The Inland Revenue in the example would lose taxable profits of £3,000 if they made the election (£6,000 as against £9,000).

It should be noted that this election will also have a consequential effect on the capital allowances computation (see Chapter 16) but the Inland Revenue do not normally take this into account in deciding whether to make the election.

It is a feature of the cessation rules that some profits will not be assessed whatever the Inland Revenue does.

Interaction of commencement and cessation rules

Where a business only exists for five years, then the application of the cessation rules takes priority over the commencement rules.

No matter how many years a business is in existence, the overall effect of the rules is that the total profits assessed over the life of the business will be different from both the total profit per the accounts and the total Schedule D Case I adjusted profit over the life of the business. The rules are such that it may or may not be advantageous to the taxpayer. This depends on the spread of the profit over the years (a typical business having small profits on commencement and larger profits at cessation may benefit). It also depends on the accounting date chosen (a careful examination of the manner in which the rules operate shows that an accounting date of shortly after 5 April can be advantageous, for instance, 30 April).

On a change in ownership of the business (including the incorporation of the business as a family company), the date of change must be decided. This will usually be the date on the vending agreement unless a different date can be shown to apply. The cessation and commencement rules would then be applied except in the following circumstances:

- On a change in the composition of a partnership, where the partners exercise certain rights (see Chapter 17).
- The Inland Revenue permit a widower continuing her deceased husband's business to continue to be assessed on the preceding year basis (extra-statutory concession).
- On the acquisition of a going concern by an existing business of the same type, where the cessation rules may be applied to the vendor but the purchaser is regarded as expanding an existing business. The profits of the acquired business will be merged with those of the existing business with no disturbance of the preceding year basis of assessment.
- Similarly, on the disposal of one of a number of branches, there is merely a contraction of the business and not a cessation.

Choice of accounting date

The choice of accounting date for a business determines the length of the interval between earning these profits and paying Schedule D Case I and II tax.

Schedule D Case I/II tax is due on 1 January in the year of assessment (50%) and 1 July following the end of the year of assessment (50%). These dates do not vary, whatever the accounting date chosen. For example, tax due for 1994/95 under a Schedule D Case I assessment will be payable 1 January 1995 and 1 July 1995 whether the accounting date is 31 March 1994 (interval 9 months) or 30 April 1993 (interval 20 months). A year ending early in the tax year is therefore advantageous in this respect.

The choice of date also influences the extent of the overlap in basis periods on commencement (depending on the trend of profits, this may or may not be beneficial) and the length of the gap (in other words, profits not assessed) on cessation.

If cessation takes place in 1994/95, the profits unassessed will be as follows:

a) 30 April accounting date: 23 months
b) 31 March accounting date: 12 months

The length of the gap is not influenced by the actual date of cessation.

Change in accounting date

To change an accounts date involves preparing accounts for an accounting period of less than 12 months or more than 12 months. One way or another, it will result in at least one non-valid accounting period and therefore a situation in which the normal basis of assessment does not apply.

The statutory situation is vague and the Statement of Practice issued by the Inland Revenue to cover the topic is very detailed. In practice anybody dealing with this topic would refer to the rules and follow them exactly. The topic is not examinable.

Special relief – farmers

These reliefs were introduced to mitigate the effects on a farmer's income tax liability of widely fluctuating profits at a time when there were high marginal rates of income tax.

They are available to any individual who alone or in partnership carries on a trade of farming or market gardening in the UK.

The time limit for making a claim under this section is two years from the end of the second of the years of assessment to which the claim relates. All claims *must* be made in chronological order.

Relief is not available in either the opening or the closing year of a business.

Full averaging

The relief is applied to the Schedule D Case I adjusted profits of two consecutive fiscal years where the adjusted profits of one of these years is 70% (or less than 70%) of the other. The adjusted profits of the two years are averaged and this average profit is substituted in the Schedule D Case I assessments of each of the two fiscal years.

It is possible to use a revised second year figure to average with a third year and so on provided in each case the profits of one year are less than or equal to 70% of the profits of the other (see Example 15.12).

It is also possible to average where the results for one of the years shows a loss – this is done by substituting 'Nil' for the figure of loss. The availability of loss relief is unaffected (see Chapter 18).

Marginal averaging

Where the profits of two consecutive years marginally fail the 70% test, a form of restricted averaging may be available.

Marginal relief is given where the adjusted profits of one year are greater than 70% and less than 75% of the adjusted profits of the other year. The amount of relief available is given by the formula below, and is deducted from the higher profits of the two years and added to the lower.

$$\text{Relief} = 3(H - L) - 3/4H \text{ or } 3 \times [75\%H - L]$$

(where H represents the higher profit and L represents the lower profit).

EXAMPLE 15.11

A farmer had the following Schedule D Case I profits:

Year ended 31 May 1991	£8,500	1992/93
Year ended 31 May 1992	£12,600	1993/94
Year ended 31 May 1993	£14,800	1994/95

Show the revised profit figures assuming that the farmer makes claims for averaging wherever possible.

a) Consider 1992/93 and 1993/94; £8,500 < 70% of £12,600, therefore full averaging is available. The average profits are £10,550 and computations for each of the years will be amended as follows:

$$
\begin{array}{ll}
1992/93 & £10,550 \\
1993/94 & £10,550
\end{array}
$$

This is provided a claim for averaging is made before 5 April 1996.

b) Next, consider 1993/94 and 1994/95; £10,550 is 71.3% of £14,800 and therefore marginal averaging only is available. Using the formula, the amount of relief is:

$$3 \times (14,800 - 10,550) - 3/4 \times 14,800 = 1,650$$
$$3 \times [(75\% \times 14,800) - 10,550] = 1,650$$

The computations for each of the years will be amended as follows:

$$
\begin{array}{ll}
1993/94 & 10,550 + 1,650 = 12,200 \\
1994/95 & 14,800 - 1,650 = 13,150
\end{array}
$$

This is provided a claim for averaging is made before 5 April 1997.

Benefits of averaging

A claim for averaging can be used to level out profits so that a farmer does not waste part of his basic rate band in one year, whilst having liability to higher-rate tax in the previous or next year. (Note that averaging may avoid the loss of personal allowances in a year in which a loss is made.)

As both years' profits must be established before a claim is made, the claim itself is likely to give rise to a repayment of tax already paid for the earlier year and an increased liability for the current year. Alternatively, it could give rise to an increased liability for the earlier year and a reduction of the current liability. In cash flow terms, therefore, there is little to be gained.

Averaging is claimed before the deduction of capital allowances, so the benefits of careful timing of capital expenditure will not be lost or diluted. The fact that the availability of loss relief is unaffected by averaging may make the loss relief claims more efficient: all the variables should be carefully studied before any claims are made.

National Insurance contributions

A self-employed individual must pay Class 2 flat rate National Insurance contributions (1994/95 a flat rate of £5.65 per week above an earnings threshold of £3,200). The earnings figure is the accounting profit for the current fiscal year before adjustment for tax purposes. There is no tax relief for this expense either in the overall income tax computation or as an allowable deduction in the Schedule D Case I or II computation (where it is regarded as an appropriation of profit).

If earnings fall below the threshold, exemption from Class 2 contributions may be claimed, but as entitlement to certain social security benefits depends on the payment of National Insurance contributions this exemption is often not claimed. Payment of Class 2 National Insurance contributions is due quarterly in arrears. Alternatively, payment may be made monthly by direct debit. The payments are made to the Department of Social Security.

The same individual must also pay Class 4 National Insurance contributions based on his or her taxable trading profits (after capital allowances, trading losses and trade charges) assessable in the fiscal year between certain limits (1994/95 7.3% on profits between £6,490 and £22,360). A deduction of 50% of the amount paid for the fiscal year will be made from total income of that same fiscal year (that is, alongside annual charges – see Chapter 1). The liability for Class 4 NIC arises and is assessed with the Schedule D case I/II income tax liability and is payable to the Inland Revenue.

EXAMPLE 15.12

T makes up accounts to 31 December annually. The accounts show the following results:

	Accounts	DI adjusted profit
Year ended 31 Dec 1993	£15,000	£17,000
Year ended 31 Dec 1994	£10,000	£11,000
Year ended 31 Dec 1995	£(8,000)	£(6,000)

You are required to calculate the 1994/95 national insurance liabilities.

Class 2 NIC 1994/95	9/12 x 10,000	7,500	
	3/12 x (8,000)	(2,000)	
		5,500	>3,240
	£5.65 @ 52 Weeks		£293.80
Class 4 NIC 1994/95	D I assessment		£17,000
	Less: lower limit		(6,490)
			10,510 x 7.3% = £767.23

National Insurance is unlikely to be a complete examination question but it is often included as part of a wider question, for example on personal business taxation.

Summary

▶ The badges of trade are a summary of the principal factors to be borne in mind when deciding whether isolated transactions giving rise to a profit are 'adventures in the nature of trade' assessable under D Case I; annual profits assessable under D Case VI; or are not assessable as income.
▶ The computation of D Case I adjusted profits is prepared for the acounting period. It is a complicated subject with an ever-increasing volume of case law. Care must be taken to ensure the basic principles are understood.
▶ Basis periods link fiscal years of assessment to accounting periods – special provisions exist to establish basis periods on commencement, cessation and change of accounting date. A sound knowledge of commencement and cessation rules must be gained.
▶ Averaging relief may be available to farmers and market gardeners with fluctuating profits.

Self test questions

1   List six badges of trade.

2   State the treatment for tax purposes of a ten-year lease acquired for £20,000.

3   State the Schedule D Case I deductible expense when a car which would cost £15,000 is leased for an annual rent of £4,000.

4   Define a valid accounting period.

5   State the time limit for a taxpayer to make an election under ICTA 1988, s. 62.

6 A trader commences a business on 1 January 1992 and prepares accounts to 31 December each year. If he makes an election under ICTA 1988 s. 62, which profits will be assessed twice?

7 A trader who made up accounts to 30 April each year ceased to trade on 30 June 1994. Assuming the Inland Revenue do not make an election under ICTA 1988, s. 63, which profits will not be assessed?

8 In November 1991 Frank Butterfield was made redundant from his job as a sales representative. He decided to go into business, employing his wife Janet, a qualified nurse, providing permanent accommodation for elderly people. They purchased a suitable large house, Ingledene, with the proceeds of the sale of their own home, Frank's redundancy money and a loan from the National and Midland Bank plc.

The first residents arrived on 1 January 1992, the date agreed with HM Inspector of Taxes as the date when trading commenced. The first accounts were made up to 30 April 1993 covering a 16 month period. 30 April was to be the permanent accounting year end date.

The summarised profit and loss account for the period ended 30 April 1993 is as follows:

	£	£
Income: resident's fees		67,530
Expenditure:		
Food, etc	9,372	
Wages	14,837	
Depreciation –building	763	
–furniture and fittings	2,441	
Soft furnishings and bedding	2,231	
Hire-purchase interest –stair lift	237	
Repairs and renewals	1,956	
Heating oil	1,570	
Water rates	130	
Telephone	654	
Gas	125	
Electricity	1,037	
Motor vehicle expenses	4,892	
Loan interest and bank charges	5,193	
Legal and professional fees	2,644	
Sundry expenses	2,104	50,186
Net profit for the period		17,344

Additional information concerning the profit and loss account is as follows:

a) Food for consumption by Frank and Janet included in the accounts was estimated at £100 per month.

b) As Frank and Janet lived on the business premises the following adjustments have to be made for the personal use of items charged in the accounts:

Heating oil	1/20
Water rates	1/6
Telephone	1/6
Gas	1/10
Electricity	1/20

c) Motor vehicle expenses comprise:

	£
Loss on sale of car	400
Hire-purchase interest	450
Depreciation	1,832
Petrol	1,131

TAX PLANNING

Servicing and repairs	519
Licenses	240
Insurance	320
	4,892

One-third of the mileage on all the cars used in the business was agreed as private.

d) Legal and professional fees comprise:

	£
Purchase of Ingledene	2,144
Accountant's fees	500
	2,644

e) There were no disallowable items charged under any other heading in the accounts.

You are required to prepare a profit statement for the period 1 January 1992 to 30 April 1993 and to calculate the Schedule D Case I assessments for all relevant years.

9 a) Explain why care needs to be taken in determining the first and permanent accounting dates in respect of unincorporated businesses.

b) H commenced trading on 1 January 1993 and is still trading. His adjusted Schedule D Case I profits for the first three years of trading are estimated as follows:

	£
Year to 31 December 1993	10,440
31 December 1994	16,200
31 December 1995	13,200

You are required to advise H whether his permanent accounting date should be arranged as 31 March or 30 April using all the information supplied.

10 G has been in business for several years and has recently been experiencing a very successful period of trading. A limited company in the same trade has made a very attractive offer for the business, which G has decided to accept.

The sale is to take place some time during the spring of 1994 and the following information relating to G's recent profits, as agreed for tax purposes, is available:

	£
Year ended 31 December 1990	8,000
Year ended 31 December 1991	24,000
Year ended 31 December 1992	36,000
Year ended 31 December 1993	48,000

G estimates that the profits for the next few months will be:

	£
Three months to 31 March 1994	6,000
One month to 30 April 1994	1,000

You are required to advise G as to whether he should dispose of the business at 31 March 1994 or 30 April 1994. Your advice should be supported by computations of the income assessable under Schedule D Case I for all of the tax years concerned under each alternative.

adapted from CIMA 3 May 1987
Answers on pages 589–591

CHAPTER 16

Unincorporated Businesses – Capital Allowances

This chapter looks at the allowances that are available to a trader in respect of his or her capital expenditure. There have been a number of changes in the legislation over recent years but for the most part this chapter should be revision.

Capital expenditure

As we discovered in the previous chapter, capital expenditure is not an allowable deduction in computing the Schedule D Case I adjusted profits of a trade. Before the introduction of capital allowances, no relief was available for such expenditure and this still holds true for expenditure to which the capital allowance legislation does not extend.

The distinction between capital and revenue expenditure is once again paramount. In the majority of cases, traders would prefer their expenditure to be classified as revenue expenditure because they would then receive 100% relief as a deduction in computing their adjusted trading profits. Few capital allowances nowadays give 100% relief.

Capital expenditure is not defined in the legislation but it is specifically stated that it cannot include:

- expenditure allowed as a deduction in computing the profits or gains of a trade, profession or vocation, office or employment, carried on by the person incurring the expenditure
- payments which are retainable annual charges.

For further discussion on this subject and case law references, refer to the previous chapter.

Capital allowances are calculated for the fiscal year and must be *claimed* in the appropriate income tax return of the trader. They are given usually 'in the taxing of a trade' – that is they are deducted from a Schedule D Case I assessable profit in a Schedule D Case I assessment. The time limit for claiming capital allowances for chargeable accounting periods ending on or after 30 November 1993 is two years. Capital allowances in excess of assessable profit in any year constitute a trading loss; they may also be used to increase an existing trading loss. In some circumstances capital allowances are given 'by discharge or repayment of tax' – this usually applies where the person receiving the allowance is not trading (for example a landlord under Schedule A) and dictates that the allowance should be deducted primarily from the relevant source of income (Schedule A). In this case any excess capital allowances over the relevant income of the year can either be carried forward and deducted from future income of that class, or an election can be made for the excess to be set against other income of the year of assessment as if it were a trading loss.

Capital allowances are available on the following categories of expenditure:

- plant and machinery
- industrial buildings
- agricultural buildings
- patents and know-how

- mineral extraction
- scientific research
- crematoria
- dredging.

These categories, apart from crematoria and dredging, will all be considered.

Date on which expenditure takes place

It is important to determine the date when expenditure was incurred as the rate or timing of allowance given may be affected. The general rule is that expenditure is treated as incurred when the obligation to pay becomes unconditional, regardless of whether payment is actually required on a later date (up to four months later). If payment is due in whole or in part more than four months later, the expenditure or that part of it is incurred when payment is made. Capital expenditure incurred prior to the commencement of trading is deemed to be incurred on the first day of trading.

Abortive capital expenditure

Capital expenditure, particularly the incidental costs preliminary to acquiring an asset, can be abortive in the sense that no asset is subsequently acquired or constructed. Under such circumstances, capital allowances will not usually be available.

Contributions towards capital costs

Generally a trader cannot obtain capital allowances on expenditure not incurred (and paid for) by him or herself. On the other hand, the person making the contribution may obtain capital allowances on the amount of the contribution provided it was for the purpose of his or her trade. There has been doubt in the past as to whether this applied for contributions to plant and machinery. The Finance Act 1990 confirmed that it does.

An exception to this rule is where the contribution takes the form of a regional development grant when capital allowances are given on the full cost of the assets.

Fiscal years and basis periods

Capital allowances for income tax are calculated for the fiscal year by reference to the basis period in which the expenditure was incurred. That is, additions and disposals of an accounting period are normally incorporated in the capital allowances computation for the fiscal year which assesses the profits of that accounting period.

EXAMPLE 16.1

B, who has been trading for many years, incurs capital expenditure of £8,000 in his accounting year ended 30 June 1993. The profits of the year ended 30 June 1993 will be assessed to income tax in the fiscal year 1994/95 and therefore any capital allowances to be given on his capital expenditure of £8,000 will be available in the first instance in 1994/95.

Opening and closing years of assessment have a special basis by reason of the commencement and cessation provisions under Schedule D Cases I and II, as does change of accounting date. The special basis applies the following rules:

- Where the basis periods of two fiscal years overlap, the earlier period has priority.
- Where there is a gap between the basis periods of two consecutive fiscal years, the gap goes with the later period unless it is the final basis period (that is, on cessation) when it goes with the earlier basis period.

If necessary, you should refer back at this stage to the section in Chapter 15 dealing with commencement and cessation and ensure that you can identify the basis period in every set of circumstances. The application of the above rules then becomes very straightforward. Every day of trading must fall into *one (and only one)* basis period for capital allowances.

EXAMPLE 16.2

T commenced a business on 1 July 1991 and subsequently made up accounts to 30 April.

1 Statutory basis

Fiscal year	Basis period for assessment	Basis period for capital allowances	Notes
1991/92	1 July 1991–5 April 1992	1 July 1991–5 April 1992	Writing down allowance restricted to 9/12
1992/93	1 July 1991–30 June 1992	6 April 1992–30 June 1992	
1993/94	1 July 1991–30 June 1992	Nil	Writing down allowance still available
1994/95	1 May 1992–30 April 1993	1 July 1992–30 April 1993	
1995/96	1 May 1993–30 April 1994	1 May 1993–30 April 1994	

2 Actual basis (election under ICTA 1988, s 62)

Fiscal year	Basis period for assessment	Basis period for capital allowances	Notes
1991/92	1 July 1991–5 April 1992	1 July 1991–5 April 1992	Writing down allowance restricted to 9/12
1992/93	6 April 1992–5 April 1993	6 April 1992–5 April 1993	
1993/94	6 April 1993–5 April 1994	6 April 1993–5 April 1994	
1994/95	1 May 1992–30 April 1993	Nil	Writing down allowance still available
1995/96	1 May 1993–30 April 1994	6 April 1994–30 April 1994	

EXAMPLE 16.3

A business, having made up its accounts to 31 December for many years, ceased trading on 30 June 1994.

1 Statutory basis

Fiscal year	Basis period for assessment	Basis period for capital allowances	Notes
1994/95	6 April 1994–30 June 1994	6 April 1994–30 June 1994	No writing down allowance – but balancing adjustments
1993/94	1 Jan 1992–31 Dec 1992	1 Jan 1992–5 April 1994	Writing down allowance 25% only
1992/93	1 Jan 1991–31 Dec 1991	1 Jan 1991–31 Dec 1991	
1991/92	1 Jan 1990–31 Dec 1990	1 Jan 1990–31 Dec 1990	

2 Actual basis (Inland Revenue elect ICTA 1988, s 63)

Fiscal year	Basis period for assessment	Basis period for capital allowances	Notes
1994/95	6 April 1994–30 June 1994	6 April 1994–30 June 1994	No writing down allowance – but balancing adjustments
1993/94	6 April 1993–5 April 1994	6 April 1993–5 April 1994	
1992/93	6 April 1992–5 April 1993	1 Jan 1991–5 April 1993	
1991/92	1 Jan 1990–31 Dec 1990	1 Jan 1990–31 Dec 1990	Writing down allowance 25% only

Plant and machinery

What is plant and machinery?

Once again, the legislation does not define the relevant terms and to get a definition we have to turn to case law and Inland Revenue practice. In its booklet on capital allowances, plant is defined as including: '... any apparatus kept for permanent employment in the trade. In addition to the things which are commonly regarded as plant, it covers fixtures and fittings of a permanent and durable nature such as an office desk or a shop counter, but does not include a shop front.' Machinery is also not defined anywhere but its existence is more obvious (as the absence of case law confirms).

The Inland Revenue's guideline is based on the findings of case law before 1973 when the booklet was published. An earlier definition (contained in the case *Yarmouth* v. *France*, 1887) is still widely referred to:

> It includes whatever apparatus is used by a business man for carrying on his business – not his stock-in-trade, which he buys or makes for sale; but all goods and chattels, fixed or movable, live or dead, which he keeps for permanent employment in his business.

Durability has also been held to be a test in determining whether an item is plant or machinery – usually a life of two or more years is considered sufficient for this purpose.

Most subsequent cases have been concerned to distinguish between plant *with which* the trade is carried on as against other items which form the setting *in which* the trade is carried on. The latter have been held to be outside the definition of plant. Generally, therefore, plant must have an active function in the trade.

It has been established that the permanent structure of the building cannot be plant unless it fulfils the function of plant in the business operations – for instance, the costs of concrete grain silos have been allowed as plant, as have the costs of excavating and concreting a dry dock. On the other hand, apparatus which has no functional purpose in the business operation, even if it attracts custom, is not plant.

The following items are accepted as plant whether by statute or under case law:

- machinery
- office furniture
- office equipment
- motor lorries
- motor vans
- motor cars
- textbooks forming a practice library (*Munby* v. *Furlong*, 1977)
- movable office partitioning (*Jarrold* v. *John Good & Sons Ltd*, 1962)
- fixtures and fittings including central heating and air conditioning and the related wiring
- lighting and the related wiring where this is specifically to create atmosphere (*Cole Brothers* v. *Phillips*, 1982)
- the cost of alterations to buildings to accommodate machinery
- the cost of creating a swimming pool at a caravan park (*Cooke* v. *Beach Station Caravans Ltd*, 1974)
- the cost of providing and installing ducting for the construction of cable television networks.

Examples of items which were not treated as plant include: the canopy over the forecourt of a garage (*Dixon* v. *Fitch's Garages Ltd*, 1975), prefabricated buildings used as classrooms in a private school, a ship used as a floating restaurant, and suspended ceilings. Plant also does not include general lighting and its wiring.

It can be seen that there is a fine dividing line between those items which are allowable and those which are not. It is worth referring to the following cases:

Cole Brothers v. *Phillips*
Jarrold v. *John Good & Sons Ltd*
St John's School v. *Ward*

The Finance Act 1994 has attempted to clarify the boundary between buildings, which the government contends should not qualify for plant and machinery allowances, and true plant. This distinction has previously been a source of great contention, as the large amount of case law on this topic testifies.

The following table, taken from the Act, sets out in column (1) those assets which are included in the definition of a building and which do not qualify for allowances.

Column (2) of the table includes items which are caught by the new legislation but which will qualify for allowances if they pass the existing case law test.

Table 16.1

(1) Assets included in the expression 'building'	(2) Assets so included, but expenditure on which is unaffected by the Schedule
A Walls, floors, ceilings, doors, gates, shutters, windows and stairs.	1 Electrical, cold water, gas and sewerage systems – a) provided mainly to meet the particular requirements of the trade, or b) provided mainly to serve particular machinery or plant used for the purposes of the trade.
	2 Space or water heating systems; powered systems of ventilation, air cooling or air purification; and any ceiling or floor comprised in such systems.
B Mains services, and systems of water, electricity and gas.	3 Manufacturing or processing equipment; storage equipment, including cold rooms; display equipment; and counters; checkouts and similar equipment.
	4 Cookers, washing machines, dishwashers, refrigerators and similar equipment; washbasins, sinks, baths, showers, sanitary ware and similar equipment; and furniture and furnishings.
C Waste disposal systems.	5 Lifts, hoists, escalators and moving walkways.
	6 Sound insulation provided mainly to meet the particular requirement of the trade
D Sewerage and drainage systems.	7 Computer, telecommunication and surveillance systems (including their wiring or other links).
E Shafts or other structures in which lifts, hoists, escalators and moving walkways are installed	8 Refrigeration or cooling equipment.
	9 Sprinkler equipment and other equipment for extinguishing or containing fire; fire alarm systems.
	10 Burglar alarm systems.

	11 Any machinery (including devices for providing motive power) not within any other item in this column.
F Fire safety systems.	12 Strong rooms in bank or building society premises; safes.
	13. Partition walls, where moveable and intended to be moved in the course of the trade.
	14. Decorative assets provided for the enjoyment of the public in the hotel, restaurant or similar trades.
	15 Advertising hoardings; and signs, displays and similar assets.

Ancillary expenditure

Where a trader incurs costs on alterations to a building which are incidental to the installation of plant and machinery, the expenditure is treated as part of the cost of plant and machinery, as are delivery charges. (The preparation of the site for such installation does not qualify.)

Costs of borrowing prior to the commencement of trading to finance the purchase of plant and machinery – while capital – were found to be a cost of obtaining funds and not of providing plant or machinery (*Ben–Odeco Ltd* v. *Powlson*). An exchange loss incurred in repaying a foreign currency loan to finance the purchase of plant was held to be a cost of providing the plant (*Van Arkadie* v. *Sterling Coated Metals Ltd*). Note that this may change when the tax treatment of exchange gains and losses is revamped following the 1993 Finance Act.

Expenditure deemed to be on plant and machinery

Certain safety expenditure is treated as plant for the purposes of capital allowances:

- Fire safety – expenditure incurred by a trader while complying with fire safety regulations in his or her business premises.
- Thermal insulation of an industrial building – where the trader occupies the premises for his or her trade or lets the building.
- Sports safety – expenditure necessary to obtain a safety certificate, expenditure at designated sports grounds and expenditure on stands at sports grounds.
- Security assets – expenditure necessary to meet a special threat to a sole trader's or partner's personal physical security arising by virtue of the trade.

If any of the above property is disposed of, the disposal value of the above expenditure is taken as nil.

Capital expenditure on the provision or acquisition, for purposes of a trade, of a right to use computer software is treated as plant and machinery for capital allowance purposes. This makes capital allowances available on computer software licences and electronically transmitted software.

Allowances

A writing down allowance is given at the rate of 25% per fiscal year (proportionately reduced if the trade was carried on for part only of that final year, for instance, on commencement, see Example 16.2) on an individual's qualifying expenditure less disposal value. For this purpose, expenditure, with a few exceptions, is pooled.

No allowance is available in the year a business ceases. An individual need not claim his full entitlement of allowances, claiming instead part or none of the allowances available according to his or her personal circumstances for the fiscal year. The result of making no claim or a reduced claim is to leave a higher balance of qualifying expenditure (see below) for carry forward to subsequent years.

The taxpayer must notify the inspector of any expenditure eligible for allowances, not later than two years after the end of the basis period in which it is incurred.

Qualifying expenditure

Qualifying expenditure is made up of the following:

- The balance of qualifying expenditure brought forward from the previous period after deducting any writing down allowances claimed for that previous period.
- Any expenditure incurred on plant and machinery wholly and exclusively, for the purpose of the trade during the current or previous periods and which did not form qualifying expenditure of any previous period.
- Any costs, during the basis period, of demolition of plant and machinery not replaced. (If replaced, this cost would be treated as part of the cost of the replacement.)

In addition, expenditure is regarded as qualifying expenditure of the period when it is incurred even if disposed of in the same period.

Disposal value

A disposal value must be brought into account whenever one of the following happens:

- The trader ceases to own an item of plant and machinery.
- The trader loses (permanently) an item of plant and machinery.
- The asset ceases to exist.
- The asset ceases to be used wholly and exclusively for purposes of the trade.
- The trade is, or is deemed to be, discontinued.

An exception to this exists where the asset is gifted such that the gift is within the scope of Schedule E legislation. No disposal value need be brought into account in this case.

The amount of the disposal value depends on the circumstances. On a sale at arm's length, the disposal value will equal the sale proceeds. Equally, on a sale below market value for any reason (say, to a connected person), the disposal value is market value (except as noted in the next paragraph). Also, on loss or destruction, the disposal value is the sum of any receipts for the remains plus any insurance or capital compensation received. The disposal value may, in no case, exceed the original cost to the trader.

Note that where an asset is transferred to another trader at less than market value, market value will not normally be substituted. This is because the buyer will be able to claim capital allowances in respect of his or her purchase (actual cost only) – it is not normally possible to transfer plant and machinery at tax written down value.

Date of disposal

A sale is treated as occurring on the earlier of the date of completion or the date when possession is given.

Suggested layout

	Pool of expenditure	Allowances
Written down value brought forward	X	
Additions during basis period	X	
	X	
Less: disposal values during basis period (Maximum original cost)	(X)	
	X	
Less: writing down allowance – Maximum 25% (provided trade carried on throughout fiscal year)	(X)	X
Written down value carried forward	X	
Total allowances claimed		X

It is recommended that this layout is followed carefully since a different result may be obtained if items are entered in a different order.

Balancing allowances and charges

Whenever the disposal values entered exceed the qualifying expenditure, there will be a balancing charge equal to the excess. This is assessed as additional trading profit of the fiscal year and itemised separately in the notice of assessment.

A balancing allowance can only arise in the fiscal year when the business ceases, or is deemed to cease, and equals the excess of qualifying expenditure over disposal value. Relief is given as for writing down allowances.

Qualifying expenditure not added to main pool

This can be divided into the following three groups.

Separate pool

This pool, referred to as FA 80 Pool or 'Cheap Car Pool', operates in the same way as the main pool for purposes of writing down allowances and balancing allowances and charges – the trade being deemed to be separate from the actual trade and any other trade, and deemed to cease when all items included in the separate pool are sold, lost and so on.

The items of expenditure which come into this pool are motor cars costing £12,000 or less.

Assets not used wholly for business purposes

A separate record of allowances must be kept for each asset not used wholly for business purposes, for example, a car with private use. (Note that cars used by employees are normally regarded as wholly for the trade albeit that they are used privately by the employee – a Schedule E charge may arise in this case – see Chapter 3.)

Writing down allowances and balancing allowances/charges given are reduced, usually in proportion to the overall percentage of private use agreed between the taxpayer and the Inspector (see Example 16.4). It is possible that a further reduction could be argued for personal choice, under the wholly and exclusively rule, for example where a trader chooses to drive a particularly expensive car not justified by the circumstances of the trade.

Motor cars costing more than £12,000

A separate record must be kept for each car in this category. The maximum writing down allowance in this case for each car is the lower of 25% of qualifying expenditure or £3,000 per fiscal year when trading has been carried on throughout. Balancing allowances/charges are calculated and treated as above.

Definition of motor car

Motor cars are all road vehicles except either:

- those of a type primarily suited for the conveyance of goods of any description (for instance, a mini-van); or
- those of a type not usually used as private cars and not suitable for such use (for instance, a Land Rover but not a Range Rover); or
- those used wholly or mainly for short-term hire to, or carriage of, members of the public as part of a trade (for instance, taxis).

all of which remain part of the main pool.

Case law must be referred to for more detailed guidelines. For example, in *Roberts* v. *Granada TV Rental Ltd* it was held that mini-vans, registered as goods vehicles but not adapted in any way, were of a type not commonly used as private vehicles and unsuitable for such use. Also cars fitted with dual controls for the purpose of driving tuition have been held unsuitable for private use, although cars used for driving tuition but not specifically adapted remain suitable for private use.

EXAMPLE 16.4

A trader, T, who has been in business for several years, makes up his accounts to 30 April each year. During the year ended 30 April 1994, he incurs the following capital expenditure:

£10,000 on machinery (1 November 1993);
£15,000 on a lorry for the delivery of goods (1 December 1993);
£15,000 on a car for the use of an employee (acquired 30 November 1993) and £15,000 on a car for himself (acquired 31 March 1994). Both are to be used privately as well as for business. He agrees his proportion of private use as 30% for the year ended 30 April 1994.

During the same year he makes the following disposals:

A machine originally costing £1,500 was sold for £2,000;
His old lorry was given a trade-in allowance of £4,000 against the cost of the new one;
His old car was sold privately to his brother for £2,500 (market value £3,500). His brother is also trading and will use the car for business. The tax written down value of the car at the date of sale was £3,375 (the proportion of private use over the period of ownership had been 30%).
T has qualifying expenditure of £25,000 brought forward from 1994/95.

TAX PLANNING

Capital allowances computation 1995/96
(Basis period – year ended 30 April 1994)

	Main pool £	Expensive car – no p.u* £	Private use cars £		Less p.u. £	All'ces £
Written down value bf	25,000		3,375	–		
Additions	25,000	15,000	–	15,000		
Less: disposals in period	(5,500)	–	(2,500)	–		
	44,500	15,000	875	15,000		
Less: balancing adjustment	–	–	(875)	–	263	612
	44,500	15,000	–	15,000		
Less: writing down allowance						
– max.	(11,125)	(3,000)	–			14,125
				(3,000)	900	2,100
Written down value c/f	33,375	12,000	–	12,000		
Total allowances						16,837

*A car for private use by an employee is not classified as a private use asset – capital allowances are not restricted.

The writing down allowances shown are the maximum available and such smaller amount as better fits an individual's circumstances may be claimed.

Short-life assets

In the system described above, an asset with a short life which is pooled with other assets does not generate a balancing allowance on its disposal – instead the balance of expenditure remains in the pool. A trader can elect for expenditure on individual items of plant and machinery, with certain exceptions, not to be pooled. Capital allowances are instead computed separately for each such asset with the result that a balancing charge/allowance may arise on its disposal. This is known as 'de-pooling'.

The legislation is clear as to what is not a short-life asset, but it does not define what is a short-life asset. The advantages of the election are, however, negated if the asset is held for more than four years following the year of purchase.

The following cannot be short-life assets:

▶ ships
▶ motor cars not forming part of the main pool
▶ assets leased otherwise than in the course of a trade
▶ assets used partly for non-trade purposes
▶ assets received by gift or brought into trade use following a period of non-trade use
▶ assets on which first year allowances are still available
▶ assets on which a subsidy is received
▶ assets leased and not used for a qualifying purpose.

A rule of thumb is that the election may only apply to assets which would otherwise form part of the main pool.

The election must be made within two years of the end of the basis period in which the expenditure is incurred, in writing, specifying the asset, the amount of expenditure and the date it was incurred. The election, once made, is irrevocable.

If no disposal value has been brought into account for the asset during the basis periods ending four years after the period of purchase, then the tax written down value of the asset is transferred to the main pool at the commencement of the following basis period.

EXAMPLE 16.5

During his accounting year to 31 December 1989, S bought two machines costing £12,000 and £10,000 respectively. Both were expected to become obsolete within four years and an election to 'depool' them was made. The first machine was scrapped in the year ended 31 December 1993 and only £500 received. The second machine is still in use for purposes of the trade at 31 December 1993 but is sold for £500 on 31 March 1994. There was qualifying expenditure on the main pool of £25,000 brought forward from 1989/90 but there have been no other additions or disposals during the period under review.

Capital allowance computation

	Pool	Machine A	Machine B	Allowances
	£	£	£	£
1990/91				
Written down value b/f	25,000			
Additions		12,000	10,000	
WDA 25%	(6,250)	(3,000)	(2,500)	11,750
Written down value c/f	18,750	9,000	7,500	
1991/92				
WDA 25%	(4,687)	(2,250)	(1,875)	8,812
1992/93				
WDA 25%	(3,516)	(1,688)	(1,406)	6,610
1993/94				
WDA 25%	(2,637)	(1,266)	(1,055)	4,958
Written down value c/f	7,910	3,796	3,164	
1994/95				
Disposal value		(500)		
Balancing allowance		3,296		3,296
WDA 25%	(1,978)		(791)	2,769
Written down value c/f	5,932		2,373	
Total allowances				6,065
1995/96				
Transfer to pool	2,373		(2,373)	
	8,305			
Disposal value	(500)			
	7,805			
WDA 25%	(1,951)			1,951
Written down value c/f	5,854			

Where a short-life asset is disposed of within the four year period to a connected person, the 'depooling' election continues in force as if the connected person had incurred the original expenditure and made the election. The trader and the connected person may also jointly elect (within two years of the end of the basis period of the transfer) to treat the asset as if transferred at tax written down value – no balancing allowance or charge will then arise. If no such election is made the asset will be deemed to have been transferred at market value where this is more than actual sale price (compare disposal values where the asset is not a short-life asset).

Modifications of the above system are acceptable in practice as the Inland Revenue recognises the difficulty in preparing computations where there are a large number of short-life assets. These modifications will usually take the form of a modified pooling system for short-life assets – Inland Revenue Statement of Practice (SP 1/86) refers.

Hire purchase and leasing

Hire purchase

An asset purchased on HP is treated as if purchased outright for the cash price at the date the agreement is entered into. The buyer may claim capital allowances on the cash price and may write off the finance charge as a revenue expense over the term of the contract. The seller is treated as having sold the asset for the cash price – the seller is not, therefore, entitled to claim capital allowances.

Leases

Leases, from an accounting point of view, are divided into two categories – operating leases and finance leases – and the accounting treatment differs accordingly.

Operating leases or rental leases are essentially short-term hire agreements where a single asset may be hired out to several different operators during its useful life. Often the lessor provides servicing facilities for the assets and may even insure it. The lessor owns the assets and obtains the capital allowances while the total hire charges paid by the lessee will normally be treated as a revenue expense. This is restricted in the case of a car costing more than £12,000 (see Chapter 15).

Finance leases are contracts which require payment of specified sums over an obligatory period which are usually sufficient in total to cancel all the lessor's outlays in respect of that asset and to give some profit. An asset is leased out to one operator for the greater part of its useful life. The purpose of the lease is to allow the lessee to avoid a large capital outlay. SSAP 21 deals with the accounting treatment of such assets – they are treated in virtually the same manner as if they were being acquired on a hire purchase contract and capitalised in the books of the lessee. However, the Inland Revenue makes no distinction between a finance lease and an operating lease and states that, notwithstanding SSAP 21, lessees are not entitled to obtain capital allowances in respect of leased plant and machinery. For tax purposes, therefore, SSAP 21 adjustments have to be reversed.

The tax position, therefore, is the same irrespective of the type of lease (unless the lease contains an option to purchase when it is treated as a hire purchase contract). Expenditure on assets for leasing is added to the main pool of expenditure of the lessor except for expenditure on motor cars which is added to the separate FA 1980 pool.

Where an item of plant or machinery is leased, it can still qualify as a short-life asset providing it is used for a 'qualifying purpose' throughout the 'requisite period' (four years after the end of the basis period in which the expenditure was incurred). A 'qualifying purpose' is one of the following:

- The asset is leased to a lessee who uses it for a trade other than leasing and if the lessee had incurred the expenditure it would have been qualifying expenditure in the main pool.
- The person who incurred the expenditure, or a person connected with him or her, uses the asset for short-term leasing.
- The asset is leased to a lessee who uses it for short-term leasing in the UK.
- The person who incurred the expenditure, or a person connected with that person, uses the asset for a trade other than leasing.
- The asset is a ship, transport container or an aircraft which does not otherwise qualify but is let on a charter to a UK trader for the purpose of his or her trade.

Successions to trades

Where a trade changes hands and is treated as discontinued, plant and machinery in use both before and after the change is treated as being sold to the successor at open market value at the date of transfer.

Where a person succeeds to a trade under the terms of a will or intestacy, that person may elect that any plant and machinery transferred to him or her be transferred at its tax written down value (if this is less than open market value). This is done at the commencement of the final period of assessment plus any additions less any disposal values during the period before death. Any subsequent disposal of an inherited asset will be entered in the capital allowance computation at disposal proceeds, maximum original cost to the deceased.

When the trade changes hands to a connected person, they may jointly elect that the trade shall not be treated as discontinued for the purpose of capital allowances. The successor then stands in the shoes of his or her predecessor with allowances being made to, and charges being made upon, him or her as if the successor were in fact his or her predecessor. A connected person is as defined for capital gains tax – see Chapter 5.

Planning considerations

The withdrawal of long-term first year allowances has greatly reduced the scope for planning tax deferral through the timely acquisition of plant and machinery.

The major advantage that can still be gained is the timing of acquisitions with disposals to avoid a balancing charge. This has the effect of seemingly increasing allowances on acquisitions as demonstrated below:

	£
Written down value b/f	5,000
Additions during basis period	10,000
	15,000
Disposals during basis period	(15,000)
Writing down allowance and Written down value c/f	Nil

A balancing charge of £10,000 has effectively been avoided by an effective 100% allowance on additions.

Careful use of the de-pooling election can also produce good results. It should be used, for example, where a balancing allowance is anticipated but not where a balancing charge is anticipated. In addition, if the main pool of qualifying expenditure is at a relatively low level and future disposals are likely to give rise to a balancing charge, it may be worth while foregoing the short-life asset election in order to inflate the main pool.

Attention should also be given to the possible benefits of not claiming the full writing down allowance. The following factors will need to be considered in this case:

- other sources of income
- charges paid
- entitlement to personal allowances
- liability to national insurance
- liability to higher rate tax
- loss reliefs (see Chapter 18).

Renewals basis

As an alternative to claiming capital allowances, the renewals basis may be used. This operates in the following way.

No capital allowances are claimed on the cost of the original asset, or on all assets of a particular class. Subsequently, on their replacement, the cost is a revenue expense deductible in arriving at the trading profits of the period in which the replacement took place (less, of course, any proceeds on disposal of the replaced asset).

This basis tends to be used for small items not individually identifiable, but there is no reason why it should not be used for larger items.

The advantage of this basis is that a 100% allowance is effectively available for replacements. A disadvantage is that it is only possible where like is replaced by like – there can be no allowance for any improvement element or additions to the original asset/assets.

This basis has not been used significantly since first year allowances were first introduced. However, with the disappearance of 100% first year allowances, it may become more attractive. There are no laid down procedures for switching from capital allowances to the renewals basis. It is possible that the attempt to make this switch might result in a deemed disposal at market value for capital allowance purposes leading to balancing charges. This would not be so attractive.

Industrial buildings

What is an industrial building?

It can be defined as any building or structure, or part thereof, which is used for a trade, or a part of a trade, which is a qualifying activity.

The following are listed as qualifying activities:

- a trade carried on in a mill or factory
- a trade which consists of the manufacture of goods or materials or the subjection of goods or materials to any process
- a transport, dock, inland navigation, water, sewerage, electricity or hydraulic power undertaking, tunnel or bridge undertaking, agricultural contractors, mining or fishing
- a trade which consists in the storage of goods or materials to be used in the manufacture of other goods or materials, or to be subjected to a manufacturing process; or the storage of finished goods for delivery to the purchaser.

In addition, the following qualify:

- buildings used for the welfare of employees in a qualifying trade above and sports pavilions for the use of employees in any trade
- qualifying hotels
- any commercial buildings in an enterprise zone (constructed within ten years of it being so designated).

In the latter instance, the Finance Act 1992 introduced a formula to calculate the amount of qualifying expenditure where part of the construction cost falls within the ten year period and part does not:

$$A \times \frac{B}{C}$$

where A is the expenditure which would otherwise qualify,
B is the part of actual cost falling within the ten-year period, and
C is the total construction cost.

A building, or part of a building, qualifies as an industrial building if used in part of a trade for a qualifying activity (provided that the part of a trade is not insubstantial).

Excluded from the above are buildings used as a dwelling-house, retail shop, showroom, or office. However, a drawing office has been held to be part of a factory for this purpose. A warehouse may cause problems – if it is ancillary to a qualifying trade, it will qualify; if it is ancillary to a retail trade, it will not qualify; if it is ancillary to a wholesale trade, it will usually qualify.

Buildings for the welfare of employees include canteens, social clubs and day nurseries. However, it must be noted that these facilities must be available to all employees or at least to manufacturing workers – buildings for office workers are regarded as ancillary to the offices.

A qualifying hotel is a building of a permanent nature which:

- has at least ten letting bedrooms
- whose rooms are not normally in the same occupation for more than one month
- is open for at least four months (120 days) in the period April to October
- provides ancillary services including breakfast, an evening meal, the cleaning of rooms and the making of beds.

Qualifying cost

Allowances are given in respect of capital expenditure incurred on the construction of a building or structure. For this purpose the costs of levelling and preparing the land and the architect's fees may be included, but not the cost of the land itself nor legal fees associated with the acquisition of the land or buildings. Preparing the site for the installation of machinery and plant also ranks for allowances if not eligible as plant and machinery. The cost of improvements and extensions used for the qualifying activity also qualify. There are the usual difficulties regarding the classification of expenditure on alterations and repairs as either capital or revenue.

That part of a building which is offices or otherwise not used for a qualifying activity is not eligible for allowances unless the total cost of the non-industrial parts (such as offices) does not exceed 25% of the total construction cost.

EXAMPLE 16.6

X, who makes up his accounts to 30 April each year, acquired a new purpose-built factory on 31 August 1992 at a cost of £300,000, of which £50,000 was for the land. The main area is used for industrial processing but it is ascertained that the cost of the administrative offices was £37,500 and the cost of the drawing office was £30,000. He brought the factory into use immediately.

The qualifying cost is £250,000 (£300,000 less the cost of the land £50,000). As the drawing office is treated as being for a qualifying purpose, the cost of the administrative offices, £37,500, is less than 25% of £250,000 (the total construction cost). Allowances will first be available in 1994/95 – the purchase was in the basis period to 30 April 1993, the profits of which will be assessed in 1994/95.

If a further £35,000 had been spent on the offices, the other costs remaining unchanged, the total cost of the building would have been £285,000. In this case the cost of the non-industrial parts is £72,500 (£37,500 + £35,000), which exceeds 25% of the total construction cost and therefore the qualifying cost would be restricted to £212,500 (£285,000 – £72,500).

Initial allowance

The initial allowance ceased to be available for expenditure incurred on all buildings, other than those in enterprise zones, after 31 March 1986. However, they were recently re-introduced for industrial buildings constructed under a contract entered into between 1 November 1992 and 31 October 1993 and brought into use for the purpose of a qualifying trade before 31 December 1994. Owing to the nature of the industrial buildings allowance and the need to refer to records 25 or even 50 years later, it is necessary to understand when the initial allowance is/was available and on what expenditure.

An initial allowance was available to the person who incurred capital expenditure on a building which that person constructed or which that person acquired *new and unused* and which was to be an industrial building occupied for the purposes of a trade carried on by the person, his or her lessee or sub-lessee.

The allowance was given in the fiscal year during the basis period of which the expenditure was incurred and was based on the 'qualifying cost' of the building. This was either the purchase price from the builder, or the original cost if self-built, or the lower of purchase price and original cost if purchased elsewhere. The allowance was also available on the cost of improvements or extensions to qualifying industrial buildings. (Details are listed above of items which may or may not be included in the qualifying cost.) Initial allowances for pre-construction expenditure were given even if no building was subsequently constructed.

The rates of allowance depend on the date the expenditure was incurred:

	%	**Expenditure incurred**
Industrial buildings and sports pavilions	50	before 11 March 1981
	75	11 March 1981–13 March 1984
	50	14 March 1984–31 March 1985
	25	1 April 1985–31 March 1986
Qualifying hotels	20	11 April 1978–31 March 1986
Qualifying hotels and commercial buildings in enterprise zones	100	after 27 March 1980
Industrial buildings	20	1 November 1992–31 October 1993 (contract) and use by 31 December 1994

(Note that these rates will be supplied in the examination if required.)

Qualifying hotels and commercial buildings in enterprise zones

It should be noted that commercial buildings in enterprise zones include buildings which, situated elsewhere, would not be qualifying industrial buildings. Plant and machinery fitted as fixtures in such buildings also qualify. A 100% initial allowance is still available.

Initial allowances can be claimed in full or in part by a trader.

Writing down allowances – first user

Since 31 March 1986, these are now the principal allowances available. They are given for the fiscal year to the person who holds the 'relevant interest' in the building or structure at the *end of the basis period*, provided it qualifies as an industrial building on *the last day of the basis period*. Writing down allowances are based upon the 'qualifying cost', that is, they are calculated on a straight line basis. (Compare writing down allowances for plant and machinery.)

Writing down allowances are first available in the fiscal year for the basis period when the building is first brought into industrial use. (In the past this may have been the same year as the initial allowance was available – if the expenditure was incurred and the building brought into use in the same basis period). They may subsequently be available for some periods and not others. This depends on whether the building qualifies as an industrial building on the last day of the basis period (ignoring temporary disuse). The writing down allowance is proportionately reduced if the trade is not carried on throughout the fiscal year (in the first year of trading for example).

The rates of writing down allowance have also been subject to change over the years:

	%	**Expenditure incurred**
Industrial buildings	4	after 5 Nov 1962
Qualifying hotels	4	after 11 April 1978
Qualifying hotels and commercial buildings in enterprise zones (if initial allowance not claimed in full)	25	after 27 March 1980

In no case can a writing down allowance exceed the residue of expenditure (see below). Where an industrial building has been extended, the expenditure on each addition (having taken place at different times) should be separately recorded.

Writing down allowances for industrial buildings are given to the person with the relevant interest (see below). There are no specific provisions allowing him or her not to claim all or part of the allowance.

EXAMPLE 16.7

S, a manufacturer with a 30 June year end, bought an unused industrial building from a builder for £120,000 (including land). The builder's construction costs were £60,000. He paid for the building on 30 April 1985 and brought it into use on 1 August 1985. The purchase price was allocated as follows:

	£	£
Land		20,000
Levelling		2,000
Architects		3,000
Building costs:		
production section	60,000	
raw materials store	6,000	
finished goods warehouse	10,000	
quality control	10,000	
administration	9,000	95,000
		120,000

During his accounting year ended 30 June 1986, his own labour added an extension to the building at a capital cost of £25,000, (£11,000 for office accommodation and £14,000 for a staff canteen), which was brought into use on 31 March 1986.

Calculate the industrial buildings allowances available.

The initial expenditure was incurred on 30 April 1985 in the accounting period to 30 June 1985, assessed 1986/87. The qualifying cost was £100,000 (excluding the cost of the land but including the administration section as this was less than 25% of the total construction costs of £100,000). An initial allowance was available in 1986/87 when the expenditure was incurred. However, writing down allowances were not available until 1987/88 when the building was brought into use.

The expenditure on the extension was incurred in the accounting period to 30 June 1986 assessed 1987/88. Providing the canteen was available to all staff, it would qualify as an industrial building. The total office costs of £20,000 (£9,000 + £11,000) would qualify, being less than 25% of the total construction costs of £125,000 (£100,000 + £25,000).

The capital allowances claimed would be:

	Industrial building		Extension		Total allowances
	£	£	£	£	£
1986/87					
Qualifying cost	100,000				
IA 25%	25,000				
		25,000			25,000
		75,000			
1987/88					
Qualifying expenditure			25,000		
IA 25%			6,250		
WDA 4%	4,000		1,000		
		4,000		7,250	11,250
Residue of expenditure		71,000		17,750	

Relevant interest

The relevant interest in a building or structure is the interest to which the person who incurs any expenditure on its construction is entitled, at the time that person incurs it. The relevant interest will be transferred on sale of the freehold, but will not pass on the granting of a subsidiary interest (for instance, a lease).

Industrial buildings allowance therefore is normally granted to the owner of the building and not the lessee. Where a building is let, however, under a long lease (more than 50 years) the lessor and the lessee may jointly elect that the grant of the lease shall be deemed to be a sale. The effect of this is that the lessee can obtain the industrial buildings allowance. This election is particularly relevant where the lessor is exempt from tax and could not use the allowances. The election must be made within two years of the date when the lease is granted.

Residue of expenditure

The residue of expenditure is the balance of the original qualifying cost remaining after the initial allowance and writing down allowances (actual and notional) given to date have been deducted. Notional writing down allowances are those allowances *not* given to the taxpayer for any year after the first – when the industrial building was not in industrial use on the last day of the basis period.

Balancing allowances and charges on disposal

For tax purposes, the life of an industrial building is deemed to be 25 years (4% writing down allowance) or 50 years, if the expenditure was incurred before 6 November 1962. Its qualifying cost, however, was often written off over a shorter period when initial allowances were available.

Balancing adjustments will only be made if the building is sold within its tax life.

No non-industrial use

Where there has been no non-industrial use during the period of ownership, the calculations are straightforward. The residue of expenditure of the vendor is compared with the sale proceeds – maximum original qualifying cost. Care must be taken to ensure that only the sale proceeds of that part of the building which qualified as an industrial building are brought into account. Note that writing down allowances are not available in the year of disposal since the building is not in use by that person on the last day of the basis period.

	£
Qualifying cost	X
Allowances given to date	(X)
Residue of expenditure	X
Sale proceeds (maximum cost)	(X)
Balancing allowance/(charge)	X

Non-industrial use

Special rules apply to the calculation of balancing allowances and charges where a building has been used otherwise than as an industrial building during the period of ownership:

- Where the sale proceeds are more than the original cost of the building, the balancing charge will be the amount of the allowances actually given.
- Where the sale proceeds are less than the original cost of the building, the 'adjusted net cost' must be calculated. If the adjusted net cost is greater than the allowances actually given, a balancing allowance arises. If the adjusted net cost is less than the allowances actually given, a balancing charge is made.

The 'adjusted net cost' is the qualifying cost less sale proceeds (net cost of ownership) reduced in the proportion that the period of time for which the building was in industrial use bears to the whole period of ownership. (This is usually calculated to the nearest month.)

$$\text{Net cost of ownership} \times \frac{\text{Period of industrial use}}{\text{Period of ownership}}$$

EXAMPLE 16.8

Y, who makes up his accounts to 31 December each year, incurred expenditure of £100,000 on 1 June 1989 on a building which qualified for industrial buildings allowance. It was brought into use immediately. It was used as an industrial building until 31 May 1991 and for non-industrial purposes until 31 May 1992. It was used for industrial purposes again until 31 May 1993 when it was sold for:

a) £110,000
b) £90,000

		£	£
Qualifying cost			100,000
1990/91	Writing down allowance 4% actual	4,000	
1991/92	Writing down allowance 4% actual	4,000	
1992/93	Writing down allowance 4% notional	4,000	
1993/94	Writing down allowance 4% actual	4,000	
1994/95	Year of sale – no allowance	—	
			16,000
Residue of expenditure			84,000

a) Sale price £110,000 (greater than cost)

	£
Residue of expenditure	84,000
Sale proceeds – maximum cost	(100,000)
Balancing charge	16,000
restricted to allowances actually granted	12,000

b) Sale proceeds £90,000 (less than cost)

	£
Qualifying cost	100,000
Sale proceeds	90,000
Net cost of ownership	10,000
Adjusted net cost:	
$10,000 \times \dfrac{3 \text{ years}}{4 \text{ years}} =$	7,500
Allowances granted	(12,000)
Balancing charge	4,500

Writing down allowances – second and subsequent users

Where a used industrial building is sold the amount of the writing down allowance available to the purchaser is based upon his or her qualifying cost (frequently referred to as residue after sale), calculated as follows:

	£
Residue of expenditure of vendor	X
Balancing charge/(allowance) of vendor, if any	X
Qualifying cost of purchaser	X

This qualifying cost is spread over the remaining tax life of the building (calculated to the nearest month).

EXAMPLE 16.9

Continuing the examples above:

a) Sale price £110,000

	£
Residue of expenditure of vendor	84,000
Balancing charge of vendor	12,000
Qualifying cost of purchaser	96,000

(Note that this is both less than the price paid (£110,000) and less than the original qualifying cost (£100,000).)

Remaining tax life of building:	
25 years less 1 June 1989–31 May 1993	21 years
Annual writing down allowance of purchaser	4,571

b) Sale price £90,000

	£
Residue of expenditure of vendor	84,000
Balancing charge of vendor	4,500
Qualifying cost of purchaser	88,500
(Note that this is less than the price paid (£90,000) and less than the original qualifying cost (£100,000).)	
Remaining tax life of building – as above	21 years
Annual writing down allowance of purchaser	4,214

Agricultural buildings

Qualifying expenditure

Capital expenditure incurred by the holder of a 'major interest' in any agricultural land on the construction of farmhouses, farm buildings, cottages, fences or other works or part thereof, will qualify for agricultural buildings allowance. No expenditure on the acquisition of, or rights in, any land will qualify. The expenditure must be for the purpose of husbandry on the agricultural land at the time the expenditure is incurred.

A maximum of one-third of any expenditure on the farmhouse is allowable (the fraction will be reduced below one-third if the size and amenities of the farmhouse are inconsistent with the farm). Where any other asset serves partly the purposes of husbandry and partly other purposes, an apportionment of the expenditure is made.

There is no provision that a farm-employee's cottage must be situated on the farm (but this could have implications on the Schedule E liability of the employee).

'Other works' are not defined but include drainage and sewerage, water and electricity installations, shelter belts of trees, greenhouses for market gardening, farmyard paving and so on.

Major interest in land

This means the freehold or agreement to acquire the freehold, or a lease. The lessee is therefore entitled to agricultural buildings allowance on qualifying expenditure incurred by him or her while the landlord is entitled to allowances on his or her qualifying expenditure.

Allowances (post FA 86)

Like industrial buildings allowance, a 4% writing down allowance on the straight line basis is given for a 25-year writing down period. The allowance cannot be reduced. Basis periods apply as for plant and machinery and industrial buildings and the allowances are given in the taxing of a trade.

In addition, a first owner is entitled to receive an initial allowance of 20% in respect of agricultural buildings constructed under a contract entered into between 1 November 1992 and 31 October 1993. This allowance can be disclaimed.

Balancing allowances/charges do not automatically arise on the transfer of assets classified as agricultural buildings. Unless an election is made, the balance of the allowances automatically passes to the purchaser. In the fiscal year in the basis period for which the transfer takes place, the transferor receives a final writing down allowance which is a fraction of the full allowance based on the period from the start of the basis period to the date of the transfer. The transferee also receives his or her first allowance proportionately reduced according to the period from the date of the transfer to the end of his or her basis period.

An election for a balancing adjustment may be made on the transfer of an asset or when it ceases to exist (demolished, destroyed and so on). It must be made jointly by the transferor and transferee on a transfer and by the original owner on any other occasion. The election must be made in writing to the inspector within two years of the end of the fiscal year in the basis period for which the event occurred.

EXAMPLE 16.10

M, who makes up his farm accounts to 31 March, incurred expenditure of £5,000 in December 1991. The asset was transferred to P, who makes up his farm accounts to 31 December, on 30 September 1993 for £10,000.

1 No election

M can claim allowances of £200 (4% of £5,000) for each of 1992/93 (year end 31 March 1992) and 1993/94 (year end 31 March 1993) and an allowance of £100 for 1994/95 (six months from April 1993 to September 1993).

P can claim £50 in 1994/95 (three months from October 1993 to December 1993) and £200 for 1995/96 *et seq*.

2 Election

			£
M	Cost December 1991		5,000
	WDA 1992/93 and 1993/94 as above		400
	Residue of expenditure		4,600
	1994/95 Sale proceeds maximum cost		5,000
	Balancing charge		400
P	Residue of expenditure		4,600
	Balancing charge of transferor		400
	Revised qualifying expenditure to be spread over 23 years 3 months (the remainder of the 25 years)		5,000
	The election must be made by 5 April 1997		

Patents

Purchasers of patent rights are entitled to writing down allowances. This includes those who buy the patent outright and those who acquire a licence in respect of a patent.

Allowances are given to a trader taxable under Schedule D Case I and to a person who is taxable in respect of income from patents.

Allowances

All capital expenditure on the purchase of patent rights is included in a pool, and writing down allowances of 25% on a reducing balance basis are made. These are proportionately reduced if the trade is not carried on for the whole of the basis period.

A balancing allowance/charge may arise on the disposal of patent rights in the same way as it does for plant and machinery. (A disposal of patent rights includes an outright sale or the grant of a licence.) The disposal value is normally the lower of the sale proceeds and the cost of the patent rights (but if the rights were originally acquired through connected persons or are sold to connected persons then special rules apply). Note that the amount by which sale proceeds exceeds cost constitutes a gain assessable under Schedule D Case VI, in six equal instalments over six years commencing with the fiscal year of sale.

Know-how

Know-how is any industrial information and techniques likely to assist in any of the activities that qualify for industrial buildings allowances. It is not protected under law, but is often commercially treated in the same way as patents.

Acquisition

Capital allowances are available for expenditure incurred in acquiring know-how for use in a trade in so far as no other relief is obtained for the expenditure. Where it is acquired with a trade or part of a trade, it is frequently treated as a payment for goodwill and no capital allowances are available (unless both parties elect otherwise).

Disposal

Know-how which is disposed of may not appear as an asset in the books of the vendor and in this case the vendor will not have received capital allowances in respect of it. In this case a receipt for the sale of know-how may be regarded as a payment for goodwill on a disposal of the business. It may also be regarded as a trading receipt if the trade still continues; otherwise it will be taxed under Schedule D Case VI. It will be taxed as income in this way where both vendor and purchaser make an election in order that the purchaser obtains capital allowances.

Allowances

All capital expenditure on the acquisition of know-how is included in a pool and writing down allowances of 25% on a reducing balance basis are made. Basis periods apply as for plant and machinery.

The allowances are reduced proportionately where the trade is not carried on throughout the basis period and are given in taxing a trade. Balancing allowances/charges operate as for plant and machinery except that disposal proceeds are deducted in full (that is, not restricted to original cost).

Scientific research

Where capital expenditure is incurred on scientific research by a trader for the purposes of his or her trade, or the trader sets up and commences a trade connected with the research, he or she is entitled to a 100% allowance given in the taxing of the trade for the 'relevant chargeable period'. The 'relevant chargeable period' for income tax purposes corresponds with the fiscal year in which the basis period in which the expenditure is incurred is assessed – except that allowances for any expenditure incurred prior to the commencement of the trade are given in the first year of assessment of the trade.

No allowances are available for the acquisition of land or the acquisition of a dwelling-house (unless it is part of a building used for scientific research and does not represent more than one quarter of the cost of the whole).

Where an asset on which a scientific research allowance has been received is disposed of, the proceeds will be treated as a trading receipt equal to the lower of the allowance given or the proceeds.

If a scientific research allowance is claimed no other capital allowances may be claimed on the same expenditure.

Mineral extraction

Qualifying expenditure on mineral extraction is capital expenditure on:

- mineral exploration and access; acquisition of mineral deposits (excluding the undeveloped land value); construction works in connection with working the mineral deposits
- pre-trading expenditure on plant and machinery disposed of
- pre-trading exploration expenditure
- provision of buildings, common services and the like for employees where the mineral extraction is overseas
- post-trading restoration expenditure.

There is an overlap between expenditure eligible under these headings and expenditure eligible as industrial buildings or plant and machinery or scientific research. A claim for mineral extraction allowance precludes other allowances.

Writing down allowances are calculated separately for each item of expenditure at a rate ranging from 10% to 25% depending on the type of expenditure. This is, however, reduced proportionately where the trade was not carried on throughout the fiscal year.

Balancing allowances/charges are made where assets are disposed of.

Summary

- Plant and machinery allowances are the biggest area but the changes to the system have not been dramatic over recent years. The principal areas are the giving of writing down allowances on the date expenditure is incurred and not when brought into use; the election for special treatment of short-life assets.
- The definition of plant will always be a difficult area. The Finance Act 1994 has attempted to clarify this area by specifying items deemed to be part of a building and thus ineligible for plant and machinery allowances.
- Industrial buildings have been affected by the temporary re-introduction of the initial allowance. The most difficult area remains the balancing adjustments on sale where there were periods of non-industrial use.
- No major changes have been made to the systems of granting allowances for agricultural buildings, patents, and know-how. Care should be taken to ensure that you are familiar with these.

Self test questions

1. Where the basis periods for a number of fiscal years overlap, to which capital allowance computation should capital expenditure be allocated?
2. What capital allowances are available in the first fiscal year of trading?
3. For what capital expenditure is the FA 80 pool used?

4   Why are motor cars costing more than £12,000 recorded individually for purposes of computing writing down allowances?

5   To what assets does the de-pooling election apply?

6   To what capital allowances is a lessee of plant and machinery entitled?

7   List four categories of building which may qualify for industrial buildings allowance.

8   When are writing down allowances for industrial buildings available?

9   An old, established manufacturing firm operates from a factory with a floor area of 30,000 square feet which had cost £10,000 in 1966. An extension to the building for use as offices was completed in April 1992, no other alterations had been made to the building in the interval. It had a floor area of 3,000 square feet and cost £20,000. The firm prepares accounts to 31 December each year. What industrial buildings allowances will be due for the years 1993/94 and 1994/95? (The original factory received an initial allowance of 15% in 1967/68 on the total cost.)

10 S, engaged for many years in manufacturing and selling containers used for transportation, has incurred the following capital expenditure during the following accounting periods:

		y/e 30 Sept 1991 £	y/e 30 Sept 1992 £	y/e 30 Sept 1993 £
1 Dec 1990	Factory heating system	7,000		
9 Jun 1991	Computer (which was sold for £150 on 5 July 1994)	2,000		
21 March 1992	Office equipment		19,000	
24 July 1992	Purchase of new freehold factory (including land costing £40,000)		240,000	
15 Sept 1992	Manufacturing plant (£1,400 was obtained for plant scrapped)		108,000	
23 Sept 1992	Purchase of patent rights		10,000	
1 Jan 1993	Car for proprietor (private use 20%)			18,000

General plant and machinery pool brought forward at 5 April 1992 amounted to £24,000. Prior to January 1993, all cars were leased.

You are required to do the capital allowances computations for the relevant years of assessment, assuming any relevant elections were made, and that all allowances and reliefs are claimed in full.

11 a) The partners of CCD Trading Co, a manufacturing concern which makes up its accounts to 31 March each year, are considering the purchase of an additional, second-hand factory on 1 April 1994. They have decided to spend £150,000 and the following details refer to four possible purchases which could each be acquired for the above sum. All are equally suitable for the company's purposes and all have been used for qualifying industrial purposes throughout their lives.

	Original cost to first owner	Date of first use
i)	£100,000	1 April 1970
ii)	£80,000	1 April 1969
iii)	£160,000	1 April 1990
iv)	£120,000	1 April 1984

Advise the partners of the amount of industrial buildings allowances which will be available to the business as a result of purchasing each of the above factories, indicating the periods for which the allowances will be available. Which building would you advise them to purchase?

b) Having acquired the above factory the partners intend to incur further capital expenditure as follows:
  i) Installation of display lighting in a showroom where customers will view the company's products.
  ii) Thermal insulation of the factory.
  iii) Construction of a canteen within the factory premises for the use of the workforce.

Advise the partners of the extent to which capital allowances will be available in respect of the above items of expenditure.

(adapted from CIMA 3 Nov 1988)
Answers on pages 591–593

CHAPTER 17

Partnerships

This chapter looks at the manner in which the profits of a partnership are assessed to tax and the effect of changes in the composition of a partnership. Once again, you will have studied much of the subject-matter in the Paper 7 syllabus. The aim here is to provide some quick revision of the basics and to develop an understanding of partnership taxation in order to appreciate the scope for tax planning in this area.

Tax status of a partnership

The Schedule D Case I or II adjusted profits of a trading partnership are computed in the manner described in Chapter 15 (see Example 15.1).

A partnership in England and Wales, however, is not a legal entity separate and distinct from its members and cannot be ultimately liable for the partnership tax liabilities. It is for administrative convenience that the Inland Revenue raises an assessment on the partnership rather than on the individual partners.

The precedent acting partner (normally the first named in the partnership agreement) is responsible for making the partnership tax return. The partnership tax return only covers the partnership income (including profit-sharing arrangements) and claims for allowances; it does not include any private income or allowances of the individual partners, which must be shown on their personal tax returns.

The partnership assessment takes into account the following:

- the firm's Schedule D Case I adjusted profits for the relevant basis period
- capital allowances
- the allowance for Class IV National Insurance contributions of each of the partners
- any business charges paid
- the personal allowances of each of the partners.

It then arrives at the total income tax liability (lower, basic and higher rate).

For this final income tax liability to be accurate, the assessable profits, the capital allowances and any business charges of the partnership are shared between the partners (in line with the profit-sharing information returned and interpreted in accordance with the Taxes Acts). Their individual deductions and personal allowances are subtracted and each individual's income tax liability is calculated, usually, as if it were their only source of income (in other words, a full lower and basic rate band is given before any liability to higher rate arises). The partnership assessment is therefore merely the sum of the partners' individual liabilities.

Any non-trading income of the partnership (for example, Schedule A or Schedule D Case III) is assessed directly on the individual partners.

The partnership Schedule D Case I assessment

The assessable profits in any fiscal year are normally based on the adjusted profits of the accounts year ending in the preceding fiscal year.

Allocation of assessable profits

Although the accounts on which the adjusted profit computation is based will show an appropriation account, this is of no relevance for tax purposes. For tax purposes, the DI adjusted profits are income of the fiscal year and must be allocated between the partners – according to their profit-sharing arrangements during that fiscal year.

If a partnership prepares its accounts to 31 December each year, the assessment for 1994/95 will be based on the adjusted profit of the accounting year ended 31 December 1993. It is irrelevant how the profits were appropriated in the 1993 accounts, for tax purposes they will be divided between the partners according to their profit-sharing arrangements in the year ended 5 April 1995.

Note that this will give rise to anomalies if the profit-sharing arrangements in the two periods are significantly different. (The appropriation account for the year ended 31 December 1993 determines what profits a partner actually receives while the profit-sharing arrangements for the year to 5 April 1995 determine the profits that partner will be taxed on.)

EXAMPLE 17.1

A, B and C are in partnership sharing profits, after partnership salaries and interest on capital, equally. The appropriation account for the year ended 31 December 1993 was as follows:

	A	B	C	Total	£
Net profit brought down					51,000
	£	£	£	£	
Partners' salaries	14,000	10,000	6,000	30,000	
Interest on capital	1,200	1,000	800	3,000	
				33,000	
Balance of profit 1:1:1	6,000	6,000	6,000	18,000	
	21,200	17,000	12,800	51,000	51,000

The Schedule D Case I adjusted profit for the year was £60,000.

The partners had a reorganisation which took effect from 1 January 1994 and would remain unchanged until 1 January 1996. The partners agreed that their salaries would become respectively £7,000, £12,000 and £12,000 per annum; the capital accounts and agreed interest rate remained unchanged; and the remaining profit sharing ratio was adjusted to 2:1:1.

1994/95 Schedule D Case I partnership profit £60,000

Division between partners – per arrangements in force during 1994/95 ie after the change.

	A	B	C	Total
	£	£	£	£
Partners' salaries	7,000	12,000	12,000	31,000
Interest on capital	1,200	1,000	800	3,000
				34,000
Balance of profit	13,000	6,500	6,500	26,000
	21,200	19,500	19,300	60,000

If you compare the amounts on which the individual partners are assessed, you will see that although the adjusted profits are £9,000 higher than the actual profits, A is assessed on the same amount while B is assessed on £2,500 extra and C is assessed on £6,500 extra.

Changes in profit-sharing arrangements during the year of assessment

In the above illustration, no change in profit-sharing arrangements took place during the year of assessment 1994/95; the change which took effect on 1 January 1994 applied throughout 1994/95.

If the change in Example 17.1 had not taken effect until 1 January 1995, then the profit-sharing arrangements which applied during 1994/95 would have been as follows:

    6 April 1994–31 December 1994   Original agreement
    1 January 1995–5 April 1995   New agreement

Again the profit-sharing arrangements in existence throughout the year of assessment are reflected.

The following example uses the previous example but adapts it in the manner described above.

EXAMPLE 17.2

1994/95 Schedule D Case I partnership profit = £60,000

	A £	B £	C £	Total £
6 April 1994–31 December 1994				
Partners' salaries (9 months)	10,500	7,500	4,500	22,500
Interest on capital (9 months)	900	750	600	2,250
				24,750
Balance of profits (9 months)	6,750	6,750	6,750	20,250
(£60,000 × 9/12)				45,000
1 January 1995–5 April 1995				
Partners' salaries (3 months)	1,750	3,000	3,000	7,750
Interest on capital (3 months)	300	250	200	750
				8,500
Balance of profits (3 months)	3,250	1,625	1,625	6,500
(£60,000 × 3/12)				15,000
	23,450	19,875	16,675	60,000

Notional losses

Note that the profit-sharing agreements are interpreted in the same way as in the appropriation account. It is therefore possible that when assessable profits are low, and one or more partners has a high partnership salary, the division of the profits according to the profit-sharing agreement may result in one or more partners showing overall a negative share of profit. While this is perfectly acceptable in the appropriation account, it is *not* acceptable for tax purposes. It is a notional loss, not a real loss.

Where there are assessable profits (no matter how low), the least that can be allocated to an individual partner is £Nil. It would therefore be necessary, in the circumstances described, to proportionately scale down the positive shares of the other partners until the notional loss/losses were removed.

EXAMPLE 17.3

D, E and F are in partnership sharing profits and losses in the ratio 3:1:1 after deducting partnership salaries for E and F of £10,000 and £9,000 respectively. The adjusted profits for the year ended 31 March 1994 are £15,000.

1994/95 Schedule D Case I partnership profit £15,000
Divided between the partners as follows:

	D £	E £	F £	Total £
Partners' salaries	—	10,000	9,000	19,000
Balance of profit	(2,400)	(800)	(800)	(4,000)
Partnership assessment	(2,400)	9,200	8,200	£15,000
Removal of notional loss	2,400			
Allocate 9,200:8,200		(1,269)	(1,131)	
Individual assessments		7,931	7,069	

Changes in the members of a partnership

Where there is a change in the members of a partnership through the death or retiral of a partner or the admission of a new partner, the business will be assessed as if it had ceased and a new business were set up at the date of change. The Schedule D Case I cessation and commencement provisions apply.

The final year of assessment for the old firm will be the one in which the date of change falls. The profits assessed will be the actual adjusted profits for the period from 6 April to the date of change. The assessments for the penultimate and the ante-penultimate years are subject to the Inland Revenue's option to revise under ICTA 1988, s. 63.

The first year of assessment for the new firm will be the one in which the date of change falls and the profits assessed will be the actual adjusted profits for the period from the date of change to the following 5 April. If any partner before the change continues to be a partner after the change, such that an 'election for continuation' (see below) could have been made then the normal commencement rules are amended.

The commencement rules are amended so that the second, third and fourth years of assessment will be assessed on the actual adjusted profits of those years. The fifth and sixth years of assessment, however, will revert to the preceding year basis unless the new firm elects (ICTA 1988, s. 62) to continue the actual basis for those years. (The time limit for such an election is seven years after the end of the fifth year of assessment.) The seventh year of assessment will always be assessed on the preceding year basis – unless, of course there has been another change of partners in the interval.

Election for continuation under ICTA 1988, s. 113(2)

On a change in the members of a partnership as described above, it is possible to elect that the business will not be treated as if it had ceased. This is provided that at least one of the partners before the change continues to be a partner after the change and that all the partners both before and after the change agree. The election must be made in writing within two years of the date of the change to the Inspector of Taxes and must be signed by all the partners immediately before and immediately after the change. (The personal representative of a deceased partner may sign on his/her behalf.) It can be revoked within the same time limit.

If this election is made, the partnership assessment for the fiscal year in which the change takes place and subsequent years will continue to be on a preceding year basis as if no change had taken place. The assessment for the fiscal year in which the change takes place must, of course, be divided in accordance with the profit-sharing arrangements throughout that year:

Fiscal year in which change takes place
6 April–Date of change   Old partnership profit-sharing arrangements
Date of change–5 April   New partnership profit-sharing arrangements

There will be circumstances when an election will be advantageous to the firm and circumstances when it will not. This is due to the gaps between basis periods on cessation and the overlaps on commencement.

One of the reasons why the legislation was amended in 1985 was to encourage partnerships to elect for continuation. The Inland Revenue believed that substantial sums escaped taxation through the manipulation of partnership provisions and commencement rules. It is now difficult for any business to determine with certainty, within the time limit for making the continuation election, if this will be the most advantageous route.

Determining if the election will be beneficial

As a rule of thumb, a continuation election will be worth while when profits over the relevant period are rising.

To evaluate whether an election is worth while, the method should be to tabulate the assessments for the years of assessment affected (eight years in all) under the premise that:

- no continuation election is made
- a continuation election is made.

The total profits assessed under each are then compared.

Note that in practice the profit figures for all these years are not available and estimates have to be made to advise a client appropriately.

EXAMPLE 17.4

F, B and I were in partnership sharing profits equally, the partnership accounts being prepared to 31 December each year. At 31 December 1990, F retired and a senior employee, N, was admitted as a partner from 1 January 1991, from which date profits were shared by B, I and N in the ratio 2:2:1.

The adjusted profits of the partnership are as follows:

		£
Year ended 31 December	1987	33,000
	1988	31,200
	1989	34,500
	1990	35,100
	1991 (estimated)	30,000
	1992 (estimated)	24,000
	1993 (estimated)	27,000
	1994 (estimated)	33,000
	1995 (estimated)	36,000
	1996 (estimated)	39,000

Advise the firm whether it should elect for a continuation.

F, B and I	No continuation election			Election continuation
	Statutory	Actual	Final	
	£	£	£	£
1988/89				
year end 31 December 1987	33,000			33,000
April 1988–5 April 1989		32,025	32,025	
1989/90				
year end 31 December 1988	31,200			31,200
6 April 1989–5 April 1990		34,650	34,650	
	64,200	66,675		
1990/91				
year end 31 December 1989 (3/4)				25,875
6 April 1990–31 December 1990			26,325	
B, I and N				
1990/91				
year end 31 December 1989 (1/4)				8,625
1 January 1991–5 April 1991			7,500	
1991/92				
year end 31 December 1990				35,100
6 April 1991–5 April 1992			28,500	
1992/93				
year end 31 December 1991				30,000
6 April 1992–5 April 1993			24,750	
1993/94				
year end 31 December 1992				24,000
6 April 1993–5 April 1994			28,500	
1994/95				
year end 31 December 1993	27,000		27,000	27,000
6 April 1994–5 April 1995		33,750		
1995/96				
year end 31 December 1994	33,000		33,000	33,000
6 April 1995–5 April 1996		36,750		
	60,000	70,500		
			242,250	247,800

Since £242,250 is less than £247,800, it looks as if the election should not be made. It should be borne in mind, however, that many of the profits were estimated – in this case it is the timing and the extent of the estimated dip in profits which makes the difference. 'How reliable are the figures?' is a question which should always be asked.

Sometimes it is not enough to show that making an election is advantageous to the firm, to persuade all partners before and after the change to sign the election. Some partners wish to be assured that it is advantageous for them as an individual. In this case it would be necessary to apportion each of the final assessments between the relevant partners for every year and then compare an individual partner's total without an election and with an election. Such a comparison can reveal some interesting results depending on how the profit-sharing arrangements have varied over the period. The comparison is made below (for Example 17.4) for the year of change only:

EXAMPLE 17.4 (continued)

	Total £	F £	B £	I £	N £
1 No continuation election					
1990/91 Actual basis					
Old partnership					
6 April 1990–31 December 1990					
(9/12 × £35,100 1:1:1)	26,325	8,775	8,775	8,775	
New partnership					
1 January 1991–5 April 1991					
(3/12 × £30,000 2:2:1)	7,500		3,000	3,000	1,500
		8,775	11,775	11,775	1,500
2 Continuation election					
1990/91 y/e 31 December 1989					
	Total £	F £	B £	I £	N £
Old partnership					
6 April 1990–31 December 1990					
(9/12 × £34,500 1:1:1)	25,875	8,625	8,625	8,625	
New partnership					
1 January 1991–5 April 1991					
(3/12 × £34,500 2:2:1)	8,625		3,450	3,450	1,725
		8,625	12,075	12,075	1,725

It should be noted that under the continuation basis the outgoing partner is not taxed on any profits arising after 31 December 1989 and the incoming partner is taxed on profits arising prior to becoming a member of the firm.

Where inequalities arise in the way profits are allocated to partners – and in order to get a unanimous decision whether or not an election should be made – it is likely that individual partners would be indemnified by the others against any additional tax liabilities resulting. This is, in fact, often incorporated in the partnership agreement.

Planning considerations on a change in partnership

The election for continuation is also available when a partnership comes into existence (that is, where a sole trader takes another person or persons into partnership) or when a partnership reverts to being a sole trader. It should be noted that the amended commencement rules applying to partnership changes detailed above do not apply in these circumstances – 'normal' commencement rules apply.

The above can be particularly useful when the husband is a sole trader and introduces his wife as a partner when the business becomes sufficiently profitable.

The continuation election can be used to advantage in any rapidly expanding firm with a rising profit trend, in a succession of partnership changes each introducing a new partner, provided the incoming partner can be persuaded to sign the election.

Where two or more partnership changes take place within a three-year period, the partners may choose to make an election for continuation on the first change but not on the second. The Inland Revenue's option to amend the assessments (on cessation) for the penultimate and ante-penultimate years of assessment to actual on the second change may be exercised – notwithstanding the previous election for continuation. A retiring partner on the first change might then become liable for an additional tax liability. It is usual for the partnership agreement to indemnify him against this.

Capital allowances

The provisions relating to capital allowances set out in the previous chapter apply equally to partnerships. This section deals with provisions peculiar to partnerships.

Assets owned by the partnership

Assets owned by the partnership qualify for allowances as if they were owned by an individual. The legislation does not state how the allowances should be apportioned between the partners. Nevertheless, common practice apportions them between the partners in accordance with the profit-sharing ratio (ignoring salaries and interest on capital) throughout the fiscal year in question.

Assets owned by individual partners

Capital allowances *may* also be due in respect of property owned by an individual partner but used in the trade carried on by the partnership.

The relevant criteria, as to relevant interest and use, are satisfied, for example, for industrial buildings allowance and agricultural buildings allowance. There is no requirement for such allowances to be apportioned between the other partners. They would normally be claimed on the individual's own tax return although, in practice, they are likely to be given in the partnership assessment in such a way as to reduce only that partner's share of the tax liability. (Where the partner leased a building to the partnership, the allowances would be deductible in the first instance from the rental income of that partner.)

The legislation specifically provides for allowances on plant and machinery in this category. The same allowances, deductions and charges are made as if the plant and machinery were partnership property. The legislation is unclear whether it is the partnership or the individual partner who should receive the allowance. It is, however, common practice for the individual to be given the full benefit of allowances due on plant and machinery provided by him or her (for instance, a motor car).

The allowance would normally be claimed alongside the partnership capital allowance computation. On the transfer of such an asset between partners (connected persons) no balancing allowances/charges arise if it continues to be used in the trade.

EXAMPLE 17.5

X and Y have been business partners sharing profits in the ratio 3:2 for many years. The firm makes up its accounts to 31 December each year. The qualifying expenditure on partnership plant and machinery brought forward from 1993/94 is £15,000; the qualifying expenditure on vans owned by X and Y brought forward from 1993/94 are

£1,000 and £4,000 respectively – both are used entirely for the partnership business. X bought a car on 15 January 1993 for £6,000 – business use is agreed at 60%.

There are no other additions or disposals in the year ended 31 December 1993 by the partnership or the partners. The adjusted profits for the year ended 31 December 1993 were £50,000.

Compute the capital allowances for 1994/95 and show how they would be incorporated in the partnership assessment for that year.

Capital Allowances Computation 1994/95
(basis period year ended 31 December 1993)

	X&Y pool £	X van £	Car 60% £	Y van £
Written down value b/f	15,000	1,000		4,000
Additions			6,000	
	15,000	1,000	6,000	4,000
WDA 25%	3,750	250	1,500	1,000
Written down value cf	11,250	750	4,500	3,000
Total allowances due	3,750	250	900	1,000

The partnership assessment and the division between the partners is as follows:

1994/95	Total £	X £	Y £
Schedule D Case I profit 3:2	50,000	30,000	20,000
Capital allowances			
Partnership property	(3,750)	(2,250)	(1,500)
Assets individual partners	(2,150)	(1,150)	(1,000)
Net assessment	44,100	26,600	17,500

Changes in members of partnership

Continuation election

Where there is a change in the members of a partnership and an election for continuation (under ICTA 1988, s. 113(2)) is made, it automatically applies to capital allowances and these continue to be calculated as if there had been no change.

No continuation election

Where no election for continuation under ICTA 1988, s. 113(2) is made, any property in use immediately before and after the change is treated as if it had been sold by the old partnership to the new partnership at its open market value.

In relation to plant and machinery only, a separate election for continuation to apply to capital allowances can be made provided at least one of the partners before the change was also a partner immediately after the change. The election must be made in writing to the inspector within two years after the change by each of the partnerships before and after the change.

EXAMPLE 17.6

S and T have been business partners for many years preparing accounts to 31 December each year. A new partner is admitted to the firm on 1 October 1993. There are three possibilities:

1 They elect for continuation under ICTA 1988, s. 113(2).
2 They make no elections at all – there will be a cessation for tax purposes on 30 September 1993 and the plant and machinery will be deemed to have been transferred to the new partnership at open market value, balancing allowances/charges arising accordingly.
3 They make no election for continuation under ICTA 1988, s.113(2) but they elect under CAA 1990 s. 77 for the trade to be treated as continuing for capital allowance purposes only.

The 1993/94 basis periods for capital allowance purposes under option 3 will be as follows:

Old partnership – year ended 31 December 1992 plus the period 1 January 1993 to 30 September 1993. The writing down allowance will be restricted to 6/12 as 30 September 1993 is half way through 1993/94.

New partnership – 1 October 1993 to 5 April 1994. The writing down allowance will be restricted to 6/12.

For 1994/95 and onwards the new partnership will be assessed on an actual basis under the commencement provisions and the basis periods for capital allowances will follow the normal rules for commencement.

Claims for reduced writing down allowances

Since the partnership is carrying on the trade, capital allowances are made to the partnership. A reduced or nil claim on plant and machinery must be made by the partnership, and cannot be made by an individual partner in respect of his or her share of the allowances. This applies also for assets which are not partnership property.

Miscellaneous partnership matters

Class IV National Insurance contributions

In partnership assessments a deduction is made for 50% of the Class IV National Insurance contribution of each of the partners in respect of the assessable profits.

Partnership charges

If the partnership pays annual charges (retainable or non-retainable) during the year of assessment, the gross amount must be apportioned between the partners in their profit-sharing ratio (ignoring salaries and interest on capital) at the time of payment.

In some instances, where a former partner has retired due to age or ill-health, the partnership agreement provides for annual payments to be made by the continuing partners to that partner or that partner's widow/dependant. Relief is available at basic and higher rates. (The annuity is treated as earned income of the recipient up to a threshold based on his or her share of the past profits of the partnership.)

Provision for income tax liabilities in the partnership accounts

It is possible merely to pay the current tax liabilities (normally based on the preceding year's profits) out of current income. However, the larger the partnership grows, the greater the need to provide for future tax liabilities from current profits is. Such a provision ensures that sufficient funds are retained in the partnership to cover its income tax liabilities and also relieves individual partners from worry about cash to pay tax liabilities on due dates.

Difficulties do arise in deciding what form the tax provision should take and what contingencies should be additionally provided for (for instance, a cessation). Another problem arises with incoming partners (for whom no reserve has been created) who can be faced with tax liabilities (resulting from profits prior to them being admitted as partners) which exceed their entitlement to profits in their first year.

Non-trading income of the partnership

Assessments are not raised on the partnership for unearned income such as bank interest (taxed or untaxed) or rent from property (Schedule A or Schedule D Case VI). Each partner is assessed as an individual on his or her share (calculated by applying the profit-sharing ratio, ignoring salaries and interest, of the fiscal year of assessment). Care must be taken in apportioning non-trading income taxed on a preceding year basis, when there is a change in the profit-sharing ratio.

Partnerships involving companies

There is no reason why a partner should not be a limited company. Where all partners are limited companies, the profit will be liable to corporation tax. Where a partnership is made up of limited companies and individuals, there is a specific procedure to follow. This topic is beyond the scope of Paper 11.

Summary

- ▶ Partnerships can be a complicated topic but they are a favourite with examiners. It is worth spending time understanding each stage of the basic computation before moving on to the special situations and elections that are possible.
- ▶ A partnership assessment is made for each fiscal year. The profits assessed (normally) are the Schedule D Case I adjusted profits of the accounts year ending in the preceding tax year.
- ▶ The partnership assessment is divided between the partners according to the profit-sharing arrangements which existed during the year of assessment.
- ▶ A change in the composition of a partnership causes the one partnership to cease at the date of change and a new partnership to commence. The cessation rules and modified commencement rules apply automatically. This can be avoided by an election for continuation which allows the partnership to continue to be assessed on the preceding year basis in spite of the change. Careful consideration will be needed to decide if this is beneficial.
- ▶ Capital allowances are available to a partnership on partnership property and on property belonging to individual partners which is used in the trade. They are shared, where appropriate, between the partners in the profit-sharing ratio of the year of assessment.
- ▶ It is possible to elect for a continuation basis for capital allowances, although no election is made for profits to be assessed on a continuing basis.
- ▶ Non-trading income of the partnership is divided between the partners in profit-sharing ratio and assessed directly on the individual partners.
- ▶ Special rules exist where one or more of the partners is a limited company.

Self test questions

1. On a change in the composition of a partnership, how are the commencement rules modified where a continuation election could be made, but is not?

2. What is the time limit for an election for continuation under ICTA 1988, s.113(2)?

3. Three partners preparing accounts to 31 December, changed the profit-sharing ratio on 1 January 1994 from 2:2:1 to 1:1:1. What profit-sharing arrangements will be applied in the 1994/95 assessment?

4. What is the effect of making an election for continuation under ICTA 1988, s.113(2)?

5. When a sole trader takes on a partner:

    a) May an election for continuation be made?

    b) If not, or if none is made, do the modified rules for commencement apply?

6. How are capital allowances on partnership assets apportioned between the partners?

7. a) John is a baker of some repute, whose business has expanded considerably during the past years. He now owns four shops in and around Bambridge and adjusted profits for the past few years have been as follows:

	£
Year ended 31 July 1990	21,750
Year ended 31 July 1991	27,360
Year ended 31 July 1992	33,500
Year ended 31 July 1993	48,000

    Profits are expected to continue to increase and are forecast to be £60,000 for the year ended 31 July 1994 and to increase at the rate of £5,000 pa for the next three years.

    b) On 1 June 1992 John married Kate who has worked for him as an assistant for five years earning a salary of £10,000. She intends to continue working in John's business.

    c) On 1 July 1993 John acquired a car costing £9,000. This will be used primarily by Kate, to visit the four shops. It is estimated that her private use of the car will be approximately 15%. Other capital expenditure comprised two ovens bought on 15 November 1993 at a cost of £6,000 each and a food mixer costing £980 bought on 10 December 1993. The pool balance brought forward at 5 April 1993 was £10,000. The tax written down value of John's car at 5 April 1993 was £10,000 and his private use had previously been agreed at 30%.

    d) John admitted Kate as a partner on 1 December 1993 and shares future profits and losses equally.

    You are required to prepare a memorandum outlining the tax implications of the information given, illustrating your answer with calculations and giving advice where necessary. Your answer should only consider the position up to and including 1995/96.

8. Peter and Paul began a trading partnership in 1975 to manufacture special machinery for the oil industry. They prepare accounts to 31 July each year and for the year to 31 July 1993 their Schedule D Case I profits were £128,000. Their profit-sharing ratio is: Peter – 40: Paul – 60.

    Their main factory, in London, was bought in June 1978 for £90,000 (including land £9,000). In December 1984 they acquired a small factory building in Scotland for £40,000 from which they conducted trade with their Norwegian customers. (Initial allowance 50%.) From 1 August 1986 until 31 July 1993 it was let to a customer company which used it as an exhibition centre and sales office.

The partners have set up a branch factory in Norway. This cost £25,000 for land, £130,000 for buildings, £2,000 for legal and architects' fees and £40,000 for drainage and site work: a grant of £30,000 was obtained from a Norwegian government agency. Their Scottish factory was sold in July 1993 for £52,000 (after expenses of sale). The partners expect that the Norwegian factory will be completed and in use before 1 September 1992.

During the year, plant and machinery costing £20,000 (August 1992) was acquired and an extension made to the development testing laboratory in London for £18,000. The tax written down value for plant and machinery at the end of 1993/94 is £18,400.

Peter is a widower aged 45 years: his son Bill, aged 22 years, was crippled in a car accident as a child and has no income. Paul is married and pays interest of £4,320 (gross) to the building society on a £36,000 mortgage (the interest is paid under the MIRAS scheme): he is also 45 years old. Each partner pays £800 per month in personal pension plan premiums.

Assuming these proposals were carried out, estimate income tax payable by each partner for 1994/95.

Answers on pages 593–595

Trading Losses

CHAPTER 18

This chapter looks at the various ways in which sole traders and members of partnerships may obtain relief for trading losses. All of the reliefs have already been studied in the Paper 7 syllabus, but from a purely computational point of view. This chapter covers the same ground for revision purposes and then requires you to consider losses as if you were giving advice regarding the most suitable loss relief to claim. This is a favourite examination area.

Schedule D Case I adjusted losses

Where the Schedule D Case I adjusted profit computation for the basis period (usually the accounting period ending in the previous fiscal year) shows a loss, there are two consequences:

- The Schedule D Case I assessment is £Nil.
- Loss relief may be claimed.

The assessment procedure, therefore, is not interrupted or upset in any way because a loss has been made. This is a common error made by students and must be guarded against. The Schedule D Case I assessments, arrived at in the way described in Chapter 15, will never be changed as a result of any action taken to relieve trade losses. The taxpayer is given relief for the loss in his or her personal tax computation.

This does not happen automatically. The various ways in which such relief is available are laid down in the Taxes Acts and are considered below, firstly for the sole trader and then at the end of the chapter, in relation to the members of a partnership. With two exceptions, all the loss reliefs considered are available only for the years of assessment in which the trade is carried on. (The exceptions are relief for losses in the opening years of a business under ICTA 1988, s. 381; and relief for losses incurred prior to the transfer of a business to a limited company under ICTA 1988, s. 386.)

Established and ongoing businesses

There are two principal ways in which relief may be given to a taxpayer who has incurred a trading loss in an established and ongoing business:

- It can be carried forward and deducted from the first available trading profits of the same trade (ICTA 1988, s. 385).
- It can be deducted from the taxpayer's statutory total income of the fiscal year in which the loss was made and/or from the next following fiscal year (ICTA 1988, s. 380).

Trading losses carried forward against future profits

Where a loss, as adjusted for Schedule D Case I, is made the trader may 'claim' under ICTA 1988, s. 385 that it is carried forward and deducted from the first available profits of the same trade irrespective of any other trades or income which the taxpayer may be carrying on or receive. A loss must be agreed with the inspector within six years of the year of the loss (statutory limitation) and, in practice once agreed, loss relief is automatically given under this section on submission of the computation unless a claim is made under ICTA 1988, s. 380 below.

EXAMPLE 18.1

M has been in business for many years as a grocer. The recent adjusted profits/losses of his business are:

	£
Year ended 30 June 1990	12,000
Year ended 30 June 1991	(9,000)
Year ended 30 June 1992	2,000
Year ended 30 June 1993	4,000
Year ended 30 June 1994 estimate	4,000

M has other income less charges amounting to £400 per annum. Assuming that he claims loss relief under s. 385 only, his Schedule D Case I assessments and loss relief will be as follows:

	1991/92	1992/93	1993/94	1994/95	1995/96
	£	£	£	£	£
Schedule D Case I	12,000	–	2,000	4,000	4,000
s. 385 relief	–	–	(2,000)	(4,000)	(3,000)
	12,000				1,000
Other income (net)	400	400	400	400	400
Statutory Total Income	12,400	400	400	400	1,400

Loss memo
Year ending 30 June 1991

	£
Loss for year	9,000
Utilised: s. 385 claim 1993/94	(2,000)
1994/95	(4,000)
1995/96	(3,000)

Note that when a claim is made under this section, relief is given to the full extent of the first available profits regardless of the other circumstances of the taxpayer (such as waste of personal allowances). No partial claim is possible. The amount of the loss relief in each year is the lower of a) the net Schedule D Case I assessment for the year or b) the balance in the loss memo.

Capital allowances

If the trading loss is being carried forward under s. 385, the related capital allowances must also be carried forward. Where losses are carried forward under s. 385 and there are other deductions available, the order of set-off is as follows:

1. capital allowances for the current year
2. capital allowances brought forward
3. trading losses under s. 385.

Remember that a loss may be created when capital allowances claimed for any year exceed the adjusted profit of the basis period. Loss relief under s. 385 is also available under these circumstances.

Trading losses set off against general income and capital gains

General principles

Where a loss, as adjusted for Schedule D Case I, is suffered by a trader a claim may be made under ICTA 1988, s. 380 in respect of the fiscal year in which the loss was made and/or of the following fiscal year. The claim must be made in writing to the inspector within two years of the end of the fiscal year for which the relief is claimed.

Therefore if a loss is suffered in the fiscal year 1994/95, a claim for loss relief by deduction from the statutory total income of 1994/95 must be made not later than 5 April 1997 while if further relief in respect of the same loss is claimed for 1995/96 (or relief is claimed for 1995/96 only) then this claim must be made not later than 5 April 1998.

Loss relief under this section is obtained by treating the loss as a deduction from statutory total income (total income less charges). The maximum relief that can therefore be given in this way in any fiscal year is the amount of the taxpayer's statutory total income for that fiscal year. To the extent that tax has already been paid for that year a repayment will be obtained, otherwise the outstanding tax liabilities for the year will be discharged in whole or in part.

From 1991/92 onwards, the taxpayer *may claim* for trading losses (remaining after set-off against statutory total income of either year) to be deducted from net capital gains of the same year, as if they were allowable losses arising in that year. No set-off against net capital gains of either fiscal year is permissible without a claim for set-off against STI of the same year. A claim must be made for the 'relevant' amount of the trading loss available for the year of assessment to be determined, usually at the same time as the s. 380 claim is made. The maximum 'relevant amount' to be treated as an allowable loss in either year is the amount on which the taxpayer would otherwise have been chargeable to capital gains tax if the annual exemption were ignored (that is, the net gains for the year less losses brought forward); note that this may result in the loss of some or all of the annual exemption.

There are two important restrictions on s. 380 relief. The first applies to all trades, professions and vocations and states that this relief will not be available unless it is shown that the trade was being carried on 'commercially with a view to profit' during the fiscal year of the claim. The second applies specifically to farmers and market gardeners and states that relief will not be available for a loss in a fiscal year if losses were incurred in each of the five previous fiscal years unless it can be shown that a profit can reasonably be expected in the next fiscal year.

Concessionary basis

By concession, the meaning of 'fiscal year in which the loss was made' is taken as the fiscal year in which the loss-making accounting period ends. In technical jargon this is stated as 'the accounting period in which the loss is made is treated as co-terminous with the fiscal year ending on the following 5 April'. For example, a loss incurred in an accounting year ended 30 April 1994 is treated as a loss of the fiscal year 1994/95 and will be relieved by deduction from the taxpayer's statutory total income of that year and/or 1995/96.

EXAMPLE 18.2

L, a trader had the following Schedule D Case I adjusted results:

		£
Year ended 31 December 1992	profit	10,000
Year ended 31 December 1993	loss	(15,000)
Year ended 31 December 1994	profit	2,000

He also had bank interest (gross) as follows:

	£
1993/94	300
1994/95	350
1995/96	200

He paid interest on a qualifying loan (gross) of £200 per annum.

His Schedule D Case I assessments would therefore be:

		£
1993/94	Year ended 31 December 1992	10,000
1994/95	Year ended 31 December 1993	Nil
1995/96	Year ended 31 December 1994	2,000

His loss of £15,000 is incurred in 1993/94, so relief under s. 380 is available in 1993/94 and 1994/95.

L 1993/94 tax computation		**Loss memo**	
	£		£
Schedule D Case I	10,000	Loss	15,000
Bank interest	300		
	10,300		
Less: charges	(200)		
Statutory total income	10,100		
Less: loss relief s. 380	(10,100)	Used	(10,100)
Taxable	Nil		4,900

L 1994/95 tax computation		**Loss memo**	
	£		£
		b/f	4,900
Schedule D Case I	Nil		
Bank Interest	350		
	350		
Less: charges	(200)		
Statutory total income	150		
Less: loss relief s. 380	(150)	Used	(150)
Taxable	Nil	Unused	4,750

The loss should be offset firstly against earned income and then against investment income. In most cases nowadays this is merely a formality.

Note that the taxpayer was unable to use his personal allowances in either year, since the loss relief wiped out his income. This was not the most efficient way of using his loss relief but it illustrates that the taxpayer cannot claim merely the amount of loss relief which suits his circumstances; the amount of the claim must be the lower of a) the statutory total income of the year or b) the balance on the loss memo.

In practice, the taxpayer in the above example may have claimed the relief in 1993/94 (if no claim was made there would almost certainly have been taxable income in that year after personal allowances and therefore a tax liability would have occurred; when business is bad, cash flow considerations may be more important than tax efficiency) but certainly he would not have done in 1994/95, as illustrated below:

L 1994/95 tax computation		Loss b/f 4,900
	£	
Schedule D Case I	Nil	
Bank Interest	350	
	350	
Less: charges	(200)	
Statutory total income	150	
Less: Personal allowances	(150)	
Taxable	£Nil	Unused £4,900

The unused loss of £4,900 (or £4,750 above) is not lost; it can be carried forward and deducted from the first available future profits of the same trade under ICTA 1988, s. 385 (that is, the profits for year ended 31 December 1994 £2,000 *et seq* – see above). Alternatively, if there were net capital gains in 1993/94, it might be worth claiming to use the losses in this way (note that the capital gains annual exemption can be wasted in the same way as personal allowances). If no claim is made against STI for 1994/95, there can be no claim against net capital gains for 1994/95.

Statutory basis

Without the concessionary basis, the 'fiscal year in which the loss is made' means the loss arising on an actual basis in the fiscal year to 5 April, and allows s. 380 relief of that amount against the statutory total income of the same fiscal year and/or the following fiscal year.

The statutory basis is best considered in four stages:

1. calculating the Schedule D Case I assessments
2. determining the amount of the loss, if any
3. deciding if a claim is to be made under s. 380 for either or both years
4. the loss memorandum.

EXAMPLE 18.3

L, a trader (see Example 18.2) had the following Schedule D Case I adjusted results:

		£
Year ended 31 December 1992	profit	10,000
Year ended 31 December 1993	loss	(15,000)
Year ended 31 December 1994	profit	2,000

He also had bank interest (gross) as follows:

	£
1993/94	300
1994/95	350
1995/96	200

He paid interest on a qualifying loan (gross) of £200 per annum.

1. His Schedule D Case I assessments would be:

		£
1993/94	Year ended 31 December 1992	10,000
1994/95	Year ended 31 December 1993	Nil
1995/96	Year ended 31 December 1994	2,000

2. The amount of the loss is determined as follows.

    The year ended 31 December 1993 falls into two fiscal years so the results of each of these years has to be computed on an actual basis.

TRADING LOSSES

1992/93 6 April 1992–5 April 1993
(9/12 × £10,000 + 3/12 × £(15,000))   £3,750

The answer is positive, meaning that no loss is made in 1992/93; therefore no claim under s. 380 can be made in 1992/93.

1993/94 6 April 1993 – 5 April 1994
(9/12 × £(15,000) + 3/12 × £2,000)   £(10,750)

The answer is negative, meaning a loss is made in 1993/94 and therefore a claim under s. 380 – maximum £10,750 – can be made in 1993/94 and/or 1994/95.

3 & 4   The loss is relieved as follows:

L 1993/94 tax computation   **Loss memo**

	£		£
Schedule D Case I	10,000	Loss	10,750
Bank interest	300	for s. 380	
	10,300	relief	
Less: charges	(200)		
Statutory total income	10,100		
Less: loss relief s. 380	(10,100)	Used	(10,100)
Taxable	Nil		650

L 1994/95 tax computation

	£		
Schedule D Case I	Nil		
Bank interest	350		
	350		
Less: charges	(200)		
Statutory total income	150		
Less: loss relief s. 380	(150)	Used	(150)
Taxable	Nil	Unused	500

All the comments made above about the advisability of a claim still apply.

As before the unused loss of £500 is not wasted. It and the part of the loss which was not eligible for the s. 380 claim £4,250 (£15,000–£10,750), that is, £4,750 in total, can be carried forward and deducted from the first available future profits of the same trade under ICTA 1988, s. 385.

There are circumstances when the statutory basis must be adopted. These are as follows:

▶ the first three years of assessment of a new business
▶ in the year of cessation
▶ in any year following a year for which a claim has been made on a statutory basis (for example, if a loss was made two years running and the statutory basis was used in respect of the first year of loss, then it must be used for the second year of loss)
▶ where there are irregular accounting periods.

Otherwise, this is the strict legal basis which the Inland Revenue or indeed the taxpayer may insist upon at any time. The Inland Revenue do not usually bother but it gives the taxpayer further flexibility.

In examinations, the concessionary basis should be assumed unless opening year or closing year provisions apply.

For the remainder of this section, the concessionary basis will be used.

Income of spouse

For 1990/91 and later years, any loss relief claimed under s. 380 can only be deducted from the statutory total income of the person who incurred the loss.

The loss is set off against the various categories of statutory total income in the following order:

1. earned income of the individual who incurred the loss
2. unearned income of the individual who incurred the loss
3. unearned income of a minor child taxed on the parent.

Any remaining loss may be set off against net capital gains of the year, as if it were an allowable loss of the year.

Summarising so far, a claim under s. 380 has some degree of flexibility, as noted below:

- A claim may be made for the fiscal year in which the loss is made and/or in the following year. Each or either of these claims is restricted to the income of the individual who incurred the loss and his or her net capital gains of the same fiscal year
- No claim need be made
- The balance of the loss which is unused after any claims above will be carried forward and deducted from future profits under s. 385.

Where losses are made in two consecutive years and claims are made under s. 380, a claim in respect of a previous fiscal year's loss has priority over one for the current fiscal year's loss.

Capital allowances

So far the adjusted trading loss only has been considered. Capital allowances (given in the taxing of a trade) may increase a loss or create a loss for the purposes of a claim under s. 380. The relevant capital allowances for this purpose are those claimed in the fiscal year for which the loss-making accounting period is the basis period.

To tailor the claim for relief under s. 380 as far as possible to his or her particular circumstances, the taxpayer must consider:

- making, where possible, no claim or a reduced claim for capital allowances (see Chapter 16)
- increasing the loss by the amount of the capital allowances
- leaving the loss unchanged, and carrying forward the capital allowances separately as if they were a trading loss under s. 385.

Examination approach

A thorough knowledge of the reliefs and elections which are available is required as well as the ability to incorporate them into a computation. Losses can be particularly confusing and a well-organised, logical approach is required. Layout is particularly important.

Using the following example for illustration purposes, a step-by-step approach and suggested layout is given below:

EXAMPLE 18.4

Mrs Swallow has been in business for a number of years as a grocer. The results of her business as adjusted for tax purposes in recent years have been as follows:

			£
Mrs Swallow year ended 30 April 1992	profit	6,500
year ended 30 April 1993	loss	17,000
year ended 30 April 1994 (esimated)	profit	6,000

Capital allowances may be claimed as follows: £
1993/94	1,000
1994/95	2,000
1995/96	1,500

Mrs Swallow also has investment income of £1,000 per annum. She pays no charges and is entitled to allowances of £4,000 per annum.

She has capital losses brought forward at 6 April 1993 of £6,000:

	1993/94	1994/95
Capital gains	10,000	13,000
Capital losses	(2,000)	(1,000)

Steps

1 Assess the scope of the question. The question revolves around the most beneficial loss claim.

2 Lay out a pro-forma tax computation for all the relevant years and include all the information given. Identify possible loss reliefs with the relevant fiscal years and total each year as far as possible.

	1993/94	1994/95	1995/96
	£	£	£
Schedule D Case I	6,500	–	6,000
Capital allowances	(1,000)	–	(1,500)
	5,500	–	4,500
s. 385 relief	–	–	? x
Other income	1,000	1,000	1,000
Statutory total income	6,500	1,000	
s. 380 relief	? x	? x	
Personal allowances	(4,000)	(4,000)	(4,000)
Taxable income			

	1993/94	1994/95
	£	£
Net capital gains	8,000	12,000
s. 380 claim	? x	? x

There are not many blanks. Five decisions have to be made:

1 A claim under s. 380 for 1993/94, or not.
2 If a claim is made, should there also be a claim against net capital gains of 1993/94?
3 A claim under s. 380 for 1994/95, or not.
4 If one is made should there also be a claim against net capital gains of 1994/95?
5 Whether any change in the claims for capital allowances should be made; (s. 385 claim 1995/96 is not really a decision since the income is not sufficiently high to merit special consideration by giving rise to a higher rate of tax liability and this figure therefore will be the loss left over).

3 Lay out the loss memo (where losses are made in more than one year use one memo for each year) and 'pencil in' the maximum loss, including capital allowances.

Loss memo
Year ending 30 April 1993

	£
Loss for year	17,000
Capital allowances (94/95)	2,000
Total loss – max imum	19,000

TAX PLANNING

4   Starting with the earliest year, analyse the options. It can be seen that the losses are adequate to cover all tax liabilities in each of the three years. The strategy thus becomes one of minimising the wastage of personal allowances and maximising losses for carry forward. However it is not desirable to increase the losses for carry forward unnecessarily as this may cause unavoidable problems in later years. Therefore
    a) A claim in 1993/94 under s. 380 should be made against STI and net capital gains.
    b) No claim in 1994/95 should be made.

	1993/94 £	1994/95 £	1995/96 £
Schedule D Case I	6,500	–	6,000
Capital allowances	(1,000)	–	(1,500)
	5,500	–	4,500
s. 385 relief	–	–	(4,500)
Other income	1,000	1,000	1,000
Statutory total income	6,500	1,000	1,000
s. 380 relief	(6,500)	–	–
	Nil	1,000	1,000
Personal allowances	(4,000)	(4,000)	(4,000)
Taxable income	Nil	Nil	Nil

	1993/94 £	1994/95 £
Net capital gains	8,000	12,000
s. 380 claim	(2,000)	(Nil)
Losses b/f. utilised	(200)	(5,800)
Annual exemption	(5,800)	(5,800)
	Nil	400

Loss memo
Year ending 30 April 1993

	£
Loss for year	17,000
(Capital allowances not claimed)	
s. 380 1993/94 STI	(6,500)
s. 380 1993/94 Net capital gains	(2,000)
s. 380 1994/95 STI no claim	
s. 380 1994/95 Net capital gains	N/A
Available for carry forward	8,500
s. 385 1995/96	(4,500)
To 1996/97	4,000

Capital allowances for 1994/95 should not be claimed (possibly also not for 1993/94 and 1995/96).

The loss deducted from the net capital gains for 1993/94 is made up as follows: Net gains of year (£8,000) less loss brought forward (£6,000) leaving a taxable amount, ignoring annual exemption, of £2,000 – this is the maximum relevant amount.

It is the peripheral aspects of questions which cannot be anticipated and yet candidates must show that they appreciate what options are available in a given set of circumstances and the consequential effects.

Planning considerations

- Preservation of personal reliefs – these cannot be carried forward.
- Cash flow – generally it is better to obtain relief earlier than later.
- Marginal rates of tax – not so critical with the reduction of higher rates. This is about saving tax early at a low marginal rate in favour of delaying the relief and saving tax later at a higher rate, or even perhaps spreading the relief over several years to save tax at higher rates in each of several years.
- Capital allowances – see above.
- The effect on relevant earnings for retirement annuities/personal pension plans.
- Chargeable capital gains in the relevant years – preservation of the annual exemption (this cannot be carried forward).

Trade charges

Where annual charges exceed total income for any reason (for example the business has made a loss in the year and there is insufficient other income; loss relief under s. 385 has similarly wiped out or reduced the trading income), an assessment under ICTA 1988, s. 350 will be raised on the excess retainable charges (see Chapter 1). Loss relief is available in respect of the excess trade charges. For this purpose, non-trade charges are deducted from the available income in priority to trade charges.

The excess trade charges can be carried forward and deducted from the first available future profits from the same trade (as s. 385).

EXAMPLE 18.5

S has been in business for many years. His recent results (adjusted) have been:

		£
Year ended 30 June 1993	profit	20,000
Year ended 30 June 1994	profit	15,000

He has losses brought forward under s. 385 of £25,000. He has other income of £1,000 per annum.

He pays trade charges (patent royalties) gross of £1,500 per annum and mortgage interest of £2,000 (gross) per annum.

	1994/95	1995/96	Loss memo	
	£	£		£
Schedule D Case I	20,000	15,000	b/f	25,000
s. 385 relief	(20,000)	(6,500)	1994/95 s. 385	(20,000)
	–	8,500		5,000
Other income	1,000	1,000	1994/95 excess	
	1,000	9,500	trade charges	1,500
Charges: non-trade	(2,000)	(2,000)	b/f	6,500
trade	(1,500)	(1,500)	1995/96 s. 385	(6,500)
Statutory total income	Nil	6,000		

No s. 350 assessment will be raised on the excess retainable charges in so far as they are made up of mortgage interest (see Chapter 1) but an assessment will be raised in respect of patent royalties in the amount of £375 (£1,500 @ 25%)

New businesses – opening years

The loss reliefs, s. 385 and s. 380, discussed above are also available in the opening years of a business. To the extent that reliefs are given in aggregation however, any relief available under s. 385 is reduced. In the case of a claim for relief under s. 380, the statutory basis must be applied. In addition, relief is available under ICTA 1988, s. 381.

The opening years of a business means the first three fiscal years of assessment, or if an election under ICTA 1988, s. 62 (actual basis in second and third years) has been made, the first four fiscal years.

Loss relief given in aggregation and under ICTA 1988, s. 385

The commencement rules require the results of a business for its initial accounting periods to be combined to find the assessable profits for the first, second and sometimes third fiscal years of assessment. This is called aggregation. To the extent that a loss is combined (aggregated) with a profit and thus causes the assessment for a fiscal year to be less than it would otherwise have been, relief is deemed to have been given for that loss.

There is no statutory provision for this rule but it has the backing of case law (*CIR* v. *Scott Adamson*). The topic is not examinable in Paper 11.

Set-off against general income (ICTA 1988, s. 380)

In the opening years of a new business trading losses will only be available for relief under s. 380 if they are calculated on the statutory basis.

The next section deals with loss relief claims under s. 381 which are also on the statutory basis and closely linked to claims under s. 380. Both will be illustrated at the end of that section.

Note that only the year in which a loss is made can be considered since the assessments for the following years may be affected by the interaction of the loss relief in aggregation and claims under ICTA 1988, ss. 380–381, which is outside the syllabus.

Start-up relief in early years of trade under ICTA 1988, s. 381

This additional relief is available for trading losses made in any or all of the first four fiscal years of assessment of a new business.

A trading loss made in a fiscal year is interpreted in the same manner as under s. 380 – that is, it is calculated on a statutory basis.

Relief for a loss is given by allowing it to be carried back and deducted from the statutory total income of the taxpayer in the three years preceding the year in which the loss is made, giving relief to the earliest year first. If, for example, a loss were made in 1994/95, it could be carried back and deducted from the statutory total income of 1991/92 and then 1992/93 and then 1993/94. Note that this is one of the two occasions when relief for a trading loss is given outside the period in which the trade is carried on. A claim under this section allows the income tax liability of a year or years prior to the trade (when the trader was employed, for example) to be reduced and a repayment obtained.

A claim for relief under s. 381 must be made within two years of the end of the fiscal year in which the loss is incurred.

The mechanics of the relief are similar to those for s. 380; capital allowances for the fiscal year for which the loss-making accounting period is the basis period may be either added to the amount of the loss or carried forward separately.

As before, when considering the statutory basis, it is wise to proceed according to the following four stages. (Remember that only the year in which a loss is made can be considered in this section since the assessments for the following years may be affected by the loss remaining for aggregation.)

1. On the statutory basis, establish if there are any fiscal years in which a loss is made
2. Make the following decisions for any fiscal year in which a loss is made
   a) Is a claim to be made under s. 381? If so, how much of the available loss will be absorbed?
   b) Is a claim to be made under s. 380? If so is it to be made for the fiscal year in which the loss is made and/or the following one? How much of the available loss will be absorbed?
3. Enter the loss relief claims in the appropriate tax computations and compute any adjustments to the tax liabilities.
4. Prepare a loss memorandum for the accounting period in which the loss is made, starting with total adjusted loss and deducting any claims made.

EXAMPLE 18.6

T commenced to trade on 1 June 1992 and makes up his accounts to 31 May. His results have been:

		£
Year ended 31 May 1993	loss	7,500
Year ended 31 May 1994	profit	16,000

An election under ICTA 1988, s. 62 would not be beneficial.

Assume that the taxpayer has substantial other income and relief is to be claimed at the earliest opportunity, for example, under s. 381/s. 380.

1. The loss available in 1992/93 is determined as follows:
   1992/93   1 June 1992–5 April 1993
              (10/12 × loss 7,500)   (6,250)
   As the loss-making period falls partly into the next year it is prudent to see if loss relief is also available for that year.
   1993/94   6 April 1993–5 April 1994
              (2/12 × loss 7,500 + 10/12 × 16,000)   £12,083
   The answer is positive – no loss is available in 1993/94
2. The taxpayer may:
   a) make a claim under s. 381 1989/90, 1990/91, 1991/92 and/or
   b) make a claim under s. 380 for 1992/93 and/or 1993/94.
   Note that relief for the loss will not be given twice but if any loss remains after the s. 381 claim then a s. 380 claim may be made if the taxpayer has substantial other income and wishes to claim as early as possible. Assume that a claim is made under s. 381 and that this will use the full amount of the loss.
3. In this example there is insufficient information to adjust the tax liabilities and compute any repayments.
   The assessment for the fiscal year in which the loss is made is:
   1992/93   1 June 1992–5 April 1993
              (10/12 × loss 7,500)   £Nil
4. The loss memorandum will read:

   Loss memo
   (year ending 31 May 1993)

	£
Loss for period	7,500
Claim s. 381 1989/90 *et seq*	(6,250)
Carry forward s. 385	1,250

An approach to questions involving trade losses in opening years

As these loss claims can become confusing, an approach to this type of question is set out below:

1. Work out the assessment for the first of the four fiscal years.
2. Establish if losses have been made in that fiscal year, on the statutory basis.
3. Decide whether to claim relief under s. 380/381 for any loss established. Remember the alternative is to carry forward the loss.
4. Prepare a loss memorandum for the accounting period in which an adjusted loss was made. This is extremely important as you can see exactly how each loss has been used and how much, if any, remains unused.
5. Repeat each of the above procedures for the second fiscal year, then the third and then the fourth year (if necessary).

Note that an election by the taxpayer under ICTA 1988, s. 62 should be considered in the second and third fiscal years but if there is a loss in the first period giving way to profits in subsequent periods then it will never be beneficial (rising trend of profits).

It is a good idea to practise this approach by using four sheets of paper – one each for assessments, establishing losses, deciding if and how much to claim and the loss memorandum. The circular, chronological approach then slots into place and errors are avoided.

Cessation of trade – closing years

Set-off against general income (ICTA 1988, s. 380)

A claim for a trading loss in the closing years of a business to be set off against general income under s. 380 of the final year of assessment may be made. No claim under s. 380 may be made for the next following fiscal year as the trade has ceased. In the year of cessation the loss is computed on the statutory basis.

Terminal loss relief under ICTA 1988, s. 388

Where a trade is permanently discontinued, any loss made in the last 12 months before the date of cessation (called the terminal loss) so far as it has not otherwise been relieved, may be carried back and set off against the trading profits (defined below), assessed in the three fiscal years preceding the year in which the cessation occurred. Relief is given first against the latest year and so on. Losses for this purpose include unrelieved capital allowances and trade charges for the 12 months before cessation.

A claim for terminal loss relief must be made within six years of the end of the year of assessment in which the trade ceased.

The profits available for set-off are the Schedule D Case I assessments for each of the years, less capital allowances, less gross annual charges (not covered by other income).

Computation of terminal loss

The amount of the terminal loss is computed in six stages by adding together the following amounts:

1. The loss in the year of assessment in which the trade is permanently discontinued so far as it has not otherwise been relieved, that is, from 6 April to the date of cessation.

2   The capital allowances for the final year of assessment permanently discontinued so far as not otherwise relieved.
3   Unrelieved trade charges for the final year of assessment.
4   The loss, if any, from the date 12 months before the date of cessation to the following 5 April; this may mean apportioning the results of two accounting periods. Only losses count towards the terminal loss – ignore a net profit.
5   The lower of: a) any unrelieved capital allowances for the preceding year of assessment and b) a fraction of the total capital allowances of the preceding year of assessment, being the proportion that the length of period in point 4 above bears to 12 months.
6   The lower of a) any unrelieved trade charges for the preceding year of assessment and b) a fraction of the total trade charges for the preceding year of assessment, being the same fraction as in point 5 above.

EXAMPLE 18.7

H had been in business for many years before she finally ceased trading on 30 June 1994. Her adjusted profits were as follows:

		£
Year ended 31 December 1990	profit	10,400
Year ended 31 December 1991	profit	8,000
Year ended 31 December 1992	profit	6,000
Year ended 31 December 1993	profit	4,800
Period to 30 June 1994	loss	(3,600)

	Capital allowances	Patent royalties (gross)
1991/92	3,000	1,200
1992/93	4,400	1,200
1993/94	5,600	1,200
1994/95	400	1,200

Ignore the Inland Revenue option under ICTA 1988, s. 63.

Assessments before terminal loss relief:

	D I £	Capital allowances £	Net £	Patent royalties £	Taxable £
1991/92	10,400	(3,000)	7,400	(1,200)	6,200
1992/93	8,000	(4,400)	3,600	(1,200)	2,400
1993/94	6,000	(5,600)	400	(1,200)	
1994/95	0	(400)	0	(1,200)	

Terminal loss computation:

1 July 1993   5 April 1994   30 June 1994
   9 months   3 months

		£
1	Loss 6 April 1994–30 June 1994 (3/6 × 3,600)	1,800
2	Capital allowances 1994/95	400
3	Unrelieved trade charges 1994/95	1,200
4	Loss 1 July 1993–5 April 1994 (6/12 × 4800 profit + 3/6 × 3,600 loss)	Nil
5	Unrelieved capital allowance lower of i) Nil ii) 5,600 × 9/12 that is,	Nil
6	Unrelieved trade charges lower of i) 800 ii) 1,200 × 9/12 that is,	800
		4,200

TAX PLANNING

The final assessments will be:

	Taxable b/f	Terminal loss	Assessable
	£	£	£
1991/92	6,200	(1,800)	4,400
1992/93	2,400	(2,400)	Nil
1993/94	Nil	–	Nil
1994/95	Nil	–	Nil

There is no requirement that a claim should be made under s. 380 (set off against general income – statutory basis in year of cessation) for the final year of assessment in priority to a terminal loss claim but it may be advantageous to do this depending on the level of other income, chargeable capital gains and on the taxpayer's marginal rates of tax in the relevant years.

Losses brought forward from outside the terminal loss period plus the balance of any unrelieved terminal losses are wasted unless the following section applies.

Business transferred to a limited company (ICTA 1988, s. 386)

The conversion of a business to a limited company constitutes a change of ownership, the vendor is assessed as if the business had been discontinued, and the company assessed as if a new business had been set up, at the date of the transfer.

The company is a separate legal entity and cannot obtain relief for losses incurred by the previous owner.

Under ICTA 1988, s. 386, if the consideration for the transfer consists wholly or mainly of shares in the company, the vendor(s) may carry forward any unrelieved losses (but not capital allowances) established prior to the transfer and deduct them from income received from the company (salaries followed by dividend income) so long as he continues to be the beneficial owner of the shares and the business continues to be carried on by the company.

Miscellaneous trading losses

Pre-trading expenditure

Revenue expenditure incurred prior to the official commencement of trade is disallowed in the Schedule D Case I computation (see Chapter 15). Relief is available for pre-trading expenditure provided that:

▶ it is incurred within seven years of the date of commencement of the trade
▶ it would have been allowable as revenue expenditure if the trade was already being carried on.

Relief is given by treating the total of such expenditure as if it were a loss arising in the year of assessment in which the trade commences. It is necessary to make a separate claim for this relief even if there is a normal trading loss for the first year of assessment.

Relief for losses in unquoted companies

Relief is available to an individual who subscribed for shares in a qualifying trading company and who incurs an allowable loss (as defined for capital gains tax purposes) on the disposal of those shares.

Relief is given by treating the loss as a trading loss in the fiscal year in which the disposal/claim takes place – it may be deducted from the statutory total income of that year and/or the following year (like a s. 380 loss) but it takes priority over both s. 380 and s. 381 relief.

A claim must be made within two years of the end of the fiscal year which the relief is claimed.

On a part disposal, where original shares were subscribed for but further shares have been acquired since, the disposal is deemed to be of the shares acquired later rather than earlier.

Qualifying trading company

A qualifying trading company is a company which has been unquoted and UK resident since its incorporation and has been:

- a trading company for a continuous period of six years ending on the date of disposal/claim or a date not more than three years prior to it (provided that from this date to the date of disposal it has not been an excluded company or an investment company); or
- a trading company for a shorter continuous period ending on the date of disposal/claim or a date not more than three years prior to it and has never since its incorporation been an excluded company or an investment company.
- This relief may also be claimed in respect of losses arising on the disposal of shares acquired under the Enterprise Investment Scheme.

Partnership losses

Where a partnership suffers an adjusted loss, each partner may decide, without reference to co-partners, how he or she will claim relief for a loss. In the established and ongoing business this will be under either s. 380 or s. 385.

A claim may be made under s. 381 in the opening years of a newly formed partnership or by an incoming partner in the first four years of assessment as a partner.

Where there is a change in members of a partnership and no election is made for continuation, a retiring partner is eligible to claim terminal loss relief while a continuing partner is not. For continuing partners, the business is not regarded as ceasing/recommencing for purposes of loss relief; loss relief continues uninterrupted, for example, under s. 385, a partner's share of a loss before the change may be set off against the partner's share of the profits after the change.

When a partnership is transferred to a limited company each partner can carry forward under s. 386 his or her own unrelieved losses.

Division of the loss

The profit-sharing arrangements of a period are applied to adjusted losses in the same way as they are applied to adjusted profits (that is, partners' salaries, interest on capital and then the increased loss in profit-sharing ratio).

Some anomalous results may be produced in practice when an adjusted loss is divided between the partners because the basis of allocation differs depending on whether a partner claims loss relief under s. 380 or under s. 385.

Claim for relief under s. 380

Relief under s. 380 is available in the first instance for the fiscal year in which the loss was made. Therefore the share of a loss belonging to a partner making a claim under

s. 380 is determined according to the profit-sharing arrangements for the fiscal year in which the loss is made.

Claim for relief under s. 385

Relief under s. 385 is given against the first available profits of the same trade, that is, the fiscal year in which the loss will be used is indefinite when the claim is made. There is no statutory provision regarding the allocation of the loss between the partners when relief is claimed under this section but in practice it is shared between the partners according to the profit-sharing arrangements for the accounting period in which the loss arose.

EXAMPLE 18.8

A, B and C are trading as partners sharing profits and losses in the ratio 3:2:1 after paying C a partnership salary of £10,000. The adjusted loss for the year ending 30 June 1994 was £14,000. On 1 July 1994 the profit-sharing ratio was amended to 2:2:1 and C's salary was not changed.

If all partners were to make a claim for relief under s. 380, the loss would be divided between them in accordance with the profit-sharing arrangements which persisted during 1994/95 as follows:

	Total £	A £	B £	C £
6 April 1994–30 June 1994				
Partners' salaries	2,500	–	–	2,500
Loss in ratio 3:2:1	(6,000)	(3,000)	(2,000)	(1,000)
Adjusted loss – 3 mths	(3,500)	(3,000)	(2,000)	1,500
Less: notional profit C				(1,500)
apportion 3:2		900	600	
		(2,100)	(1,400)	
1 July 1994–5 April 1995				
Partners' salaries	7,500	–	–	7,500
Loss in ratio 2:2:1	(18,000)	(7,200)	(7,200)	(3,600)
Adjusted loss – 9 mths	(10,500)	(7,200)	(7,200)	3,900
Less: notional profit C				(3,900)
apportion 2:2		1,950	1,950	
		(5,250)	(5,250)	
Total	(14,000)	(7,350)	(6,650)	Nil

On the other hand, if all partners were to make a claim under s. 385 then the loss would be divided between them according to the profit-sharing arrangements during the accounting period.

	Total £	A £	B £	C £
Year ended 30 June 1994				
Partners' salaries	10,000	–	–	10,000
Loss in ratio 3:2:1	(24,000)	(12,000)	(8,000)	(4,000)
Adjusted loss	(14,000)	(12,000)	(8,000)	6,000
Less: notional profit C				(6,000)
apportion 3:2		3,600	2,400	
		(8,400)	(5,600)	
Total	(14,000)	(8,400)	(5,600)	Nil

The anomaly arises if some partners wish to claim under s. 380 and other partners wish to claim under s. 385: the apportionment in the accounting period forms the upper limit for loss relief. Therefore A may claim £7,350 under s. 380 leaving £1,050 for relief under s. 385 or A may claim £8,400 under s. 385. On the other hand B may claim £6,650 under s. 380 with none remaining for carry forward under s. 385, or may claim £5,600 under s. 385.

Limited liability partners

A limited partner's liability for partnership debts is limited, usually to the capital introduced by him or her, and as a result he or she cannot take part in the management of the business.

If a partnership with a limited liability partner makes a loss, the amount of loss relief to which the limited liability partner is entitled is restricted to the amount of capital he or she introduced to the partnership, plus undrawn profits.

Summary

▶ A detailed knowledge of all loss claims is essential. Answers to questions should be tackled in simple steps, preferably in chronological order. Layout is very important.
▶ An established business making a loss in any year may claim
   – for it to be relieved by offset against general income and net capital gains in that year and/or in the next following year under ICTA 1988, s. 380
   – for any balance of loss remaining, or the whole of the loss if no claim was made under s. 380, to be carried forward under ICTA 1988, s. 385 and deducted from the first available profits of the same trade.
▶ Capital allowances, if claimed, may be added to a loss, or used to create a loss, for purposes of a s. 380 claim for loss relief. Alternatively, they may be kept separate and carried forward for deduction from the first available profits of the same trade.
▶ Unrelieved trade charges may be added to trading losses carried forward for deduction from the first available profits of the same trade under ICTA 1988, s. 387.
▶ In the opening years of a new business, claims for loss relief may be made:
   – under ICTA 1988, s. 381 (carry back for set-off against general income of the preceding three years)
   – under s. 380 detailed above
   Losses remaining after these or any combination of these claims, or the whole loss if none of these claims are made, will be reduced by any relief given in aggregation and the balance carried forward under ICTA 1988, s. 385 for deduction from the first available profits of the same trade.
▶ Losses for claims under s. 380 are usually calculated on the concessionary basis but for purposes of a claim in the opening years or a claim under s. 381, the statutory basis must be used.
▶ In the final year of a business, claims for loss relief may be made:
   – under s. 380 detailed above (calculated on the statutory basis)
   – under ICTA 1988, s. 388 for terminal loss relief where any loss in the final 12 months of trading may be carried back and deducted from the trading profits assessed in the three years preceding the final year
   – under both s. 380 and 388.
   Losses remaining are generally wasted unless the business is being transferred to a

limited company when they can be carried forward and deducted from any income, earned or unearned, from the company.
▶ Care must be taken with claims for losses made by members of a partnership.

Self test questions

1. What is the time limit for a loss relief claim under ICTA 1988, s. 380?
2. How are capital allowances which have been claimed dealt with when a loss is made?
3. What is meant by the 'concessionary basis' for purposes of a claim under ICTA 1988, s. 380?
4. Describe business 'start-up' loss relief.
5. What is the time limit for making a claim for business 'start-up' loss relief?
6. Describe the six elements which make up the terminal loss.
7. Describe the relief available for accumulated losses when a business is transferred to a limited company.
8. What is the relief for losses on shares subscribed for in unquoted companies available under ICTA 1988, s. 574?
9. a) Boris, Steffi and Ivan are partners in a leisurewear business which has been established for several years. Until 30 June 1994, the partners shared profits in the ratio 3:3:1, after paying a salary of £2,000 to Ivan. After that date, the partners shared profits in the ratio 4:3:2, after charging a salary of £10,000 to Ivan. Recent partnership profits/(losses) after making all necessary tax adjustments are as follows:

    Year to 31/10/93   £28,000
    Year to 31/10/94   (£30,000)

    You should assume that the partners' individual assessable shares of profits in 1996–97 will be £30,000, £35,000 and £40,000 respectively. You should also assume that 1994/95 tax rates and allowances apply for *all* relevant years of assessment.

    Ivan, who is single, has no other income apart from his partnership profits. He is anxious to know how to make best use of his share of the loss incurred in the year to 31 October 1994. He understands that he has a choice between a claim against total income under s. 380, ICTA 1988, or alternatively against future trading profits under s. 385 ICTA 1988.
    i) Compute the partnership profits assessable in respect of each of the partners for 1994/95.
    ii) Compute the loss relief available to each of the partners under s. 380 and s. 385 respectively.
    iii) Advise Ivan whether he should claim relief under s. 380 or s. 385 taking both income tax and NIC considerations into account. Show all supporting calculations.
    b) Boris (who is aged 25) and his wife Martina enjoy the following income in addition to his partnership profits:

	Year ended	
	5/4/94	5/4/95
Self	£	£
Interest received on National Savings Bank ordinary account	200	230
Interest received on building society deposit account	9,700	10,740
Interest on National Savings Certificates	100	120
Wife		
Unfurnished rental income	200	300

Boris intends to claim relief under s. 380 in respect of the earliest year possible.

Compute Boris's income tax and Class 4 NIC liabilities for 1994/95, indicating clearly any items on which he is not taxable.

c) Boris has paid pension contributions so as to obtain the maximum amount of relief for all years of assessment up to 1992/93. He paid no contributions in respect of 1993/94, when his share of profits was £9,643.

Advise Boris as to the maximum relief he can claim in respect of the payment of personal pension contributions for the years 1994/95 to 1996/97 inclusive.

Answers on pages 595–598

Finance Act 1994 – the new current year basis of assessment

CHAPTER 19

This chapter considers the provisions in the Finance Act 1994 which fundamentally change the basis of assessment for the self-employed. The preceding year basis of assessment is to be abolished and all income is to be taxed on a current year basis.

The earlier chapters of this textbook covered the old rules which still apply to established sources of income and are therefore still examinable. This chapter considers the new rules which apply immediately to sources of income commencing after 5 April 1994, and from 1997-98 to existing sources of income.

The new Schedule DI assessment rules

Self-employed people will continue to be able to make up their accounts to any date they choose. They will be assessed under Schedule D case I on the profits for the accounting year ending in the year of assessment.

EXAMPLE 19.1

N has been in business for many years, making up accounts to 31 August. The adjusted Schedule D Case I profits for the year ended 31 August 1998 will be assessed to tax in the fiscal year 1998–99.

In the first year of the business, the profits to be assessed will be those arising in the year to 5 April. The normal current year basis of assessment will apply from the second year of assessment onwards. If the accounts ending in the second year of assessment cover less than 12 months, the second year's assessment will be based on the profits of the first twelve months of trading.

EXAMPLE 19.2

C commenced trading on 1 January 1995 and decided to make up accounts to 31 December. The adjusted profits for the first two accounting periods are as follows:

Year ended 31 December 1995	£24,000
Year ended 31 December 1996	£30,000

C's schedule DI assessments will therefore be:

1994–95	£24,000 x 3/12 =	6,000
1995–96	A/cs to 31/12/95	24,000
1996–97	A/cs to 31/12/96	30,000

Schedule DI assessments cease in the fiscal year in which the business ceases. The profits assessable in the final year of assessment are those arising from the end of the basis period assessed in the penultimate year of assessment until the date of cessation.

EXAMPLE 19.3

Continuing the previous example, assume C ceases trading on 30 June 1997 and has adjusted profits from 1 January 1997 to 30 June 1997 of £8,000.

The final year of trading is 1997–98. The penultimate year of assessment (1996–97) charged the profits up to 31 December 1996. In 1997–98 C will therefore be assessed on the profits arising from 1 January 1997 to 30 June 1997, namely £8,000.

As you can see, the new cessation rules do not give rise to a gap. However, the commencement rules still mean that it is possible for some profits to be taken into account in more than one year of assessment. In C's case, the adjusted profits earned over the life of the business amount to £62,000 (24,000 + 30,000 + 8,000), yet the assessments amount to £68,000 (6,000 + 24,000 + 30,000 + 8,000).

The intention of the new legislation is that over the lifetime of the business the adjusted profits should be taxed in full, once and only once. In order to achieve this, any profits which are taken into account more than once will be eligible for a relief, known as overlap relief. This relief will be given either when the business ceases, or for any earlier year of assessment for which the basis period is longer than twelve months.

EXAMPLE 19.4

Continuing the previous examples, the period 1 January 1995 to 5 April 1995 is an overlap as the profits for this period were assessed in both 1994–95 and 1995–96. The profits qualifying for overlap relief are £6,000 and this figure will be deducted from the 1997–98 assessment, thus reducing it to £2,000 (8,000 – 6,000). The Schedule DI assessments will now equate to the adjusted profits earned over the lifetime of the business.

If a business changes its accounting date, the procedure to be followed will depend on whether the accounts to the new date are made up for a period of more or less than twelve months:

- If the accounts are made up for a period of less than twelve months, the basis period will be the 12 months to the new accounting date.
- If the accounts are made up for a period of more than twelve months, they will form the basis period. The profits are not restricted to a 12 month period.

If the basis period does exceed 12 months, overlap relief may be given. The relief is restricted by the following formula:

$$\text{Overlap relief} \times \frac{X - 12}{\text{Overlap period (in months)}}$$

X refers to the number of months in the basis period.

EXAMPLE 19.5

K starts in business on 1 July 1994. The accounts to 30 June 1995 show an adjusted profit of £24,000. The next accounts cover the fifteen months to 30 September 1996 and show an adjusted profit of £37,500.

K's schedule DI assessments will be as follows:

		£	£
1994-95	£24,000 x 9/12 =		18,000
1995-96	A/cs to 30/6/95		24,000
1996-97	A/cs to 30/9/96	37,500	
	Less overlap relief:	(6,000)	31,500

The overlap relief has been computed as follows:

$$£18,000 \times \frac{15-12}{9} = £6,000$$

The remaining £12,000 of overlap relief will be given either on cessation or in any other year for which the basis period is longer than twelve months.

Capital allowances

Under the new rules, capital allowances will be treated as trading expenses and balancing charges as trading receipts. This means that allowances will be deducted in computing the Schedule DI profit, in the same way as currently applies for corporation tax purposes.

Capital allowances will be calculated in respect of accounting periods rather than basis periods. Thus where accounts are drawn up for less than twelve months, any writing down allowance will need to be proportionately reduced. Similarly, where accounts are drawn up for more than one year, any writing down allowance will need to be proportionately increased.

EXAMPLE 19.6

Continuing with example 19.5, assuming that K has assets with a written down value of £15,000 as at 1 July 1995, the capital allowances due for 1996–97 will be £15,000 x 25% x 15/12 = £4,688.

Losses

Relief under s380 will be available against income of the year of the loss, and/or income of the preceding year. Relief is given for current year losses in priority to relief for losses carried back.

The loss belongs to the year it would have been assessed in if it had been a profit.

Similar changes apply to the rules allowing relief for losses on unquoted shares.

EXAMPLE 19.7

L makes up accounts to 30 November annually. The accounts for the year ended 30 November 1998 show an adjusted loss of £8,000.

The loss relates to 1998–99 as this is the year any profit for the accounts to 30 November 1998 would have been assessed in. L can claim relief under s380 against income for 1998–99 and/or 1997–98.

This can be compared to the position under the old system, under which relief could have been claimed under s380 against income for 1998–99 (the year of the loss) and 1999–2000 (the following year).

Partnerships

With effect from 1997–98, partnerships will no longer be assessed on the profits of the partnership. Instead, each individual partner's share of the profits will be assessed on him or her individually. The share will be allocated by reference to the period of account rather than by reference to the year of assessment.

A change in the members of a partnership, where there is at least one partner common to both the old and the new partnerships, will no longer be regarded as a cessation for tax purposes. These new rules will apply immediately to any new partnership commencing, or deemed to commence, after 5 April 1994.

EXAMPLE 19.8

J and M have been in partnership for many years, making up their accounts to 30 September annually. They have always shared profits and losses equally. Their accounts for the year ended 30 September 1998 show an adjusted profit of £90,000.

Assuming that they decide to change their profit sharing ratio to J 60% and M 40% on 1 April 1998, their profit for the year ended 30 September 1998 will be allocated as follows:

	Total £	J £	M £
1/10/97 – 31/3/98	45,000	22,500	22,500
1/4/98 – 30/9/98	45,000	27,000	18,000
	90,000	49,500	40,500

If the change in the profit sharing ratio was to occur instead on 1 October 1998, the accounts to 30 September 1998 would be shared equally. The new profit sharing ratio would apply to the 1999-2000 assessment.

Summary

▶ The new current year basis of assessment has immediate effect for businesses starting after 5 April 1994. Existing businesses move to the new basis for the tax year 1997–98.

▶ The new rules mean that over the lifetime of the business the adjusted profits are taxed in full, once and only once.

- Under the new rules a basis period can be longer than 12 months and, in such cases, any writing down allowance due will be proportionately increased.
- Individual partners will receive their own individual assessment on their share of a partnership's profits. These profits will be allocated according to the profit sharing ratio in force for that period of account. This will remove the current anomaly whereby a partner can be assessed on a figure of profit different to that actually earned by him.

Self test questions

1   Jason commenced trading on 1 August 1994 and ceased trading on 31 January 1998. His adjusted profits are as follows:

	£
Year ended 31 July 1995	12,000
Year ended 31 July 1996	11,000
Year ended 31 July 1997	15,000
Period to 31 January 1998	9,000

Show Jason's Schedule DI assessments for all the years affected by the above information.

2   D makes up his accounts to 30 June annually. In 1998/99 he decides to change his accounting date and draws up accounts for the nine months to 31 March 1999. Which months' profits will his 1998/99 Schedule DI assessment be based on?

3   How does the computation of capital allowances under the new rules differ from the computation under the existing rules?

4   How does s380 relief under the new rules differ from the relief under the existing rules?

5   Identify three ways in which the assessment of partnerships under the new rules differs from the old rules.

Answers on page 598

CHAPTER 20

The Disposal and Replacement of Business Assets

This chapter deals with the taxation implications of the disposal and replacement of business assets in an integrative manner. These come principally under the heading of capital gains tax and the principles considered in Chapters 5 to 7 are applied specifically to businesses. The interaction with income tax and the Schedule D Case I rules and capital allowances are covered as well as the reliefs which are available for replacement of business assets. Some of these aspects will already have been covered independently in Paper 7 and will therefore be revision. It is important now to be able to consider all the taxation implications of an individual topic since this is the way in which tax problems arise in practice.

Business assets

Where a cost has been treated as an allowable deduction for income tax, it cannot be an allowable cost for capital gains tax – income tax always takes precedence over capital gains tax. Capital expenditure of a business is disallowed in the Schedule D Case 1 computation and is therefore eligible to be an allowable cost for capital gains tax – it may also however be expenditure on which capital allowances are available. Whenever there is a disposal of a business asset both aspects must be considered.

There will be a gain or loss for capital gains tax purposes and a balancing adjustment for capital allowances purposes. The computation of balancing adjustments for capital allowances has already been fully considered in Chapter 16 and does not vary to accommodate capital gains tax. Where the two systems meet, therefore, it is necessary for the capital gains tax system to make provision for its interaction with capital allowances. In general, assets used in a business are treated for capital gains tax purposes like any similar asset not used in business. Certain assets and transactions are peculiar to businesses and are considered below. Tangible movable property (chattels) which are wasting assets need special consideration.

Goodwill

Goodwill is a chargeable asset. Where it was not acquired for a consideration, it is treated on its disposal as acquired for nil consideration at the time the business was set up.

Trading stock

Assets forming part of the trading stock, which are appropriated for any other purpose, are treated as being acquired at the value credited to the trade for purposes of income tax.

Assets purchased otherwise than as trading stock, which are subsequently appropriated into trading stock, are treated as disposed of and immediately reacquired at market value. In this way a chargeable disposal arises for purposes of capital gains tax.

Tangible movable property which is a wasting asset

This type of asset was considered in Chapter 6. To recap: in non-business circumstances, this type of asset is exempt from capital gains tax whatever consideration is received on disposal. The exemption is lost or restricted, if the asset is used in a trade such that capital allowances could have been claimed (whether or not they were claimed). The chattel exemption for small disposals (consideration and allowable deductions of £6,000 or less) and the marginal relief rules may apply.

The type of business asset which falls within this section is plant and machinery, office furniture and the like. (Note that all plant and machinery is tangible movable property.) Motor cars are always exempt.

Since they are wasting assets, it is unlikely that sale proceeds will exceed cost but insurance proceeds based on replacement value could give rise to a gain. The gain would be the disposal value less allowable cost (see below) and indexation allowance. The disposal value and allowable cost of any asset used partly for the trade and partly for other purposes are apportioned by reference to the business use percentage for capital allowances, and treated as two separate disposals of which the non-business disposal is exempt.

Interaction with capital allowances affects the allowable cost (see below).

Interaction of capital gains tax and capital allowances

For capital gains tax purposes, the allowable deductions are not reduced for expenditure in respect of which capital allowances have been claimed except where, if no adjustment were made, an allowable loss would arise. The purpose of the provisions is to prevent double relief being obtained for expenditure through both obtaining a balancing allowance (capital allowance provisions) and an allowable loss (capital gains provisions).

Restriction of allowable losses

Where, if no adjustment were made, a loss (unindexed) would arise the allowable deductions are reduced by the net capital allowances received (that is, capital allowances granted less balancing charges).

Plant and machinery

Where, if no adjustment were made, a loss (unindexed) would arise and the disposal is of property in respect of which capital allowances have been or could have been claimed, the capital allowances are deemed to be the difference between the expenditure incurred and the disposal value. It is necessary to deal with it in this way, as the pooling provisions for plant and machinery make it difficult to establish the capital allowances in respect of individual assets.

EXAMPLE 20.1

An industrial building was bought in January 1982 at a cost of £100,000 (including land £20,000). It was sold in January 1995 for £90,000 (including land £20,000). The building was used for a qualifying industrial purpose throughout the period of ownership.

Capital gains computation 1994/95

	£	£
Proceeds		90,000
Cost	100,000	
Less: net capital allowances received	(10,000)	
(80,000 – 70,000)		
		(90,000)
Unindexed gain/loss		Nil

Remember that indexation can no longer create or increase an allowable loss, but is available as an indexation loss.

EXAMPLE 20.2

a) Fixed plant and machinery, purchased in January 1988 for £7,000, was disposed of in January 1995 for £5,000.

Capital gains computation 1994/95

	£	£
Proceeds		5,000
Cost	7,000	
Less: capital allowances (deemed)	(2,000)	
(7,000 – 5,000)		(5,000)
Unindexed gain/loss		Nil

b) If the fixed plant in a) above had been tangible moveable property, it would have been classed as a chattel and the computation would have become:

	£
Consideration (marginal loss rules substitute £6,000 for actual sale proceeds)	6,000
Cost (as above)	(5,000)
Unindexed gain/loss	1,000
Indexation allowance	
$\dfrac{144.7 - 103.3}{103.3}$ (0.401 × 5,000) = £2,005	
Indexation allowance (restricted)	(1,000)
	–

Indexation loss £1,005

Partnership disposals

There are few references to partnerships in the capital gains legislation. The taxation of partnership gains is based on Inland Revenue practice allied to the general capital gains tax principles.

The partnership assets are owned jointly by the members of the partnership but because a partnership is not a legal entity (as discussed in Chapter 17), a capital gains tax assessment cannot be raised on the partnership in respect of any gains arising on their disposal. Each partner must be assessed separately on his or her share of the proceeds less his or her share of the cost. A partner's share for this purpose is the share in surplus assets on a winding up or, if not specified, his or her share according to the treatment in the accounts.

It would seem at first glance that this method of assessing a gain or loss separately for each partner could be bypassed by simply calculating the overall gain or loss and dividing it between the partners. This is so in some cases but not in others. For example, the question of elections arises. Are elections to be made by the partnership as a whole or by each individual partner?

It is understood that each partner has a separate right of election applying to partnership assets held on 31 March 1982 and disposed of after 5 April 1988 (Finance Act 1988 election for universal 31 March 1982 values) and that an election made by a partner for his or her personal assets will also apply to his share of disposals of partnership assets.

EXAMPLE 20.3

A, B and C are in partnership sharing all profits and losses equally. On 30 March 1995 they close down a branch office and dispose of the premises for £120,000 (original cost £30,000 in 1980, value at 31 March 1982 £27,000). We need to show the chargeable gain arising to each of the partners.

	31 March 1982 value	Old rules
	£	£
Disposal value (1/3)	40,000	40,000
Less acquisition cost (1/3)		(10,000)
31 March 1982 value (1/3)	(9,000)	
Unindexed gain	31,000	30,000
Less: indexation allowance:		
$\dfrac{145.0 - 79.4}{79.4} = 0.826$		
10,000 × 0.826	(8,260)	(8,260)
Gain	22,740	21,740

The chargeable gain would normally be the lower of the gain using the 31 March 1982 value (£22,740) and the gain arising under the old rules (£21,740) that is, £21,740. However, if one of the partners had made an election for universal re-basing to 31 March 1982, that partner's gain would be the unindexed gain of £31,000 less the indexation allowance of £7,434 (9,000 × 0.826), that is, £23,566.

EXAMPLE 20.4

In the above example, if the property had been transferred to A at its market value (£120,000) instead of being sold externally what would have happened?

A chargeable disposal would have been made by each of B and C to A of their 1/3 shares in the asset. Gains would have been assessed on them as above. A would not have made any disposal but would have acquired 1/3 of the asset from each of B and C. A's base cost would be made up as follows:

	£
Acquisition cost (1/3) 1980	10,000
Acquisition cost from B (1/3) 30 March 1995	40,000
Acquisition cost from C (1/3) 30 March 1995	40,000
	90,000

Partners are connected persons and all transactions between them are normally deemed to be at market value. Relief from these provisions is available to acquisitions and disposals of partnership assets if they are as a result of bona fide commercial arrangements. Most transactions concerning a partnership's business assets and the interests of the partners are therefore outside the rule (however, if the partners are otherwise connected such as, father and son, the market value rule may still apply).

Inheritance tax implications

Where the transaction is of a commercial nature between connected persons (such as partners) it is necessary to show non-gratuitous intent, that is, that the transaction is on commercial terms.

To show non-gratuitous intent between unconnected persons it is only necessary to show that the transaction is at arm's length, but to show non-gratuitous intent between connected persons, the taxpayer will need to show that the transaction is such that it might have been expected to be made between unconnected persons.

The terms must therefore be commercial but also the nature of the transaction and the manner in which the terms were arrived at should be carried out in a commercial manner (for example, by obtaining independent advice).

Replacement of business assets

When assets which are used exclusively for a trade are disposed of and all the proceeds are re-invested in other assets also to be used exclusively for the trade, the taxpayer may claim to defer the capital gains tax arising by deducting the chargeable gain arising from the acquisition cost of the newly acquired asset. The procedure can be repeated as long as one business asset is replaced by another. This is called 'roll-over' relief.

A number of conditions must be met before this relief can be claimed:

- Both of the assets must be within one of the following groups (not necessarily the same group):
  a) land and buildings occupied solely for the purpose of the trade
  b) fixed plant and machinery not forming part of the buildings (defined as a depreciating asset)
  c) ships, aircraft, hovercraft
  d) satellites, space stations and spacecraft
  e) goodwill
  f) milk quotas, potato quotas, and EC agricultural quotas for the premium given to producers of ewes and suckler cows.
- The re-investment must take place within the period 12 months before the disposal to 36 months after the disposal or such longer time as the Inland Revenue may allow.
- Both assets must be used by the taxpayer for the purposes of a trade, not necessarily the same trade. The trades may be carried on concurrently or successively.
- Where the asset disposed of has not been used in the trade for the whole period of ownership, the gain is apportioned and only the part of the gain relating to the period of trading may be 'rolled over'.

The trade referred to need not be in the UK. The letting of furnished holiday accommodation also qualifies as a trade as does a profession or vocation.

The relief must be claimed within six years of the end of the year of assessment in which the chargeable disposal arises.

EXAMPLE 20.5

A freehold building was bought in April 1982 at a cost of £100,000. It was sold in May 1985 for £150,000. A replacement building was bought in February 1985 for £200,000. This building was subsequently sold in January 1995 for £350,000.

1 Disposal July 1985

	£
Disposal value	150,000
Less: allowable deductions	(100,000)
	50,000

Less: indexation allowance:

$$\frac{95.2 - 81.0}{81.0} = 0.175$$

100,000 × 0.175	(17,500)
Gain to be 'rolled-over'	32,500

2 Disposal January 1995

		£
Disposal value		350,000
Less: allowable deductions: cost	200,000	
less rolled over gain	(32,500)	
		(167,500)
		182,500

Less: indexation allowance:

$$\frac{144.7 - 91.9}{91.9} = 0.575$$

167,500 × 0.575	(96,313)
Chargeable gain unless proceeds again re-invested	86,187

Proceeds not wholly re-invested

If the proceeds of disposal of the original asset are not wholly re-invested in a replacement asset, the amount of the gain which can be rolled over is restricted by the amount of any proceeds not re-invested.

The chargeable gain, under these circumstances, is the lower of:

- the full gain
- the proceeds not re-invested.

EXAMPLE 20.6

The information is the same as for Example 20.5, except that the replacement building was purchased in February 1985 for £130,000.

1 Disposal July 1985

	£
Total gain as above	32,500
Less: proceeds not re-invested (150,000 – 130,000)	(20,000)
Gain available for 'roll-over'	12,500
Chargeable gain assessable 1985/86	20,000

2	Disposal January 1995		£
	Disposal value		350,000
	Less: allowable deductions: cost	130,000	
	less rolled over gain	(12,500)	
			(117,500)
			232,500
	Less: indexation allowance:		
	$\dfrac{144.7 - 91.9}{91.9} = 0.575$		
	117,500 × 0.575		(67,563)
	Chargeable gain unless proceeds again re-invested		164,937

Asset not used exclusively for the trade

If an asset has not been used exclusively for the trade throughout its ownership, the gain arising on its disposal must be apportioned between the part used in the trade and the non-trade part. Only the part of the gain attributable to the part of the asset used in the trade may be rolled over. Similarly if the proceeds were not all re-invested, then they must be apportioned in the same way and only the part of the proceeds attributable to the part of the asset used in the trade may be rolled over.

EXAMPLE 20.7

The information is the same as for Example 20.6, except that 20% of the building was used for non-trade purposes throughout its ownership. Calculate the amount of the gain eligible for roll-over relief.

Disposal July 1985

	Total	Trade use	Non-trade
	£	£	£
Total gain as above	32,500	26,000	6,500
Less: proceeds not re-invested	(20,000)	(16,000)	(4,000)
Gain available for roll-over		10,000	
Chargeable gain assessable 1985/86:			
The gain from non-trade use in full			6,500
Proceeds from part used in trade not re-invested			16,000
			22,500

Re-investment in depreciating assets

If the replacement asset is a depreciating asset, roll-over relief as described above is not available (as the cost must be diminished over time, the gain rolled over against the cost would be reduced and the tax liability would disappear instead of being deferred).

Instead the gain is 'held over' (postponed) until the earliest of the following events:

- ten years from the date of acquisition of the replacement asset
- the disposal of the replacement asset
- the cessation of trade or the cessation of use of the replacement asset in the trade.

It will be deemed to arise in the fiscal year of the earliest of the above events. It will be assessed to capital gains tax in that year.

A depreciating asset is an asset which is a wasting asset or one which will become a wasting asset within ten years (that is, it has a life of 60 years or less). Fixed plant and machinery will always be a depreciating asset, freehold land will never be a depreciating asset.

Identification of replacement asset

Although the time limit for claiming relief is generous and the replacement asset may be acquired within the period 12 months before the disposal to 36 months after the disposal; there may be some urgency (for example, cash flow) to identify a replacement asset before the tax initially becomes payable (normal due date is 1 December following the end of the year of assessment).

In these circumstances, the taxpayer may claim to have reinvested in a convenient depreciating asset although it is his intention to acquire a non-depreciating asset at a later date. Provided that the non-depreciating asset is acquired before the held-over gain accrues, it is possible to transfer the held-over gain and to 'roll it over' against the cost of the non-depreciating asset.

Finance Act 1988 re-basing provisions

Where an asset, acquired after 31 March 1982 but the subject of a rollover or holdover claim from a previous disposal, is disposed of after 5 April 1988 the deferred gain is halved if it is wholly or partly attributable to a gain arising before 31 March 1982. This relief must be claimed on the earliest such occasion within two years of the end of the year of assessment in which either the asset is disposed of or the deferred gain accrues.

Partnership roll-over relief

Roll-over relief may be available to a partner who disposes of:

- partnership assets
- an asset owned privately but used by the partnership.

Roll-over relief on the disposal of partnership assets is given to individual partners in respect of their individual gains.

Where an asset is owned personally by the partner, it must be used exclusively by the partnership for the purpose of the trade for roll-over relief to be available.

Gift of business assets

Capital gains tax

When business assets used for the purposes of a trade, or shares in either an unquoted or family trading company are transferred from one individual to another, gift relief applies (see Chapter 5). If all the assets of a business are transferred the tax reliefs described in Chapter 21 apply.

As described in Chapter 5, if consideration is received, the amount of the gain which may be held over is restricted by the amount the consideration received exceeds the total allowable deductions. The transferee is deemed to acquire the asset at its market value less the held-over gain.

The Finance Act 1988 re-basing provisions must be taken into account and a claim may be made on the subsequent disposal of that asset, as above, for the deferred gain to be halved where the gift took place, after 31 March 1982 and before 6 April 1988, and the asset was acquired before 31 March 1982.

Inheritance tax

Inheritance tax is irrelevant to a transaction which is entirely commercial.

Where there is gratuitous intent, inheritance tax has already been covered in depth in Chapters 8 to 10, as have the principal reliefs which are available, that is, business property relief and agricultural property relief.

Summary

- Wasting chattels used in a business are chargeable assets but are eligible for the chattel relief for small disposals and the marginal relief for gains and losses.
- Capital allowances are ignored in the computation of chargeable gains but where an allowable loss would otherwise arise the allowable cost is reduced by the net capital allowances received.
- In addition to the general provisions for deferring gains covered in Chapter 5, additional provisions are available to businesses. These are particularly important as the withdrawal of funds from the business for capital gains tax liabilities might otherwise severely impede the expansion of the business. The principal provisions are for the replacement of business assets and the transfer of a business to a limited company (see Chapter 21).
- As a partnership is not a legal entity in England, capital gains tax assessments cannot be made on the partnership and must therefore be made on the individual partners. Each partner is regarded as owning a part of every partnership asset determined with reference to the ratio in which he or she would share in surplus assets on a winding up of the partnership.
- Roll-over relief applies to partners and partnership assets in much the same way as it applies to sole traders.
- Inheritance tax applies in the manner described in Chapters 8 to 10 where transactions have a gratuitous intent or are of a non-commercial nature between connected persons. This is particularly important in respect of transfers of assets between partners.

Self test questions

1. A fire in the basement of A's business premises caused stock worth £10,000 and plant which had cost £2,000 in April 1986 to be destroyed. A was insured and made a claim against the insurers for the cost value of the stock and replacement value (£2,800) of the plant. This was paid in full on 5 July 1994. Calculate the unindexed gain for capital gains tax purposes.

2. B, a manufacturer, occupied and used industrial buildings which she acquired new in 1980 for £20,000. She claimed all allowances and reliefs available. Due to staff problems, she ceases trading and sells the property for £18,000 on 15 August 1994. Show the allowable loss that will arise.

3. To claim roll-over relief on the replacement of business assets, must the replacement asset be within the same group as the original asset?

4. For purposes of roll-over relief, when must re-investment in the replacement asset take place?

5   A leasehold business property is sold for £30,000 and replaced by a smaller property costing £20,000. The gain arising on the disposal is £5,000. How much of the gain may be rolled over?

6   Fixed plant acquired in June 1982 for £30,000 was sold in November 1987 for £50,000. The proceeds were re-invested in:

   a) freehold land and buildings acquired in January 1987 for £75,000 and sold in January 1995 for £120,000
   b) leasehold land and buildings (65-year lease) acquired in January 1987 for £40,000 and sold in January 1995 for £50,000
   c) fixed plant and machinery acquired in December 1987 for £40,000 and sold in January 1995 for £25,000.

   In each of the above cases compute the capital gains arising.

Answers on pages 598–599

CHAPTER 21

Disposal of All or Part of a Business; Retirement

This chapter deals with the taxation implications of disposing of all or part of a business. This includes transfers of partnership share between partners, the outright disposal of the business (including disposal to a limited company) and the relief available if this coincides with retirement. Where the disposal is by way of gift, inheritance tax and the inheritance tax reliefs must also be considered. Once again it is important that all taxation aspects of a particular situation are considered.

Transactions between partners

Partners are connected persons and all transactions between them are normally deemed to be at market value. As seen in the previous chapter, relief from these provisions is available to acquisitions and disposals of partnership assets if they are as a result of bona fide commercial arrangements.

There are two occasions when disposals between the members of the partnership normally take place:

- changes in the composition of the partnership
- changes in the profit-sharing ratio or ratio for sharing surplus assets.

Where changes of this type occur, each partner is treated as acquiring or disposing of a part or the whole of a share in each partnership asset – represented by the increase or decrease in the share of the asset.

The disposal consideration of each chargeable asset will be the appropriate fraction of the current balance sheet value and therefore could be less than, equal to or more than the acquisition cost of the asset depending on whether or not any revaluation adjustments have been made in the accounts.

No adjustments in the accounts

In this case the current balance sheet will reflect the original balance sheet values (that is, cost) and the disposal consideration will be deemed to equal indexed cost for purposes of capital gains tax and no capital gains tax liability will arise.

EXAMPLE 21.1

A and B have been partners since 1984, sharing all profits and losses equally. They admit C into the partnership on 30 March 1995 and agree to share all profits and losses in the ratio 5:4:1. No payment is made by C for admission to the partnership and no adjustments are made to the value of the partnership assets in the accounts. The partnership assets per the balance sheet on 30 March 1995 are as follows:

	£
Freehold property (at cost April 1984)	80,000
Plant and machinery (at cost April 1984)	20,000
Less: provision for depreciation	(16,000)
Net current assets	16,000
	100,000
Capital accounts	100,000

A originally had a 50% interest in each asset and still has a 50% interest while B's 50% interest in each of the partnership assets has been reduced to 40% with C being given a 10% interest. He has made a chargeable disposal of 10% of each of the assets on the balance sheet for 10% of the balance sheet value. As no adjustment has been made to the balance sheet values, his disposal value is deemed equal to his share of the indexed acquisition cost and neither a chargeable gain nor an allowable loss will arise.

Revaluation in the accounts

Where the assets in the balance sheet are revalued to reflect their market values at the date of the change, a capital gains tax liability can arise as the disposal values now differ from the original cost.

EXAMPLE 21.2

(Using the information in Example 21.1.) Before admitting C as a partner A and B revalue the assets leaving the balance sheet as follows:

	£
Goodwill	20,000
Freehold property	150,000
Plant and machinery (at cost April 1984)	20,000
Less: provision for depreciation	(16,000)
Net current assets	16,000
	190,000
Capital accounts	190,000

As above, A has made no disposal and is unaffected by the introduction of C to the partnership while B has disposed of 10% of each of the partnership assets to C. The computation of the gain/loss arising on the disposal is as follows:

		£	Gain
a)	Goodwill: Disposal value (1/10)	2,000	
	Less: acquisition value	–	
	Unindexed gain	2,000	
	Less: indexation allowance		
	$\dfrac{145.0 - 88.6}{88.6} = 0.637$		
	Nil × 0.637	–	
			2,000
b)	Premises: Disposal value (1/10)	15,000	
	Less: acquisition value (1/10)	(8,000)	
	Unindexed gain	7,000	
	Less: indexation allowance		
	8,000 × 0.637	(5,096)	
			1,904
c)	No chargeable gains/allowable losses arise on any of the other assets.		
			3,904

DISPOSAL OF ALL OR PART OF A BUSINESS; RETIREMENT

Partnership – roll-over relief

Roll-over relief may be available to a partner who disposes of a partnership share.

Roll-over relief also applies to the situations outlined in the previous section where the disposal results from an adjustment in the profit-sharing ratio.

Inheritance tax

Inheritance tax is irrelevant to a transaction which is entirely commercial. On disposal of a partnership share or on retirement of a partner, many of the disposals will fall into this category (partners being connected for transactions outside the partnership but not for transactions within the partnership) although others may be on commercial terms to a connected person or by way of gift.

To show non-gratuitous intent between unconnected persons it is only necessary to show that the transaction is at arm's length, but to show non-gratuitous intent between connected persons, the taxpayer will need to show that the transaction is such that it might have been expected to be made between unconnected persons.

The terms must therefore be commercial but also the nature of the transaction and the manner in which the terms were arrived at should be carried out in a commercial manner (for example, by obtaining independent advice).

The disposition should not be part of a transaction intended to confer gratuitous benefit (it must be considered in the light of the associated operations legislation) and it must be remembered that a disposal can be deemed to arise by the omission to exercise a right.

In a family partnership there may be a risk that the disposal of the partnership interest of a retiring partner is not for full consideration or that the payment to a retiring partner is gratuitous.

If the disposal of the partnership interest of a retiring partner is wholly or partly by gift, there is a risk of creating a gift with reservation if the partnership is to pay an annuity on a partner's retirement.

The principal reliefs available are business property relief, agricultural property relief and woodland relief. These have all been considered in the earlier chapters covering inheritance tax (especially Chapter 9). The reduction in value for both business property relief and agricultural property relief is made before deducting the annual exemption and any other exemptions that apply. Neither relief requires a claim. If agricultural property relief applies, it is given first. Business property relief cannot therefore apply to the part of the value transferred in respect of which agricultural property relief has been given (or would have been given if it were not restricted by taking into account the lower value of a previous property to fulfil the minimum qualifying period of ownership).

Disposal of a business

Where an unincorporated business is disposed of, the sale proceeds are apportioned between the assets of the business, and include goodwill (whether or not on the balance sheet). The gain or loss for capital gains tax on disposal of the business is the sum of the gains and losses on the individual assets' computations.

The heading 'disposal of a business' is also used to describe the disposal of shares or securities in a personal trading company.

The sections which follow outline circumstances in which the overall gain or loss arising may be held over for capital gains tax and/or actually reduced.

Commercial transactions

As stated above, inheritance tax is irrelevant to transactions which are entirely commercial.

To show non-gratuitous intent between unconnected persons, it is only necessary to show that the transaction is at arm's length. To show non-gratuitous intent between connected persons, the taxpayer will need to show that the transaction is such that it might have been expected to be made between unconnected persons. The terms must therefore be commercial but also the nature of the transaction and the manner in which the terms were arrived at should be carried out in a commercial manner (for example, by obtaining independent advice).

This section is extremely important when the transfer of shares in an unquoted company is considered such that the transferor's holding is reduced from a majority holding to a minority holding. If inheritance tax becomes involved, it is the loss to the transferor's estate that is the value transferred and this might be far in excess of the price freely negotiated at the time of the sale. Price has been held to mean only money and therefore where an exchange of assets takes place, the section may not apply.

It may be possible to seek clearance from the Inland Revenue in advance.

Note that connected persons for inheritance tax purposes are defined as they are for capital gains tax purposes (see Chapter 5) but more widely. A relative includes not only brother, sister, ancestor or lineal descendant but also includes uncle, aunt, nephew and niece. The definition of settlement is also much wider (see Chapter 8) as is the definition of settlor and trustee.

Transfer of business to a limited company

Where an individual transfers his or her business to a limited company and certain conditions are satisfied, the chargeable gain (all or part) is automatically held over for capital gains tax purposes (no claim is necessary).

The conditions to be satisfied are as follows:

- The business must be transferred as a going concern.
- All the assets of the business (or all assets other than cash) must be transferred.
- The transfer must be made wholly or mainly in exchange for shares.

If the transfer is wholly in exchange for shares, the whole of the gain is deferred by deducting it from the acquisition value of the shares.

If the transfer is only partly in exchange for shares, only the part of the gain given by the formula:

$$\frac{\text{Value of shares}}{\text{Total consideration for business}} \times \text{Total gain on transfer}$$

is deferred. The remainder of the gain on transfer is chargeable in the fiscal year of the transfer.

The company is deemed to acquire the assets at their market value at the date of the transfer.

EXAMPLE 21.4

A transferred her business to A Ltd on 1 January 1995 in exchange for 150,000 £1 shares at par and £10,000 in cash. The market values of the assets of the business at the date of transfer to A Ltd were:

	Value 1 Jan 1995 £	Acquisition Cost £	Date	31 March 1982 Value £
Goodwill	5,000	Nil	n/a	2,000
Premises	142,000	10,000	1978	25,000
Car	8,000			
Current assets	15,000			
	170,000			
Current liabilities	(10,000)			
	160,000			

The total gain on transfer is calculated by summing the gains on disposal of the individual chargeable assets as follows:

		£	Gain £
a)	Goodwill: Disposal value	5,000	
	Less: 31 March 1982 value	(2,000)	
	Unindexed gain	3,000	
	Less: indexation allowance		
	$\frac{144.7 - 79.4}{79.4} = 0.822$		
	$2,000 \times 0.822$	(1,644)	
			1,356
		£	
b)	Premises: Disposal value	142,000	
	Less: 31 March 1982 value	(25,000)	
	Unindexed gain	117,000	
	Less: indexation allowance		
	$25,000 \times 0.822$	(20,550)	
			96,450
c)	Other assets: the car is not a chargeable asset and the others are not capital items		—
	Total gain on transfer		97,806
	Less: gain to be held over $97,806 \times \frac{150,000}{160,000}$		(91,693)
	Chargeable gain 1994/95		6,113
	Base cost of shares in A Ltd:		
	Value at 1 January 1995		150,000
	Less: gain held over		(91,693)
			58,307

If the shares given in exchange are of more than one class, the deferred gain is apportioned between them in proportion to the market value of each class at the time of the transfer.

As in the previous section, the Finance Act 1988 re-basing provisions must be taken into account. Where the transfer of the business to a limited company took place after 31 March 1982 and before 5 April 1988 (incorporating assets acquired before 31 March 1982), a claim may be made for the deferred gain to be halved on the disposal of the shares after 5 April 1988.

Planning considerations

The transferor may have income tax trade losses at the date of the transfer, or he or she may have capital losses. He or she will also want if at all possible to use his or her capital gains annual exemption. The principal condition for the relief to apply is that the consideration is wholly or partly for shares. Provided this is the case, it is worthwhile planning carefully to extract the maximum amount of cash at the date of transfer without incurring tax liabilities. The gain attributable to the cash consideration should be matched with the sum of the transferor's capital losses for the year of assessment and brought forward together with the annual exemption. In future years shares can be sold, realising on each occasion sufficient gains to use the annual exemption.

Income tax trade losses can be deducted from the income (remuneration and/or dividends) derived from the company (see Chapter 18).

Many examination questions focus on this area.

Retirement relief

Retirement relief is available to an individual whose age is 55 or more when he or she makes a material disposal of business assets (including the disposal of shares or securities in a personal trading company) provided certain conditions are satisfied throughout a qualifying period of at least one year.

Retirement relief is also available when a partner who satisfies the relevant conditions disposes of an interest or part of that interest in a partnership as if it were the whole or part of a business. It also includes assets owned personally by the partner but used by the partnership when their disposal is associated with the partner's material disposal of business assets.

It is not necessary for the individual to actually retire at the date of the disposal. However, if a material disposal of business assets takes place at an earlier age and the reason for the disposal is retirement resulting from ill health, retirement relief may also be available but, in this case, the individual must actually retire from the business concerned (and the relief must also be claimed within two years after the end of the fiscal year in which the disposal took place).

Conditions to be satisfied in respect of the disposal of assets in an unincorporated business

A material disposal of business assets in an unincorporated business amounts to the disposal of the whole or part of a business.

Retirement relief exempts all or part of the gains 'qualifying for relief' from capital gains tax provided the conditions are satisfied throughout the qualifying period. Where the qualifying period is ten years or more, maximum retirement relief is available, that is, the first £250,000 of the gain plus half of any gain between £250,000 and £1,000,000. If the qualifying period is less than ten years but at least one year, the relief is reduced proportionately.

EXAMPLE 21.5

A taxpayer disposes of her business on 1 October 1994 at the age of 59, making a gain on disposal of chargeable business assets of £350,000. The relevant conditions have been satisfied throughout a qualifying period of eight years. How much retirement relief is available to her?

For a qualifying period of eight years, the lower threshold becomes £200,000 (8/10 of £250,000) and the upper limit becomes £800,000 (8/10 of £1,000,000). The retirement relief available is therefore:

£200,000 + 1/2 (£350,000 − £200,000) = £275,000

Retirement relief is available to each of husband and wife if they individually meet the conditions.

Qualifying period

The qualifying period is the period ending with the date of disposal throughout which the business was owned by the individual disposing of it.

If an individual has been involved in two businesses consecutively, the qualifying periods in each business may be aggregated, provided the gap between the businesses is not more than two years.

EXAMPLE 21.6

X has owned his current business for four years when he decides to dispose of it at age 55. Prior to acquiring his current business, he had taken a year off after disposing of his previous business which he had had for six years.

In the ten years prior to the disposal of his current business, nine out of ten of those years qualify; he therefore has a qualifying period of nine years.

Gains qualifying for relief

Gains qualifying for relief are the aggregate gains (net of allowable losses) on the disposal of the business's chargeable business assets. Chargeable business assets are those chargeable assets used for the purpose of the trade (that is, goodwill is included but shares and securities and other assets held as investments are excluded). An asset is not a chargeable business asset if a gain on its disposal would not give rise to a chargeable gain. Plant and machinery are therefore chargeable business assets if either the cost or market value is greater than £6,000.

Disposal of the whole or part of an unincorporated business

Note that for retirement relief to apply, the disposal must be of the entire or a 'stand alone' part of the business (that is, the disposal of chargeable business assets does not necessarily qualify as the disposal of part of a business).

EXAMPLE 21.7

Y has been trading since 1 July 1980 and has decided to dispose of his business and retire on 31 March 1995. He is 58 years old. He disposes of the business for £100,000, attributable to the assets as follows:

	31 March 1995	31 March 1982 Value
	£	£
Goodwill	15,000	5,000
Freehold premises	50,000	15,000
Shares held as investment	10,000	2,000
Net current assets	25,000	
	100,000	

Calculate the gains accruing to Y on the disposal of the above assets, assuming he has made an election for universal 31 March 1982 re-basing and show the amount of retirement relief available.

			£	Gain £

a) Goodwill: Disposal value — 15,000
Less: 31 March 1982 value — (5,000)
Unindexed gain — 10,000
Less: indexation allowance:
$$\frac{145.0 - 79.4}{79.4} = 0.826$$
$5,000 \times 0.826$ — (4,130)
      5,870

b) Premises: Disposal value — 50,000
Less: 31 March 1982 value — (15,000)
Unindexed gain — 35,000
Less: indexation allowance:
$15,000 \times 0.826$ — (12,390)
      22,610

c) There are no other chargeable business assets
Total gains qualifying for retirement relief — 28,480
Retirement relief is lower of:
   a) Gains qualifying for relief — 28,480
   b) Maximum available — 250,000
      (28,480)

Chargeable gains after retirement relief — –
Add gains not qualifying for retirement relief
Investments: Disposal value — 10,000
Less: 31 March 1982 value — (2,000)
Unindexed gain — 8,000
Less: indexation allowance
$2,000 \times 0.826$ — (1,652)
      6,348

Chargeable gain — 6,348

Conditions to be satisfied in respect of the disposal of shares or securities in an incorporated business

Retirement relief is available in respect of the disposal of the shares or securities in a personal trading company held throughout a qualifying period. Maximum relief as above, is available for a qualifying period of ten years or more. If the qualifying period is less than ten years but at least one year, the relief is proportionately reduced.

Qualifying period

The qualifying period in this case is the period ending with the date of disposal, throughout which period the business was owned by a trading company which is (or the holding company of which is) the individual's 'personal company' of which the individual is a full-time working officer or employee.

Personal company

A personal company is one in which the director or the employee personally holds not less than 5% of the voting rights.

Full-time working officer or employee

A full-time working officer is an employee who must devote a substantial part of his or her time to the service of the company or companies. Case law has shown that between 25 and 30 hours per week should be sufficient to constitute 'full-time'.

Disposal of shares or securities in a personal trading company

Note that to qualify for retirement relief, the individual must both own the relevant shares and be a full-time working director (or employee) throughout the qualifying period. Relief is given for the shorter of these two periods.

EXAMPLE 21.8

Y disposed of his 30% holding (30,000 £1 shares) in Y Ltd for £200,000 (indexed gain £150,000) on 31 March 1995 when he reached the age of 60. He had been a full-time working director of the company for the previous four years and had owned the shares for the same period. Chargeable business assets of the company at that date were valued at £400,000 while chargeable assets amounted to £500,000. Show the retirement relief available and the amount of the chargeable gain arising.

		£	£
Indexed gain on disposal of shares			150,000
Less: Retirement relief is lower of:			
a) attributable to chargeable business assets:			
$150,000 \times \dfrac{400,000}{500,000}$		120,000	
b) maximum relief available			
lower/upper limits $\dfrac{4}{10} \times 250,000/1,000,000$			
100,000 + 1/2(120,000 − 100,000)		110,000	
			(110,000)
Chargeable gain			40,000

Retirement relief on successive disposals

Where qualifying disposals are made at different times, the retirement relief on later disposals is restricted by the amount of relief already given, as follows:

Retirement relief on latest disposal limited to A − B

	£
A is lower of	
i) Gains qualifying for relief on the latest disposal	X
Add retirement relief given on previous disposals	X
Total gains qualifying for relief	X
ii) Maximum retirement relief available by reference to qualifying period calculated to date of latest disposal	X
B aggregate relief given on previous disposals	X

TAX PLANNING

Other disposals where retirement relief is available

Retirement relief may also be available for disposals on retirement of:

- assets owned personally by a partner or director but used in the business
- trust property (shares or assets of the business) if the beneficiary has an interest in possession in the trust and is a full-time working officer or employee of the personal company
- assets provided by an employee for use in an office or employment (the employment must have been his or her full-time employment for a qualifying period of at least one year prior to the disposal of the asset)
- assets used in letting furnished holiday accommodation provided the necessary conditions are satisfied.

Assets owned personally by partner or director

Retirement relief is given on the disposal of assets owned personally by a partner or director if:

- the partner or director qualified for retirement relief on the disposal of his or her entire partnership interest/shares in the family company; and
- the asset was used for purposes of the partnership/company's trade; and
- the asset was so in use immediately before the disposal of the partnership interest/shares in the family company.

The qualifying period is the same as for the retirement relief above irrespective of the period of ownership of the asset itself.

Gift of all or part of a business

In this case there is both capital gains tax and inheritance tax to consider. The capital gains tax provisions for the disposal of a business have been considered above and the inheritance tax provisions were considered in Chapters 8 to 10. Each tax operates independently of the other, each with its own exemptions and reliefs as previously considered.

Transfer of business between husband and wife

The transfer of a business or shares in a personal company from husband to wife or vice versa is deemed to be a 'no gain, no loss' disposal for capital gains tax (see Chapter 5).

Where the transfer takes place on the death of either husband or wife, the survivor may elect to be treated for purposes of retirement relief as having owned the business or shares in the family company from the date of acquisition of the transferor.

Where the transfer does not take place on death the periods of ownership may also be aggregated, but if the business or shares are disposed of to a third party during the lifetime of the transferor, this treatment must be the subject of an election. The maximum relief available will be restricted to the entitlement of the transferor if the inter-spouse transfer had not taken place.

For inheritance tax purposes a transfer between husband and wife is exempt; as above, if the transfer takes place on death, the period of ownership for business property relief and agricultural property relief is taken from the date of acquisition of the transferor.

Interaction of retirement relief and gift relief (capital gains tax)

When a material disposal of business assets takes place and retirement relief is available, retirement relief must be deducted first from the gain and the balance of the gain is available for hold-over relief.

If consideration is received for the transfer then the amount by which the consideration received exceeds the sum of the allowable cost and the retirement relief is immediately chargeable, further restricting the gain eligible for hold-over relief.

Re-investment relief

This relief was introduced in the Finance Act 1993 and substantially extended by the Finance Act 1994. The gain arising on any asset disposed of on or after 30 November 1993 can be deferred if a qualifying investment is acquired with the sale proceeds.

Qualifying investment

The re-investment must take place within one year before or three years after the date of disposal of the asset. A qualifying investment is the acquisition of ordinary shares in a qualifying company. There is no requirement for the investor to take a minimum holding.

A qualifying company is an unquoted company existing for the purpose of carrying on one or more qualifying trades either itself or as a holding company of a trading group. This requirement must be satisfied throughout the three years following the acquisition. A qualifying trade is one conducted on a commercial basis with a view to the realisation of profits and not an excluded activity. Excluded activities include dealing in land and commodities, financial and leasing businesses.

Roll-over

The re-investment criteria is generous in that the re-investment is effectively treated as the top slice of the gain.

Roll-over relief is therefore obtained in full provided that the amount of the gain is re-invested (that is, unlike other roll-over reliefs, it is not necessary to re-invest the full sale proceeds to obtain full roll-over relief).

The amount rolled-over may be restricted to a sum specified in the claim. Annual exemptions for capital gains tax need not therefore be wasted.

The interaction of retirement relief with re-investment relief

Where both retirement relief and re-investment relief are due, re-investment relief applies before retirement relief. However, the re-investment relief claim should be restricted to any gains which are not covered in full by retirement relief.

Re-investment relief is not restricted to the gain arising in respect of chargeable business assets. This means that it can be used to defer gains which are not eligible for either retirement relief or gift relief.

EXAMPLE 21.9

J is 56 years old. He holds 75% of the shares in C Ltd, an unquoted trading company in which he has been a full-time working director for 2 years. J purchased the shares in October 1989 for £75,000; he sold them in October 1994 for £230,000, realising a chargeable gain of £135,500.

In October 1994, the assets and liabilities of C Ltd were as follows:

	£
Freehold premises	100,000
Fixed plant and machinery	80,000
Goodwill	40,000
Investment property	50,000
Stock	25,000
Debtors	15,000
Bank	20,000
Creditors	(22,000)

This was J's only disposal during 1994–95. He has capital losses brought forward of £8,000.

J proposes to invest part of his sale proceeds in T Ltd, an unquoted manufacturing company recently set up by a friend.

The gain eligible for retirement relief is that in respect of the chargeable business assets:

	Chargeable assets £	Chargeable business assets £
Freehold premises	100,000	100,000
Plant and machinery	80,000	80,000
Goodwill	40,000	40,000
Investments	50,000	–
	270,000	220,000

The gain eligible for relief is therefore:

£135,500 × 220,000/270,000 = £110,407

As J has only been a full-time working director for 2 years, he will be restricted to 20% of the maximum limits. His gain after retirement relief will therefore be:

		£
Gain		135,500
Less retirement relief:		
In full on £250,000 × 20% =	50,000	
50% × (110,407 – 50,000) =	30,204	80,204
Chargeable gain		55,296

As J is entitled to an annual exemption of £5,800 and capital losses of £8,000 he should therefore invest £41,496 (£55,296 – 5,800 – 8,000) of his disposal proceeds in T Ltd. This will ensure that he has no capital gains tax liability in respect of this disposal. The investment must be made by October 1997.

Withdrawal of relief

The gain will subsequently become chargeable if:
- the new shares are sold without being replaced
- the individual becomes non-UK resident
- within 3 years of the reinvestment, the company in which the shares are held ceases to carry on a qualifying trade.

Summary

► Whenever there is a change in the profit-sharing arrangements or a change in the members of a partnership, fractional adjustments must be made in the ownership of each partnership asset and, to the extent that these assets are chargeable assets, capital gains tax liabilities may arise.

► The transfer of a business to a limited company is an ideal opportunity for realising tax-free capital gains.

► Retirement relief (capital gains tax) is important in tax planning. Consideration should always be given to the viability of delaying a disposal until the taxpayer reaches 55 years of age or, if the conditions are satisfied, until the qualifying period reaches ten years. Remember that the relief is available to both husband and wife if both satisfy the conditions.

► Retirement relief applies to partners and partnership assets in much the same way as it applies to sole traders.

► Inheritance tax principally affects the unincorporated business on the retirement or death of the sole trader or partner. It should therefore be considered as part of retirement planning.

► Where there is no gratuitous intent between connected persons care must be taken to create evidence that the transaction was conducted on a commercial basis.

► For inheritance tax purposes, care should be taken that the necessary qualifying periods for ownership and/or occupation are fulfilled in relation to both business property relief and agricultural property relief.

► Woodland relief (inheritance tax) is only available on death. It is not directly relevant to retirement planning but may add attraction to forestry as an investment.

► Gains arising on the disposal of any assets on or after 30 November 1993 may be deferred if re-invested in an unquoted trading company.

Self test questions

1. What is the time limit for claiming to defer a gain on the transfer of a business to a limited company?

2. What is the minimum qualifying period of ownership for business property relief?

3. What is the minimum qualifying period of owner-occupation for agricultural property relief?

4. A owns 4,000 shares in B Ltd. The other shares are owned as follows: A's wife 2,000; A's 2 grandchildren have 2000 each; X (unconnected to A) has the remaining 10,000 shares. Is B Ltd a family company for purposes of A's entitlement to retirement relief?

5. Does the gift of an interest in a partnership constitute a material disposal of business assets for purposes of retirement relief and if so, would gift relief also be available?

6. Jeremy Thompson is a client of the firm of certified accountants you work for. On 9 December 1994 he attended a meeting with you, at which the following information was supplied.
    a) Jeremy and his wife have recently seen, and decided to buy, a freehold cottage near the coast which they will use as a holiday cottage, until they move into it when Jeremy retires on his 55th birthday on 28 May 1995. The Thompsons have made an offer of £120,000 for the cottage, which has been accepted, and at the request of the present owners, have agreed a completion date of 15 May 1995.

b) Jeremy and his wife already own a leasehold holiday flat near the coast which they are now selling. They bought the flat on 1 August 1971 for £38,000 plus stamp duty of £200 and legal fees of £400, when the lease had an unexpired term of 42 years. They have accepted an offer of £78,000 for the flat and completion date has been fixed for 31 January 1995. Legal fees on sale are estimated at £600 and estate agent's fees £1,600. The value of the flat has not changed over the past 13 years.

c) The additional money required to pay for the cottage will be obtained from the planned disposal by the Thompsons, in mid-April 1995, of the following:

i) 8,000 shares in Westbank plc. Jeremy has built up his holding of shares over a number of years, as follows:

7 June 1971	Received 2,000 shares on the death of his aunt, when their value was £5.84 each.
21 October 1980	Bought 7,000 shares at £5.68 each.
31 March 1982	Bought 3,000 shares at £5.40 each.
15 May 1983	Received a lifetime gift of 1,000 shares from his mother when their value was £5.20 each. No election was made to postpone the gain arising to his mother.
1 December 1986	Bought 2,000 shares for £5.10 each.
9 February 1988	Bought 1,000 shares for £5.00 each.

The price of the Westbank plc shares has been steady at £4.00 each for the past few months.

ii) 4,000 shares in Thompson Engineering Ltd to the company's production director for £5.00 each. Jeremy took over the company on 1 January 1970 when he acquired 18,000 £1 ordinary shares at par. The assets of the company, and their values in April 1995, are expected to be:

	Cost		Market value April 1995
	£		£
Goodwill	–		30,000
Freehold factory	30,000	(1966)	50,000
Plant and machinery			
Large plant (2 items)	15,000	(1981)	10,000
Small plant – cost less than £2,000 per item	12,000	(1984)	10,000
Trading stock	8,000	(1987)	10,000
Investment in supplier company	4,000	(1975)	10,000

The shares in Thompson Engineering Ltd were valued at £4.00 each in March 1982.

iii) An antique piece of furniture. Jeremy bought this in June 1982 for £3,500. At an auction recently, the highest bid was £1,500 and no sale took place. The bidder has contacted Jeremy privately and offered £1,700, which Jeremy is likely to accept, the sale taking place in May 1995.

d) Mrs Thompson plans to cash National Savings Certificates to cover the cost of new curtains and carpets. The certificates were acquired in 1981 for £3,000 and their realisable value in May 1995 is expected to be £6,400.

Compute the capital gains/losses which will arise if the Thompsons carry out the above transactions, as planned.

Answers on pages 600–601

CHAPTER 22

Value Added Tax

This chapter aims to give an appreciation of the system of value added tax both in its basic concepts and its impact, particularly as regards the requirements it imposes on businesses and the manner in which it interacts with other taxes. Much of the content will have been covered in the Paper 7 syllabus and will therefore be revision.

The scope of value added tax

Value added tax (VAT) is an indirect tax on general consumer expenditure and constitutes a significant proportion of central government taxation revenue.

The tax was first introduced into the UK on 1 April 1973. Since then substantial amendments have been made to the law. Now the legislation is contained in the Value Added Tax Act 1983 (VATA 1983) as amended by subsequent Finance Acts. However the overriding law on VAT comes from the European Community Directives which are binding on member states and which specify the result which the legislation in a member state must produce. The member states themselves can decide upon the form and method of compliance. Where any of the provisions in the EC Directives are mandatory, EC law takes precedence if there are inconsistencies with UK law.

The tax is administered by HM Customs and Excise, who publish guidance booklets on all aspects of VAT. These do not in general have any legal standing but set out how Customs and Excise interpret the law.

Value added tax is charged on the supply of goods and services in the UK and on the importation of goods into the UK. The basic principle is for VAT to be added at each stage of production of goods (and services) – the supplier only accounting for VAT added to selling price less VAT suffered on purchases and expenses – so that the whole of the tax is passed to and borne by the final consumer who is unable to recover VAT on expenditure. The collection of the tax is made on the other hand via instalments payable at each stage of production.

The principle is simple but in practice there are exemptions, two rates of tax, special schemes and so on.

For any particular transaction to be within the scope of VAT and therefore chargeable to tax, it must be: 'a taxable supply of goods and services made by a taxable person in the course of his business'.

Supply of goods and services

Supply is not defined by the legislation but covers everything that is done for consideration unless specifically excluded, as well as gifts of business assets (except single gifts costing less than £10; gifts of industrial samples, in a form not available to the public, to customers or potential customers; and gifts of services) and the private use of business assets. Some transactions, however, are regarded as supplies of neither goods nor services and are outside the scope of VAT (examples are the services of an employee to an employer – whether a person is employed or self-employed for VAT purposes will in general be determined by his position for income tax purposes; transfer of a business as a going concern; the assignment of rights under an HP or similar contract to a bank or financial institution).

Taxable supply

A taxable supply is any supply in the UK of goods or services that is not an exempt supply. Exempt supplies are listed in the legislation and include most supplies in connection with land, insurance, postal services, betting, finance, education and health.

Taxable person

A taxable person is a person who makes or intends to make taxable supplies while he or she is, or ought to be, registered.

For this purpose, a person may be a sole trader, a partnership, a limited company, a club and so on.

In the course of business

Business is not defined in the legislation but there are indications as to its scope. It includes any trade, profession or vocation. In general it is regarded by the Customs and Excise as meaning any recurrent activity which involves, wholly or mainly, making supplies to other people for consideration. There is no requirement to have a profit motive. Clubs and associations have been defined as businesses for VAT purposes where the members are provided with facilities or other advantages in return for a subscription or other form of consideration. Recreational activities and hobbies, on the other hand, have been excluded from the definition where the making of taxable supplies is incidental to the general activity.

The provisions of membership benefits by clubs and associations is a business activity unless they are of a type listed below. Therefore, if the taxable turnover (including subscriptions and other sales) exceeds the registration limits, the organisation must be registered for VAT. The exceptions are subscriptions to charitable associations and organisations of a political, religious, philanthropic, philosophical or patriotic nature, where the subscriptions give the members no benefits other than rights to annual reports and accounts, and to vote at general meetings.

Compulsory registration/deregistration

Registration is evidenced by a registration number.

A person who makes or intends to make taxable supplies in the course of a business must be registered whenever he or she satisfies either one of two tests:

- at the end of any month, his or her taxable supplies over the 12 months then ending, exceed a specified limit (1994: £45,000)
- at any time there are reasonable grounds for believing that taxable supplies in the next 30 days will exceed the limit (1994: £45,000).

Because it is the person who must register and not the business, one registration applies to all of a person's business activities. Therefore if a number of businesses are carried on by the same person, although the taxable supplies of each are under the specified limit, the person will be required to be registered if the aggregate of all his or her taxable supplies exceeds the limit.

Any person not registered, who, at the end of any month, has exceeded the limit in the 12 months just ended, need not register if he or she can demonstrate that his or her cumulative taxable supplies for the next 12 months will not exceed the limit for the 12 months beginning (1994: £43,000 see below). This is often difficult to demonstrate.

In determining whether a trader should be registered under the above provisions, disposals of fixed assets which have been used in the business are ignored.

The specified limits for the current and recent years are as follows:

Date from which effective	Per 12 months just ended £	Per 12 months beginning £
19 March 1991	35,000	33,600
11 March 1992	36,600	35,100
16 March 1993	37,600	36,000
1 December 1993	45,000	43,000

Where a person exceeds the retrospective limit, he or she must notify the Customs and Excise within 30 days of the end of the month (referred to as the 'relevant month'). He or she will be registered with effect from the end of the month following the 'relevant month'; for example, if taxable turnover for the 12 months to 31 January is over the limit, the date of registration will be 1 March or earlier if mutually agreed.

Where a person expects to exceed the limit in the next 30 days, he or she must notify the Customs and Excise and will be registered from the date the grounds for the belief first existed.

Failure to notify the Customs and Excise will incur a penalty for late notification and, in addition, will result in the registration being backdated to the appropriate date (and VAT being payable whether or not collected).

A trader who is registered must notify Customs and Excise within 30 days if he or she permanently ceases to make taxable supplies (temporary interruption of trade does not apply) and state the date of cessation. His or her registration is then cancelled from that date or later date if mutually agreed.

On cessation, goods forming part of the business are deemed to be self-supplied either at cost or, if not new, at market value (stocks and capital items are an example). The purpose of this is to allow output tax to be collected prior to deregistration. No VAT need be charged if:

▶ the business is transferred as a going concern (see Chapter 27 – *note*: applies to individuals and companies)
▶ the tax on the deemed supplies is £250 or less
▶ no input tax was recovered on original supply.

Where only one of several businesses ceases, such that the thresholds above are no longer exceeded, compulsory deregistration will not take place (voluntary deregistration may be requested).

If the status of the taxable person changes (for example, from sole trader to partnership) then the one registration is cancelled from the date of change (notified to the local VAT office within ten days) and a new registration takes its place.

Voluntary registration/deregistration

A trader is entitled to register in the following circumstances:

▶ If he or she satisfies the Commissioners that he or she makes or intends to make taxable supplies in the course of business – objective evidence is required to substantiate the claim – provided he or she notifies the Commissioners if he or she ceases to make or to intend to make taxable supplies. It is not necessary to expect to exceed the registration limit. The registration is effective from the date the request is made or earlier by mutual agreement.
▶ If he or she neither makes nor intends to make taxable supplies but satisfies the following conditions:

- he or she is UK resident or has a business establishment in the UK; and
- he or she makes or intends to make supplies which would be taxable if made in the UK.

Note that before this, voluntary registration was at the discretion of the Commissioners and subject to conditions imposed by them.

Similarly the deregistration provisions were changed so that the Commissioners must deregister a trader who is not, or has ceased to be, liable to be registered if he or she so requests (that is, the tax exclusive turnover in the next 12 months will be less than £43,000 – the reduction not being due to planned cessation of trade or temporary interruption of the trade). It will be cancelled from the date of the request or later if mutually agreed.

Planning considerations

There are a number of reasons why a person may voluntarily register for VAT or not deregister when the opportunity presents:

- Input tax can be recovered and therefore the business expenses are reduced.
- Customers who are registered can reclaim the output tax charged.
- Credibility – a VAT registration may create the impression of a bigger or more well-established business.
- It avoids the risk of not registering at the correct time:
  - penalties (see below)
  - interest (see below)
  - input tax is only recoverable on services received in the six months prior to registration (and on goods on hand at the date of registration)
  - output tax is payable whether it is charged to the customers or not, from the date that registration should have taken place.

The deemed self supply prior to deregistration and consequent VAT liability may be a deterrent to deregistration.

Administration

VAT invoice

If a taxable person is to obtain relief for input tax suffered, he or she must have a VAT invoice. A taxable person is therefore required to give an invoice showing specific information whenever he or she makes a taxable supply (and retain a copy). The information which must be shown is as follows:

1. invoice identification number
2. tax point (see below)
3. supplier's name, address and VAT registration number
4. customer's name and address
5. type of supply (for example, sale, hire purchase, loan, exchange, hire/lease/rental, sale or return)
6. description of goods or services supplied
7. for each item supplied – quantity, rate of VAT, and the amount payable excluding VAT in sterling
8. total payable excluding VAT in sterling
9. rate of any cash discount offered
10. the total VAT chargeable at each rate (note that this is calculated on the total payable after deducting cash discount, whether or not it is claimed) in sterling
11. the total VAT chargeable in sterling.

Credit notes require a similar amount of detail plus a cross-reference to the original invoice.

Retailers

A retailer is not required to provide a tax invoice unless requested by a customer who is also a taxable person. Where such a request is made, he may issue an invoice with less detail if it is for goods (plus VAT) amounting in total to no more than £100. Only items 2, 3, 6, and 7 above need be shown plus the invoice total including VAT. Such an invoice should not include zero-rated or exempt supplies but special rules apply to invoices for petrol and diesel fuel.

Self-billing

It is not always practical to issue a tax invoice to the customer. The Customs and Excise may approve a system of self-billing whereby, for example, a customer prepares the tax invoice – instead of the supplier and sends it with payment to the supplier. This is the system used by publishers in respect of royalties. This counts as a taxable supply of the author.

If an error is made in the tax invoice, the person issuing the invoice is responsible for making good any understatement of VAT and may be so assessed by the Customs and Excise.

Tax point

The time at which a supply is treated as taking place is called the tax point and this determines the rate of VAT applicable (where a change in rates has taken place) and the accounting period in which the VAT must be accounted for.

The basic tax point is the date on which the goods are delivered or made available to the purchaser but it is overridden when payment is made or the invoice is issued earlier than that date, the earlier date then becomes the actual tax point.

If the supplier issues the tax invoice within 14 days after the basic tax point, this becomes the actual tax point unless the trader has notified the Commissioners that he does not wish this rule (known as the 14-day rule) to be applied. An extension to the 14-day rule may be requested if invoices are regularly prepared monthly, making the tax point either the last day of the month or the date the invoice is prepared – whichever is chosen must be implemented consistently.

The basic tax point in the case of services is the date when the service is performed.

Some special situations are listed below with the relevant rules for determining the tax point:

- Goods supplied on sale or return. The tax point is the time when the goods are adopted by the customer or, if sooner, 12 months after their issue on sale or return.
- Continuous supply of services. Where services are supplied over a period of time, and payment is received periodically, a tax point arises every time a payment is received or a tax invoice is issued, whichever is the earlier.

Accounting periods, the VAT return and the EC Sales List

Every taxable person must complete and submit a VAT return with any tax payable in respect of each accounting period within 30 days of its end. All supplies with a tax point falling within the accounting period must be included in the VAT return. In addition, businesses with a turnover greater than £59,000 or making EC supplies greater than £10,000 must submit an EC Sales List with the VAT return.

The accounting period for VAT is normally three months ending on a date determined by the Customs and Excise by reference to the particular trade (notified usually in the certificate of registration). This allows Customs and Excise to stagger the returns over the year.

Exceptions to the three month accounting period are as follows:

- A one month accounting period may be permitted if repayments are expected (for example, if supplies are zero-rated). If a trader registered voluntarily then monthly tax returns will not be allowed.
- An optional scheme for an annual accounting period for small businesses (taxable turnover below £300,000) exists whereby an estimated annual assessment is agreed with the Customs and Excise and the trader pays nine instalments of one-tenth of the estimate spread over the year. The tenth instalment – the balance due – would be paid with the annual return within two months of the end of the accounting period. (The accounting period for VAT will not necessarily coincide with the trader's financial year – but see below).
- The first period after registration and the final period before deregistration may vary in length, also any other period affected by a change in the return date. The Customs and Excise give special consideration to applications requesting return periods to coincide with the business's financial year or any other reasonable request.
- Large VAT payers (over £2 million per annum) are allowed to make quarterly returns, but must make monthly payments on account.

The information to be given in the return includes details of the total output tax and input tax for the period as well as statistical information of total inputs and outputs excluding VAT (see specimen return Figure 22.1).

Where a return is not completed for a period or where the Customs and Excise consider for any reason that there has been an under-declaration of VAT (for example, after a control visit), the Commissioners may issue an assessment for the tax underpaid. This is payable within 30 days and leave to appeal is normally only given if the disputed amount is deposited with the Commissioners beforehand.

Accounting records

Accounting records require some modification to deal with VAT. The legislation states that 'every taxable person must keep such records as the Commissioners may require'. Despite this, the Customs and Excise state that it is not necessary for accounting records to be kept in any special form for VAT purposes provided sufficient detail is recorded to enable:

- the tax payable or repayable to be calculated
- the VAT returns to be prepared
- the Customs and Excise officer to check the completeness and accuracy of the VAT return if he or she so requires.

All records must be kept up to date and must be available to Customs and Excise officers on request, and if there is more than one place of business, a list of all branches must be kept at the principal place of business.

The Commissioners may require records to be preserved for a period up to six years although permission may be given to retain some of the records for a shorter period. Records may be preserved on microfilm and microfiche provided there are adequate facilities for Customs and Excise to view. They may also be kept on computer tape or disk provided 'they can be readily converted into legible form and made available to Customs on request'.

The VAT account

Every taxable person must keep and maintain an account known as the value added tax account. It must be divided to show the tax payable and tax allowable for each VAT accounting period. The purpose is to establish the 'true amount of tax' for the accounting period. Errors identified in a later period must be referenced to the period in which the error was made:

- If net errors do not exceed £2,000 they may be corrected in the VAT account (and therefore the return) by adding or subtracting from the true tax for the period in which the error is discovered.
- If net errors exceed £2,000, or the taxpayer chooses, the local VAT office should be notified in writing. A special voluntary disclosure form may be used.

Computer records

Where records are kept on a computer, Customs and Excise must be informed and must have access to it and must be able to check its operation and the manner in which information is stored. They can also ask for the help of anyone concerned with the operation of the computer or its software. As a condition of approval the Commissioners are able to impose any requirement they feel is reasonable to secure that the information will be as readily available to them as it was originally.

Problems may be encountered when a computer system is changed or improved regarding the obligation to retain VAT records for six years.

Retailers' schemes

Special records are necessary where the taxable person is operating one of the special retail schemes. The detail of these schemes is not examinable.

Confidentiality of information

The Customs and Excise and the Inland Revenue are authorised to help each other with their enquiries and, in so doing, may disclose information to each other. Exchange of information will take place at a local level particularly where tax evasion is suspected. Information may also be exchanged with other EC countries, or other government departments. The consent of the registered person is required for information to be given to any person or organisation other than those listed above.

The charge to tax

Rates of tax

VAT is charged on taxable supplies at one of two rates:

- standard rate – currently (1994) 17.5%
- zero rate – 0%.

The rate of tax depends on the type of goods or services supplied. Standard rate applies unless the supplies are specifically zero-rated (described below).

HM Customs and Excise

Value Added Tax Return

For the period
01 02 94 to 30 04 94

For Official Use

Registration Number | **Period**

You could be liable to a financial penalty if your completed return and all the VAT payable are not received by the due date.

Due date: 31 05 94

For Official Use

Your VAT Office telephone number is 071-865 3000

ATTENTION
If you are using Retail Scheme B1, D or J, please remember to carry out your annual adjustment at the appropriate time.

Before you fill in this form please read the notes on the back and the VAT leaflet *"Filling in your VAT return"*. Fill in all boxes clearly in ink, and write 'none' where necessary. Don't put a dash or leave any box blank. If there are no pence write "00" in the pence column. **Do not** enter more than one amount in any box.

For official use

	Box	£	p
VAT due in this period on **sales** and other outputs	1		
VAT due in this period on **acquisitions** from other **EC Member States**	2		
Total VAT due **(the sum of boxes 1 and 2)**	3		
VAT reclaimed in this period on **purchases** and other inputs (including acquisitions from the EC)	4		
Net VAT to be paid to Customs or reclaimed by you (Difference between boxes 3 and 4)	5		
Total value of **sales** and all other outputs excluding any VAT. **Include your box 8 figure**	6		00
Total value of **purchases** and all other inputs excluding any VAT. **Include your box 9 figure**	7		00
Total value of all **supplies** of goods and related services, excluding any VAT, to other **EC Member States**	8		00
Total value of all **acquisitions** of goods and related services, excluding any VAT, from other **EC Member States**	9		00

Retail schemes. If you have used any of the schemes in the period covered by this return, enter the relevant letter(s) in this box.

If you are enclosing a payment please tick this box. ☐

DECLARATION: You, or someone on your behalf, must sign below.

I, ...declare that the
(Full name of signatory in BLOCK LETTERS)
information given above is true and complete.

Signature ....Date ....19..........
A false declaration can result in prosecution.

S

CD 2859/N3(08/93) F 3790 (JANUARY 1993)

VAT 100

Figure 22.1 A specimen VAT return.
This form is Crown copyright and is reproduced by kind permission of the Controller of Her Majesty's Stationery Office.

Notes

These notes and the VAT leaflet *Filling in your VAT Return* will help you fill in this form. You may also need to refer to other VAT notices and leaflets.

If you need help or advice please contact your local VAT office. Their telephone number is shown over the page.

If you are using the 'cash accounting scheme', the amounts of VAT due and deductible are for payments you actually receive and make, and not on invoices you receive and send out.

If you put **negative figures** in boxes 1 to 4, put them in brackets.

Amounts not declared correctly on previous returns

1. If any of your previous returns declared too much or too little VAT that has not yet been accounted for, you can correct the position using boxes 1 and 4 for net amounts of **£2000 or less**.

2. If the net amount is **over £2000**, tell your local VAT office immediately. Don't include the amount on this return.

If you do not follow these instructions you could be liable to a financial penalty.

How to pay your VAT

Cross all cheques and postal orders "AC Payee Only" and make them payable to "H M Customs and Excise". In your own interest do not send notes, coins, or uncrossed postal orders through the post.

If you wish to pay by 'credit transfer', ask your local VAT office. Pre-printed booklets of credit transfer slips will then be sent to you.

Please write your VAT registration number on the back of all cheques and credit transfer slips.

Where to send this return

You must make sure your completed form and any VAT payable are received by the 'due date' (shown over the page) by:

**The Controller
VAT Central Unit
H M Customs and Excise
21 Victoria Avenue
Southend-on-Sea X
SS99 1AA.**

CD 2859/R/N3(08/93)

Box 1
Show the VAT due on all goods and services you supplied in this period.

Box 2
Show the VAT due (but not paid) on all goods and related services you acquired in this period from other EC Member States.

Box 3
Show the total amount of the VAT due ie the sum of boxes 1 and 2. This is your total **Output** tax.

Box 4
Show the amount of VAT deductible on any business purchases including acquisitions of goods and related services from other EC Member States. This is your **Input** tax.

Box 5
If this amount is under £1, you need not send any payment, nor will any repayment be made to you, but you must still fill in this form and send it to the VAT Central Unit.

Boxes 6 and 7
In box 6 show the value excluding VAT of your total outputs (supplies of goods and services). Include zero rated, exempt outputs and EC supplies from box 8.

In box 7 show the value excluding VAT of all your inputs (purchases of goods and services). Include zero rated, exempt inputs and EC acquisitions from box 9.

Boxes 8 and 9
EC TRADE ONLY

Use these boxes if you have supplied goods to or acquired goods from another EC Member State. Include related services such as transport costs where these form part of the invoice or contract price. The figures should exclude VAT.

The other EC Member States are: Belgium, Denmark, France, Germany, Greece, Netherlands, Ireland, Italy, Luxembourg, Portugal and Spain.

You must tell your local VAT office about any changes in your business circumstances (including changes of address).

Printed in the U.K. for H.M.S.O. 10/93 Dd. 8368001 C108800 13110

Zero-rated supplies

The main categories of zero-rated supplies are:

- food and drinks (except principally those supplied as part of a catering business, pet food and non essentials)
- sewerage services and water excluding supplies to industry
- books, brochures, newspapers, periodicals, music, maps, but not stationery
- news services, for example, supplied by agencies or freelance journalists (excluding photographs)
- construction and sale of new buildings/protected buildings
- international services – sundry professional type services performed or deemed to be performed outside the UK
- transport – but not hire cars or taxis
- caravans/houseboats designed for permanent habitation
- drugs, medicines supplied on prescription, and specially adapted aids for the handicapped
- exports; but see below
- sundry supplies to charities, fundraising and for educational purposes
- clothing and footwear only suitable for young children and protective head and footwear.

Fuel and power for domestic and charity use will become standard rated following the Finance Act 1993. From 1 April 1994 VAT will be charged at 8%, rising to 17.5% from 1 April 1995.

Type of supply

A transaction made up of several supplies is called a 'mixed supply', while a transaction involving various goods/services making up one single supply is called a 'composite supply'.

Mixed supply

Where a mixed supply takes place the whole may be charged at a single inclusive price but for VAT purposes it is a supply of the component parts. If all the parts are standard rated, output tax may be calculated in the normal way; however, if some of the parts are zero-rated or exempt the tax value of the component parts must be calculated to arrive at the output tax. Any apportionment of the total price between the various components should be done fairly and be able to be substantiated. (Correspondence courses, for example, are mixed supplies being made up of textbooks (zero-rated) and tuition (standard rated).)

Composite supply

Where a composite supply takes place it too will be charged at a single inclusive price but for VAT purposes it is regarded as one single indivisible supply with one rate of VAT applicable. No apportionment is made for a composite supply.

Output and input taxes

VAT is chargeable on each taxable supply by a taxable person. The taxable person must add the appropriate rate of VAT (output tax) to his own selling price and collect this amount on behalf of Customs and Excise. The person is, however, allowed to deduct from the total of the output tax for which he or she is accountable, as much of any tax suffered on his or her purchases of goods and services (input tax) as is attributable to his or her taxable supplies and supplies outside the UK which would otherwise have been taxable supplies. The net amount, the excess of output tax over input tax, represents ideally the appropriate rate of tax on the value added by his or her business and he or she must account for this periodically to the Customs and Excise. In cases where the total input tax for the period exceeds the total output tax for the same period, the amount is reclaimable from the Customs and Excise. No distinction is made for the purposes of VAT between capital and revenue transactions. Output tax is charged on the disposal of fixed assets and input tax is reclaimable on the cost of fixed assets for use in the business (see below for an exception).

EXAMPLE 22.1

To illustrate the impact of VAT in various circumstances, assume that A sells goods to B who is a wholesaler, who sells the same goods to C who is a retailer, who sells them to D who is a member of the public. Consider four situations:

1. VAT does not exist
2. VAT @ 17.5% and A, B, and C registered for VAT
3. VAT @ 17.5% and A and B are registered for VAT but C is not
4. VAT @ 17.5% and A, B and C registered for VAT but C exports the goods and they are therefore zero-rated.

		A	sells to B	sells to C	sells to D
Situation 1 No VAT					
	SP	100	Cost 100 + SP 200 + Profit 100	Cost 200 + SP 300 + Profit 100	Cost 300
Situation 2 VAT 17.5% A,B & C registered	SP +VAT	100 17.5	Cost 100 + 17.5 SP 200 + 35.0 Profit 100 | 17.5	Cost 200 + 35.0 SP 300 + 52.5 Profit 100 | 17.5	Cost 300 + VAT 52.5 352.5
To C & E		17.5	17.5	17.5	
Situation 3 VAT 17.5% A & B registered, C not registered	SP + VAT	100 17.5	Cost 100 + 17.5 SP 200 + 35.0 Profit 100 + 17.5	Cost 235 SP 300 Profit 65	Cost 300
To C & E		17.5	17.5	Nil	
Situation 4 VAT 0% VAT 17.5% A, B & C registered	SP + VAT	100 17.5	Cost 100 + 17.5 SP 200 + 35.0 Profit 100 | 17.5	Cost 200 + 35 SP 300 + 0 Profit 100 (35)	Cost 300
To/(from) C & E		17.5	17.5	(35)	VAT 0 300

Note that when VAT is introduced universally as in Situation 2 (that is, when all traders are registered) they do not suffer loss of profit; they merely collect the standard rate tax on their value added so that throughout the various stages from manufacture to receipt by member of the public the Customs and Excise collects £52.50 VAT, which is reflected in the increased price paid by the public.

Situation 3 reflects the situation any new business might be in when its taxable supplies are below the threshold for VAT registration or the position of any trader who makes exempt supplies (see above) and is therefore not liable/entitled to register. Because C is not registered, she cannot recover the VAT suffered on the purchases and expenses of the business and profit is reduced *unless* she puts prices up to say £335 in order to maintain profit – in this case the public still pay higher prices. It looks here as if C is still in a reasonably competitive situation compared with VAT-registered competitors but if the realities of the situation are considered, she has set up a new business with all the extra costs entailed, she is a small business and probably cannot take advantage of bulk purchase discounts and so forth. Her costs are therefore probably considerably higher than those of her competitors.

C has a number of alternatives: either she registers voluntarily (reverting to situation 2) or

- she puts up her prices as far as she can to maintain profit
- she leaves her selling price as low as she can in an effort to sell more by undercutting the prices of competitors.

This illustrates one of the cases for voluntary registration. When this is combined with the possibility that some of her customers are themselves registered for VAT then voluntary registration becomes even more attractive. (A registered business will pay £352.50 to another VAT registered business knowing it can recover £52.50 input VAT, in preference to paying £352.50 to a non-registered business with nothing recoverable).

Situation 4 illustrates that there is no penalty suffered where a registered trader makes zero-rated supplies. Input tax is fully recoverable from the Customs and Excise. The final price remains attractive to the final consumer.

The VAT fraction

Normally tax is calculated by adding the standard rate of VAT to the tax exclusive price, and the separate amounts are shown on the tax invoice. Sometimes, (for example in a less detailed invoice) the VAT has to be calculated from the tax inclusive price and this is done by applying the VAT fraction, calculated as follows:

$$\text{VAT fraction} = \frac{\text{Rate of tax}}{100 + \text{rate of tax}}$$

Where standard rate VAT is 17.5%, the VAT fraction is:

$$\frac{17.5}{117.5} = \frac{7}{47}$$

Valuation of supplies

The tax value of a supply is the VAT exclusive price.

Where consideration is paid wholly in money in a bargain made at 'arm's length', the tax value will be the consideration less the tax. There are no provisions to ensure that the consideration received in these circumstances is adequate.

Where the supply is not for a consideration or the consideration is not, or not wholly, in money, the value of the supply is the amount in money which, with the addition of the tax chargeable, is equivalent to the consideration. Examples where this applies are part exchange agreements, and interest-free loans where these are granted to a club as a condition of membership, gifts of business assets other than those under £10 and in the course of the business but including goods for the personal use or consumption of the trader or his employees.

If consideration paid wholly in money is less than the open market value and the person to whom the supply is made is a connected person, the Customs and Excise may direct that the tax value of the supply is the open market value.

Where a discount is offered for prompt payment the tax value of the supply is the value of the supply less the discount, whether or not this is claimed.

VALUE ADDED TAX

Where a gift voucher is purchased, the tax value of the supply is the amount over and above the face value of the voucher less tax thereon. When the voucher is exchanged tax will be accounted for on the tax inclusive value of the voucher.

Sale of a motor car used in business

VAT need only be accounted for when a car which has been used in the business is disposed of for more than its purchase price unless the car is such that VAT was reclaimable on its acquisition (see below). VAT is accounted for on the excess which is deemed to be tax inclusive. Purchase price includes all accessories fitted at the time of purchase on which VAT was not reclaimable (see below). A tax invoice must not be issued.

Private motoring – use of vehicle

Charge made for use
If a charge of any kind (direct payment, deduction from wages, salary reduction) is made to an employee, director or partner, VAT must be accounted for on the charge as if it were tax inclusive. If the charge covers fuel as well, they must be separated.

No charge made for use
By concession no VAT is due on a car which was purchased/leased for use in the business and which is used for private motoring free of charge. Tax must be accounted for on the private use of a vehicle other than a car (based on the cost of making the vehicle available).

Fuel for private motoring

Charge made equal to or exceeding the cost
If a charge is made for fuel used for private motoring which equals or exceeds the cost (inclusive of VAT) of the fuel supplied, VAT must be accounted for on the charge as if it were tax inclusive.

Supplied free or charge less than cost
If no charge is made equal to the cost of the fuel supplied, the trader has two options. He may either:

▶ account for VAT using the scale charges, or
▶ not reclaim input tax on any fuel whether used for business or private motoring.

1994/95 Quarterly returns	Petrol scale £	VAT £	Diesel scale £	VAT £
Up to 1,400 cc	160	23.83	145	21.60
1,401 cc to 2,000 cc	202	30.09	145	21.60
Over 2,000 cc	300	44.68	187	27.85

Connected persons

The definition of connected persons is as defined for income tax and capital gains tax (see Chapter 5).

An individual is connected to his spouse, any relative of himself or his spouse, and with the spouse of any relative; to a partner and his partner's spouse and relatives; to a company controlled by himself; to a trustee of a settlement if he is the settlor or connected to the settlor.

Relative means brother, sister, ancestor or lineal descendant.

Self-supply

The term self-supply is commonly used to refer to the supply of goods by the business to the proprietor. The statutory reference for this term applies only where *specified* goods or services (for example, motor cars and stationery) are acquired or produced by a person in the course of business and are not supplied to another person directly or indirectly, but are used in the business, the goods are treated for purposes of VAT as being supplied for the purpose of the business and supplied by the trader in the course of the business. That is, he or she is treated as having made a taxable supply to him or herself of an amount equivalent to the original cost of the goods or services. The purpose of the legislation is to cancel any tax advantage.

If he or she is not a taxable person (for example, his principal supplies are exempt) then he or she would have to take this supply into account for the purpose of deciding liability to register. If he or she is a taxable person the input tax is non-deductible.

EXAMPLE 22.2

Explain the principle of 'self-supply' as it applies to a manufacturer/dealer in motor-cars.

Self-supply occurs when specified goods or services are acquired or produced by a person in the course of his or her business and are not supplied to another person directly or indirectly, but are used by the business. The goods are treated for purposes of VAT as being supplied to him or her for the purpose of the business and supplied by him or her in the course of the business. That is, he or she is treated as having made a taxable supply to him or herself.

A manufacturer is likely to be a taxable person who has reclaimed all input tax during the production of the motor car. Similarly a dealer in motor cars is able to reclaim VAT as input tax on unused cars acquired for the purpose of the business. Any other person who acquires a motor car for the purpose of their business cannot reclaim the VAT suffered on purchase. Self-supply cancels the advantage that the car manufacture/dealer would otherwise have for any cars retained by them for use in their business.

The supply to themselves would be a taxable supply and they would account for VAT while the 'purchase' would be of a car for use in the business and VAT would not be reclaimable. The tax point would be when the vehicle is transferred from new car sales stock into some other business use. The value of the supply would be the original VAT exclusive cost of the car (including the cost of any accessories fitted).

Capital items such as computers, computer equipment and land and buildings exceeding specified values, will be excluded from the above rules and will be dealt with by the Capital Goods Scheme (see below).

Bad debt relief

A supplier accounts for the VAT on his or her taxable supplies whether or not he or she has received payment for the debt. Bad debts relief provides that VAT can be recovered on any debt more than six months old, which has been written off in the trader's accounts. If, subsequently, the debt is recovered the relief obtained will be repayable to Customs and Excise.

Input tax – special circumstances

A taxable person is entitled to credit at the end of each VAT quarter for allowable input tax. Allowable input tax is defined as that input tax on supplies and imports in the period which is attributable to his or her taxable supplies and supplies outside the

UK which would be taxable supplies if made in the UK (anything relating to exempt supplies is not recoverable). Input tax on goods and services used partly for the business and partly for other purposes must be apportioned and only the portion relating to the business use is reclaimable (an example is telephone expenses).

The following rules relate to particular circumstances:

- *Pre-registration.* A claim may be made to reclaim VAT suffered on goods and services prior to registration, in the first VAT return. The goods must not have been sold or consumed before the date of registration and services should not have been received more than six months before this date. The claim must be able to be substantiated.
- *Motor fuel bought by employees.* Where employees are reimbursed for the actual amounts paid, the VAT paid by the employees may be treated as input tax even if the fuel is for private motoring (but see output tax on this element). Where employees are paid a mileage allowance for business mileage, input tax is calculated by applying the VAT fraction to the fuel element of the allowance provided certain conditions are met.
- *Motor expenses where there is some private motoring.* The costs of leasing, hiring, repair and maintenance, and accessories need not be apportioned between private and business use of the employee, proprietor or partner; the whole of the VAT is recoverable.
- *Post de-registration.* A taxable person may claim input tax on an invoice for supply of services to him or her after deregistration if he or she can show that they relate to a taxable supply before that date.

Non-deductible input tax

Input tax on the following goods and services cannot generally be reclaimed:

- Goods and services not obtained for business purposes. This includes items for solely private use, for another person's business, for another person or for a non-business activity even when paid for by the taxable person
- Motor cars (except by a car dealer, private taxi, self-drive hire firms, driving schools and businesses leasing cars to such firms) and fitted accessories
- Goods and services used or to be used for the purpose of business entertaining. The provision of entertainment for employees solely is not included under the heading of business entertainment nor are subsistence expenses of the employer or employee
- Self-supplies (see above)
- Repairs, refurbishments and other expenses relating to domestic accommodation provided by businesses for use by directors and their families.

Imports and exports

VAT is charged on goods and services (with some exceptions) imported into the UK as if it were a customs duty, whether or not the importer is a taxable person. The importer, being the customer, pays the supplier for the goods but must account for VAT to Customs and Excise, usually at the time of entry (for which he receives either a VAT copy of the customs entry or a certificate of VAT paid). The amount of VAT is based on the price of the goods plus (if not included) all taxes, duties and so on levied on importation, plus all costs of commission, packing, transport and insurance as far as the place of importation.

If the importer is a taxable person, the VAT on postal imports is treated as a supply to himself and shown as a taxable supply in the appropriate VAT quarter. All VAT paid by an importer is also input tax and is allowable subject to the restrictions already described.

Goods and services which are exported are zero-rated.

The European Community – the Single Market

Goods and services are not regarded as being imported/exported when the transaction takes place between EC countries, but as 'acquisition of goods in the UK from' and 'supplies of goods from the UK to' other member states.

- Where VAT registered traders in one EC country despatch goods to registered traders in another EC country: i) the supply will be zero-rated; and ii) the customer will be expected to account for VAT, on his VAT return, both as a taxable supply and as input tax at the rate in force in the country of receipt (similar to the postal system described above). This is known as **the destination system**.
- Where VAT registered traders in one EC country despatch goods to unregistered traders in another EC country, suppliers will charge VAT at the rate in force in the country of despatch. This is known as **the origin system**.

Supplies of goods from the UK to other member states

Supplies to registered traders, will be zero-rated, if certain conditions are satisfied. The principal conditions are:

- that the supply involves both the goods leaving the UK and their acquisition by a registered trader in another member state
- that the supplier obtains the customer's VAT registration number (with a country prefix code) and shows it on the sales invoice
- that the supplier has documentary evidence that the goods have left the UK.

The supplier's VAT registration number must show the prefix GB on the tax invoice to confirm UK registration (this prefix may also be shown on UK tax invoices, if required).

If these conditions are not met, the supply cannot be zero-rated and VAT must be accounted for at standard rate (the origin system described above).

EC sales statements must be submitted by VAT-registered traders making supplies in another EC member state alongside the normal VAT return (that is, quarterly).

There are additional registration requirements in respect of 'distance selling'. This occurs where a supplier in one EC country supplies goods (and is responsible for their delivery) to any person in another EC country who is not registered for VAT (for example, private individuals, public bodies, charities, small businesses). An example of this type of supply is mail order. The origin system above applies in principle, but once the value of distance sales to an individual member state exceeds an annual threshold, subsequent sales are taxed in that member state: the supplier (UK) is liable to register in that member state or appoint a tax representative who will account VAT in the member state on his behalf (destination system).

The annual threshold adopted by member states may be either 35,000 ECU (£24,500) or 100,000 ECU (£70,000).

Acquisitions of goods in the UK from other member states

For most transactions between VAT-registered traders in different member states, the liability to pay VAT is triggered by the acquisition or receipt of the goods by the customer. A UK customer has to account for this VAT on his or her VAT return as a supply – often he or she may recover the VAT as input tax in the same quarter.

Time of acquisition

The time of acquisition from other member states is the earlier of:

- the 15th day of the month (following that in which the goods were first removed)
- the date of issue of an invoice containing the requisite details.

Distance selling by suppliers in other member states to the UK

This is the converse of the system described above which applies to UK suppliers. The annual threshold adopted by the UK is 100,000 ECU (£70,000).

A person who is not registered in the UK and not otherwise liable to be so registered, becomes liable to be registered under these provisions if in the period beginning 1 January in the year, he or she makes 'relevant supplies' to a value exceeding £70,000.

Cash accounting

As part of an initiative to help small businesses with the burden of VAT, regulations have been introduced allowing certain small businesses to account for VAT on the basis of cash paid and received rather than on an invoice basis.

The scheme is optional. It is open to all businesses with an annual taxable turnover (exclusive of VAT) not greater than £350,000 provided they have a 'clean' VAT record over the previous three years. Returns must be up to date and all outstanding VAT debts should not exceed £5,000. Once approved, businesses are expected to implement the scheme for the whole of their business.

The scheme must be started at the beginning of an accounting period for VAT, and any receipts or payments from that date on transactions already accounted for must be identified and kept separate (otherwise VAT may be accounted for twice).

The tax point for output tax will be the day on which payment is received or the date on a cheque if later. The effective date for input tax will be the date on which payment is made or the date on the cheque if later.

There is no relaxation in the requirements for record-keeping, retention of records or in the obligation to produce tax invoices.

The main advantages of the scheme are automatic bad debt relief and the easing of cashflow as the date for accounting for VAT is postponed where customers are slow to pay.

Leaving the scheme

Customs and Excise must be notified within 30 days if the taxable turnover for the previous year, at the end of any accounting period, has exceeded £437,500 and is expected to exceed £350,000 for the following year or there is reason to believe that taxable supplies in the year beginning will exceed £437,500.

Second-hand schemes

The basis of second-hand schemes is that VAT is accounted for on the profit margin of a transaction by a registered person, and not the selling price.

EXAMPLE 22.3

A second-hand car dealer purchases a car for £4,000 and sells it for £5,880. The gross margin is £1,880 and the output tax due is £280 (7/47 × £1,880).

The purchaser cannot reclaim input tax on goods purchased for resale under these schemes. If repairs or alterations to the goods are made prior to resale, any VAT incurred can be reclaimed in the normal way. A condition of using a second-hand scheme is that a comprehensive stock record system is maintained. Second-hand goods schemes exist for cars, works of art, antiques, caravans, boats, aircraft, horses and ponies.

Retail schemes

This topic is not examinable. A brief overview of the schemes and their background is provided for information purposes. The Customs and Excise have recognised the fact that it is not practical for retailers (particularly shopkeepers) to keep the detailed records maintained by other businesses.

This does not present a problem where all the goods dealt in are subject to one rate of VAT. Output tax may be calculated by applying the VAT fraction to the total takings in the VAT accounting period.

The complication arises where more than one rate of VAT is applicable; here it is not possible to apply a constant VAT fraction to the total takings to calculate the output tax.

A number of schemes (currently A to J) have been introduced, each applying to trades of different types and sizes. The essence of all the schemes is to provide an approved means (through estimation and approximation) of arriving at an amount of output tax.

Retailers may not be able to use a particular scheme because of the conditions attached to it, but in most cases they will have a choice of schemes. The Customs and Excise have published guidelines and the local VAT office will give information and advice but, because the different schemes may result in different tax liabilities, the final choice must be made by the retailer.

Whichever scheme is used, a daily record of gross takings is a fundamental requirement which may then be adjusted for specific types of transactions.

Partial exemption

A person making wholly exempt supplies is not liable/entitled to be registered for VAT. He or she cannot charge VAT on supplies or recover input tax. Where a taxable person makes both taxable and exempt supplies, he or she is 'partially exempt' and may not be able to deduct/reclaim all of his input tax. Input tax paid is only recoverable if incurred in respect of taxable supplies.

There are provisions to determine the amount of the allowable input tax in these circumstances.

No restriction on the amount of input tax allowable is made where in any VAT quarter (and for purposes of the annual adjustment – see below), the exempt input tax is less than £600 per month on average. This is known as the de minimus rule.

The standard method of attributing input tax to taxable supplies will normally apply but in certain circumstances the Customs and Excise may approve a special method.

Standard method

The input tax is initially attributed to the taxable supplies for a VAT quarter. This is done as follows:

- All input tax relating to importation and supplies in the period which are wholly for the purpose of making taxable supplies, is allowable.
- All input tax relating to importation and supplies in the period which are wholly for the purpose of making exempt supplies, is not allowable.
- The remaining input tax, not directly attributable, is allowable to the extent that a proportion of the importation and supplies to which it relates is used for the purpose of making taxable supplies. This is done by applying a percentage based on the formula:

$$\frac{\text{Taxable outputs (net of VAT)}}{\text{Total outputs (net of VAT)}}$$

An alternative formula might be:

$$\text{Remaining input tax} \times \frac{\text{Input tax wholly re: taxable supplies}}{\text{Total input tax}}$$

Certain specified items must be excluded from the fraction. An annual adjustment is then made. The steps above are repeated over the annual totals to ensure that seasonal fluctuations have not distorted the fraction in any quarter. Any difference between the amount of allowable input tax calculated on the annual basis and the total amount of input tax provisionally deducted in each of the quarters is an over- or under-declaration of VAT and it must be entered on the first VAT return for the following year.

Enforcement

VAT is administered by the Commissioners of Customs and Excise via a VAT administration directorate in London and a VAT control directorate in Southend. There is a network of local VAT offices throughout the UK, which deal with the administration of VAT in their area. They do not issue VAT returns or collect the tax (this is done from Southend). VAT is a self-assessed tax and businesses are responsible for computing the tax due and submitting a cheque in payment. Besides giving advice and dealing with enquiries, the local VAT offices are responsible for making 'control visits' to local businesses to check that their records are in order and that their VAT returns are complete and accurate.

As mentioned above, the Commissioners have the power to issue assessments where a taxable person has failed to complete a return or where they believe that there has been an under-declaration of VAT. Interest may also be charged on unpaid or under-declared tax. Time limits for making such assessments are two years after the end of the VAT quarter or, if later, one year after the evidence comes to their notice, with an overall maximum of six years after the end of the VAT quarter (20 years where there has been fraudulent evasion of tax). The taxpayer may appeal but must deposit the disputed tax with the Commissioners unless hardship can be proven.

Appeals may be discussed and settled in the first instance with the local VAT office; otherwise they are heard by a VAT tribunal (all VAT returns due to date must have been made) which is a completely independent body. Appeals beyond the tribunal may be made, on a point of law only, to the High Court, Court of Appeal and House of Lords under normal procedure.

Varying degrees of penalties are imposed for non-compliance with the VAT regulations. For certain offences criminal proceedings may be instituted by the Customs and Excise. In other cases, civil penalties are imposed. These penalties are in addition to the raising of assessments for tax actually due.

Criminal offences and penalties

- *Fraudulent evasion of tax.* Conviction on indictment leads to an unlimited penalty and/or imprisonment of up to seven years; summary conviction leads to maximum statutory penalties (currently £2,000) or, if greater, three times the tax and/or imprisonment up to six months.
- *Knowledge that evasion is intended.* This leads to maximum statutory penalties or, if greater, three times the tax payable.
- *Bribery and obstruction of officers.* Bribery leads to a fine of £500 while obstruction may lead to an unlimited penalty or to imprisonment up to two years or both.

Civil penalties

It should be noted that only default surcharge, serious misdeclaration, and default interest are examinable in detail.

- *Tax evasion involving dishonesty.* This may lead to a penalty equal to the tax but may be reduced if the trader co-operates with Customs & Excise.
- *Serious misdeclaration penalty.* This will take place when a return understates the liability to tax by underdeclaring VAT or overclaiming VAT or an assessment is made which understates the liability to tax and steps are not taken to correct it within 30 days and the tax which would have been lost amounts to the lesser of:
  a) 30% of the gross tax throughput for the period (output tax plus input tax); or
  b) £1 million
  The maximum penalty is 15% of the tax which would have been lost.
  It will not normally be imposed for tax errors of less than £2,000 in any period nor in the period from the end of the VAT period to the due date of the next return nor when a misdeclaration has been corrected by a compensating misdeclaration in the following period (with no loss of tax).
- In the case of *persistent misdeclarations* resulting in understatements or overclaims, a penalty will be incurred if:
  - a material inaccuracy occurs in any VAT quarter (the tax which would have been lost amounts to the smaller of 10% of the gross tax throughput or £500,000, and
  - further such inaccuracies occur so that in three out of twelve consecutive accounting periods there are misdeclarations and in at least two of those periods a penalty liability notice had been issued (this specifies a penalty period of two years from the date of the notice).

  The maximum penalty is 15% of the tax which would have been lost.
- *Late registration or failure to notify changes.* This leads to a penalty of 10% of the tax for delays of nine months or less, 20% for delays between nine and 18 months and 30% for delays over 18 months, the minimum amount of the penalty being £50.
- *Breaches of regulations* involving inadequate records, failure to give information and so on, lead to a written warning and, subsequently, to daily penalties of £5 per day for a further offence in the two year period, £10 for two offences, £15 in other cases, with a maximum charge for 100 days but a minimum penalty of £50.
- *Default surcharge results from failure to submit returns or pay tax by the due date.* This gives rise to the issue of a surcharge liability notice. A further default within a 12 month period leads to the issue of a further default surcharge liability notice. Each notice is valid for 12 months. The late payment of tax within the notice period results in the imposition of a default surcharge which increases according to the number of defaults within the notice period. The surcharge is 2% of VAT unpaid for the first default, increasing to 5% for the second and rising by 5% for subsequent offences to a maximum of 15% of the outstanding tax. No surcharge

assessment will be issued for amounts less than £200, unless the rate applicable is 10% or more.

The surcharge liability notice will be cancelled whenever four consecutive returns are submitted on time with payment of the tax shown, in full. Late submission of nil and repayment returns will constitute a default resulting in the extension of the notice period but not an increase in the rate of surcharge.

Most of these offences can be avoided if it can be shown that there was reasonable excuse, that is that all reasonable steps were taken to avoid committing the offence or that there was voluntary disclosure.

Interest payable on tax

Default interest provisions exist whereby VAT due in certain circumstances will carry interest from the reckonable date until the date of payment. The reckonable date is the latest date on which a return is required for the accounting period to which the amount assessed or paid relates. Liability is now limited to three years. The rate varies in line with commercial rates and the interest is not deductible for income or corporation tax purposes.

Repayment supplement

For any VAT quarter where deductible input tax exceeds output tax, a supplement of 5% of the repayment due or £50, if greater, is due to the taxable person provided that:

- the return is received by the Commissioners not later than the due date
- the Commissioners fail to issue written instructions directing the payment to be made within 30 days of the end of the quarter or, if later, 30 days from the date the return was received
- the return must not contain errors amounting to more than £250 or 5% of the amount of the repayment claim.

For purposes of the second point above, the 30 days will exclude days spent following any reasonable enquiry relating to the return or any time spent awaiting the submission of documents and so on. Certain credits may also be excluded from the calculation of the supplement.

There is a right of set-off of amounts due from the Commissioners against amounts due to Customs & Excise (whether tax, penalties, interest or surcharges).

Partnerships

Because a partnership is not a legal entity in English law an application for registration for VAT must be accompanied by a form showing the names and addresses of all partners and it must be signed by each of them.

Apart from this, the registration for VAT may be in the name of the partnership and all changes in the members of the partnership will be ignored for purposes of VAT.

Where any notice is required to be given by the partnership, it is the joint and several responsibility of all the partners to give it.

Where the individual partners each carry on separate businesses from the partnership, separate registrations apply.

The Customs and Excise have powers to treat two or more traders as one taxable person if it appears that a business is being artificially split into smaller firms in order to avoid VAT registration. An order may be made that all such persons carrying on the separate parts of the business be treated as carrying on the business in partnership together – and the business must then register for VAT.

Limited companies

A company or any unincorporated association may be a taxable person and as such is required to be registered for value added tax in the same way as any other taxable person.

Divisional registration

A company which is divided into several individual units which are autonomous for accounting purposes can apply for divisional registration.

The separate divisions do not become separate taxable persons and the company is still liable for the VAT. Each division must be registered although their turnover may individually be below the registration limits. Interdivisional transactions may be ignored.

The advantages accruing from divisional registration are administrative cost-saving rather than VAT-saving when considered in terms of centralising the VAT information for entry on one VAT return and the difficulties which may be encountered in meeting the 30-day time limit for its submission.

EXAMPLE 22.4

A married couple are considering extending their business interests. The husband runs a health food shop in a nearby town. He wishes to commence a counselling and healing practice – he considers that this activity would complement the health food shop and, in addition, his wife, who has a psychology qualification, would be able to become involved. The health food shop is registered for VAT purposes, but the husband would prefer not to register the practice, because the additional cost for a consultation might make the service unattractive. Can the two businesses be run separately, and, if so, how?

The husband cannot run two businesses without them being treated as one for VAT purposes, as it is the person who is registered, and not the business. However, it may be possible for the second business to be run as a partnership between husband and wife (a partnership is a separate taxable person from the individual partners) or for the wife to run the second business. Whether either of these alternatives would satisfy the Customs and Excise will depend upon the facts: it would be necessary to show that the business operated entirely separately (premises, bank accounts and so on should be separate). For instance, it may be necessary to acquire another business address for the new business, or operate it from home. If it is operated from the shop it would almost certainly be deemed to be part of the same business.

Interaction with other taxes

Schedule D Cases I or II

For the purposes of arriving at Schedule D Case I or II profits of a taxable person, the revenues and expenses are treated as being the VAT-exclusive amounts, provided that the input tax was allowable (and output tax in the case of bad debts recovered). If not, the expenditure inclusive of VAT is taken into account (and the bad debt inclusive of VAT is written off). Any input tax not allowable under the partial exemption rules must be allocated back to the various expense payments. The expenses of a person who is not taxable will be VAT inclusive.

For purposes of stock valuation, the costs of taxable persons are VAT exclusive but in cases of partial exemption the VAT not allowable should be reflected in the valuation of trading stock.

Capital allowances

Similar rules apply for the computation of capital allowances. Where VAT is accounted for, the eligible expenditure/sale proceeds are VAT exclusive.

Schedule E

Benefits in kind to employees to be declared on the annual P11D return, need to be declared gross of VAT whether or not the employer has recovered the relevant input tax. Where an employer gives staff the option of having a car for a lower salary, this salary sacrifice will not be treated as consideration for the use of the car and no VAT will arise on provision of the car.

Capital gains tax

Where VAT is paid on a capital asset but is recovered by a taxable person, cost for capital gains tax purposes is VAT exclusive; if the VAT is not recovered then cost for capital gains tax is VAT inclusive. On the disposal, VAT charged on the supply is disregarded for purposes of the consideration on sale. A partially exempt trader should be able to allocate a proportion of his or her non-allowable input tax to capital purchases.

Summary

- VAT is chargeable when a taxable supply of goods or services is made by a taxable person in the course of a business carried on by him or her.
- Taxable supplies are all supplies other than exempt supplies (it includes standard rate and zero-rated supplies).
- A taxable person is a person who makes/intends to make taxable supplies while he or she is required to be registered for VAT. Registration may be compulsory or voluntary.
- Allowable input tax is recoverable by a taxable person.
- A taxable person who makes both taxable and exempt supplies is partially exempt and special rules apply to determine the amount of allowable input tax.
- VAT is normally accounted for on an invoice basis but recent legislation has introduced an optional scheme which will allow small businesses to account for VAT on a cash basis.
- Special schemes are available to assist retailers to account for VAT.
- Severe penalties are levied for failure to comply with the VAT regulations.

Self test questions

1. When may a person register voluntarily for VAT?
2. What is the basic tax point and why is the tax point important?
3. List the exceptions to three-monthly accounting periods for VAT.
4. For how long must VAT records be preserved?

5 How is VAT for fuel on private motoring dealt with?

6 When is input tax non-deductible?

7 Which businesses are eligible for 'cash accounting'?

8 Which penalties require notice before they can be enforced?

9 Roger has been registered for VAT for many years. His VAT year ends on 31 December and he accounts for VAT on a quarterly basis. Unfortunately, Roger made his bookkeeper redundant on 31 January 1994 and decided not to replace him. As a result, since then he has submitted a number of his VAT returns late. The history of his returns since then has been as follows:

		VAT payable £	Timing of submission and payment
1994	1st Quarter	800	Late
	2nd Quarter	1,100	Late
	3rd Quarter	400	Late
	4th Quarter	900	On time
1995	1st Quarter	1,000	On time
	2nd Quarter	800	Late
	3rd Quarter	750	On time

You are required to explain the following to Roger:
i) How the default surcharge regime operates.
ii) Which liabilities he has incurred under it.
iii) What he must do to escape from it.

Answers on pages 601–602

CHAPTER 23

Tax Management

The purpose of this chapter is to look more closely at the administrative procedures followed by the tax authorities in assessing and collecting the foregoing taxes and to consider the Inland Revenue inquiry and investigation procedures. The Finance Act 1989 completed the introduction of the Keith Committee's recommendations on the reform of the enforcement powers of the Revenue departments. It is only by understanding this environment that it is possible to deal effectively and efficiently with the Inland Revenue.

The organisation of the Inland Revenue

An understanding of the procedures followed by the tax authorities is helped by a knowledge of how the Inland Revenue is organised. This is outlined in Table 23.1:

Table 23.1 Board of Inland Revenue

Seven members known as the Commissioners of Inland Revenue. They are permanent civil servants under the direction of the Treasury and administer all direct taxation.

Policy and technical divisions Specialist offices	Operations division
1 **Capital Taxes Offices** (London, Edinburgh, Belfast) Inheritance tax and share valuations	A **Assessment** **Inspectors of Taxes** (organised in tax districts)
2 **Metropolitan Valuation and Stamp Offices** (London, Edinburgh, Belfast) Stamp duty and property valuation	Functions: 1 issue returns 2 examine returns 3 assessments
3 **Oil Taxation Office**	4 deal with appeals
4 **Claims Branch** Trusts, settlements, charities and matters of residence	5 PAYE code numbers 6 correspond with taxpayers
5 **Inspector of Foreign Dividends** Interpretation and implementation of double tax agreements	B **Collection** **Collectors of Taxes** (also organised in tax districts)
6 **Pension Schemes Office (PSO)** Approval of pension schemes	
7 **Public Departments** Tax liabilities of central and local government servants, police and armed forces	Functions: 1 Collection of tax assessed 2 Enforcement procedures
8 **Solicitor's Office**	
9 **Enquiry Branch and Special Office** Fraud and tax evasion	

Tax districts

Originally tax districts were geographically based, the local tax district being responsible for all the taxpayers in the area (employees were dealt with by their employer's tax district). Nowadays, administrative convenience is the criterion.

District offices (managed by a district inspector) can be found in most large towns. Many offices have lost their Schedule E cases to special Schedule E districts meaning that the tax affairs of most employees are dealt with long distance. The Schedule E districts were the first to computerise but most other districts have now computerised.

There used to be a Collector of Taxes for each tax district, to facilitate liaison, but most routine collection is now computerised and has been centralised in Accounts Offices (principally Shipley and Cumbernauld).

Administration of income tax and capital gains tax

Tax returns

At the beginning of every fiscal year, Inspectors of Taxes issue tax return forms to taxpayers 'on their books', that is individuals, partnerships (to be completed by the first named or precedent acting partner – see Chapter 17) and trusts (to be completed by a trustee). These should be completed within the time stipulated (30 days) although in practice at the moment, this time limit is not enforced.

The tax return asks for information under three main headings: income, outgoings and allowances. The return issued in April 1994 required the following information:

- income for the year ended 5 April 1994 (including chargeable gains if appropriate – see Chapter 5)
- details of expenses and outgoings in the year ended 5 April 1994 for which tax relief may be available (for example, interest paid)
- the personal allowances claimed for the year ended 5 April 1995 according to the taxpayer's circumstances at the beginning of the year.

The style of tax return issued in April 1994 has been fully revised. There are two types of tax return currently in use, depending on whether the individual's main source of earned income is from employment or self-employment. All returns are accompanied by 'notes for completion'.

A return is not regarded as completed until all relevant computations are also submitted (for example the adjusted Schedule D Case I profits or the computation of chargeable gains). Detailed tax accounts are not required from individuals and partnerships with a turnover of less than £15,000 a year. These businesses still need to keep detailed business records but only a 'three line account' (total turnover, total business purchases and expenses, and the resulting net profit) is required with their tax returns.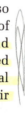

Any person chargeable to tax for any year who has not received a tax return for any reason or otherwise declared all his or her income and chargeable gains, must notify the Inland Revenue that he or she is so chargeable within one year after the end of the fiscal year concerned, except in certain specified circumstances. Failure to do so can give rise to a penalty equal to the tax liability arising from such undeclared income.

Often tax returns are not issued every year to taxpayers whose only income is from employment (taxed under PAYE) and from savings taxed at source. Provided all the income of these taxpayers has been taken into account in arriving at their liability to tax or under PAYE, they are within the exceptions referred to above.

Assessments

Where income arises in circumstances where it is not taxed at source or under PAYE, it must be assessed to tax. The Inspector of Taxes issues a separate 'notice of assessment' for income taxable under each Schedule or Case. A taxpayer who has more than one source of income may therefore have more than one assessment for a fiscal year.

The assessment is based on the information received by the Inspector in the tax return unless no return has been received. In this case, the assessment will be estimated by the Inspector if he believes there is a liability to tax. The tax is due under some Schedules (for example, Schedule A) before the fiscal year has ended and in this case, he will also estimate the current year's income based on information from the previous year. Reliefs and allowances are usually given against the taxpayer's main source of earned income in the first instance, that is, principal employment or trading income (see Chapter 1).

Notices of assessment are sent to the person assessed. (There is provision also for a copy to be sent to the taxpayer's personal advisor if the taxpayer so requests.)

An assessment must normally be raised within six years of the end of the fiscal year unless the special rules for neglect and default apply (see back duty and investigations below).

In circumstances where the taxpayer's only income is a social security pension (such is the case with pensioners) which exceeds the single personal allowance, no assessment will be raised if the amount of tax due is £30 or less unless an assessment is being issued in any case (for example, by request of the taxpayer). The only reason for this is cost effectiveness.

Once issued, a notice of assessment can only be reduced in accordance with specific provisions in the Taxes Acts: namely by appeal, commencement/cessation provisions, error or mistake claims. An assessment is final and conclusive if determined on appeal (see below) or not appealed against.

Additional assessment

If the Inspector 'discovers' that profits, income or gains have not been assessed to tax, or that allowances or reliefs have been obtained to which a person is not entitled, the Inspector may make an assessment for such further amounts as he considers ought to be charged.

'Discovery' has a very wide meaning. It exists where the Inspector merely comes to the conclusion that there has been an under-assessment, or when there has been an error (including arithmetical) or change of opinion. It is not necessary therefore for new facts to come to light. However, if a matter has been specifically adjudicated in the determination of an appeal (see below), the Inland Revenue cannot re-open the matter.

The six-year time limit referred to above applies to discovery. However the time limit is extended by one year for taxpayers affected in order to allow them to make claims or vary reliefs, provided the 'discovery' did not result from an offence by the taxpayer.

Appeals and postponement of tax charged

The taxpayer has a right of appeal if the assessment is not, in his or her opinion, correct.

If he or she decides to appeal, notice must be given in writing to the Inspector within 30 days of the date of issue of the notice of assessment. The grounds for appeal must be specified. Late appeals will be accepted provided there was reasonable excuse and that the appeal has otherwise been made without delay. Notice of acceptance of a late appeal must be given by the inspector in writing.

If the tax charged by the assessment is excessive, it is necessary to apply for postponement of some or all of the tax charged (in addition to the appeal). This must also be in writing, within 30 days of the date of the issue of the notice of assessment; the grounds for applying for postponement and the amount of tax remaining due must be stated.

Determination of appeal by agreement

The Inspector will normally try to reach agreement with the taxpayer informally and if he does so, the matter is treated as if it had been determined on appeal provided verbal agreements are confirmed in writing by both parties.

Although an appeal, once made, cannot be withdrawn, it is usually possible at this stage to agree with the Inspector not to proceed and to treat it as if settled by agreement.

If the Inspector cannot reach agreement with the taxpayer, he will pass the details of the appeal to the Clerk to the Commissioners who will list the appeal for hearing and notify both parties of the time, date and place.

General and Special Commissioners

An appeal is made to the General or the Special Commissioners (they must be distinguished from the Commissioners of Inland Revenue who make up the Board).

Both the General and the Special Commissioners are appointed by the Lord Chancellor to hear appeals against assessments to tax or against the refusal by the Inland Revenue to grant allowances or accept claims. The General Commissioners are local professional or business people who are part-time and unpaid (apart from expenses). They have a legally qualified clerk to assist them and the proceedings are informal (they usually sit in pairs). The Special Commissioners are barristers or solicitors of at least ten years' standing. They are full-time civil servants based in London who go 'on circuit' round the rest of the country. The proceedings are formal and only one Special Commissioner need be present – their clerk is only a minute clerk and takes no part in any decisions.

The General Commissioners usually take those cases concerned with fact and requiring common sense without any detailed knowledge of tax law. The Special Commissioners tend to take the more complicated or technical cases. Generally appeal is to the General Commissioners unless the taxpayer elects for the Special Commissioners. The Inland Revenue can direct which division of the Commissioners will hear the appeal provided the taxpayer does not object within 30 days.

Determination of appeal by Commissioners

There is no set procedure laid down but the following has emerged over the years for hearings before the General Commissioners.

- Appellant or his representative opens the case.
- Appellant's evidence is adduced – written or oral.
- Appellant's witnesses are cross-examined.
- Appellant's witnesses are re-examined by the appellant or his or her representative.
- Inland Revenue opens its reply to the appellant's case.
- Inland Revenue adduces evidence for its reply.
- Summing up and submission by appellant or his or her representative.
- Commissioners attempt to reach a decision.

The Commissioners should know nothing of the case until it comes before them and the onus of proof is on the taxpayer unless the Inland Revenue is contesting a new precedent.

After hearing the evidence the Commissioners can reduce, confirm or increase the assessment.

The taxpayer or the Inspector can express dissatisfaction with the decision immediately after it has been given if it is considered to be 'erroneous in point of law'. The decision of the Commissioners on a question of fact is final.

Appeals to higher courts

When either party to the appeal is dissatisfied on a point of law, having immediately expressed dissatisfaction, he or she should give notice in writing to the Clerk to the Commissioners within 30 days for a case to be stated by the Commissioners for the opinion of the High Court (enclosing a £25 fee).

Before the taxpayer can proceed any further, all tax due under the determined appeal must be settled.

In due course, the appeal will be heard and a decision reached. The dissatisfied party may again express dissatisfaction – further appeals will go to the Court of Appeal and thereafter to the House of Lords.

Costs

Costs may be awarded by the courts in the normal way – the loser pays all the costs of both parties. (In certain cases, where a new precedent is being tested, for example, the Inland Revenue may undertake to pay the costs.)

If appellants conduct their own case before the Commissioners and win, they may still incur legal costs if the Inland Revenue appeals to the High Court, or higher, and eventually wins the case. In such circumstances, the taxpayer will have to pay the considerable costs incurred by the Inland Revenue. (Usually costs of appearing before the Commissioners are not awarded but there may be costs incurred in stating a case for the High Court.)

The rules of procedure for tax appeals, referred to above, will give the Special Commissioners powers to award costs where either party has acted wholly unreasonably in making, pursuing or resisting an appeal. As before, costs will not be awarded in hearings before the General Commissioners, allowing taxpayers to have an appeal heard with no risk of costs being awarded against them.

Error or mistake claim

The taxpayer may make a claim in writing within six years of the end of the year of assessment, for relief to be given against any over-assessment of tax due to his or her error or mistake either in his or her tax return or any statement submitted by him or her.

Due date for payment of tax

Tax is due for payment on:

the later of a) normal due date (NDD), or
b) actual due date (ADD).

This is except where it relates to Schedule E, when it is usually deducted at source under the PAYE system by the employer. If additional tax is assessable under the PAYE system, it is due for payment 14 days after being requested by the Collector.

Normal due date

This is the statutory due date as laid down in the statutes and is as follows:

Table 23.2

▶ UK trading profits assessed under Schedule D Case I and II and on foreign trading profits assessed under Schedule D Case V	Half 1 January in year of assessment. Half 1 July following end of year of assessment
▶ Other income received gross (Schedule A, D Cases III, IV, V and VI)	1 January in year of assessment
▶ Income from which basic rate income tax is deducted at source – liability at higher rate only	1 December following end of fiscal year
▶ Chargeable gains assessed to capital gains tax	1 December following end of fiscal year

In each case, if a date 30 days after the date of issue of the assessment is later than the statutory date then this will be the normal due date.

Actual due date

The actual due date for tax assessed above will be *30 days after the date of issue of the assessment* unless an appeal is made and an application to postpone some or all of the tax assessed is submitted.

When the appellant applies for some or all of the tax to be postponed, none of the tax is payable until the amount of tax not postponed is determined and notice of the determination is issued to the taxpayer. The actual due date for the tax not postponed is *30 days after the date of issue of the notice of tax postponed* (that is, the date of agreement to postpone).

When the appeal is finally determined, the actual due date for any further tax due (irrespective of whether it was originally postponed or is additional to the original assessment) is *30 days after the date of issue of the notice of the total amount payable*.

Interest on overdue tax

Interest on overdue tax is charged on each assessment at the rate or rates applicable at the time and is the aggregate of the interest on each instalment of tax payable. Interest runs from the reckonable date appropriate to that instalment (even if it is a non-business day) to the date the tax is paid.

Interest rates are now fixed according to a formula and change automatically to follow changes in market rates of interest – the formula is the average base lending rate of specified High Street banks plus 2.5%, less basic rate income tax. The examination will always use 10%.

The interest is payable gross and is not deductible from profits or income for tax purposes.

Reckonable date

The calculation of the reckonable date depends on whether or not an application is made to postpone the tax arising on the assessment. The reckonable date is worked out for each separate instalment of the tax payable as follows.

a) No appeal, or appeal but no application to postpone tax.	Later of	a) Normal due date (NDD), or b) Actual due date (ADD).

b) Appeal and application to postpone	Later of	a) Normal due date (NDD), or
		b) earlier of:
		   i) Actual due date (ADD), or
		   ii) Table date.

It should be noted that the reckonable date may be sooner than the actual due date, that is, in circumstances where there has been an appeal and application for postponement and the actual due date is later than the table date, interest runs from the table date despite the fact that at that point the taxpayer did not know how much tax was due.

The table date is six months after the normal due date or statutory date described above, except for Schedule D Case I where there is only one table date, which is 1 July following the end of the fiscal year of assessment.

EXAMPLE 23.1

The 1994/95 estimated Schedule A assessment was issued on 18 November 1994 for an amount of £25,000, tax payable £6,250. It was thought to be excessive and therefore a notice of appeal was submitted together with an application to postpone £2,250 tax on 30 November 1994. The inspector of taxes agreed to the postponement on 16 December 1994. The non-postponed tax (£4,000) was paid on 19 January 1995. The appeal was finally determined on 14 August 1995 in an amount of £30,000 and notice of the total tax due (£7,500) was issued on 19 August 1995. The balance of the tax was paid on 31 August 1995.

Normal due date (Schedule A 1994/95):		1 January 1995
Actual due date:		
1)	Non-postponed tax (Date postponed tax is agreed with the Revenue + 30 days)	15 January 1995
2)	Postponed tax (Date notice of total tax due is issued + 30 days)	18 September 1995
3)	Additional tax (Date notice of total tax due is issued + 30 days)	18 September 1995
Table date (6 months after normal due date)		1 July 1995

Reckonable date of non-postponed tax £4,000

Later of	a) (NDD), or		1 January 1995
or	b) earlier of	i) (ADD)	15 January 1995
		ii) Table date	1 July 1995
The reckonable date is		15 January 1995	
Tax paid		19 January 1995 that is,	4 days' interest on £4,000 @ 10% = £4.38

Reckonable date of postponed tax and additional tax £3,500

Later of	a) (NDD), or		1 January 1995
	b) earlier of	i) (ADD)	18 September 1995
		ii) Table date	1 July 1995
The reckonable date is	1 July 1995		
Tax paid	31 August 1995 that is, 61 days' interest on £3,500 @ 10% = £58.49		

Total interest on assessment	£62.87

Penalty interest

Penalty interest under s88 TMA 1970 is charged when an assessment is raised for the purpose of making good tax lost .through:

- a failure to give a notice, make a return, or provide a document or other information, or
- an error in any information or return supplied.

In order to impose a charge to penalty interest the Inland Revenue must issue a notice of determination. Penalty interest runs from the normal due date of payment. The alternative later date of 30 days after the issue of an assessment is not relevant. If penalty interest is charged, interest on overdue tax is not charged.

Certificates of tax deposit

Certificates of tax deposit are available to individuals to meet their tax liabilities. The initial deposit must be a minimum of £2,000 but subsequent deposits may be made of £500 or more. The certificates earn interest at one of two rates and may be 'cashed in' (lower interest rate) or used to settle a tax liability (higher interest rate): the intention does not have to be specified at the time of purchase. Interest accrues daily and is taxable under Schedule D Case III.

To settle a tax liability, a certificate may be used in a number of ways.

- *Pre-paying tax.* Interest is earned from the date the certificate is purchased to the 'deemed due date' for payment of the tax liability (maximum six years). The deemed due date is the normal due date. Whether the assessment is raised at this date or not, interest does not accrue beyond this date.
- *Estimated assessments.* Where taxpayers wish to protect themselves from interest on overdue tax while an appeal (and application for postponed tax) is being determined as in the above example, it is possible to purchase a certificate of tax deposit (for example, on the table date) for the amount of tax which may potentially become payable. If the appeal is lost and the tax does become payable, the certificate is surrendered – no interest is earned on the money but no interest is charged on the tax outstanding. If the appeal is won, the taxpayer has a certificate which may be encashed or held to satisfy a future tax liability.

Repayment supplements

A repayment of tax to a taxpayer (or set-off against a separate and later tax liability) which is repayable more than 12 months after the end of the fiscal year to which it relates, is supplemented by interest. The interest paid is called a repayment supplement and is tax free.

The rate of interest is the same as that for interest on overdue tax.

Interest is calculated for complete tax months (from the 6th of one month to the 5th of the next and so on) to the end of the tax month in which the repayment is made from a date determined as follows.

		Interest commences
a)	Original tax paid > 12 months after end of year of assessment.	6 April following the date the original tax was paid.
b)	Original tax paid in year of assessment or < 12 months after end of year of assessment.	First anniversary of 6 April following end of year of assessment in which the original tax was paid.

If a repayment relates to tax paid in more than one year of assessment, it is treated as relating to later years rather than earlier years for purposes of the repayment supplement.

EXAMPLE 23.2

Schedule A tax of £1,500 was paid for 1992/93 on 1 January 1993. £700 was repaid on 15 August 1994. The repayment supplement will be calculated from 6 April 1994 to 6 September 1994 (that is, five months) on £700.

Fraudulent or negligent conduct

The term 'evasion' does not appear in the legislation. Assessments are made for 'fraudulent or negligent conduct'. This offence is very widely defined and, in considering the areas covered, it is useful to look at the offences it replaced, namely: fraud, wilful default and neglect.

Neglect was defined as 'negligence, or failure to give any notice, make any return or to produce or furnish any document or other information required by or under the Taxes Acts'. Neglect amounts to omission to take some action.

Fraud, on the other hand, is active and deliberate evasion.

Wilful default may be described as persistent neglect rather than deliberate evasion.

Assessments may be made at any time not later than 20 years after the year of assessment to which they relate to recover tax lost due to fraudulent or negligent conduct. The reason the offence was changed was because the onus of proving fraud or wilful default was on the Crown and this was difficult; now the onus is on the taxpayer to prove the assessments are excessive.

Penalties may be charged as below in addition to the tax liability and any interest on overdue tax.

Penalties

Table 23.3

Failure to notify chargeability (within one year after the end of the tax year in which the income arose)	Amount of the tax liability (maximum) under assessments made more than 12 months after end of the year.
Failure to submit a return	£300 (maximum) plus £60 per day if failure continued after the penalty has been imposed plus amount of tax liability (if failure continues beyond the end of the tax year following the year in which the return was issued).
Incorrect returns: neglect	The lost tax (maximum).
Incorrect returns: fraud	The lost tax (maximum).

Penalties are based on 100% of the tax and mitigated according to the seriousness of the offence (see below).

However, note that a fixed limit penalty exists for delay. Penalties are being phased in for delays until, by 1995, it is intended to impose an automatic fixed penalty. The Inland Revenue may take proceedings before the Appeal Commissioners to force the taxpayer to complete an overdue return (either a personal Tax Return or an information return from a business). The initial penalty and the daily amount are fully mitigable.

Inland Revenue inquiry and investigation

The Inland Revenue makes inquiries and investigations where it suspects tax may have been lost due to a taxpayer's fraudulent or negligent conduct.

The main area of Inland Revenue investigation work is concerned with the omission of business profits, covered separately below. There are far fewer opportunities for the evasion of tax in other areas.

Most of the problems in these other areas stem from a failure to notify a source of income (such as casual earnings – 'moonlighting' – or investment income from the National Savings Bank). There are other individuals unknown to the Inland Revenue or for whom the Inland Revenue has no tax files – 'ghosts' whose residence, for example, is doubtful. Equally serious is the falsification of claims to allowances and other deductions.

The local district is usually responsible for 'personal' investigations (some districts for example have units specialising in directors) but in cases of serious fraud, the Inquiry Branch is involved and this usually results in criminal prosecution. The Special Office may become involved where artificial avoidance schemes have been used or there are problems as to whether Schedule E or Schedule D should apply. They also select for investigation areas of the economy which appear to them to be worth investigating.

Methodology

The previous year's tax return may be studied and all available information collated. Any apparent discrepancy with the current tax return may prompt an inquiry. The usual form that this takes is to ask the taxpayer to review the return and verify that all the entries are correct and complete. The particular source of income in doubt is not disclosed in case there are also discrepancies in others. The taxpayer should consider carefully before replying. The reply may settle the matter or disclose further irregularities.

Where income is omitted, the source of the underlying capital is often of interest to the Inland Revenue. Common explanations include betting winnings, legacies and gifts. For these to be acceptable, it is necessary for the taxpayer to produce corroboration.

Sources of information

Information sources fall into two categories: official and others.

Official sources of information include the Capital Taxes Office, the Customs and Excise (information about vessels), the Special Office (information on acquisitions of aeroplanes and expensive cars) the District Valuer (large property transactions), and returns from banks, building societies and other financial institutions.

Other sources of information come from the local knowledge of the Inland Revenue officers themselves, voluntary disclosure by taxpayers themselves, newspaper advertisements, 'Yellow Pages', specialised press covering personalities, and sundry anonymous sources (in particular spouses, disgruntled ex-employees, neighbours and business associates).

Examination of business accounts (see also Chapter 15)

The District Inspector no longer simply follows up as many cases as possible. The approach is structured with the District Inspector having to carry out a programme of detailed investigations in order to reach specified targets for tax collection. Selected accounts are scrutinised in detail (frequently the original records are examined) and compared with average gross profit figures for the trade as a whole. The Inspector, after taking into account local conditions, may seek to amend the receipts figure to bring the gross profit into line. Alternatively, where this approach is unsatisfactory, understated profits, if any, may be derived from the increases in capital from year to year.

If local investigation discloses serious fraud (understatement of profits in excess of £50,000) it will usually be referred to the Inquiry Branch.

Scrutiny of one set of business accounts may also lead to the discovery of other defaulters (such as employees or non-employees).

Capital statements

A capital statement is drawn up:

- by adding together an individual's spending for the year (both on personal assets and estimated living expenses) and his or her savings for the year and then deducting known income and known capital receipts. Without evidence to the contrary, the balance is presumed to represent omitted taxable profits. For example:

Living expenses (estimated)	X	
Other expenditure	X	
Total spending		X
Savings for the year		X
Total cash received		X
Less: Known income	X	
Known receipts	X	(X)
Omitted income		X

or

- the capital of the taxpayer at the end of the year (that is, his or her total wealth less any liabilities by way of loans, overdrafts and so on) less the capital at the beginning of the year gives the net increase in wealth to which is added the estimated living expenses. Any known income and receipts can then be deducted leaving a balance of unexplained income. For example:

Capital at end of year	X	
Capital at beginning of year	(X)	
Net increase in wealth over year	X	
Add: Living expenses (estimated)	X	
Total cash received in year		X
Less: Known income	X	
Known receipts	X	(X)
Omitted income		X

Powers

Returns from third parties

The Inland Revenue has the power to request returns from various third parties in order to obtain information about certain categories of income or persons who may be chargeable. There is a general time limit on such returns – they should not require information for any year of assessment ending more than three years before the date of the request.

Returns may be required of lodgers, employees, copyright, interest paid, grants and subsidies given, licences granted, lessees and the payment of fees and commissions by, for example, clubs to entertainers, by relevant parties and also of clients by auctioneers or stockbrokers.

The penalties for incomplete or false returns are a maximum of £3,000 for each offence. Failure to complete the return will occur penalties for delay as set out above.

Production of documents

Subject to having the Board's authority and the consent of a General or Special Commissioner, Inspectors may, in writing, require the taxpayer to deliver to them any documents which they have reason to believe contain information related to the taxpayer's tax liability. The taxpayer may also be required to give written answers to written questions of fact.

A similar request may be made to the taxpayer's spouse or child or to any person carrying on a business or to any company where the tax liability which is the subject of inquiry relates to that business or company.

Documents may also be required relating to an unnamed taxpayer. An example of its use, quoted by the Inland Revenue, might be to obtain information from the sponsors of a tax avoidance scheme which is considered ineffective, regarding the taxpayers who made use of the scheme.

Documents include 'books, accounts, any other document or record whatsoever' (there are special provisions regarding computer records), but personal records (such as those defined in the Police and Criminal Evidence Act 1984) and journalistic material are specifically excluded.

- The Revenue cannot require any document to which a barrister, advocate or solicitor can claim professional privilege without the taxpayer's consent. In addition any documents required of barristers, advocates and solicitors must be requested by the Board and not by the inspector.

The Revenue hold powers under TMA 1970 to call for the papers of a tax accountant where he or she has been:

- convicted of a tax offence, or
- subject to a penalty for assisting in the preparation of an incorrect return.

The Finance Act 1994 substantially extends these powers so that it is now only necessary for an inspector to have reasonable grounds for believing that an accountant has knowingly assisted in the giving of information which he or she had reasonable grounds to believe would be used for tax purposes and to be incorrect. This power can only be exercised with the consent of a Special Commissioner who must be satisfied that the inspector is justified in proceeding in this way.

Except in certain serious cases where notice is given by the Board, at least 30 days must be allowed for the documents or information to be produced.

Falsification of documents

There are criminal sanctions against the falsification or destruction of documents. A person is released from the obligation to preserve the document:

- on its sight by the Inland Revenue
- six months after the initial informal request for access has been made, unless the request is renewed
- two years after the formal request
- on release from the obligation following application for release by the taxpayer to the Revenue or the Appeal Commissioners.

Search and seizure

Where tax fraud is reasonably suspected, a warrant may be obtained by the Board to enter premises and search and seize anything which may be evidence. These powers are restricted to serious fraud and are brought into line with police and VAT search powers.

Information for foreign tax authorities

Under the 1977 European Directive, member countries have been required to provide each other with information about taxpayers. This has previously been interpreted as applying to information on record but it now appears that it applies to other information. The Inland Revenue may obtain information required solely by a foreign tax authority. In addition, the European Directive may be extended to taxes on gifts.

Certificate of full disclosure

If there is a case to answer before a settlement is finally reached the taxpayer will usually be required to agree a computation of lost tax and sign a certificate of full disclosure to cover the specified period. This takes the place of the declaration on the tax return and if incorrect, it is tantamount to fraud.

Interest on unpaid tax and penalties

At the settlement interview with the Inspector, there is an opportunity for the taxpayer to be given a warning plus an opportunity to agree the degree of culpability. The way in which the irregularities came to light, their gravity, size and the degree of co-operation given by the taxpayer during the inquiry will affect the Inspector's conclusion. The taxpayer may offer an amount in settlement of the liability to tax, interest and penalties.

Although maximum penalties are rarely given, the Inspector is subject to scrutiny by his superior officers as regards the settlement reached. The offer in settlement must be made voluntarily by the taxpayer and if it is less than the normally acceptable amount, it should be accompanied by a statement of assets.

Further interest may be charged at the normal rates (see above) from the contracted payment date to the date actually paid.

If the taxpayer does not co-operate, the case will be listed for the Commissioners and in this case the taxpayer might be advised to take out a certificate of tax deposit against the interest arising on tax paid late (see above).

Default interest

Where tax is assessed late as a result of an offence by a taxpayer, interest is charged from the date the tax would have been due if it had been assessed at the correct time. Default interest is charged on any tax which is assessed late as the result of an incorrect return, eliminating the advantage the taxpayer otherwise enjoyed over a taxpayer who completed his or her return correctly.

Administration of inheritance tax

Inheritance tax is administered by the Capital Taxes Office of the Inland Revenue (see above), but unlike the other direct taxes, there is no system of regular returns. There is instead a 'duty to report' on death and whenever a chargeable lifetime transfer takes place.

Duty to report

On death, the personal representatives of the deceased person and every person liable to tax (if any arises) as transferee or trustee of a settlement are obliged to deliver an account to the Capital Taxes Office specifying to the best of their knowledge the property transferred and its value. The account must be delivered within 12 months following the end of the month in which death occurred. This time limit is extended for personal representatives to three months after their appointment if this is a later date. For this purpose, delivery of the account by the personal representatives to a probate registry is deemed to be delivery to the Board.

On chargeable lifetime transfers, the responsibility to deliver an account is likely to fall on the transferor and must be made within 12 months of the end of the month in which the transfer is made or, if later, within three months of the date the liability to tax arises. Note that the tax can be due (see below), and therefore interest can be chargeable, before the return is due.

If any errors in an account subsequently come to light (that is, the account is discovered to be defective) a further account must be delivered within six months of the discovery. Similarly, if any claims have been made for conditional exemptions (such as woodlands and heritage property) and tax subsequently becomes chargeable, an account must be delivered within six months of the end of the month in which the tax liability arises.

Powers

The Board of Inland Revenue, subject to prior approval by an Appeal Commissioner, may require anyone to furnish any information it may need. Such a request must be in writing.

The power does not apply to barristers and solicitors where professional privilege may be claimed unless the client consents. Solicitors may, however, be obliged to disclose the name and address of a client.

Where tax or interest is unpaid (see below) a charge may be imposed for that amount on any property to which the tax is attributable.

Determinations and appeals

When a transfer of value has been made, the Board issues a notice of determination showing the value of the transfer and the tax chargeable. A notice of determination has much the same function as the notice of assessment for income tax. If an account has been delivered and is correct, the notice of determination will be in accordance with the account, but otherwise the notice of determination will be made by the Board to the best of its judgement.

A person who receives a notice of determination may appeal against it within 30 days of the date of issue. It must be in writing and state the grounds of appeal. A late appeal may be accepted if reasonable excuse for the delay is shown.

An appeal will generally be heard by the Special Commissioners whose decision is final except on a point of law, but in certain circumstances it may be heard by the Lands Tribunal or go direct to the High Court. The procedures thereafter are similar to income tax appeals.

Due date for payment of tax

The due date for payment of tax is six months after the end of the month of transfer or death except where a chargeable lifetime transfer takes place after 5 April and before 1 October, when the tax is not due until 30 April following.

On death, however, personal representatives must pay the tax on delivery of the account at a probate registry. As a grant of probate cannot in general be obtained until this is done, this date may be before the due date.

In some cases, works of art, historic buildings and the like may be accepted in lieu of tax.

Instalment option

An election may be made for the tax to be paid in ten equal instalments (the first instalment being payable on the due date as above) where the transfer takes place on death or where the donee is paying the tax on a chargeable lifetime transfer.

The main transfers to which the instalment option applies are:

- land
- shares and securities in a company under the control of the transferor prior to the transfer
- unquoted shares or securities which, together with other items to which the instalment option applies, amount to 20% or more of the total tax liability by that person or where the Board is satisfied that the tax on the shares cannot be paid without causing undue hardship
- unquoted shares with a value greater than £20,000 and being at least 10% of the issued share capital of the company
- a business or an interest in a business.

Interest on overdue tax

Interest is charged on overdue inheritance tax from the due date to the date the tax is paid. The interest is payable gross and is not deductible.

No interest is charged on instalments paid unless the property is land on which agricultural property relief is not available.

The examination will normally use an interest rate of 10%.

Interest on repayments

Non-taxable interest is given on repayments.

Penalties

Penalties are chargeable for failures to comply with inheritance tax legislation as follows:

▶ Failure to render an account/failure to supply information required	£50(max)/ £10 per day if failure continues after declared by court/commissioners
▶ Incorrect returns: – neglect (by person liable)	The lost tax (maximum) + £50
– fraud	Twice the lost tax (maximum) + £50 per year
▶ Incorrect returns: – neglect (by person not liable)	£250 (max)
– fraud	£500 (max)

Organisation of Customs and Excise

The Customs and Excise has a great many other responsibilities other than simply overseeing VAT. An outline of the organisation of that part of Customs and Excise which is responsible for VAT may help give an understanding of the procedures adopted by it.

Table 23.4 Board of Commissioners of Customs and Excise

Administration Directorate	Control Directorate
London	Southend
(Policy and technical matters)	(Collection of VAT – organised on a regional structure)
Specialist divisions	
	Assistant collector
Computers	(per region)
Fraud and investigations	
	Surveyor
	(per district)
	Senior officer
	(3 – 4 per district)

The Customs and Excise operates very differently from the Inland Revenue. In particular, although the trader may have a professional adviser who prepares and presents the returns, Customs and Excise generally insists on dealing with the trader directly and usually at the trader's place of business.

The most senior official is the Assistant Collector who is responsible for up to ten districts. He or she rarely has any direct dealings with traders. Each district has a surveyor and within each district there will be a number of VAT offices or VAT sub-offices, each responsible for the administration of VAT for the traders in their area (they do not issue VAT returns or collect the tax). It is the VAT officers from these offices with whom the trader most often comes into contact.

Administration of value added tax

Self-assessment

VAT is a self-assessed tax and the onus is on traders to ensure that they are registered and submit their returns and pay over any tax on time.

General

Chapter 22 has dealt in detail with the enforcement procedures where a trader fails to register or submit VAT returns, including the appeal procedures and penalties.

Powers of Customs and Excise

The Customs and Excise has considerable powers, including the right to enter business premises at any reasonable time, to inspect records and to ask questions. Officers have the right to take away relevant records and samples of products. Where fraud is suspected they may obtain a search warrant to enter and search premises and if criminal offences are suspected, they may arrest without warrant.

Generally VAT officers make appointments rather than take full advantage of their powers.

Professional advice is usually a taxable supply and therefore a VAT officer has the right of access to confidential communications with professional advisers.

Summary

- ▶ It is the responsibility of taxpayers to ensure that the Inland Revenue is notified that they are chargeable to income or capital gains tax for any year, if they have not received a tax return. Penalties may be imposed if this is not done.
- ▶ An assessment, once issued, can only be reduced in certain specified circumstances, but additional assessments can be issued within the six year time limit as a result of 'discovery' (20 years if due to an offence by the taxpayer). Discovery has a very wide meaning.
- ▶ Taxpayers have the right of appeal against any assessment which is not, in their opinion, correct, and if it is excessive, the separate right to apply for postponement of the tax charged.
- ▶ Appeals may be determined by the Inspector, the General or Special Commissioners, or, on questions of law, by the courts.
- ▶ There are severe penalties for fraudulent or negligent conduct.
- ▶ The Inland Revenue has many sources of information to check the completeness and accuracy of a taxpayer's return, and wide powers to require information from third parties.
- ▶ Many business accounts are accepted by the Inspector without detailed

examinations. A selected sample is scrutinised thoroughly, the emphasis being on a fast and efficient approach to meet targets for collection of back duty.

▶ For inheritance tax also, it is the duty of the taxpayer to 'deliver an account' where he or she is or may be liable to do so. Penalties are chargeable for failure to do so or for rendering incomplete or fraudulent returns.

▶ Value added tax is a self-assessed tax with severe penalties for both delayed and incomplete returns. It is administered by the Customs and Excise which has even wider powers than the Inland Revenue.

Self test questions

1 If A starts doing 'odd jobs' in the evenings in September 1994, when must he inform the Inland Revenue of his chargeability to tax?

2 What is the penalty for not notifying chargeability in the previous example?

3 What is the time limit for appealing against an assessment?

4 What is the statutory due date for a higher rate income tax liability on income from which basic rate income tax was deducted at source?

5 What is the reckonable date?

6 What is the time limit for raising assessments where fraudulent or negligent conduct is suspected?

7 State the rules for interest on overdue inheritance tax.

8 On 1 November 1994, Bob received a tax assessment on business profits for 1994/95, based on his return of income for the previous year. As he believed the assessment to be correct he did not appeal against it and paid the tax charged on the due dates.

Outline the circumstances under which i) Bob and ii) the Inspector dealing with Bob's case could obtain an alteration to the amount assessed at a later date. You should note any relevant time limits which may apply.

9 Paul made a chargeable capital gain of £18,000 in June 1994; disposal proceeds were £30,000. His brother Hugh made a chargeable capital gain of £2,600 in January 1995; disposal proceeds were £7,000.
   a) Advise Paul of his responsibility for reporting his gain to his Inspector of Taxes:
      i) assuming that the Inspector issues a tax return in respect of 1994/95
      ii) assuming that the Inspector does not issue a tax return in respect of 1994/95.
   b) Advise Hugh in the same way of his responsibility for reporting his gain:
      i) assuming that the Inspector issues a tax return in respect of 1994/95
      ii) assuming that the Inspector does not issue a tax return in respect of 1994/95.

State briefly the penalties (other than interest charges) which may be imposed for failure to discharge these responsibilities. Assume that neither Paul nor Hugh are liable to income tax for 1994/95.

Answers on pages 602–603

Question Bank – Personal Business Taxation

1. Mr Simple, a single man aged 54, has been trading as a consultant since 1 July 1974. His trading profits (losses) (as adjusted for tax purposes) for recent years are as follows:

	£
Period to 30/6/89	12,000
30/6/90	14,000
30/6/91	15,000
30/6/92	11,000
30/6/93	8,000
30/6/94	5,000
31/12/94	(40,000)

The loss for the period ended 31 December 1994 was largely attributable to an exceptional bad debt. Mr Simple intends to continue to run his business for the next ten years and he expects it to make approximately £15,000 per annum in future years. Mr Simple has no other income apart from annual rents of £2,700.

Mr Simple has decided at today's date (which you may assume to be 31 December 1994) to incorporate his business immediately by selling it to a newly formed company, Sadcake Ltd. Mr Simple's summarised balance sheet at 31 December 1994 is as follows:

		£
Fixed assets:		
Plant and machinery (NBV)		6,000
Motor car (NBV)		9,000
		15,000
Current assets:		
Debtors		5,000
Bank		3,000
Net current assets		8,000
Total assets		23,000
Financed by:		
Mr Simple – capital account		23,000

All of the assets in the balance sheet will be sold to Sadcake Ltd at their book value, which also represents their current market value. In addition, goodwill currently valued at £18,000 will be sold to Sadcake Ltd. The market value of the goodwill at 31 March 1982 was £4,000. Mr Simple has decided *not* to elect that assets eligible for capital allowances should be deemed to be transferred at their tax written-down value. The written-down value of assets eligible for capital allowances were as follows as at 1 July 1988:

	£
Pooled expenditure	34,667
Motor car	14,000

There have been no purchases or sales of assets since 1 July 1988, apart from the purchase of a machine for £1,000 on 1 August 1992. Private use of the motor car by Mr Simple has been agreed at 25%.

Mr Simple will receive annual remuneration of £9,000 from Sadcake Ltd payable at the commencement of each month. However, Mr Simple would also like to be able to extract further amounts of profit from the company in a tax-efficient manner in approximately three to four years time. Mr Simple had originally intended that Sadcake Ltd should acquire his business wholly in exchange for shares issued to Mr Simple. However, he has since been told that it is also possible for the company to acquire the business partly for shares, with the balance of the purchase price being left unpaid as a loan from Mr Simple to the company. Mr Simple is unsure whether this would be a preferable course of action from a tax viewpoint, and if so what value of shares ought to be issued.

a) Calculate Mr Simple's *total* income for the tax years 1990/91 to 1994/95 inclusive, taking into account any loss relief to which Mr Simple may be entitled.

b) Discuss whether Sadcake Ltd should acquire the business only *partly* for shares and if so, what value of shares should be issued. You should bear in mind the immediate consequences for capital gains tax and for any claims for loss relief, as well as any longer-term tax implications which may be relevant.

2   Jennifer, born in 1916, has been running her own wool retail and mail order business since April 1966, shortly after the death of her husband. The business is run through a company, Woolway Limited, in which Jennifer holds 9,000 £1 ordinary shares, the other 1,000 shares being held by her granddaughter, Helen. The shares were subscribed for at par value early in April 1966.

Early in 1995, Jennifer decided to retire and in March agreed to sell her shares to Caridigan plc for a consideration of £450,000 to be satisfied by the payment of £337,500 cash and the issue of 45,000 shares in Cardigan plc valued at £2.50 each.

Information regarding the assets of Woolway Limited is as follows:

	Cost	Value 31 March 1982	Value 31 March 1995
	£	£	£
Goodwill	–	80,000	100,000
Freehold shops	15,000	100,000	255,000
Equipment	40,000	25,000	30,000
Investment in 1972 in Supplier Ltd	10,000	20,000	85,000
Stocks	14,000	8,000	13,000
Debtors less creditors	9,000	5,000	9,000
Bank and cash		2,000	8,000
		240,000	500,000

Each item of equipment cost less than, and at 31 March 1995, is worth less than £6,000.

The sale was completed on 31 March 1995 and on that day, Jennifer gifted 30,000 shares in Cardigan plc to her son.

On 1 April 1995 Jennifer
– gifted £10,000 cash to Helen in consideration of her forthcoming marriage
– gifted £30,000 cash to the NSPCC, a recognised charity
– settled £200,000 cash into a discretionary trust
– lent £80,000 cash to her grandson at a market interest rate of 8% gross, payable quarterly in arrears.

Jennifer has made no earlier gifts and is to pay any inheritance tax on the above transfers.

Assuming Jennifer claims all available exemptions and reliefs, explain clearly, using computations, the tax consequences of the transactions carried out by Jennifer on 31 March and 1 April 1995, and compute any capital gains and inheritance tax payable.

3   a) Bruce, employed full-time a with a local garage as a motor mechanic, and his wife Madeline, are both motor car enthusiasts. A few years ago they read a newspaper article on the lower prices payable for cars in certain European countries compared to the UK. As a result, Bruce obtained a bank loan and visited Germany where he bought a second-hand, left-hand drive sports car which he drove back to the UK. He then carried out the necessary work to convert the car to right-hand drive.

A short while later, Madeline became pregnant and the sports car soon became unsuitable. A friend who admired the car offered to buy it, and Bruce sold it a market value which resulted in a profit of £1,000. He used the proceeds to buy an estate car in the same way.

Discuss whether this profit might be assessable on Bruce:
▶ as income
▶ as a capital gain.

b) Due to pregnancy, Madeline will shortly cease working, resulting in a considerable reduction in their income. Bruce is considering supplementing their income by visiting Germany six times a year, on each occasion buying and driving back to the UK a left-hand drive car. He would carry out the necessary conversion work and advertise the car for sale in local newspapers. He would expect a profit of £1,000 on each of the six cars sold during the year.

State whether your answer in a) would still apply, and if not, why it would differ.

c) An alternative which Bruce is considering is to resign from his employment, and form his own business as a sole trader. He would emply a driver to visit European countries, buying second-hand cars and driving them back to the UK. Bruce would then carry out conversion work while Madeline would deal with sales to customers.

He accepts that the profits of such a full-time business would be assessable to income tax but is uncertain regarding the VAT position. He expects that sales of cars will result in a yearly sales figure of £250,000 and an adjusted profit for tax purposes of £25,000 after paying a modest wage to Madeline.

You are required to advise Bruce:
i) whether he is required to register for VAT and why.
ii) whether, assuming he is required to register, the failure to do so would result in any penalty becoming payable.
iii) whether he would be required to charge VAT on the second-hand cars he sells
iv) regarding the advantages of the VAT scheme applicable to second-hand cars

v) whether he would be charged, and whether the could claim as input tax, VAT on:
- cars imported
- second-hand cars bought from private individuals
- parts bought for conversion work.

d) You are required to state concisely the recommendations contained in SSAP5 (Accounting for value added tax)) regarding:
- ▶ whether turnover shown in the profit and loss account should include VAT
- ▶ whether expenditure shown in the profit and loss account should include any irrecoverable VAT
- ▶ whether amounts due to or from Customs & Excise in respect of VAT should be disclosed separately or should be included in creditors/debtors.

4 a) Jack, a self-employed architect, has been in business since the late 1970s. Almost all his clients are private houseowners whose main source of income is from employment or a pension. Jack's gross income in the years ending 30 April 1991, 1992 and 1993, amounted to £17,500, £18,000 and £19,500 respectively, with allowable expense giving a tax adjusted profit of approximately £2,000 less than the above figures. He is not registered for VAT. The results of the business in later accounting periods have not yet been determined.

You are required to advise Jack whether or not he should register for VAT, giving your reasons.

b) Jack has recently been approached by Howard, also a self-employed architect, whose accounting year end is 30 June. Due to a number of years of ill-health Howard's expenses and capital allowances have for the past few years exceeded his income. He is now fully recovered and has approached Jack and suggested that their two businesses might merge on 1 May 1994, with accounts of the new partnership being prepared to 30 April.

Assuming the merger takes place, you are requested to advise Jack:
i) regarding the basis of assessment applicable to himself and Howard in the tax years preceding, during and following the merger and what options are open to them
ii) what set-off would be available for Howard's unrelieved losses
iii) what effect the merger would have on their VAT position.

5 You have recently been appointed by an individual running her own business to act on her behalf in a back duty investigation. Following preparation of a capital statement for a number of years, you have agreed with the District Inspector handling the case the additional amounts to be assessed, and calculations showing the amounts of tax, interest on overdue tax and penalties arising on the additional amounts assessable.

Your client is puzzled as to how the back duty investigation began. She has also asked whether the Inland Revenue will accept a settlement of less than the full amount.

You are required to write a letter to your client advising her:
a) what sort of information the Inspector might have received which resulted in an investigation into her affairs
b) of the circumstances of the case which the Inland Revenue might take into consideration in deciding whether to accept a payment of less than the full amount due.

6 The Inland Revenue has recently finished an investigation into the taxation affairs of Stephen Harrison aged 34, who owns and manages a supermarket. The investigation concerned Stephen's accounts for the year ended 31 July 1993. These were submitted to the Inland Revenue on 1 February 1994, and showed a tax adjusted profit of £52,000. In view of the investigation, the Inland Revenue issued an estimated assessment for 1994/95 on 15 October 1994 as follows:

	£	£
Schedule D (estimated)		55,000
Class 4 NIC relief (50%)	580	
Personal allowance	3,445	
		(4,025)
		50,975
Income tax due:		
£3,000 at 20%		600
£20,700 at 25%		5,175
£27,275 at 40%		10,910
		16,685
Class 4 NIC due:		
(£22,360 – £6,490) × 7.3%		1,159
		17,844

The assessment was appealed against on 1 November 1994. However, no application was made to postpone the income tax and class 4 NIC payable, and this was paid by the relevant due dates.

The Inland Revenue investigation revealed the following:
(a) Since 1 October 1992, Stephen has been operating a cafeteria in a corner of his shop, the profits from which have not been declared in his accounts. The Inland Revenue has agreed that during the year ended 31 July 1993 the income from the cafeteria amounted to £9,500, whilst the related figure for purchases was £4,600. All of the cafeteria sales were standard-rated, all of the purchases were zero-rated. No entries have been made in respect of these purchases or sales on Stephen's VAT returns.
(b) Stephen's accounts show no adjustment for own consumption for the year ended 31 July 1993. An adjustment for goods, all of which are standard-rated, costing £2,900 with a retail price of £4,100 has now been agreed by the Inland Revenue. The cost of these goods had been included in Stephen's purchases figure for the year, and the related input tax has been reclaimed. However, he has made no entries on his VAT returns in respect of the own consumption.

All of the figures in (a) and (b) are inclusive of VAT where applicable.

On 10 October 1995 the Inland Revenue amended the assessment for 1994/95 in respect of the above discoveries, and Stephen paid the additional amounts of tax due on 28 October 1995.

Required:
(a) Calculate Stephen's additional VAT, income tax, and class 4 NIC liabilities in respect of the accounts year ended 31 July 1993 as a result of the Inland Revenue's investigation. Use 1994/95 rates and legislation throughout. Ignore interest on overdue tax and penalties.

(10 marks)

(b) (i) State the conditions which must be met if penalty interest is to be charged by the Inland Revenue under s88 TMA 1970, and whether or not it will be applied in this case.
   (ii) Assuming that the Inland Revenue do not charge penalty interest under s88 TMA 1970, calculate the interest on overdue tax that Stephen will be charged. Use an interest rate of 10%.
   (iii) State the maximum amount of the penalties that Stephen could be charged by the Inland Revenue, and the factors that will be taken into account when deciding the actual amount.

(11 marks)

(c) Explain how the payment of a personal pension premium by Stephen could reduce his liability to the Inland Revenue. Your answer should state by what date such a payment should be made.

(4 marks)
(25 marks)

7   You have been asked to provide advice at today's date (which you should assume is 6 April 1994) to Andrew Hope. Andrew is due to commence self-employment running a catering business on 1 July 1994. Andrew's wife Hilda will also be involved on a full-time basis in running the business. Both Andrew and Hilda are 45 years old, and they plan to transfer the business to their son in about 10 years. Projected profits (before charging depreciation and any possible wages to Hilda) are as follows:

	£
Period ended 30/4/95	33,000
Year ended 30/4/96	48,000
Year ended 30/4/97	36,000

No adjustments to these figures for tax purposes are anticipated.

Andrew will acquire second-hand equipment from his brother costing £25,000 on 1 July 1994, and new equipment costing £15,000 on 1 June 1995.

Andrew also has the following sources of income:
i) £125,000 in a building society account producing interest of £10,000 gross.
ii) An unfurnished property worth £90,000 which produces an income, net of expenses, of £9,000 per annum. Andrew is considering selling this property within the next five years, and the sale would give rise to a substantial capital gain.

Hilda currently has no income or assets in her own right.

a) Calculate Andrew's projected Schedule D Case 1 profits and capital allowances for 1994/95 to 1997/98 inclusive, assuming that he wishes to minimise his assessable profits.
b) Outline the tax implications of Andrew employing Hilda until 30 April 1985, and then bringing her into partnership as an equal partner from 1 May 1985 onwards. Your explanation should include a consideration of income tax, NIC, CGT and IHT.
c) Assuming that the strategy in b) is followed, discuss other tax planning measures that Andrew and Hilda could take in order to minimise their overall tax liability. Your discussion should include a consideration of income tax, CGT and IHT. You should assume that future Schedule D Case 1 profits, net of capital allowances, will not exceed £45,000 per annum.

(ACCA Pilot Paper)

Answers on pages 603–611

The Computation of Profits Liable to Corporation Tax

CHAPTER 24

This chapter covers the scope of corporation tax. It deals with the various elements which determine the profits liable to corporation tax and the format of the computation. Students must be thoroughly familiar with the computation and aware of means available to the taxpayer to influence the profits liable to corporation tax.

Background to corporate taxation

The imputation system of corporation tax was introduced on 1 April 1973.

Corporation tax is charged on the profits and then dividends are declared out of the 'after tax profits'. The dividends declared, however, are, in the hands of the shareholders, a net dividend with lower rate income tax imputed as paid while advance corporation tax (ACT), equivalent in amount to lower rate income tax on the gross dividend, is paid to the Inland Revenue by the company (on account of the corporation tax liability for the accounting period *in which* the dividend is paid).

Shareholders receive the dividend net of lower rate tax and account to the Inland Revenue for any higher rate tax liability through their personal tax computation.

EXAMPLE 24.1

A company with profits of £200 (no adjustment needed for tax purposes) suffers corporation tax at 25%. It is decided to retain 50% of the remaining profits and distribute 50%. The shareholders (husband and wife) are liable to higher rate income tax at 40% (assume basic rate income tax is 25%).

	£	Shareholders
		£
Profits of company	200	
Less: Corporation tax 25%	(50)	
Profits after tax	150	Net of
Dividend paid (50%)	(75)	lower rate 75
Retained profit	75	
ACT payable by company on gross equivalent of dividend	19	
(£75 × 20/80)		
on account of future CT liability		
Higher rate liability £75 × $\frac{100}{80}$ × (40–20%)		(19)
Shareholders' dividend after tax		56

Shareholders could be said to have an interest in 50 per cent of the '*underlying profits*', that is, £100; after taxation they have £56 which is an effective overall tax rate of 44%.

The advance payment of corporation tax (ACT) is necessary to fund the lower rate income tax credit imputed to the shareholders but is not lost to the company since the corporation tax liability of the period in which it is paid is correspondingly reduced.

Any shareholder who is not liable to pay income tax may obtain repayment of the tax credit.

Scope and general principles of corporation tax

Liability to account for tax

Corporation tax is chargeable on the worldwide profits of a company resident in the UK and of a UK branch or agency of a company not resident in the UK.

For purposes of corporation tax a company is not just a body registered under the Companies Acts, but also includes any body corporate or unincorporated association (except a partnership, charity, local authority, trade or housing association). Most formal associations of people are unincorporated associations and therefore assessable (examples are sports clubs, societies and residents' associations).

Building societies and life assurance companies are subject to special rules.

Residence

The Finance Act 1988 introduced new rules for company residence the effect of which, from 1993, is:

- All new and existing companies incorporated in the UK will be resident in the UK for tax purposes except for some companies (having previously received Treasury consent to 'migrate') which will remain non-resident unless or until they cease to carry on business or otherwise cease to be taxable outside the UK.
- Companies not incorporated in the UK continue to be treated as UK resident for tax purposes if their central management and control is in the UK.

Prior to this, a company was generally regarded as being resident (for UK tax purposes) in the country where its central management and control was exercised. Determining residence in this way rests on a question of fact. In practice, the country in which central management and control was exercised often meant the country in which the board of directors met. Abuses of this practice latterly led to the Inland Revenue investigating further and actually considering whether the board exercised control in practice.

The principles concerning the location of a company's central management and control are still relevant in certain cases (and are studied further under Overseas Activities).

The Finance Act 1994 introduced new provisions whereby companies which are resident in the UK, but which would be regarded as resident in another country for the purposes of a double taxation agreement, will in future be treated as not resident in the UK.

Accounting periods

An accounting period for purposes of corporation tax normally coincides with the company's period of account. However, *the maximum length of an accounting period is 12 months*. Therefore if the company's period of account is longer than 12 months, it must be split into two accounting periods for purposes of corporation tax: the first will be for 12 months from the beginning of the period of account; the second will commence after the first ends and finish at the end of the company's period of account.

Corporation tax assessments are raised for chargeable accounting periods. Technically, an accounting period commences:

- when the company first comes within the charge to corporation tax by acquiring a source of income or by becoming UK resident
- when a previous accounting period ends and the company is still within the charge to corporation tax.

An accounting period finishes:

- 12 months after it commences; or
- at the end of the company's period of account; or
- when the company commences/ceases to trade; or
- when the company begins/ceases to be UK resident; or
- when the company ceases to be within the charge to corporation tax.

EXAMPLE 24.2

A company, A Ltd, was formed on 1 October 1993 and shares were subscribed for and allotted on 31 October 1993. The subscription monies received were placed on deposit on 1 November 1993. The company commenced trading on 1 January 1994. Accounts were prepared for the period to 30 September each year. The accounting periods of A Ltd are as follows:

1. 1 November 1993 (when a source of income was first acquired) to 31 December 1993 (when the company commenced to trade).
2. 1 January 1994 to 30 September 1994 (the date to which the company prepares its accounts).
3. 1 October 1994 to 30 September following.

Where a company is to be wound up, an accounting period ends and a new one begins at the commencement of the winding up. During the winding up period, accounting periods are 12 months in length until the winding up is complete.

Financial years

Corporation tax rates are fixed for financial years which run from 1 April to the following 31 March. A financial year is identified by the calendar year in which it begins. For example, the financial year 1994 (FY 1994) means the year from 1 April 1994 to 31 March 1995.

If the company's period of account runs from 1 January 1994 to 31 December 1994, the profits chargeable to corporation tax for the accounting period from 1 January 1994 to 31 December 1994 are *apportioned on a time basis* so that the rate for FY 1993 is applied to the period from 1 January 1994 to 31 March 1994 and the rate for FY 1994 to the period from 1 April 1994 to 31 December 1994.

EXAMPLE 24.3

A company prepares its accounts for the 15 month period from 1 October 1993 to 31 December 1994.

```
                    1 October 1993                              31 December 1994
Period of account   |_____ 15 months _____|

                    1 October 1993           1 October 1994    31 December 1994
Accounting periods  |_____ 12 months _____|___ 3 months ____|

Financial years     |   6 months    |   6 months    |  3 months     |
                        FY 1993         FY 1994         FY 1994
```

Corporation tax rates

	Financial year			
	1991	**1992**	**1993**	**1994**
Standard rate	33%	33%	33%	33%
Small companies rate	25%	25%	25%	25%
Lower limit	£250,000	£250,000	£250,000	£300,000
Upper limit	£1,250,000	£1,250,000	£1,250,000	£1,500,000
Marginal relief fraction	1/50	1/50	1/50	1/50

The Chancellor normally sets in advance the rates of corporation tax (FA 1994 set the rates for FY 1994) to help 'companies plan ahead'. These rates may, however, be adjusted retrospectively (the Finance Bill 1991 downwardly adjusted the rate for FY 1990).

The charge to corporation tax

The outline of the computation of the profits chargeable to corporation tax for an accounting period is set out below:

	£
Schedular income (A, D)	X
Investment income from which income tax is deducted at source	X
Chargeable gains	X
	X
Annual charges (gross)	(X)
Profits chargeable to corporation tax	X

There are similarities to income tax but note the following differences. They are fundamental in the approach to corporation tax.

1. *Corporation tax is levied entirely on a current basis.* This even applies to the schedular income. There is no preceding year basis of assessment.
2. *Assessments to corporation tax are made on the total profits* chargeable to corporation tax in an accounting period and not on the individual sources of income.
3. *There are no adjustments for private use.* A company cannot use its assets privately. If an employee uses an asset belonging to the company privately, there is no adjustment of the expenses relating to that asset in the company's accounts but the employee may be charged to tax under Schedule E on such a benefit (see Chapter 3).
4. *Dividends received* from other UK companies (referred to as franked investment income (FII) when grossed up) are exempt from the charge to corporation tax.

As already mentioned with reference to the imputation system of taxation, the liability to corporation tax may be discharged in two parts.

If the company makes any distributions of income during an accounting period, it is obliged to account for advance corporation tax (ACT) shortly after payment of the distribution irrespective of whether it expects to have an actual liability to corporation tax at the end of the accounting period. The rate of ACT for FY 1994 is 20% (previously 22.5%) on the gross equivalent of a distribution.

To the extent that the company has a liability to corporation tax for an accounting period, any ACT paid or payable as a result of distributions during the accounting period may, subject to certain limits, be set off against that liability. Any liability then remaining is called mainstream corporation tax (MCT). It is payable nine months after the end of the accounting period.

Sources of income

The legislation provides that:

> Except as otherwise provided by the Taxes Acts, the amount of any income shall for purposes of corporation tax be computed in accordance with income tax principles, all questions as to the amounts which are or are not to be taken into account as income, or in computing income, or charged to tax as a person's income, or as to the time when any such amount is to be treated as arising, being determined in accordance with income tax law and practice as if accounting periods were years of assessment.

This means that all statutory and case law rules about assessable profits for income tax will apply for corporation tax unless specifically excluded.

A company which is resident in the UK is liable to corporation tax on its income from all sources except dividends from other UK companies.

Some of the schedules which apply to income tax also apply to corporation tax but in a modified form – there is no preceding year basis of assessment and the schedules do not dictate the method or date of payment of the tax.

Each of the above sources of income will be considered in detail as it applies for corporation tax purposes.

Schedule D Case I – trading profits

Adjusted profit computation for period of account

It is necessary to prepare a Schedule D Case I adjusted profit computation in the same way as was done for unincorporated businesses, although on this occasion income omitted from the accounts but taxable under Schedule D Case I is unlikely to apply.

Capital allowances are deducted in arriving at the Schedule D Case I profit (a balancing charge is added) for purposes of corporation tax.

Suggested layout

	£
Net profit (before tax) per accounts for period	X
Add: Expenses per accounts not deductible Schedule DI	X
	X
Less: Income per accounts not taxable Schedule DI	(X)
Less: Expenses not in accounts deductible Schedule DI	(X)
Less: Capital allowances	(X)
Schedule D Case I adjusted profit/(loss) for period	X

Before continuing further you should ensure that you are fully conversant with the rules described in Chapter 15 for computing Schedule D Case I adjusted profits for unincorporated businesses. *Remember there is no adjustment for private use.*

As regards the Schedule D Case I computation for corporation tax purposes, the following are expressly stated not to be deductible:

- dividends or other distributions
- yearly interest, annuity or other annual payments within the definition of annual charges. This section, however, specifically does not prevent the deduction of yearly interest payable in the UK on an advance from a UK-resident bank to the extent that such interest is deductible as a business expense in arriving at the Schedule D Case I profits (*Wilcock* v. *Frigate Investments Ltd* 1981). Debenture interest, on the other hand, is always treated as a charge.

Pre-trading expenditure of a company in the seven years before commencement of that trade is treated as having been incurred on the first day of trading and is deductible provided that it would have been allowable if incurred after the trade had commenced. This provision includes interest which counts as a charge (see above).

The costs of setting up employee share schemes are also a deductible expense.

Where the adjusted profit computation shows a loss, £Nil must be shown for Schedule D Case I. The reliefs available for trading losses are dealt with later.

Basis of assessment

The basis of assessment for corporation tax is the profits of the current accounting period (maximum length 12 months). Where the company's period of account is longer than 12 months, it is necessary to divide the Schedule D Case I adjusted profits *before capital allowances* between the two accounting periods, as demonstrated above. This is done on a time basis.

Capital allowances

These are calculated for an accounting period and not for a period of account (that is, maximum of 12 months). As corporation tax is assessed entirely on a current basis, there are no problems with overlaps and gaps in basis periods. Where an accounting period is shorter than 12 months, writing down allowances must be scaled down proportionately. They are normally deducted as if they were a trading expense in arriving at the Schedule D Case I profit. This apparently small difference between income tax and corporation tax has a significant effect, for example, when losses arise.

Where, however, the allowances are of a type given by discharge or repayment of tax (such as those claimed by a lessor of buildings or plant and machinery), they are primarily given by deduction from the letting income. But if this is insufficient, they may be:

- Carried forward against similar income in succeeding accounting periods
- deducted from other profits of that or an earlier accounting period (equal in length)
- set off under s. 242 against surplus franked investment income (see below).

EXAMPLE 24.4

The accounts of B Ltd for the 15 months to 31 December 1994 show a profit of £145,000 after deducting depreciation of £20,000 and debenture interest of £15,000 gross (£5,000 paid on each of 31 December 1993, 30 June 1994 and 31 December 1994). The balance brought forward in the plant and machinery pool at 1 October 1993 was £16,000. On 1 November 1994 a car costing £15,000 was bought for the managing director. It was estimated that his private use would amount to 25%. No other additions or disposals of fixed assets took place during the period.

*Schedule D Case I adjusted profit computation
for the fifteen months to 31 December 1994*

	£	£
Profit per the accounts		145,000
Add: Depreciation	20,000	
Debenture interest	15,000	
		35,000
Trading income before deducting capital allowances		180,000

	12 months to 30 Sept 1994 £	3 months to 31 Dec 1994 £
Trading income before deducting capital allowances (12:3)	144,000	36,000
Capital allowances (see below)	(4,000)	(1,500)
Schedule D Case I profit	140,000	34,500
Other income	–	–
Total profit	140,000	34,500
Less: charges paid (debenture interest)	(10,000)	(5,000)
Profits chargeable to corporation tax	130,000	29,500

Capital allowance computation

	Pool £	Expensive Car £	Allowances £
12 months to 30 September 1994			
Balance brought forward	16,000		
Additions during period	–		
Disposals during period	–		
	16,000		
Writing down allowance (25%)	(4,000)		4,000
Balance carried forward	12,000		
3 months to 31 December 1994			
Additions during period	–	15,000	
Disposals during period	–	–	
	12,000	15,000	
Writing down allowance (3 months) 25%	(750)		750
£3,000 Max × 3/12		(750)	750
Balance carried forward	11,250	14,250	1,500

Notes
1 The writing down allowance on the car is not restricted for private use. The director will be assessed under Schedule E benefits in kind.
2 Gross charges are deductible in the accounting period in which they are paid.

As demonstrated, the format and the principles of the capital allowance computation are unchanged when applied to the accounting period of a company except for there being no private use of company assets.

There have been a number of changes to the system of capital allowances given to a company consequent upon the introduction of Pay and File (see Chapter 25). The following are applicable for accounting periods ending after 1 October 1993:

▶ *Plant and machinery.* A company need not claim a writing down allowance in full or in part. The effect is to leave an increased balance in the pool and therefore increase the potential allowances in a future accounting period.

- *Industrial buildings.* The initial allowance of 100% on commercial buildings in an enterprise zone may be disclaimed in whole or in part within two years after the end of the accounting period. A writing down allowance of 25% straight line is available on the balance.

  Writing down allowances in general on industrial buildings are given on the straight line basis and therefore there would be little advantage in not claiming them all or in part, since there is no chance to increase the allowance in a future year. Care must also be taken since the life of a building is specified as 25 years and allowances cannot be given beyond the end of an asset's life.
- *Agricultural buildings and scientific research.* Allowances cannot be claimed in part.
- *Patents and know-how.* It is probable that these allowances can be disclaimed in whole or in part since the pool system is used.

Claims and variations and withdrawals of claims must be made within two years of the end of an accounting period (within three years for chargeable accounting periods ending prior to 30 November 1993) or such later date as either a) a corporation tax assessment for the period becomes final and conclusive, or b) the date on which a determination for the period of an amount of losses affected by the claim becomes final. Adjustments to a claim may be accepted after this date at the inspector's discretion up to six years after the end of the period.

Schedule D Case III

Interest arising in the accounting period is liable to corporation tax. The term 'arising' means the interest credited to the account and it arises on the date it is credited or due to be credited. Since the figure included in the accounts is very often an accrued amount, adjustments usually need to be made.

The interest paid by banks and building societies to company account holders is paid gross and taxable under Schedule D Case III.

Other Schedular income

The other Schedules and Cases (excluding Schedules E and F) are applied for corporation tax in the same way as for income tax, merely substituting chargeable accounting period for fiscal year (for example, under Schedule A the amount taxable will be the 'rent receivable less expenses paid' in the chargeable accounting period as adjusted for losses brought forward from the previous accounting period under Schedule A).

Where the period of account is greater than 12 months, Schedule D Case VI income may need to be apportioned between the accounting periods on a time basis. The gross amount of foreign income computed under Schedule D Cases IV and V must be included. The manner in which it is allocated to accounting periods within one period of account will depend on the source of the income. Relief may be available for all or part of the foreign tax credit (See Overseas Activites)

Unfranked investment income

Income received net of basic rate income tax by a company is commonly called unfranked investment income (UFII). The term is not used in the legislation but in practice it serves to distinguish such income from franked investment income described below.

Income is said to be 'franked' when it is paid out of profits which have been charged to corporation tax. The loan interest or charge on income being received has been deducted from the total profits of the paying company before arriving at profits chargeable to corporation tax, that is, it is paid out of pre-tax profits and is 'unfranked'.

It is the gross amount of such income which is chargeable to corporation tax. Building society interest is now received gross. The company obtains relief for the income tax deducted at source in one of three ways:

1. by set-off against income tax it has deducted from annual charges paid during the accounting period (see Chapter 25)
2. by set-off against the mainstream corporation tax liability of the accounting period
3. if 1 and 2 do not apply it will be repaid to the company on agreement of the corporation tax computation.

Chargeable gains

Chargeable gains/capital losses are computed according to the rules applying to capital gains tax (see Chapters 5 to 7) but are included in the profits chargeable to corporation tax of a company in the chargeable accounting period in which they are realised. Indexation losses and the annual exemption do not apply to companies.

Chargeable gains and capital losses of the current chargeable accounting period are set off against each other. A net capital loss may be carried forward and deducted from chargeable gains of future chargeable acounting periods. Capital losses cannot be set off against profits other than chargeable gains nor can capital losses be carried back and deducted from chargeable gains of earlier accounting periods.

Chargeable gains after deducting any allowable capital losses are included in the profits chargeable to corporation tax.

There are, however, a number of slight modifications to the computation:

▶ Most new legislation is effective for individuals from 6 April while, for companies, the relevant date is 1 April (for example, the Finance Act 1988 re-basing provisions).
▶ There is no annual exemption.
▶ The identification rules for the disposals of shares are slightly modified.

Identification rules for the disposal of shares within a short period of acquisition

Where companies own 2% or more of the shares of that kind in issue, disposals are matched (after same day acquisitions) with shares acquired within one month before or after the disposal (Stock Exchange transactions) or six months (other transactions) before being matched with 'Pool A' (see Chapter 7).

Franked investment income

A dividend or other distribution received from a UK company together with the related tax credit is called franked investment income (FII). As indicated above, income is franked when paid out of profits which have been charged to corporation tax. Since it has already been subjected to corporation tax, it is not taxable on the recipient company.

Charges on income

Charges are defined separately for purposes of corporation tax and cover:

▶ yearly interest (capital or revenue in nature), annuity or other annual payment (including those that require basic rate income tax to be retained, such as royalties, debenture interest, deeds of covenant)
▶ any other interest paid to a bank, stockbroker or discount house carrying on business in the UK.

In many cases, interest paid will be deductible as a trading expense, but will also meet the criteria to be a charge on income – under these circumstances the taxpayer may choose whichever relief is appropriate.

In other cases interest is not deductible as a trading expense (for example, debenture interest) and may therefore be deducted from total profits, provided it meets the conditions below.

Briefly, the conditions which must be met by any annual payment for deduction as a charge are as follows:

- It must be borne by the company claiming relief.
- It must have been paid in the period (that is, accrued charges per the company accounts will not obtain relief until actually paid).
- The definition of a charge includes covenanted donation to charity (capable of continuing for more than three years) and qualifying donations to charity (see below). With these exceptions, an annual payment must have been for valuable and sufficient consideration.

Annual payments described above to non-UK residents are only deductible as a charge if the company is resident in the UK and:

- income tax at basic rate (or such lower rate as is authorised by the Inspector of Foreign Dividends – see Overseas Activities) is retained from the payment and accounted for to the Inland Revenue, or
- the payment is interest and is paid outside the UK or for the purposes of a trade carried on outside the UK or is paid in a currency other than sterling, or
- the payment is of interest on quoted Eurobonds. Such interest is paid gross.

Any annual charge paid subject to deduction of income tax at source may be described as an unfranked payment (UFP). The manner of accounting for the income tax retained is described in the next chapter. It is the gross amount of any such charges that is deductible from total profits.

Trade charges and non-trade charges

It is necessary for some purposes (see losses) to distinguish between trade charges and non-trade charges. Covenanted and qualifying donations to charity are non-trade charges but the other payments mentioned above are normally trade charges.

Qualifying donations to charity

UK-resident companies may claim relief as a charge on income for 'qualifying donations' to charity. A qualifying donation is a single payment made to a charity other than

- a covenanted donation (see above)
- a payment otherwise deductible (such as under Schedule D Case I) in computing profits for corporation tax purposes.

For 'close' companies a qualifying donation is a single gift of not less than £250 (net of tax) (£450 before 16 March 1993). It would appear that there is no minimum limit to single gifts by 'non-close' companies (see Chapter 26).

The company must deduct basic rate income tax from qualifying donations, give the donee a completed form R 240(SD) and account to the Inland Revenue for the income tax retained (see Chapter 25). They are treated, in the hands of the recipient, as income having had basic rate income tax deducted at source.

Deep-discount securities

Relief may be obtained by companies issuing deep-discount securities (see Chapter 4) in respect of the discount to redemption at issue. The relief is given on the income

TAX PLANNING

element for any income periods ending in the accounting period, as a deduction from total profits. It is generally treated as a charge on income provided that certain conditions are fulfilled.

Trading losses

There are a number of ways in which a trading loss for corporation tax may be relieved. It is the alternatives and the 'knock-on' effects of loss relief which sometimes give the appearance of being difficult.

The example set out below will be used to illustrate each of the alternatives in turn.

EXAMPLE 24.5

Lock Ltd commenced trading on 1 January 1990 and has had the following results:

Year ended 31 December	1990	1991	1992	1993	1994
	£	£	£	£	£
Schedule D I profit/(loss)	25,000	30,000	(100,000)	45,000	50,000
Schedule A	15,000	15,000	16,000	20,000	21,000
Chargeable gains less losses	–	–	–	(5,000)	1,000

Carry forward of trading losses

A trading loss may be carried forward and deducted from the first available profits of the *same trade* in subsequent accounting periods (under s. 393(1) ICTA 88). It may be carried forward indefinitely until it is exhausted by set-off against trading profits.

This alternative is often less attractive than the others, in the first instance, since no immediate benefits are reaped.

EXAMPLE 24.5 (Continued)

Corporation tax computations

Accounting periods Year ended 31 December	1991	1992	1993	1994
	£	£	£	£
Schedule D Case I	30,000	–	45,000	50,000
Less loss relief s. 393(1)		-	(45,000)	(50,000)
	30,000	–	–	–
Schedule A	15,000	16,000	20,000	21,000
Net chargeable gains	–	–	–	–
Total profits	45,000	16,000	20,000	21,000

Loss memo
31 December 1992

	£
Loss for year	100,000
Less s.393(1) year ended 31 December 1993	(45,000)
	55,000
Less s.393(1) year ended 31 December 1994	(50,000)
Loss to cf to 1995	5,000

THE COMPUTATION OF PROFITS LIABLE TO CORPORATION TAX

	Capital loss 31 December 1993 £
Loss for year	5,000
Used year end 31 December 1994	(1,000)
Carried forward to 1995	£4,000

Note that the net capital loss for the accounting period 31 December 1993 has been carried forward and deducted from the net chargeable gains of the accounting period 31 December 1994 leaving no chargeable gains taxable for that accounting period. The balance of the capital loss £4,000 will be carried forward to 1995 et seq until exhausted.

Set-off against other profits

A trading loss may be set off against the total profits (before deduction of charges) of the same chargeable accounting period in which the loss was made under ICTA 88, s.393 A(1)(a). The amount of the loss so relieved is the lower of:

- the amount of the loss for the accounting period as determined (see Pay and File, Chapter 25), or
- the amount of the total profits.

The time limit for electing to use the loss relief in this way is two years from the end of the accounting period in which the loss was made. In practice, entry at the appropriate line on the CT 200 corporation tax return will normally be accepted as satisfying the claim requirements.

Any remaining loss may be set off under ICTA 88, s.393A(1)(b) against the total profits (before deduction of charges) but without disturbing the set-off of trade charges of chargeable accounting periods falling within 36 months preceding the accounting period in which the loss is incurred. The set-off is in later accounting periods in priority to earlier ones and set off in each accounting period is the lower of:

- the amount of loss remaining, or
- the amount of the total profits less trade charges which would otherwise be relieved.

This is subject to the proviso that the company had been trading throughout this period. This additional claim is subject to the same time limit as above.

These alternatives have the advantage that an immediate liability to corporation tax may be cancelled as well as the possibility of a repayment of corporation tax already paid for the preceding accounting periods.

This relief is only available provided that the trade is carried on in a commercial manner with a view to the realisation of profits. If the trade is one of farming or market gardening, further restrictions apply: if a loss has been made in each of the five years preceding the current loss, then no relief for the current loss is available under this section.

EXAMPLE 24.5 (Continued)

Corporation tax computations

Accounting periods year ended 31 December	1990 £	1991 £	1992 £	1993 £
Schedule D Case 1	25,000	30,000	–	45,000
Less: loss relief s.393(1)	–	–	–	–
	25,000	30,000	–	45,000
Schedule A	15,000	15,000	16,000	20,000
Net chargeable gains	–	–	–	–
Total profits	40,000	45,000	16,000	65,000
Less: Losses s. 393A(1)(a)			(16,000)	
Losses cb s. 393A(1)(b)	(39,000)	(45,000)		–
Profits chargeable to Corporation Tax	1,000	–	–	65,000

Loss memo
31 December 1992

	£
Loss for year	100,000
Less s. 393A(1)(a) y/e 31 December 1992	(16,000)
s. 393A(1)(b) y/e 31 December 1991	(45,000)
s. 393A(1)(b) y/e 31 December 1990	(39,000)
Further carryback N/A (No trade)	
Losses to carry forward to y/e 31 Dec 1994	Nil

EXAMPLE 24.6

Stock Ltd prepares its accounts to 31 January each year. On 1 February 1993 it decided to change its accounting date to 30 April each year. The results of Stock Ltd are given below:

Year ended 31 January	1991 £	1992 £	1993 £	3 months 30 April 1993 £	Year to 30 April 1994 £
Schedule D I profit/(loss)	25,000	30,000	35,000	15,000	(150,000)
Schedule A	5,000	5,000	6,000	2,000	7,000
Chargeable gains less losses	–	–	–	(5,000)	1,000

Corporation tax computations

Accounting periods year ended 31 January	1991 £	1992 £	1993 £	3 months 30 April 1993 £	Year to 30 April 1994 £
Schedule D Case 1	25,000	30,000	35,000	15,000	–
Less: loss relief s. 393(1)	–	–	–	–	–
	25,000	30,000	35,000	15,000	–
Schedule A	5,000	5,000	6,000	2,000	7,000
Net chargeable gains	–	–	–	–	–
Total profits	30,000	35,000	41,000	17,000	7,000
Less: Losses s. 393A(1)(a)				–	(7,000)
Losses cb s 393A(1)(b)	(22,500)	(35,000)	(41,000)	(17,000)	
Profits chargeable to Corporation tax	7,500	–	–	–	–

	Loss memo
	30 April 1994
	£
Loss for year	150,000
Less: s. 393A(1)(a) year ended 30 April 1994	(7,000)
Less: s. 393A(1)(b) 3 months 30 April 1993	(17,000)
s. 393A(1)(b) year ended 31 January 1993	(41,000)
s. 393A(1)(b) year ended 31 January 1992	(35,000)
s. 393A(1)(b) year ended 31 January 1991	(22,500)
Losses to carry forward	27,500

The loss may be carried back and deducted from the total profits of the 36 months preceding the loss-making period (relief is given in later periods before earlier ones) after being set off against the total profits of the chargeable accounting period in which the loss was incurred. Note that in this example, the period to 31 January 1991 commences 39 months prior to the loss-making accounting period and therefore the set-off of the losses in that period is restricted to the lower of the balance on the loss memo or 9/12 of the total profits for that period.

Carry forward of excess trade charges

If trade charges exceed total profits for any reason (including the consequential effects of loss relief claims under ICTA 1988, s. 393A(1)(a) but not s. 393A(1)(b)) the excess may be added to any losses being carried forward under s. 393(1) or, if none, carried forward on its own and deducted from the first available trading profits of the same trade.

EXAMPLE 24.7

Assume example 24.7 is amended as follows:

Year ended 31 January	1991	1992	1993	3 months 30 April 1993	Year to 30 April 1994
	£	£	£	£	£
Schedule D I profit/(loss)	25,000	30,000	35,000	15,000	(150,000)
Schedule A	5,000	5,000	6,000	2,000	7,000
Chargeable gains less losses	–	–	–	(5,000)	1,000
Debenture interest gross	2,000	2,000	2,000	1,000	2,000

Corporation tax computations

Accounting periods year ended 31 January	1991	1992	1993	3 months 30 April 1993	Year to 30 April 1994
	£	£	£	£	£
Schedule D Case 1	25,000	30,000	35,000	15,000	–
Less: loss relief s. 393(1)	–	–	–	–	–
	25,000	30,000	35,000	15,000	–
Schedule A	5,000	5,000	6,000	2,000	7,000
Net chargeable gains	–	–	–	–	–
Total profits	30,000	35,000	41,000	17,000	7,000
Less: Losses s. 393A(1)(a)				–	(7,000)
Losses cb s. 393A(1)(b)	(22,500)	(33,000)	(39,000)	(16,000)	
Less: charges	(2,000)	(2,000)	(2,000)	(1,000)	(2,000)
Profits chargeable to corporation tax	5,500	–	–	–	–
unrelieved trade charges added to loss per loss memo					2,000

Loss memo
30 April 1994

	£
Loss for year	150,000
Less: s. 393A(1)(a) year ended 30 April 1994	(7,000)
Less: s. 393A(1)(b) 3 months 30 April 1993	(16,000)
s. 393A(1)(b) year ended 31 January 1993	(39,000)
s. 393A(1)(b) year ended 31 January 1992	(33,000)
s. 393A(1)(b) year ended 31 January 1991	(22,500)
(see Note 1)	
Losses to carry forward	32,500
Add: unrelieved trade charges y/e 30 April 1994	2,000
(see Note 2)	
Carry forward	34,500

Notes

1. As before, the loss may be carried back and deducted from the total profit of the 36 months preceding the loss-making period after being set off against the total profits of the chargeable accounting period in which the loss was incurred. As before the period to 31 January 1991 commences 39 months prior to the loss-making account period and therefore the set off of the losses in that period must be restricted.

   There is some doubt as to the amount of the loss which may be set off in the above example. The most probable is the one illustrated, that is, the lower of:
   - the remaining loss; or
   - total profits × 9/12 (£22,500) provided that the remaining profits £7,500 (total profits × 3/12) are sufficient to cover the trade charges £2,000 as in this case.

   The alternative interpretation is that the amount of the loss which may be set off should be calculated as the lower of:
   - the remaining loss, or
   - (total profits less trade charges) × 9/12, that is, £21,000 [(30,000 – 2,000) × 9/12]

   Until the matter is clarified, either will be accepted in the examination. This study text will use the first alternative.

2. Excess trade charges in the loss-making accounting period are excluded from losses available for carryback and should not therefore be included in the loss memo until the end.

Suggested procedure for examination questions

Where an examination question involves a series of results at annual or other intervals, with trading losses, it is necessary to approach the question in logical steps.

1. Set out the computations for all accounting periods side by side (see examples above) taking care to note prominently the length of each accounting period.
2. Enter the Schedule D Case I taxable profits for each accounting period (losses are entered as Nil) and open up a loss memo for each loss.
3. Leave some space after the Schedule D Case I profits and then enter all other known taxable income (including chargeable gains) for each accounting period, *having first dealt with any losses arising from these sources.*
4. Commencing with the earliest accounting period in which a loss was made and working backwards, compute the total profits (before charges).
5. Decide whether a loss relief claim under s. 393A(1)(a) is to be made; if yes, consider also if the claim is to be extended to the profits of preceding accounting periods under s. 393A (1)(b). Factors to be considered:
   a) amount of non-trade charges for which relief would be lost

b) the level of current and future profits and whether tax can be saved at standard rate or higher rate as against small company's rate (see Chapter 25)
c) cash flow
d) interaction with DTR and ACT set-off (see Chapter 25)
e) group considerations (see Chapter 27).

6 Show loss claims decided upon in computations and in the loss memo.
7 Complete computations for these years adding any excess trade charges for the year in which the loss was incurred to any remaining losses to be carried forward.
8 Deduct losses for carry forward from the Schedule D Case I profits of subsequent accounting periods. *Note the carry forward of losses from previous years takes priority over losses of later years.* Enter details in loss memo.
9 Go to next accounting period in which a loss is made and repeat steps 4 to 8 above and so on.

Terminal loss relief

Terminal losses which are incurred prior to the cessation of trade will be carried back under the rules above, namely s. 393A (1) (a) and (b) with one small amendment.

Where the company has made a trade loss in an accounting period immediately prior to the cessation of trade, the company can increase the trade loss for carry back purposes by including any excess trade charges incurred in the final accounting period (ICTA 88 s. 393A(7)).

EXAMPLE 24.8

B Ltd had been a trading company for many years. It permanently ceased to trade on 31 March 1995. It had always made up accounts to 31 December. It has had the following results:

	Years ended 31 December				3 months 31 March
	1991	1992	1993	1994	1995
	£	£	£	£	£
Schedule D Case I	10,000	20,000	16,000	8,000	(50,000)
Schedule A	2,000	4,000	2,000	2,000	2,000
Charges paid: trade	1,500	1,500	2,000	2,000	500
Charges paid: non-trade	–	–	500	500	500

Corporation tax computations

Accounting periods to 31 December	1991	1992	1993	1994	3 months 31 March 1995
	£	£	£	£	£
Schedule D Case I	10,000	20,000	16,000	8,000	–
Schedule A	2,000	4,000	2,000	2,000	2,000
Total profits	12,000	24,000	18,000	10,000	2,000
Less: loss relief s. 393A(1)	n/a	(22,500)	(16,000)	(8,000)	(2,000)
	12,000	1,500	2,000	2,000	–
Less: charges	(1,500)	(1,500)	(2,000)	(2,000)	–
Profits chargeable to CT	10,500	Nil	Nil	Nil	Nil

Loss memo
(3 months 31 March 1995)

	£
Loss per accounts	50,000
Less: s 393A(1)(a) 3 months to 31 March 1995	(2,000)
Add: Excess trade charges for 3 months	500
	48,500
Less: s. 393A(1)(b) year ended 31 December 1994	(8,000)
Less: s. 393A(1)(b) year ended 31 December 1993	(16,000)
Less: s. 393A(1)(b) year ended 31 December 1992	(22,500)
Wasted (as no carryforward on cessation)	2,000

Note that there is no set-off for non-trade charges in these circumstances.

Other reliefs for trading losses

In addition to those reliefs listed above, there are two more reliefs available for trading losses:

- set off against surplus franked investment income; this is dealt with in Chapter 25.
- group relief; this is dealt with in Chapter 27.

Anti-avoidance

The carry forward of losses incurred prior to a change in ownership under ICTA 1988, s. 393(1) to accounting periods after the change in ownership is prevented by ICTA 1988, s. 768 under certain circumstances, as follows:

- within any period of three years there is both a change in ownership of a company (whenever a person/persons acquire more than half the ordinary share capital of the company) and a major change in the nature or conduct of the company's trade or business; or
- at any time after a company's business has become small or negligible and before any revival there is a change in ownership.

A major change in the nature or conduct of the company's trade or business covers, for example, a major change in customers, outlets or markets or a major change in the property, services or facilities provided.

The carry back of losses under ICTA 1988, s. 393A (1)(b) to accounting periods prior to a change in ownership is also prevented under similar circumstances.

Other losses

Capital losses

Capital losses may be set against capital gains of the same accounting period. Where capital losses exceed capital gains in any accounting period the excess capital losses are carried forward and deducted from capital gains in subsequent accounting periods. The only exception to this rule is capital losses suffered by an investment company on shares in a qualifying trading company (see below).

Schedule A losses

Schedule A losses may be set off against Schedule A income of the current or subsequent accounting periods subject to the restrictions on set-off between different types of leases (see Chapter 4).

Schedule D Case VI

Where a company makes a loss in a transaction (which would have been liable to be brought into charge to tax under Schedule D Case VI if a profit had been made), the company may claim to set off the loss against other Schedule D Case VI income of the same or first available following accounting period. The claim must be made within six years of the end of the accounting period in which the loss was incurred whether or not there is or has been any Schedule D Case VI income against which it can be set off.

Schedule D Case V

Losses incurred in a trade carried on and controlled outside the UK must be carried forward and deducted from the first available future profits of the same trade.

Examination format

It is useful to have a pro-forma layout to work to in examinations. This has to be sufficiently abbreviated in order not to waste time but also sufficiently comprehensive to serve as an *aide-memoire* for order of set-off of the various reliefs. Some of the items listed will not be expanded upon until later chapters. The layout suggested in Figure 24.1 is Part A; the second section, Part B, is given in the next chapter. You are advised to learn and use this layout.

Planning considerations

To the extent that claims for relief are made for current or earlier accounting periods, loss relief claims normally result in a repayment of corporation tax already paid or the elimination of a liability to corporation tax. Therefore, a claim for the carry forward of a loss for future relief is likely to be less attractive to a company than claims giving an immediate advantage.

Other planning considerations are linked to the consequential effects of a change in 'profits liable to corporation tax' on the overall corporation tax liability such as:

- amount of non-trade charges for which relief would be lost
- the level of current and future profits and whether tax can be saved at standard rate or higher rate against small company's rate (see Chapter 25)
- cash flow
- interaction with DTR and ACT set-off (see Chapter 25)
- group considerations (see Chapter 27).

These points should be reconsidered after you have studied the next three chapters.

Figure 24.1 Corporation tax computation – Worksheet part A

Accounting period from .... to .... *

	£	£
Schedule D Case I (if loss enter NIL)	X	
Less: losses and excess trade charges bf s. 393(1) and s. 393(9) and s. 242(5)	(X) (X)	
		X
Schedule D Case III		X
Schedule D Cases IV and V	X	
Less: losses brought forward	(X)	
		X
Schedule D Case VI	X	
Less: losses brought forward	(X)	
		X
Unfranked investment income		X
Income from which basic rate income tax *not* deducted at source by group election		X
Schedule A	X	
Less: losses brought forward	(X)	
		X
Chargeable gains	X	
Less: capital losses current year	(X)	
Less: capital losses brought forward	(X)	
		X
Total profits		X
Less: trading losses CY s. 393A(1)(a)		(X)
Less: charges paid (1) non-trade	(X)	
Less: charges paid (2) trade	(X)	
		(X)
Less: group relief s. 402		(X)
Less: **trading losses cb s. 393A(1)(b)		(X)
Profits chargeable to corporation tax (= Basic profit)		X (= I)

Basic profit + franked investment income (excluding group companies)
= Profit; (I + FII = P)

* Maximum period: 12 months.

** Note the position of this relief has been altered from that used in examples above – this is the *effective* order of set-off of reliefs against total profit. Remember trading losses carried back are deducted from total profit of previous accounting periods but without disturbing the set-off of *trade* charges of those periods. Group relief has priority over trading losses carried back. Make sure you are familiar with the computation of the amount of trading loss which can be relieved by carry back.

Summary

- A period of account is any period for which a company prepares accounts for filing with the Registrar of Companies.
- A chargeable accounting period is a period in respect of which a corporation tax assessment is raised. It must not be longer than 12 months.
- Profits liable to corporation tax are computed according to income tax principles unless the legislation provides otherwise.
- The main exceptions to income tax principles are:
  - current basis of assessment
  - capital allowances are treated as an expense in arriving at the Schedule D Case I profits
  - no private use adjustments
  - bank interest paid may be treated as an expense or a charge
  - dividends from UK companies (FII) are not taxable
  - chargeable gains are liable to corporation tax.
- A company making a trading loss in any year may claim:
  - for it to be relieved against total profits (pre charges) of that accounting period and if applicable, the profits (pre non-trade charges) of the 36 months immediately preceding such accounting period under ICTA 1988, s. 393A provided the company was trading throughout
  - for any loss remaining, or the whole of the loss if no claim was made under s. 393A, to be carried forward under ICTA 1988, s. 393(1) for deduction from the first available profits of the same trade.
- Unrelieved trade charges of the accounting period in which the loss was incurred may be added to the trading losses carried forward for deduction from the first available profits of the same trade.
- Corporation tax is assessed on the profits as a whole rather than on individual sources of income or profit
- Corporation tax rates are set for a financial year which runs from 1 April to 31 March, the year being designated by the calendar year in which April falls.
- Advance corporation tax (ACT) is payable whenever a company makes a distribution whether or not it expects to have profits chargeable to corporation tax for the accounting period.
- Mainstream corporation tax (MCT) comprises the remainder of the corporation tax liability after deducting, subject to certain restrictions, any ACT paid.

Self test questions

1. A Ltd changes its accounting date and prepares accounts for 1 December 1993 to 31 March 1995. How will its trading profits be assessed to corporation tax?

2. B Ltd was formed and shares were allotted on 1 August 1992 when a deposit account was opened. Trading commenced 1 November 1992. Accounts were prepared to 31 December 1993. It ceased trading 30 April 1994. A liquidator was appointed 1 June 1994. What are the accounting periods of B Ltd?

3. Summarise the principal provisions relating to residence of a company.

4. What do you understand by central management and control?

5. A Ltd prepares its accounts for the twelve months to 31 December 1994. State the financial years which affect this accounting period.

6. A company commenced trading on 1 October 1993. It purchased a car for £15,000 for the use of the director (private use approximately 25%). Compute the capital allowances for the accounting period ended 30 June 1994.

7   B Ltd, a trading company, purchased a 20-year lease on new business premises for £30,000 on 1 August 1994. B Ltd prepares accounts to 31 December each year. How will the purchase of the lease be treated for tax purposes?

8   C Ltd, a trading company, prepared accounts to 31 December each year. On 1 January 1994 a car is hired with a cost price of £15,000 at a cost of £7,000 per annum. What is the allowable Schedule D Case I expense?

9   Define franked investment income.

10 What is the latest date by which a claim for loss relief under ICTA 1988, s. 393A(1)(a) must be made in respect of a trading loss suffered in the year ending 30 June 1994?

11 List the various types of relief for trading losses available to a company (not ceasing to trade).

12 The records of Scotia Circuits Ltd, a manufacturing electronics company, contain the following information for the year to 30 September 1994

Trading profit	£311,000
after debiting:	£
Audit fees	6,200
Depreciation	27,800
Plant hiring charges (note 1)	18,000
Property expenses (note 2)	8,800
Legal expenses (note 5)	9,550
Directors' remuneration	95,000
and after crediting:	
UK company dividends (cash received)	12,600
Rental income (note 2)	16,400
Insurance recovery (note 4)	36,800
Profit on sale of shares	16,000

Notes

	£
1 Hiring charges – general machinery	10,000
– car	8,000

(the car, costing £30,000, was hired for the use of the managing director).

2   Property charges – Scotia Circuits Ltd purchased an office block as an investment for £80,000 in August 1993. It was leased to tenants at £4,100 per calendar quarter from 1 September 1993. The rental payments due in June and September 1994 were not received until 20 October 1994. The roof was damaged in a storm in January 1994: estimated repair costs were £1,800. The company, however, expended a total of £4,200 including extensions to the attic storage space. Rates and insurance were £4,600.

3   Scotia Circuits Ltd had the following dealings on the United Kingdom Stock Exchange in the shares of British Dynamics plc:

   10 February 1982   purchased   12,000 shares for £24,000
   6 September 1988   purchased   4,000 shares for £8,000
   14 January 1994   sold   16,000 shares for £48,000

Value of shares at 31 March 1982 was estimated at £1.75 each.

4   Insurance recovery – a London showroom was damaged by fire in April 1994; the full amount received was:

   Building   £20,000
   Plant/machinery   £1,800
   Stock in trade   £15,000

5   Legal expenses   £
    Expenses of insurance claim   1,600
    Purchase of let property – under-provided 1993   1,500
    Purchase of Liverpool (Speke) building   4,000
    Contracts of service for directors   1,000
    Expenses of debenture issue on 29 September 1994:

	£
Solicitor's expenses	600
Printing	210
Broker's fee	190
Stamp duty	450
	1,450

6   Scotia Circuits Ltd completed a showroom and administration office in Liverpool (Speke), an enterprise zone, on 3 May 1994 for £35,000.

7   The written down value for capital allowances at 30 September 1993 was – plant and machinery £17,800 and cars £8,400. Plant and similar purchased on 7 March 1994 was £24,000.

Compute the profits chargeable to corporation tax.

13 Barrel Ltd prepares its accounts to 31 December each year. It was decided to change the accounting date of Barrel Ltd to 31 March each year commencing with a fifteen-month period to 31 March 1992.

The results of Barrel Ltd are given below:

	15 months 31 March 1992	Year 31 March 1993	Year 31 March 1994	Year 31 March 1995
	£	£	£	£
Schedule D Case I profit/loss	40,000	30,000	25,000	(90,000)
Schedule D Case III	2,500	1,000	4,000	500
Chargeable gains less losses	–	2,000	10,000	–
Debenture interest paid 31 December (gross)	5,000	5,000	5,000	5,000
Charitable deed of covenant paid 31 December (gross)	500	500	500	500

Calculate the profits chargeable to corporation tax in each of the above years, assuming all reliefs are claimed as early as possible.

Answers on pages 611–613

Computation of the Corporation Tax Liability and its Collection

CHAPTER 25

This chapter deals with the second and final stage in the corporation tax computation. The gross corporation tax liability on the profits chargeable to corporation tax is computed, and the manner in which it will be discharged under Pay and File is considered in conjunction with the penalties for overdue tax and the repayment supplement. Once again a thorough understanding of the company decisions which may influence this computation is essential to students who may then use this knowledge to best advantage in tax planning.

Liability to corporation tax

The rates of corporation tax as set out in Chapter 24 are repeated below:

	Financial year 1991	Financial year 1992	Financial year 1993	Financial year 1994
Standard rate	33%	33%	33%	33%
Small companies rate (SCR)	25%	25%	25%	25%
Lower limit	£250,000	£250,000	£250,000	£300,000
Upper limit	£1,250,000	£1,250,000	£1,250,000	£1,500,000
Marginal relief fraction	1/50	1/50	1/50	1/50

Remember that the rates are applied for the financial year which runs from 1 April to 31 March.

EXAMPLE 25.1

A Ltd has the following results for the year ended 31 December 1994:

	£
Schedule D Case I	1,600,000
Schedule A	20,000
Chargeable gains	50,000
Debenture interest (gross) paid	10,000

Worksheet – Part A (See Figure 24.1)

	£
Schedule D Case I	1,600,000
Schedule A	20,000
Chargeable gains	50,000
Total profits	1,670,000
Less: Debenture interest	(10,000)
Profits chargeable to CT	1,660,000

Corporation tax liability

		£
FY 1993	(1 January 1994 – 31 March 1994)	
	£1,660,000 × 3/12 × 33%	136,950
FY 1994	(1 April 1994 – 31 December 1994)	
	£1,660,000 × 9/12 × 33%	410,850
		547,800

Note that as the rates for both years have remained the same, an acceptable (and easier) alternative would be: £1,660,000 × 33% = £547,800.

Small company rate

The small company rate is applied to the 'basic profits' of a company whose 'profits' fall below a certain limit (FY 1994 £300,000) for a 12-month accounting period. If the company is part of a group of companies (see later chapter), the limit is shared equally between all members of the group (companies dormant throughout the accounting period are ignored).

▶ Basic profits (I) are the profits chargeable to corporation tax (refer to Worksheet – Part A in previous chapter)
▶ Profits (P) are the basic profits above plus franked investment income (FII).

For this purpose any franked investment income from a group company (see Chapter 27) is ignored.

EXAMPLE 25.2

B Ltd, not a member of a group, has the following results for the nine-month accounting period to 31 December 1994:

	£
Schedule D Case I	55,000
Schedule A	10,000
Chargeable gains	2,000
Franked investment income	10,000
Debenture interest (gross) paid	5,000

Worksheet – Part A

	£
Schedule D Case I	55,000
Schedule A	10,000
Chargeable gains	2,000
Total profits	67,000
Less: Debenture interest	(5,000)
Profits chargeable to CT	62,000

Basic profits (I) = Profits chargeable to CT = £62,000
Profits (P) = Profits chargeable to CT+FII = £72,000
limit for small companies rate £300,000 × 9/12 = £225,000
P (£72,000) less than £225,000; therefore SCR applies to I

Corporation tax liability

	£
FY 1994 (1 April 1994–31 December 1994)	
£62,000 × 25%	15,500

Marginal relief

Small companies rate does not apply to companies whose profits (*P*) exceed the annual limit of £300,000 (FY 1994). To lessen the impact of the differential between small companies rate and standard rate, there is a relief for companies whose profits (*P*) fall between defined limits (FY 1994 £300,000 and £1,500,000) for a 12-month period per group of companies. Relief is given by charging basic profit (I) to tax at standard rate corporation tax and calculating and deducting taper relief according to the formula:

$$(M - P) \times \frac{I}{P} \times \text{marginal relief fraction}$$

- where *M* is the upper limit (that is £1.5 million for the 12-month accounting period, with the company not a member of a group)
- where *I* is the basic profits
- where *P* is the basic profits + franked investment income
- where marginal relief fraction is the fraction for the financial year as stated in the relevant Finance Act.

EXAMPLE 25.3

C Ltd, not a member of a trading group, has the following results for the year ended 31 March 1995.

	£
Schedule D Case I	300,000
Unfranked investment income	10,000
Chargeable gain	15,000
Franked investment income	25,000
Debenture interest paid (gross)	5,000

Worksheet – Part A

	£
Schedule D Case I	300,000
UFII	10,000
Chargeable gain	15,000
Total profits	325,000
Less: Debenture interest	(5,000)
Profits chargeable to CT	320,000

Basic profits (*I*) = Profits chargeable to CT = £320,000
Profits (*P*) = Profits chargeable to CT + FII = £345,000
Lower limit: £300,000
Upper limit: £1,500,000
£300,000 less than *P* (£345,000) < £1.5 million therefore standard rate CT applies to *I* with taper relief.

Corporation tax liability

		£
FY 1994 (1 April 1994–31 March 1995)		
£320,000 × 33%		105,600.00
Less: taper relief		
FY 1994: $(1,500,000 - 345,000) \times \dfrac{320,000}{345,000} \times \dfrac{1}{50}$		(21,426.09)
		84,173.91

Where the accounting period falls into more than one financial year (when the upper and lower limits may change as well as the rates of tax and the taper relief fraction) and the company is a member of a trading group or the period of account is less than 12 months, the calculations can become quite cumbersome. The following example illustrates the strict procedure which should be followed. Note that in financial years where only some of the abovementioned variables change there are shorter methods.

EXAMPLE 25.4

D Ltd, a member of a trading group with one other group member, has the following results for the year ended 31 December 1994:

	£
Schedule D Case I	300,000
Unfranked investment income	10,000
Chargeable gain	15,000
Franked investment income	25,000
Debenture interest paid (gross)	5,000

Worksheet – Part A

	£
Schedule D Case I	300,000
UFII	10,000
Chargeable gain	15,000
Total profits	325,000
Less: Debenture interest	(5,000)
Profits chargeable to CT (basic profit)	£320,000

	FY 1993	FY 1994
	£	£
Basic profits (l) = £320,000	80,000	240,000
Profits (P) = basic profit + FII = £345,000	86,250	258,750
Lower limit £250,000 × 3/12 × 1/2	31,250	
£300,000 × 9/12 × 1/2		112,500
Upper limit £1,250,000 × 3/12 × 1/2	156,250	
£1,500,000 × 9/12 × 1/2		562,500

FY 1993 P £86,250 > £31,250 but < £156,250
FY 1994 P £258,750 > £112,500 but < £562,500
therefore standard CT rate applies to l with taper relief in both cases.

Corporation tax liability

	£
FY 1993 (1 Jan 1994–31 Mar 1994) £80,000 × 33%	26,400.00
FY 1994 (1 Apr 1994–31 Dec 1994) £240,000 × 33%	79,200.00
	105,600.00
Less: Taper relief	
FY 1993 (156,250 − 86,250) × $\dfrac{80,000}{86,250}$ × $\dfrac{1}{50}$	(1,298.55)
FY 1994 (562,500 − 258,750) × $\dfrac{240,000}{258,750}$ × $\dfrac{1}{50}$	(5,634.78)
	98,666.67

When profits (P) lie between the lower and upper limit, it is important to appreciate the implications in terms of the marginal tax rate.

Corporation tax, unlike income tax, is not a progressive rate of tax. This means that once the upper limit has been exceeded, all profits, not just those in excess of the upper limit, are taxable at standard rate corporation tax. Therefore, the average rate of tax gradually increases from 25% to 33% for profits between the lower and upper limit; for FY 1994 this gives an effective marginal tax rate of 35% (FY 1993 35%) for profits within this band if the company has no franked investment income.

EXAMPLE 25.5

If a company's basic profits are £350,000 with no franked investment income, illustrate for the financial year 1994 the net cost of making a further £10,000 contribution to the company pension scheme.

Financial year 1994	Before £		After £
Taxable profit	350,000	Taxable profit	340,000
Corporation tax 33%	115,500	Corporation tax 33%	112,200
Taper relief: $(1,500,000 - 350,000) \times \frac{1}{1} \times \frac{1}{50}$	(23,000)	Taper relief: $(1,500,000 - 340,000) \times \frac{1}{1} \times \frac{1}{50}$	(23,200)
	92,500		89,000
Tax saving £3,500	Pension cost £10,000		Net cost £6,500
Marginal rate of tax	$\frac{92,500 - 89,000}{10,000} = 35\%$		

Significant advantage can therefore be obtained through judicious timing of payments (such as an employer's contributions to a pension scheme) to a particular accounting period or the judicious use of loss relief, in order to save tax at a high marginal rate.

Payment of the corporation tax liability

The payment of the corporation tax liability may be split in two main parts:

- advance corporation tax (ACT)
- mainstream corporation tax (MCT) – the balance.

The payment of ACT is solely dependent upon the amount of distributions made and received in the accounting period and has nothing at all to do with the existence or non-existence of profits chargeable to corporation tax. The factors affecting the payment of ACT and the timing thereof are considered below.

Any ACT paid or payable in respect of an accounting period may, within limits, be deducted from the total corporation tax liability alongside a number of other reliefs. The remaining liability is known as mainstream corporation tax (MCT). The method and timing of this payment is considered below.

Pay and file

The system for paying corporation tax and for filing corporation tax returns is known as Pay and File. This system began on 1 October 1993 and is effective for all accounting periods ending on or after 1 October 1993.

Pay and file is designed largely to do away with the need for estimated assessments, appeals and delay hearings before the General Commissioners. It is also intended to improve the Revenue's cash flow. The aim is to put onto companies the onus to pay their corporation tax (estimated, if necessary) by the due and payable date, without prior assessment. A regime of automatic interest and penalties is triggered for delays beyond this.

The corporation tax return

The corporation tax return (CT200) is computational in style. Companies are required to make the return on receipt of notice (usually served about three months after the end of the accounting period). The filing date for the return is usually 12 months from the end of the accounting period. If a company has profits chargeable to tax for the accounting period but has not been served notice, it has an obligation within 12 months of the end of the accounting period to notify the Inspector. Companies must use the return form provided by the Inland Revenue or have a substitute version officially approved. The form is several pages in length with detailed guidance notes for completion, but the level of detail required does not amount to more than the standard corporation tax computation done by practitioners under the previous arrangements. Accounts and schedules to support individual entries on the return must be submitted. The CT200 should be signed by an authorised company official.

If final figures are not available by the time the return is due, the company should enter its best estimates with a covering letter. This will be regarded as satisfying its filing obligation. Final figures should be submitted as soon as they become available.

Capital allowances and group relief

Pay and file introduced a new system for claiming capital allowances (see Chapter 24) and group relief (see Chapter 27). Claims are made in the corporation tax return and must be for an exact amount; if they need to be revised or withdrawn this must be done in an 'amended return form' before the time limit for the claim has expired.

The normal time limit will be the later of:

- two years from the end of the accounting period of the claimant company
- the date on which the profits for the accounting period are finally determined (maximum 6 years after the end of the accounting period).

Normal due date for payment of mainstream corporation tax

The mainstream corporation tax liability for an accounting period is due and payable nine months and one day after the end of the accounting period.

Companies are expected to estimate and pay the corporation tax liability by this date – a payslip and envelope will normally be sent to the company about three months after the end of an accounting period. Reminders will also be issued as the normal due date approaches.

If the company subsequently finds that the amount paid was too small, it should make a further payment as soon as this becomes apparent without waiting for a demand or assessment to be issued.

Issue of assessments

If the tax has not been paid when the return is submitted, the Inland Revenue will take formal proceedings to collect the declared liability. If the Inspector considers that the liability should be more than this, he must issue an estimated assessment. He will also issue an estimated assessment if:

- the company fails to submit a return within 18 months of the end of the accounting period
- there is a dispute about the tax due which needs to be referred to the Commissioners
- the six-year time limit for making assessments is about to pass.

The general provisions for appealing against assessments and applying to postpone tax as already examined under income tax apply to appeals against assessments to corporation tax, payments on account and applications for postponement of tax assessed.

Determination of loss

Once the amount of the loss is agreed, a notice of determination of the amount will be issued to the company (and agent) by the Inspector. This fixes the amount of the loss and any claims for its use cannot exceed this amount. The amount determined will take into account claims submitted in the normal manner for loss relief under s. 393A (1) (a) and (b).

The company will have a right of appeal against the 'determination of loss'.

If the Inspector 'discovers' that the loss determination is excessive, he can issue a direction to reduce the amount in the determination of the loss notice. This is the equivalent of issuing a further assessment.

Interest and penalties

Interest

Interest on underpayments will be calculated from the normal due date to the date paid and interest on overpayments will be paid from the normal due date (or date of payment if later) irrespective of whether an assessment has been raised. The repayment rate of interest (linked to the average return on lending) will be at a lower rate than that on late payments (linked to the average rate of borrowing). Groups of companies (see Chapter 27) will be able to transfer tax overpayments from one group company to another with the same accounting date and therefore minimise the group loss through the differential rates. Where claims are subsequently made which amend a corporation tax liability but also have consequential effects re other set-offs (such as carry back of losses under s. 393 A(1)(b) – see Chapter 24) the interest rules will reflect the original liability outstanding up to the date for the later period when the loss claim arose. A repayment of corporation tax arising from a s. 393 A claim is treated as arising as follows:

- Where the trading loss is carried back under s. 393A and set off wholly against the 12 month accounting period preceding the loss-making period, the repayment is treated as being of that earlier period's corporation tax.
- Where the trading loss is carried back under s. 393A and set off outwith the 12 month period preceding the loss-making period, the repayment is deemed to be a repayment of tax for the loss-making accounting period.

Penalties

Penalties are chargeable for late filing and will arise automatically with no need for proceedings in court or before the Commissioners to implement them. These cannot be mitigated but a 'reasonable excuse' claim may be accepted. The amount of the penalty will depend on a number of factors:

- how late the return is
- the amount of tax paid
- the company's previous history of filing returns on time.

A penalty will not be exacted if the company has permission to file late with the Registrar of Companies (the tax regime will adopt the same date), additional time for submission has previously been agreed with the Inspector, or reasonable excuse exists (this would need to be exceptional in view of the time allowed for filing).

The fixed penalties are as follows:

- Up to 3 months late: £100
- Over 3 months late: £200

These amounts are increased to £500 and £1,000 for returns delivered late for the third successive accounting period.

Tax-geared penalties in addition to the fixed penalty will be levied where the return is later than 18 months after the end of the accounting period and the filing date has passed. This could amount to 10% of the unpaid tax for periods up to 24 months and 20% for periods over 24 months. Unpaid tax is the corporation tax unpaid less credit for income tax deducted at source which can be set off against that liability. If the tax has already been paid and it is merely the return that has not been submitted, then there will be no tax-geared penalty.

The penalties for fraudulent or negligent returns are as outlined in Chapter 22.

Company distributions

Whenever a company makes a qualifying distribution (often referred to as an income distribution) it must account for advance corporation tax at the appropriate rate to the Inland Revenue.

The meaning of qualifying distribution for this purpose is necessarily wide and aims to cover *all* payments to members other than repayments of capital (in other words, distributions are not simply dividends). The legislation lists those payments not regarded as qualifying distributions rather than specifically defining qualifying distributions.

Non-qualifying distributions

A non-qualifying distribution is one which potentially, but not immediately, depletes the assets of the company. It does not lead to the payment of ACT (but the Inspector of Taxes must be informed within 14 days). An example would be a bonus issue of redeemable shares. The effect on the assets of the company would be nil on issue but on their redemption, there would be a qualifying distribution.

The following are specifically excluded from being qualifying distributions:

- bonus issues and repayments or reductions of capital when carried out independently (but note that when they are coupled together a qualifying distribution may arise)
- distributions made in respect of shares during the winding-up or liquidation of a company (these are capital distributions and from the shareholder's point of view represent disposals of his or her shares for capital gains tax)
- purchase of own shares if the circumstances fit those approved by s. 219–229 ICTA 1988 (see Chapter 28)
- distributions made as a result of an approved demerger.

Qualifying distributions

The following are examples of qualifying distributions:

- dividends
- distributions in specie from a company's assets in respect of shares other than capital repayments

- issue of redeemable shares or securities unless new consideration is received for the issue
- interest payments over and above a reasonable commercial rate
- other payments not satisfying the conditions for non-qualifying distributions above.

Advance corporation tax (ACT)

Franked payments (FP)

A company making a qualifying distribution must account for advance corporation tax (ACT) at the rate of 20/80 (1/4) of the amount of distributions from 6 April 1994 to 5 April 1995 (the rate was previously 22.5/77.5 in FY1993, and 25/75 in FY1992). The total of the distribution and the ACT is called a franked payment. The rate of ACT, previously, linked to the basic rate of income tax at the date of payment, is now after 5 April 1994 linked to the lower rate of income tax such that the proportion of ACT in the franked payment equals the lower rate of income tax.

EXAMPLE 25.6

X Ltd pays a dividend of £30,000 in September 1994
ACT would be due of (30,000 × 20/80) = £7,500
Franked payment would be (£30,000 + £7,500) = £37,500
It should be noted that ACT may be calculated in one of two ways:

- by applying the appropriate fraction to the amount of the distribution thus:

    1994/95 $\dfrac{\text{Lower rate income tax}}{100 - \text{lower rate income tax}}$ $\dfrac{(20)}{(80)}$

- By taking the appropriate percentage of the franked payment, that is; 1994/95 20%.

Franked investment income (FII)

As already mentioned, this is the term applied to the total of a qualifying distribution received from another UK company and the tax credit. It is so called because it is paid out of profits which have been 'franked', that is, charged to corporation tax. Franked investment income must be determined on two separate occasions for corporation tax purposes. Franked investment income is not chargeable to corporation tax in the hands of the recipient company since it is regarded as already having suffered corporation tax. The tax credit will normally on both occasions be equal to the amount of advance corporation tax paid by the company in respect of the distribution (1994/95 20/80 of the distribution) but for 1993/94 this was not the case. In 1993/94 companies paid ACT at the rate 22.5/77.5 of the distribution, but the tax credit given to the recipient (and for determining individuals' income tax liabilities) was 20/80 of the distribution.

EXAMPLE 25.7

	£
Dividend received from a UK company September 1993	30,000
Tax credit (20/80 × 30,000)	7,500
Franked investment income (for the purposes of determining 'P')	37,500

The tax credit, however, to be set off against the company's liability to pay advance corporation tax in 1993/94 or in a subsequent accounting period will normally match (and therefore cancel) the advance corporation tax payable on an equivalent dividend paid on the same date. For this purpose, therefore, for 1993/94 only the tax credit is deemed to be 22.5/77.5 of the distribution received. For 1994/95 it is 20/80 of the distribution received.

EXAMPLE 25.7 (continued)

	£
Dividend received from a UK company September 1993	30,000
Tax credit (22.5/77.5 × 30,000)	8,710
Franked investment income (for purposes of determining ACT payable)	38,710

It is important to understand at this stage the role played by the tax credit and whether the company gains any real benefit and if so, exactly how.

EXAMPLE 25.8

X Ltd expects to have a corporation tax liability of £50,000 based on its profits for the year ended 31 March 1995. As a result of paying a dividend of £30,000 it has a liability for advance corporation tax of £7,500. Consider the mainstream corporation tax liability if:

a) X Ltd has no UK dividend income during the year, or
b) X Ltd has UK dividend income of £10,000. Tax credit for ACT offset purposes £2,500 (10,000 × 20/80) and therefore FII for this purpose will be £12,500.

	(a) £			(b) £		
Corporation tax liability			50,000			50,000
Less: FII	37,500			37,500		
less tax credit	–			(12,500)		
ACT paid	37,500	@ 20%	(7,500)	25,000	@ 20%	(5,000)
Mainstream corporation tax			42,500			45,000

This example illustrates that although the tax credit reduced the ACT liability by £2,500, the result was a corresponding increase in the mainstream corporation tax liability of £2,500. Since ACT is payable very much earlier than MCT, the benefit from the tax credit on franked investment income is merely a cash flow advantage. There is no permanent reduction in the overall tax burden unless the ACT that would otherwise have been payable would be 'irrecoverable'(see below).

Accounting for advance corporation tax

A company is required to account for ACT on the calendar quarters (31 March, 30 June, 30 September, and 31 December) and if one of these dates does not coincide with the company's year end, then on the year end date also. The Inland Revenue form used for this purpose is called a CT61Z. The form must be submitted within 14 days of the end of the return period and, where ACT is payable, a cheque should accompany it. Interest on unpaid tax arises on payments made after the due date.

For any return period the amount of ACT payable/(recoverable) is given by:

Cumulative FP for accounting period to date	X
Less: Cumulative FII for accounting period to date	(X)
Less: Surplus FII b/f from previous accounting period	(X)
Excess of FP over FII for accounting period	X
@ 25/22.5/20% as appropriate* gives:	
ACT due for year to date	X
(if FP not greater than FII, ACT due = nil)	
Less: ACT already paid in year to date	(X)
ACT payable/(repayable) for current return period	X

* previously this line could have been described as 'basic rate income tax' and from 5 April 1994 it is described as 'lower rate income tax' but in FII 1993, neither description fits.

At the end of the accounting period the net ACT due for the year (that is, incorporating any amount payable/(repayable) 14 days after the year end), if any, may be set off against the corporation tax liability for the year within certain limits (see below). If no ACT is due and FII for the year plus any amount brought forward from the previous year exceeds FP for the year, the excess, called surplus FII, must be carried forward to the next accounting period.

EXAMPLE 25.9

A company which makes up its accounts annually to 31 January made and received the following distributions in the year ended 31 January 1995 (assume that the rate of ACT throughout was 20%):

			£
15 March	Received dividend from X Ltd		8,000
30 June	Paid final dividend year ended 31 Jan 1994		16,000
22 Nov	Received dividend from X Ltd		9,600

Return period	FP	FII	Cumulative net (FP–FII)	ACT due to date @ 20%	ACT paid	ACT payable/ (repayable)
1 February–31 March	–	10,000				
	–	10,000	(10,000)	Nil	Nil	Nil
1 April–30 June	20,000	–				
	20,000	10,000	10,000	2,000	Nil	2,000 (14 July)
1 July–30 September	–	–	Nil Return			
1 October–31 December	–	12,000				
	20,000	22,000	(2,000)	Nil	2,000	(2,000)
1 January–31 January	–	–		Nil Return		
	20,000	22,000	(2,000)	Nil	Nil	Nil

For the year ended 31 January 1995, franked investment income (FII) exceeded franked payments (FP) by £2,000. This is surplus FII and will be carried forward to the next accounting period. Meanwhile, ACT paid on or before 14 July 1994 was repaid (or is repayable) sometime after 14 January 1995, and therefore no ACT was due for the year ended 31 January 1995.

EXAMPLE 25.10

A company which makes up its accounts annually to 31 December made and received the following distributions in the year ended 31 December 1994 and had surplus FII brought forward at 1 January 1993 of £5,000. Assume again that the rate of ACT was 20% throughout:

		£
15 March	Received dividend from X Ltd	8,000
30 June	Paid final dividend year ended 31 Dec 1993	24,000
2 Nov	Received dividend from X Ltd	9,600

Return period	FP	FII	Cumulative net (FP–FII)	ACT due to date @ 20%	ACT paid	ACT payable/ (repayable)
b/f	–	5,000				
1 January–31 March	–	10,000				
	–	15,000	(15,000)	Nil	Nil	Nil
1 April–30 June	30,000	–				
	30,000	15,000	15,000	3,000	Nil	3,000 (14 July)
1 July–30 September	–	–		Nil return		
1 October–31 December	–	12,000				
	30,000	27,000	3,000	600	3,000	(2,400)

For the year ended 31 December 1994, franked payments (FP) exceeded franked investment income (FII) by £3,000 and therefore ACT of £600 (£3,000 @ 20%) was due for the year ended 31 December 1994. An amount of £3,000 had been paid on or before 14 July and part of this (£2,400) would be repayable by the Inland Revenue upon receipt of the return for the period ended 31 December (due to be submitted on or before 14 January 1995).

Change in rate of ACT

Where the rate of income tax to which ACT is linked changes on 6 April following the Budget, a corresponding adjustment must be made to the rate of ACT. In 1993/94 and 1994/95 the changeover from linking ACT to basic rate income tax to linking it to lower rate income tax follows the same procedure.

The period 1 April to 5 April is treated as a separate return period and ACT is accounted for cumulatively from:

▶ the beginning of the accounting period to 5 April
▶ 6 April to the end of the accounting period

as if 5 April were the end of an accounting period. Franked investment income received after 5 April cannot cause ACT paid before 6 April to be repaid. If franked investment income before 6 April exceeds franked payments before 6 April then the 'surplus FII' is carried forward to the period after 5 April.

EXAMPLE 25.11

This example uses the same information as the previous example, but assumes ACT at the rate of 22.5% to 5 April and 20% thereafter.

Return period	FP	FII	Cumulative net (FP–FII)	ACT due to date @ 22.5%	ACT paid	ACT payable/ (repayable)
b/f		5,000				
1 January–31 March	–	10,323				
	–	15,323	(15,323)	Nil	Nil	Nil
1 April–5 April	–	–		Nil return		
	–	15,323	15,323	Nil	Nil	Nil
b/f		15,323		@ 20%		
6 April–30 June	30,000	–				
	30,000	15,323	14,677	2,935	Nil	2,935 (14 July)
1 July–30 September	–	–		Nil return		
1 October–31 December	–	12,000				
	30,000	27,323	2,677	535	2,935	(2,400)

For the period to 5 April, the franked investment income (FII) was added to the surplus FII brought forward at 1 January and the new total was able to be carried forward to the 6 April as it would be if 5 April were the end of an accounting period. Note that it is very important to carry forward FII and not the dividends received or the individual tax credits as the new tax rate is applied to the surplus FII carried forward.

EXAMPLE 25.12

A company which makes up its accounts annually to 31 December made and received the following distributions in the year ended 31 December 1994 (ACT at the rate of 22.5% applies to 5 April and 20% thereafter).

		£
31 March	Paid final dividend year ended 31 Dec 1993	31,000
15 April	Received dividend from X Ltd	8,000
22 Nov	Received dividend from X Ltd	9,600

Return period	FP	FII	Cumulative net (FP–FII)	ACT due to date @ 22.5%	ACT paid	ACT payable/ (repayable)
1 January–31 March	40,000					
	40,000	–	40,000	9,000	Nil	9,000 (14 April)
1 April–5 April		–	–			Nil return
	40,000	–	40,000	9,000	9,000	Nil
				20%		
6 April–30 June	–	10,000				
	–	10,000	(10,000)	Nil	Nil	Nil
1 July–30 September				Nil Return		
1 October–31 December	–	12,000				
	–	22,000	(22,000)	Nil	Nil	Nil

COMPUTATION OF THE CORPORATION TAX LIABILITY AND ITS COLLECTION

The ACT paid for the period to 5 April cannot be repaid when franked investment income is received after 5 April. There is therefore ACT paid in the accounting period which can be set off against the corporation tax liability for the accounting period and there is surplus franked investment income to carry forward to the following accounting period.

Income tax

As for individuals, companies who pay retainable annual charges must deduct basic rate income tax at source from the payment and subsequently pay it over to the Inland Revenue. We saw in the previous section that for the purposes of accounting for advance corporation tax each accounting period is divided into quarterly return periods. The return of retainable annual charges and income tax payable is made by reference to the same return periods and is made on the same Inland Revenue form (CT61Z). As with ACT, the return form and any income tax payable are due 14 days from the end of the return period. Interest on unpaid tax arises on payments made after the due date.

The company is liable to pay to the Collector income tax at basic rate which has been deducted from any relevant payments (UFP) made but, it may claim to set off against this amount any income tax which the company has suffered by deduction from its unfranked investment income (UFII).

Typical payments and receipts by a company which are subjected to retention of basic rate income tax at source are debenture interest, government stock interest, patent royalties, covenanted payments and qualifying donations to charity.

If a company pays income tax to the Collector in respect of an unfranked payment in one return period and in a subsequent return period *within the same accounting period* suffers income tax deduction at source on unfranked investment income, the company may claim a repayment of income tax on form CT61Z (limited to the amount of income tax already paid in the accounting period). Any income tax suffered on unfranked investment income on which a repayment is not claimed through form CT61Z (because it is in excess of the income tax paid in the accounting period) may be deducted at the end of the accounting period from the mainstream corporation tax liability. (See above – definition of unpaid tax 'Pay and File')

No amounts of income tax or UFII or UFP are carried forward to the next accounting period.

EXAMPLE 25.13

A company prepares accounts to 31 March each year. On 25 April 1994, it pays debenture interest on £10,000 nine per cent debentures and on 5 September 1994, it receives interest on £15,000 eight per cent Treasury Stock.

Return period	UFP	UFII	Cumulative net (UFP–UFII)	IT due to date @ 25%	IT paid	IT payable/ (repayable)
1 April–30 June	900	–				
	900	–	900	225	–	225 (14 July)
1 July–30 September	–	1,200				
	900	1,200	(300)	Nil	225	(225)
1 October–31 December						Nil Return
1 January–31 March						Nil Return
	900	1,200	(300)	Nil	Nil	Nil

The situation for the accounting period as a whole is shown by looking at the totals. Unfranked payments (UFP) £900 were less than unfranked investment income (UFII) £1,200, meaning that all income tax retained on payments and paid to the Collector on or before 14 July has been reclaimed (and hopefully repaid) against the income tax suffered on unfranked investment income and there is a further £300 which has suffered income tax deducted at source, on which the income tax has not yet been recovered (£300 @ 25% = £75). This will be deductible from the corporation tax liability for the accounting period ended 31 March 1995.

The computation of MCT

Mainstream corporation tax is the corporation tax liability remaining after all possible double tax relief, advance corporation tax (ACT), and income tax suffered by deduction at source have been set off.

Set-off of double tax relief

The computation of the amount of double tax relief available in any situation is dealt with in the section on overseas matters. However, once calculated, it must be deducted from the corporation tax liability attributable to the relevant source of income and it is restricted to that amount. (The company may choose the source of income against which it deducts charges paid and other reliefs.)

EXAMPLE 25.14

W Ltd is a UK company which conducts business in the UK and through an overseas branch. Its results for the year ended 31 March 1995 are as follows, assuming that standard rate corporation tax applies:

	£
Schedule D Case I (UK)	500,000
Schedule D Case I (foreign branch) (foreign tax £40,000)	100,000
Profits chargeable to CT	600,000

	UK trade	Foreign branch trade	Total
	£	£	£
Trading income	500,000	100,000	600,000
	£	£	£
Corporation tax 33%	165,000	33,000	198,000
Double tax relief deducted from relevant income	–	(33,000)	(33,000)
	165,000	–	165,000

Set-off of advance corporation tax

ACT is a payment in advance of mainstream corporation tax. It is reasonable to expect that the full amount of ACT paid by reference to a particular accounting period would automatically be set off against the corporation tax liability of the same accounting period. This is not always the case. In certain circumstances the amount of ACT that may be deducted is restricted.

Maximum set-off

The maximum permissible ACT set-off is an amount which when added to a qualifying distribution equals the profits chargeable to corporation tax (*I*) for that accounting period.

Expressed another way, the maximum ACT that can be set off in arriving at a company's mainstream corporation tax liability is an amount equal to the profits chargeable to CT (*I*) for the accounting period at the appropriate ACT rate.

The set-off is further restricted to the amount of corporation tax payable on each individual source of a company's taxable profits. This may be illustrated by continuing Example 25.14.

EXAMPLE 25.14 (continued)

Profits chargeable to CT	600,000
Maximum permissible ACT set-off (600,000 @ 20%)	120,000

But when the individual sources of income are considered, a further restriction arises as a result of double tax relief already having been given:

	UK trade	Foreign branch trade	Total
	£	£	£
Trading income	500,000	100,000	600,000
	£	£	£
Corporation tax 33%	165,000	33,000	198,000
Double tax relief deducted from relevant income	–	(33,000)	(33,000)
	165,000	–	165,000
Maximum act set-off			
500,000 @ 20%	100,000		
100,000 @ 20%		Nil	100,000

No ACT can be set off against the tax due on the foreign income as the double tax relief given reduces the liability on this source of income to nil.

If the above company had received dividends of £3,000 and paid a dividend of £420,000 during the accounting period, the ACT paid in relation to the accounting period would be:

525,000 (FP) – 3,750 (FII) @ 20% £104,250

Since this is greater than the maximum permissible set-off, £4,250 (104,250 – 100,000) would remain. This amount is called 'surplus ACT' (see below).

Change in rate of ACT during the accounting period

The computation of the maximum ACT set-off for any accounting period is further affected by a change in rate of income tax and consequently, in the rate of ACT during the accounting period. The 1993/94 and 1994/95 changes to the rate of ACT result in the same procedure. The result can be illustrated as follows:

Corporation tax liability (year end 31 December 1994)		
FY 1993 (3 months) $I \times 3/12$ @ 33%		X
FY 1994 (9 months) $I \times 9/12$ @ 33%		X
		X
Less: ACT		
Maximum FY 1993 $I \times 3/12 \times 22.5\%$	X	
Maximum FY 1994 $I \times 9/12 \times 20\%$	X	
A	X	
Paid in year 1/1/94–5/4/94 (FP–FII) 22.5%	X	
6/4/94–31/12/94 (FP–FII) 20%	X	
B	X	
Set off lower of above amounts (A or B)		(X)

EXAMPLE 25.15

ABC Ltd makes up its accounts to 30 September. In the year to 30 September 1994, the company had trading profits of £1,032,000 and in addition made and received the following distributions:

		£
15 January	Paid dividend for year ended 30 September 1993	620,000
31 March	Received dividends from X Ltd	77,500
30 April	Received dividends from Y Ltd	96,000

Return period	FP	FII	Cumulative net (FP–FII)	ACT due to date @ 22.5%	ACT paid	ACT payable/ (repayable)
1 October–31 Dec	800,000	–				
	800,000	–	800,000	180,000	Nil	180,000
1 January–31 March	–	100,000				
	800,000	100,000	700,000	157,500	180,000	(22,500)
1 April–5 April	–	–		nil return		
	800,000	100,000	700,000	157,500	157,500	Nil
				20%		
6 April–30 June	–	120,000	(120,000)	Nil	Nil	Nil
1 July–30 Sept	–	–				
	–	120,000	(120,000)	Nil	Nil	Nil

Corporation tax computation – year ended 30 September 1994

Schedule D I		1,032,000
Profits chargeable to coporation tax (*I*)		1,032,000
FII (77,500 × 100/80)	96,875	
(96,000 × 100/80)	120,000	216,875
'Profits' (*P*)		1,248,875

Standard rate CT with taper relief applied.

				£
CT liability				
FY 93	1,032,000 × 6/12 × 33%			170,280
FY 94	1,032,000 × 6/12 × 33%			170,280

Less: Taper relief

FY 93 $\quad \dfrac{6}{12} \times (1{,}250{,}000 - 1{,}248{,}875) \times \dfrac{1{,}032{,}000}{1{,}248{,}875} \times \dfrac{1}{50}$ $\qquad$ (9)

FY 94 $\quad \dfrac{6}{12} \times (1{,}500{,}000 - 1{,}248{,}875) \times \dfrac{1{,}032{,}000}{1{,}248{,}875} \times \dfrac{1}{50}$ $\qquad$ (2,075)

$\qquad\qquad\qquad\qquad\qquad\qquad\qquad\qquad\qquad\qquad\qquad\qquad$ 338,476

Less: ACT

Maximum	FY 93 1,032,000 × 22.5% × 6/12	116,100	
	FY 94 1,032,000 × 20% × 6/12	103,200	
		219,300	
Paid	1/10/93–5/4/94 (800,000 –100,000) 22.5%	157,500	
	6/4/94–30/9/94 (0 – 120,000) 20%	Nil	
		157,500	
Set-off			(157,500)
MCT			180,976

Surplus FII £120,000 to carry forward.

Foreign Income Dividend Scheme (FIDS)

The Finance Act 1994 introduced the new Foreign Income Dividend Scheme. From 1 July 1994, companies can elect to pay a FID out of foreign source profits. The election must be made before the dividend is paid and the FID must be matched to foreign profits of the same, the previous or subsequent years. Foreign source profits are income or gains forming part of a company's chargeable profits, on which double taxation relief is available.

The aim of the FID is to help companies with surplus ACT problems (see next section). ACT is still payable on the FID, but any surplus ACT resulting from its payment will now be recoverable. The ACT due in respect of a FID is calculated on the amount by which the FID paid exceeds any FID received.

The shareholder receiving the FID will be treated as receiving income net of 20% tax and, as for normal dividends, there will be no further liability for lower and basic rate taxpayers. Higher rate taxpayers will be required to account for the difference between the lower and higher rates of tax. However, non-taxpayers will not be able to reclaim any tax as the FID does not carry a tax credit as such.

Companies falling within the definition of an International Headquarters Company (IHC) will not be required to pay ACT on foreign income dividends at all. An IHC is a company with none of its shareholders owning less than 5% of its share capital and at least 80% of its shares being held by non-UK residents. The aim of this rule is to increase the attractiveness of the UK as a base for multinational companies.

Surplus ACT

Whenever more ACT has been paid with reference to an accounting period than it is permissible to set against the corporation tax liability for that accounting period, surplus ACT arises.

Relief for surplus ACT may be given in one of four ways:

▶ *It may be carried back* and set off against the corporation tax liability for accounting periods beginning in the six years preceding the accounting period in which the surplus arises (claims being made for later periods before earlier periods); and then/or

- *It may be carried forward* indefinitely and set off against the first available corporation tax liability in future accounting periods; or
- *It may be surrendered* to a group company (see Chapter 27).
- *It may be repaid* to the company if it relates to a Foreign Income Dividend

A surplus of ACT which is carried forward to a subsequent accounting period will be set off *after* any ACT which is actually paid in respect of that subsequent accounting period while a surplus of ACT which is carried back to an earlier accounting period will be set off *after* any ACT which was actually paid in that earlier accounting period *and after* any ACT brought forward to that earlier accounting period from a previous accounting period.

The claim to carry back the surplus must be made within two years after the end of the accounting period in which the surplus arose and results in a repayment of corporation tax by the Inland Revenue for the period in which the mainstream corporation tax was paid. Usually no repayment supplement will be available as the repayment is deemed to relate to the accounting period in which the surplus arose.

EXAMPLE 25.16

The following information relates to C Ltd for the three years since trading commenced on 1 April 1992. Assume the rate of corporation tax to have been 33% for all years and the rate of ACT to have been 20%.

	31 March 1993	31 March 1994	31 March 1995
	£	£	£
Trading profits	80,000	130,000	100,000
Rent receivable	20,000	–	–
Chargeable gains	–	20,000	–
Franked investment income	40,000	40,000	40,000
Franked payments	150,000	150,000	150,000

Corporation tax computations

Worksheet – Part A

	31 March 1993	31 March 1994	31 March 1995
	£	£	£
Schedule D Case I	80,000	130,000	100,000
Schedule A	20,000	–	–
Chargeable gains	–	20,000	–
Total profits	100,000	150,000	100,000
Less: Charges paid	–	–	–
Profits chargeable to CT (I)	100,000	150,000	100,000
Corporation tax liability			
Basic profits @ 33%	33,000	49,500	33,000
Less: ACT			
MAX I @ 20%	20,000	30,000	20,000
PAID FP–FII @ 20%	22,000	22,000	22,000
ACT set-off	(20,000)	(22,000)	(20,000)
Mainstream corporation tax	13,000	27,500	13,000
Surplus ACT (paid but not set off)	2000	–	2,000

Since the year ended 31 March 1993 is the first year of trading, the surplus ACT cannot be carried back and must be carried forward to set off against the first available corporation tax liability of later accounting periods. The first available corporation tax liability is in the year ended 31 March 1994, where ACT of £30,000 could have been set off against the corporation tax liability but only £22,000 had been paid. The surplus ACT from year ended 31 March 1993 (£2,000) can be absorbed in year ended 31 March 1994 as follows:

Basic profits @ 33%	33,000	49,500
Less: ACT		
Maximum I @ 20%	20,000	30,000
Paid FP–FII @ 20%	22,000	22,000
Surplus ACT bf	–	2,000
	22,000	24,000
ACT set-off	(20,000)	(24,000)
Mainstream corporation tax	13,000	25,500

The surplus ACT for year ended 31 March 1995 may be carried back or it may be carried forward and deducted from the first available corporation tax liability. It is usually preferable to carry back the surplus ACT since this gives relief earlier and often a cash flow advantage in the form of a lower mainstream corporation tax liability or tax repayments.

To carry back the surplus ACT (£2,000) for the year ended 31 March 1995, it is necessary to work chronologically back through each accounting period (for a maximum of six years). In this case the surplus ACT can be absorbed in the year ended 31 March 1994 as the maximum ACT set-off for that year was £30,000 and to date only £27,500 has been relieved.

	31 March 1993	31 March 1994	31 March 1995
Basic profits @ 33%	33,000	49,500	33,000
Less ACT			
Max I @ 20%	20,000	30,000	20,000
Paid FP–FII @ 20%	22,000	22,000	22,000
Surplus ACT b/f	–	2,000	–
Surplus ACT c/b	–	2,000	–
	22,000	26,000	22,000
ACT set off	(20,000)	(26,000)	(20,000)
Mainstream corporation tax	13,000	23,500	13,000
Surplus ACT remaining	–	–	–

If any surplus ACT should arise in subsequent years, a further £4,000 can be absorbed in the year ended 31 March 1994 which will result in the mainstream corporation tax liability being further reduced to £19,000 (the £4,000 will therefore be repaid to the company).

Repayments of tax as a result of surplus ACT carried back, for purposes of the repayment supplement, are treated as repayments of tax for the accounting period in which the surplus ACT arose.

Anti-avoidance

Where a company has surplus ACT accumulated over a number of years, this represents an asset, albeit an unuseable one, while the company is unable to set it off against its corporation tax liability (compare the accounting position where it is described as irrecoverable ACT and written off to profit and loss account – strictly the write-off represents a provision reducing the asset to its current net realisable value).

Such a situation could arise when a company has experienced a decline in its business over a period of years such that trading losses have been incurred but the company has continued to pay dividends.

The surplus ACT might be regarded as a desirable asset to another company acquiring this company with a view to turning the business around and making it profitable once again. There is anti-avoidance legislation which prevents surplus ACT being 'bought' or 'sold' as an asset in certain circumstances.

Surplus ACT paid prior to a change in ownership of a company in the following circumstances cannot be set off against the corporation tax liabilities of accounting periods after the change in ownership. In the same way, ACT paid after a change of ownership of a company in the same circumstances cannot be carried back for set-off against corporation tax liabilities arising before the change in ownership.

The circumstances are:

▶ that within any period of three years there is both a change in ownership of a company (whenever a person/persons acquire more than half the ordinary share capital of the company) and a major change in the nature or conduct of the company's trade or business; or
▶ that at any time after a company's business has become small or negligible and before any revival there is a change in ownership.

A major change in the nature or conduct of the company's trade or business covers, for example, a major change in customers, outlets or markets or a major change in the property, services or facilities provided.

Trade losses carried back and ACT set-off

Since the introduction of provisions for the carry back of trade losses for 36 months prior to the loss-making accounting period and the consequential effect on the ACT set-off in these accounting periods, some doubt has arisen about the scope which exists for claims for ACT set-off to be made or varied. The problem arises from the time limits for each claim.

EXAMPLE 25.17

A trading loss incurred in the year ended 31 December 1994 can be carried back and offset against profits for the years ended 31 December 1993, 1992 and 1991, provided a claim is made by 31 December 1996.

ACT offset in any of the above accounting periods may therefore be upset. (The profits chargeable to corporation tax reduced or eliminated, will reduce or restrict the amount of ACT which can be offset). An example is the year ended 31 December 1992. Ideally ACT thus disturbed should be carried back further (ACT can be carried back six years) but this is prevented because ACT carry back must be claimed within two years of the end of the accounting period in which the surplus arose (31 December 1994 has passed). The question arises whether, if a claim had previously been made for ACT of the accounting year ended 31 December 1992 to be carried back, the amount for carry back could be increased. There are indications in case law that a claim must be for a specified amount and cannot be varied.

It has also been suggested that the ACT set-off disturbed in the year ended 31 December 1992 could be carried forward and as such would be per the legislation 'treated as ACT paid' in the next accounting period, and therefore a claim could be made at this point for any surplus of that accounting period to be carried back.

Set-off of income tax

The income tax section above dealt with the occasions on which income tax had to be paid over to the Collector of Taxes and the circumstances when any such income tax paid with reference to an accounting period might be repaid during the same accounting period through accounting for income tax on forms CT61Z. It was pointed out that any repayment in this way was restricted to the amount of income tax already paid with reference to the accounting period. Any further repayment of income tax to which the company is entitled is achieved by set-off against the mainstream corporation tax liability for the same accounting period or, if this is nil, by repayment on submission of the corporation tax computation.

There is no limit to the amount of income tax which may be set off in this way. The calculation is simply unfranked investment income (UFII) for the accounting period less unfranked payments (UFP) at basic rate income tax. If unfranked investment income does not exceed unfranked payments, no repayment of income tax is due.

Examination format

It is useful to have a pro-forma layout to work to in examinations which is sufficiently abbreviated in order not to waste time but also sufficiently comprehensive to serve as an *aide-mémoire*. The layout suggested in Figure 25.1 is Part B of the format given in the previous chapter. You are advised to learn and use this layout.

Figure 25.1 Corporation tax computation – Worksheet part B

```
Corporation tax liability                                              £      £
FY............ P............ I............ at...... %                  x
FY............ P............ I............ at...... %                  x
                                                                       ___
                                                                              X
(Compare P with upper/lower limits for FY pro rata
number of months)
Less marginal small companies relief    FY........         (x)
                                        FY........         (x)
                                                           ___
                                                                             (X)
Less double tax relief (deduct from relevant income)                         (X)
Less advance corporation tax
    Maximum I @ appropriate ACT rate              A    x
                                                       ═══
      (Further restricted to the lower of the
      appropriate ACT rate on each source of income
      or CT on that source of income)
    Operative where double tax relief

    Surrendered by group companies                B    x
    Paid in year (FP–FII) @ ACT rate              C    x
    Surplus ACT b/f from previous years           D    x
    Surplus ACT of later years carried back       E    x
                                                  F    x
                                                       ═══
        Set off lower of A and F                                             (X)
                                                                              ___
                                                                              X
Less income tax (UFII-UFP) @ basic rate IT                                   (X)
Mainstream corporation tax/(income tax repayable)              X
                                                                              ═══
```

It is particularly important that the computation proceeds in this order when double tax relief is involved since it may restrict the amount of ACT which can be set off.

Surplus franked investment income

It has already been demonstrated that franked investment income (FII) has no effect on the overall corporation tax liability (it is not taxable) other than in determining the rate of corporation tax but that it reduces the amount of advance corporation tax that has to be paid and therefore aids 'cash flow'. If franked investment income in an accounting period exceeds the amount of franked payments, there is a surplus of franked investment income.

Surplus franked investment income can be carried forward from one accounting period to the next and set off against franked payments in that accounting period as if it were franked investment income of that period, thus reducing the ACT in that accounting period. If surplus FII again arises, the new surplus is carried forward to the following accounting period and so on until the surplus is absorbed by franked payments in some future accounting period. A company not making franked payments, for any reason, will not be able to absorb its franked investment income.

Surplus franked investment income may not be carried back to earlier accounting periods.

An alternative to the carry forward of surplus franked investment income as described above, is for the company to make a claim under ICTA 1988, s. 242. Where the company makes such a claim, the surplus franked investment income of the accounting period, excluding surplus franked investment income brought forward, is treated as if it were trading profits chargeable to corporation tax. The company may then set off against these profits, various types of losses and expenses, particularly:

- trading losses of the current accounting period over and above those that would be absorbed on a ICTA 1988, s. 393A(1)(a)/(b) claim
- charges – both trade and other – of the current accounting period
- excess management expenses of the current accounting period in the case of an investment company.

The tax credit inherent in the franked investment income is then repaid.

Before this relief is looked at in detail, it should be noted that this relief is unlike other reliefs in that the repayment outlined above may, under certain circumstances, require to be repaid to the Inland Revenue at some future date. This is because franked investment income is only a 'cash flow' relief and of a temporary nature, the duration of which depends on the individual circumstances. Once the relief is repaid to the Inland Revenue, the company is returned to its original position.

Set-off of losses against franked investment income (ICTA 1988, s. 242)

A claim under ICTA 1988, s. 242 gives some relief to a company in the situation where:

- there is surplus FII in the current accounting period (excluding surplus FII brought forward from previous accounting periods) and/or in earlier accounting periods for which s. 393 A(1)(b) claim has been made
- there are surplus reliefs in the current accounting period (excluding surpluses brought forward from previous accounting periods) because there is insufficient income to absorb them, for example:
  - unrelieved trading losses after making a s. 393A(1)(a) claim and if desired, an s. 393 A(1)(b) claim for the previous 36 months
  - excess charges
  - unrelieved management expenses in an investment company
  - capital allowances allowed primarily by discharge or repayment of tax.

Claims for relief of surplus FII against a trading loss or capital allowances must be made within two years of the end of the accounting period in which the loss was incurred while the time limit for claims for relief in relation to charges and management expenses is six years from the end of the accounting period in which they were incurred/paid.

A claim under this section is normally made for earlier years before later years if a trading loss were made in each of the years 31 March 1994 and 31 March 1995, and there was surplus FII in each of the years, then an s. 242 claim would normally be made for 1994 prior to making a claim for 1995. The amount of the repayment as a result of a claim is calculated at the tax credit rate (25% to 31 March 1993 and 20% thereafter) on the smaller of the surplus FII or the available reliefs.

EXAMPLE 25.18

D Ltd, which prepares accounts annually to 31 March, has had the following results:

	31 March 1994	31 March 1995
	£	£
Trading profits/(losses)	25,000	(40,000)
Bank interest received	2,000	900
Debenture interest paid	5,000	5,000
Franked investment income	10,000	10,000
Franked payments	4,000	4,000

No surplus FII arose prior to the above accounting periods nor can the trading loss be absorbed prior to year ended 31 March 1993.

Assume a corporation tax rate of 33% and ACT at 22.5% for the year ended 31 March 1994 and 20% for the year ended 31 March 1995.

Corporation tax computations

Worksheet – part A

	31 March 1994	31 March 1995
	£	£
Schedule D Case I	25,000	Nil
Schedule D Case III	2,000	900
Total profits	27,000	900
Less: loss relief s. 393A(1)(a)		(900)
s. 393A(1)(b)	(22,000)	
Less: trade charges	(5,000)	
Profits chargeable to CT	Nil	Nil

Loss memo

	31 March 1995
Loss for year	40,000
Less: s. 393A(1)(a) year ended 31 March 1995	(900)
s. 393A(1)(b) year ended 31 March 1994	(22,000)
Losses for c/f to 19963	17,100
Add excess trade charges y/e 31 March 1995	5,000
	22,100

Under s. 393A(1)(b) the remaining loss of £17,100 should be carried back to the years ended 31 March 1993 and 1992. As this is not possible in this instance, the loss may be relieved under s. 242.

Claims under ICTA 1988 s. 242 are possible in both years as follows:
- ▶ 31 March 1994 Surplus FII (6,000) Trading loss carried back from 31 March 1995 under s. 393A(1)(a)/(b) (17,100). If there had been surplus FII in the years ended 31 March 1993 and 1992 then claims would also be possible for these years.
- ▶ 31 March 1995 Surplus FII (6,000) Trading loss of current year (remaining) + excess charges for year (5,000).

Claim under ICTA 1988, s. 242

	31 March 1994	Loss memo		s. 242 Loss memo
FII	10,000	bf	17,100	
FP	4,000			
Surplus FII	6,000	(year ended 31 March 1994)		
s. 242	(6,000)	s. 242	(6,000)	6,000
Surplus FII cf	Nil	Repayment £6,000 @ 20% £1,200		
	31 March 1995			
FII	10,000	bf	11,100	
FP	4,000	+ charges	5,000	
Surplus FII	6,000	(year ended 31 March 1995)		
s. 242	(6,000)	s. 242	(6,000)	6,000
Surplus FII cf	Nil	Repayment £6,000 @ 20% £1,200		
		c/f	10,100	c/f 12,000

The claim stops both the FII and the available reliefs being available for use. The amount of the various claims under ICTA 1988, s. 242 are noted and carried forward separately as above.

In a subsequent accounting period, if franked payments arise in excess of the franked investment income of that subsequent accounting period, causing ACT to be payable which would not have been payable if the s. 242 claim had not been made, this is regarded as the tax credit repayment being repaid to the Inland Revenue. This ACT repayment is ignored in the computation of MCT and the trading loss/other reliefs involved in the s. 242 claim are reinstated.

EXAMPLE 25.18 (continued)

For the year ended 31 March 1996, D Ltd had the following results:

	31 March 1996
	£
Trading profits	30,000
Bank interest	100
Debenture interest paid	5,000
FII (grossed @ 20%)	6,000
FP	8,000

Assume a corporation tax rate of 33% and a basic rate of income tax of 25% throughout. The ACT is 20%.

During the year, ACT will have been accounted for as follows:

FP	8,000
FII	6,000
FP–FII	2,000
ACT paid 2,000 @ 20%	400

The excess of franked payments over franked investment income causes a partial reversal of the s. 242 claim (2,000 of the total 12,000).

	31 March 1996	**Loss memo**	**s. 242**
	£	£	**Loss memo** £
		bf 10,100	bf 12,000
Schedule D Case I	30,000		
Less: loss relief s. 393(1)	(10,100)	1994 (10,100)	
Less: s. 242 loss reinstated and relieved in 1996	(2,000)		(2,000)
	17,900		c/f 10,000
Schedule D Case III	100		
Total profits	18,000		
Less: charges paid	(5,000)		
Profits chargeable to CT	13,000		
Corporation tax liability			
13,000 @ 33%			4,290.00
Less: ACT paid			
FP		8,000	
FII		(6,000)	
s. 242 reversed		(2,000)	
Set off			–
Mainstream CT liability			4,290.00

A reversal of the s. 242 claims will take place in each subsequent accounting period whenever franked payments in the accounting period exceed franked investment income until the remainder of the claim £10,000 has been reversed and £10,000 @ the appropriate rate is repaid to the Inland Revenue.

Planning considerations

▶ There are effectively three rates of corporation tax which must be considered when alternative tax reliefs/strategies are evaluated: FY 1994 – SCR 25%, standard rate 33% and the marginal SCR of 35%.
▶ The timing of qualifying distributions (principally dividends) can materially affect cash flow. A distribution delayed a few days from the end of one return period to the beginning of the next will delay the payment of ACT for three months. Similarly, a distribution timed to coincide with franked investment income in a return period will reduce the ACT payment.
▶ The level of qualifying distributions should also be considered with reference to the maximum amount of ACT set off in any accounting period – particularly when double tax relief is involved – and whether there is any scope for carry back of surplus ACT.

Summary

▶ Corporation tax is payable on 'profits liable to corporation tax' or 'basic profits' (this does not include franked investment income) but the rate of corporation tax which applies depends on the level of 'profits' (which is basic profit plus franked investment income).
▶ Advance corporation tax (ACT) is due on the cumulative excess of franked payments over franked investment income of the accounting period calculated at three-monthly intervals over the year – 31 March, 30 June, 30 September and 31

December – and on the last day of the accounting period if this is different. ACT payable is arrived at by deducting the amount already paid in the year to date from the amount due.
- ACT due with reference to an accounting period (note that it may not actually have been paid on the last day of the accounting period if the distribution took place during the final return period) may be deducted from the corporation tax liability on the profits of the same accounting period subject to certain restrictions.
- The corporation tax liability which results is called mainstream corporation tax (MCT).
- The introduction of Pay and File for accounting periods ending on or after 1 October 1993 means that companies cannot wait for an estimate of the mainstream corporation tax liability to arrive, but must take care to make a best estimate of this liability and to pay it prior to the normal due date (nine months after the year end). Heavy penalties and interest apply for late returns and payments.
- Surplus ACT arises when ACT paid exceeds the maximum amount of ACT set off.
- Surplus ACT may be carried back for up to six years and any ACT still unrelieved may be carried forward to set against the first available corporation tax liability.
- Surplus FII arises when franked investment income exceeds the franked payments in an accounting period.
- Surplus FII may be carried forward and treated as franked investment income of the following accounting period or it may be used in a ICTA 1988, s. 242 claim.
- Any income tax deducted at source on unfranked investment income and not recovered at the end of the accounting period may be set against the mainstream corporation tax liability. If it exceeds the mainstream corporation tax liability, it will be repaid.

Self test questions

1 State the formula for the calculation of taper relief.

2 C Ltd, a company with no associated companies, has the following results for the nine months to 31 December 1994:

	£
Schedule D Case I	196,000
Chargeable gains	14,000
Franked investment income	24,000
Debenture interest paid	4,000

Calculate the taper relief, if applicable.

3 Define basic profits (I).

4 Define profits (P).

5 A Ltd prepared accounts to 31 March each year until 31 March 1989 when the accounting date was changed and the next accounts were prepared for the period to 30 September 1990. In the year ended 30 September 1994 there was surplus ACT. What is the earliest accounting period to which it can be carried back?

6 Explain how ACT is paid.

7 What is surplus FII and is it of value to the company?

8 When may ICTA 1988, s. 242 loss relief be claimed?

9 What is a FID and how does it differ from a normal dividend?

10 What is an IHC? What is the significance of being an IHC?

11 MA Ltd, a company with no associated companies, provides the following information in respect of the two 12-month accounting periods ended 30 September 1994.

	12 months to 30 September 1993 £	12 months to 30 September 1994 £
Income		
Adjusted trading profits (losses)	180,000	(120,000)
Schedule A income	4,000	2,000
Bank deposit interest	5,000	4,000
Chargeable gains (losses)	(6,000)	12,000
(date of gain – 30 June 1994)		
Dividends received		
30 June 1993	3,100	
30 June 1994		6,400
Charges paid		
Debenture interest (gross)	8,000	4,000
Charitable covenant	1,000	1,000
Dividends paid		
30 April 1993	17,980	
30 April 1994		14,600

a) Compute the mainstream corporation tax payable by MA Ltd in respect of the year ended 30 September 1993, before any claims are made in respect of the loss incurred for the year ended 30 September 1994.

b) Compute the amount of corporation tax repayable in respect of the year ended 30 September 1993, assuming all possible claims are made at the earliest opportunity in respect of the year ended 30 September 1994.

c) Show any amounts available for carry forward at 30 September 1994.

(adapted from CIMA 3 Nov 1988)
Answers on pages 614–615

Investment Companies and Close Companies

CHAPTER 26

This chapter deals with special classes of company liable to corporation tax. These companies follow the general principles of corporation tax but further provisions apply in each case. Unincorporated associations, investment companies and close companies are all considered.

Clubs and associations

The Taxes Act defines a company as any body corporate or unincorporated association. A typical example of such an unincorporated association is a members' club such as a golf club. Much of the club's income is termed 'mutual income' in so far as it arises from trading with its members and is therefore not taxable. Where, however, the club trades other than 'mutually' or receives interest on bank deposits or other investments, this is chargeable to corporation tax in the normal way.

Investment companies

Definition

An investment company is one 'whose business consists wholly or mainly in the making of investments and the principal part of whose income is derived therefrom'.

Assessment

An investment company does not have trading income from which to deduct its day-to-day running expenses (referred to usually as 'management expenses'). It is, however, permitted to deduct its management expenses, capital allowances and charges on income when arriving at its profits chargeable to corporation tax (they are deductible from total profit before charges).

The principal sources of income chargeable to corporation tax are likely to be Schedule D Case III, Schedule A and unfranked investment income (UFII) – remember that franked investment income (FII) is exempt.

Management expenses are principally the expenses of maintaining an office and staff not otherwise deductible in arriving at the taxable profits of a particular Schedule or case. Management expenses includes commissions as well as, specifically, employers' national insurance, statutory redundancy pay and additional payments, payments to approved pension schemes, incidental costs of obtaining loan finance, discounts and so forth on bills of exchange and certain training costs. The following expenses also generally qualify as management expenses: accounts; share register and AGM costs; registered office expenses; valuation costs. Excessive director's remuneration will not, however, be allowable, not being a true expense of management (see *LG Berry Investments Ltd* v. *Attwooll*). The restrictions on business entertainment expenditure apply and brokerage and stamp duty on investment changes are not allowed, being capital expenditure.

Capital allowances for corporation tax purposes are normally given as a trading expense, and in respect of non-trading activities, are normally deducted from the source of income to which they relate. An investment company may make a once and for all election for capital allowances on plant and machinery used in its business to be deducted from its business income, that is, total profit chargeable to corporation tax. The computation is then as normal.

Surplus allowances

If the management expenses, unrelieved capital allowances and trade charges exceed the amount of profits then the excess may be carried forward and treated as management expenses of the next accounting period and so on – they are therefore effectively relieved against total profits of the current and all subsequent accounting periods.

Alternatively, the excess may be set off against surplus FII of the accounting period under ICTA 1988, s. 242 (see Chapter 25).

Loss on unquoted shares in a trading company

An investment company which incurs a loss on the disposal of shares (as computed for capital gains tax purposes) for which it subscribed and which were qualifying shares in a qualifying trading company, may claim to deduct the loss from income rather than from its chargeable gains. Relief must be claimed within two years after the end of the accounting period in which the loss is made. Relief is given by deducting the loss from income before management expenses and charges of the accounting period in which the loss is made. Any remaining loss may be carried back and deducted from income before management expenses and charges of the 12 months preceding the accounting period in which the loss is made.

Close companies

Close companies are a special class of company to which all the corporation tax provisions covered so far apply. There are, however, further provisions which apply only to close companies.

A close company is one which is under the control of five or fewer participators, or any number of participators who are directors.

Background

This special class of company originates from anti-avoidance legislation. A company may be formed by a single individual or by a married couple and as such will have an independent identity. The individual or couple could run a business without incorporation and be subject to the income tax legislation while the same individual or couple could form a company and run the same business through the medium of the company and be subject to the corporation tax legislation. In the past and to a lesser extent, at present at high income levels there are significant differences between the marginal income tax rates and corporation tax rates; this can lead to opportunities for tax avoidance through the manipulation of the company's affairs to personal advantage.

Close company legislation was first introduced by the FA 1922 and has been with us to a greater or lesser extent ever since. The primary purpose of the close company legislation was and is to counter the avoidance, mitigation or deferral of liability to income tax.

The legislation originally operated in two principal directions:

▶ Where domestic or personal benefits were provided for participators, who were not employees, out of the resources of a close company, the cost of their provision could be treated as a distribution for income tax purposes.

▶ Where profits available for distribution were retained and accumulated within a close company, the amount by which the company's distribution policy fell short of a distribution standard was apportioned (for tax purposes only) among the shareholders with all the tax consequences as if it were an actual dividend.

Apportionment has now been abolished, but the legislation still treats benefits to participators as distributions.

Before the consequences of being found to be a close company can be looked at in greater depth, it is first necessary to return to the definition of a close company and expand upon the terminology used. (These definitions and the steps taken to determine close company status are included as briefly as possible for background information purposes only – only the consequences of being a close company will be examined.)

Definition

A close company is one which is under the control of five or fewer participators, or any number of participators who are directors.

Although a company may fall within the basic definition of a close company outlined above, it may not be a close company under the legislation. The main exceptions are quoted companies (the shares must have been dealt in on a recognised Stock Exchange within the previous 12 months) where at least 35% of the voting shares are held by the public and the principal members between them do not possess more than 85% of the total voting power.

It is necessary to define some terms before progressing.

Control

The definition of control is the usual one – that which is obtained by possessing or being entitled to acquire the greater part of:

▶ the share capital/issued share capital/voting power, or
▶ any distribution if the whole of the income were distributed, or
▶ any distribution of assets in the event of winding up or any other circumstance,
  or by any other means or the ability to acquire such means.

Participator

For most practical purposes a participator is taken to be a shareholder, but the actual definition is less specific and therefore wider – a person who has 'a share or interest in the capital or income of the company' is a more accurate definition.

Associate

In deciding whether control exists, each participator or director has attributed to them the interests of their nominees, associates, and companies controlled by them and their associates.

An associate is defined as:

▶ a relative – spouse, parent or remoter forebear, child or remoter issue, sibling
▶ a partner
▶ the trustees of any settlement set up by the participator or his or her relatives
▶ the trustees of any trust holding shares in the company if the participator also has an interest in those shares.

Principal member

A principal member is a person who, with his or her associates, owns more than 5% of the voting power and is one of the five largest voting shareholders.

Determination of close company status

A person plus his or her associates are counted as a single participator. Where a number of participators are associated, it is necessary to group them in such a way to produce the smallest number of participators in order to establish whether the company is under the control of five or fewer participators.

Distributions – extended meaning for close companies

The following items of expenditure are treated as a distribution when paid by a close company and are therefore not deductible when computing the profits of the company for corporation tax purposes, nor are they allowed as charges on income.

Benefits provided to participators or their associates

Any benefit which is provided by a close company to a participator or his or her associate is a distribution equal to the cash equivalent of the benefit provided (as defined for assessing benefits on directors and higher-paid employees). However, benefits taxable under Schedule E on directors and higher-paid employees are excluded, as is living accommodation provided by reason of his or her employment to any employee. Pensions and gratuities to the wife or children of a former director or employee are also excluded from this section.

Since benefits taxable under Schedule E cover not only the benefits provided to the director or higher-paid employee but also to a member of his or her family or household, this section is only likely to apply to a participator who is not a director, or an employee, or a family or household member of either.

The effect of such benefits being distributions is that the cost will be disallowed in the Schedule D Case I computation and the company will be required to account for ACT on the amount of the distribution in the normal way. The disallowed expense and the distribution will not necessarily be the same amount. The participator will be charged to income tax on the distribution plus the tax credit.

The distribution is treated as made in the accounting period in which the expense is incurred by the company.

Where the recipient of the benefit is a UK-resident company which is a subsidiary or a fellow subsidiary of the close company, no distribution shall arise on the transfer of assets/liabilities from one to the other. There is however, anti-avoidance legislation dealing with back-to-back arrangements whereby each benefits the other's shareholders.

EXAMPLE 26.1

Broomwell Ltd is a close company. When the company premises are being redecorated, the house belonging to Mrs Dickie, who is a shareholder, is also redecorated. Mrs Dickie is not an employee.

The cost of the redecoration will be a disallowable expense to the company and will be a distribution to Mrs Dickie on which the company will be required to pay advance corporation tax. The distribution plus the tax credit will be included in Mrs Dickie's income.

Loans to participators or their associates

A loan by the close company to a participator or his or her associate is a means of making cash available without the tax consequences of making a distribution. However, to counter any possible advantage, an amount equivalent to ACT on the amount of the loan must be paid to the Inland Revenue (called henceforth notional ACT) and this amount will not be repayable to the company until the loan itself is repaid.

This notional ACT is kept separate from normal ACT and is not deductible from the liability to corporation tax. It is not accounted for through the quarterly return but is due within 14 days of the end of the accounting period in which the loan is made. The loan is not deemed to be income of the participator nor does any tax credit accrue to him or her.

This section is often encroached upon by accident where, for example, directors maintain current accounts. Remuneration and fees are credited to the account while the director's drawings are debited to this account. If the director's drawings exceed the amounts credited, such that the account becomes overdrawn, the company may be liable to account for tax. If the liability is overlooked, but subsequently comes to the attention of the Inspector of Taxes, the tax is assessable together with interest on overdue tax although the loan has since been repaid. It should be noted, however, that 'participator or his associate' refers not only to individuals but also to companies acting in a 'representative capacity' and non-resident companies.

Debts incurred for goods supplied in the normal course of business are ignored (unless the credit given or taken is excessive – usually more than six months), as are loans which do not exceed £15,000, to a full-time director or employee of the company who does not have a material interest (more than 5% of the ordinary share capital).

When a loan which has been charged to tax in this way is repaid wholly or in part, the relevant tax will be repaid. A claim to the Inland Revenue must be submitted within six years of the end of the financial year in which the repayment of the loan occurs.

If the repayment of all or part of a loan is waived, there will be no refund of ACT to the company or set-off against MCT and the participator is treated as having received income of an amount equal to the amount written off, grossed up for lower rate income tax, in the year of assessment in which the waiver was made.

EXAMPLE 26.2

Broomwell Ltd is a close company. It advanced £10,000 to George Davis, a shareholder, on 30 April 1994. He has a 15% interest in the ordinary share capital of the company but is not a director or an employee. On 1 September 1995, he repaid £4,000. On 31 March 1996, the company, with his agreement, wrote off the balance of the debt. Assume that 1994/95 rates continue to apply.

Tax consequences:
- Notional ACT on £10,000 (20/80 × £10,000) would be due by the company 14 days after the end of the accounting period in which the loan is made.
- The repayment of £4,000 will allow the company to claim repayment of tax on £4,000 (20/80 × £4,000).
- The writing off of £6,000 will result in income of £7,500 (£6,000 × 100/80) being included in George Davis's total income for 1995/96. The tax credit (£1,500) is not repayable under any circumstances.

Further consequences of being a close company

- Annual payments, other than interest, which if made by an individual would not be deductible, will no longer be deductible by a close company (FA 1989).

▶ A transfer of value for inheritance tax purposes, made by a close company, may be treated as if made by its participators, that is, the company is 'looked through'. Such a deemed transfer of value cannot be a PET and therefore would automatically be a fully chargeable transfer (see Chapter 8).

Close investment-holding companies (CICs)

The Finance Act 1989 introduced the concept of a close investment-holding company (CIC). The small companies rate of corporation tax will not be available to these companies.

The purpose of abolishing close company apportionment and substituting this system is to simplify the way in which undistributed profits are taxed while still ensuring that non-trading companies are not used by higher-rate taxpayers to avoid tax.

Definition

A close company is not a close investment-holding company if it exists wholly or mainly for the purpose of trading or is a member of a trading group.

The trade must be carried on on a commercial basis.

The definition of a member of a trading group includes a holding company of a trading group as well as group companies which hold property for trading subsidiaries or provide them with services.

Rate of corporation tax

A CIC will not be eligible for the small companies rate of corporation tax.

Other consequences of being a CIC

A recipient of a dividend from a CIC will not be entitled to have the tax credit attaching to those dividends repaid in certain circumstances (such as the purchase of its own shares by a CIC) where there would otherwise be a tax advantage and this is considered to be a main purpose of the arrangement.

Summary

▶ Investment companies may deduct management expenses in arriving at their profits chargeable to corporation tax. Excess management expenses may be carried forward and treated as management expenses of the next following accounting period.
▶ The definition of a close company is wide and complex. A company caught under any one of its provisions will be a close company unless it is of a type excluded from being close.
▶ The principal consequence of being a close company is that the meaning of distributions is extended to cover benefits and loans to participators and their associates who are not directors or employees. The associated costs are therefore not allowed as Schedule D Case I expenses and a liability to ACT arises.
▶ The Finance Act 1989 introduced the concept of a close investment-holding company (CIC) which will not be eligible for small companies rate of corporation tax.

Self test questions

1. List two common examples of an investment company.

2. Is an investment company eligible to claim capital allowances?

3. Describe the way in which the meaning of distribution is extended in the context of close companies.

4. What are the consequences of making a loan to a participator?

5. The Isla Mill Co Ltd has an issued share capital of 40,000 £1 shares and is a close company in which J. Thomson (chairman) has a 38% interest (including associates), L. Bishop has a 10% interest, and D. Knight, the chairman's nephew has a 6% interest. D. Knight is an apprentice engineer employed by the company at a salary of £4,750 per annum.

    J. Thomson and L. Bishop are partners in a certified accountants practice and jointly own the entire share capital of Interface Systems (Mercia) Ltd.

    The Isla Mill Company's trading profit, Schedule D Case I, for the year to 30 September 1994 is £260,000.

    The Isla Mill company's records for the year show the following information:

    a) 21 January 1994 sale of a surplus showroom for £130,000 (purchased May 1976 for £50,000 (March 1982 value £80,000)).

    b) various dates; £1,000 car expenses, including petrol, for a 1,600 cc company car (cost £12,000 May 1991) used solely by D. Knight; it is used for business for 8,000 miles being 60% of its total use in the year.

    c) 7 June 1994 a loan of £7,000 to Mr G. Bishop, son of L. Bishop, to assist him in purchasing a racing yacht; he will pay interest at a commercial rate in November and May each year.

    d) dividends – final 1993; paid 21 December 1993   12.5p per share
       interim 1994; paid 16 April 1994   7.5p per share
       final 1994; paid 13 November 1994   7.5p per share

    All relevant payments of ACT are made within the due time limits.

You are required to compute the mainstream corporation tax for the year to 30 September 1994, briefly explaining your reasons for the treatment of the above transactions.

Answers on pages 615–616

CHAPTER 27

Groups and consortia

Each individual company is chargeable to corporation tax on its profits but in some circumstances, the corporation tax legislation looks beyond the individual company to the companies 'associated' with that company. The recognition of these 'associated' companies brings both penalties and benefits. This chapter looks at the consequences of being part of a 'group' or consortium for corporation tax purposes.

Overview

The penalties suffered by companies which are members of a group are generally the restricting or limiting of reliefs. For example, the lower limit of profits for small companies rate of corporation tax to apply is shared by all members of the group. These are anti-avoidance measures to discourage a company from splitting up its business among several companies so that each should benefit from the reliefs.

By contrast there are five common benefits enjoyed by companies which are members of groups:

▶ Dividends payable by a subsidiary company to a parent company may be paid without accounting for advance corporation tax and interest payable by one group company to another may be paid without deducting income tax at source
▶ Advance corporation tax paid by a parent company may be surrendered to a subsidiary and treated as if paid by that subsidiary
▶ The trading losses of one group member may be set against the profits of another group member (ICTA 1988, s. 402)
▶ Assets may be transferred between members of the same group of companies without any immediate capital gains implications.
▶ Roll-over relief on the replacement of business assets within a group treats group companies as a single company with a single trade.

Unfortunately, the group structure requirements for each of these penalties and reliefs must be looked at separately; that is, the degree of control exercised by the parent on the subsidiary determines the extent of the taxation consequences of being a 'group' for tax purposes.

It is convenient to identify five principal structures:

▶ associated companies
▶ 51% groups
▶ capital gains group
▶ 75% groups
▶ consortiums.

Each of these group structures will be studied in turn and the implications for tax purposes of each one will be outlined. It is important to note and understand the definition of each type of group.

TAX PLANNING

Associated companies

Definition

Two companies are regarded as 'associated' with one another for tax purposes if, at that time or at any time within the accounting period, one is under the control of the other or they are both under common control.

Control means, for this purpose, the ability to acquire or exercise control over (directly or indirectly) more than 50% of the share capital, the voting rights, the income or the net assets on a winding up.

Companies are under common control if they are under the control of the same person or persons (not necessarily a company).

Note that this definition is not restricted to UK-resident companies. To establish the number of associated companies, the worldwide group structure must be considered. Any associated company which did not carry on a trade or business during the accounting period (that is, which was dormant) is ignored.

Consequences of being associated companies

The upper and lower limits for small companies' rate of corporation tax and taper relief (FY 1994 £300,000 and £1.5 million) are divided equally between the associated companies.

EXAMPLE 27.1

Company A had a 51% interest in each of companies B and C throughout the accounting period for the year ended 31 December 1994. During the first three months of the year it also had a 51% interest in company D which it disposed of on 31 March 1994. On 1 September it acquired a 51% interest in company E. All companies carried on business during the relevant parts of the accounting period.

Although companies D and E were associated with company A at different times in the accounting period, there were five associated companies during the accounting period.

FY93   Lower limit $\dfrac{250,000}{5} \times \dfrac{3}{12}$ = £12,500 each A, B, C, D, and E

FY94   Lower limit $\dfrac{300,000}{5} \times \dfrac{9}{12}$ = £45,000 each A, B, C, D, and E

51% groups

Definition

In this case the relationship of parent company and subsidiary company must exist. Two companies resident in the UK are regarded as members of a 51% group, where one company owns more than 50% of the ordinary share capital of the other or the share capitals of both are more than 50% owned by the same UK-resident parent. The shareholdings may be either direct or indirect, but any shareholdings via a non-resident are ignored (the stock shareholdings of a share-dealer company are also ignored). In addition, the parent must be beneficially entitled to more than 50% of the profits available to the equity shareholders and more than 50% of the assets available to the equity shareholders on a winding-up of the subsidiary.

The ordinary share capital of a company is taken to be all the issued share capital not bearing a fixed rate of dividend.

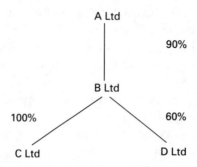

Figure 27.1 51% groups

Provided that all the companies are UK resident, they form a 51% group. If B Ltd were non-resident, there would not be a 51% group.

Companies being members of a 51% group will also inevitably be associated companies as defined above.

Note that when a company goes into liquidation any assets held by it are technically held in trust for the creditors and not owned by the company. Where shares are held in a subsidiary, therefore, the group relationship is broken. In the above figure, if B Ltd were to go into liquidation, C Ltd and D Ltd would be associated companies but they would not be in a group relationship with B Ltd. A Ltd and B Ltd would still form a group, however.

Reliefs available to members of a 51% group

Two reliefs are available to members of a 51% group:

- They can elect not to account for:
    - advance corporation tax on dividends that pass between them (group income); and/or
    - income tax on annual charges that pass between them (group charges).
- Unused advance corporation tax can be passed between the companies (subject to the further restrictions listed below).

Group income and group charges

The members of a 51% group may *jointly* elect that:

- dividends (not other qualifying distributions) payable by one to the other, may be paid without accounting for ACT thereon. Since dividends are not payable by a parent to a subsidiary, the dividends covered by the group income election would be those payable horizontally or vertically (in the above example, horizontally between C and D (if applicable) or vertically from both C and D to B and from B to A); and/or
- payments that are charges on income payable by one to the other, may be paid without the deduction of basic rate income tax at source. This election applies to such payments, whether payable horizontally, vertically or downwards (Figure 27.1: horizontally between C and D; or vertically from both C and D to B and from B, C and D to A; or downwards from A to B, C, or D, or from B to C or D).

A separate election is required for each. There is no prescribed form for making the election other than that it should be in writing to the Inspector of Taxes. The elections are valid three months after they are made or, if earlier, the date the Inspector acknowledges receipt of the valid election. The elections continue in force until revoked.

The principal advantage of the elections is cashflow in the short term, but problems of surplus ACT arising in a subsidiary company may also be avoided in this way.

EXAMPLE 27.2

A Ltd and its 55% subsidiary SA Ltd both prepare accounts to 31 March each year. In the year ended 31 March 1995 the following distributions take place:

 14 April 1994 SA Ltd pays a dividend of £50,000
 31 August 1994 A Ltd pays shareholders a dividend of £30,000.
 The appropriate ACT rate is 20/80

a) **Group income election**
The dividend, £27,500, from SA Ltd to A Ltd is group income and no ACT need be accounted for. SA Ltd will account for ACT on 14 July 1994 of £5,625 (22,500 × 20/80).

A Ltd must account for ACT on the dividend of £30,000 to its shareholders on 14 October 1994 (£30,000 × 20/80) £7,500.

b) **No group income election**
SA Ltd must account for ACT on 14 July 1994 (£50,000 × 20/80) £12,500.

A Ltd then has FII of £34,375 (£27,500 × 20/80). If it pays a dividend of £30,000 to its shareholders, this is a FP of £37,500 and it must account for ACT [(£37,500 − £34,375) × 20%] £625 on 14 October 1994.

Note that the total ACT paid is the same in both cases (£13,125)

Although an election is in force in the case of dividends, it may be temporarily set aside and a company may account for ACT on any dividend if it chooses to do so for any reason. This may happen if the subsidiary has FII which it wishes to transfer to the parent company.

EXAMPLE 27.3

A Ltd and its 100% subsidiary SA Ltd both prepare accounts to 31 March each year. In the year ended 31 March 1995, the following distributions and receipts take place:

 14 April 1994 SA Ltd receives a dividend of £20,000
 25 May 1994 SA Ltd pays a dividend of £20,000
 31 August 1994 A Ltd pays a dividend of £30,000
 The appropriate ACT rate is 20/80

a) **Group income election**
The dividend £20,000 from SA Ltd to A Ltd is group income and no ACT need be accounted for. SA Ltd will have surplus FII to carry forward of £25,000 (£20,000 × 100/80)

A Ltd must account for ACT on the dividend of £30,000 to its shareholders on 14 October 1994 £7,500 (£30,000 × 20/80).

b) **No group income election**

SA Ltd must account for ACT on 14 July 1994. It has FII of £25,000 (as above) and FP of £25,000 (£20,000 × 100/80).

£NIL ACT is payable.

A Ltd then has FII of £25,000 which it can set against its FP of £37,500 (£30,000 × 100/80) and it must account for ACT of £2,500 [(37,500-25,000) × 20%].

Note that, in this case, total ACT paid is lower if no group income election is utilised (£2,500 against £7,500). This is because the FII in SA Ltd has effectively been transferred to A Ltd.

Surrender of ACT

Advance corporation tax paid on dividends (not other qualifying distributions) in the current accounting period may be surrendered *down* by the parent to a 51% subsidiary subject to the restrictions set out below. The parent company may surrender all or part of its ACT to one or more of its subsidiaries – there is no requirement for the parent to first set off ACT against its own corporation tax liability.

The surrendered ACT is treated as having been paid by the subsidiary in respect of a distribution made by that subsidiary on the date when the actual dividend was paid by the parent company. It is therefore available for set-off against the corporation tax liability of the subsidiary subject to the normal maximum set-off rules. If the subsidiary is unable to use the full amount of surrendered ACT in the current accounting period, the surplus may be *carried forward* by the subsidiary and set against corporation tax liabilities of future accounting periods provided that the subsidiary is still a 51% subsidiary throughout the whole of the accounting period for which its use is claimed. Surrendered ACT cannot be carried back.

The time limit for the claim to surrender ACT is six years from the end of the accounting period to which the claim to surrender relates. The claim to surrender ACT must be made by the surrendering company but the consent of the subsidiary/ies to which it is being surrendered is also required.

Payment for surrendered ACT is ignored for corporation tax purposes up to the amount of the surrendered ACT.

EXAMPLE 27.4

S Ltd is a wholly owned subsidiary of H Ltd. Both companies prepare accounts to 31 March each year. They have the following results for the year ended 31 March 1995. (Assume corporation tax rate 33% and the ACT rate 20/80.)

	H Ltd	S Ltd
	£	£
Schedule D Case I	300,000	15,000
Chargeable gains	10,000	
Group income (dividend from S)	15,000	
Dividend paid	279,000	15,000
ACT paid	69,750	Nil

Corporation tax computation for H Ltd

Worksheet – Part A	£
Schedule D Case I	300,000
Chargeable gains	10,000
Profits chargeable to corporation tax	310,000

Corporation tax liability 33%		102,300
Less: ACT Max 310,000 @ 20%	62,000	
Paid	69,750	(62,000)
Surplus surrendered	7,750	
Mainstream corporation tax		40,300

Corporation tax computation for S Ltd

		£
Schedule D Case I		15,000
Profits chargeable to corporation tax		15,000
Corporation tax liability 33%		4,950
Less: ACT Max 15,000 @ 20%	3,000	
Surrendered by H	7,750	(3,000)
Surplus to cf	4,750	
Mainstream corporation tax		1,950

Priority of set off of surrendered ACT

If in any accounting period a subsidiary has both surrendered ACT and ACT of its own, the surrendered ACT will be set off against the subsidiary's corporation tax liability in priority to ACT paid on its own dividends. This leaves its own ACT available to be carried back and set against the corporation tax liabilities of prior years (see Worksheet – Part B; Chapter 25).

EXAMPLE 27.5

SA Ltd is a 51% subsidiary of A Ltd. Both companies prepare accounts to 31 March. In the year ended 31 March 1995, A Ltd surrendered ACT of £15,000 to SA Ltd. SA Ltd paid a dividend of £12,000 in the year ended 31 March 1995 (and paid ACT of £3,000). The results of SA Ltd for the years ended 31 March 1994 and 31 March 1995 were as follows: (assume corporation tax rate 33% and ACT rate 20/80 in FY 1994 and 22.5/77.5 in FY 1993.

		31 March 1994		31 March 1995
		£		£
Schedule D Case I		80,000		50,000
Profits chargeable to CT		80,000		50,000
Corporation tax liability				
Profits chargeable to CT @ 33%		26,400		16,500
Less: ACT Max @ 22.5%/20%	18,000		10,000	
Surrendered	–		15,000	
Set off	–		10,000	(10,000)
Available cf	–		5,000	
Paid in year			3,000	
Carried back	3,000		(3,000)	
		(3,000)		
Mainstream corporation tax		23,400		6,500

Pay and file

Companies within a group are in the same position as single companies for interest purposes on a refund of tax under the ACT surrender provisions.

Restrictions on surrendering ACT

To enable ACT to be surrendered to a subsidiary, the subsidiary must have been a member of the 51% group *throughout the whole of the accounting period* in which the dividend to which the ACT relates was paid. To enable surrendered ACT to be used, the subsidiary must have been a member of the 51% group *throughout the whole of the accounting period* in which the use of the surrendered ACT is claimed.

For illustration of the effects of the above see Chapter 28.

Capital gains groups

Definition

A group for capital gains purposes is defined as a 75% group. Unfortunately the capital gains legislation does not use the same definition as corporation tax. A group for capital gains purposes is the parent company and its 75% subsidiaries and their 75% subsidiaries, except that any 75% subsidiary which is not 'an effective 51% subsidiary' of the principal company is excluded. A 75% subsidiary is one where at least 75% of the ordinary share capital is owned directly or indirectly by a UK-resident parent. Although a non-resident company cannot be a member of the group, a UK-resident 75% subsidiary of a non-resident company can be a member of the group of which its non-resident parent was a 75% subsidiary.

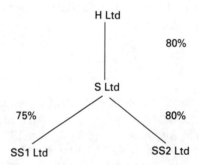

Figure 27.2 A capital gains group

An effective 51% subsidiary is one where the principal company (H Ltd in Figure 27.2) has more than a 50% interest in the profits and the assets of the group member. A company can not be a member of more than one group. All four companies above form a capital gains group.

Transfer of assets within a capital gains group

Companies within a capital gains group are 'connected persons' and therefore, in the absence of special relief, all transfers of chargeable assets between them would be deemed to be at market value. The market value rules are however not applied.

Where chargeable assets are transferred from one group company to another, the acquisition by the transferee company is deemed to be at a value which ensures that 'no gain, no loss' occurs to the transferor company (usually base cost plus indexation allowance). When the chargeable asset is eventually disposed of outside the group, the capital gain will be calculated by reference to the difference between the disposal proceeds and the original cost to the group. The intention of the legislation is that all companies within a capital gains group should be treated as if they were a single entity.

Note that for transfers of assets held on 31 March 1982, and transferred on a 'no gain, no loss' basis after 1 April 1988, an election for universal re-basing at 31 March 1982 made by the group transferor company applies to the ultimate disposal of the asset by the transferee company.

EXAMPLE 27.6

In Figure 27.2 above company SS1 Ltd can transfer a chargeable asset to H Ltd without any capital gain arising to SS1 Ltd.

EXAMPLE 27.7

A Ltd and B Ltd prepare accounts to 31 December each year. On 10 June 1973, A Ltd acquired retail shop premises for £50,000. The premises were transferred to B Ltd, a wholly owned subsidiary, on 25 August 1989, when the market value was £100,000 (March 1982 value, £75,000). Legal costs of £1,000 were incurred in the transfer. The indexation allowance amounted to £34,350, based on the higher of cost and March 1982 value. B Ltd disposed of the premises outside the group on 12 December 1994 for £175,000.

No capital gains arise until the accounting period for the year ended 31 December 1994, when B Ltd has a disposal for capital gains purposes. The date of acquisition of the asset to B Ltd is deemed to be the acquisition date to the group (10 June 1973) at the March 1982 value/cost to the group of £50,000 plus allowances as follows:

		Cost	31 March 1982 Value
		£	£
Original cost (March 1982 value) to the group		50,000	75,000
Add: legal fees (Aug 89)	1,000		
indexation allowance	34,350		
		35,350	35,350
		85,350	110,350

In addition to this B Ltd will be entitled to a further indexation allowance from 25 August 1989 to 12 December 1994.

There are a number of specific exceptions to the 'no gain, no loss' transfer of assets within a capital gains group and in these instances, a chargeable disposal will arise:

- if the intra-group transfer is in whole or part satisfaction of a debt
- if it is a disposal (upon their redemption) of redeemable shares in a group company
- on the deemed disposal of an interest in shares that is a capital distribution
- if the transferee company is a 'dual resident' company such that no chargeable gain will arise on the subsequent disposal of the asset (by virtue of a double tax treaty)

Certain transfers of shares which form part of a reorganisation are not regarded as transfers within a capital gains group as there is deemed not to be a disposal by the transferor (see Chapter 28). In addition, a chargeable gain will arise if a company leaves the group having received a group asset within the previous six years (see Chapter 7).

Intra-group transfers of assets to trading stock and trading stock to assets

Where a fixed asset of one group member becomes trading stock of the other group member, the transfer is treated as being of a fixed asset and the transferee company is then deemed to appropriate the fixed asset to its trading stock. This will be a chargeable disposal.

The chargeable gain or allowable loss will be the difference between the market value and the sum of the 'no gain, no loss' price and any further indexation allowance due, unless an election is made under TCGA 1992, s. 161(3). In this case, the market value at the time of appropriation (for Schedule D Case I purposes) will be reduced by the amount of the chargeable gain or increased by the amount of the allowable loss.

Where trading stock of one group company becomes a fixed asset of another group company, the transferor company is treated as having appropriated the asset to capital immediately before the transfer. The acquisition cost for capital gains purposes is the disposal value brought into the accounts.

Depreciatory transactions

There is anti-avoidance legislation governing what are known as 'depreciatory transactions'. These occur when, within a group, assets are transferred from one company to another at less than market value, or there is otherwise a deemed disposal, causing the value of the shares held in that company to be materially reduced such that a capital loss would arise on the disposal of those shares. Under such circumstances, the capital loss arising on the disposal of the shares may be restricted by the inspector to an amount which is 'just and reasonable'. Meanwhile, if the transferee company disposes of the asset in question outside the group within six years, and as a result of the depreciatory transaction (the no gain, no loss group transfer) makes a chargeable gain, this will also be reduced, as is 'just and reasonable'.

Election for FA 1988 re-basing provisions

In the case of 75% groups, this election must be made by the principal company in the group on behalf of the whole group.

Roll-over relief

As all the trades of a capital gains group are treated as a single trade, roll-over relief may be claimed on the disposal of a qualifying asset by one group company against the cost of assets acquired by another group member. The Finance Act 1990 denies a roll-over relief claim where the company acquiring the replacement asset is a dual resident company in which the replacement asset will be exempt from UK tax on any gains by virtue of a double tax treaty.

A recent case, *Campbell Connelly & Co. Ltd* v. *Barnett* (1992), denied rollover relief, however, where the replacement asset was acquired in two stages by different members of the capital gains group (the purchase of the original freehold and the acquisition of the under lease). The grounds were that although trades of group members were treated as a single trade, there is no provision for the members of a group to be treated as a single person. The government has since announced its intention that existing practice should be continued regardless of the outcome of the case.

75% groups

Definition

Again the relationship of parent company and subsidiary company must exist. Two companies resident in the UK are regarded as members of the same 75% group, where one company owns at least 75% of the ordinary share capital of the other or the share capitals of both are at least 75% owned by the same UK resident parent. The shareholdings may be either direct or indirect, but any shareholdings via a non-resident company are ignored (also the stock shareholdings of a share-dealer company are ignored).

Ordinary share capital is all of the issued share capital not bearing a fixed rate of dividend.

In addition to the above provisions, the parent must at least be entitled to a 75% share in the distributable profits available to the equity shareholders and a 75% share in the assets of the subsidiary on a winding up.

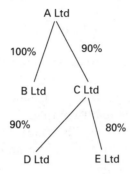

Figure 27.3   A 75% group

A Ltd is treated as owning 81% of D Ltd and 72% of E Ltd. Therefore provided that all the companies are UK resident, A, B, C and D form one 75% group, while C, D and E form another, separate, 75% group. Although C and D are common to both groups there is not a 75% group relationship between E and either A or B. In contrast, all companies (A, B, C, D, and E) would be members of one capital gains group.

If a company has a direct holding in another company plus a number of indirect holdings in the same company through one or more 'chains' of companies, the total percentage of ordinary share capital held in that company is found by multiplying the percentages in each chain and adding together the results.

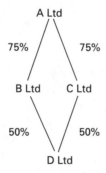

Figure 27.4   A 75% group (2)

A owns indirectly through B Ltd (75 × 50)% 37.5% of D Ltd and through C Ltd (75 × 50) % 37.5% of D Ltd that is, in total 75% of D Ltd. Therefore A, B, C, and D together form a 75% group.

A non-resident company is wholly disregarded. Any shares owned by a non-resident company in a UK company cannot be taken into account for the purposes of establishing indirect control.

It should be noted that companies being members of a 75% group will also inevitably be associated companies (see above), members of a 51% (see above) and members of a capital gains group (see above).

Additional reliefs available to members of a 75% group

One additional relief is available to members of a 75% group:

▶ Group relief may be claimed (subject to the further restrictions listed below).

Group relief (ICTA 1988, s. 402)

There are four different kinds of group relief available to members of a 75% group:

▶ group relief for trading losses
▶ group relief for excess charges
▶ group relief for certain capital allowances given by way of discharge or repayment of tax
▶ group relief for excess management expenses of an investment company.

The company in which the relief arises is called the 'surrendering company' and is said to surrender the relief. The company against whose profits the reliefs are claimed is called the 'claimant company'. The reliefs surrendered under a group relief claim must be deducted from the claimant company's total profits in the 'corresponding accounting period'. The maximum that may be surrendered to any one group company is the amount of the relief or the amount of the claimant company's *chargeable profits*, whichever is the less. The reliefs may be surrendered horizontally, vertically or downwards.

A claim for group relief must be made within two years of the end of the surrendering company's accounting period in which the relief arose and must be made by the claimant company (with the agreement of the surrendering company). Note that under pay and file, precise claims to group relief must be submitted with the corporation tax return and should be accompanied by a letter of consent from the surrendering company (the surrendering company must also submit details of amounts surrendered and copy of letter of consent). The loss available for surrender will then be determined. Companies within a group will be treated in the same way as single companies for interest on a refund of corporation tax under the group relief provisions.

It is not necessary for payment to be made for reliefs surrendered but, especially where there are minority interests in the surrendering company, it is usual to do so. Such payments are ignored for purposes of the corporation tax computation up to the amount of the relief surrendered.

Trade losses

Where a company is a member of a 75% group, group relief is available to a company with a trading loss. The trading loss can not only be used against the company's own profits as described in Chapter 24 but it can be set against the total profits of companies in the same group. The loss may be surrendered in whole or in part (that is, irrespective of minority interests and to suit the circumstances of both surrendering and claimant company) and may be surrendered in precedence to a claim under ICTA 1988 s. 393A. It may be offset against the total profits of the claimant company of the corresponding accounting period *after* deducting any s. 393A loss claims and after charges for the current year but before deducting s. 393A(1)(b) claims for the carry back of losses from a subsequent accounting period (see Worksheet – Part A; Chapter 24).

EXAMPLE 27.8

SH Ltd is the wholly owned subsidiary of H Ltd. Both companies make up accounts to 31 December each year. The following are their results for the years ending 31 December 1993 and 1994:

	H Ltd		SH Ltd	
31 December	1993	1994	1993	1994
	£	£	£	£
Schedule D Case I	40,000	50,000	80,000	(200,000)
Schedule A	7,500	10,000	–	–
Chargeable gains	–	60,000	–	–
UFII	10,000	10,000	10,000	10,000
Debenture interest paid	5,000	5,000	–	–

The amount of trading loss of SH Ltd available for group relief for the year ending 31 December 1994 is £200,000. Assume that SH Ltd cannot absorb any losses in years prior to 1993. The amount however which may be claimed by H Ltd is limited to the profits chargeable to tax in H Ltd for the year ended 31 December 1994 as follows:

	£
Schedule D Case I	50,000
Schedule A	10,000
Chargeable gains	60,000
UFII	10,000
	130,000
Less: Charges	(5,000)
Profits available for relief	125,000

SH Ltd may choose to take as much relief as it can against its own profits before surrendering its losses for group relief. In this example, SH Ltd may make a claim for loss relief under ICTA 1988 s. 393A before surrendering the balance for group relief. This involves a claim initially under s. 393 A(1)(a) with the possibility of extending it under s. 393 A(1)(b) to the 36 months prior to the period of the loss. In this example, no losses can be absorbed prior to 1993.

	SH Ltd	
	1993	1994
Schedule D Case I	80,000	Nil
UFII	10,000	10,000
Total profits	90,000	10,000
Less: Loss relief s. 393A	(90,000)	(10,000)
Profits chargeable to CT	Nil	Nil

	Loss memo
Loss for year	200,000
s. 393A year ended 31 Dec 1994	(10,000)
s. 393A year ended 31 Dec 1993	(90,000)
	100,000
Less: Amount surrendered to H Ltd	(100,000)
Loss remaining for carry forward	–

If, due to ACT paid in the accounting period, H Ltd did not want the whole of the £100,000, then H Ltd would only claim that part of the loss that it did want.

In practice SH and H would probably look at the marginal rates of tax suffered by each of them in the accounting periods in which the loss could be relieved. On the basis of this examination, losses would be allocated in order to maximise the tax savings.

Excess charges

A group company may surrender to any other group company, so much of its charges as exceed its profits in any accounting period (for the purpose of arriving at a figure of profits all losses or reliefs derived from earlier or later accounting periods must be ignored).

Corresponding accounting periods

In the examples considered so far, the accounting periods of the surrendering company and the claimant company have coincided and there has been no need to make adjustments to the reliefs surrendered to coincide with the profits of the corresponding accounting period.

Where the accounting periods of the surrendering and the claimant company do not coincide, only the profits of the claimant company earned in the part of the year which corresponds with the period in which the group relief arose, may be reduced by group relief.

EXAMPLE 27.9

S Ltd and H Ltd are members of a 75% group. S Ltd incurred a trading loss of £100,000 in the year ended 31 December 1994. H Ltd makes up accounts to 31 March and had the following results:

Year ended 31 March 1994: £60,000 profit
Year ended 31 March 1995: £140,000 profit

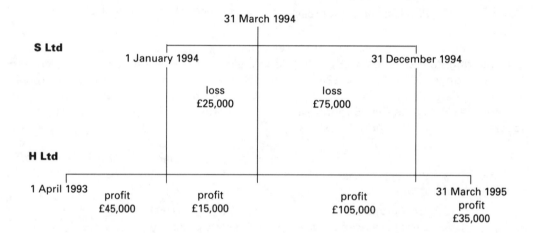

Figure 27.5

Corresponding period a) 1 Jan 1994–31 Mar 1994 group relief restricted to lower of £25,000 or £15,000
b) 1 Apr 1994–31 Dec 1994 group relief restricted to lower of £75,000 or £105,000

Anti-avoidance

From the date that arrangements exist to transfer ownership of a company out of a group, group relief ceases to be available.

Consortia

Definition

A company may be defined as a consortium company if it is a UK-resident company of which at least 75% of the ordinary share capital is owned beneficially by other UK-resident companies, (each having at least 5% and none having 75% or more of the ordinary share capital and each being beneficially entitled to at least 5% of the profits available to the equity shareholders and at least 5% of the assets available to the equity shareholders on a winding-up of the subsidiary). A 90% subsidiary of such a company, directly or indirectly, is also regarded as a consortium company.

The company should be a trading company, or a holding company, or a holding company with a trading company as its 90% subsidiary.

EXAMPLE 27.10

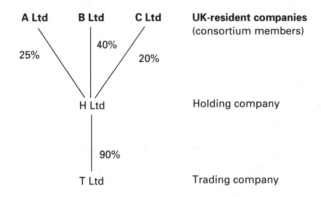

Figure 27.6

H Ltd and T Ltd are consortium companies as 75% of the ordinary share capital of H Ltd is owned by A Ltd, B Ltd and C Ltd.

Relief available in a consortium

There are two reliefs available in a consortium situation:

- group relief
- group income and charges elections.

Group relief

Although the legislation refers to a 'consortium claim', there is no reference to consortium relief. The relief is referred to as group relief and is computed in the same way as for 75% groups; in other words it is made up of:

- trading losses
- excess charges on income
- capital allowances given by way of discharge or repayment of tax
- excess management expenses.

It must be related to the corresponding accounting period and must be claimed within two years of the end of the surrendering company's accounting period in which the relief arose.

Group relief may be passed up or down between the consortium members and the consortium companies:

1. The amount of the relief which may be claimed by or surrendered to a consortium member is limited to the proportional interest of that consortium member in the ordinary share capital of the consortium company. The consortium company is, however, deemed to have used the loss to make the maximum possible claim under s. 393A.

In Example 27.10 above, A Ltd, B Ltd and C Ltd could each claim respectively a maximum of 25%, 40% and 20% of any trading losses of T Ltd or excess management expenses of H Ltd.

2 Conversely, if one of the consortium members had, for example, trading losses, then the amount of group relief that could be claimed by the consortium company would be limited to the proportional interest of that consortium member applied to the profits of the corresponding accounting period in the consortium company. In Example 27.10 above, any trading losses of B Ltd for example, could be claimed by T Ltd to a limit of 40% of T Ltd's profits chargeable to corporation tax for the corresponding accounting period.

A claim for group relief need not be for the full amount available and requires the consent of all the consortium members and of the surrendering company.

Group income and charges

The provisions relating to group income and group charges outlined for 51% groups are extended to consortium companies namely:

1 A consortium company (H Ltd or T Ltd in Example 27.10) may pay dividends to any consortium member (A Ltd, B Ltd or C Ltd in Example 27.10) without accounting for ACT.
2 A consortium company (H Ltd or T Ltd in Example 27.10) may pay charges to any consortium member (A Ltd, B Ltd or C Ltd in Example 27.10) without deducting income tax.

Link companies and group/consortium companies

A link company is a company which is both a member of a 75% group and a member of a consortium.

EXAMPLE 27.11

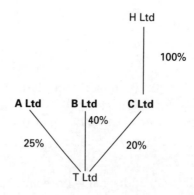

Figure 27.7

H Ltd and C Ltd form a 75% group. C Ltd is also a consortium member and is therefore a link company.

A group/consortium company is a company which is both a member of a 75% group and a consortium company. In Example 27.10, H Ltd was a group/consortium company.

There are provisions extending group relief in this type of structure. These are not examinable.

Groups and value added tax

Two or more companies may apply to be treated as a group provided that one of them controls the other or they are under common control (either by an individual or a body corporate); that is, in terms of the definitions for corporation tax purposes discussed above, associated companies may form a VAT group. Group treatment is also available where two or more individuals, in partnership, control two or more companies.

Associated companies may establish as many VAT groups as they wish. This is to say that each company may only belong to one VAT group but it is not necessary for all associated companies to belong to the same VAT group.

Care should be taken to establish efficient groups.

Group registration

One company, called the representative member, is registered for VAT (any existing registrations are cancelled) and is responsible for submitting returns and for payment of the tax on behalf of the group. (Application must be made by that company or by the person controlling them, at least 90 days before it is to take effect).

An application may only be refused if it is to protect the revenue and this refusal may be appealed against. Subsequently the group registration may be amended as follows:

- to add additional companies
- to remove companies
- to split the group into a number of separate groups
- to change the representative member
- to discontinue the group.

There has been some concern by the Customs and Excise about the use of VAT groups to reduce VAT liabilities and there has been a move to tighten up on the availability of group registration. Unless or until new legislation is introduced for the purpose, this can only be done through the enforcement of the existing legislation, that is, by refusal of group registrations and adherence to the 90 day rule.

Effect of group registration

The effect of group registration is that all businesses carried on by members of the group are treated as being carried on by the representative member. The output tax charged on the taxable supplies of the group as a whole may be set off against the input tax suffered by the group as a whole whilst transactions within the group (inter-company purchases and sales) are not taxable supplies, that is, no VAT is charged.

All members of the group are jointly and severally liable for any tax due by the representative member. In the event that the representative member is unable to meet the VAT debt of the group, the Customs and Excise will hold each group member liable for the amount of the debt arising while they were members of the group.

Planning considerations

The structure of the group needs to be planned carefully.

To achieve an efficient group, the membership of the group needs to be considered. A company supplying management services, for example, should be in the same group as companies receiving those management services – VAT does not need to be charged and this in itself may give a cash flow advantage. A company making large quantities of exempt supplies probably ought to be excluded from the group as should a company making predominantly zero-rated supplies which is able, outside the group, to submit monthly repayment claims. Any company supplying the public directly where turnover is below the registration limit should also be excluded.

The inclusion of companies which make a proportion of exempt supplies must be considered to ensure that the group as a whole does not suffer as a result of the partial exemption rules – their inclusion may even improve the partial exemption calculation.

Reorganisations

The VAT consequences of the reorganisations discussed in the next chapter should not be overlooked particularly where the movement of assets is involved. Many of the consequences are avoided if the transferor and the transferee are members of the same VAT group.

The transfer of a business or a trade may be regarded as a 'going concern' transfer and this has a special status for VAT purposes being treated as not being a supply, provided that certain conditions are satisfied:

▶ The purchaser must be liable to be registered or must actually become registered (that is, voluntarily).
▶ The purchaser must intend to use the assets for the same kind of business after the transfer.
▶ If only part of a business is being transferred, that part must be capable of independent operation.

If VAT is charged incorrectly it must be paid over to the Customs and Excise but cannot be recovered by the purchaser (except at the discretion of Customs and Excise). The VAT must also be refunded to the purchaser by the vendor. Conversely, if the transaction is incorrectly treated as qualifying, the vendor must account for the VAT to the Customs and Excise although he or she may not be able to recover it from the purchaser.

A clearance procedure is available where there is doubt whether the transaction will qualify. Where the transaction qualifies, there is an obligation to transfer all the value added tax records with the business.

If the VAT group to which the business is transferred is partly exempt, the representative member will be deemed to have made a 'self supply' (see Chapter 22). Any items included in the transfer of the business which are covered by the capital goods scheme (see Chapter 22) must be excluded from the self supply charge.

Planning considerations

The existence of a group increases the number of alternative courses of action available to a company in a given set of circumstances. In some circumstances options available become so numerous as to be confusing. Companies evaluate their options according to their own individual sets of priorities which may be claiming relief at the earliest opportunity (cashflow), or saving tax at the highest possible rates (commonly referred to as tax rate arbitrage).

For students, a knowledge of the various alternative reliefs is essential, along with an understanding of the consequential effects in terms of the interaction of reliefs, the effect on the corporation tax rate, double tax relief and ACT set-off.

Summary

▶ The penalties and benefits of companies being linked together in the form of groups depend on how closely they are linked.
▶ The following are possible consequences of being a group:

a) The thresholds for small companies rate of corporation tax are shared equally between the companies
b) Group companies may jointly elect to pay dividends between themselves without accounting for ACT and/or to pay charges between themselves without deducting income tax
c) Parent companies may surrender ACT to subsidiary companies
d) Group relief for trading losses, excess charges, capital allowances and excess management expenses is available
e) Assets may be transferred to other group companies without any capital gains implications
f) Roll-over relief for replacement of business assets is available on a group basis.

▶ Where one company controls another, or they are both controlled by the same person – not necessarily a company – they are called associated companies. Small company thresholds apply.
▶ Where control is through companies, such that a parent/subsidiary relationship exists, there is said to be a 51% group. a), b) and c) above apply.
▶ Where control is 75% or more, the companies are members of a 75% group – a), b), c), d), e) and f) above apply but note the slight difference in the definitions for capital gains groups and groups for purposes of group relief.

Note the flexibility of group relief. Group relief is the only loss relief which may be claimed 'in whole or in part' dependent upon the whims of the surrendering/claimant companies.

▶ Where a company is owned by a consortium, b) and d) above apply.
▶ Value added tax applies to companies just as it does to individuals.
▶ There are additional provisions relating to companies which are intended to aid administration either where a company is very large and geographically spread out or where a company operates through a number of subsidiary companies: these are divisional registration and group registration respectively.
▶ Because of the flexibility of the group registration, tax savings may be made with properly planned VAT groups.

Self test questions

1   What is the order of set-off of the following: trade charges; non-trade charges; loss relief under s. 393A(1)(a) and (b); group relief?

2   Describe the conditions to be satisfied for a parent to surrender ACT to a subsidiary.

3   What is meant by the group income election?

4   What is the priority of set-off of ACT, that is, own ACT paid in the current year, brought forward from a previous year, or carried back from a subsequent year or surrendered ACT?

5   How much ACT may be surrendered?

6   Describe the conditions to be met for group relief to be claimed.

7   What is the time limit for claiming group relief and who makes the claim?

8   What reliefs are available to a consortium?

9   What conditions must exist for companies to apply for group registration for VAT purposes?

10 What is the time limit for group registration?

11 Define a group for capital gains purposes.

12 What are the consequences of being a group for capital gains purposes?

13 H Ltd owns 80% of the ordinary share capital of S Ltd. Neither company has any other associated companies and both companies have been trading since 1978.

The following information relates to the two most recent accounting periods of each company:

H Ltd

	12 months to 31 December 1993 £	9 months to 30 September 1994 £
Adjusted Schedule D I	25,000	(45,000)
Schedule A	3,000	4,000
Loan interest paid (gross)	2,000	2,000

S Ltd

	12 months to 31 March 1994 £	12 months to 31 March 1995 £
Adjusted Schedule D I	52,000	250,000
Schedule D III	8,000	10,000
Loan interest paid (gross)	5,000	5,000

Neither company paid or received any dividends in any of the above periods.

Compute the MCT payable by each company for each of the above accounting periods and show any loss carried forward by H Ltd.

14 H Ltd acquired the whole of the share capital of S Ltd on 1 April 1994. Neither H Ltd nor S Ltd has any other associated companies.

The following information relates to the year ended 31 March 1995.

	H Ltd £	S Ltd £
Income:		
Trading profits	36,000	133,000
Bank deposit interest	4,500	15,000
Debenture interest (gross)	6,000	7,500
Franked Investment Income	18,000	28,500
Chargeable capital gains	4,500	13,500
Charges paid:		
Loan interest (gross)	7,500	6,000
Charitable covenant (gross)	1,500	1,500
Dividends paid:		
Final in respect of year ended 31 March 1994		
– paid 30 June 1994	43,900	–
Interim in respect of current year		
– paid 31 December 1994	10,950	–

a) Compute the mainstream corporation tax payable by each company, assuming advantage is taken of any reliefs available.

b) Advise the directors of H Ltd of the effect of S Ltd paying a dividend to H Ltd.

c) Discuss the implication of H Ltd having acquired the assets, liabilities and business of S Ltd and winding it up, instead of acquiring its share capital. (Assume that the above profits and gains of both companies are earned by H Ltd and that H Ltd pays all the above charges.)

CIMA May 1988

15 The following diagram represents the relationships, in terms of ordinary share capital held, between the companies shown:

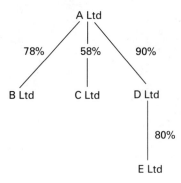

Figure 27.8

The following information relates to the year ended 31 March 1995:

	Schedule DI	Schedule DIII	Loan interest paid (gross)
	£	£	£
A Ltd profit	76,000	–	3,000
B Ltd loss	24,000	3,000	1,000
C Ltd profit	90,000	15,000	4,000
D Ltd profit	65,000	–	2,000
E Ltd loss	12,000	–	–

None of the above companies had any other income or gains.

a) Compute the corporation tax payable by each company, assuming group relief is claimed in the most efficient manner.
b) Explain the circumstances in which a group of companies should set aside an existing group income election.

CIMA May 1988

16 The directors of a public company have decided that a number of subsidiaries will be acquired and that the business will engage, for the first time, in export activities.

Draft a report to the board on the VAT implications of the above proposals.

CIMA May 1989

Answers on pages 617–620

CHAPTER 28

Reorganisations

The purpose of this chapter is to look at the taxation implications of setting up some of the more common commercial business structures and of reversing the process at a later date once the commercial need for them has disappeared.

Background

Within the section on unincorporated businesses we have already looked at the transfer of an unincorporated business to a company and the effect this has:

- on trading losses brought forward
- on the transfer of the business assets for capital allowance purposes
- on the capital gains tax position of the sole trader or partnership.

Tax reliefs are available in all of these areas for a bona fide commercial transaction. Once a company is in existence it may be taken over or merged with another company and this also will usually be without penalty. Where the acquisition is effected by the issue of shares in the acquiring company to the shareholders in the amalgamating company, it is treated as a share-for-share exchange with no disposal having occurred for capital gains tax purposes. The only restrictions may be on the carry forward of losses and in both the carry forward and carry back of ACT where in any period of three years there has been both a change in ownership and a major change in the nature or conduct of the trade, or prior to the change in ownership the scale of activities in the company's trade had become small or negligible (see Chapters 24 and 25). Provisions also restrict the use of pre-entry capital losses.

A change of ownership is disregarded if both before and after the change the company is a 75% subsidiary of another company; this prevents the loss of ACT, trading losses and capital losses where there is a group reorganisation, under which the ultimate ownership of the company does not change. Remember that the definition of a 75% subsidiary ensures that a 75% subsidiary is one in which the parent is entitled to a 75% share in the profits available to the ordinary shareholders and a 75% share of the assets of the subsidiary on a winding-up. If there is a change in ownership of a company, there will be deemed to be a change of ownership of any shares (rights or powers) held by that company.

This chapter will look at each of the following commercial arrangements and outline the related tax implications:

- a company joins or leaves a group
- share-for-share amalgamations
- capital reductions and purchase of own shares
- disincorporation
- liquidations.

A company joins or leaves a group

Group relief

When a company begins or ceases to be a member of a 75% group, a notional accounting period is treated as beginning or ending on that date and the profits/losses of the accounting period are apportioned over the respective notional accounting periods (for the purpose of computing group relief only). If apportionment on a time basis appears to be unreasonable, any other method of apportionment which appears to be reasonable may be used.

Group relief is then available for the corresponding accounting periods.

EXAMPLE 28.1

A Ltd is a trading company with two wholly owned subsidiaries, B Ltd and C Ltd. All three companies make up their accounts to 31 March each year. C Ltd left the group on 30 June 1994. The results of the three companies for the year ended 31 March 1995 were as follows:

	A Ltd £	B Ltd £	C Ltd £
Schedule D Case I profit/(loss)	600,000	120,000	(200,000)
Schedule D Case III	10,000		

Assume A Ltd is the claimant company for group relief.

Both A Ltd and C Ltd are treated as having a notional accounting period ending on 30 June 1994. Assuming that time apportionment is reasonable, profits and losses are apportioned to the notional accounting periods as follows:

	A Ltd	C Ltd
1 April 1994–30 June 1994	(1/4) 152,500	(1/4) (50,000)
1 July 1994–31 March 1995	(3/4) 457,500	(3/4) (150,000)

As C Ltd left the group on 30 June 1994 only the loss for the notional accounting period from 1 April 1994 to 30 June 1994 is available for group relief ie £50,000. A Ltd is able to absorb the whole of this amount as its profits for the same notional accounting period were £152,500.

The corporation tax computations of the companies are then:

	A Ltd £	B Ltd £	C Ltd £
Schedule D Case I profit	600,000	120,000	–
Schedule D Case III	10,000	–	–
Total profits	610,000	120,000	–
Less: group relief	(50,000)	–	–
Profits chargeable to CT	560,000	120,000	–

	Loss memo
Schedule D Case I loss	200,000
Less: utilised group relief	(50,000)
Balance of loss for carry forward	150,000

In the above example it was assumed that the loss was surrendered to A Ltd but it could equally have been surrendered to B Ltd. In that case the maximum claim by B Ltd would have been £30,000 (B's profits for the notional accounting period, that is, 1/4 of £120,000) and C Ltd could have surrendered its remaining loss for the notional accounting period £20,000 (£50,000 – £30,000) to A Ltd. This latter course of action may have been the better course when the companies' marginal rates of tax are considered The lower limit is £100,000 (£300,000 ÷ 3) therefore B Ltd will be suffering standard rate tax with taper relief – a marginal rate of 35%. Whereas the upper limit is £500,000 (£1,500,000 ÷ 3) thus A Ltd will be suffering tax at the standard rate only. The optimal solution is to transfer sufficient loss to B to take it down to the small companies rate, with the balance to A. B therefore needs £20,000 (£120,000 – £100,000).

ACT surrendered to a subsidiary

When a company begins or ceases to be a member of a 51% group, the surrender of ACT by the parent is likely to be restricted. The company must have been a subsidiary throughout the whole of the accounting period in which the dividend to which the ACT relates, was paid. Any ACT not used immediately by the subsidiary could be carried forward by the subsidiary for use in a subsequent accounting period but the company must also have been a subsidiary throughout the whole of the accounting period in which the surrendered ACT is used.

EXAMPLE 28.2

A Ltd surrendered ACT to C Ltd in the year ended 30 September 1993. C Ltd was unable to use it all in that year and carried forward £20,000 to year ended 30 September 1994.

C Ltd left the group on 31 December 1993 and therefore was not a subsidiary throughout the whole of year ended September 1994. ACT surrendered by A Ltd could not be offset (even if there had been profits) and would be wasted.

If both companies are subsidiaries of a third company for the remaining part of the period the company is not treated as leaving the group and ACT can continue to be carried forward

Z Ltd is able to use the surrendered ACT of Y Ltd.

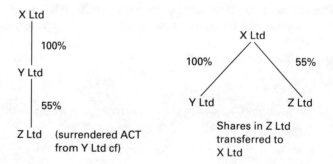

Figure 28.1

No gain, no loss intra-group transfers of assets

When a group member leaves the 75% group and:

▶ within the six years prior to leaving has received a chargeable asset from another group company which was deemed, for capital gains tax purposes, to have been transferred at no gain, no loss (that is, usually at original cost plus an indexation allowance to date of transfer),

▶ it still has the asset (or a replacement asset under the roll-over provisions)

the group member will be deemed to have sold the asset and immediately reacquired it at market value at the date of the original transfer.

The gain will be deemed to arise at the beginning of the accounting period in which the company leaves the group, although it is computed according to the accrual transfer date.

EXAMPLE 28.3 (Example 28.1 continued)

In March 1990, A Ltd transferred a building to C Ltd which it had acquired in January 1985 for £50,000. The market value of the building in March 1990 was £100,000. C Ltd still occupied the building in June 1994 when it left the group. The market value at that date was £120,000.

In March 1990 A Ltd would have transferred the asset on a no gain, no loss basis to C Ltd. C Ltd would have a deemed acquisition date of January 1985 and a deemed acquisition cost of:

```
Cost (January 1985)                              50,000
Indexation allowance
  (121.4 − 91.2) / 91.2  = 0.331 × 50,000        16,550
                                                 ──────
                                                 66,550
```

On leaving the group in June 1994. C Ltd will be deemed to have sold the asset and reacquired it at March 1990 at market value at that date:

```
                        £
MV                   100,000
Deemed cost           66,550
Chargeable gain       33,450    assessable year ended 31 March 1995 (the
                                year in which C Ltd leaves the group)
```

There are a number of exemptions to this charge: for example, leaving the group on a winding up or in consequence of certain mergers (see below).

Collection of outstanding corporation tax

The Finance Act 1994 introduced new rules to prevent the avoidance of corporation tax on a change in ownership of a company, known as the 'tax-payer company'.

If corporation tax remains unpaid six months after the date on which it was assessed, the Inland Revenue may now recover the outstanding tax from any person who had control of the tax-payer company immediately prior to the change in ownership or, from any company of which that person had control.

In order for these provisions to apply, any one of the following conditions must be fulfilled:

▶ the activities of the tax-payer company either ceased or became small or negligible within the three years prior to the change in ownership of the tax-payer company, and no significant revival of the activities occurred before the change in ownership
▶ as a result of arrangements made before the change in ownership, the activities of the tax-payer company became small or negligible after the change in ownership
▶ there is a major change in the nature or conduct of the trade of the tax-payer company, due to the transfer of assets to the person having control of the company or to any person connected to him. These transfers must have occurred within the three years preceding the change in ownership or after the change in ownership but under arrangements made before that change.

Anti-avoidance

The value-shifting provisions cover situations where arrangements have been made to artificially reduce the value of a subsidiary before its sale.

Capital losses

The set off of capital losses brought into a group of companies as a result of a company joining the group is restricted. Specifically:

- pre-entry losses will not be able to set off a gain on a post-entry acquisition
- no restriction will be placed on a set-off where two or more companies join the group at the same time
- allows the set off of pre-entry losses against gains accruing when shares were exchanged for qualifying corporate bands pre-entry
- excludes from the restrictions, reconstructions where a new holding company is inserted in a group without a change in ownership.

Share-for-share amalgamations

Where all or part of a company's business is transferred in exchange for an issue of shares by the transferee company to the shareholders of the transferor company, the shareholders will not be treated as having realised a chargeable gain on the exchange of shares provided that:

- the exchange of shares is entered into in connection with a scheme of reconstruction or amalgamation (or by concession, demerger)
- the transferee company issues shares as closely as possible in proportion to the original holdings in the transferor company (the shares in the transferor company are cancelled).

The purpose of these provisions is to facilitate reorganisations for bona fide commercial reasons which would otherwise be expensive in terms of tax and which, although they alter the form of an undertaking, result in substantially the same business being run by substantially the same persons. Such a scheme may be one which requires the approval of the directors and shareholders only or one which requires the approval of the court. It is necessary under these sections for the transferor company to be dissolved or wound up as otherwise the distribution of shares by the transferee company would constitute a distribution on which ACT would be payable.

Clearance

It is advisable to obtain Inland Revenue clearance in advance for any scheme of reconstruction under each of the above sections. The application may be made by either the company issuing the shares or the company being acquired. More details may be requested by the Inland Revenue within 30 days and the clearance decision must be made within 30 days of either the application or the receipt of the further information.

EXAMPLE 28.4

As part of a scheme of reconstruction involving company A, shares in company B are issued to the shareholders of company A in proportion to their shareholdings in company A as a result of which the shares in company A are subsequently cancelled.

The new shares in company B are deemed to have been acquired at the cost or base value of shares in company A. This would normally happen on a reconstruction with the consent of the court and company A would be dissolved without a formal winding up; it could also happen on a voluntary liquidation.

Capital reduction and purchase of own shares

Capital reduction

A company may repay surplus capital with the permission of the court. This is not normally a qualifying distribution, but would be treated as a part disposal for capital gains tax.

Purchase of own shares

With the introduction by the Companies Act 1981 of provisions for a company to purchase its own shares, amendments to the tax legislation were needed for it to be an attractive proposition.

Before this a company could only purchase its own shares if these were issued as redeemable preference shares. This was not a qualifying distribution unless the shares were originally issued as bonus shares or the redemption price exceeded the amount originally subscribed.

The purchase by a company of its own shares is not a repayment of capital (to the extent that the redemption or purchase is financed out of profits, the company's fixed capital must be preserved by a transfer to capital redemption reserve), nor is it a distribution on account of share capital on a winding up, and therefore it would normally be a qualifying distribution for tax purposes (that is, ACT would be due).

Provisions were introduced by Finance Act 1982 which, if satisfied, allow the purchase of own shares to be treated as a disposal by the shareholder for capital gains tax purposes rather than as a qualifying distribution.

The provisions to be satisfied are as follows:

- The company must be an unquoted trading company or member of a trading group (unquoted means not listed and not a 51% subsidiary of a listed company).
- The purpose must be wholly or mainly for the benefit of the trade (not as part of a scheme of tax avoidance) or to allow the vendor to meet inheritance tax liabilities which would otherwise cause undue hardship (in which case no further provisions need to be satisfied).
- The vendor must be resident and ordinarily resident in the UK when the shares are purchased.
- The vendors or their spouses must in most cases have owned the shares throughout the period of five years preceding the date of purchase.
- As a result of the purchase of the shares by the company, the vendor's interest (together with that of associates) must be substantially reduced (vendor's interest constitutes both his or her percentage of the share capital and the percentage share of the distributable profits and substantial means by at least 25%).
- After the purchase of the shares by the company, the vendor must cease to be connected with the company or any company in the same 51% group (connected means generally owning with associates more than 30% of the issued ordinary share capital).

For the benefit of the trade

The Inland Revenue have stated that they will accept that the purchase of shares will benefit the company's trade in the following different sets of circumstances:

- A dissident shareholder is having an adverse effect on the running of the company's trade.
- The majority shareholder is retiring to make way for new management.
- An outside shareholder is withdrawing his investment.
- The personal representatives of a shareholder who has died do not wish to keep the shares.

Clearance

It is possible to apply for clearance before a company purchases its own shares, in order to confirm whether or not the above provisions are satisfied. As with other clearances the application must be in writing and the Inland Revenue have 30 days from receipt of the application or receipt of further particulars to give or refuse clearance.

EXAMPLE 28.5

The shareholders of X Ltd are as follows:

X	1,200	} 70%
Brother of X	200	
Y	600	
	2,000	100%

If the company purchases 800 of X's shares, the shareholdings in X Ltd would become:

X	400	} 50%
Brother of X	200	
Y	600	
	1,200	100%

X's holding has been substantially reduced (that is, by 28.5% – 20/70 × 100).

However, X is still connected with the company as his interest is greater than 30% of the share capital. Unless the company purchases a greater number of its own shares to satisfy this provision, the purchase of the shares will be treated as a distribution on which ACT will be due to be paid by the company. Provided the company has profits chargeable to corporation tax for the period sufficient to set off the ACT arising, the only consequence of the treatment as a distribution from the company viewpoint is cash flow.

As far as X is concerned, he will be deemed to have income equal to the proceeds less original cost × 100/80 (in 1994/95) which will be liable to income tax as his top slice of income less the tax credit. If the disposal had qualified to be treated as a capital gain only the excess of the proceeds over the cost price of the shares (plus indexation) would be taxable. It would qualify for the capital gains annual exemption and the balance would be chargeable at the marginal rate of income tax.

Disincorporation

The converse of converting a business into a company is disincorporation. This can normally only be achieved by putting the company into liquidation. There is at present no legislation to facilitate a move from running a business in a company to running it as a sole trader or partnership, for example, in respect of deferring shareholders' capital gains and transferring a company's trading losses.

A company may be wound up by members' voluntary liquidation, by creditors' voluntary liquidation or by the court as a compulsory liquidation. It is also possible to enter into a court-approved reconstruction, when the transferor company is dissolved without a winding up. Alternatively, it may be struck off the register by the Registrar of Companies.

Liquidation

Cessation of accounting periods

An accounting period for corporation tax ends whenever any of the following occur:
- the cessation of trading (if prior to the appointment of a liquidator)
- commencement of the winding up (that is, the appointment of the liquidator)
- 12-monthly intervals from passing of resolution to wind up
- anticipated completion of the winding up (agreed in advance by liquidator and Inland Revenue for tax liabilities to be settled)
- 12-monthly intervals from date of anticipated completion of winding up as above
- actual completion of the winding up.

Where tax rates are not known for the final financial year involved when the liquidator is ready to settle final tax liabilities, the rates for the previous financial year are used.

Taxation consequences of the appointment of a liquidator

- A trading loss brought forward under ICTA, 1988 s. 393(1) prior to the liquidation may be carried forward and set off against trading income while the liquidator continues to trade.
- Group membership is effectively lost for group relief purposes if the parent company goes into liquidation and it is not possible for group relief to be surrendered or claimed.
- Plant and machinery sold after the cessation of trade is deemed to be sold on the last day of trading.
- Terminal loss relief may be claimed on the cessation of trade when this takes place.
- Post-cessation trading expenses may be deducted from post-cessation receipts – it is normal to ensure that the final accounts of the trade include claims for all trading expenses.
- Capital losses brought forward prior to the liquidation may be set off against net capital gains during liquidation.
- The group relationship for capital gains purposes is not lost; therefore intra-group transfers of assets may continue to be made and no company is deemed to have left a group as a result of a liquidation.
- Surplus ACT brought forward prior to the liquidation may be set against the mainstream corporation tax liability in the liquidation period, subject to the usual limits.
- Group membership is lost for purposes of group income elections and surrender of ACT if the parent company goes into liquidation. Any surrendered ACT brought forward in a subsidiary company is lost.

Distribution in a liquidation

Distributions in a winding up are specifically excluded from being qualifying distributions even if they are in respect of income during the liquidation period.

Liquidation distributions are part disposals for capital gains tax purposes.

Summary

▶ It can be seen from the above pages that the tax implications of commercially acceptable reorganisations are found simply by looking at what is in fact being done and applying the provisions of each of the taxes separately to that situation. A thorough working knowledge of each of the taxes is necessary before this can be attempted.

▶ Additionally, there may be special tax arrangements for particular types of reorganisations satisfying specific conditions. It is always necessary to ensure that none of the anti-avoidance legislation is infringed.

▶ The Inland Revenue clearance procedures are invaluable in checking that a particular reorganisation will work as planned.

Self test questions

1   Company A makes up its accounts to 31 December each year and in the year to 31 December 1994 it incurs a trading loss of £50,000. It acquired 80 per cent of the share capital of company B on 1 July 1994. B has a trading profit of £40,000 for the six months to 31 December 1994. How much group relief is available?

2   If ACT of £10,000 were available for surrender by A in the above circumstances (Question 1) for the year end 31 December 1994, how much could be surrendered?

3   Describe the consequences of a company leaving a capital gains group in possession of an asset transferred to it by another group company at 'no gain no loss'.

4   Explain the purpose of applying for 'clearance'.

5   What provisions (the main ones) must be satisfied if the purchase of its own shares by a company is to be regarded as a capital gains disposal for the shareholder?

6   Where a company purchases its own shares the vendor is required substantially to reduce his or her holding in the company if the transaction is to qualify for relief from distribution charges.

Explain briefly three tests that determine whether the vendor has substantially reduced his or her holding.

7   Harry's shareholding in Rosefield Ltd, an unquoted UK trading company, is 4,000 ordinary £1 shares and 800 preference £1 shares. The total issued share capital is 4,800 ordinary £1 shares and 3,200 preference £1 shares.

It is proposed that Rosefield Ltd will purchase 3,250 £1 ordinary shares from Harry for £2 each.

The preference shares have a fixed dividend of 12%. Rosefield's undistributed reserve are £8,000 before the purchase.

Compute whether this proposal will qualify for relief from distribution charges.

Answers on page 620

Tax Planning and Tax Avoidance

CHAPTER 29

This chapter considers in general terms the steps which may be taken to minimise a tax liability and identifies the principal tax benefits and costs of incorporation. The manner in which tax planning may be affected by both anti-avoidance legislation and developments in the approach to tax avoidance adopted by the courts when interpreting the legislation is considered.

Tax planning in general

Before any thought can be given to tax planning, it is necessary to have a firm grasp of the tax legislation as it affects a given situation or a particular transaction. This involves an appreciation of the impact of each of the foregoing taxes and their interrelationship with each other.

It is not sufficient to be able to do computations mechanically when faced with a given set of circumstances. Familiarity with the situations in which they may be required is necessary as well as a working knowledge of the conditions which must be satisfied before allowances, exemptions and reliefs may be claimed.

Planning involves anticipating a set of circumstances and identifying of opportunities to minimise or defer tax liabilities. At its simplest it involves arranging affairs to ensure that the maximum allowances, exemptions and reliefs are available. Cashflow and the marginal tax rates of consecutive fiscal years should also be considered. Timing is an important element as has been shown in earlier chapters particularly in relation to acquisitions, disposals, the choice of accounting date, and the date of cessation of trade.

For your examination, you are expected to be sufficiently familiar with the legislation to advise taxpayers about the options available at a given time and to identify situations where a minor alteration in the timing of anticipated events may be to their advantage. Throughout the book an effort has been made to consider the opportunities for tax planning which may be available in given situations.

The first major decision made at the commencement of any business, however, is about the business medium. This decision is often not made in the context only of the taxation consequences (nor should it be) but has a fundamental impact on the subsequent liabilities to taxation for the parties involved. It is important that you have an overall view of the taxation of each type of business medium.

Comparison of a limited company with an unincorporated business

There are many factors, both legal and financial, to be considered when a business medium is chosen. Not the least of these are the tax considerations.

As an unincorporated business is not a legal entity, its profits belong entirely to its owner/owners and are liable to income tax in their hands. Companies are a separate legal entity and are liable to corporation tax on the profits remaining after remuneration has been paid to the 'owner' (director). The 'owner' of a limited company may also receive remuneration or dividend or a combination of both and is liable to income tax thereon.

The other difference between an unincorporated business and a company is the legal requirement for companies to have their accounts audited. These requirements are being relaxed slightly.

Companies with a turnover below £90,000 will no longer be required to have an audit. Companies with a turnover between £90,000 and £350,000 will now be required to have a 'compilation report' rather than a full audit.

Remuneration

One of the key considerations of individuals who intend to set up in business will be their personal tax position. If they set up in business as a sole trader or in partnership with others, they will be self-employed. If, on the other hand, they set up a company, they will be an employee (albeit a director) of that company. The personal taxation of an individual under Schedule D Case I and under Schedule E has been fully considered elsewhere in this text. It is relevant here to recap on a number of points. From the point of view of the company it is also important to appreciate the cost to the employer.

A remuneration package may consist of salary, fees, bonuses and so forth and benefits in kind. Some of the benefits may not be taxable on the employee but their cost to the company is deductible in the company's Schedule D Case I computation. These are obviously the most valuable benefits. The most important one from the director's point of view is pension scheme contributions. Other benefits in kind, although taxable on the employee, are also deductible in the company's Schedule D Case I computation and are a relatively tax-efficient means of paying remuneration to a company director. The principal such benefit is a company car (although its tax efficiency has been reduced over the last few years with the increased scale benefit and the employer's NIC liability thereon). The income tax treatment of the car benefit was reformed from April 1994 and as benefits are now based on a percentage of list price (including vintage cars) the former advantages of this type of remuneration are virtually cancelled out.

In the unincorporated business, the market value of goods taken by the proprietor is taxable and the costs associated with any private use of assets by the proprietor are disallowed. Any salary taken by the proprietor is an appropriation of profit and is also disallowed.

In both cases if the spouse is employed, the salary must be justifiable as reasonable in relation to the work done. However, there is added flexibility to the sole trader or partnership, where the spouse may be taken in as an active partner taking whatever share in profits the partners choose.

National Insurance

National Insurance contributions are a major cost to all employers. Class I contributions are payable by both the employer and the employee as shown in Chapter 3.

The maximum cost to an employee is therefore £38.44 per week (£56.99 @ 2% per week plus £373 @ 10%) or £1,998.88 per annum; but the cost to the employer, although tax deductible, is unlimited. The liability is calculated on the gross earnings of employees before their superannuation contributions are deducted. NIC contributions are therefore paid on overtime, commissions, fees, bonuses and sick payments to the employee by the employer but are not charged on benefits in kind (other than on a company car and fuel), gratuities not paid by the employer, and expenses incurred in employment reimbursed by the employer. For directors, the NIC liability cannot be reduced by opting to pay the greater part of the remuneration in the form of annual lump sums (that is, fees and bonuses) since for directors the lower and upper earnings limits are applied on an annual basis (£2,964 and £22,360 per annum).

The national insurance liability may be mitigated by the payment of dividends rather than remuneration although the effectiveness of this depends on where the share ownership lies.

A sole trader or partner, on the other hand, must pay a weekly flat rate Class 2 National Insurance contribution of £5.65 (£293.80 per annum) if annual profits exceed £3,200. This amount is not tax deductible. In addition, Class 4 contributions at 7.3% are payable on the slice of profits falling between £6,490 and £22,360 for 1994/95. The maximum Class 4 contribution is thus £1,158.51, and one-half of these are an allowable deduction for income tax purposes.

EXAMPLE 29.1

a) Director paid £22,360		b) Profits of sole trader or partner £22,360	
	£		£
Class 1 employee	1,998.88	Class 2	293.80
Class 1 employer	2,280.72	Class 4	1,158.51
	4,279.60		1,452.31
Deductible (CT)	2,280.72	Deductible (IT)	579.26

This is a very significant cost differential which gets bigger the larger the remuneration/profits figure used although it should be borne in mind that some social security benefits are not available to the self-employed.

Dividends

The payment of remuneration and benefits reduces the profits liable to corporation tax (and may affect the rate of corporation tax) but, as illustrated above, the National Insurance costs are high. The payment of a dividend does not reduce profits liable to corporation tax but does not involve the payment of National Insurance nor does it provide a pension on retirement. Advance corporation tax is payable but this may be offset against the mainstream corporation tax liability. A record of substantial dividend payments may inflate the share value on a subsequent disposal for inheritance and capital gains tax purposes as will retained profit (note that BPR may mitigate the inheritance tax effect). A combination of remuneration and dividend usually gives the best result. (Note that this is only an option if the directors own the shares in suitable proportions).

EXAMPLE 29.2

A company has profits chargeable to corporation tax of £20,000 before paying either remuneration or dividends. Consider a single director's financial position if:
a) the profit is paid out as remuneration
b) the profit is paid out as dividend
c) the profit is paid out half in remuneration and half in dividend.

	(a)	(b)	(c)
Cost to company	£	£	£
Salary	18,149	–	9,294
Employers NIC (10.2%)	1,851	– (7.6%)	706
	20,000	–	10,000
Profits	20,000	20,000	20,000
Profits chargeable to CT	–	20,000	10,000
CT liability 25%	–	5,000	2,500
Cash dividend payable	–	15,000	7,500
ACT (deduct from CT) 20/80	–	3,750	1,875
MCT	–	1,250	625
Net cash outflow	20,000	20,000	20,000
Effect on director	£	£	£
Tax position			
Schedule E	18,149	–	9,294
Dividend 100/80	–	18,750	9,375
	18,149	18,750	18,669
Personal allowance	(3,445)	(3,445)	(3,445)
Taxable income	14,704	15,305	15,224
Income tax 20%/25%	3,526	3,061.00	3,187.25
Less: tax credit dividend (20%)	–	(3,750.00)	(1,875.00)
	3,526	(689.00)	1,312.25
Net cash inflow			
Salary	18,149	–	9,294
Employee's NIC 2%/10%	(1,578)	–	(692)
Dividend	–	15,000	7,500
Tax (payable)/repayable	(3,526)	689	(1,312)
	13,045	15,689	14,790

It should be noted that where no national insurance contributions are made this would adversely affect the right to social security benefits.

Pensions

Company pension arrangements for employees, including directors, may be more generous than those possible for the self-employed.

The small company may contribute to a small self-administered scheme of which the director himself is trustee. Often the scheme is able to reinvest the funds back into assets used by the company. The director may contribute up to 15% of earnings into the scheme (tax deductible) but the only limit to the amount that the company may contribute is that the contributions should not be more than is necessary to give the maximum approved level of benefits to the director on his retirement (2/3 final remuneration (max. £76,800) after 20 years service).

Where remuneration is given in the form of benefits in kind (to reduce the liability to National Insurance for example) this may adversely affect the maximum approved level of retirement benefits payable by the fund (since benefits in kind may not be included for purposes of establishing final remuneration for pension purposes). Similarly, if the decision is taken to pay dividends instead of remuneration, there may be a consequential effect on retirement benefits.

A sole trader or partner may contribute into a personal pension plan up to 17.5% (or more if he or she is over 35 years of age at the beginning of the tax year). This is often insufficient to provide benefits comparable with a company pension scheme.

Loss reliefs

Trading losses incurred by a company are locked into the company (or group companies); they cannot be set against the proprietor's income under any circumstances.

If trading losses are incurred in the early years of trading as a company, they will be made worse by the impact of National Insurance contributions where the director is remunerated but if he or she opts to take dividends, ACT must be paid and the company will not be able to utilise this immediately because the mainstream corporation tax liability is insufficient. If an overall loss is incurred there may be no dividends available.

One of the principal advantages of starting up in business as a sole trader or partnership is the 'startup' relief for trading losses which may be carried back and deducted from income earned prior to the commencement of the trade giving an immediate tax repayment. Otherwise trading losses may be set off against total income of the year in which the loss was incurred. Unfortunately, unless there is substantial other income, the use of this relief may cause personal allowances to be wasted.

Rates of tax

For companies, corporation tax of 25% applies on profits up to £300,000. If profits exceed £1.5 million, the rate of corporation tax is 33% with an effective rate of 35% applying on profits between £300,000 and £1.5 million. The director will be liable to income tax on any remuneration and dividends paid to him or her but there is some flexibility to leave profits in the company, since the company's marginal rate of tax (probably 25% as it is a new company) will be less than the directors' (25 or 40%). Retained profit can be taken at a later date (when marginal rates of tax are less) or an eventual disposal of some or all of the shares. The gain in this case is reduced by the indexation allowance and annual exemption.

For the sole trader or partner in 1994/95, income tax rates vary from 20 to 25% (on taxable income up to £23,700) to 40% (on taxable income exceeding £23,700). They will be taxed on the whole of the profits of the trade after deducting personal allowances regardless of how much they withdraw. Husband and wife each have lower and basic rate tax bands and personal allowances – the flexibility of the unincorporated business allows them to take advantage of this. Investment income and capital gains are assessed directly on the sole trader or partner. Individuals are exempt from tax on the first £5,800 of capital gains in 1994/95.

Due dates for payment of tax and NIC

Companies are assessed on their income and chargeable gains of the accounting period and this is payable nine months after the end of the accounting period. The employee's income tax and NIC and the employer's NIC are due 14 days after the end of the tax month when salaries are paid, and ACT is due 14 days after the end of a return period whenever dividends are paid.

The unincorporated business enjoys considerable advantages in this area. For businesses which commenced prior to 6 April 1994, profits in the opening years (usually lower than average in the early years) are taxed twice or even three times. The use of the opening/closing year rules for partnership change and the preceding year basis (on a continuation election including admission of spouse) can give tax savings. The preceding year basis of assessment gives an interval of between nine and 20 months before the first instalment of tax and Class 4 NIC is due. The second instalment is due six months later. There is no tax or NIC due on any drawings made during the accounting period, the only outlay being Class 2 NIC. For businesses commencing on or after 6 April 1994, many of these advantages are lost as the new current year basis of assessment applies.

Chargeable gains

A company's chargeable gains have been charged to corporation tax at the same effective rate as its other profits, that is 25%, 33% or 35% (see above), with the added flexibility that trading losses may be set off against any chargeable gains included in total income.

An individual's chargeable gains, subject to the first £5,800 being exempt, are chargeable to capital gains tax at the individual's marginal rate of income tax: that is, 20/25% or 40%. The tax liability can be reduced by trading losses.

It may be worth considering holding assets used by the business outside the company and charging a rent for them. If the assets are appreciating assets, this will avoid the corporation tax charge to the company on disposal plus the IT/CGT charge to the shareholder when extracted from the company. This would depend on whether any direct tax advantage would be lost or if any of the reliefs listed below would be lost.

Both a company and an unincorporated business are entitled to roll-over relief on the replacement of business assets.

Retirement relief is available on the disposal of shares in a family company as it is on the disposal of a business.

To the extent that tax is payable on the disposal of shares, a double charge to tax arises. The profits retained within the company were charged to corporation tax when they arose and are liable to a further charge to capital gains tax to the extent that they are reflected in the value of the shares unless removed by the payment of dividends prior to the disposal of shares. This charge to tax is one that should not be ignored if it is expected to retain a high level of profits within the company and then dispose of the company in the short term.

Inheritance tax

Shares in a company are an easier asset to dispose of in parcels than a business is.

Business property relief of either 100% or 50% (depending on the size of the shareholding) will be available as it will on business assets owned outside the business by a controlling shareholder.

Business property relief of 100% is available on the transfer of all or part of an unincorporated business. Difficulty arises however, in transferring part of a business and usually takes the form of admitting a partner whose partnership share is gradually increased. Note that relief is not available on the transfer of individual business assets.

Loans

Close companies must account for ACT whenever loans are made to participators (apart from specific excluded situations) and this is lost to the company if the repayment of the loan is waived – see Chapter 26. The Companies Act 1985 prohibits loans to directors in excess of £2,500.

No such restriction applies to the unincorporated business.

Sources of finance

The availability and choice of long-term and permanent sources of finance to companies is considerably greater than that available to the unincorporated business. Limited companies must choose between issuing additional share capital or loan capital when raising long-term funds – only public companies can tap the large financial markets, smaller family companies (like unincorporated businesses) rely on relatives, friends and business contacts. Often the formality of the arrangements with a limited company is more attractive. However, an equity share issue dilutes the interests of existing shareholders and dividend payments are not tax deductible but there is nevertheless the advantage that no fixed return to shareholders is required and there is no fixed repayment period. On the other hand, a debenture issue increases the gearing ratio, has a fixed repayment period but interest payments are tax deductible. It is useful to compare the cost to the company of raising £1,000 from the issue of 10% preference share with raising £1,000 from the issue of 10% debentures.

For the company, the cost of raising loan finance is significantly less than the cost of raising share capital:

	£		£
Preference dividend	100	Debenture interest	100
ACT recoverable	Nil	Tax saving (assume 25%)	(25)
Net cash outflow	100	Net cash outflow	75

The investor, however, is worse off with the loan finance than with the preference shares:

	£		£
Received	100	Received	75
Tax credit (20/80)	25	Deducted at source	25
Gross income	125	Gross income	100
IT liability (40%)	(50)	IT liability (40%)	(40)
Net cash inflow	75	Net cash inflow	60

The introduction, from 1 January 1994, of the Enterprise Investment Scheme should make it easier for unquoted trading companies to raise new equity finance. The scheme enables companies to raise up to £1 million a year. Investors receive tax relief at 20% on investments of up to £100,000 a year.

Retained profit is often mentioned as an internally generated source of long-term finance – this would apply to both types of business medium although that retained by a limited company is likely to be after tax of only 25% (SCR applies up to profits of £300,000) while the retained profit of an unincorporated business may well be after tax at 40%. When the profit is finally distributed by the company, however, or realised as a capital profit on the sale of shares, there will be an income tax or capital gains tax liability (in other words, there is a double charge to tax).

Medium-term sources of finance include leasing, hire purchase and loans. These are in general available to both limited companies and unincorporated businesses, as are the short-term sources such as trade credit, factoring and bill finance. There are many government-backed sources of funds available to limited companies (the venture capital scheme is an example) and unincorporated businesses (enterprise allowance). Under the Loan Guarantee Scheme the government guarantees up to 80% of medium-term loans made by participating institutions to sole traders, partnerships or limited companies.

Conclusion

The decision to incorporate or not is inevitably bound up with an individual's personal circumstances and the manner in which he or she wishes to provide for the future as well as his or her current lifestyle.

Although it is relatively easy to incorporate, it is not so easy to disincorporate, as was seen in the previous chapter.

Further aspects of tax planning

Tax planning on occasions goes beyond the basic techniques mentioned above and also requires:

▶ an ability to interpret tax legislation and apply it to particular circumstances (possibly identifying 'loopholes')

- a knowledge of tax shelters and a willingness to use them
- a willingness to use available tax planning 'schemes'
- a knowledge of the attitude of the Inland Revenue and the courts to tax shelters and tax planning schemes to assess the likely outcome of any steps taken.

The above have been used to minimise or defer tax liabilities; that is, they are concerned with tax avoidance. This is the process of arranging affairs within the law to reduce the tax payable and as such it differs from tax *evasion* which is knowingly breaking the law to reduce a tax liability.

The high rates of UK taxation in past years encouraged the taxpayer to go to great lengths to minimise or defer tax liabilities. In particular, the use of artificial schemes has led to anti-avoidance legislation and developments in the approach adopted by the courts to tax avoidance when interpreting tax law.

For your examination, you are not expected to be familiar with tax shelters and tax 'schemes'.

Anti-avoidance

Anti-avoidance legislation which was brought into existence to counteract artificial tax avoidance schemes is not examinable. The paper will deal with anti-avoidance legislation relating to normal transactions and to a certain extent with the non-statutory anti-avoidance principles established in the cases of *Ramsay* v. *CIR* 1981 (54 TC 101), *Furniss* v. *Dawson* 1984 (55 TC 324) and *Craven* v. *White* 1988 (STC 476).

Non-statutory anti-avoidance provisions

The approach of the courts over the years has undergone a number of changes, as follows:

- strict construction of the letter of the law
- form versus substance
- the new approach.

Strict construction of the letter of the law

This is the historic approach and means that the law, including the anti-avoidance provisions in the legislation, should be interpreted literally. It was said that equitable interpretation of the legislation was not the role of the courts: a person was taxable if he was within the letter of the law but could not be taxed if the Inland Revenue could not bring him within the letter of the law even if he was within the spirit of the law.

In the case of *Ayrshire Pullman Motor Services* v. *CIR* (1929), Lord Clyde stated that:

> No man in this country is under the slightest obligation, moral or other, so to arrange his legal relations to his business or to his property as to enable the Inland Revenue to put the largest possible shovel into his stores. The Inland Revenue is not slow – and quite rightly – to take every advantage which is open to it under the taxing statutes for the purpose of depleting the taxpayer's pocket. And the taxpayer is, in like manner, entitled to be astute to prevent, so far as he honestly can, the depletion of his means by the Revenue.

Since that time the quantity of anti-avoidance legislation has significantly increased and rather than put the onus on the Inland Revenue to prove that the taxpayer is clearly within the charge to tax, the courts have tended to try to put into effect what they think is the purpose of the various statutes.

Form versus substance

In an early case, *CIR* v. *Duke of Westminster* (1935), where a deed of covenant was used as a tax-efficient means of payment of wages, Lord Tomlin stated:

> Every man is entitled, if he can, to order his affairs so that the tax attaching under the appropriate Acts is less than it otherwise would be. If he succeeds in ordering them so as to secure this result, then however unappreciative the Commissioners of Inland Revenue or his fellow taxpayers may be of his ingenuity, he cannot be compelled to pay an increased tax.

Therefore, merely because a greater tax liability would have arisen if the transaction had been carried out in another way, this did not justify the transaction being set aside by the substance over form argument.

The courts have tended over the years to follow form to the exclusion of substance until recently, when in cases of blatant tax avoidance, substance has prevailed over form.

The cases of *Ramsay* v. *CIR* and *Furniss* v. *Dawson* were responsible for developing the principle that transactions, or parts of transactions, that are undertaken for purely tax avoidance motives may be ignored or overturned. In other words the courts will look to the substance, rather than the form, of a transaction.

In *Ramsay* v. *CIR*, the scheme was circular and self-cancelling, and as a whole no gain or loss arose, the principle was therefore established that the substance of the transaction could be looked at in isolation from the intermediate steps and if there was no 'real' loss any 'paper' loss could be ignored.

In *Furniss* v. *Dawson*, it was held that where steps inserted in a pre-ordained series of transactions had no commercial or business purpose (other than the avoidance of tax), they could be ignored for tax purposes regardless of whether the transaction as a whole had a valid commercial purpose. In addition, the existence of these two factors – the pre-ordained series of steps and the absence of commercial purpose – should be questions of fact to be decided by the General or Special Commissioners.

The new approach

The above cases, looking at substance over form, are the basis of the 'new approach' to the interpretation of tax law by the courts. The stated intention was to put an end to the tax-avoidance industry.

As a result of the above judgements, however, there is now considerable uncertainty exactly as to how and in what situations these principles should be applied. There have also been considerable reforms to the tax system which have changed the climate in which the tax avoidance industry flourished.

A recent report by the Special Committee of Tax Law Consultative Bodies concluded that the courts have so far not been able to define the limits of the 'new approach' so as to achieve a balance between:

- the taxpayer's need for certainty, and
- unacceptable tax avoidance.

There appears to be a will to distinguish between what might be called 'genuine' or legitimate tax planning, that is tax mitigation, whereby an individual takes a course of action that may lead to the minimisation of a tax liability, and tax avoidance, for example by the use of 'schemes', which is not genuine and is illegitimate. In any of the cases referred to there has been no question of improper action (tax evasion).

In the meantime, questions have been raised with the Inland Revenue and replied to regarding certain transactions. As regards individuals, on the subject of inter-spouse transfers for both capital gains tax and inheritance tax, the Inland Revenue have confirmed that most such transactions in this area would not be caught, but it is still necessary to consider the nature of the transaction as a whole and its result.

Tax legislation, at least in theory, should still be construed according to its written meaning. Taxpayers are still, in principle, entitled to arrange their affairs so as to reduce their tax. However, the tax planning exercises which are outside the Ramsay principle, particularly in the light of the decision in *Furniss* v. *Dawson*, are limited.

Recent cases have sought to clarify the situation. In *Craven* v. *White*, the House of Lords indicated that for this principle to be followed, all the transactions in a series have to be pre-ordained with a sufficient degree of certainty that, at the time of earlier transactions, there is no practical possibility that the transactions would not take place – the 'practical likelihood' test. The pre-ordained test was also failed in *Bayliss* v. *Gregory* and *IRC* v. *Bowater* on similar grounds.

The position will be clarified in due course as more cases pass through the courts.

Statutory anti-avoidance provisions

The government's approach to anti-avoidance legislation is somewhat inconsistent.

Generally the practice has developed of inserting into any legislation that gives relief from tax, sections to prevent relief being available where the transactions form part of a scheme, or other arrangements, whose main objective is the avoidance of tax.

Other approaches have been to insert specific provisions in legislation for specific types of transaction to prevent anticipated abuse or to counteract existing abuses of the legislation. These provisions typically cover:

- transactions between connected persons
- circumstances where there is control over another person
- transactions not at arm's length
- close companies
- schemes approved by the Inland Revenue.

Other examples include income which has previously been tax free being brought into charge to tax (such as offshore funds legislation) or income previously chargeable to capital gains tax being brought into charge to income tax (such as deep-discount securities). In this text, where applicable, these have been considered in relation to the subject to which they apply or as separate topics where appropriate.

There are no *general* anti-avoidance provisions contained in UK tax legislation.

Tax planning has therefore developed in the knowledge that there is a time lag between the development and implementation of schemes and the legislation to counteract them. Although retrospective legislation has always been a possibility, it has not generally been used.

The main anti-avoidance provisions relating to the migration of companies, transfer pricing and controlled foreign companies are dealt with in the overseas section of this book.

Summary

- There are many factors to be considered when choosing whether to set up a business as a limited company or as a sole trader/partnership. The decision is very much linked with the individual's total personal financial planning.
- If incorporation is chosen, further thought must be given to striking the balance between paying remuneration and paying dividends.
- Anti-avoidance provisions now come in two forms:
  - non-statutory
  - statutory.
- The developments in case law over recent years, where substance has prevailed over form, have left some areas of tax planning, in particular the use of 'schemes', very much up in the air.

Self test questions

1 List some of the income tax implications involved in deciding when a trade commences.

2 Jean wishes to give her mother (aged 68) £10,000 to invest in a building society, to give her income to supplement her state retirement pension which is her only income. What are the tax implications of this?

3 What factors should be taken into consideration when purchasing a second-hand industrial building?

4 Outline the National Insurance contributions associated with an employee and with a self employed trader.

5 Why is a company pension scheme a tax efficient benefit?

6 Why is it better to start as an unincorporated business when trading losses are expected in the early years?

7 Distinguish between tax avoidance and tax evasion.

8 Two recent cases have established the principle that the courts should look to the substance rather than the form of a transaction. What were the two cases?

9 In the UK tax legislation, are there any general anti-avoidance provisions?

10 What is the 'new approach'?

11 The issued share capital of Slowman Limited, a very prosperous unquoted investment company is owned as follows:

	'A' ordinary shares	'B' ordinary shares
Mr T. Slowman	8,000	–
Mrs S. Speedy	–	2,000
	8,000	2,000

Mrs Speedy is Mr Slowman's sister.

The 'A' ordinary shares and 'B' ordinary shares rank pari passu in all respects except that only the 'A' shares carry voting rights. Mr Slowman now proposes that Slowman Limited should pass a resolution whereby the 'B' shares will also be granted voting rights, but only the 'B' shares will be entitled to receive any dividends. Mr Slowman has left his shares to his wife in his will.

Explain the potential inheritance tax consequences for Mr Slowman only of passing the proposed resolution and why these arise. Ignore annual allowances and exemptions, but refer to any other claims for relief which might be made.

12 Mr Greaves is proposing to transfer very valuable assets to a new discretionary trust in which the potential beneficiaries include his wife and his children. It is anticipated that the trust would enjoy substantial income and capital gains in the coming years. The trustees would probably make some income distributions to Mr Greaves's children, who are all very young.

Explain the potential income tax, inheritance tax and capital gains tax consequences for Mr Greaves only of the proposed transfer, and why these arise. Ignore annual allowances and exemptions, but refer to any other claims for relief which might be made.

13 Describe briefly the development of the attitude of the courts towards tax avoidance and the implications of this for tax planning.

Answers on pages 620–622

Question Bank – Corporate Taxation

1. Stacker Ltd, a non-close company, has been manufacturing and selling containers used for storage and transportation since 1958.

    The accounts for recent years show:

	Year ended 30 Sept 1992 £	Year ended 30 Sept 1993 £	Year ended 30 Sept 1994 £
Net profits per accounts	18,150	5,725	87,875
After charging:			
Depreciation	5,200	6,900	28,200
Debenture interest	6,750	9,000	9,000
Legal expenses	2,000	2,200	2,700
General expenses	3,500	3,200	3,400
And after crediting:			
Investment income	11,500	15,250	5,875

    a) The £100,000 9% debentures were issued on 1 January 1992 with interest being payable every six months in arrears.

	Year ended 30 Sept 1992 £	Year ended 30 Sept 1993 £	Year ended 30 Sept 1994 £
b) Legal expenses relate to debt collection apart from:			
issue of debentures	800		
renewal of lease of showroom for a term of 21 years		650	
raising finance for plant			200
issue of shares			1,200
c) General expenses include:			
charitable donation paid to Oxfam on 30 June under deed of covenant (gross)	200	200	200
installation costs of plant		900	
costs of registering new patent		800	

    d) Capital expenditure incurred is:

Date	Item	£
1 December 1991	Factory heating system	7,000
9 June 1992	Computer (sold for £150 on 15 July 1994)	2,000
1 October 1992	Office equipment	19,000
10 October 1992	Purchase of new freehold factory (including land costing £40,000)	240,000
31 October 1992	Manufacturing plant (£1,400 was obtained for plant scrapped)	108,000
23 September 1993	Purchase of patent rights	10,000
1 January 1994	Car for managing director (private use 20%)	18,000

    General plant and machinery pool brought forward at 1 October 1991, amounted to £24,000. Prior to January 1994, all cars were leased.

TAX PLANNING

		Year ended 30 Sept 1992 £	Year ended 30 Sept 1993 £	Year ended 30 Sept 1994 £
e)	Investment income comprises:			
	Dividends from unconnected UK companies			
	Received 3 July 1992	7,500		
	4 January 1993		3,750	
	15 August 1993		7,750	
	3 May 1994			1,935
	Taxed interest (gross)			
	30 June	2,000	2,000	2,000
	31 December	2,000	2,000	2,000
f)	Dividends paid were:			
	1991 final – paid November 1991	14,600		
	1992 interim – paid August 1992	6,000		
	1994 interim – paid August 1994			26,710

A final dividend for 1994 of £7,500 is due to paid on 1 December 1994.
At 30 September 1991 there was surplus franked investment income of £2,000.

Prepare corporation tax computations for each of the above accounting periods, assuming:
a) all reliefs and allowances are claimed as early as possible
b) all claims beneficial to the company are made
c) that all possible claims for an earlier accounting period are made before dealing with a later period.

Note: quarterly accounting for income tax and ACT is not required, but you should state the date that any MCT is payable.

2 Maura Ltd is a private trading company which makes annual taxable profts of approximately £350,000. It is wholly owned by Mr Hugh McIntyre, who is the full-time managing director of the company. Mr McIntyre acquired his shares in 1985. You act as tax adviser to both the company and Mr McIntyre. Mr McIntyre is a married man aged 54 and currently receives annual earnings of £55,000 from Maura Ltd. He has no other income, and no other assets apart from his private residence. Maura Ltd currently trades from a rented office but the owner at the office is now anxious to sell it, together with a small adjoining flat (valued at £5,000), for a total sum of £70,000. Mr McIntyre's bankers have agreed to provide 100% mortgage loan finance for the acquistion of the property, including the flat.

Mr McIntyre is unsure whether the property should be acquired by Maura Ltd or by himself personally. In the latter case, Mr McIntyre will charge a market rent of approximately £5,000 per annum to Maura Ltd for the property. As this amount will be insufficient to cover his repayments of principal and interest to the bank, which are estimated to be £8,500 per annum, he intends also to draw either additional remuneration or dividends from Maura Ltd to finance the shortfall. Mr McIntyre wishes to know which option is preferable from a tax viewpoint. Mr McIntyre also intends that various members of his family should live in the flat adjoining the shop rent free. He is concerned whether this will give rise to tax consequences. The property will be acquired shortly after today's date (which you should assume is 6 April 1994).

a) Describe the corporation tax implications which would arise for Maura Ltd if i) Maura Ltd and ii) Mr McIntyre acquires the property. Under ii), ignore Mr McIntyre's financing of the shortfall on his loan repayments.
b) Describe the income tax and NIC implications which would arise for Mr McIntyre if i) Maura Ltd and ii) Mr McIntyre acquires the property. Under ii), ignore Mr McIntyre's financing of the shortfall on his loan repayments.
c) Indicate whether Mr McIntyre should draw out either additional remuneration or dividend to finance his shortfall, taking into account the tax effects on both Mr McIntyre and Maura Ltd. Show all supporting calculations.
d) Advise Mr McIntyre as to the CGT implications if he acquired the property personally and in seven years' time sold both the company and the property.
e) Set out the due dates applicable to any potential income tax and NIC liabilities arising in respect of Mr McIntyre.

3 You act as tax adviser for Mr J. Snow, a bachelor of 36, who has traded for many years as a general building contractor. A number of Mr Snow's competitors have recently been made bankrupt and Mr Snow (who owns a valuable private residence but no other non-business assets) has decided to incorporate his trade into a new company, Snow Limited, on 30 June 1994.

The following information is available:

i) Adjusted trading profits

	£
Year ended 30 June 1990	13,000
1991	22,000
1992	29,000
1993	33,000
1994	38,000

The figure for the year to 30 June 1994 has been estimated without reference to the proposed incorporation.

ii) Capital allowances

The written down value of pooled expenditure on plant was £3,000 as at 30 June 1989. No purchases or disposals of plant have taken place since then other than the acquisition of a second-hand cement mixer for £1,500 on 3 April 1992. Maximum allowances have always been claimed. The open market value of the pooled assets at 30 June 1994 was £8,000; each asset had a market value and price below £2,000.

iii) The summarised closing balance sheet of the business at 30 June 1994 is estimated to be as follows:

Fixed assets	£	£
Premises (at cost)	52,000	
Plant (NBV)	8,000	
		60,000
Current assets		
Stocks	3,000	
Debtors	1,500	
Cash at bank	2,400	
	6,900	
Less: Current liabilities		
Creditors	(4,400)	
Net current assets		2,500
		62,500
Financed by:		
Capital account – J. Snow		37,500
Bank loan		25,000
		62,500

iv) The business is currently valued at £65,000. It was acquired in January 1980, and its value at 31 March 1982 was £60,000

v) The value of goodwill is currently estimated at £100,000. It had a nil value at 31 March 1982.

vi) The company will acquire the stock at its market value of £8,000.

vii) Mr Snow has unused capital losses of £15,000 as at 6 April 1994. Of these £1,500 were incurred prior to 31 March 1982.

viii) It has been agreed that the most viable procedure is for the entire business (including cash) to be incorporated in exchange partly for shares in Snow Limited, the balance to remain outstanding on loan account. The amount of the loan is to be calculated so that it allows Mr Snow the maximum opportunity to withdraw cash from the company free of tax, but without incurring additional personal tax liabilities on the incorporation. The loan will be interest free.

ix) Mr Snow, although he does not have a mortgage, had undertaken other substantial financial commitments and wishes to draw out approximately £24,000 per annum from the company net of tax. He has asked you to advise him as to whether it would be a good idea for the company to pay him dividends as well as gradually repaying his loan.

a) Advise Mr Snow on the income tax, capital gains tax and VAT consequences of incorporating his business. Describe fully the conditions which must be met before any relevant reliefs may be claimed.

b) Advise Mr Snow on his optimum strategy regarding dividend payments from the company.

4 The Streamdriven Computer Company Ltd has faced a declining market in recent years as at today's date (which you should assume is 1 November 1994) it is expected to make a net unadjusted trading loss of £11,750 in the six months ending on 31 March 1995. Results for the previous three years (before any adjustments for tax purposes) have been as follows:

	Trading profits	Bank interest
Year ended 30 September 1991	–	–
Year ended 30 September 1992	10,000	–
Year ended 30 September 1993	3,000	–
Year ended 30 September 1994	4,000	400

The projected balance sheet at 31 March 1995 on a going concern basis is as follows:

Fixed assets	£	£
Office (at valuation)		120,000
Fixed plant and machinery	50,000	
Less: Depreciation	(30,000)	20,000
		140,000
Current assets		
Trading stock	34,000	
Cash	500	
Less: Creditors (including 1993 corporation tax)	(4,000)	
Net current assets		30,500
Total assets		170,500

	£	£
Financed by:		
Share capital		50,000
Retained profits		95,500
		145,500
10% Debenture		25,000
		170,500

The projected profit and loss account for the 6 months to 31 March 1995, again on a going concern basis, is as follows:

	£	£
Sales		97,000
Opening stock	37,000	
Purchases	60,000	
Less: Closing stock	(34,000)	(63,000)
Gross profit		34,000
Less: Staff and administrative costs	42,050	
Depreciation	2,500	
Debenture interest	1,250	
Bank interest received	(50)	(45,750)
Net loss		(11,750)

Mr Ludd, who owns 99.9% of the company's issued share capital, proposes that the company should sell all of its assets on 31 March 1995 for cash to an unconnected third party for a total amout of £131,000, attributable as follows:

	£
Goodwill	–
Office	100,000
Plant and machinery	2,000
Trading stock	29,000
	131,000

Immediately after the assets are sold the company would cease trading and the liquidation of the company would commence. The company would pay all of its current liabilities and distribute the balance of cash to its shareholders shortly afterwards. Mr Ludd is unsure which of three alternative methods the company should adopt:

a) to distribute all of the cash before 6 April 1995
b) to distribute all of the cash after 6 April 1995
c) to make distributions both before and after 6 April 1995.

The company is expected to agree and receive any repayments of corporation tax, including any arising out of its trading loss, by 7 June 1995. It is estimated that these amounts will just be sufficient to cover the liquidator's fees so that no further cash will be distributed to the company's shareholders.

The following information is also available.

i) The 10% debenture was issued in January 1962 to finance the company's trading activies.
ii) All of the plant machinery was acquired on 1 April 1989. The company has claimed maximum writing-down allowances (but no other allowances) in respect of this expenditure.
iii) In computing depreciation for accounts purposes the company uses a straight line basis and applies the same depreciation rate to all of the plant and machinery.
iv) The company has no associated companies and has not paid dividends for several years.
v) In February 1988 the company had disposed of an asset acquired in May 1980, giving rise to a chargeable gain of £300. The company elected that the gain should be held over by reference to the expenditure on plant and machinery noted in (ii) above. The company has made no chargeable disposals since February 1988.
vi) The disposal of the office will give rise to nil gain/nil loss position for CGT purposes.
vii) Mr Ludd inherited his shares in the company in March 1982, when they had a probate value of £50,000.
viii) Mr Ludd, who is single and aged 40, will have total income of £30,000 in 1994/95 and total income of £10,000 in 1995/96. He plans to retain all of his existing capital assets (except his shares in the company) for the foreseeable future.
ix) You should assume that all staff and administrative expenses are fully allowable.

a) Compute the final corporation tax liabilities of the company in respect of the periods commencing 1 October 1991 and ending 31 March 1995.
b) Compute the total amount which should be repaid to the company by the Inland Revenue on 7 June 1995.
c) Advise Mr Ludd as to which alternative method of distributing cash by the company is preferable.

Assume that 1994/95 rates and allowances continue to apply in 1995/96

5   You are to assume that you have received the following letter from a social acquaintance of yours:

Hackney Way,
LONDON

A. Lincoln Esq.
Lincoln, Fields & Co.
Certified Accountants, LONDON   4 June 1994

Dear Mr Lincoln

As I mentioned in our recent telephone conversation, I have been unable to find any acceptable employment since losing my £30,000 a year job on 30 April 1994. I am anxious to start a business, using my redundancy pay of £52,000 (including my statutory redundancy payment of £7,000).

I am planning to set up a small chain of five snooker leisure clubs within the next few months, possibly on 1 September 1994. I have found suitable premises on which I can obtain short-term leases without payment of a premium. I will, however, need to invest £200,000 in snooker tables and equipment, and intend using my redundancy money and a bank loan of £148,000. I have spoken to my bank manager who is prepared to provide the finance, which will be secured on my home, subject to a report on my likely cashflow position in the first two years of the business.

Budgeted figures show a profit, before depreciation but after all other charges £20,000 for the first year, increasing by 50% a year in each of the next four years to a profit of about £100,000 in year five.

I am uncertain, as yet, whether to run my business as a sole trader, or form a company in which I would own the majority of the shares, and be managing director.

I have already received financial advice on this venture and would now appreciate a letter dealing with any tax aspect of my proposals. In particular:

a) whether my redundancy pay together with the bank loan of £148,000 will be adequate to finance the purchase of the snooker tables
b) how expenditure and income of the business would be determined and assessed
c) how tax relief will be obtained for the capital expenditure of £200,000 and whether this relief will reduce tax liability or give rise to a repayment of tax
d) how my expenditure and income as an individual would be determined and assessed.
e) whether any capital gain, if the business is a success, will be assessable or whether the allowance now given for inflation would eliminate any gain.

In dealing with each of these points, I would appreciate if you would clearly show the differences in the tax position if:

a) the business is run by myself as a sole trader; or
b) the business is run by my company.

Yours sincerely,
I. Davis

Draft a reply to Mr Davis's letter. You are not required to deal with pensions or National Insurance in your answer.

6   Xerxes Ltd is a manufacturing company which owns all of the issued share capital of its own manufacturing subsidiaries, Bella Ltd and Donna Ltd. The accounting profits of the group of companies were as follows:

Year ended 31 December 1994
Profit (loss)
£

Xerxes Ltd	(71,000)
Bella Ltd	349,000
Donna Ltd	317,000

Donna Ltd paid dividends to Xerxes Ltd as follows: £220,000 on 6 February 1994 and £15,000 on 1 July 1994. Xerxes Ltd paid a dividend of £280,000 to its shareholders on 15 March 1994. Xerxes Ltd made a loan of £450,000 to Bella Ltd on 1 July 1994, with interest payable at 10% per annum on a monthly basis. The loan was used for trading purposes. No elections were made in respect of any of the above inter-group payments. The interest payments were not included in the calculation of the accounting profits set out above.

On 9 August 1994, Bella Ltd sold part of an office building for £72,000 less solicitors' fees of £3,000. It had acquired the entire building on 31 March 1981 for £20,000 plus legal fees of £2,000. In May 1984 the part of the building which was being sold had been extended at a cost of £9,000. The value of the entire building on 31 March 1982 was £40,000 and the current value of the part retained was £33,000. The gain was not included in the accounting profits set out above.

In all cases, depreciation charges in the accounts and capital allowances claimed are identical in amount, except in respect of the purchase of a factory for £90,000 by Xerxes Ltd from an unconnected manufacturing company, Nugent Ltd, on 1 August 1994. Nugent Ltd had acquired the factory new on 1 May 1984 from a builder at a cost of £50,000, of which £15,000 related to land. The current value of the land in August 1994 was estimated at £25,000 and the estimated useful life of the building was 50 years. No other tax adjustments to the accounting profits were required.

It has been suggested that the staff of Xerxes Ltd should in future undertake market research for Bella Ltd, and that a management charge of £10,000 per annum should be made for this service. All the turnover of the group companies is standard rated for VAT purposes, except for 30% per annum of Bella Ltd's turnover, which is exempt. The companies are not registered as a group for VAT purposes.

a) Calculate the tax position of each of the group of companies for the year ended 31 December 1994 on the basis that all claims for relief are made in the most favourable manner. Assume that no relief can be claimed for periods prior to 1994. Explain briefly your reasons for selecting the claims actually made.

b) Comment on the VAT consequences of the proposed management charge and indicate the likely cost to the group if the proposal is adopted.

7   James Joyce, who is aged 42, owns all of the issued share capital of Bloom Ltd, a company which normally makes up its accounts to 31 March. The company sells goods on the UK market, all of which are liable to VAT at the standard rate. The summarised balance sheet of Bloom Ltd, together with a note of current market values, at today's date (which you should assume is 30 September 1994) is as follows:

Fixed assets	At cost/valuation £	At current valuation £
Factory	250,000	900,000
Plant	100,000	10,000
	350,000	910,000
Goodwill	–	–
Net current assets		
Stock	400,000	500,000
Others	30,000	30,000
Net assets	780,000	1,440,000
Financed by:		
Share capital	25,000	
Retained profits	755,000	
	780,000	

The following information is also available regarding the tax position of Mr Joyce and Bloom Ltd:

i) The factory was acquired for £40,000 (of which £10,000 related to land) in October 1979. The tax written-down value of the factory was £5,000 on 1 April 1994. The current market value of the land is £100,000 and of the factory building is £800,000. At 31 March 1982, the market value of the land was £40,000 and the market value of the factory building was £310,000.

ii) The tax written-down value of the plant (the expenditure on which is all pooled) was £45,000 on 1 April 1994.

iii) The company had surplus ACT of £150,000 at 1 April 1994. No dividends have been paid or declared since that date.

iv) The company's trade is expected to make insignificant taxable profits for the year to 31 March 1995.

Ulysses Ltd is a large company which sells similar goods to those sold by Bloom Ltd; 70% of these are exported out of the UK. Ulysses Ltd's accounting year end is also 31 March. Ulysses Ltd has offered to acquire the business of Bloom Ltd for a cash at today's date. It is prepared to either i) buy the shares of Bloom Ltd from Mr Joyce, or ii) buy the net assets of the company from Bloom Ltd. In each case, the price would reflect the market value of the net assets in Bloom Ltd. Ulysses Ltd has no subsidiaries at today's date.

a) Set out the various tax consequences for Bloom Ltd:
   i) assuming that Ulysses Ltd buys the net assets of Bloom Ltd
   ii) assuming that Ulysses Ltd buys the shares in Bloom Ltd.

b) Set out the various tax consequences for Ulysses Ltd:
   i) assuming that it buys the net assets of Bloom Ltd
   ii) assuming that it buys the shares in Bloom Ltd.

In all cases, assume that the purchases take place on 30 September 1994.

8   Sally Jones has been a shareholder and the managing director of Zen Ltd since its incorporation on 1 January 1988. Zen Ltd is a UK-resident company manufacturing computer equipment. Sally is 58 years old and has been a widow since her husband died on 12 May 1993. Following her husband's death she has decided to retire as managing director of Zen Ltd on 31 December 1994, and plans to dispose of most of her shareholding on the same date.

Zen Ltd has a share capital of 60,000 £1 ordinary shares of which Sally holds 31,000. The remaining shares are held by the other directors who are not related to Sally. She would like to dispose of 20,000 of her shares but none of the other directors are in a position to purchase them. However, Zen Ltd currently has surplus funds and is prepared to purchase 20,000 of Sally's shares at their market value of £230,000. This will result in a chargeable gain for her, after indexation but before any reliefs, of £200,000.

Sally is paid directors' remuneration of £24,000 per annum, and she also receives an annual bonus based on Zen Ltd's annual results. For the year ended 31 March 1994 the bonus was £4,200, and for year ended 31 March 1995 it is expected to be £5,700. The bonuses are agreed by the directors prior to the relevant year end, and then paid on the following 30 April. Zen Ltd is also to give Sally an *ex gratia* lump sum upon her retirement of £40,000, which she is not contractually entitled. This is to be paid in two equal instalments on 31 March 1995 and 31 March 1996.

Sally has no other income or outgoings apart from a pension of £950 per month that will commence upon her retirement. She has an adopted child aged 17 who is currently studying full-time at college.

a) Outline the conditions to be met for the purchase of Sally's shares by Zen Ltd to qualify for the special treatment applying to a company's purchase of its own shares. Your answer should indicate whether or not these conditions are met.

b) Assuming that the purchase of Sally's shares qualifies for the special treatment,
   i) calculate her taxable income for 1994/95
   ii) calculate her capital gains tax liability for 1994/95

   Your answer should include an explanation of the treatment of Sally's annual bonuses and *ex gratia* payment.

c) What deductions will Zen Ltd be entitled to when calculating its corporation tax liability for the year ended 31 March 1995 in respect of the payments and emoluments provided to Sally. Your answer should include a consideration of NIC.

Answers on pages 622–635

Overseas Aspects of Personal Taxation

CHAPTER 30

This chapter defines the terms 'residence', 'ordinary residence' and 'domicile' and considers their significance. The ways in which overseas income and gains are charged to tax are looked at, particularly income from overseas employments and the reliefs available and the taxation of trades conducted overseas. The way in which UK income and gains of non-UK residents is brought within the charge to tax and the tax collected is also considered.

Residence, ordinary residence and domicile

The residence status of an individual is important in determining his liability to UK income tax.

Generally, UK residents are liable to UK income tax on their worldwide income while non-UK residents are only liable to UK income tax on UK source income. However, domicile and ordinary residence influence the taxation treatment and must also be considered.

Residence is equally important for capital gains tax while domicile is the critical factor for inheritance tax.

Residence

There is no statutory definition of residence. The question of who is and who is not resident in the UK, however, is comprehensively dealt with in the Inland Revenue free explanatory leaflet IR 20.

It is not a question of establishing residence in one country or another. It is possible to be resident for a fiscal year in more than one country or even not to be resident in any country.

Residence for tax purposes in the UK is a question of fact and will normally be determined for the fiscal year as a whole (that is, a person is either resident or non-resident throughout the fiscal year). Any decision by either the General or Special Commissioners on a question of residence will be final.

A person is regarded as resident in the UK for a fiscal year in the following circumstances:

- if he or she is physically present in the UK for a period of six months (183 days) or more in the fiscal year. Normally days of arrival and departure are excluded. This is the only statutory provision and as such, residence in this case would be automatic.
- if he or she visits the UK on a regular annual basis and the visits in each case are substantial. An average of 90 days or more would be regarded as substantial and a regular pattern would be established if such visits took place every year for four years (Inland Revenue leaflet – IR 20).

These are the principal factors establishing residence but other factors may be taken into account: for example, the person's intentions, nationality, the purpose of the visits and previous history regarding residence. There is one further situation where a person is generally regarded as UK resident:

- A person who is ordinarily resident in the UK (see below) and is temporarily abroad (that is more than six months but less than one full tax year).

It is evident that if these are the factors establishing residence, and that if every country were to use the same factors, a person may readily be resident in more than one country.

Visits extended because of exceptional circumstances

A Statement of Practice (SP2/91) was issued by the Inland Revenue following the Gulf Crisis in March 1991. Any days spent in the UK because of exceptional circumstances beyond an individual's control, such as illness, will be excluded from the calculation in the second test above to determine UK residence. Each case will be considered on its merits.

Ordinary residence

Again no statutory definition of ordinary residence exists but the term denotes a degree of permanence or continuity greater than that implied by residence. A person is ordinarily resident in the UK if he or she is habitually resident here.

Residence and ordinary residence are together used to determine degrees of residence. It is possible to be resident (R) and not ordinarily resident (OR) or vice versa as well as both (R and OR) or neither (not R not OR).

A person who is resident in the UK for more than four consecutive fiscal years (whatever the original intention) is regarded as ordinarily resident after four years.

Extra-statutory Concession (A11) – Residence

It was stated above that a person must be either resident or non-resident for the whole of a fiscal year.

In practice, residence or ordinarily resident status may run:

- from the date of arrival if a person is entering the UK permanently, or
- to the date of departure if a person is leaving the UK permanently, or
- to the date of departure and from the date of return if the person is going abroad to take up full-time employment for a period greater than one tax year.

This means that a person may be resident for a part of a fiscal year and non-resident for the remainder, or vice versa.

Persons coming to UK

The following table attempts to set out how the above provisions will be applied in a variety of situations:

Table 30.1 Residence status for tax purposes

		Resident status
1	A visitor to UK for less than six months with no intention of establishing residence	not R not OR
2	A visitor to UK for less than or greater than six months with the intention of establishing residence (for example, through regular annual visits or acquisition of accommodation); *evidence* of intention required.	R and OR (date of arrival)
3	A visitor to UK for greater than six months with no intention of establishing residence	R not OR (whole tax year)
4	A visitor to UK to work for greater than two years	R not OR (date of arrival)
5	A visitor to UK to work for greater than two years actually works for more than four years	As 4 above but OR from start of tax year following 3rd anniversary
6	A visitor to UK to work for more than two years decides to remain permanently	R from date of arrival and OR from earlier of date of decision or from start of tax year following third anniversary.

Persons coming to the UK to study full time will be resident and ordinarily resident from the date of arrival if the period of study is expected to last for more than four years. If the period of study is not expected to be more than four years, he or she will be regarded as resident but whether or not he or she will be regarded as ordinarily resident will depend on other factors, such as accommodation available, intentions on completion of period of study, and proposed visits in future years.

Persons leaving the UK

The following table attempts to set out how the foregoing provisions will be applied when a resident and ordinarily resident person leaves the UK in a variety of situations:

Table 30.2 Resident status for persons leaving the UK

		Resident status
1	Absence from the UK for short periods (less than one fiscal year)	remains R and OR
2	Absence from the UK with the intention of remaining abroad (non-residence claimed); *evidence* will be required (such as sale of house in UK and/or purchase of house abroad)	provisionally not R not OR (date departure)
3	Absence from the UK with the intention of remaining abroad (non-residence claimed); *no evidence* to support claim	not R (date of departure) but OR for three years (review+adjusted retrospectively)
4	Absence from the UK for full-time work abroad for period greater than one complete fiscal year (all duties abroad or UK duties incidental)	not R not OR for period of absence

Once resident status is lost, it is important that the visits to the UK do not exceed the limits specified in the section headed 'residence' above namely more than six months in any fiscal year or more than three months on average in successive fiscal years.

Domicile

Domicile follows the common law rules. The general principle is that a person may only have one country of domicile at any time. This is normally the country where she has her permanent home. A person acquires a domicile of origin at birth (usually from the father or person on whom she is legally dependent) but, later, when majority has been attained, may change it to her domicile of choice provided this is established by her conduct (for instance, by the acquisition of a burial plot). If any later action demonstrates that this domicile of choice has been abandoned, domicile of origin will automatically be reacquired.

The domicile of a dependent person is determined by the domicile of the person on whom they are dependent and therefore if that person's domicile changes then the dependent's domicile will also change. This now affects children and mentally disabled people. From 1 January 1974 a married woman may have a domicile independent from that of her husband – it will be determined according to the same factors as for any other person but a woman, already married at that date, will retain her husband's domicile until she acquires another one (domicile of choice) or revives a previous one.

Domicile is an important concept, not least because of the tax benefits to immigrants. An individual, for example, who has a domicile of origin outside the UK and who lives in the UK for the greater part of his life but who vaguely indicates that one day he intends to return home may retain his domicile of origin.

Overseas income of UK residents

Generally UK residents (R and OR) are liable to income tax on their worldwide income. However, a UK resident (R and OR or R and not OR) who is not domiciled in the UK is only liable to income tax on non-UK income to the extent that it is remitted to the UK (but see exception Schedule E Case I).

Income from employment overseas

The cases of Schedule E

Schedule E is actually divided into three cases and the case under which a taxpayer is assessed depends on whether he or she is resident, ordinarily resident and/or domiciled in the UK in the year for which the remuneration is earned, as well as whether he or she performs the duties in or outside the UK.

Taxpayers who are not in the UK permanently will need to consider their residence status for the year in which the emoluments were earned in order to decide the amount taxable. Once the taxable amount is established, tax will be charged in the year of receipt.

EXAMPLE 30.1

A bonus of £6,000 earned in 1993/94 when the employee was resident and ordinarily resident in the UK will be chargeable under Schedule E Case I for 1994/95 when it is received even if following a move abroad, the employee is not resident in 1994/95.

Table 30.3 summarises the situation:

Table 30.3

Residence status	Duties wholly or partly in the UK		Duties wholly outside the UK
	UK duties	Non-UK duties	
R and OR	I	I 100% relief for 365 days' qualifying	I non-foreign emoluments – 100% relief for 365 days' qualifying
			III foreign emoluments (remittances)
R not OR	II	III (remittances)	III (remittances)
not R	II	None	None

Note: foreign emoluments are emoluments earned by a non-UK domiciled individual employed by a non-UK resident employer.

The emoluments of persons resident and not ordinarily resident in the UK and of persons not resident in the UK are considered later in this chapter.

365-day qualifying period

Individuals resident and ordinarily resident in the UK, taxable under Schedule E Case I who spend long periods abroad may be entitled to special relief if they have a '365-day qualifying period'.

The emoluments of the individual during a 365-day qualifying period enjoy 100% tax relief.

A qualifying period is made up of successive periods of absence from the UK while working abroad plus the intervening periods in the UK provided that the intervening periods in the UK fulfil certain criteria:

▶ They are not more than 62 days in length, and
▶ No period together with previous intervening periods in the UK is more than one-sixth of the total qualifying period to date.

A qualifying period will terminate immediately before the beginning of an intervening period which fails either of the above tests.

A day counts as a day in the UK if the individual is in the UK at midnight. Therefore, the day of arrival counts as a day in the UK but the day of departure counts as a day of absence.

EXAMPLE 30.2

Doctor X leaves the UK on 1 May 1993 and takes up a post in the United States. He returns to the UK on 1 August 1994.

Since he has been absent for more than 365 consecutive days, his US earnings will be subject to a 100% deduction (equivalent to exemption).

Note that the 365-day qualifying period does not have to coincide with a year of assessment and indeed if it did coincide the employee would be non-resident for that year (see 'Residence').

EXAMPLE 30.3

Doctor X above leaves the UK as before, on 1 May 1993 but returns to the UK on 21 November and leaves again on 1 January 1994. Due to family circumstances, he is forced to return to the UK on 15 March and he leaves again on 25 March returning as before on 1 August 1994.

Doctor X is absent from May until November (204 days) and from January until March (73 days) and from 25 March to the end of July (129 days). The two intervening periods in the UK total 41 days and 10 days respectively. So:

a) No intervening period exceeds 62 days;
b) The first period in the UK, as a proportion of the total period to date is as follows:

$$\frac{41 \text{ days}}{(204 + 41 + 73) \text{ days}} = \frac{41}{318} \text{ that is, less than } \frac{1}{6}$$

The period from 1 May 1993 to 15 March 1994 therefore qualifies.

The second period in the UK must be tested:

$$\frac{(41 + 10) \text{ days}}{(204 + 41 + 73 + 10 + 129) \text{ days}} = \frac{51}{457} \text{ that is, less than } \frac{1}{6}$$

The whole period from 1 May 1993 to 31 July 1994 therefore qualifies.

EXAMPLE 30.4 (continuing Example 30.3)

If Doctor X's salary is £25,000, his emoluments will be taxed as follows:

		£	£
1993/94			
Before departure: 6 April 1993 to 30 April 1993			
1/12 × £25,000			2,083
Overseas: 1 May 1993 to 5 April 1994			
11/12 × £25,000		22,917	
	100%	(22,917)	
			–
Assessable			2,083
1994/95		£	£
Overseas: 6 April 1994 to 31 July 1994			
4/12 × £25,000		8,333	
	100%	(8,333)	
			–
After return: 1 August 1994 to 5 April 1995			
8/12 × £25,000			16,667
Assessable			16,667

Note: in practice, the fractional apportionments would be based on the number of days, but for examination purposes you are only required to make apportionments in months.

Insurance policies are available to cover the risk of additional tax liabilities, should an early return to the UK be necessary for any reason.

Slightly more generous criteria apply to the intervening period in the UK for British seafarers. A seafarer may have a 365-day qualifying period provided that the intervening periods in the UK do not individually exceed 183 days (previously 90 days) and cumulatively, half of the qualifying period to date (previously a quarter). The rules are relaxed also for persons returning early to the UK because of the Gulf Crisis, so that they should not suffer financially.

Travelling expenses

The cost of travel to and from an overseas employment together with the cost of travel between overseas employments is an allowable expense. Board and lodging outside the UK, provided or reimbursed by the employer, is also deductible (provided it is included in assessable emoluments). This provision is unaffected by the introduction of a ceiling on tax-free relocation packages.

If duties are partly in the UK and partly outside the UK, travel costs (to and from the UK, however frequent) provided or reimbursed by the employer for the performance of the duties of the employment are deductible (so far as assessed). In addition, where there is an absence from the UK for a period of 60 days or more, the travel costs of spouse and children under 18 if incurred/reimbursed by the employer are also allowable (maximum two outward and two inward journeys per person per fiscal year).

Similarly, return trips home by a non-UK domiciled individual during the first five years in the UK are allowable as well as visits to the UK by his or her family (limited as above). (Any new arrival in the UK who has been resident in the UK in any of the previous five years is excluded.)

Medical insurance while overseas is an allowable expense.

Remittance basis

Emoluments are treated as received in the UK if they are paid, used or enjoyed in, or are in any form or manner transmitted to the UK.

There are many transactions which are construed as remittances. For example, emoluments arising outside the UK are treated as received in the UK (and are therefore assessable) if used outside the UK by an individual ordinarily resident in the UK in or towards the satisfaction of a debt (or interest thereon) which arose in the UK.

It is necessary to keep capital and income held abroad separate in order to be able to show whether it was capital or income remitted.

Schedule D Cases IV and V

Schedule D Case IV assesses income from foreign securities, that is, income from interest-bearing investments.

Schedule D Case V assesses income from foreign possessions which include:

- rent from foreign property
- foreign pensions
- profits from overseas trades
- dividends from overseas companies if not paid through a UK paying agent. These are taxed at the lower rate of 20% (as is applicable to dividends from UK companies) unless the remittance basis applies.

Basis of assessment

The normal basis of assessment is the income arising in the preceding fiscal year. The rules for opening and closing years are as the same as for Schedule D Case III (see Chapter 4). Note that for sources of income commencing after 6 April 1994 the new current year basis of assessment will apply. These rules apply only to persons resident and domiciled in the UK.

The remittance basis applies to:

- persons resident but not domiciled in the UK; and
- British subjects or Eire or Commonwealth citizens not ordinarily resident in the UK.

Foreign pensions

Where a UK-domiciled and -resident individual receives a pension or annuity from abroad, it is taxed on the arising basis of assessment (that is, income arising in the preceding tax year) and is reduced by a 10% deduction (only 90% is taxable).

Overseas trades

A trade is said to be carried on in the country in which it is managed and controlled irrespective of where the daily business activities are conducted. A trade carried on in the UK is taxed under Schedule D Cases I and II, while a trade carried on abroad is taxed under Schedule D Case V.

Where the trade is conducted by a sole trader resident in the UK, it has been held that although he or she took no part in the management and control, since he or she could have done so at any time, the business would be taxable under Schedule D Case I (*Ogilvie* v. *Kitton* (1908) 5 TC 338). Where a trade is carried on is a question of fact. It is easier to establish a trade carried on abroad for a partnership, particularly if the partnership is managed and controlled abroad.

Assessment is on a preceding year basis with profits being computed using the Schedule D Cases I and II rules. Therefore, in the majority of cases it makes little difference under which case it is assessed. There are, however, two points to note:

- Loss relief under Schedule D Case V can only be set off against other overseas income:
  - carried forward against future overseas profits, or
  - set off against specific overseas income of the fiscal year in which loss was incurred or the next following fiscal year (overseas emoluments, overseas pensions, other trading profits)
- The remittance basis will be applied to Schedule D Case V profits of a non-UK domiciled individual and in this case it becomes important where the trade is actually carried on.

A deduction may be claimed for expenses incurred in a business carried on abroad (and not assessed on the remittance basis), for travelling between anywhere in the UK and anywhere the business is carried on:

- by the individual, provided his or her absence is wholly and exclusively for the purpose of the trade (board and lodging costs overseas are also deductible), or
- where the absence is for a continuous period of 60 days or more for the spouse and any children under 18 who accompany him on his outward journey or visit him during the period (maximum of two outward and two return journeys per person per year of assessment).

If more than one overseas business is carried on at a location, travel expenses and so on are apportioned between them. The cost of travel between overseas business locations is normally allowable.

Double taxation

Just as the UK brings a UK resident's worldwide income into charge to UK tax as well as UK source income of non-UK residents, other countries follow the same approach. The result is that income may be taxed twice.

Double tax relief in the UK is available in two principal ways:

- under a double tax agreement, or
- by unilateral relief.

These methods of obtaining relief are mutually exclusive. Treaty relief has priority and overrides unilateral relief.

Double tax agreements

A double tax treaty is an agreement between two countries which sets out a reciprocal policy for dealing with situations where double taxation might take place through the operation of domestic legislation in the respective countries. Double tax agreements vary but the usual result is that each country agrees to give credit for tax paid to the other country in calculating the tax liability to itself. Alternatively, one country may agree to exempt certain income (which would otherwise be taxable) in certain circumstances from taxation in that country and the other country would reciprocate with a corresponding exemption. The possibility of double taxation is therefore avoided.

Double tax treaties vary one from the other and from time to time. A detailed knowledge of the content of specific double tax treaties is outside the scope of the syllabus.

In 1977 the Organisation for Economic Cooperation and Development (OECD) published a model double tax treaty, on which most modern tax treaties are based. It is this model which laid down the foundations for dealing with the following matters between partner countries:

- provisions to ensure that specific types of profits are taxed in one country but not the other
- provisions for the availability of overseas tax credits
- arrangements to permit dividends and/or interest to be paid without deduction of tax
- a definition of permanent establishment.

Unilateral relief

Unilateral relief is available where there is no double tax agreement between the relevant countries, or where the double tax agreement which exists does not cover the particular situation.

Unilateral relief for individuals gives a credit for the overseas withholding tax.

The foreign income is included in the individual's income tax computation gross and a UK tax liability calculated. Double tax relief is then the lower of the foreign tax and the UK tax on the foreign income (calculated as the top slice of the individual's total income). Where dividend income is involved, the dividends should be treated as the top slice of income for the purpose of calculating the UK liability. However, the overseas income should be treated as the top slice for the purpose of computing double tax relief as this gives a higher figure of credit relief.

The tax credit for the married couple's allowance is given before any double tax relief due.

EXAMPLE 30.5

A, a married man, has the following income in 1994/95:

	£
Salary	20,000
UK dividends (net)	16,000
Foreign dividends (net of tax 20%)	5,000

Assuming maximum double tax relief is claimed, calculate the UK tax liability.

Income tax computation 1994/95

			£
Schedule E			20,000
UK dividends (16,000 × 100/80)			20,000
Schedule DV (5,000 × 100/80)			6,250
			46,250
Personal allowance			(3,445)
Taxable income			42,805

Income tax due:

On non dividend income	3,000	at 20%	600
	13,555	at 25%	3,389
(20,000 − 3,445)	16,555		
On dividends (part)	7,145	at 20%	1,429
	23,700		
On dividends (balance)	19,105	at 40%	7,642
	42,805		13,060

Less: MCA relief £1,720 at 20%			(344)
Less: double tax relief the lower of:			
a) Foreign tax £6,250 at 20% =		£1,250	
b) UK tax £6,250 at 40% =		£2,500	(1,250)
UK tax liability			11,466

Overseas gains of UK residents

UK residents are taxable on capital gains arising on disposal of assets, wherever they are situated. To the extent that capital gains are taxed in another country, relief for double taxation should be available as above, either under the terms of a double taxation agreement or under unilateral relief.

Inheritance tax and gift of non-UK property by UK residents

Residence is not relevant to the computation of inheritance tax. Domicile is the critical factor and this is dealt with fully in Chapter 8.

To the extent that a person may be required to pay inheritance tax, or a tax of a similar type, on the same property, both in the UK and in another country, relief for double taxation may be available as above, under the terms of a double taxation agreement between the countries; if there is no such agreement, tax would be paid under the unilateral double tax relief arrangements in the UK.

Unilateral double tax relief

Unilateral double tax relief for inheritance tax is available where no relief can be obtained under a double tax agreement or where more relief can be obtained.

The calculation of the relief depends on where the property is situated. The relief is the whole of the overseas tax, if the property is situated overseas and not situated in the UK. If the property is situated in a third country (not in the overseas country or the UK) or in both the overseas country and the UK, only partial relief is given for the overseas tax according to the formula:

$$\frac{A}{A+B} \times C$$

where A is the amount of the inheritance tax
B is the amount of the overseas tax
C is the lower of A or B.

UK income of non-UK residents

A non-resident (not R not OR) individual is liable to UK income tax only on income arising in the UK and as a rule, is not entitled to personal allowances. Full personal allowances may be available in a few special cases (see below) for 1990/91 and subsequent years of assessment.

In all cases, the rules set out below apply subject to the provisions of individual double tax agreements.

Trading in the UK

Although in the previous chapter it was stated that a trade is deemed to be carried on in the country from which it is managed and controlled, a non-resident is liable on the profits of a trade physically present in the UK even if it is managed and controlled from abroad.

A non-resident trading in the UK normally does so through a UK agent or branch. The agent (or person in charge of the branch) is personally chargeable on all the profits arising whether he or she receives them or not. He or she is, however, entitled to retain the tax out of funds in his charge.

This does not prevent the non-resident being assessed directly where a notice of assessment can be served.

If the profits cannot readily be ascertained, the assessment will be on a percentage of turnover. (The agent is obliged to disclose this information). The normal appeal provisions apply. The anti-avoidance provisions relating to trading at artificial prices apply where the agent controls the non-resident or vice versa (this applies more commonly to companies and is covered more fully in Chapter 31)

Trade 'with' the UK or 'within' the UK?

In considering the question of whether a trade is carried on within or outside the UK, an important factor is where the sales contract is completed. If a sales contract between a UK purchaser and a non-resident company is made outside the UK this would be regarded as trading with the UK and no liability to UK tax would normally arise.

Employment in the UK

An individual who is non-resident (not R) or if resident, not ordinarily resident (R not OR), in the UK, is chargeable to tax as follows:

- Emoluments for duties performed in the UK are assessed under Schedule E Case II.
- Emoluments for duties performed outside the UK:
  - If the taxpayer is non-resident in the UK are not liable to UK income tax
  - If the taxpayer is resident but not ordinarily resident (R not OR) in the UK, he or she is assessable under Schedule E Case III to the extent that they are remitted to the UK (the remittance basis).

Where the duties of a single employment are performed both inside and outside of the UK, it is necessary for the emoluments to be apportioned for the above assessments. Time apportionment based on the number of working days inside and outside the UK is normally applied. However, where part of the emoluments are paid in the UK, provided this represents a reasonable apportionment for the UK duties, the Inland Revenue will accept it and only make assessments under Schedule E Case III on any further amounts remitted by residents.

Payment of rent and other annual sums to non-residents

Rent (less expenses paid), copyright royalties and interest paid to non-residents by or through any person in the UK must be paid net of basic rate income tax. An agent is entitled to deduct commission from the amount collected before deduction of tax.

The Inland Revenue may ask for a return detailing all payments made.

Collection of tax

Although a notice of assessment may be served abroad on a non-resident, there are difficulties in collection. This is the reason why arrangements are made to collect the tax in the UK before the income is remitted to the non-resident.

Interest on most UK government securities is exempt from UK income tax if the recipient is not ordinarily resident (included are 3.5% War Loan, all funding loans and most issues of Treasury Loan Stock and Exchequer Loan Stock).

Note also that a person not ordinarily resident in the UK may make a declaration to that effect to a bank or a building society and the interest will continue to be paid gross. The person concerned must undertake to notify the bank or building society of any changes in circumstances. By extra-statutory concession, this income is also treated as exempt.

Personal allowances

In general, non-residents are not entitled to personal allowances. There are, however, a few special cases when personal allowances will be given. Excess allowances, given in these circumstances cannot be transferred from husband to wife unless the wife also qualifies for full allowances in her own right.

UK income

UK income is any income arising in the UK except for interest on certain government securities which is exempt (see above). Any income eligible for double tax relief is also left out of account.

UK gains of non-UK residents

A non-resident (not R not OR) individual is liable to capital gains tax if he or she carries on a trade, profession or vocation in the UK through a branch or agency on the profits of which he or she is chargeable to UK income tax, and disposes of business assets situated in the UK.

In this case the non-resident will be assessed in the name of the branch or agency which is held responsible under the Taxation of Chargeable Gains Act 1992. The person so charged is entitled to retain the tax out of funds in his or her charge.

The unrealised gains are charged to tax if:

- the UK branch or agency ceases, or
- the assets are removed from the UK and roll-over relief for the replacement of business assets will only be available if the replacement asset is within the UK tax charge.

Inheritance tax and non-UK residents

Residence has no significance for inheritance purposes except, in certain circumstances, to extend the meaning of domicile. A non-UK domiciled individual is liable to inheritance tax on all dispositions of assets situated in the UK.

Summary

- Legislation provides for residence to be determined for the fiscal year as a whole, but Extra-statutory Concession A11 allows in limited circumstances, residence to commence from the date of arrival in the UK or cease from the date of departure from the UK.
- 'Ordinarily resident' is the term applied to a person who is habitually resident in the UK (usually established from the start of the tax year following the third anniversary of arrival in the UK).
- An individual may have a domicile of origin or a domicile of choice or a domicile of dependency.
- The taxation of overseas income from employment is a complex area. Which Case of Schedule E applies depends on the residence status of the individual as well as where the duties of the employment are performed.
- Where an individual chargeable under Schedule E Case I has long periods of absence abroad performing the duties of his or her employment, he or she will be entitled to a 100% deduction from his or her emoluments if he or she has a 365-day qualifying period.
- A resident and ordinarily resident non-UK domiciled individual receiving foreign emoluments for duties performed wholly abroad will be taxed under Schedule E Case III on the remittance basis.
- Overseas trades are taxable under Schedule D Case V.
- Overseas dividends are taxable at 20%.
- Double tax relief is available for income or gains taxed twice.
- Non-resident individuals are liable to income tax on UK source income but generally are not entitled to personal allowances.
- Collection of tax from non-residents is difficult and wherever possible, the person in the UK through whom the payment is remitted is made responsible for deducting basic rate income tax at source.
- Non-residents are only liable to capital gains tax on disposals of business assets situated in the UK.
- Residence is not relevant for inheritance tax.

Self test questions

1. Describe three situations when an individual coming to the UK may be resident from the date of arrival.
2. Is it possible to be resident in more than one country?
3. How are foreign pensions taxed?
4. What tests do the intervening periods in the UK have to satisfy for there to be a 365-day qualifying period?
5. Does a 365-day qualifying period have to be a complete tax year?
6. For the travel costs of a spouse and children visiting during a period when duties are being performed abroad to be tax deductible, what criteria must be satisfied?

7   Where is a trade carried on?

8   A informs you that he has been offered a job in America by the UK-resident company which currently employs him. He has been offered a contract for five years from 1 December 1994, during which time all his duties will be performed in the United States.

Prepare a memorandum outlining how his residence position will be determined for 1994/95 onwards and how this will effect his tax position in each of these years. Your answer should cover the effect of spending his annual leave in the UK.

9   Dr Freda Footloose, who is resident, ordinarily resident and domiciled in the UK, provides you with the following information regarding her journeys to and from the UK whilst she is employed as a doctor in a hospital in Brazil:

Left UK to take up appointment	12 April 1994
Returned to UK	15 May 1994
Left UK	9 June 1994
Returned to UK	27 September 1994
Left UK	29 October 1994
Returned to UK	28 March 1995
Due to return finally to UK	7 September 1995

Dr Footloose comes to see you on 15 April 1995 during her visit to the UK regarding her 1994/95 tax affairs. She intends to return to Brazil on 1 May to complete her contract.

You are required to advise her whether she qualifies for the 100% deduction from overseas earnings and of any further action she must take.

10 Consider the following individuals:
    a) An American, resident in London, who has a directorship with a Paris-based company.
    b) An English citizen who has worked in Rome for many years is sent by her employer to London on a two-year contract. The job involves both UK and overseas duties.

Write notes in preparation for an interview with each person, outlining their possible positions with regard to UK taxation and listing any further information that would be required.

Answers on pages 635–636

Company Residence and its Implications

CHAPTER 31

The purpose of this chapter is to look at the factors which affect the residence of a company and consider the implications, particularly in terms of the anti-avoidance legislation necessary in the UK to back it up.

Residence

New rules for company residence were introduced with effect from 15 March 1988. The current position is therefore:

- All companies incorporated in the UK are resident in the UK for tax purposes
- Companies not incorporated in the UK are treated as UK resident for tax purposes if their central management and control is in the UK.

The Finance Act 1994 introduced new provisions whereby companies which are resident in the UK, but which would be regarded as resident in another country for the purposes of a double taxation agreement, will in future be treated as not resident in the UK.

At 15 March 1988 there were some companies incorporated in the UK which were non-resident (having received Treasury consent to 'migrate'); they will remain non-resident unless or until they cease to carry on business or otherwise cease to be taxable outside the UK.

Prior to this date, for UK tax purposes, a company was regarded as being resident in the country in which its central management and control was exercised – the country of incorporation was irrelevant.

The new rules have extended the scope of UK corporation tax significantly: Companies incorporated in the UK are UK resident as well as any other company which has its central management and control in the UK.

Central management and control

The location of a company's central management and control continues to be relevant for companies incorporated outside the UK. It is considered to be a question of fact.

Central management and control is the highest level of control of the company's business: that is, policy and strategy decisions rather than the day-to-day control of the business operations.

It must first be ascertained whether the directors exercise this central management and control and, if so, *where* they exercise it (this is not necessarily where they meet). If all the directors live outside the UK and meet outside the UK, it is unlikely that the company could be said to be resident in the UK. Where some of the directors live in the UK, the majority should live outside the UK and it would be necessary to show that the UK-resident directors did not exercise the central management and control on their own. The place where the board meetings are held is significant only if it can be shown that the board exercises the central management and control of the company.

If the directors do not exercise the central management and control of the company, it must be established who does exercise it and from where. The residence of a wholly owned subsidiary is not normally determined by the residence of the parent unless the authority of the board of the subsidiary is undermined by the parent company.

The residence of a company is a question of fact in any particular case. Emphasis is given to establishing the reality of the situation rather than accepting those factors that exist merely to obtain taxation advantages. Note that double tax agreements often address the problem of residence and therefore in many cases, the problem does not arise.

The implications of UK residence

A company that is UK resident is liable to UK corporation tax on its worldwide profits. The UK tax authorities are anxious to protect the revenue to which they are entitled and as a result have introduced many anti-avoidance provisions in this area, the most important of which are outlined below.

There have been many periods in the past when the burden of UK taxation has been heavier than in most other countries and it was tempting for companies which conducted a large part of their business outside the UK to 'move their residence' in order to escape UK taxation (by making sure that their central management and control resided outside the UK). Legislation was therefore enacted to prohibit this unless it was carried out with the Treasury consent. The 1988 amendments made a change of residence possible (for those companies not incorporated in the UK) upon them being subjected to an 'exit charge' (see below).

With the growth of multinational groups of companies, it is possible for a UK company to be 'connected with' companies resident in other countries. Where any inter-company trading is carried on there is an opportunity for profits to be moved from one country to another in order to minimise the tax burden of the group as a whole. The tax authorities of both the acquiring and the vending companies will be anxious to ensure that the transfer prices at which such transactions are carried out are not artificially fixed to enable the profits of either company to be manipulated in this way.

Becoming non-resident in the UK

As a result of the new residence rules this section will only apply to those companies not incorporated in the UK but who have their central management and control in the UK.

If a company no longer wishes to be UK resident after 15 March 1988, it must give to the Board of Inland Revenue the following:

▶ notice of its intention to cease to be UK resident together with its anticipated date of cessation
▶ a statement of all tax estimated due and payable up to that date (the following taxes must be included in addition to corporation tax on chargeable profits for all periods up to the anticipated date of cessation: PAYE, income tax deducted at source from unfranked payments, tax collected from payments to subcontractors)
▶ a statement of the arrangements which will be made to secure the payment of that tax.

The Inland Revenue must approve the arrangements to secure payment and be satisfied that the statement of tax is complete and accurate.

At the date the company becomes non-UK resident:

▶ it is deemed to dispose of all its assets at market value and immediately reacquire them at that same value

▶ no roll-over relief will be available beyond this date on earlier disposals of assets on which roll-over relief had been claimed.

A significant chargeable gain is therefore likely to accrue in the final accounting period; this has been referred to as the 'exit charge'. In certain circumstances the charge is modified.

One such circumstance is where the company retains a branch or an agency in the UK. Those assets in the UK used by the branch or agency for the purposes of its trade are not deemed to be disposed of and roll-over relief will continue to be available against replacement assets so situated and used.

A second circumstance arises to the extent that the assets deemed to be disposed of are foreign assets (that is those assets outside the UK used for the purposes of a trade outside the UK). A postponement of the gain arising on the deemed disposal of such assets is available if the company, immediately after becoming non-UK resident, is a 75% subsidiary of a UK-resident company (termed the 'principal company') and both companies so elect within two years of the company becoming non-UK resident. The postponement will operate as follows:

▶ The *net gains* arising on the deemed disposal of the foreign assets are treated as a single chargeable gain which may be postponed.
▶ If all or some of these assets (on which gains arose) are disposed of within six years, the whole or an appropriate proportion of the postponed gain will accrue to the principal company at the date of the disposal.
▶ The postponed gain or the remainder thereof will also crystallise to the principal company if, at any time, the company ceases to be a 75% subsidiary of the principal company or the principal company ceases to be UK resident.
▶ Whenever any of the postponed gain becomes chargeable on the principal company, the principal company and the subsidiary company may jointly elect for any unrelieved capital losses of the subsidiary to be set against that gain (this election must be expressed in writing within two years).

EXAMPLE 31.1

A Ltd is the principal company of B Ltd which ceased to be UK resident on 31 December 1990. At that date a gain was deemed to accrue on B's foreign assets. There were three foreign assets with gains respectively of £50,000, £90,000 and £60,000, giving a total of £200,000. Both A Ltd and B Ltd elected for the gain to be postponed.

On 30 September 1992 one of the above assets (with a gain included above of £50,000) was disposed of. A further such asset was disposed of on 31 December 1994 (gain included above of £60,000).

Gains will arise to the principal company on the appropriate proportion as follows:

30 September 1992

$$\frac{50,000}{50,000 + 90,000 + 60,000} \times 200,000 \text{ (postponed gain)} \qquad £50,000$$

31 December 1994

$$\frac{60,000}{90,000 + 60,000} \times (200,000 - 50,000) \qquad £60,000$$

Anti-avoidance legislation (ICTA 1988, ss. 765–766)

In order to prevent companies 'migrating', these sections make certain transactions by companies unlawful if carried out without Treasury consent.

The two transactions which require Treasury consent before they may be undertaken by a UK-resident company are:

- causing or permitting a non-resident company, directly or indirectly controlled by it, to create or issue shares or debentures
- causing or permitting the transfer to any person of shares or debentures which it owns in a non-resident company, directly or indirectly controlled by it (except to qualify that person to act as director).

The current legislation can therefore be summarised as follows:

- A company incorporated in the UK is UK resident (except for those companies with Treasury consent at 15 March 1988) and cannot migrate.
- A company not incorporated in the UK but with its central management and control in the UK is UK resident but can migrate on payment of an 'exit charge'.
- A company resident in the UK, but regarded as resident in another country for the purpose of a double taxation agreement, will be treated as not UK resident.

In addition, a UK-resident company which has a controlling interest in a non-resident company (that is, a non-resident subsidiary) needs Treasury consent before:

- the subsidiary can issue shares or debentures
- it disposes of all or any part of its interest in that company.

Control of the subsidiary cannot therefore be given up or diluted without permission.

The Treasury gives either general consent or special consent and may attach conditions to any consent granted.

A special consent applies to a specified transaction or transactions.

A general consent is a consent in principle to a particular company undertaking a specified type of transaction. It may be revoked.

Severe penalties (a maximum fine of £10,000 or three times the tax liability on its total profits arising in the 36 months preceding the offence and/or two years' imprisonment) may be imposed for offences under this section.

Movements of capital within the European Community

Where the non-resident subsidiary referred to above is resident in another EC member state, Treasury consent is not required, but the UK parent must make the appropriate returns.

Trading at artificial prices

This is another anti-avoidance section. Whenever any trading transactions take place between a UK-resident body of persons and a non-UK-resident connected body of persons, the UK tax authorities may look at the transactions to ensure that:

- sales are not made by a UK company at an undervalue
- purchases are not made by a UK company at an overvalue.

If the Inland Revenue consider that either or both of these circumstances are arising, market value (that is, an 'arm's-length price') may be substituted for the purpose of establishing the profits chargeable to corporation tax. Note that if the opposite were happening (sales were being made at an overvalue and purchases at an undervalue) no adjustment would be made. Profits chargeable to corporation tax may be increased but not decreased under this section.

Connected persons

For the purpose of this section, 'connected' means that one body of persons is under the control of the other or both are under the control of a third person or persons.

A body of persons may include a company or a partnership.

Control in this sense is separate and distinct from 'central management and control' for the purpose of determining residence, and it reflects the ability to exercise control, either directly or indirectly, through the size of the shareholding or the number of votes exercised.

To establish direct or indirect control, persons are attributed with the powers of:

1. their nominees
2. their spouses
3. brother, sister, lineal ancestor or descendant of themselves or their spouses
4. the spouse of anybody in 3 above
5. their partners or the persons connected with them above
6. the nominees of the above.

Transactions to which this section applies

This section applies not only to trading transactions but also to the purchase and sale of fixed assets and other property, to the letting and hiring of property, the granting of licences and the provision of business facilities. It therefore includes loan interest, patent royalties and management charges.

Procedures

The Inland Revenue employs a specialist team to carry out investigations in this field. There are many ways in which this team may become interested in a particular taxpayer, including referral by his Inspector.

The taxpayer may be required to furnish within a specified time (minimum 30 days) information related to a transaction which is or appears to be:

- one (or connected to one) to which this section may apply
- relevant in determining whether this section should or should not be applied
- relevant to determining the market price of a transaction.

The Inspector of Taxes will make such enquiries as are warranted and wherever possible will seek to come to an agreement with the taxpayer by correspondence or discussion if it appears that an adjustment of transfer prices is necessary.

The Inland Revenue may give notice requiring access to the books and records of any parties to the transaction. The companies are entitled to appeal against such a notice to the Board and subsequently to the Special Commissioners. The normal rights of appeal exist against an assessment raised under this section.

The European Community

The EC Convention on the elimination of double taxation in connection with the adjustment of profits of associated enterprises will require (when ratified) member states to adopt specific procedures and refer disputes relating to transfer pricing adjustments to an advisory commission. It will override domestic legislation.

Summary

- The residence rules for companies were changed in 1988, with the result that the majority of companies incorporated in the UK will be resident in the UK.

- The central management and control test which previously applied to all companies is still relevant in determining the residence of non-UK incorporated companies.
- Owing to varying levels of taxation in countries, it has been necessary to police those elements which determine the level of profits chargeable to corporation tax in companies, namely changes of residence and inter-company transfer pricing.
- The situation regarding change of residence has altered substantially as a result of the Finance Act 1988. A company incorporated in the UK cannot normally be non-UK resident. A company not incorporated in the UK may now become non-resident in the UK upon being subjected to an 'exit charge'. The anti-avoidance legislation has largely been repealed in this area.
- The 'exit charge' may in certain circumstances be postponed.
- Where the UK tax authorities discover that profits chargeable to corporation tax are understated due to international pricing policies between connected persons, an arm's length price may be substituted for the purpose of assessing the profits chargeable to corporation tax.

Self test questions

1. Outline the rules for determining whether a company is resident in the UK following the Finance Act 1988.

2. Outline the principles applied in determining where a company's central management and control lies and indicate whether these have any relevance following the Finance Act 1988.

3. List the taxation consequences of a company migrating after 14 March 1988.

4. Under what circumstances will the tax charge under question 3 above be deferred or postponed?

5. Explain why the Inland Revenue is concerned when transactions take place other than at market value.

Answers on page 636

Outward Investment by UK Companies

CHAPTER 32

The purpose of this chapter is to consider the UK tax treatment of income arising from overseas investment by UK-resident companies including the reliefs available for double taxation.

Overview

A UK-resident company is chargeable to corporation tax on its worldwide profits.

In an international context, it will often happen that two countries will charge the same profits to tax. For example, the profits of an overseas branch operated by a UK-resident company will invariably be charged to tax under Schedule D Case I in the same way as a UK branch of the same trade. In addition to being charged to UK corporation tax the profits of the overseas branch will usually be charged to tax in the overseas country. Without provision for relief, the profits would be taxed twice; this would be excessive. To provide relief the UK has entered into numerous double tax treaties with other countries, which override the effect of domestic legislation in the respective countries.

Although the majority of overseas investment is undertaken by UK companies for commercial reasons, it is unrealistic to suppose that low rates of tax and other benefits are not either the primary or a secondary concern of at least some of the companies. The UK is not alone in its concern about the loss of tax revenue which has occurred with the removal of exchange controls and the growth of international movements in capital and there is a vast area of anti-avoidance legislation which has been in existence for some time (the main elements of this legislation were considered in Chapter 31). More recent anti-avoidance legislation concerns controlled foreign companies (CFCs) which are companies resident in low-tax areas and controlled by UK residents. These are considered later in this chapter.

Operations overseas

A UK company which carries on a trade through a branch or agency overseas will be chargeable to corporation tax under the appropriate schedules on the profits arising which in the case of a trading branch will be either Schedule D Case I or Case V. A branch or agency means any factorship, agency, receivership, branch or management. If it is controlled from the UK, Schedule D Case I applies while if it is controlled abroad Schedule D Case V will apply. The question of where control lies is one of fact.

Where Schedule D Case I applies the computation of profits, relief for capital allowances and so on, will proceed as normal, and any losses of the branch, being part of the UK company's results, will be available to set off against the total profits of the UK company for the accounting period or even for group relief purposes to other group members (UK). Disposals of the overseas assets of an overseas branch will be chargeable disposals for capital gains purposes but roll-over relief will be available.

Where, for example, an agency is set up overseas, and controlled overseas, the profits of the agency will be chargeable to corporation tax under Schedule D Case V. The rules of computation of profits under Schedule D Case V are the same as for Schedule D Case I. However, any trading losses incurred in an accounting period may only be carried forward and set off against profits of the same trade arising in future accounting periods.

The profits of an overseas subsidiary will not, it is assumed, be subject to corporation tax because it will be set up in such a way that it is non-UK resident. Dividends from the subsidiary will be assessed under Schedule D Case V. The following consequences are suffered where a group of companies includes an overseas subsidiary:

- Trading losses incurred by an overseas subsidiary are not eligible for group relief nor may losses of other group companies be surrendered to an overseas subsidiary.
- The transfer of assets from a UK group company to an overseas group company is not eligible to be transferred on a 'no gain, no loss' basis and may therefore generate a chargeable gain.
- Dividends paid by an overseas subsidiary cannot be group income; overseas companies cannot make group income and charges elections.
- Overseas subsidiaries count as associated companies for purposes of reducing the upper and lower limit for the small companies rate of corporation tax.

Income from foreign securities is taxable under Schedule D Case IV.

Double tax relief

Double tax relief in the UK is available in two principal ways:

- under a double tax agreement
- by unilateral relief.

These methods of obtaining relief are mutually exclusive.

Treaty relief has priority and overrides unilateral relief. Unilateral relief when available is not mandatory and may be disclaimed by election. If unilateral relief is disclaimed or, for any other reason, is not allowable, the foreign tax will be allowed as an expense deductible from the foreign income.

Double tax treaties

A double tax treaty is an agreement between two countries which sets out a reciprocal policy for dealing with situations where double taxation might take place through the operation of domestic legislation in the respective countries. Double tax agreements vary but the usual result is that each country agrees to give credit for tax paid to the other country in calculating the tax liability to itself. Alternatively one country may agree to exempt certain income (which would otherwise be taxable) in certain circumstances from taxation in that country and the other country would reciprocate with a corresponding exemption. The possibility of double taxation is therefore avoided.

Double tax treaties vary one from the other and from time to time. A detailed knowledge of the content of specific double tax treaties is outside the scope of the syllabus.

The OECD's model double tax treaty, published in 1977 is the framework on which most modern double tax treaties are based.

Unilateral relief

Unilateral relief is available where there is no double tax agreement between the relevant countries, or where the double tax agreement which exists does not cover the particular situation.

Unilateral relief takes two forms, the most common of which is for withholding taxes.

Withholding taxes

When foreign income is received net of foreign tax, the foreign tax is called 'withholding tax'. The gross amount of such income is charged to tax in the UK. Therefore the profits of an overseas branch controlled in the UK plus the foreign tax charged on those profits (that is the taxable profits before tax), will be assessable under Schedule D Case I. The profits of an overseas branch controlled outside the UK plus the foreign tax charged on those profits will be assessable under Schedule D Case V. Interest from overseas securities plus the withholding tax will be assessable under Schedule D Case IV while dividends from overseas investments plus the withholding tax will be assessable under Schedule D Case V.

The amount of double tax relief available is limited to the amount of corporation tax charged on the foreign income. In arriving at the amount of foreign income chargeable to corporation tax, all deductions (charges, losses, group relief and management expenses, if applicable) may be set off in whatever proportions against whatever source of income the company wishes, that is, whatever is most advantageous to the company to maximise its double tax relief and other reliefs. Double tax relief is deducted from corporation tax in priority to ACT (see Worksheet – Part B, Chapter 25).

If the amount of overseas tax is greater than the liability to corporation tax on the foreign income, then some of the overseas tax will be unrelieved. Unrelieved overseas tax cannot be carried forward.

EXAMPLE 32.1

A Ltd is a UK company with six associate companies. All companies prepare their accounts to 31 December. A Ltd's results for the year ended 31 December 1994 are as follows:

	£
UK trading profits	175,000
Overseas dividends gross (foreign tax 50%)	50,000
Chargeable gains	10,000
Group income	40,000
Debenture interest paid (gross)	35,000

Worksheet – Part A	£	United Kingdom	Overseas
Schedule D Case I	175,000	175,000	
Schedule D Case V	50,000		50,000
Chargeable gains	10,000	10,000	
	235,000	185,000	50,000
Less: charges	(35,000)	(35,000)	
Profits chargeable to CT	200,000	150,000	50,000

Worksheet – Part B	£	£	£
Corporation tax liability 33%	66,000	49,500	16,500
Double tax relief – Maximum	(16,500)		(16,500)
	49,500	49,500	–
Foreign tax paid			25,000
Relieved			(16,500)
Unrelieved			8,500

In this case the unrelieved tax is effectively the difference in the rates of tax between the UK and the overseas country. When the rate of tax in the overseas country is higher than that in the UK, there will always be unrelieved foreign tax and tax planning is unlikely to be able to alleviate the situation. The situation above would have been more pronounced if, for example, SCR had applied. The company may consider increasing the taxable profits – for example, where trading losses are involved, consideration must be given to surrendering them to a group company.

The effect of the set off of double tax relief on the limit for set off of ACT should be revised at this stage (covered in Chapter 25). The maximum ACT set off in the above example is the ACT percentage on the profits chargeable to CT, further restricted to the CT liability on each source of income:

		£	£
UK income	(150,000 × 3/12 × 22.5%)		
	(150,000 × 9/12 × 20%)		30,938
Overseas income			
lower of 1)	(50,000 × 3/12 × 22.5%)		
	(50,000 × 9/12 × 20%)	10,313	
2)	CT liability	Nil	
			Nil
Maximum ACT set-off			30,938

Generally, charges and loss reliefs should be allocated to UK sources of income in preference to overseas sources of income where double tax relief is involved in order to minimise the wastage of the double tax relief and the restriction on the ACT set-off. Group relief for losses eases the situation, as does the surrender of ACT.

The restriction of the ACT set-off is a very real problem for multinational companies based in the UK whose overseas income represents a substantial proportion of total profit from year to year. The payment of dividends is expected by shareholders but results in 'irrecoverable ACT', which effectively increases the company's overall level of taxation. The reduction in the ACT rate over 1993/4 and 1994/5 will help to reduce the problem. The Foreign Income Dividend Scheme introduced in the Finance Act 1994 is aimed at eliminating the problem.

Underlying taxes

In some cases, in addition to relief for withholding taxes, relief is also available for underlying tax.

Relief for underlying tax is available when a UK company receives dividend income from an overseas company in which it controls at least ten per cent of the voting power (directly or indirectly). See Figure 32.1 for a graphic explanation.

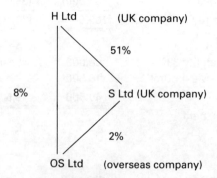

Figure 32.1 H Ltd controls 10% of the voting power of OS Ltd.

Underlying tax is the tax suffered relating to the profits out of which the dividend has been paid. Profits means accounting profits and not taxable profits of the overseas company (*Bowater Paper Corporation Ltd* v. *Murgatroyd* 1969). The tax suffered is the overseas tax eventually paid (not that provided in the accounts). The formula for calculating the amount of the underlying tax applicable to the dividend is as follows:

$$\text{Dividend} + \text{withholding tax} \times \frac{\text{Overseas tax paid on profits of accounting period}}{\text{Relevant profits (available for distribution per accounts)}}$$

EXAMPLE 32.2

The profit and loss account (in sterling) of an overseas company for the year ending 31 March 1995 is as follows:

	£
Profits before taxation	200,000
Taxation (estimated liability)	(80,000)
Profits after taxation (available for distribution)	120,000
Dividends (subject to a withholding tax of 10%)	(60,000)
	60,000

The tax liability on the profits of the year was finally agreed at £75,000.

If A Ltd has two associated companies and owns 10% of the voting power of this overseas company and its only other income is trading income of £500,000, A Ltd's corporation tax computation will be as follows:

Worksheet – Part A	£	United Kingdom	Overseas
Schedule D Case I	500,000	500,000	
Schedule D Case V	9,750		9,750
Profits chargeable to CT	509,750	500,000	9,750

Worksheet – Part B	£	£	£
Corporation tax liability 33%	168,217	165,000	3,217
Double tax relief: Maximum	(3,217)		(3,217)
	165,000	165,000	–

Notes		£
Dividend received from overseas company		5,400
Add withholding tax (10/90 5,400)		600
		6,000
Add underlying tax $(6,000 \times \frac{75,000}{120,000})$		3,750
Schedule D Case V		9,750
Foreign tax available for DTR (9,750 – 5,400)		4,350
Relieved		(3,217)
Unrelieved		1,133

Expense relief

Where for any reason there is no liability to corporation tax (when there are trading losses for example) no relief for foreign tax will be available above. Under these circumstances, the foreign tax can be deducted from the foreign income as an expense, and has the effect of increasing the amount of UK tax losses available.

EXAMPLE 32.3

A Ltd has a trading loss for the year ending 31 December 1994 of £20,000 and received dividends from an overseas company of £8,500 (withholding tax of 15% was suffered). A Ltd's computation is done a) with unilateral relief claimed and b) with expense relief:

			£
a)	**Unilateral relief**		
	Schedule D Case I		Nil
	Schedule D Case V		10,000
	Total profits		10,000
	Loss relief s. 393A		(10,000)
	Profits chargeable to CT		Nil
	Loss Memo		£
	Loss for year		20,000
	Claimed s. 393A		(10,000)
	Loss for c/b s. 393A or cf		10,000
b)	**Expense relief**		£
	Schedule D Case I		Nil
	Schedule D Case V	10,000	
		(1,500)	
			8,500
	Total profits		8,500
	Loss relief s. 393A		(8,500)
	Profits chargeable to CT		Nil
	Loss Memo		£
	Loss for year		20,000
	Claimed s. 393A		(8,500)
	Loss for c/b s. 393A or cf		11,500

Therefore by claiming expense relief when unilateral relief is not available the losses for carry forward are increased by the amount of the withholding tax. Of course a claim under s. 393A need not have been made, allowing unilateral relief to be claimed against the corporation tax liability of £2,500 (£10,000 @ 25% assuming SCR) leaving a tax liability of £1,000 and losses for carry forward of £20,000. This alternative depends on the cash flow situation, the comparative rates of withholding tax and corporation tax and the availability of future profits.

Controlled foreign companies

It was generally advantageous from a taxation point of view to accumulate income in a foreign company resident in a country where the tax rates were lower than in the UK rather than suffer the higher rates of UK corporation tax which existed in this country prior to the present regime. During the early 1980s, there was evidence of concern within government and the Inland Revenue about the growth in the use of 'tax haven countries' for tax avoidance companies and, in particular, the use of those companies for the accumulation of profits and investment income of UK groups.

One proposal for tackling the problem is to apportion the profits of specific defined foreign companies resident in tax havens to their corporate shareholders resident in the UK and impose a UK taxation charge on the apportioned income.

Definition

A controlled foreign company (CFC) is:

- resident outside the UK
- controlled by persons resident in the UK
- subject to a lower level of taxation in the country in which it is resident.

A lower level of taxation is defined as less than three-quarters of the corresponding UK tax (a list has been published in an Inland Revenue press release of the countries which, for the time being, are not regarded as low tax countries – note that Hong Kong is within the definition of low tax countries).

Application

The legislation giving effect to these provisions is very bulky and is mostly concerned with detailed anti-avoidance legislation which is beyond the scope of this syllabus.

The apportionment provisions apply to UK companies which, together with their associates, have at least a 10% interest in the controlled foreign company. 'Interest' is as widely defined for this purpose as control is for close companies (see Chapter 26). The 'chargeable profits' (excluding chargeable gains) of the CFC, together with the 'creditable tax', are apportioned to UK-resident corporate shareholders and brought into charge to UK corporation tax in the accounting period in which the CFC's accounting period ends (subject to relief for double taxation).

Subject to the normal restrictions, apportioned profits brought into charge to tax in this way will be able to be relieved by the set-off of trading losses, charges, management expenses, group relief and so forth to the extent that the reliefs cannot be used against the company's other profits.

When dividends are subsequently paid by the CFC out of profits that have been apportioned, the UK tax that has already been paid will be treated as foreign tax paid by the CFC and be eligible for double tax relief.

The legislation is not mandatory and only applies in cases where the Board of Inland Revenue directs. Four principal circumstances are detailed in which no direction will be made.

The intention is that bona fide commercial investments in tax havens will not be subject to statutory apportionment.

EXAMPLE 32.4

R Ltd owns 20% of the equity in Y, a company resident in a tax haven country where the rate of tax is 10% on profits. A and B, UK residents, also own 20% of the share capital of Y. During the year ended 31 December 1994, Y made profits after tax of £50,000 but no dividends were paid.

In the year ended 31 March 1995, R Ltd had profits chargeable to corporation tax of £50,000.

Y is a controlled foreign company which does not have an acceptable distribution policy. As R Ltd owns more than 10% of its share capital, it will be deemed to have received £11,111 (20% of £50,000 × 100/90). R Ltd basic profit will be £61,111 and the corporation tax liability (SCR) will be £15,278 less double tax relief of £1,111 that is £14,167.

Excluded circumstances

The provisions will not be applied if any of the following are satisfied:

- *The profits of the CFC are less than £20,000* for a 12-month accounting period (rateably reduced for shorter accounting periods)
- *The CFC has an 'acceptable distribution policy'*. For a trading company this means at least 50% of its accounting profits have been distributed as a dividend within 18 months of the end of the accounting period. A trading company has a wider definition than usual and includes companies dealing in securities, land and commodities. The acceptable percentage for a non-trading company is 90% of its taxable profits.
- *The activities of the CFC are exempt.* If the CFC has a business establishment in the country of its residence which is effectively managed and controlled in that country and certain other detailed conditions are satisfied as to the nature of that business, the activities will be deemed to be exempt
- *The CFC has a public quotation.* If at least 35% of the ordinary share capital is held by the public and has been dealt in on a recognised Stock Exchange within the accounting period
- *The motive* for setting up the CFC and the transactions which took place satisfy the Board that the reduction of a tax liability was not the primary consideration.

Clearance

There is no formal advance clearance procedure to ascertain whether a particular company will be treated as a CFC. However, the company may appeal to the Special Commissioners against a 'notice of direction' and there is a technical unit of the Inland Revenue available to give advice.

Branch or subsidiary?

Very often non-tax considerations will determine whether a branch or a subsidiary overseas is the better business outlet. However, an awareness of the following tax considerations is also necessary:

- Where a foreign branch is merely an extension of the UK business, relief is available to the UK company for set-up costs and losses. The losses of an overseas subsidiary are not available to the UK parent.
- There is a cashflow advantage when profits are taxed in the UK as dividends from an overseas subsidiary, since these will be declared and paid with respect to an accounting period sometime after the end of the accounting period and will be subjected to corporation tax in the period in which they are received. The profits of a branch, on the other hand, will be charged to tax in the accounting period in which they are earned.
- An overseas company can choose whether to pay a dividend (subject to the CFC rules) and so avoid generating foreign tax credits in an accounting period when there is no corporation tax liability against which they can be offset.
- Capital gains of a foreign branch are taxable in UK while capital gains of an overseas subsidiary are not.
- Difficulties may be encountered in establishing the non-UK residence of an overseas subsidiary (that is, that the central management and control are not in the UK).

Starting up as an overseas branch and transferring the overseas business to a subsidiary (non-UK resident) once the business has become profitable would appear to be the most advantageous route. However, there are a number of consequences of incorporating an overseas branch which could give rise to tax charges both overseas and in the UK.

The UK consequences will be:

- an 'exit charge' from the UK under the FA 1988 on the transfer of all or part of the trade of a UK-resident company (not incorporated in the UK) to a non-UK resident company. Treasury consent would be required in respect of a UK-incorporated company (see Chapter 26).
- balancing adjustments on capital allowance computations
- capital gains may arise on the disposal of the trade but may be postponed if the consideration for the disposal consists wholly or partly of shares in the overseas company such that the transferor holds at least 25% of the ordinary issued share capital of the transferee company
- trade is deemed to be discontinued – stock will be valued at market value
- any trading losses of the branch being carried forward will be lost;

but there may also be balancing adjustments, capital gains and transfer taxes overseas.

Summary

- Profits from an overseas branch or agency controlled from the UK; Schedule D Case I

    Income from foreign securities; Schedule D Case IV

    Income from overseas possessions; Schedule D Case V
    - dividends from overseas subsidiaries;
    - profits from an overseas branch or agency controlled overseas;
      capital gains on disposal of assets held overseas.
- In all the above cases, the income or profits, is likely to suffer tax both overseas and in the UK
- Where tax is suffered twice on the same profits, double tax relief will normally be available.
- Double tax relief may be given:
    - under a double tax agreement (this is mandatory if available)
    - unilateral relief – either withholding tax only or withholding tax and underlying tax if relating to a 10% or greater investment by a UK company in an overseas company
    - expense relief – which is often useful if advantage cannot be taken of the other reliefs.
- There is specific anti-avoidance legislation for controlled foreign companies (CFCs)
- Care needs to be taken in deciding whether to operate through a foreign branch or subsidiary and the various advantages and disadvantages must be weighed up. The cost of a later transfer from foreign branch to subsidiary must be considered.

Self test questions

1. List the consequences to the group where a 75% group of companies includes an overseas subsidiary.

2. Where, in the computation of the mainstream corporation tax liability, is double tax relief given?

3. What is underlying tax?

4. What is the formula for calculating the underlying tax relating to particular dividends?

5   Briefly define a controlled foreign company (CFC).

6   What is the consequence of a UK company having a 10% or greater interest in a CFC?

7   P Ltd, a company resident in the UK, owns 90% of Q(USA) Inc, a company resident in America.

   The directors of P Ltd are considering changing the residence of Q(USA) Inc to a far eastern country where the rate of corporation tax is 5%.

   You are required to draft a memorandum to the board of P Ltd concerning the taxation implications of this proposal.

CIMA May 1988

8   MN Ltd, a UK-resident company, has the following holdings of ordinary voting shares in other companies, which, apart from O Ltd, are all UK resident.

   65% in B Ltd
   80% in C Ltd
   90% in O Ltd (a foreign resident company)
   80% in D Ltd

   D Ltd holds 90% of the ordinary shares of E Ltd, A Ltd holds 12% of the shares in B Ltd and O Ltd holds 5% of the shares in E Ltd.

   The trading results for each company for the year ended 31 March 1995 were as follows:

		£
A Ltd	Loss	60,000
B Ltd	Profit	70,000
MN Ltd	Profit	22,000
C Ltd	Loss	10,000
D Ltd	Profit	105,000
E Ltd	Loss	5,000
O Ltd	Loss	10,000

   No company had any other income.

   a) Assuming the above losses are used in the most efficient manner, compute the corporation tax payable by each of the above companies for the chargeable accounting period, that is the 12 months ended 31 March 1995;
   b) Outline the reliefs which may be available to any of the above companies in respect of inter-company transfers of assets.

CIMA May 1989

9   Bristol Adventurers Ltd, a UK-resident company, provides the following information in its accounts:

	£
Trading profits (after adjustments for taxation)	46,000
Cash dividend from Adelaide Adventurers Ltd, a wholly owned subsidiary registered abroad; dividend before the 15% withholding tax under the treaty was £92,000	78,200
Dividends paid in year	105,000

   The subsidiary suffered tax of 40% on its profits in its own country.

   Compute the mainstream corporation tax, after allowing double tax relief, for the accounting year to 31 March 1995.

Answers on pages 636–638

Inward Investment

CHAPTER 33

The purpose of this chapter is to consider the UK tax treatment of income arising to a foreign resident company from investment in the UK. A foreign resident company may invest in the UK by setting up a UK-resident subsidiary company or by itself investing directly in the UK, for example through a branch or an agency.

UK-resident subsidiary

A UK-resident subsidiary of a foreign resident company will be subject to UK corporation tax. The profits of the subsidiary will be remitted to the parent company by dividend.

The UK subsidiary will normally be required to account for ACT on the dividend. The general rule is that a shareholder outside the UK is not entitled to a tax credit on a dividend from a UK company but will not, on the other hand, be assessable to income tax on that dividend. However, depending on the terms of the double tax agreement between the two countries, a part (usually 50%) of the tax credit may be repayable to the foreign resident company. In these circumstances the UK subsidiary may be permitted to pay to the foreign resident company the dividend plus one-half of the tax credit and so discharge a corresponding amount of its liability to account for ACT. A withholding tax may be provided for in the agreement in such a case. (The Inspector of Foreign Dividends oversees such payments and must give permission for the provisions of a double tax agreement to be implemented.)

The Finance Act 1994 introduced the International Headquarters Company (IHC). The definition of an IHC is a company with none of its shareholders owning less than 5% of its share capital, and at least 80% of its shares being held by non-UK residents.

An IHC does not have to pay ACT on any foreign income dividends it pays (see Chapter 25). The aim of the new legislation is to increase the attractiveness of the UK as a base for companies, for example the European base of a multinational company.

If trading losses are incurred by the UK subsidiary, then such losses may be set off against the total profits of the UK subsidiary under ss. 393A(1)(a) and (b) or carried forward and deducted from future profits of the same trade under s. 393(1). Where there are other UK subsidiaries, group relief will only be available if they form a UK group for this purpose (that is, they are all subsidiaries of a UK holding company).

Payment of management charges to the foreign resident company may be made gross but payments of patent royalties and interest must normally be made under deduction of basic rate income tax unless the double tax agreement permits some modification (see below).

Direct investment in the UK

A non-UK-resident company is liable to corporation tax on its chargeable profits if it carries on a trade in the UK through a branch or an agency in the UK.

A non-UK-resident company which does not trade through a branch or agency in the UK is not liable to corporation tax. If it has income arising in the UK, such income will be liable to income tax (this will usually be deducted at source); examples are royalties, interest, dividends and rent.

The question of whether a non-UK resident company is carrying on a trade in the UK is therefore fundamental.

Trade 'with' the UK or 'within' the UK?

In considering the question of whether a trade is carried on within or outside the UK, an important factor is where the sales contract is completed. If a sales contract between a UK purchaser and a non-resident company is made outside the UK this would be regarded as trading with the UK and no liability to UK tax would normally arise. Where contracts are completed in the UK by an agent of a non-resident company, this would be regarded as trading within the UK and the profits would be liable to corporation tax.

Branch, agency or permanent establishment?

Branch or agency?

The UK tax legislation refers to trading through a 'branch or agency' in the UK. For this purpose the trading profits arising as a result of a visiting employee of an overseas resident company concluding contracts in the UK may be construed as arising from an agency in the UK.

Permanent establishment

Although the UK tax legislation refers to a 'branch or agency', the provisions of the Organisation for Economic Co-operation and Development (OECD) Model Double Tax Agreement use the term 'permanent establishment'. A permanent establishment is defined as follows:

- a place of management
- a branch
- an office
- a factory
- a workshop
- a mine, quarry and similar sites for extraction activities
- a long-term construction site.

Therefore where a double tax agreement applies, only trading carried on from a fixed place of business is subject to UK corporation tax (double tax agreements override the internal tax legislation of the respective countries). This excludes sales made through independent agents acting in the ordinary course of their business and by visiting employees, which will not be regarded as trading within the UK.

Various activities are excluded from the definition of permanent establishment: storage and display facilities, an establishment for the purchase of goods or collection of information and advertising.

Chargeable profits

The profits chargeable to corporation tax are the trading profits of the branch or agency (or, if a double taxation agreement applies, the trading profits of the permanent establishment restricted to those profits which might be expected if it were an independent enterprise) wherever they arise (even if from trading transactions outside the UK), plus any other income arising to the branch from property in its possession. Any unrealised gains on assets of a UK branch or agency (or permanent establishment) are chargeable to tax if the UK business ceases or the asset is removed from the UK. Similarly, roll-over relief will only be available where the replacement asset is within the charge to UK tax.

Generally these profits will be taxed as if the branch were a UK resident. The small companies tax rate (with the rules about associated companies) will apply if the worldwide company profits are below the prescribed limit. There is no problem about remitting the profits of the branch to the foreign resident company.

Where trading losses are incurred by the branch they may be allowed against the profits of the foreign resident company (depending on the tax legislation of that country), or they may be carried forward by the branch and deducted from future trading profits of that branch.

Failure by a non-resident company to meet its liability on branch or agency gains may cause other companies in the same group or controlling directors to be held liable.

No branch or agency in the UK

A UK resident who makes payments to a resident of another country of patent royalties, interest or rent is normally required to deduct basic rate income tax at source. If a double tax agreement exists between the countries which wholly or partly relieves that income, such income may be paid gross or under deduction of tax at a specified lower rate on receipt of notice from the Inland Revenue (Inspector of Foreign Dividends).

UK branch or subsidiary?

Once a foreign resident company intends to establish trading in the UK, the question arises as to whether this should be by means of a branch or a subsidiary. The profits of either would be liable to corporation tax. The decision depends on a number of factors, and not merely the taxation consequences.

The taxation considerations however are relevant and are outlined below:

- If there are likely to be trading losses on commencement, it may be advantageous to start as a branch and thus get loss relief against the overseas company's other profits. If it is subsequently decided to incorporate the trade of the branch this can be done without loss of loss relief (reconstruction without change of ownership). Assets can also be transferred on a no gain, no loss basis. There is less flexibility once trade as a subsidiary has commenced since there are, at the present time, no similar concessions on disincorporation.
- If there are other UK subsidiaries, any new company incorporated could become a member of a UK group with a UK holding company and thus obtain loss relief.
- The need to remit the profits of the branch/subsidiary must be considered, as should any existing double tax agreement would affect any such arrangements.
- A UK subsidiary may be regarded as a close company. A foreign resident company cannot, however, be a close company even if it carries on a trade in the UK.

Summary

- A non-UK company may trade in the UK via a subsidiary or a branch or agency.
- Both a UK subsidiary and a UK branch or agency are liable to corporation tax on the chargeable profits of the UK establishment.
- If there is no trade carried on within the UK via a branch or agency any profits arising in the UK will be liable to income tax deducted at source.
- Any reliefs on the taxation positions described above depend on the particular double tax agreement which applies.

Self test questions

1. What activities will render a non-UK company liable to UK corporation tax?

2. Define a UK branch or agency.

3. How is corporation tax assessed on a UK branch or agency?

4. Describe the role of double tax agreements.

5. Explain the meaning of the term 'permanent establishment' in a double taxation agreement and say why it is important.

6. Warren Iron Company Inc (Warren), registered and controlled in Delaware USA, owns 10,750 ordinary £1 shares in Gwent Metals Ltd (Gwent), a trading company resident in the UK. Gwent's issued share capital is 14,000 ordinary £1 shares and its profit for the year to 31 March 1995 is expected to be £152,000. Warren proposes to purchase the entire share capital of the Denny Trading Co Ltd (Denny), a UK-resident company, on 1 January 1995. On 1 May 1994 the accumulated trading losses of Denny for corporation tax purposes total £90,000, and it is forecast to lose a further £54,000 in the year to 30 April 1995. Warren will probably have a trading profit of $750,000 in its year to 31 December 1995.

    The Executive Board of Warren is undecided as to whether it should hold the shares directly or, alternatively, form a UK subsidiary to hold its UK investments.

    Explain the group structure necessary so that the losses of Denny may be most effectively relieved, illustrating how these losses may be set off.

    Answers on pages 638–639

Question Bank – Overseas Activities

1. Mr JPW is Chairman and managing director of JPW Textiles Limited. His annual salary is £25,000. The company is taken over by Western Tweeds plc, a public company, on 31 October 1994. Two months later JPW is asked to resign in an administrative restructuring. He is awarded a compensation payment of £40,000 on 5 January 1995 and appointed Chairman of Industrial Fabrics Limited, a small specialist subsidiary company of Western Tweeds plc. His salary is £800 per month.

    It is necessary that he should review the company's operations in the Far East. To do so he moves to Jakarta, Indonesia on 1 March 1995. His review completed JPW returns to the UK on 6 August 1995.

    During the period abroad his salary is increased to £1,000 per month. The company pays a special medical insurance premium for his overseas trip of £1,250 on 26 February 1995. His wife Jill visits Jakarta at the company's expense from 26 March to 21 April 1995; her travel costs are £1,935. JPW pays mortgage interest of £1,620 gross to the Abbefax Building Society in the year to 31 March 1995. The interest is paid under the MIRAS scheme.

    Compute the income tax payable by JPW for 1994/95, including explanations of your treatment of income and expenses.

2. Mr Poirot is a French oil engineer who is employed by a French company. From 1 March 1994 he worked almost totally in the UK. His salary was paid in the UK which with benefits in kind totalled £45,000. He opened a bank account in London on 7 April 1994: interest credited on 28 February 1995 was £722. Investment income arising in France was £3,500 (when converted into sterling) and was paid into his account in France: no remittance was made to him in the UK. His wife accompanied him to the UK; their only previous visits had been three short holidays between 1972 and 1984. (Ignore non-UK tax).

    Compute his liability to UK income tax for 1994/95, outlining in your answer:

    a) Mr Poirot's residence etc status for UK tax; and
    b) the basis on which his income is assessed.

3. William, a single man, has lived in the UK since birth. In June 1994, at the age of 43, he was made redundant. Since then, in spite of applying for numerous jobs, he has been unemployed.

    He owns the house he lives in, on which there is a mortgage, and some shares in UK quoted companies which he had bought over a number of years. In 1988 his mother died, leaving him the cottage she lived in, and certain United Kingdom Government Securities.

    William let the cottage in 1988, receiving rental income.

    Following a recent interview, William has been offered, and has accepted, an offer of employment, all the duties of which will be carried out overseas. The contract is initially for five years, though, as it is likely to be renewed, William expects to work outside the UK until the age of 65, when he will retire and return to the UK to live.

    He has appointed a UK agent to let his house, and to collect the rent, pay expenses, mortgage interest and so on, on both the house and the cottage. The cottage is already let on a long lease as William does not wish to occupy it in the future. His house will be let furnished, as William plans to re-occupy it on his retirement. Both the cottage and the house are freehold properties.

    William plans to buy a house overseas once he has settled down in his job, and will probably sell some shares to raise the necessary finance.

    He will remain a British subject whilst abroad, but does not expect to spend more than one month in any year in the UK during the next 20 years.

    He requires advice on the tax implications of his proposed emigration.

    a) Define, clearly and fully, the meaning of the terms, 'residence, ordinary residence and domicile'.
    b) Explain:
        i) William's income tax position on both UK and overseas sources of income whilst he is abroad.
        ii) His capital gains tax and inheritance tax position on both UK and overseas assets;
            – whilst he is living and working abroad
            – on his retirement and return to the UK.

    In all cases your answer should deal only with the UK tax position.

4. Alpha Ltd, which began trading in 1958, has always made up amounts annually, to 30 November each year. It operates an international distribution service with a fleet of leased vehicles and for the year ended 30 November 1994, its accounts show:

	£	£
Net trading profit:		250,000
After charging:		
Entertaining overseas suppliers	8,000	
Entertainng the UK agent of an overseas customer	5,000	
Gifts of food hampers to UK customers	7,000	
Gifts of Alpha Breakdown Kits to customers costing £9 each	9,000	
Costs of staff outing	6,000	
Profit on sale of fixed assets:		
Plot of land		177,000
Bought in March 1980 for	100,000	
and sold in January 1994 for	277,000	
The land was estimated to have increased in value for each of the first four years of ownership by 10% of its value at the start of the year		
Estate car		1,000
Bought at auction in February 1994 for £5,000 and sold in May for £6,000		
Gilt-edged securities		15,760
Bought December 1989 for £40,000		
Half of the holding was sold in March 1994 for £25,760 and the other half in October 1994 for £30,000		
Dividends received:		
From UK companies – excluding tax credit (received 10 April 94)		24,500
From an overseas company in which Alpha Ltd holds 2% of the shares. The dividend is after deducting a withholding tax of 15%. The company suffers overseas tax on profits at the rate of 40%		10,200
Dividends paid:		
On 15 February 1994 – final re 1993		133,000
On 3 September 1994 – interim re 1994		73,500
Dividend proposed:		
Final re 1994 – due for payment in February 1995		161,000

Alpha Ltd has no associated company and does not maintain a deferred taxation account. At 30 November 1993 Alpha Ltd has surplus ACT of £3,000. Its mainstream corporation tax liability, based on the profit for the year ended 30 November 1993, was agreed in August 1994 at £42,000, and it will be paid on the due date.

For the year ended 30 November 1995 its trading profit, as adjusted for tax, is estimated at £200,000, dividends from UK companies are estimated at £7,000 and no dividend is expected from the overseas company.

a) Compute the corporation tax liability of Alpha Ltd for the year ended 30 November 1994, based on the information given.
b) Show, in accordance with SSAP 8 (The treatment of taxation under the imputation system in the accounts of companies) the amounts which will appear in the profit and loss account for the year ended 30 November 1994, or the balance sheet at the year end, of Alpha Ltd in respect of:
  i) UK or overseas taxation
  ii) dividends received, paid or proposed.

5 a) Domo Ltd is a trading company resident in the UK. The majority of its business is carried on from its UK headquarters but it also has a branch in Norland, a country which imposes taxation at the rate of 30% on the profits of companies resident there and profits arising there.
    The information at the top of page 531 relates to Domo Ltd for the year ended 31 March 1995.

Compute the mainstream corporation tax of Domo Ltd for the year ended 31 March 1995, showing clearly, with explanations, your workings and stating the schedule and case under which each source of income is assessable. Domo Ltd has not elected to treat its dividend payment as a Foreign Income Dividend.

	£
Trading income – UK headquarters	120,000
– Norland branch (before deducting tax suffered in Norland)	30,000
Investment income:	
Dividend on a holding of 15% of the ordinary shares in Fjord Norland Ltd (after deducting 15% withholding tax)	11,900
Dividend on a holding of 12% of the ordinary shares of Supplier UK Ltd	7,100
Interest on a holding of 12% of the debentures of Lake Norland Ltd (after 20% withholding tax)	12,000
Dividend on a holding of 8% of the ordinary shares of Valley Norland Ltd (after deducting 15% withholding tax)	10,200
Capital profit on land in Norland bought for £20,000 in May 1987, sold in May 1994 for £36,000 – tax suffered in Norland £4,800	16,000
Royalties paid to Inventa UK Ltd (net)	10,650
Dividend paid – January 1995 – final for year ended 31 March 1994	113,600

b) Domo Ltd is considering acquiring a substantial holding of shares in a company resident and operating in a tax haven country. Such an acquisition might bring the foreign company within the rules for controlled foreign companies.

Prepare a concise summary explaining briefly what is a controlled foreign company, what are the consequences, and in what circumstances the rules will not apply.

6 a) Multinat plc, a UK-resident public company liable to corporation tax at 33%, owns all of the issued share capital of Haven Limited. Haven Limited is resident in the country of Ruritania, where it carries on a trade of manufacturing. Ruritania, which does not have a double tax treaty with the UK, imposes tax at 5% on taxable trading profits. Haven Ltd made pre-tax accounting profits of £150,000 in the year ended 31 December 1994 (this is the year end for all group companies). For Ruritanian tax purposes, taxable profits, after making all necessary adjustments under Ruritanian tax rules, were £165,000. If Haven Ltd had been resident in the UK its profits chargeable to UK corporation tax, after making all necessary adjustments under UK tax rules, would have amounted to £160,000.

The directors of Multinat plc have learnt from the Inland Revenue that they regard Haven Ltd as a 'controlled foreign company'. The directors understand that unless Haven Ltd pays a dividend equivalent to a least 50% of its distributable profits for the year ended 31 December 1994, an apportionment will be made under the appropriate legislation. The directors have been advised that there is no point in appealing against the Revenue's direction. Ruritania does not impose any withholding taxes on dividends. Assume that today's date is 1 February 1995.

i) Explain what is meant by a 'controlled foreign company' and describe *two* sets of circumstances under which Revenue will *not* direct an apportionment to be made in the case of such a company (apart from the 'acceptable distribution' criterion).

ii) Calculate the corporation tax consequences for Multinat plc:
▶ assuming that Haven Ltd does not pay a dividend
▶ assuming that Haven Ltd pays a dividend equal to 50% of its distributable profits on 1 April 1995.

b) Multinat plc also intends to send one of its senior executives, Mrs Noble, to Ruritania in order to carry out strategic planning duties for Haven Ltd. Mrs Noble would continue to be employed and paid by Multinat plc. She would leave the UK on 8 December 1994 and would take up her post in Ruritania for either 14 or 18 months depending on circumstances. Mrs Noble intends to return to the UK on holiday for an average of at least two weeks every three months, but probably more frequently than this. However, she has heard that the frequency of these visits could result in her earnings from Haven Ltd becoming liable to UK taxation. She understands that different considerations will apply depending on the overall length of her stay in Ruritania. Multinat plc has also agreed to reimburse her the costs of her return visits to the UK and Mrs Noble is concerned that if she becomes liable to UK tax on her earnings, then these payments will also be taxable. Multinat plc is also anxious that it should obtain a tax deduction for the salary and expenses paid to Mrs Noble while she is working in Ruritania. Ruritania does not impose any taxes on individuals.

i) Discuss Mrs Noble's potential liability to UK taxation while working in Ruritania:
▶ assuming that she stays in Ruritania for 14 months
▶ assuming that she stays in Ruritania for 18 months.

ii) Give your views as to whether or not Multinat plc would obtain a tax deduction for Mrs Noble's salary and expenses.

Answers on pages 639–645

CHAPTER 34

How to Tackle the Tax Planning Examination

The purpose of this chapter is to consider the examination paper and suggest strategies for tackling it and subsequently to illustrate the manner in which key tax planning topics are examined and should be answered.

General strategy

The fundamental difference between Paper 7 and Paper 11 is that Paper 7 usually deals with the tax computation based on a set of circumstances that are fact (which have actually happened) and therefore cannot be altered while Paper 11 will ask you to deal with the tax computations based on one or more events that may happen on a specified future date – suggestions for changing these events (such as timing or sequence) can therefore be made.

Format of the paper

There are six equally weighted questions on the examination paper of which you have to answer four over a period of three hours; you will have 45 minutes per question. Tax rates and allowances will be given at the front of the paper – you should make yourself aware of the figures you will be given and those you will not be given. As a general rule, all the information given at the back of this book is given to you in the examination.

The examination

Multi-tax approach

Paper 11 aims to consider the inter-relationship of the various taxes. The majority of the questions therefore involve more than one tax. Sometimes a question specifies which taxes are to be considered and on other occasions it will simply ask for the taxation implications of a particular situation.

If the taxes are specified you should ensure that you confine your answer to the taxes required – the examiner has obviously confined the answer for good reason and you should pay heed to this even when there may be some seemingly irrelevant aspects of the situation which have been asked about. If not specified, you must consider each tax in turn to check whether there are any implications in the situation under review. If none you should state none. Do not forget VAT and National Insurance as well as the mainstream taxes.

Many students find it more difficult to answer a question which does not specify the taxes to be considered. In reality, this should make no difference because you should go into the examination armed with a checklist of taxes about which you are supposed to know.

You should prepare for the examination by ensuring that you have a broad basic knowledge of each tax rather than a detailed knowledge of specific narrow areas. Having done this, some topics are obviously more important than others – this is usually a reflection of their respective importance in everyday life.

The time factor

Three hours is not long to score enough marks to pass. The questions are quite long and detailed and reading time must be sparingly allocated and yet you need to decide which questions to answer. Often, reading the requirements of each question is sufficiently informative and quicker than a detailed reading of each question. You should avoid starting one question and then deciding to answer another.

Your time should be allocated fairly equally between the questions. You will score more marks starting a new question than finishing off an existing one.

As it takes time to settle down in the examination, many people advocate that you should start with your second 'favourite' question choice. Once you have relaxed you stand to make the best possible attempt at your first choice of question. You must stick to your time allowance, however!

Answering the questions

Make sure you read each question properly. It is advisable to plan your answer.

Examination questions come in a number of styles but most of them come down to a basic format – one or more options open to the taxpayer and the taxation implications of each. Each option must be broken down into its constituent parts and each part analysed for its tax implications. I recommend a 'spreadsheet approach' when planning the answer: each tax should be listed along the top and the constituent parts of the option down the left-hand side. This allows notes to be made in each 'box'. A methodological approach such as this ensures that your answer is structured and covers all possibilities.

Take care with the layout of your answer. It helps you as well as the examiner. Computations, for example over a period of years or for each company in a group, should be done in a columnar layout as this minimises your writing and saves you turning backwards and forwards through your examination booklet. Double line spacing is also recommended – if you omit anything it is easy to go back and add it.

If the answer requires a conclusion as to which option should be recommended from a taxation viewpoint, it is simply necessary to sum the tax costs for each option. It is usual to balance any recommendations of this type with a comment on the respective cashflows and timing.

Illustrations of key tax planning topics

Remuneration packages

Remuneration packages affect both the employee and the employer. The employer will ideally want to pay the employee as much as possible at the least possible overall cost while the employee will want the maximum amount of remuneration with the least possible tax liability.

Employees can be remunerated in quite a number of different ways. To recap, consider the following list:

- salary and bonuses
- profit-related pay
- pension provision
- benefits in kind
- expense allowances
- profit share schemes } incl
- share option schemes } ESOPs
- payments on termination of office.

The employee will want security of employment and a sustainable level of remuneration. He or she will be particularly concerned with the rate at which tax is deducted and the total tax payable.

The employer on the other hand will be concerned with the actual cost of the remuneration package (for instance inclusive of Class 1 employer's NIC), tax reliefs and incentives available.

The tax planning opportunities as regards salary and bonuses are limited – they will always attract National Insurance and will always be taxable in full on the employee. Only the timing can be altered: the timing, for instance, of bonuses to employees other than directors, may delay a higher-rate liability until the following year; it may reduce National Insurance contributions of the employee where the upper earning limit for the year will not be reached. Payment of remuneration in ways other than salary may well save both employee and employer NIC.

Some benefits in kind are taxable according to a formula which does not represent the value of the benefit (in terms of expenditure saved) to the individual and these are obviously good value – provided the cost is not excessive to the employer. It should be remembered that all benefits are gross, and therefore even where the amount assessable represents a fair value it will usually be better than receiving the cash and paying for the benefit out of net income. The cost of providing benefits will always be deductible to the employer under Schedule D Case I.

Pension provision is a long-term benefit to the employee which is not always immediately appreciated. It also provides a great deal of flexibility to the employer when used to keep profits within the small companies rate of corporation tax.

In this way you should be able to state how any item in a remuneration package will be taxed upon an employee and how it will be treated in the employer's books. When you can do this you should try the following question from the June 1990 examination paper:

Case study

Mr Hodges is the financial controller (but not a director) of Cecil Ltd, a manufacturing company in which he does not own any shares. At today's date (which you should assume is 1 April 1994) he earns £30,000 per annum and he has held his employment for the last 15 years. It has previously been the policy of Cecil Ltd to provide only a fixed monthly salary to its employees. The company is now considering various possible additional means of remunerating Mr Hodges only: all other employees would continue under their present arrangements. The proposals under consideration are as follows:

i) Acquiring a new 1600 cc motor car from 6 April 1994 at a cost of £14,000 (inclusive of VAT) and allowing Mr Hodges to use it for both business and personal purposes. Mr Hodges would travel 16,000 miles of which 14,000 would relate to personal use. The full cost of petrol for all 16,000 miles (estimated at £950) would be borne by Cecil Ltd.

ii) Awarding a special bonus to be paid in respect of Mr Hodges' performance during each accounting year of the company. The first bonus would be calculated and paid 10 months after the year ended 31 October 1995. A payment of £1,000 on account of the bonus would be made on 31 March 1995. The amount of £1,000 plus a preliminary estimate of the balance payable to Mr Hodges would be debited in the accounts for the year ended 31 October 1995.

iii) Providing a flat in Leeds for Mr Hodges from 6 April 1994 so that he could live closer to his work. Mr Hodges believes that it is necessary for him to do so in order to carry out his duties properly. Cecil Ltd would pay £67,000 to acquire a 45-year lease on the property. It would also pay an annual rent of £5,000. The gross rateable value of the flat would be £3,000 per annum. The flat would not be available for Mr Hodges during the months of July, August and September when it would be used to provide holiday accommodation for foreign customers of the company. Mr Hodges would be expected to contribute £200 per month to Cecil Ltd towards its rental costs for the remaining nine months. The value of the flat if it were to be sold on the open market would be £150,000. Mr Hodges has heard that a special income tax charge applies to property with a value in excess of £75,000.

iv) Issuing a special class of 2,000 20p shares to Mr Hodges, which would be subject to various restrictions. The likely value of these shares at the date of issue would be £1.30 per share, but Mr Hodges would only be required to pay 20p per share. The restrictions would be removed in three years' time, if Mr Hodges still remained an employee at that date. It is expected that the value of the shares at that date would be £3.40 if they were still subject to the restrictions, and £3.90 if the restrictions were removed. Legal costs of £500 would be incurred in connection with the share issue.

a) Explain the income tax implications for Mr Hodges of each of the above proposals. Indicate the circumstances in which any tax due would be collected under the PAYE system. (12 marks)

b) Explain the corporation tax and value added tax implications for Cecil Ltd of each of the above proposals. (13 marks)

As you can see this question tells you exactly what is required; it mentions employee implications and employer implications and even refers you to the taxes which you should consider. If the question had asked you to:

'Consider the taxation implications of each of the above remuneration packages' (25 marks)

the answer would be the same. As you cannot rely upon the exact requirements always being spelled out (in practice they certainly would not be!) you should get used to 'translating' any question you do while preparing for the examination: one that tells you in detail what to do should be made less specific than that above and one that is less specific should be rewritten in detail.

The detailed question should form the plan for your answer – it is very important (when the examiner has given a detailed question) to present the answer in the format requested. Do not try to reorganise it. If, on the other hand you have created the detailed question from a less specific one, rewrite the question in the format in which you want to answer it – that is, if it does not form a good question written that way, then the answer following that plan would probably not follow a logical order. Alternatively your answer may be thought of in terms of the spreadsheet approach mentioned above.

A sample answer is reproduced below

a) **The employee position**

Mr Hodges is an employee of Cecil Ltd and as such would be taxable under Schedule E. Schedule E assesses emoluments from an office or employment – emoluments include all salaries, wages, bonuses, fees, commissions and profits whatsoever whether payable in cash or convertible to cash. In addition, certain benefits not convertible into cash, received by reason of a person's employment, may also be assessable under Schedule E on all or certain categories of employee. Where possible, income tax on Schedule E earnings is collected under the PAYE system.

Mr Hodges earns £30,000 per annum at 1 April 1994 and will therefore be subject to the benefit in kind rules applying to employees earning more than £8,500 per annum. The PAYE rules would currently be applied to his monthly salary.

Proposal 1

The value of the benefit derived from the provision of a motor car for Mr Hodges' personal use would be established initially by reference to the list price of the car. A new car, 1600 cc, costing £14,000 would have a benefit of £4,900 (£14,000 × 35%). This figure is the benefit for a full fiscal year for a car which does less than 2,500 business miles.

Similarly, a benefit in kind will arise from fuel provided for private motoring of an employee, the cost of which is not paid for in full by the employee. The amount of the benefit is established by reference to a Fuel Benefit Table which gives the benefit for a full fiscal year of £810.

The total benefits in kind (£5,710) should be notified by Cecil Ltd to the Inland Revenue on a form P11D some time after 5 April 1995. A copy of the P11D should be given to Mr Hodges and entered by him on his 1995/96 Tax Return. When Mr Hodges' 1994/95 Schedule E Assessment is done, an underpayment of tax will result. This will probably be collected in 1995/96 or later years by adjustment of his code number. In addition his code number for 1995/96 and subsequent years will be adjusted to include an estimated benefit in kind for that year (on the assumption that Mr Hodges will also have a car and fuel for private use in those years). In this way, tax due for car benefits is collected under the PAYE system.

Proposal 2
A bonus is assessable to income tax in the fiscal year in which it is received. For any employee who is not a director, 'received' is defined as the earlier of the time when payment is made or the time when entitlement to payment occurs. In Mr Hodges' case, the £1,000 will be assessable when paid as will the balance of the bonus, that is, £1,000 in 1994/95 (paid 31 March 1995) and the balance in 1996/97 (entitlement arises 10 months after the year end, that is, 31 August 1996 unless actual payment takes place before this). The estimate in the accounts is ignored for a non-director.

PAYE is deductible at the time when payment is made, that is 31 March 1995 and 31 August 1996 or such other time as payment is made.

Proposal 3
The provision of living accommodation is a benefit taxable on all employees irrespective of their earnings, unless its provision is job related. Since Mr Hodges has been in the job for 15 years and has not previously had accommodation provided, it will not be possible to claim that the accommodation is job related (necessary for the proper performance of the duties of the employment and is customary, or as part of special security arrangements) unless there has been a fundamental change in circumstances of which we have not been informed. The basic benefit is the gross rateable value of the property or, if greater, the rent paid by the employer for the property. This is then reduced by any contribution made by the employee. In this case the gross rateable value is £3,000 while the rent paid by Cecil Ltd is £5,000 per annum. The amount of the benefit will therefore be 9/12 of £5,000 (the proportion of the year when the accommodation is available) less £200 per month for 9 months, that is £1,950.

The additional benefit chargeable on the provision of living accommodation arises when the cost of provision of the property (including improvements) exceeds £75,000. In this case the cost of the property to the company is £67,000, that is, less than £75,000. The value of the property on the open market (£150,000) is assumed to be the value of the freehold and this is irrelevant – the value of the leasehold on the open market is also irrelevant unless the property has been owned by the employer for six years prior to the employee's occupation.

Further benefits may be assessable if the flat is provided furnished or if Cecil Ltd pays any other expenses associated with the accommodation.

Income tax will become due and PAYE will become chargeable on any assessable benefit in the same way as under Proposal 1.

Proposal 4
In general, a Schedule E benefit arises if an employee is given shares or is sold them at an undervalue. The amount of the benefit is calculated at the date of acquisition of the shares as the difference between the market value of the shares and the consideration given, if any – in this case £1.10 per share (£1.30 – 20p). A Schedule E benefit also arises whenever a chargeable event such as the removal

of restrictions on a class of shares takes place – in this case £0.50 per share.

Income tax will become due and PAYE will become chargeable on any assessable benefit in the same way as under Proposal 1.

b) **The company position:**

Proposal 1

The VAT on the acquisition of a motor car is not deductible input tax for value added tax purposes and therefore must be treated as part of the cost of the car for accounting purposes. The acquisition of a car is capital expenditure by Cecil Ltd and therefore neither the cost of the car (inclusive of VAT) nor the depreciation charged in the accounts is deductible for Schedule D Case I purposes. The cost of the car (inclusive of VAT) will, however, qualify for capital allowances on plant and machinery. The writing down allowance is 25% per annum on the reducing balance restricted each year to a maximum of £3,000. This will be deducted in arriving at the Schedule D Case I profits of Cecil Ltd as charged to corporation tax. Cecil Ltd must also account for NIC Class 1A on the car benefit to the employee, that is, per the income tax car benefit (this would however be a deductible Schedule D Case I expense), payable at the end of the fiscal year.

The VAT on petrol cost is deductible input tax for value added tax purposes but the provision of fuel for private use is deemed to be a taxable supply for value added tax, and output tax per quarter in accordance with a fuel benefit table (corresponding to the income tax fuel benefit table) must be accounted for to Customs and Excise. The petrol cost net of input and output tax is deductible for Schedule D Case I purposes (see above). Cecil Ltd must pay Class 1A NIC on the fuel benefit.

Proposal 2

There is no value added tax implication in paying a bonus. As accounts are prepared on the accruals basis and this is accepted by the Inland Revenue for Schedule D Case I purposes, a bonus will be deductible for Schedule D Case I purposes in the period to which it relates provided that it is paid within nine months of the year end. In this instance payment takes place of the balance, 10 months later and will not be deductible until year end 31 October 1996.

Proposal 3

Any input tax on the legal costs associated with the acquisition of the leasehold will be deductible as input tax. The net cost (exclusive of VAT) will be capital expenditure and therefore no allowable deduction will arise in the Schedule D Case I computation for the cost of the property or for depreciation. Capital allowances will not be available as a flat does not meet the definition of plant and machinery or of industrial building.

The annual rental would normally be an allowable deduction for Schedule D Case I purposes but in this case the issue is complicated by the use of the flat to provide holiday accommodation for foreign customers during July, August and September. This will be regarded as entertainment if provided free of charge and therefore will be disallowed along with any other expenses incurred by Cecil Ltd in providing the accommodation. Only the rent for the nine months occupied by Mr Hodges will be allowed as an expense less his contribution of £200 per month. If the foreign customers pay rent then a Schedule D Case VI computation would be required treating the rent received as income and deducting the rent paid for the three months and any other expenses which arise over the three months (no allowance would be available for the premium on the lease as subletting does not count as a trade and it does not qualify as furnished holiday accommodation).

Proposal 4

Any input tax on the legal costs of the share issue will be deductible as input tax. The legal costs net of VAT will not be deductible for Schedule D Case I purposes as they will be capital expenditure. The share issue itself has no direct implications for Cecil Ltd for corporation tax and value added tax.

Employment *vis-à-vis* self-employment

A question of this type compares Schedule E and Schedule D Case I/II. To recap, the principal differences are:

- the definitions of allowable expenses
- the bases of assessment
- the timing of the tax liabilities
- National Insurance contributions
- pension provision
- tax reliefs (capital allowances, losses, retirement relief, rollover relief)
- treatment of private use of assets
- VAT.

If you can outline the treatment of each of the above under each of Schedule E and Schedule D Case I, you should consider the following question which was in the June 1989 examination.

Case study

Bruno Zapp left university at the end of July 1993, aged 22. He lives at home with his parents. On 1 January he was approached by his cousin, a guitarist in a rock band, who has asked him if he would be willing to organise the band's touring arrangements for the next 12 months, starting on 1 May 1994.

The band has offered to pay Mr Zapp a lump sum of £6,500 in return for his agreeing to undertake this responsibility, together with further amounts of £2,500 per month, over the period. Mr Zapp has just bought a new 1,600cc car for £7,500 and the band have agreed to pay him a mileage allowance as he will be required to visit numerous locations in the United Kingdom. The mileage allowance is expected to amount to at least £7,500 for the year.

a) Draft a report for Mr Zapp setting out the principal income tax, NIC and VAT implications for him if he were to be regarded as:
   i) employed
   ii) self-employed.
   You are not required to consider tax liabilities arising after 5 April 1995.
   (13 marks)
b) Describe the criteria which are used to distinguish between employment and self-employment.
   (12 marks)

Again this question is fairly detailed and gives you quite a lot of help. It could simply have been written:
'Advise Mr Zapp whether he is likely to be treated as employed or self-employed and set out the taxation implications of each'.
(25 marks)

This is another example of where a spreadsheet approach would work. You should plan the main headings to be considered for each tax. For example, for income tax, restricting yourself to the information in the question, the main subdivisions are:

- basis of assessment
- sums assessable (including treatment of lump sum and expenses and benefits received)
- expenses deductible.

It is important that this outline is followed for each of Schedule E and Schedule D Case I so that Mr Zapp can make a comparison between them.

a) Report to Mr Zapp on the income tax, National Insurance and VAT implications of being either employed or self-employed.

TAX PLANNING

Income tax

If you are regarded as employed, you will be taxed under Schedule E on your earnings from the performance of the duties of the employment in that year. This will include all emoluments whether in cash or some other form such as benefits in kind (at cost to your employer as you will be higher paid – earning more than £8,500 per annum).

The lump sum of £6,500, in return for agreeing to undertake the responsibility, will also be taxable under Schedule E as remuneration for future services unless it can be shown that it represents compensation for some right or asset given up on taking up the employment. The mileage allowance may also be regarded as a taxable emolument. The rate of mileage allowance paid would be compared with the rate allowed under the fixed profit car scheme. If the rate is in line with this, no return of the amount paid would be made to the Inland Revenue and it would not be included in gross pay for PAYE purposes. If a higher rate of mileage allowance is paid, the mileage allowance would be regarded as a taxable emolument in the first instance – details of amounts paid would be returned to the Inland Revenue on form P11D.

From these gross emoluments you will be able to claim as deductible all expenses which are wholly, exclusively and necessarily incurred in the performance of the duties of the employments. This is quite a stringent provision but it would cover travel expenses (if included initially as a taxable emolument, see above) – although it should be noted that expenses of travel from home to your normal place of work will not be allowed. Travel expenses would normally be the business proportion of total expenses and loan interest plus capital allowances if the car can be shown to be wholly, exclusively and necessarily for the purpose of the performance of the duties of the employment. Where reimbursement rates are in line with the fixed profit car scheme no action is necessary for normal car running expenses unless the business proportion of these is higher than the amount reimbursed when a claim for the excess may be made. In addition, tax relief may be claimed for any interest paid on a car loan as this element is not allowed for in the FPCS rate. All cash emoluments paid will be subjected to PAYE, meaning that you will only receive the net amount.

If you are regarded as self-employed you will be assessable to income tax under Schedule D Case I on your trading profits after deducting all expenses wholly and exclusively incurred for the purpose of the trade. Once again, the lump sum of £6,500 by way of retainer and the subsequent payments would be taxable, including the mileage allowance. You would be permitted to deduct your motoring costs for business trips (once again, travel from home to your normal place of work will not be treated as a business trip). The normal procedure is to agree with the Inland Revenue a percentage of your total mileage as being for business purposes and then apply this percentage to your total motoring costs. The resulting net profit will be taxable in 1994/95 based on your earnings from 1 May 1994 to 5 April 1994. The following year will be based on your earnings in the first 12 months and subsequently you will be assessed on the profits of the accounting period ending in the year of assessment.

Capital allowances would also be available on your car at the rate of 25% per annum reducing balance – restricted in 1994/95 to 11/12 of 25% (representing the eleven months from 1 May 1994 to 5 April 1995 and also to the percentage of business use agreed (see previous paragraph).

National Insurance contributions

As an employee, you would be liable for Class 1 contributions which in 1994/95, on a salary of £2,500 per month, would amount to approximately £154 (maximum £38.44 per week for four weeks) per month. Your employer would have to pay 10.2% on the whole £2,500 in addition.

As a self-employed person, you would pay a flat rate Class 2 stamp of £5.65 per week plus a Class 4 contribution of 7.3% on earnings between £6,490 and £22,360. The Class 2 contributions are not tax deductible but one half of the Class 4 contribution is an allowable deduction for income tax.

Value added tax

If you are employed, you do not need to consider VAT. If you are regarded as self-employed, you will need to consider VAT.

The type of service which you will be offering will be a taxable supply and therefore if you make or expect to make taxable supplies in excess of specified limits you must register for VAT. The limit is specified per total for 12 months (£45,000) and any person who exceeds this limit must register unless he can show that his cumulative total for the 12 months then beginning will not exceed the limit (£43,000).

Your figures, including the £6,500 and the mileage allowance of £7,500, are approaching the 12-month limit in the fourth quarter and therefore you should keep a close check on your turnover to ensure that you do not accidentally exceed the registration limit of £45,000. It may be to your advantage to register voluntarily, this would largely depend on whether your clients were themselves registered. Registration is effective 30 days after notification or earlier if agreed with Customs and Excise but late notification will incur a penalty and be backdated to the appropriate date – VAT will be payable whether collected or not.

If desired, the report could have been written in point format rather than narrative format provided you remembered that it was requested as a report and therefore too abbreviated an answer would not have been appropriate.

b) The main criterion which is used to make the distinction is whether the relationship between the person paying for the service and the person performing the service is a 'contract of service' (in which case the person is 'employed') or a 'contract for services' (in which case the person is 'self-employed').

In determining which of these applies, a number of factors are taken into account:

i) any control exercised by another person over the manner in which the work is performed
ii) the ability to delegate to another person the work which is the subject of the contract
iii) the extent to which the person performing the service is free to determine the price for the job
iv) whether the person performing the service takes any financial risk, that is, whether he or she keeps the profits or bears the losses
v) whether the person performing the service provides his or her own tools and equipment
vi) whether the person for whom the work is done lays down regular and defined hours of work
vii) whether both parties agree 'employment' or 'self employment'
viii) the right of action available to the person for whom the work is done if it is not performed satisfactorily, for example, whether payment can be withheld
ix) the extent to which services are performed wholly or mainly for one business
x) the place where the duties are performed
xi) entitlement to a pension as a result of contributions by those for whom the services are performed.

None of these factors is conclusive in itself but they are points which have in the past influenced the courts in their decisions. A leading case in the field is *Fall* v. *Hitchin* (1972) in which a theatrical artiste held a contract with a theatre management which allowed work to be performed for others but the nature of the contract was such that it was nevertheless held to be a contract of service. A non-practising barrister in *Sidey* v. *Phillips* (1987), who lectured part-time on legal subjects while holding two other separate sources of earnings, was held to be an employee. In *Nethermere (St Neots) Ltd* v. *Taverna* (1984), persons working at home but almost exclusively for one person using sewing machines provided by that person, were held to be employees.

Inheritance tax/capital gains tax planning

Questions of this type usually ask for advice on how an estate can best be passed to the next generation; in particular they ask how much can be done during the transferor's lifetime, incurring as few tax liabilities as possible.

There is a conflict between inheritance tax, which may not arise on a lifetime transfer (because it is a PET) but will certainly arise on death, and capital gains tax which arises on lifetime disposals but not on death. It is important that a strategy is developed to reconcile the two.

These questions are relatively easy once you come to terms with the principles. If a lifetime transfer is not to incur a capital gains tax liability, then one or more of the following apply:

- Assets are exempt from capital gains tax.
- Any gains arising are covered by reliefs (for example retirement relief).
- Any gains arising will be covered by losses arising in the same fiscal year.
- Any gains arising will be covered by losses brought forward.
- Any gains arising will be covered by the annual exemption.

Once it is appreciated that avoiding a capital gains tax liability does not mean avoiding the realisation of capital gains, the question becomes very much simpler – which assets should be transferred? Often the starting point here is to calculate the gains and losses which would arise on each asset if it were disposed of.

The next part is to minimise inheritance tax. Excluded property can be transferred at any time with no inheritance tax implications. Full use should be made of lifetime exemptions and reliefs as these remove the possibility of an inheritance tax liability arising. If the transferor survives seven years from the date of the transfer, no inheritance tax will arise on any PETs made; if the transferor does not survive seven years then taper relief will reduce any tax which does arise (and this will not be payable by the transferor's estate). The problem is what not to transfer. The aim here is to minimise the inheritance tax liability on death, the limiting factor will be the capital gains tax position:

- Appreciating assets should be transferred in preference to depreciating assets.
- Care must be taken when transferring assets qualifying for business property relief and agricultural property relief as the transferee must still hold the asset in virtually the same form at the date of the transferor's death (within seven years) if the relief is to be retained on death.

Once you are happy with the above principles try the following question which was set in December 1989.

Case study

Mr Gregory is a 68-year-old single man for whom you act as tax adviser. He comes to see you on 30 June 1994 and tells you that he has just been informed by his doctor that he has only three months left to live. He intends that all his wealth should pass on to his only son Neil (who will be his sole executor). He has heard that in some circumstances it might be advantageous to either transfer some of his assets immediately to Neil as a gift or alternatively to sell some of his assets and then to transfer the sale proceeds to Neil as a gift.

Mr Gregory is not currently in a position to make cash gifts as he has just drawn out the last of his savings from his bank account. He provides you with the following information concerning his assets:

i) He owns 2,000 shares in Bingo plc, a quoted company, currently valued at £500. He had originally acquired 1,000 shares in Little plc for £12,500 in December 1984. On 15 February 1988 Bingo plc acquired the shares in Little plc on the basis of two ordinary shares in Bingo plc and 80p for every ordinary share in Little plc. The shares in Bingo plc were valued at 90p per share on 15 February 1988.

ii) Mr Gregory had acquired 20,000 £1 shares at par out of an issued share capital of 200,000 shares in Peck Limited, a retail company, in February 1988. Mr Gregory's shares have been valued recently at £1.20 each.

iii) Mr Gregory had acquired 10,000 £1 shares out of an issued share capital of 100,000 shares in Zingo Limited, a quoted land dealing company, for £10.57 each in April 1987. The shares are currently worth £20 per share.

iv) All tax liabilities have been agreed and paid on time up to 5 April 1994. Mr Gregory does not expect to have any liabilities outstanding on his death, as his income should be just enough to cover his outgoings up to that time. It is estimated that the income tax computation up to the date of his death will show a repayment due of £300.

Other relevant information is as follows:

v) He had taxable capital gains in the previous four years of assessment as follows (taking into account the transaction of 15 February 1988 noted in (i) above):

	1990/91	1991/92	1992/93	1993/94
	£	£	£	£
Net gains	6,900	7,800	–	9,000
Less: Annual exemption	(5,000)	(5,500)	(5,800)	(5,800)
Taxable gains	1,900	2,300	Nil	3,200

(The rate of capital gains tax was 25%).

vi) In January 1987 he made an outright gift of his principal private residence to his son Neil who now resides there. Mr Gregory went to live with his brother. The value of the residence at that time was £50,000 but it has since risen to £120,000. Neil has now suggested that Mr Gregory should come and live with him rent-free. Mr Gregory has refused to go and live with Neil partly on personal grounds, but also because he believes that if he does, problems might arise in connection with inheritance tax. The gift of his residence is the only gift which Mr Gregory has made during his lifetime to date.

vii) His son Neil is due to get married shortly and has indicated that he will need to convert any assets which he receives from his father into cash by 31 December 1994 at the latest, in order to invest in his new business.

a) Advise Mr Gregory on the optimum tax strategy regarding lifetime transfers of value. Show all supporting calculations. (13 marks)

b) Assuming that Mr Gregory had in fact gone to live with Neil in his former private residence, advise him on the inheritance tax consequences which would have arisen. Detailed calculations are not required. (5 marks)

c) Assuming that Mr Gregory adopts your advice under a) above, calculate the inheritance tax liability arising to the estate on the basis that he dies on 30 September 1994. (7 marks)

Note: Assume that the rate of interest on underpaid and overpaid tax is fixed at 10% per annum.

As indicated above the first step is to examine the various capital gains implications of realising each of the assets. Then it is a case of selecting which ones can be combined in order to avoid a tax liability and be consistent with the overall inheritance tax strategy of minimising the liability on death.

a) Dear Mr Gregory

Your optimum strategy regarding lifetime transfers of value revolves primarily around the income tax and capital gains tax liabilities which would arise since any lifetime transfers to your son would be potentially exempt transfers under inheritance tax. These are set out below:

i) Bingo plc

	Number of shares	Cost	
		£	
Little plc: Dec 84	1,000	12,500	
	2,000	8,654	$12,500 \times \dfrac{2 \times 90}{(2 \times 90) + 80}$
Sale June 94	(2,000)	(8,654)	

	£
Disposal value June 94	500
Cost	(8,654)
Allowable loss – CGT 94/95	(8,154)

ii) Peck Limited

	£
Disposal value June 94	24,000
Cost February 88	(20,000)
	4,000
Indexation allowance	
$\dfrac{143.0 - 103.7}{103.7} \times £20,000 = £7,580$	(4,000)
	–

iii) Zingo Limited

	£
Disposal value per share	20.00
Cost per share (April 87)	(10.57)
Indexation per share	
$\dfrac{143.0 - 101.8}{101.8} \times 10.57$	(4.28)
Chargeable gain per share	5.15

On sale or gift of all shares the gain would therefore be £51,500.

As there is no capital gains tax on death, it is wise to dispose of any assets on which allowable losses will arise prior to death. However, as a disposal to a son is a disposal to a connected person, any loss thus arising could only be carried forward and deducted from gains on future disposals to the same connected person. The shares in Bingo plc should therefore be sold and the cash transferred to Neil. The loss arising can then be carried back three years prior to death and deducted from net gains assessed in those years as follows:

	1991/92	1992/93	1993/94	Loss June 94
Net gains	7,800	–	9,000	8,154
Loss c/b	(2,300)	–	(3,200)	(5,500)
Annual exemption	(5,500)	–	(5,800)	–

Remaining loss available to cover gains in the period prior to death	
	2,654

Indexation loss also available (not calculated).

A capital gains tax repayment of £1,375 (£2,300 @ 25% and £3,200 @ 25%) will be due together with a repayment supplement from 6 April 1993 to the date of death on £575 (£2,300 @ 25%), that is, £86.25 (£575 @ 10% for 18 months). Refer to Chapter 23 if you have forgotten the rules for calculating repayment supplements.

It would be inadvisable to dispose of all the shares in Zingo Limited prior to death as no capital gains tax liability arises on death. However, no business property relief is available to reduce any inheritance tax liability arising on death and therefore there is no disadvantage in disposing of shares to absorb the remaining allowable loss of £2,654 on the sale of Bingo plc shares plus the indexation loss plus the 1994/95 annual exemption of £5,800: numbers of shares to be used = losses plus annual exemption/£5.15. This would give a lifetime transfer of value (numbers of shares sold @ £20 each) either in cash or shares. Lifetime transfers of value are exempt up to £11,000 (annual exemption 1994/95, 1993/94 £3,000 each and marriage exemption £5,000) and any transfer exceeding this amount will add to the cumulative transfers. You may wish to restrict the lifetime transfer of value to 550 shares (£11,000/£20). Either the shares or cash may be transferred.

b) There is a danger that if Mr Gregory goes to live with his son within the seven years prior to his death, the gift of his principal private residence will be deemed to have been a gift with reservation. The effect of this would be that the current value of the residence would be deemed to be part of his estate on death and the original transfer would be ignored for purposes of calculating inheritance tax. This would cause a higher inheritance tax liability. Mr Gregory may, however, qualify for exemption on the grounds that this is reasonable provision for a relative unable to support himself through old age or infirmity. Further medical information would be required in this case.

c) Inheritance tax on death 30 September 1994

		£	£	£
Value of estate:	Bingo plc – cash			500
	Peck Limited 2,000 @ £1.20		24,000	
	Less: BPR 50%		(12,000)	
				12,000
	Zingo Limited 9,450 @ £20			189,000
	Income tax repayment			300
	Capital gains tax repayment and			1,375
	supplement			86
				203,261
Lifetime transfer (£50,000 – AE £6,000)				44,000
				247,261

Inheritance tax payable on death by estate:
£106,000 (150,000 – 44,000) @ Nil   Nil
£97,261 @ 40%   £38,904
                                                     £38,904

Note that the tax liability arising on the lifetime PET now chargeable, will not be borne by the estate but by his son, the transferee.

Sources of finance

Questions under this heading are relatively new but because this is a tax paper, you can be sure that it will be tax implications, in principle, which will be examined – although a little bit of revision from Paper 8 will not go amiss.

The following question was set in June 1992.

Case study

Nile Ltd, a manufacturer of soft drinks, has run into severe financial problems and urgently needs to raise additional finance. The company's normal credit facilities are exhausted, so the directors are considering two alternative methods of raising the required finance. Whichever one is chosen will be completed on 31 March 1995.

Nile Ltd has two subsidiaries, Amazon Ltd and Ganges Ltd. Amazon Ltd has been a wholly owned subsidiary since 1 April 1982. Ganges Ltd has been a wholly owned subsidiary since 31 May 1986 when Nile Ltd acquired the remaining 40% of its share capital for £100,000. The original holding of 60% had been acquired on 1 April 1984 for £75,000.

The two alternatives are:

1) An offer of £500,000 has been made for Ganges Ltd by Congo Ltd, a rival drinks manufacturer. However, the directors consider Ganges Ltd to be worth £625,000 as follows:

	£
Factory	300,000
Office	140,000
Net current assets	185,000
	625,000

Both the factory and office were originally acquired by Amazon Ltd on 1 July 1982 for £40,000 and £18,000 respectively. The factory was sold to Ganges Ltd on 1 April 1986 for £125,000, and the office was sold to Ganges Ltd on 1 April 1989 for £90,000; both sales were at market value.

2) Danube Ltd, a property company, is prepared to enter into a 'sale and leaseback' arrangement on a factory owned by Nile Ltd. Under the arrangement the factory would be sold to Danube Ltd for its current market value of £550,000, and then leased back to Nile Ltd for 10 years at £50,000 per annum payable in advance. The lease is at the current market rate. The factory cost £300,000 on 1 April 1988 as follows:

	£
Land	80,000
Architect's and legal fees	10,000
Factory	140,000
Canteen	20,000
General offices	50,000
	300,000

The current market value includes £150,000 re the land, £50,000 re the canteen, and £75,000 re the general offices. The factory had replaced a smaller factory sold on 31 December 1988 for £220,000, realising a chargeable gain of £140,000.

Each of the group companies has a 31 March year end, pays corporation tax at the full rate, and is currently profitable. However, both Nile Ltd and Ganges Ltd have substantial trading losses brought forward from the past two years, and these are unlikely to be fully utilised in the near future. All the group's factories qualify for Industrial Buildings Allowance, and it is group policy to claim roll-over relief wherever possible. All the companies mentioned are UK resident.

a) Advise the directors on the taxation implications for each of the two alternatives. Your answer should include the due date of any tax liabilities. You should *only* consider the implications for the Nile group of companies.
(15 marks)

b) Comment briefly on the non-tax factors which Nile Ltd should take into account in deciding between the two alternative methods of financing. (4 marks)

c) i) State whether Congo Ltd would be able to benefit from the unrelieved trading losses of Ganges Ltd, and if so, how.
ii) Given the additional information that Amazon Ltd has unused capital losses and has recently bought fixed plant and machinery, suggest one tax planning point that could apply to each alternative method of financing.
(6 marks)

Again this is a fairly detailed question which gives you a lot of help in planning the answer. It could have read:

'Evaluate the two proposals from the point of view of the Nile group of companies, taking into account both tax and non-tax factors'. Part c) ii) of the question could either have been added on the end or built into the background information.

a) i) Sale of Ganges Ltd by Nile Ltd

	£
Sale proceeds 31 Mar 95	500,000
Cost 1 April 84	(75,000)
Cost 31 May 86	(100,000)
	325,000
Indexation	
$\dfrac{145.0 \times 88.6}{88.6} \times 75,000$	(47,743)
$\dfrac{145.0 \times 97.8}{97.8} \times 100,000$	(48,262)
Chargeable gain year ended 31 Mar 95	228,995

This chargeable gain will result in an additional corporation tax liability to Nile Ltd of £75,568 (£228,995 @ 33%) which will be due on or before 1 January 1996. Trading losses of Nile Ltd brought forward cannot be set off against chargeable gains.

At the same time, chargeable gains will also result to Ganges Ltd itself, to the extent that there had been intra-group transfers of assets (that is, on a no gain, no loss basis for capital gains tax purposes) within the previous six years. Ganges did not become a 75 per cent subsidiary of Nile until 31 May 1986 and it is therefore assumed that the disposal of the factory by Amazon to Ganges would not have been done as an intra-group transfer. The sale of the office, on the other hand, would have been an intra-group transfer within six years of Ganges leaving the group.

Office

	£
Market value (also sale proceeds) 1/4/89	90,000
Cost 1/7/82	(18,000)
Indexation:	
$\dfrac{114.3 - 81.8}{81.8}$ (0.397) × 18,000	(7,146)
Chargeable gain	64,854

The gain will be deemed to arise at the beginning of the accounting period in which the company leaves the group, that is 1 April 1994, although the gain is computed according to the actual transfer date, namely April 1989. The gain will give rise to a corporation tax liability of £21,402 (£64,854 × 33%), due on or before 1 January 1996. This liability should have been taken into account by Congo in the purchase price of £500,000.

ii) **Factory sale and leaseback Nile/Danube**

The disposal of the factory by Nile will have capital allowance and capital gains implications as follows:

Industrial Buildings Allowance

	£
Qualifying cost (1/4/88)	220,000
(offices <25% total building cost £210,000)	
writing down allowances 4% × 220,000 × 6 years	(52,800)
Residue of expenditure	167,200
Sale proceeds (Maximum original qualifying cost)	(220,000)
Balancing charge year ended 31 March 1995	52,800

Capital gain computation	£	£
Sale proceeds		550,000
Cost 1/4/88	300,000	
Less: rolled-over gain 31/12/88	(140,000)	
		(160,000)
Indexation $\dfrac{145.0 - 105.8}{105.8}$ (0.371) × 160,000		(59,360)
Chargeable gain year ended 31 March 1995		330,640

The balancing charge should not result in an additional corporation tax liability as it will be covered by the trading losses brought forward. The chargeable gain of £330,640 will result in an additional liability to corporation tax of £109,111 (330,640 @ 33%) due on 1 January 1996. (Sale and leaseback agreements can be treated as part disposals for capital gains tax under anti-avoidance legislation – this is beyond the scope of the examination).

The rent under the lease of £50,000 per annum would be a Schedule D Case I deduction provided it is at a commercial rate. This would therefore increase Nile's trading losses for carry forward.

b) The non-tax factors to be considered would be:
   i) The finance is raised without incurring future liabilities;

   The products, expertise, customers and future profits of Ganges are given up and there is a risk that Congo will gain inside information about the Nile group.

   The sale of a subsidiary may alert creditors, customers, shareholders and others to the serious financial situation which may have more long-term implications.

   ii) The sale and leaseback arrangement commits the group to £50,000 per annum for ten years.

   It may not be easy to escape from this agreement if this was necessary – the factory became too large, or too small or otherwise unsuitable.

   After 10 years, there is no guarantee that the factory would be available to the group if required – this would then involve a move.

c) i) Congo would not be able to use the brought forward trading losses of Ganges as group relief because only current year losses can be used in this way. In addition, if the change in ownership is accompanied by a major change in the nature and conduct of the trade within three years, the losses will not be available for carry forward and future use by Ganges.

   ii) *Sale of Ganges Ltd*

   Nile could transfer its shares in Ganges to Amazon prior to the sale as a (no gain, no loss) intra-group transfer and the sale of Ganges would then be negotiated between Amazon and Congo. In this way the brought forward losses in Amazon could be set against the chargeable gain on disposal of Ganges.

   Sale and leaseback

   The gain on disposal of the factory by Nile could be held over against the fixed plant and machinery recently acquired by Amazon as they are members of a capital gains group. Fixed plant and machinery is a depreciating asset but it will nonetheless have the effect of deferring the gain.

Extracting profit from a company

Profit can be extract from a company in three principal ways:

- remuneration
- dividends
- capital (on disposal of the shares).

Usually questions centre on two of these, that is:

▶ the ongoing company situation where the choice is between remuneration and dividend
▶ the company cessation/sellout situation where the choice is between final distributions as dividend or capital.

The methodology is simply to try it both ways considering all aspects and evaluate which is the cheaper in terms of tax. The following question was set in the December 1991 examination and is on the second of the above situations. (You will remember that the first of the above situations was covered in Chapter 29.)

Case study

a) Mr Don Atello, who is 40, is the managing director of Snake Ltd, a trading company. He owns all of the shares in the company. It is proposed that Snake Ltd will sell its trade to Guru Ltd, a company which is not associated with either Mr Atello or Snake Ltd. Snake Ltd is registered for VAT and has made no exempt supplies. The sale will take place one month from today's date (which you should assume is 1 April 1994).

The sale of the trade will involve the disposal of the following assets: equipment, goodwill, investments, stock and debtors.

   i) State which of the disposals of assets noted above would normally be treated as taxable supplies for VAT.

   ii) Describe the conditions which must be met in the present case for such disposals to fall outside the scope of VAT. (5 marks)

b) Immediately following the sale of its trade, Snake Ltd will be liquidated. Shortly after this, the proceeds of the liquidation will be paid to Mr Atello. The base cost of Mr Atello's shares (including the indexation allowance) is £80,000. The net proceeds of liquidation are currently estimated at £250,000. Mr Atello does not intend to make any further disposals of assets during the year. Mr Atello has heard that it may be advantageous for him to declare a dividend before liquidating the company as this would result in a corresponding reduction in his capital gain (you should assume that any such dividend will be declared on 20 April 1994). Mr Atello will receive nothing else from the company apart from a bonus of £5,000 paid to him on 15 April 1994 in respect of his services as managing director for the year ended 31 March 1994. You may assume that Mr Atello will have no other taxable sources of income, and that he will make no disposals of assets other than his shares in Snake Ltd in 1994/95.

The following details of Snake Ltd's tax situation from the date of its incorporation on 1 April 1987 are available.

	Case I profit/(loss)	Capital gain/(loss)	Patent royalties paid (gross)	Covenant to charity (gross)	Dividends paid (net)	Dividends received (net)
30/4/94	26,000	5,000	–	–	–	800
31/3/94	15,000	–	(300)	(1,000)	–	–
31/3/93	(34,000)	–	(300)	(1,000)	16,000	–
31/3/92	1,000	–	–	(1,000)	–	–
31/3/91	12,000	(2,000)	–	(1,000)	–	–
31/3/90	25,000	–	–	–	–	–
31/3/89	70,000	–	–	–	–	750
31/3/88	20,000	–	–	–	–	–

Snake Ltd has three associated companies. Claims for relief for the loss in the accounting period ended 31 March 1993 have been made as follows:

Loss year ended 31/3/93	34,000
Surrendered to group company	(18,000)
Add trade charges unrelieved year ended 31/3/93	300
Loss carried forward @ 31/3/93	16,300

    ii) Compute the corporation tax payable by Snake Ltd for all accounting periods, before setting off any payments of ACT.

    ii) Compute the maximum amount of the dividend which can be paid by Snake Ltd on 20 April 1994 without incurring irrecoverable ACT. You should assume that any surplus ACT in respect of the dividend declared on 20 April 1994 will be carried back in priority to the surplus ACT arising in the accounting period ended 31 March 1993.

    iii) Show the maximum amount of tax which can be saved by paying a dividend on 20 April 1994.   (20 marks)

The following CT rates should be used in answering the question:

Financial year	Full rate %	Small companies rate %	Taper relief fraction	ACT fraction	Upper limit £	Lower limit £
1987	35	27	1/50	27/73	500,000	100,000
1988	35	25	1/40	25/75	500,000	100,000
1989	35	25	1/40	25/75	750,000	150,000
1990	34	25	9/400	25/75	1,000,000	200,000
1991	33	25	1/50	25/75	1,250,000	250,000
1992	33	25	1/50	25/75	1,250,000	250,000
1993	33	25	1/50	22.5/77.5	1,250,000	250,000
1994	33	25	1/50	20/80	1,500,000	300,000

a)   i) The disposal of equipment and trading stock would normally be regarded as taxable supplies. In addition, the transfer of goodwill is also regarded as a taxable supply – since it is for consideration and is not tangible it is regarded as a supply of a service. The transfer of debtors and investments would be exempt supplies.

    ii) The transfer of a business as a going concern may be outside the scope of VAT if:
      a) The purchaser is registered already for VAT, is liable to be registered for VAT or if not so liable, if he registers voluntarily.
      b) The purchaser intends to use the assets transferred for a similar trade following the transfer.

b)   i) It is important to keep one's head doing a question of this sort which in fact looks much more complicated than it is. Marshalling the figures for all the different years is perhaps the biggest problem and the method set out in the text should be followed: i.e. slot all the figures given into pro forma computations first before worrying about what they all mean.

Snake Ltd – Corporation tax computations

	1 month 30/4/94 £	31/3/94 £	12 months to 31/3/93 £	31/3/92 £
Schedule D I	26,000	15,000	–	1,000
Less: s. 393(1) loss	(1,600)	(15,000)		
Net Capital gain	5,000			
Less: loss bf	(2,000)			
Total profit	27,400	–	–	1,000
Less: s. 393A1(a) loss				–
s. 393A1(b) loss				
Less: trade charges		(300)	(300)	–
non-trade charges		(1,000)	(1,000)	(1,000)
Profit chargeable CT	27,400	–	–	–
FII (£800 × 20/80) + £800	1,000	–	–	–
Profits	£28,400	–	–	–
Trade charges C/F		300	300	–
CT @ 33%	9,042 (W1)			
Less: SCR taper relief (W2)	(55)			
CT payable	8,987	–	–	–

(W1) FY94 Upper limit $1,500,000 \times 1/12 \times 1/4 = 31,250$
Lower limit $300,000 \times 1/12 \times 1/4 = 6,250$

(W2) $(31,250 - 28,400) \times \dfrac{27,400}{28,400} \times \dfrac{1}{50} = 55$

NB. There are four companies in the group

	30/3/91 £	12 months to 31/3/90 £	31/3/89 £	31/3/88 £
Schedule DI	12,000	25,000	70,000	20,000
Less: s. 393(1) loss				
Net capital gain				
Less loss bf				
Total profit	12,000	25,000	70,000	20,000
Less: s. 393A1(a) loss				
s. 393A1(b) loss				
Less: non-trade charges				
trade charges	(1,000)			
Profit chargeable CT	11,000	25,000	70,000	20,000
FII (750 × 100/75)	–	–	1,000	–
Profits	11,000	25,000	71,000	20,000
CT @ 25% (SCR)	2,750			
@ 25% (SCR)		6,250		
@ 35%			24,500	
@ 27% (SCR)				5,400
Less: SCR taper relief (W3)			(1,331)	
CT payable	2,750	6,250	23,169	5,400

(W3) FY88 $(125,000 - 71,000) \times \dfrac{70,000}{71,000} \times \dfrac{1}{40} = 1,331$

ii) The payment of a dividend on 20 April 1994 will cause ACT to be paid at a rate of 20/80 which will be able to be set off against the CT liability of the month ended 30 April 1994 and then the surplus ACT will be able to be carried back and set off against the CT liabilities of accounting periods commencing in the six years prior to the accounting period in which the surplus

ACT arose (claims being made for later periods before earlier periods). This means that surplus ACT can be carried back to year ending 31 March 1989.

ACT has already been paid in respect of the year ended 31 March 1993 as follows:

	£	
FP 16,000 × 100/75 =	21,333	
FII bf from 31 March 1989	(1,000)	
	20,333	ACT @ 25% £5,083

This ACT was unable to be relieved in the accounting period in which it was paid and therefore it, too, would be surplus ACT carried back. It would originally have been carried back to year ended 31/3/91 and year ended 31/3/90 but interaction with the surplus ACT in respect of the dividend paid on 20 April 1994 will cause its set off to be adjusted and it will be carried back as far as possible, that is, to the commencement of trading year ended 31 March 1988 where it will be wholly relieved (profit chargeable to CT £20,000 – maximum ACT set off 20,000 @ 27% = £5,400).

The amount of surplus ACT which can be set off will dictate the maximum dividend to be paid on 20 April 1994.

	£
Year ended March 1989 70,000 @ 25%	17,500
Year ended March 1990 25,000 @ 25%	6,250
Year ended March 1991 11,000 @ 25%	2,750
Year ended March 1992 – 25%	–
Year ended March 1993 – 25%	–
Year ended March 1994 – 22.5%	–
Period to 30 April 1994 27,400 @ 20%	5,480
	31,980

A dividend of £127,920 (31,980 × 80/20) will generate ACT of £31,980 and this can be increased by £800, the amount of the dividend received in that accounting period. Maximum dividend for tax efficiency is £128,720.

iii) In Snake Ltd the payment of ACT is cancelled by repayments of CT for earlier periods – there is therefore no tax cost to Snake Ltd.

Mr Atello, assuming no dividend, will pay capital gains tax on a gain of £170,000 (£250,000 – £80,000) less his annual exemption for 1994/95 of £5,800 with income of only £5,000, the capital gains tax liability will be:

	£		£
3,000 – (5,000 – 3,445) =	1,445	@ 20%	289
	20,700	@ 25%	5,175
	142,055	@ 40%	56,822
Gain (170,000 – 5,800)	164,200		62,286

Assuming maximum dividend, Mr Atello will pay income tax and reduced capital gains tax as follows:

	£	£
Bonus	5,000	
Dividend 128,720 × 100/80	160,900	
Less: personal allowance	(3,445)	
Taxable income	162,455	
3,000 @ 20%		600
20,700 @ 20% (as dividend income)		4,140
138,755 @ 40%		55,502
Income tax liability		60,242
Less: tax applicable to bonus (5,000 – 3445) @ 20%		(311)
Less: tax credit on dividend		(32,180)
Additional income tax		27,751
Liquidation proceeds of Snake (as above)		250,000
Less: cash paid in dividend		(128,720)
Liquidation proceeds after dividend		121,280
Base cost of shares + indexation		(80,000)
Revised capital gain		41,280
Capital gains tax @ 40%		16,512
Total tax liabilities if dividend paid		44,263
Total tax liabilities if no dividend paid (as above)		62,286
Saving by paying dividend		18,023

Other tax planning topics

The above are not an exhaustive list of key tax planning topics and you should identify others for yourself – a study of the exam and exam-style questions in the question banks may give you some ideas. Once you have identifed the topics you should try to think through the main elements of each. Here are one or two further suggestions:

- husband and wife
- the purchase/disposal of either a company's net assets or its share capital
- group planning
- investment of funds

Good luck!

Answers to End of Chapter Questions

CHAPTER 1 *Self test questions*

1. Fiscal year; year of assessment.

2. Expenses wholly, exlusively, necessarily incurred in the performance of the duties of the employment.

3. Rent receivable less expenses paid in the fiscal year.

4. No – voluntary allowance from a relative.

5. Interest of £3,000 will be eligible for relief (£40,000 × 10% × 30,000/40,000). Relief will be given by means of a tax credit: £3,000 × 20% = £600.

6. Charitable deeds of covenant.

7. Gross.

8. Age allowance – basic £4,200 – 1/2 (15,000 – 14,200) i.e. £3,800
   – married £2,705 –[1/2 (15,000 – 14,200) – 400]= £2,705

9. No.

10. Yes, basic personal allowance.

11. C. Dickens – computation of total income – 1994/95.

	£	Unearned and earned income £	Tax collected at source £
Schedular Income			
Schedule D Case II – y/e 31 December 1993 (accounts ending in 1993/94)		20,000	
Schedule A – income y/e 5 April 1995 (rents receivable less expenses paid)		2,246	
Schedule D Case VI – income y/e 5 April 1995 (rent receivable less expenses paid)			
Furnished letting		640	
Holiday letting		1,816	
Schedule D Case III – income y/e 5 April 1994		100	
Schedule F – income y/e 5 April 1995			
Dividends received	1,600		
Tax credit (20/80)	400		
		2,000	400.00

		Unearned and unearned income £	Tax collected at source £
Income taxed at source – y/e 5 April 1995			
Discretionary trust (gross – 35%)		1,400	490.00
Building society interest	720		
Income tax (25/75)	240		
		960	240.00
Total income		29,162	1,130.00
Less: personal allowance		3,445	
Taxable income (Dividends £2,000 Other income £23,717)		25,717	
Tax borne	£		
20%	3,000	–	600.00
25%	20,700	–	5,175.00
40%	17	2,000	806.80
	23,717	2,000	6,581.80
Tax liability			6,581.80
Less: tax paid			(1,130.00)
Tax payable			5,451.80

12 Dear John,

Thank you for your recent letter.
You asked for advice on two matters:

a) Monthly allowance

Unfortunately, the payment of a monthly allowance is not deductible from total income of the payer for income tax purposes. It must therefore be paid out of 'after tax' income.

b) Gift of lump sum to Mary's mother

Mary's mother is entitled to a personal allowance of £4,370 in 1994/95 as she is over 75. Since her only income, currently, is the state retirement pension, additional income, up to £1,666 per annum would not result in any additional tax liability. However, most investment income suffers basic rate income tax at source. It would be necessary therefore for Mary's mother to claim to have the tax, deducted at source, repaid to her each year, or alternatively to apply to have interest paid to her gross – most banks and building societies will do this.

The second alternative would seem to be the best from a cash point of view since you would be liable to tax at 40% on any income arising on the lump sum, if it is retained by you and invested, and any allowance you make to Mary's mother would be out of your net income.

I trust this is of help to you. Please do not hesitate to contact me if I can be of further assistance.

Yours sincerely,

13 a) Management or employee buy-out

This is the acquisition, by employees or management or both, of a substantial interest in the business for which they work. The complexity of these transactions varies considerably.

The acquisition may be achieved either by the purchase of the underlying assets of the business or by the purchase of shares. A well-known example was the buy-out in 1982 of the National Freight Company by a large group of employees and management.

The taxation implications depend upon the particular circumstances. In many cases the business acquired in this way will have been making losses for a number of years and will have substantial accumulated losses. Where the assets are acquired, the new company would not be able to make use of the accumulated losses but capital allowances would still be available. Where the shares are acquired there is no interruption to capital allowances, but again the losses will probably not be available if the buy-out results in a major change in the nature and conduct of the trade.

b) Eligible interest

The money borrowed must be in the form of a loan not an overdraft and must be used to buy shares in a company controlled by its employees. Tax relief will be available provided a number of conditions are satisfied:

i) the shares acquired are ordinary shares
ii) more than 50% of the ordinary shares and voting power is held by full-time employees or their spouses
iii) the shares are acquired no later than 12 months after the company became employee controlled
iv) the company is an unquoted trading company (or a holding company of a trading group)

v) Oliver must be a full-time employee throughout the duration of the loan (relief, however, continues for 12 months after cessation of employment).

If the buy-out is by management only, the conditions are stricter and, in addition to the above, the company must be a close company (see Chapter 26) and Oliver must have control of more than 5% of the ordinary share capital or must have an interest in the company and spend the greater part of his time during the period for which he requires tax relief, in the management of the company.

14 Grant – income tax computation – 1994/95

	£
Schedule E	40,000
Schedule A (note 1)	19,470
Bank interest (note 2)	
£1,750 × 100/75 × 1/2	1,167
	60,637
Interest on let property (note 1)	(19,000)
Deed of covenant (note 4) £3,000 × 100/75	(4,000)
Statutory total income	37,637
Personal allowance	(3,445)
Taxable income	34,192
Tax borne:	
£3,000 at 20%	600.00
£20,700 at 25%	5,175.00
£10,492 at 40%	4,196.80
	9,971.80
Add: retained on deed £4,000 × 25%	1,000.00
	10,971.80
Less: mortgage relief (note 3)	
(£6,000 × 30,000/50,000) = £3,600 × 20%	(720.00)
Less: MCA relief £1,720 × 20%	(344.00)
	9,907.80

Notes

1. Rents receivable £29,145 (28,695 + 450) less expenses paid £9,675 gives £19,470 assessable. Interest paid is eligible interest and is a charge on income. No tax would be deducted at source.

2. Bank interest is assessable on the amount arising in the current year and would be deemed to have suffered basic rate income tax at source. (It is assumed that it did not arise on a National Savings Bank account.) Where accounts are held in joint names, they are treated as owned by husband and wife in equal shares and the interest arising is divided equally between them unless a declaration is made to the contrary.

3. Although the mortgages overlap, the interest on both will be eligible for relief as the overlap was not greater than 12 months. The first mortgage must be under the MIRAS arrangement because it was only £30,000 and it was from a qualifying lender. It has therefore been ignored in the above computation. Relief on the second mortgage is restricted to interest on £30,000.

4. The deed of covenant, £3,000, is given as the amount paid and it has been assumed therefore that this is the net amount. It is to a charity and therefore is eligible for relief at both basic and high rates.

5. School fees are not an allowable deduction.

6. The tax deducted at source (£291.75) is not shown as a deduction from the income tax liability because the question did not require the amount of income tax payable.

CHAPTER 2 *Self test questions*

1. From the 6th of one month to the 5th of the next.

2. The declaration is only effective if received by the Inland Revenue within 60 days of being made and is only effective for income arising on or after that date.

3. Both husband and wife.

4. 1,720 − (8/12 × 1,720) = £573.

5. a) and b). Only to the extent that it is mortgage interest under an 'allocation of interest' election.

6 Both husband and wife within 12 months of the end of the tax year to which it applies.

7 Personal allowance £3,445.
Married couple's allowance £2,705 − (2/12 × 2,705) = £2,254.

8 Payer: no deduction (only eligible if to former spouse).
Recipient: not taxable.

9 Personal allowance £3,445.
Married couple's allowance £1,720 (that is, in full).

10 Income tax computation 1994/95 estimate

	David Knight Unearned and earned income		Carol Harris Unearned and earned income	
	£	£	£	£
Schedular income				
Schedule E (Note 1)				15,000
Schedule D Case (Note 2)		24,000		–
Less: personal pension premium (Note 3)		(1,800)		
Schedule D Case III (Note 4)		30		
Schedule F Dividend	512			
Tax credit (20/80)	128			640
Income taxed at source				
Building society interest	180			
Income tax (25/75)	60			240
Total income		22,230		15,880
Less: charges paid				
Deed of covenant (Note 5)		(1,000)		
Statutory total income		21,230		15,880
Less: personal allowance		(3,445)		(3,445)
Taxable income: Dividends	Nil		640	
Other income	17,785		11,795	
	17,785			12,435
Tax borne				
20% 3,000		600.00	3,000 + 640	728.00
25% 14,785		3,696.25	8,795 –	2,198.75
17,785		4,296.25	11,795 640	2,926.75
Less: APA relief (£1,720 × 20%)		(344.00)		
		3,952.25		

Notes

1 Child benefit and the additional benefit for single parents are exempt.

2 A partnership is assessable under Schedule D Case I on the adjusted profit of the accounts ending in the previous fiscal year. As David is entitled to a one-third share of the profits, he will be taxed on one-third of the amount assessable in 1994/95, that is, 1/3 × 72,000.

3 A personal pension premium is a deductible expense from Schedule D Case I income (amount paid in the year of assessment). The normal limit is 17.5% of net relevant earnings (1,800 < 17.5% × 24,000) and this percentage increases with the age of the taxpayer (see Chapter 4)

4 National Savings Bank interest is paid and assessed under Schedule D Case III on the amount arising in the preceding year. As it is an ordinary account the first £70 is tax free (100 − 70).

5 Charitable deed of covenant is a retainable charge deductible for both basic and higher rate tax. The amount is assumed to be the gross figure (£750 actually paid).

6 No deduction is available for the gardener's salary or the housekeeper's salary (housekeeper allowance was withdrawn by FA 1988).
   No deduction is available for the amount paid to Carol's mother (dependent relative relief was withdrawn by FA 1988).

7 David could have claimed a married couple's allowance of:

1,720 − 8/12 × 1,720 = 573

He is better off not claiming married couple's allowance and claiming the additional personal allowance.

11 Edward – income tax computation – 1994/95 (to date of death – 4 January 1995)

				Unearned and earned income £	Tax collected at source £
Schedular income					
Schedule E (Note 1)				22,787	Not known
Schedule F (Note 4)					
£7,300 × 100/80				9,125	1,825
				31,912	1,825
Less personal allowance				(3,445)	
Taxable income:	Dividends		9,125		
	Other income		19,342	28,467	
Tax borne:					
On non-dividend income		3,000	× 20%	600.00	
		16,342	× 25%	4,085.50	
		19,342		4,685.50	
On dividends (part)		4,358	× 20%	871.60	
		23,700			
On dividends (balance)		4,767	× 40%	1,906.80	
		28,467		7,463.90	
Less MCA relief		1,720	× 20%	(344.00)	
Income tax liability				7,119.90	
Less tax paid				(1,825.00)	
Income tax payable				5,294.90	

The mortgage interest has been omitted from the calculation as it receives tax relief through the MIRAS scheme.

Frances – income tax computation – 1994/95

	Unearned and earned income £	Tax collected at source £
Schedular income		
Schedule E (Note 1)	1,200	Not known
Schedule D Case I (Note 2)	13,500	–
Less: capital allowances (Note 2)	(2,660)	
Schedule D Case III (Note 3)	80	–
Income taxed at source		
Building society interest	1,533	
(550 + 600) × 100/75		383
Total income	13,653	383
Less personal allowance	(3,445)	
Taxable	10,208	
Tax borne		
£3,000 × 20%	600.00	
£7,208 × 25%	1,802.00	
	2,402.00	
Less APA relief (£1,720 × 20%)	(344.00)	
Less WBA relief (£1,720 × 20%)	(344.00)	
	1,714.00	
Less tax collected at source	(383.00)	
	1,331.00	

Geraldine – income tax computation – 1994/95

	£	Unearned and earned income £	Tax collected at source £
Schedular income			
Schedule D Case III (Note 3)		500	
Income taxed at source			
dividends	730		
tax credit (20/80)	183	913	183
Statutory total income		1,413	183
Less: personal allowance	(3,445)	(1,413)	
Taxable income		Nil	
Tax borne and income tax liability		Nil	
Less: tax paid		(183)	
Income tax payable		(183)	

Notes

1 Salary (9 × £1,500) — £13,500
   Bonus paid in year (1,400 + 1,700 + 1,500 + 1,800)
   (amount paid 31 January was due to Edward at date of death) — 6,400
   Car per scale benefit (to date of death) (11,000 × 35% × 9/12) — 2,887
   Total — 22,787

   The ex-gratia payment being less than £30,000 is exempt. The lump sum from the company's superannuation fund is exempt. Pension received by Frances (3 × 400) = £1,200.

2 Accounting period ending in previous fiscal year is 28 February 1994 – £13,500.
   Capital allowances:

	£	£		
	4,800			
Additions		12,200		
Sale proceeds	(4,000)			
	800	12,200		
balancing allowance	(800)		× 70% =	560
WDA		(3,000)	× 70% =	2,100
	Nil	9,200		
				2,660

3 It has been assumed that the National Savings Bank account has been open for many years. The preceding year basis of assessment applies (£150) with the first £70 exempt (ordinary account). Similarly, it has been assumed that Geraldine's account has been open for some time.

4 Dividends received are assessed on the amount arising in the current tax year – in this case those received to the date of death. The remaining dividends would be the property of Edward's estate, and taxable there to be passed on as taxed income to Geraldine.

CHAPTER 3 *Self test questions*

1 False.

2 Yes – £400.

3
	£
Car benefit £12,000 × 35% =	4,200
Less 2/3 discount	(2,800)
	1,400

Fuel benefit £810.
The contribution of £300 cannot be deducted because it is implied he did not pay for all private fuel.
Note: If the contribution had been towards the car, the benefit would have been reduced by £300.

4 No.

5 Yes. Whether he is a higher-paid employee or not, the market value of the car is £1,500 and he has only paid £1,000, leaving a benefit of £500.

6 The statutory redundancy pay is exempt but counts towards the £30,000. Anne is therefore taxable on £9,000. (Subject to the IR statement, re pension 'relevant benefits'.)

7 The lower of £4,000 or 20% of total pay.

8 £3,000 or 10% of salary (maximum £8,000).

9 a) Tax consequences of proposed remuneration package from Delta Ltd.

	£	
Salary	40,000	
Medical insurance	1,250	(Note 1)
Profit-sharing scheme shares - value £3,500	–	(Note 2)
Beneficial loan interest	4,000	(Note 3)
Higher cost housing allowance	1,000	
Expenses for duties abroad	950	(Note 6 and 1)
Car	10,750	(Note 7)
	56,450	

b) Tax consequences of proposed remineration package from Kappa Ltd.

	£	
Salary	37,500	
Accommodation	36,500	(Note 8)
Car	5,089	(Note 9)
Education fees	6,750	(Note 10)
Share option scheme	2,500	(Note 11)
	88,339	

Less: subscriptions of £145 deductible in each case.

Compensation for loss of office – £50,000 – appears to be contractual and as such would be fully taxable under Schedule E, when paid, without relief under ICTA 1988, s. 148.

Notes

1 Director/higher paid employees – general rules. Medical insurance to cover treatment abroad while performing the duties of the employment is not taxable (see Chapter 29).

2 Under a profit-sharing scheme approved under ICTA 1988, s. 185, shares with a market value of up to 10% of an employee's salary (minimum limit of £3,000 and maximum limit of £8,000) may be appropriated to him in any fiscal year. Salary is defined as that for PAYE purposes (net of pension contributions) excluding any taxable benefits for that year. There is no charge to income tax when shares are appropriated to an employee but a charge arises on any unauthorised shares (shares in excess of the limit to an eligible employee or any shares to an ineligible employee) at the market value on the earlier of: the date of disposal; the release date; or death. A charge also arises on the disposal of authorised shares (shares within the limit) before the release date based on a percentage of the lower of the initial market value or the market value at the date of disposal.

3 The loan of £80,000 is an assessable benefit. The charge is based on the difference between the interest due at the official rate and the interest paid: £80,000 × (10% – 5%) = £4,000. Mr King will also be treated as having paid loan interest of £4,000. Thus he will also be entitled to a tax credit of £800 (£4,000 × 20%).

4 Removal expenses are not a taxable benefit up to £8,000.

5 Contributions by employers to extra costs incurred by employees moved to higher cost housing areas are taxable from 6 April 1993.

6 Subsistence expenses while performing the duties of the employment are not taxable. As the foreign visits exceed 60 continuous days, the travel costs of a visit by his family are not assessable. The cost of accommodation will be assessable (see Chapter 29)

7	Car benefit	£
	£30,000 × 35%	10,500
	Less two-thirds discount (18,000 miles)	(7,000)
		3,500
	Fuel benefit	750
	Chauffeur's wages	6,500
		10,750

8	Gross annual value	25,000
	Additional benefit (150,000–75,000) @ 10%	7,500
	Furniture annual value-Cost (20,000) @ 20%	4,000
		36,500

			£
9	Car benefit		
	£25,000 × 35% =		8,750
	Less one-third discount (2,500)		(2,917)
			5,833
	Fuel benefit:		1,200
			7,033

10 Education fees or scholarships paid to children of employees are assessed as a benefit in the hands of a director or higher-paid employee unless the scholarship was open to non-employees and the fact that it was awarded to the child of an employee was entirely fortuitous.

11 This share option is of a type approved under FA 1984, which exempts any benefit from income tax unless the option price is significantly less than the market value at the time the option is granted. In this case there may be an assessable benefit of £2,500 [2,500 × £ (6 − 5)].

12 Payment to an employment agency is not deductible because it is not incurred in performing the duties of the employment but was incurred prior to the employment in order to obtain employment.

13 Subscriptions to recognised professional bodies are specifically allowable if relevant to the employment.

14 Golf club subscription is not allowable as it is not incurred in the performance of the duties of the employment (*Brown* v. *Bullock*) nor is it a subscription to a recognised professional body.

15 Clothing cost is not deductible as the expenditure is not wholly, exclusively and necessarily incurred in the performance of the duties of the employment (*Hillyer* v. *Leeke*).

CHAPTER 4 *Self test questions*

1 £8,000 (4 × £2,000).

2 One which, taking one year with another, is sufficient to cover the landlord's expenses.

3 1 January in year of assessment.

4 Profits and losses on all landlord's repairing leases are pooled. Any net losses can be carried forward to the following year's pool.

5 Seven years.

6 £6,300 [15,000 − 2% × (30 − 1) × 15,000]

7 Two years from the end of the year of assessment for which the claim is made.

8 70 days and 140 days.

9 It is treated as dividend income deemed to be taxed at source @ 20%. The imputed tax credit can be repaid.

10 Actual.

11 Sources commencing after 5 April 1994 are assessable on the current year basis.

12 Redeemable securities; issued at a discount greater than 15% or 1/2% per annum; taxable D III.

13 Interest on fixed interest securities is treated as accruing on a day-to-day basis. On purchase and sale, an interest adjustment must be made to the disposal proceeds; charges and reliefs which accrue are netted against each other and net charges are assessed under D VI.

14 It may be carried forward for six years only and if not used will be lost.

15 John Brown – Schedule A assessment – 1994/95.

Leases not at a full rent	2	5
	£	£
Rent receivable	500	100
Less: expenses paid – water etc	(480)	(800)
maintenance	(800)	–
Losses to carry forward to be deducted from future profits on the same lease of the same property.	(780)	(700)

	Tenant's repairing leases	3
		£
	Rent receivable (Note 1)	12,000
	Less: expenses paid – rates etc	(2,920)
	maintenance and repairs	(8,000)
	agent's fees	(2,400)
		(1,320)
	Extension to warehouse treated as premium Chargeable under Schedule A	
	18,000 – 2% × (30 – 1) × 18,000	7,560
		6,240

	Landlord repairing leases		Pooled
			£
	Rent receivable –	property 1	3,600
		property 4 (Note2)	6,400
		property 6	4,800
	Less: expenses paid –	water etc (900 + 1,600 + 800)	(3,300)
		maintenance and repairs (600 + 2,000 + 2,200)	(4,800)
		agent's fees (360 + 640 + 480)	(1,480)
		rent paid	(1,800)
			3,420
	Schedule A assessment –	tenant repairing leases	6,240
		landlord repairing leases	3,420
			9,660

Notes

1 The warehouse was not let until 5 October 1994. The lease provided for payments in advance, and therefore quarterly payments of £4,000 would be received on 5 October, 5 January, and 5 April.

2 Rent is chargeable when due whether received or not.

16 Schedule D Case VI assessment – 1994/95

			£
Rents receivable			2,450
Less: expenses paid – re tenants			
advertising		98	
cleaning		340	
			(438)
– to be apportioned to tenants			
council tax		592	
insurance		150	
repairs to structure		268	
repairs to contents		110	
wear and tear of contents (note 1)		186	
		1,306	
$\frac{44 \text{ weeks}}{52 \text{ weeks}} \times 1,306$			(1,105)
Schedule D Case VI assessment			907

Note

1 Allowance for wear and tear of contents calculated as 10% of net rent (that is, rent less council tax) × 10% (2,450 – 592) = £186.

17

Age	Year	Net relevant earnings	Maximum	% in year	Paid relief	Unused relief	Cumulative relief 1993/94
		£	£	£	£	£	£
35	1987/88	12,000	2,100	17.5	1,500	600	600
36	1988/89	15,000	3,000	20	1,500	1,500	2,100
37	1989/90	15,000	3,000	20	1,500	1,500	3,600
38	1990/91	15,000	3,000	20	1,500	1,500	5,100
39	1991/92	18,000	3,600	20	1,500	2,100	7,200
40	1992/93	18,000	3,600	20	1,500	2,100	9,300
41	1993/94	18,000	3,600	20	1,500	2,100	11,400
42	1994/95	20,000	4,000	20	1,500	2,500	

Unused relief available in 1994/95 will be £2,500 plus £11,400 brought forward, as shown above, less £600 for 1987/88 (six year limit exceeded) ie £13,300 may be paid for 1994/95.

Alternatively, if the lump sum is paid before 5 April 1995, part of it can be treated as paid in 1993/94.

Unused relief available in 1993/94 will be £11,400. A further £2,500 can then be paid with respect to 1994/95 ie £13,900 in total.

There is no point in paying more than this amount as a lump sum as no tax relief will be available on the excess. The remaining funds should be invested and used to top up your existing premium in future years.

CHAPTER 5 *Self test questions*

1. Net chargeable gains 1994/95 – 3,900 (1,000 + 4,000 – 500 + 200 – 800).

   Losses for carry forward – 1,000 (3,900 less exempt 5,800; losses b/f are unused) and indexation loss unused.

2. 1 December following end of year assessment.

3. a) Hardship – instalments over eight years or, if less, the period until the last of the consideration is due
   b) Gifts of land, controlling shareholdings, minority holdings in unquoted companies in instalments over ten years.

4. 199p (lower of i) 197 + 1/4(205 – 197) and ii) 1/2 (195 + 205).

5. i) Individual to his spouse and their relatives.
   ii) Trustee to settlor and persons connected with them.
   iii) Partner to partners and their spouses and other persons connected with them.
   iv) Companies to a controlling company or individual, and to other companies under the same control.

6. They may only be set off against gains on future transactions with the same connected person.

7. 3.

8. If it gives a greater loss, greater gain, or a gain when the old rules show a loss or vice versa.

9. Before 6 April 1990 or, if later, within two years of the end of the year assessment in which the first disposal of such an asset takes place.

10. Two years from the end of year assessment in which the disposal takes place or the deferred gain accrues.

11. Mr and Mrs Herriot – capital gains tax computation.

	Mr Herriot £	**Mrs Herriot** £
Gains	8,700	800
Less: losses	—	—
Taxable amount	8,700	800
Less: losses brought forward	—	—
Less: annual exemption	5,800	(800)
Net taxable amount	2,900	Nil
Tax on 200 @ 25%	50.00	
2,700 @ 40%	1,080.00	
2,900	1,130.00	

    Note: Mr Herriot's sister-in-law is a connected person and therefore the loss cannot be set off against other chargeable gains but may only be carried forward and deducted from future chargeable gains on transactions with the same connected person. It is assumed that an indexation loss on the same transaction will be similarly restricted.

    The loss brought forward belongs to Mrs Herriot.

12. Richard's income tax computation shows that he has statutory total income in 1994/95 of £3,254 and is entitled to an age allowance of £4,370. His taxable income and his income tax liability are £Nil.

    His chargeable gains of £10,500 are reduced by the annual exemption of £5,800 and the net taxable amount (£4,700) falls within the lower rate and basic rate band. His capital gains tax liability is therefore £1,025 (£3,000 @ 20%, £1,700 @ 25%).

13 Reginald

a)

	Value 31 March 1982 £	Old rules cost £	Gains/(Loss) £
Disposal value 31 January 1995	26,500	26,500	
Incidental cost disposal	(610)	(610)	
Acquisition cost – October 1974		(2,500)	
Enhancement cost – June 1976		(1,000)	
31 March 1982 value	(15,000)		
Unindexed gain	10,890	22,390	
Less: indexation allowance $\frac{144.7 - 79.4}{79.4} = 0.822$			
March 82 value > cost			
15,000 × 0.822 (restricted)	(10,890)	(12,330)	
	–	10,060	

The indexation allowance in the March 1982 column has been restricted as it cannot create an allowable loss. There will therefore be no gain and no loss on the disposal of the holiday cottage.

b) Gift to wife – exempt – on a 'no gain, no loss' basis.

	£
Deemed cost of land to Joan will be:	12,000
Plus: indexation allowance	
$\frac{144.4 - 89.2}{89.2} = 0.619 \times 12,000$	7,428
	19,428

c) Gains on foreign currency purchased for personal use are exempt from capital gains tax.

CHAPTER 6 *Self test questions*

1 Useful life of 50 years or less.

2 Disposal value and allowable deductions less than £6,000.

3 Lower of the normal gain and 5/3 (disposal value – £6,000).

4 Substitute 6,000 for disposal value and compute as normal.

5 Copyright, trademarks, life interests and leases (not land).

6 Elizabeth

a)

	Value 31 March 1982 £	Old rules Cost £	Gain/(Loss) £
Disposal value 6 January 1995	69,000	69,000	
Acquisition cost – April 1969		(2,000)	
31 March 1982 value	(35,000)		
Unindexed gain	34,000	67,000	
Less: indexation allowance $\frac{144.7 - 79.4}{79.4} = 0.822$			
March 1982 value > cost			
35,000 × 0.822	(28,770)	(28,770)	
	5,230	38,230	5,230

Principal private residence exemption is available on one half.

	£
Gain as above	5,230
Principal private residence exemption	(2,615)
Gain attributable to letting	2,615
Less: letting relief – lower of:	
i) exemption PPR £2,615	
ii) £40,000 Max	(2,615)
Chargeable gain	Nil

b) The gain on diposal of the clock will be that computed under the normal rules restricted to that given using chattel relief.

There is insufficient information given to compute the gain under the normal rules but it is evident from the information given that chattel relief will give the lower gain.

	£	
Disposal value	6,600	
Deemed cost	(6,000)	
× 5/3	600	= £1,000

c)

	31 March 1982 value £	Old rules cost £	Gain/ (Loss) £
Disposal value of lease	75,000	75,000	
Less: allowable cost			

Original cost × $\dfrac{\% \text{ re 33 yrs}}{\% \text{ re 55 years}}$

$32,000 \times \dfrac{90,280}{100}$ → (28,890)

31 March 1982 Value × $\dfrac{\% \text{ re 33 yrs}}{\% \text{ re 46 yrs}}$

$50,000 \times \dfrac{90,280}{98,490}$ → (45,832)

Enhancement expenditure × $\dfrac{\% \text{ 33 yrs}}{\% \text{ 44.625 yrs}}$

$20,000 \times \dfrac{90.280}{97.595 + 7.5/12\,(98.059 - 97.595)}$ → (18,446)   (18,446)

	31 March 1982 value	Old rules cost	Gain/(Loss)
Unindexed gain	10,722	27,664	
Less: indexation allowance			

$\dfrac{145.0 - 79.4}{79.4} = 0.826$

March 1982 value greater than cost
£45,832 × 0.826 = 37,857 → (10,521)   (27,664)
On enhancement expenditure

$\dfrac{145.0 - 85.7}{85.7} = 0.692$ → –   –

18,446 × 0.692 = 12,764
Loss → –   –

Total chargeable gains for 1994/95	£ 1,000

Note

1. In part c), the amortisation table percentage must not only be applied to cost but also to 31 March 1982 value and any enhancement expenditure. The indexation allowance is only given on the 'amortised' cost and so on.
2. Indexation loss of 22,957 (37,857 + 12,764 – 27,664) arises.

CHAPTER 7 *Self test questions*

1. 1,000 shares disposed of out of Pool A (500 + 800 + 1,000).

2. Acquisition or disposal of shares of same class in same company, affecting Pool A.

3. Not specified.

4. Pool value × $\dfrac{RE - RL}{RL}$ where RE is RPI for this operative event and RL is RPI for last operative event.

5

	Pool A			Pool B	
	No of shares		No of shares	Cost at 31.3.82	Cost at 10.10.90
		£		£	£
	800	1,000	500	500	–
Bonus			500	–	–
Indexed rise		358*			
	800	1,358	1,000	500	–
Rights	200	220	250		275
10 October 1990	1,000	1,578	1,250	500	275

*Indexed rise (130.3-95.9)/95.9 × 1,000.

6   Value of new holding: 200 preference shares @ £2.00   400
                            800 ordinary shares @ £3.00   2,400
                                                                2,800

Cost of ordinary shares 2,400/2,800 × 1,500 = £214
Cost of ordinary shares 2,400/2,800 × 1,500 = £1,286.

7   a) Suzanne

	31 March 1982 value £	Old rules cost £
Disposal value	15,000	15,000
Less: March 82 value/cost	(4,000)	(3,500)
	11,000	11,500
Less: indexation allowance on 31 March 1982		
$\frac{144.7 - 79.4}{79.4} = 0.822$		
4,000 × 0.822	(3,288)	(3,288)
Gain	7,712	8,212
Chargeable gain 1994/95	7,712	

b) Frances
    Matching rules – disposal of 11,000 shares in The Hastings Hardening Company plc.

    2,000 shares 19 September 1982
    2,000 shares 17 January 1985   Pool A 6,000 – 6,000 sold
    2,000 shares 12 December 1985

    2,000 shares 16 March 1968   Pool B 6,000 – 5,000 sold
    2,000 shares 29 June 1980
    2,000 shares 3 November 1967

Pool A	No of shares	Value £
19 September 1982	2,000	1,700
Indexation to 5 April 1985		
$\frac{94.8 - 81.9}{81.9} \times 1,700$		268
17 January 1985	2,000	6,000
Indexation to 5 April 1985		
$\frac{94.8 - 91.2}{91.2} \times 6,000$		237
Value of holding at 5 April 1985	4,000	8,205
Operative event December 1985		
Indexation 8.205 × $\frac{96.0 - 94.8}{4.8}$		104
Acquisition December 1985	2,000	5,500
	6,000	13,809

Pool A	No of shares	Value £
Operative event February 1995		
Indexation $13,809 \times \dfrac{144.9 - 96.0}{96.0}$		7,034
		20,843
Disposal February 1995	(6,000)	(20,843)
Sale proceeds $30,000 \times \dfrac{6,000}{11,000}$		16,364
Less: indexed cost (restricted)		(16,364)
Chargeable gain		–

Indexation loss 4,479 (20,843 – 16,364)

Pool B	No of shares	Value £
3 November 1967	2,000	1,000
16 March 1968	2,000	1,000
29 June 1980	2,000	1,300
	6,000	3,300
Disposal 17 February 1995	(5,000)	(2,750)
Carried forward	1,000	550

	31 March 1982 Value £	Old rules Cost £
Sale proceeds $30,000 \times \dfrac{5,000}{11,000}$	13,636	13,636
Less: 31 March 1982 value/cost		(2,750)
$(5,000 \times 75p)$	(3,750)	
Unindexed gain	9,886	10,886
Less: indexation allowance on 31 March 1982 value		
$\dfrac{144.9 - 79.4}{79.4} = 0.825 \times 3,750$	(3,094)	(3,094)
Gain	6,792	7,792
Chargeable gain	6,792	

Net gains 1994/95 = £6,792

8 Paul

a) Disposal of shares in XY Ltd – Pool A

	No of shares	Value £
B/f at 5 April 1985	–	–
Acquisition May 1985	2,000	3,500
Bonus issue	500	–
	2,500	3,500
Operative event May 1988		
Indexation $3,500 \times \dfrac{106.2 - 95.2}{95.2}$		404
		3,904
Disposal May 1988	(1,000)	
£3,904 × 1000/2500		(1,562)
	1,500	2,342
Operative event March 1995		
Indexation $2,342 \times \dfrac{145.0 - 106.2}{106.2}$		856
		3,198
Disposal March 1994		
£3,198 × 1000/1500	(1,000)	(2,132)
Carry forward	500	1,066

TAX PLANNING

	£
Disposal value	2,600
Less: indexed cost	(2,132)
Chargeable gain	468

b) Disposal of preference shares in CD Ltd.
   Market value of holding in CD Ltd after re-organisation.

	£
2,500 ordinary shares of 50p @ 80p	2,000
2,000 10% preference shares of £1 @ 90p	1,800
£1,000 debentures @ 90p £1	900
Total	4,700

Cost of original holding is apportioned to the above items in proportion to their respective values after the re-organisation.

	£
Disposal value of 1,500 preference shares	2,100
Less: cost $4,500 \times \dfrac{1,800}{4,700} \times \dfrac{1,500}{2,000}$	(1,292)
Unindexed gain	808
Less: indexation allowance	
$\dfrac{145.2 - 96.7}{96.7} = 0.502$	
$1,292 \times 0.502$	(649)
Chargeable gain	159

c) The racehorse is a wasting chattel and is therefore exempt from capital gains tax.

Total gains for 1994/95 (468 + 159)   £627

No entry is necessary on Paul's tax return.

CHAPTER 8 *Self test questions*

1. A transfer of value is any disposition made by a person (the transferor) as a result of which the value of his estate immediately after the disposition is less than it would be but for the disposition.

2. Dispositions with non-gratuitous intent; for family maintenance; allowable for IT and CT; to trust for the benefit of employees.

3. Property other than chargeable property, that is, outwith scope of IHT.

4. Includes persons domiciled in UK in previous three years + persons resident for IT in UK in 17 of the last 20 fiscal years.

5. Transferor may make any number of lifetime gifts of (maximum) £250 per person per fiscal year.

6. Transferor must have sufficient income remaining to maintain a normal standard of living: here 'normal' implies some degree of regularity or pattern.

7. The average rate of tax suffered on the estate on death.

8. Where more than one party is responsible for paying the tax on the estate, each part of the estate suffers tax at the average rate rather than one part being preferred to another and bearing tax at a lower rate.

9. No.

10. Valuation reliefs, transferee reliefs, then transferor reliefs.

11. Yes, including the annual exemption.

12. £3,000 deducted chronologically from transfers in fiscal year after all other exemptions. Unused portion may be carried forward to next fiscal year and used after annual exemption of that year.

13. Dear Mr and Mrs Alderson,
    Thank you for your recent enquiry.

    a) Under inheritance tax, lifetime gifts fall into three categories:
       i) exempt;
       ii) potentially exempt; or
       iii) chargeable.

Exempt lifetime gifts

These are gifts which are not chargeable for inheritance tax purposes and include gifts to spouses, for the public benefit and to charities. It also includes a small gifts exemption and exemption for normal expenditure out of income.

Potentially exempt lifetime gifts

These are outright gifts by one individual to another (or to certain types of trusts including an accumulation and maintenance trust and an interest in possession trust but not including a discretionary trust) which are not otherwise exempt. They will not be liable to tax when made and will not become liable to tax provided that the donor survives seven years after making the gift. They are potentially exempt transfers (PETs) as they will become chargeable if the donor dies within seven years.

Chargeable lifetime transfers

These are transfers by an individual which are not exempt and which are not PETs. They include gifts to discretionary trusts. A tax liability will arise at the time of the gift at half the rate of tax that would apply on death. The rate of tax is determined by the cumulative total of such transfers over the previous seven years. The value of the transfer is the amount by which the estate of the donor is depleted. There is an annual exemption and other exemptions and reliefs which apply on specified occasions. If the donor dies within seven years, there will be an additional charge to tax based on the difference between the tax that would arise on the death scale at the date of death and the tax that arose at the date of the gift.

Death

On the death of an individual, tax is calculated on:

i) the cumulative total of both chargeable and potentially exempt transfers within the seven years prior to death; and
ii) the estate at the date of death;

using the full tax rates at the date of death.

Any relief given to lifetime transfers will be retained, although, in some cases, there may be amendments such as business and agricultural property relief. There is provision for the transfer values to be amended in certain circumstances if the value of the property has materially changed.

All transfers are charged to tax chronologically so that the earlier ones will bear a lower rate of tax than the later ones. A reduction is available (taper relief) for transfers more than three years before death and in all cases, any tax paid at the date of the original gift will be set off against this liability. Death is the final transfer.

b) Proposed gifts

Both the gift to your granddaughter and the transfer into the accumulation and maintenance trust will be PETs. Providing Mr Alderson lives for seven years from the date of the gift, there will be no liability to tax.

The gift to the charity is exempt and there are no inheritance tax implications.

The transfer into the discretionary trust is chargeable and if the amount transferred after deducting any exemptions available (such as the annual exemption) exceeds the nil rate band – £150,000 currently – inheritance tax will be payable. If you intend to make this transfer as well as those mentioned above, this transfer should be made first to ensure best use of the annual exemption.

I hope this summarises the position for you.

Yours sincerely,

14 a) Norman

		£	Gross gift £	Tax £	Net gift £
Brought forward at December 1994			80,000		
Tax/Net restated @ 1994/95 rates				Nil	80,000
3 December 1994 Cash to Peter		10,000	–	Nil	–
Less: annual exemption 1994/95		(3,000)			
annual exemption 1993/94		(3,000)			
PET		4,000			
			80,000	Nil	80,000
5 December 1994 Discretionary trust		80,000	82,500	2,500	80,000
Net transfer (Norman to pay tax)					
70,000 @ Nil = Nil					
10,000 @ 20/(100–20) = 2,500					
Carried forward			162,500		

				Gross gift £	Tax £	Net gift £
18 December 1994	Car to wife – exempt (spouse)			–	–	–
				162,500	–	–
21 December 1994	Watch to grandson – exempt as small gift (under £250)			–	–	–
		c/f		162,500	–	–

b/f £162,500

			£	Gross gift £	Tax £	Net gift £
23 December 1994	Flat to interest in possession trust	PET	35,000	–	–	–
30 December 1994	Cash to god-daughter		2,000			
	Marriage exemption		(1,000)			
		PET	1,000	–	–	–
Carried forward				162,500		

b) Assumed death – March 1998

	£
Chargeable transfers brought forward	162,500
Less: February 1988 transfer outwith seven years	(80,000)
	82,500
PET's now chargeable (4,000 + 35,000 + 1,000)	40,000
Estate on death	180,000
	302,500

IHT on death – lifetime transfers

	£	£
Brought forward		80,000
3 December 1994 Cash to Peter		4,000
		84,000
Tax @ Nil%	Nil	
5 December 1994 Discretionary trust (as above)		82,500
		166,500
Tax @ rate applicable on death		
66,000 @ Nil%	Nil	
16,500 @ 40%	6,600	
	6,600	
Taper relief 3–4 years 20%	(1,320	
	5,280	
Less: tax paid originally	(2,500)	
Payable by trustees	2,780	
18 December 1994 exempt		–
21 December 1994 exempt		–
23 December 1994 PET now chargeable		35,000
		201,500
Tax @ rate applicable on death		
35,000 @ 40%	14,000	
Taper relief 3–4 years 20%	(2,800)	
	11,200	
Less: tax paid originally	–	
Payable by trustees	11,200	
30 December 1994 PET now chargeable		1,000
		202,500
Tax @ rate applicable on death		
1,000 @ 40%	400	
Taper relief 3–4 years 20%	(80)	
	320	
Less: tax paid originally	–	
Payable by god-daughter	320	
Less: transfer in February 1988		(80,000)
		122,500
IHT on death – estate		180,000
		302,500
27,500 @ Nil%	Nil	
152,500 @ 40%	61,000	

Payable by executors of estate.

c) The inheritance advantages of making further lifetime gifts would include the following:
   i) the use of the annual, small gifts and other exemptions;
   ii) possible use of normal exemption out of income for assets that would otherwise increase the value of the estate;
   iii) appreciation in value of assets from date of lifetime transfer to death is kept out of estate even if death does occur within seven years;
   iv) taper relief if death more than three years after gift.

CHAPTER 9 *Self test questions*

1 £3,225 [£10,000 @ 30.5) + (6/12 x 3.5% × 10,000)] with an income tax liability of 25% or 40% of £175.

2 Lower of quarter-up value (165p) and average of high/low marked bargains (164p), that is, 164p.

3 Number of shares of transferor as a proportion of total number of shares including related property.

4 No claim can be made unless the difference between the sale proceeds and the probate value is at least £1,000 or 5% of the probate value, if less.

5 APR @ 50% × 30% of 50% × 200,000 = 15,000
   BPR @ 100% × 50% × 200,000 = 100,000
   Whether BPR would be available on the excess of the value of agricultural property (£100,000) over the agricultural value (£30,000) will depend on the nature of the company's business.

6

	Gross gift £	Tax £	Net gift £
Brought forward at April 1984	173,000		
Tax/Net restated @ 1990/91 rates		9,000	164,000
128,000 @ Nil% = Nil			
45,000 @ 20% 9,000			

23 April 1990 Cash to Tom		£82,000		
AE 1990/91		(3,000)	Nil	
PET		79,000		
1 July 1990 Shares to Bob			173,000	9,000	164,000
(120,000 – 50,000)		70,000		
Business property relief 100%		(70,000)		
PET (Note 1)		Nil		
Carried forward			173,000	
Less: transfers at 5 April 1984			(173,000)	
Carried forward			Nil	
10 April 1992 Shares to Jack (Note 2)		100,000		
Business property relief 100%		(100,000)		
PET		Nil		
25 May 1992 Cash to daughter –		25,000		
marriage exemption		(5,000)		
AE 1992/93		(3,000)		
1991/92		(3,000)		
PET		14,000		
			Nil	

Death – May 1994 £
Chargeable transfers brought forward –
PETs chargeable (79,000 + 14,000) 93,000
Estate on death 160,000
  253,000

IHT on death – lifetime transfers £
Brought forward 173,000
23 April 1990: cash to Tom 79,000
  252,000
Tax @ rate applicable on death
79,000 @ 40% 31,600
Tapier relief 4–5 years 40% (12,640)
Tax originally paid
Payable by Tom 18,960

1 July 1990: shares to Bob (as above)
  (assuming further conditions satisfied) 252,000
Less: transfers at 5 April 1984 (173,000)
  79,000

TAX PLANNING

		£
b/f		79,000
10 April 1992: shares to Jack (as above)		
(assuming further conditions satisfied)		Nil
		79,000
25 May 92: cash to daughter		14,000
		93,000

	£
Tax @ rate applicable on death 20,000 @ Nil%	Nil
Tapier relief 0–3 years 0%	
Less: tax paid originally	
Payable by daughter	Nil

		£
IHT on death – estate		160,000
57,000 @ Nil%		253,000
103,000 @ 40%	41,200	
Less: quick succession relief original tax × 60%	(9,900)	
(death within 2–3 years) Note 3		
Payable by executors	31,300	

Notes

1. As hold-over relief was claimed no capital gains tax liability arises. If a liability to capital gains tax had arisen, no account of it would have been taken for inheritance tax purposes, in determining the amount by which the transferor's estate was diminished.
2. The related property provisions do not apply when the people concerned are siblings.
3. When original transfer is on death, the transferee's estate is increased by the full amount of the legacy and therefore the restriction (net transfer/gross transfer) is not necessary.

7 a) **Related property**

Property is related property if it is owned by the individual's spouse or if it has been the subject of an exempt transfer to a charity, political party or national heritage body, by the individual or his spouse and is, or has been owned, by that body at any time within the previous five years.

For inheritance tax purposes, property which is related is valued as a proportion of the total value of all related property, if this gives a higher value than its unrelated value.

Business property relief

For business property relief to apply, the property must:
i) be relevant business property; and
ii) have been owned by the transferor through the two years preceding the transfer or have replaced similar property which would have qualified for relief – together they must have been owned for at least two out of the five years preceding the transfer.
iii) Further conditions apply if the original transfer was a PET and death occurs within seven years (and if the original transfer was chargeable and additional tax becomes due): the transferee must still own the property (unless he or she has died in the interim) and the property must still be relevant business property.

b) **Cornworthy Ltd**

Transfer by Brenda Cornworthy

	Before		After	
	No shares	Value £	No shares	Value £
Shares held by Brenda	3,000		750	
Shares held by trust				
(Brenda life tenant)	2,250		2,250	
Shares held by Alan	6,000		6,000	
	11,250	252,000	9,000	172,800
	(75%)		(60%)	

Value of Brenda's holding

			£
Before transfer	$\frac{5,250}{11,250}$ × 252,000		117,600
After transfer	$\frac{3,000}{9,000}$ × 172,800		57,600
			60,000
Less: business property relief 100%			(60,000)
			Nil

	£
Death of Henry Cornworthy.	
No related property – 2,250 shares (15%)	34,500
Less: business property relief 50%	(17,250)
	17,250

ANSWERS TO CHAPTER 9

Death of Alan Cornworthy

	Before		After	
	No shares	Value £	No shares	Value £
Shares held by Brenda	750		750	
Shares held by trust (Brenda life tenant)	2,250		2,250	
Shares held by Alan	6,000		–	
	9,000 (60%)	172,800	3,000 (20%)	38,800
Value of Alan's holding	$\frac{6,000}{9,000} \times 172,800$		115,200	
Less: business property relief 100%			(115,200)	
			Nil	

CHAPTER 10 *Self test questions*

1 a) If full consideration is given for the interest enjoyed.

   b) If the property is an interest in land and his present enjoyment of it is not by virtue of interest reserved but as a result of a change in his circumstances and is voluntarily provided as provision for a dependent relative.

2 No, with the exclusion of the annual exemption and normal gifts out of income.

3 On a claim to the Board by the taxpayer.

4 a) If an undertaking is not observed.
   b) If the person beneficially entitled dies or disposes of the property.

5 An election must be made within two years from death.

6 a) As the first candelabrum was sold to Mary at market value, this could be argued to be a disposition such as would take place between unconnected persons in a bargain at arm's length. However, upon the gift of the second candelabrum being made, it is likely that they would be treated as associated operations.

   Both transfers would be deemed to take place at the date of the later transfer, and a transfer of value of £12,000 (20,000 – 8,000) would be deemed to be made at that date. However, as it is a gift from one individual to another, it will be a PET and no tax will be chargeable unless death occurs within seven years.

   b) If they continue to live in the house after it is gifted to their son it will be treated as a PET.

   On John's death the house will be included in his estate. If it ceased to be subject to a reservation in the seven years prior to death, a PET will be treated as made at this date, which will become chargeable at the date of death. A potential double charge to tax may arise if the original transfer also becomes chargeable – there are provisions to avoid this.

   c) There would be no gift with reservation in the following cases:
   i) James gives full consideration for his occupation of the cottage by paying a full market rent for the use of it.
   ii) James's occupation of the cottage results from an unforeseen change in his circumstances at a time when he is unable to maintain himself through old age or infirmity and is reasonable provision by the donee for the care of the donor.

7 a) Paintings – National Heritage property
   The sale in 1989 constituted a breach of undertaking for purposes of the conditional exemption.
   The painting donated to the National Gallery would be exempt as a gift for the public benefit, the National Gallery being a recognised body.
   The painting given to his daughter would be a PET.

   b) William – estate on death.

		£
Personalty		240,000
Land for forestry		100,000
Timber	60,000	
Conditionally exempt	(60,000)	–
		340,000
Gift to charity		(50,000)
Estate on death		290,000

CHAPTER 11 *Self test questions*

1 This is best explained with a table:

	Short term	Medium term	Long term
Low risk	Savings	Savings	
Medium risk		Investment	Investment
High risk	Speculation		

2 Almost. Regular savings and lump sum investment are catered for together with targeted investment – foreign, sector, growth or income – all of which enable diversification. The fluctuation in the unit values may make them unacceptable to the risk-averse investor.

3 All have their uses but it is the endowment policy which provides growth and security for the regular investor.

4 The ability to make withdrawals up to 5% tax free from the fund.

5 Advantages; instantly available, regulated under the Consumer Credit Act, fixed rate of interest. Disadvantages; expensive, inflexible.

6 No entitlement exists except by arrangement. With prior arrangement – reasonable interest rate. No prior arrangement – penal interest rate.

CHAPTER 12 *Self test questions*

1 Accountants may register with an SRO such as FIMBRA or direct with the SIB. Such separate arrangements are unlikely.

2 Yes, but only if the accountant is a sole practitioner. Individuals within firms will not be authorised.

3 Not necessarily. Clients peceived as 'sophisticated' will not require the same standard of care as the likely general client.

4 Yes. Sufficient enquiries should be made to be satisfied that the money is legitimately obtained. If doubt remains the authorities should be informed.

CHAPTER 13 *Self test questions*

1 The marginal tax positions will have a considerable effect on the range of suitable investment which could be considered.

2 It is important because existing holdings may be inappropriate; disposals may attract capital gains tax for the wealthier investor; the overall portfolio must be considered in order to achieve balance and not just the addition.

3 They are investments which can be turned into cash within a reasonable time – a notice period of possibly up to a year will usually attract better returns.

4 Diversification of investments should ensure that the failure of one sector will be compensated for by investments in other sectors. This is an essential feature of any portfolio.

CHAPTER 14 *Self test questions*

1 35%

2 Trust administration expenses are deductible: a) from dividend income (leaving it chargeable to tax at 20%; and b) from other income (leaving this income chargeable to tax at 25%)

3 a) The beneficiaries must become absolutely entitled or get an interest in possession before attaining the age of 25.
   b) No interest in posession must currently exist in the property.
   c) Either not more than 25 years must have elapsed since the trust was created or all the beneficiaries must have a common grandparent.

4 Principal charge – on each tenth anniversary.
  Exit charge – whenever funds leave the trust.

5 Income from settlements, where the settlor or the settlor's spouse retains an interest in the settled property, will be treated as income of the settlor.

6   At the time when the trust was created in 1984, the transfer of the share portfolio and cash by A to a discretionary trust was a gift at market value of £200,000. A liability to both capital gains tax (gift relief may have been available) and capital transfer tax would have arisen – depending upon the size of the shareholdings and the type of investments, business property relief may have been available.

When half of the shares were allocated to a sub-trust (interest in possession) in 1988, this did not constitute a chargeable disposal by the trustees for capital gains tax as Alan did not gain absolute entitlement. The creation of an interest in possession is, however, a chargeable transfer for purposes of inheritance tax. Business property relief may be available. As it is a discretionary trust, A's cumulative position in 1984 immediately prior to the creation of the trust (over the previous seven years) for capital transfer tax becomes the trust's opening position. The value of the transfer into the trust (£200,000) is treated as an 'assumed chargeable transfer of value' and the effective rate of tax is calculated using the lifetime rates applicable in 1988 at the time the sub-trust was created (the tax as a percentage of £200,000). This rate at 30% is then applied to the chargeable transfer of value and restricted by x/40ths where x is the number of quarters (periods of three months) from creation of the trust to the date of transfer.

The transfer to Alison would give rise to both a capital gains liability (at 35% after annual exemption of £2,500) and an inheritance tax liability – calculated as described above but using 1989 lifetime tax rates. The grossing up provisions may apply depending on whether the trustees or Alison is to pay the tax.

The death of Alan represents the death of a life tenant in an interest in possession trust. The remainder will go to his children at the age of 25. This is not a disposal for capital gains tax purposes (death of a life tenant plus the funds still remain settled) but the value of the assets will be uplifted to market value at date of death. The underlying value of Alan's life interest would form a part of Alan's estate on death but the inheritance tax (at his 'estate rate') would be payable by the trustees from the sub-trust.

QUESTION BANK – *personal taxation and financial planning*

1   a)   Taxation notes on employment package.
   1   **Approved contributory pension scheme.** Contribution payable by Deborah is deductible from her salary for tax purposes.
       The employer's contribution is not assessable on Deborah as additional emoluments.
   2   Company car. This would be regarded as a benefit in kind (additional emoluments) to Deborah since her emoluments from employment will be in excess of £8,500. The amount of the benefit in kind will be determined by reference to the manufacturer's list price of the car at the time it was first registered. The full value of the benefit is 35% of the list price. This is then discounted by one-third where business mileage exceeds 2,500 miles per annum, and by two-thirds if business mileage exceeds 18,000 miles per annum. If the car is four years old or more by the end of the year of assessment, the benefit is then reduced by one-third. The benefit covers the provision of the car and all running expenses except fuel for private mileage. Any contributions made by the employee for the private use of the car will reduce the benefit on a pound for pound basis.
       If fuel is provided for private mileage, this gives rise to an additional benefit. The charge is calculated by reference to a table and varies according to the cylinder capacity of the car and whether the fuel is petrol or diesel. The table benefit is unaffected by the amount of business mileage undertaken.
   3   **Staff canteen.** Provided that the canteen is open to all staff on the same basis, the cost of meals is not an assessable benefit to Deborah.
   4   **Suggestion scheme.** Any amounts paid under such a scheme are not assessable as emoluments provided that taking part in the scheme is not part of the contract of employment and that the amounts paid are reasonable.
   5   **Reimbursement for business entertaining.** Business entertaining costs identifiable in the employer's records are disallowed to the employer. The reimbursement will however be regarded as a taxable emolument to Deborah in the first instance unless the employer has a dispensation. This means that the employer will enter the amount of reimbursed expenses on form P11D and Deborah will need to make a claim under ICTA 1988 s. 198, for expenses incurred wholly, exclusively and necessarily in the performance of the duties of the employment in her tax return at the end of the fiscal year (both these actions are avoided if the employer has a dispensation).
   6   **Removal expenses.** Provided that they do not exceed £8,000, removal costs, including legal fees and estate agents' fees, will not be taxable on Deborah. Subsidised costs of moving to a higher- cost area are taxable from 1993/94.
   7   **Provision of company flat.** Deborah's occupation of the flat will not be 'representative' and therefore a taxable benefit will arise to Deborah.
       The amount of the benefit per fiscal year will be the gross rateable value of the flat together with the day-to-day expenses of the flat, if any, met by the firm. An additional charge arises if the cost of the accommodation exceeds £75,000. The additional benefit is computed by multiplying the excess over £75,000 by the official rate of interest in force at the start of the fiscal year.

8 **Beneficial loan**. A loan at nil or low interest rates is a taxable benefit.

   The amount of the benefit will be calculated as the difference between the official interest rate – estimate 10% – and the actual interest rate paid on the loans.

   Lower rate tax relief in respect of the interest paid on the first £30,000 of the loan to purchase your principal private residence will be given by means of a tax credit.

b) Estimated Schedule E assessment 1994/95

	£	£
Salary	13,750	
Less: 6% superannuation	(825)	
		12,925
Employer's superannuation 4%		–
Canteen (see above)		–
BUPA		260
Company car:		
£7,200 × 35% =	2,520	
Over 4 yrs (2,520 × 1/3)	(840)	
Running expenses	–	
Contribution (£20 × 12)	(240)	
	1,440	
Private fuel – paid in full	–	
		1,440
Flat – gross rateable value	500	
cleaning costs	320	
Furniture – 3,000 @ 20%	600	
Video – 700 @ 20%	140	
		1,560
Course and examination fees		–
Removal expenses		–
Overseas travel, subsistence and medical insurance		–
		16,185
Less:		
Subscription to professional body	70	
Subscription to City Club (Note 1)	–	
Professional clothing	–	
Travel home	–	
Hotel bills for holiday	–	
		(70)
Schedule E assessment		£16,115

Note 1 Disallowable as not wholly, exclusively and necessarily incurred in performance of duties

2 i) **Event giving rise to a charge**

   The sale or gift of chargeable assets, other than cash, during a persons's lifetime may give rise to a chargeable gain on which capital gains tax may result. In certain specified cases (such as business assets), on gift, the gain can be held over.

   The gift of any asset, including cash, during lifetime or on death which is not an exempt or a potentially exempt transfer may give rise to an inheritance tax charge.

ii) **The amount chargeable**

   For capital gains tax, the amount chargeable is the chargeable gain, which is in most cases the difference between the value at disposal and the value at 31 March 1982, or if acquired later, the cost, less an allowance for inflation since 1982.

   For inheritance tax the amount chargeable is the amount by which the donor's estate is diminished by virtue of the gift. This is increased by the amount of any inheritance tax if this is borne by the donor.

iii) **The rates of tax**

   Capital gains tax is charged at the individual's marginal rate of income tax in the fiscal year on net gains exceeding £5,800, that is, as if it were the individual's top slice of income.

   Inheritance tax is charged at 20% on chargeable lifetime transfers and at 40% on assets transferred on death or within seven years of death (although taper relief exists to reduce the tax if the gift is more than three years before death). No inheritance tax arises on the first £150,000 of cumulative chargeable transfers.

iv) **Main exemptions and reliefs**

   For capital gains tax the main exemptions include private motor cars, chattels with a value at sale of less than £6,000, and the taxpayer's principal private residcence. There is also an annual exemption of £5,800 per fiscal year.

   Retirement relief is available to reduce the gains arising on the sale or transfer of businesses and shares in a family company (exempt up to £250,000 and half of any excess between £250,000 and £1,000,000).

For inheritance tax, gifts to charities, political parties, or of assets to national bodies for the public benefit are exempt without limit. There is an annual exemption of £3,000 per fiscal year and, if not used, this can be carried forward to the next fiscal year. There is an exemption for gifts on marriage and an exemption for small gifts (maximum £250 per person per fiscal year). Any gifts which constitute normal expenditure out of income are exempt.

In addition, there is business property relief of 50 or 100% for transfers of business assets or shareholdings in certain companies.

v) **Phasing of disposals**

Phasing of disposals for capital gains tax purposes can be useful to make use of annual exemptions which cannot be carried forward or back. It may also be useful to gain maximum advantage from any losses arising which can only be carried forward and never back.

Similarly for inheritance tax, the phasing of disposals is useful to take advantage of the annual exemption which can only be carried forward one year. Gifts are cumulated over a seven-year period and therefore the exempt band of £150,000 renews itself after seven years. It may be useful to spread gifts over a period of years to make maximum use of this feature. A gift that is made regularly may also be established as a normal gift out of income and therefore not liable to inheritance tax.

vi) **Lifetime or death disposals**

For capital gains tax there is no advantage in making lifetime gifts. Even in the few instances where gift relief is still available, the effect is merely to postpone the tax liability and transfer it to the donee – it will eventually crystallise. Disposals on death are not chargeable and the beneficiary inherits the asset at market value with no associated tax liability.

For inheritance tax it is advantageous to make lifetime gifts as the majority of these are not chargeable when made and become completely exempt if the donor survives the date of the gift by seven years. Even if the donor does not survive the full seven years, the value transferred is the value at the date of transfer and not the value at death – there is a saving for all appreciating assets – as well as the possibility of taper relief on any tax becoming chargeable.

Any chargeable lifetime transfers only suffer tax at half the death rates and no further tax becomes chargeable if the donor survives seven years. If he or she does not survive seven years taper relief is available on any further tax liability.

Certain exemptions are not available on death; examples are marriage and the annual exemption.

vii) **Emigration**

For capital gains tax purposes it would be beneficial to become not resident and ordinarily resident in the UK as he would not then be chargeable on disposals of property situated in the UK after the date of permanent departure.

For inheritance tax purposes residence and ordinary residence do not matter, it would be necessary to become not UK domiciled. Domicile has a special definition for inheritance tax purposes and Charles would remain UK domiciled for at least three years after his departure. At that time any property still located in the UK would remain chargeable to inheritance tax.

Possible actions to take

i) The dispositions in his wife's will may be varied, so that the property (in total within the nil rate band) passes to a beneficiary of his choice. This would use her exempt band and would not result in any inheritance tax being chargeable. No liability to capital gains tax would arise. The time limit is two years from the date of death.
ii) Making dispositions from Charles's own estate using the nil rate band and annual and other exemptions. If the assets disposed of were those exempt from capital gains tax no liability would arise to capital gains tax – car, chattels, cash, principal private residence.
iii) A gift of the shareholding in the family trading company. The capital gains tax would probably be covered by retirement relief. There would be an entitlement to 100% business property relief providing the relevant conditions were satisfied and inheritance tax would not be chargeable immediately as the transfer would be a PET. In addition the shareholding is likely to be an appreciating asset and therefore the earlier it is transferred the better from the inheritance tax point of view.
iv) Gifts to charity may be made at any time.
v) Business property relief may also be available on the shares in the supplier company providing the relevant conditions are fulfilled, although these would attract a capital gains liability if transferred during his lifetime which could be deferred by claiming gift relief.

3 a) i) If Ms Needle makes an immediate outright gift of the shares to Mr Simper, the gift would be a disposal for capital gains tax purposes and a lifetime transfer for inheritance tax purposes.

Capital gains tax

The gift would firstly give rise to a chargeable gain of £356,000 (370,000 – 14,000).

Ms Needle would be eligible for retirement relief in full because she is a full-time director of the company and has been one for more than ten years; the company is a family trading company – she owns personally more than 5% of the equity; and she is over 55. Retirement relief is given on the proportion of the gain reflected by the ratio of chargeable business assets to chargeable assets of the company as follows:

	Chargeable business assets £	Chargeable non-business assets £
Buildings	160,000	–
Plant and machinery (exempt chattels)	–	–
Investments	–	80,000
Working capital (exempt assets)	–	–
Goodwill	100,000	–
	260,000	80,000

Retirement relief will therefore be available on 76.47% (260,000/340,000) of the gain.

Ms Needle will also be eligible for gift relief – being a gift of shares in an unquoted family trading company to a UK resident individual – that is, the chargeable gain on the business proportion of Mildew's chargeable assets remaining after retirement relief can be held over if both Ms Needle and Mr Simper make a joint claim. The held-over gain will be deducted from Mr Simper's base cost: that is, from £240,000.

Gain eligible for retirement relief	£
£356,000 × 76.47%	272,233
Retirement relief: first £250,000	(250,000)
	22,233
50% of balance	(11,117)
Chargeable	11,116
Held over	(11,116)
Gain not eligible for retirement relief	83,767
(356,000 – 272,233)	
Total chargeable 1994/95	83,767
Less: Losses brought forward	(50,000)
Less: Annual exemption	(5,800)
	27,967

Mr Simper would acquire the shares at their market value at the date of the date of the gift less the held-over gain, that is, £358,884 (370,000 – 11,116) and any inheritance tax he subsequently becomes liable to as a result of the gift will be deductible for capital gains tax purposes on a disposal of the shares.

Inheritance tax

The transfer is a PET; therefore there would be no inheritance tax liability unless Ms Needle were to die within seven years (before 1 January 2002). As the shares are a controlling interest in an unquoted trading company, 100% business property relief will be available except on the proportion of their value attributable to non-business and excepted assets.

	£
Total assets (300,000 + 100,000)	400,000
Non-business assets (investments)	(80,000)
Eligible for 100% BPR	320,000
Value of shares transferred	370,000
BPR 100% × 320/400 × £370,000	(296,000)
	74,000
Annual exemption 1994/95	(3,000)
PET 1 January 1995	71,000

Ms Needle has already made a PET on 1 February 1994
The amount of PET would be:

Gift 1 February 1994	107,000
Marriage exemption	(2,500)
Annual exemption 1993/94	(3,000)
Annual exemption 1992/93	(3,000)
PET 1 February 1994	98,500

If Ms Needle were to die before 1 February 2001 the inheritance tax position would be as follows:

	£
Chargeable lifetime transfers	Nil
PETs now chargeable (BPR as above providing Mr Simper still owns shares) (71,000 + 98,500)	169,500
Estate on death	?
Value on which inheritance tax chargeable at date of death	

The nil rate band of £150,000 would be entirely used against the PETs now chargeable, leaving £19,500 of later PET to be charged to inheritance tax at 40%, that is, £7,800 less taper relief at the appropriate rate depending on the number of years which have elapsed from 1 January 1995 to the date of death (payable by Mr Simper).

If Ms Needle were to die after 1 February 2001 but before 1 January 2002, the PET on 1 February 1994 would no longer be cumulated (seven years having elapsed).

	£
Chargeable lifetime transfers	Nil
PET's now chargeable (BPR as above providing Mr Simper still owns shares)	71,000
Estate on death	?
Value on which inheritance tax chargeable at date of death	

The PET would be entirely within the Nil rate band and no inheritance tax would be payable by Mr Simper in respect of the gift.

ii) If the shares were held by Ms Needle until her death on 31 March 1996, there would be no capital gains tax implications as no capital gains tax would arise on death. Mr Simper will be deemed to acquire the shares at probate value. The value of the shares is however likely to have increased given the upward trend of the Mildew's profitability – it is assumed that Mr Simper has not yet become involved in the management of the company since he does not have the shares in the company.

The value of the shares will be included in Ms Needle's death estate less 100% business property relief on all assets except the investments – the increase in the value of the shares will probably be reflected in the value of goodwill.

	£
Chargeable lifetime transfers	Nil
PETs now chargeable (1 February 1994)	98,500
Estate on death (including shares less BPR)	?
Value on which inheritance tax chargeable at date of death	

The nil rate band of £150,000 will be set initially against the PET with the balance (£51,500) available for offset against the estate on death, the balance of the death estate being chargeable at 40%.

b) By making a lifetime gift, Ms Needle reduces her death estate by the value of the shares (net of BPR). If she survives seven years there will be no inheritance tax, saving 40% of this value. If she dies within seven years, any inheritance tax liability will be reduced by the value of the shares at the date of gift being lower, the annual exemptions available and taper relief.

From a capital gains point of view, the lifetime gift does not give rise to any immediate tax liabilities. The earlier date of transfer and the held-over gain reduce Mr Simper's base cost but the heldover gain will not crystallise until Mr Simper disposes of the shares which seems many years away and is likely to be covered by his retirement relief in any case.

From a tax point of view the lifetime gift seems preferable. Other considerations would be Ms Needle's health and presumably her need to retire from the company. The delay in Mr Simper receiving the shares may prevent him from becoming involved in the management of the company.

4 a) Mr Gog will be resident and ordinarily resident in the UK in 1994/95, since he has been here since 1979 and does not appear to leave the UK for any significant periods. The fact that he intends to return to Ruritania would imply that his domicile remains Ruritanian for income tax purposes (domicile of origin).

The implications of being UK resident and ordinarily resident but non-UK domiciled are that his liability to UK income tax is restricted where the income arises from foreign possessions or securities (assessed under Schedule D Case IV and V), to sums actually remitted to the UK out of such income or gains. Assuming that the duties of his employment are carried out wholly or in part in the UK and/or that his employer is UK resident, then his Schedule E liability will be under Case I on the amount arising.

a) **Mr Gog – Income tax liability 1994/95**

	£
Schedule E Case I	29,350
Schedule D Case I	–
Schedule D Case III (note 1)	2,800
Schedule D Case V (interest not remitted)	–
Schedule D Case V (note 2)	500
Statutory total income	32,650
Less: Personal allowance	(3,445)
Taxable income	29,205

Tax due:

	£
£3,000 at 20%	600
£20,700 at 25%	5,175
£5,505 at 40%	2,202
	7,977
Double tax relief, lower of:	
a) UK tax £500 at 40% = £200	
b) Foreign tax £100	(100)
PAYE tax suffered	(7,500)
	377

Notes

1. Depending on when income first arose on the 3.5% War Loan (1992/93 or 1993/94), 1994/95 will be either the second or third year of assessment. The second year of assessment will be on actual while the third year of assessment will be on preceding year basis with the option to elect for actual. As actual equals preceding year income, it is immaterial. £80,000 @ 3.5% = £2,800.

2. Assessments would normally be made on an established source of income under Schedule D Case V on remittances in the preceding tax year. In this case the source of income ceased in 1994/95 and therefore the assessment must be on actual remittances in 1994/95.

	£
2 (30 April and 31 May) × £300	600
Ruritanian tax 600 × 20%	(120)
Net income	480
Remitted (2 × £200)	400
Tax credit 120 × 400/480	100
Schedule D Case V	500

b) **Mr Gog – domicile (for IHT purposes)**

Domicile for inheritance tax purposes follows the common law rules except on certain occasions when it has a special definition. Under these common law principles, Mr Gog will have a domicile of origin in Ruritania – he has never exercised his right to have a domicile of choice in the UK. Under inheritance tax, domicile is extended to include any person who at the relevant time was:

a) domiciled in the UK at any time within the previous three years:
b) resident (for income tax purposes) in the UK for at least 17 out of the 20 fiscal years then ending.

The UK includes Scotland and Mr Gog currently appears to have been resident in the UK since 1979/80. As it is now 1994/95, he has been UK resident for 16 out of 20 years. For inheritance tax purposes, he is currently therefore non-UK domiciled.

If he remains in the UK, he will be caught under (b) above and will be regarded as UK domiciled for inheritance tax purposes. This will happen in 1995/96. By this time, he will have been UK resident for 17 out of the 20 fiscal years up to and including 1995/96.

c) **Mr Gog – transfer of assets 5 April 1995**

A non-UK domiciled person is only liable to UK inheritance tax on assets situated in the UK. Assets situated outside the UK belonging to a non-UK domiciled individual are excluded property. (The definition of excluded property also includes reversionary interests, and certain other specified property belonging to persons not UK domiciled not ordinarily resident in the UK. Mr Gog has no other assets fitting this definition.) As Mr Gog wishes to avoid any possibility of inheritance tax arising either immediately or on death within seven years, he must limit consideration of which assets to gift to

a) those situated outside the UK; or
b) those situated within the UK which would not exceed the 'nil rate band' for inheritance tax purposes.

Mr Gog also wishes to avoid capital gains tax. A non-UK domiciled but UK-resident individual is liable to capital gains tax on chargeable gains arising from the disposal of UK-situated assets and foreign assets if the gains are remitted to the UK. As he intends to gift the assets to his son, no gains are realised for remittance to the UK. His strategy must therefore be to gift assets which

a) are situated outside the UK; or
b) if situated in the UK will not give rise to a chargeable gain.

Mr Gog's only asset outside the UK is the deposit account with National Bank of Ruritania (£60,000) and this could be transferred into his son's name with no inheritance tax or capital gains tax consequences.

UK assets which are likely not to give rise to a chargeable gain are his bank account, 3.5% War Loan (exempt asset), the Ruritanian antique vase (chattel < £6,000: exempt) and the Scottish farm (see workings).

The inheritance tax 'nil rate band' is £150,000 and he has not yet used his annual exemptions for 1993/94 and 1994/95 of £3,000 per annum – he can therefore make transfers of value up to £156,000. The Scottish farm, tenanted, should attract agricultural property relief of 100% making the transfer value £Nil (100% of £116,000). The other assets will count at their current value and may total £156,000: with cash from UK account, and with the disposal of shares in Bah plc using the capital gains tax exemption (see workings).

Computation of gain on disposal of farm 5 April 1995

	31/3/82 £	Cost £
Disposal proceeds – MV	116,000	116,000
Allowable deductions	(40,000)	(95,000)
Unindexed gain	76,000	21,000
Less: indexation		
$95,000 \times \dfrac{145.2 - 79.4}{79.4}$ (0.829)	(76,000)	(21,000)
	–	–

The indexation (£78,755) has been restricted as it cannot create an allowable loss. There is an indexation loss of £2,755.

Computation of gain on disposal of shares in Bah plc 5 April 1995:

Consideration for 10,000 shares	150,000
Less: cost	(20,000)
Unindexed gain	130,000
Less: indexation	
$£20,000 \times \dfrac{145.2 - 95.5}{95.5}$	(10,408)
Total gain	119,592
Gain per share	11.96

The transfer will therefore be limited to 715 shares: (£5,800 + £2,755/£11.96).

d) **Mr Gog – inheritance tax on death before 6 April 2002**

Lifetime transfer 5/4/95	
Farm (assume owned by son at date of death	116,000
Less: APR 100% (untenanted)*	(116,000)
	Nil
3.5% War Loan	27,000
Antique vase	6,000
Shares in Bah plc 485 × £15	7,275
Cash	23,000
PET now chargeable	63,275
AE 1994/95	(3,000)
1993/94	(3,000)
Chargeable @ nil	57,275
Lifetime transfers:	57,275
Estate at death:	
Bah plc shares	
(10,000 – 715) × £15	139,275
	196,550
nil rate band	(150,000)
Chargeable at 40%	46,550
IHT due: £46,550 at 40%	18,620

This IHT will not be due if he transfers at least £50,000 to charity under his will.

100% APR is available if the transferor has vacant possession or the right to obtain it within the next 12 months.

5 a) The two gifts (1 September 1991 and 1 July 1992) which Richard had made in the seven years prior to his death were both potentially exempt transfers. On his death on 2 November 1994 they become chargeable transfers, bearing IHT as follows:

1 September 1991	£	£
Chargeable transfers bf		90,000
Current transfer of value	111,000	
Less: marriage exemption	(5,000)	
		106,000
		196,000
IHT at rate applicable @ death		
(150,000 – 90,000)	60,000 @ Nil	
	46,000 @ 40%	18,400
Less: taper relief 3-4 yrs 20%		(3,680)
Payable		14,720
1 July 1992		
bf		196,000
Current transfer of value	120,000	
(use sale price as lower than transfer price)		
Less: mortgage	(55,000)	
Less: APR (sold prior to death)	Nil	
	65,000	(150,000 – 55,000) 95,000
		291,000
IHT at rate applicable @ death		
	65,000 @ 40%	26,000
Less: taper relief 2-3 yrs	–	–
Payable		26,000
2 November 1994		
b/f (291,000 less 90,000 transferred Sep 1985)		201,000
Estate at death		321,000
IHT @ 40% × 321,000	128,400	522,000

b) If the personal representatives sell quoted shares within 12 months of Richard's death, then the aggregate selling price (before deducting costs of sale) can be substituted for the relevant probate values. If both the shares in Bluechip plc and in Giltedge plc were sold, the loss in value in Bluechip would be counteracted by the profit in Giltedge and no IHT saving would result. However, if the shares in Giltedge were retained for more than 12 months and those in Bluechip were sold the sale value would be £5,000 less than the probate value and an IHT saving of £5,000 @ 40% (£2,000) would result. No relief is available on the disposal of shares in Nobody Ltd as these are unquoted shares.

If the personal representatives sell land within four years of Richard's death, then the aggregate selling price is substituted for the relevant probate values. If both the private residence and the holiday home were sold there would be no overall reduction in probate value and therefore no tax saving. However, if only the holiday home is sold then the sale value would be £15,000 less than the estate value and an IHT saving of £6,000 (15,000 @ 40%) would result.

Realising assets to achieve a reduction in IHT is only usually worth while if the value of the asset has permanently fallen. It is probable that the executors would not be able to use the CGT losses (probate value plus indexation less sale proceeds) – if the asset had been passed directly to a beneficiary, the beneficiary would be able to realise capital losses in his own right with a consequential personal tax saving at the marginal rate of income tax.

c) If Boris and Christian varied Richard's will so that a proportion of the estate, equal to the exempt band, is transferred to Maria (£150,000) then IHT of £60,000 would be saved on Richard's death and on Maria's subsequent death the assets would presumably transfer to them IHT free (using her exempt band).

The main conditions which must be satisfied for the variation to be effective for IHT purposes are as follows:

▶ The variation must be within two years of death.
▶ It must be signed by all beneficiaries surrendering rights under the will.
▶ A written election for the variation to apply for IHT purposes must be made to the Inland Revenue within six months of its execution.
▶ No consideration must be received by the surrendering beneficiaries in respect of the variation.

d) Nigel must deliver an account to the Inland Revenue within 12 months of the end of the month of death, by 30 November 1995. The account should specify all the property comprised in the estate at the date of death. Probate cannot be granted until such an account has been delivered and the IHT due (other than that eligible for instalment relief) has been paid. Interest will run on IHT due from the end of the sixth month after death to the date of payment.

Instalment relief is available on land and certain holdings in unquoted companies, but interest still runs on unpaid IHT if the land/shares are not used for business purposes.

If Nigel does not pay the IHT due then the Inland Revenue may have recourse to the beneficiaries to the extent that they have received assets under the will; purchasers of land if the Inland Revenue have registered a charge against the land for IHT due; anybody who acts as an executor of an estate even if not so officially (executors de son tort).

6 a) Capital gains tax
Share in Bod Limited:

	Shares	Cost	Sale proceeds	Gain/loss
		£	£	£
Pool A (post 31 March 1982)				
At 5/4/85	1,200	1,800		
Indexation $\dfrac{94.8 - 86.7}{86.7}$		167		
		1,967		
Operative event 18 August 1985				
Indexation $\dfrac{95.5 - 94.8}{94.8}$		14		
Acquisition	600	3,000		
	1,800	4,981		
Operative event 5 April 1995				
Indexation $\dfrac{145.2 - 95.5}{95.5}$		2,592		
		7,573		
Disposal	(1,800)	(7,573)		
Disposal value (60% holding) 1,800 @ £25			45,000	37,427

	Shares	Cost	31 March 1982
		£	£
Pool B (pre 31 March 1982)			
6 September 1976	1,200	1,000	4,000
Disposal 5 April 1995	(200)	(167)	(667)
Carry foward 1,000	1,000	833	3,333

	31 March 1982	Cost	
	£	£	£
Disposal value (60% holding)			
200 @ £25	5,000	5,000	
MV 31 March 1982			
Cost	(667)	(167)	
	4,333	4,833	
Indexation			
$\dfrac{145.2 - 79.4}{79.4}$ (0.829) × 667	(553)	(553)	
	3,780	4,280	3,780
Carried forward			41,207

Brought forward £41,207			
Assignment of lease	£	£	£
Disposal value 1/5/94	210,000	210,000	
Cost 100,000 × $\dfrac{91,912}{99,289}$ (note 1)		(92,570)	
Value 31/3/82 120,000 × $\dfrac{91,912}{98.902}$	(111,519)		
Unindexed gain	98,481	117,430	
Indexation			
$\dfrac{142.9 - 79.4}{79.4}$ = 0.800 × £111,519	(89,215)	(89,215)	
	9,266	28,215	9,266
Brought foward (41,207) + 9,266)			50,473
Less: annual exemption			(5,800)
Chargeable gains 1994/95			44,673
Assuming a marginal rate of income tax of 40%			
Capital gains tax liability			17,869

TAX PLANNING

	Inheritance tax		Gross	Tax	Net
	Lifetime transfers		–	–	–
	Brought forward 1 May 1994				
	Lease	210,000			
	AE 94/95	(3,000)			
	AE 93/94	(3,000)			
					204,000
	Tax at 150,000 at Nil =	Nil			
	54,000 at 20/80 =	13,500			
		13,500	217,500	13,500	
			217,500	13,500	204,000
	Shares 5 April 1995 (note 2)	92,010			
	Cash paid	(10,000)			
					82,010
	BPR (note 3) 100%	(82,010)			
	PET	Nil	–	–	–

b) Capital gains tax gift relief is available on the assignment of the lease and on the transfer of the shares.

Lease

This is a gift to a discretionary trust on which there is an immediate inheritance tax liability. Both the donor and donee must jointly claim for the capital gain to be held over as no consideration was given, the whole gain (£9,266) can be held over, deducted from the donee's acquisition value (£210,000 – £9,266) for capital gains tax purposes. The gain will therefore crystallise when the donee disposes of the lease and in this case the inheritance tax liability on the transfer will be deductible from any gain on the subsequent disposal (it cannot turn a gain into a loss).

Shares

These are shares in an unquoted family company and are therefore also eligible for gift relief. In this case, consideration of £10,000 changed hands and therefore only part of the gain may be held over as follows:

		£
Gain on disposal of shares		37,427
		3,780
		41,207
Chargeable: Consideration	10,000	
Allowable deductions (excluding indexation)	(4,800)	
	(667)	
		(4,533)
Available for hold over		36,674

c) Inheritance implications – death 20 April 1995

		£
Cumulative lifetime transfers		217,500
PETs now chargeable		
Chargeable estate		
Shares 1,000 (see note 2)	20,000	
BPR (>25%) 100%	(20,000)	
	Nil	
Cash (assuming IHT £13,500 paid)	40,000	
		40,000
		257,500

	Gross	Tax		TPR £	Paid £	Payable £
1 May 1994	217,500	150,000 @ Nil =	Nil			
		67,500 @ 40% =	27,000			
			27,000	–	13,500	13,500
Death	40,000	@ 40%	16,000	–	–	16,000
	257,500					

d) Tax is payable six months after date of death in all cases, that is, 31 October 1995. It is possible to pay tax on transfers of land in ten equal instalments. The first instalment would be payable on the due date above.

Notes

1 Period of lease remaining at 1 May 94 was 34 years and 11 months: lease percentage is 91.156 + 11/12 (91.981 – 91.156) = 91.912

2 Related property provisions apply to value of shares

	Before shares	£	After shares	£	Transfer
His	3,000	75,000	1,000	16,000	59,000
Wife	1,000	16,000	1,000	16,000	
Related	4,000	146,680	2,000	36,000	110,680

Transfer value is the greater of the figures above, that is, £92,010.

$$(59{,}000 \text{ and } \frac{3{,}000}{4{,}000} \times 146{,}680 - \frac{1{,}000}{2{,}000} \times 36{,}000 = 92{,}010)$$

Death on 20 April 1995 would result in a transfer value of £36,000 − £16,000, that is, £20,000.

3 Business property relief has been put in at this point because no claim is necessary.

7 **George Rowe**

a) i) The gift of the shares into an accumulation and maintenance trust will be a potentially exempt transfer of value (PET). No inheritance tax liability will arise at the date of transfer or at a later date provided that George survives for seven years after the date of transfer. In these circumstances, the transfer will also be disregarded for IHT calculations on subsequent transfers of value or on death.

If George dies within the seven-year period, IHT will be payable as follows:

		£
Value of transfer		160,000
Less: AE 1994/95	3,000	
AE 1993/94	3,000	
		(6,000)
PET now chargeable		154,000

Assume rates at death = 1994/95
£150,000 @ Nil
4,000 @ 40%   £1,600
Less: taper relief if death 3–7 years
       after date of gift   (?)
       (20%/80% × 1,600)

The gift of shares into an accumulation and maintenance trust is a chargeable disposal of chargeable assets. It will be a transfer to a connected person (a person is connected to the trustees of a trust of which he is settlor) and as such will be deemed to take place at market value. It is assumed that the capital gain of £35,000 on disposal of the shares takes this and the indexation allowance into account. No holdover relief will be available for the gift as no inheritance tax liability arises on the transfer and the shares are not eligible for business property relief. The capital gains tax liability will be at George's marginal rate of income tax, that is £14,000 (£35,000 @ 40%).

ii) The gift of the shares into a discretionary trust will be a chargeable transfer of value. As George is to pay any taxes on setting up the trust it is assumed that he will pay the inheritance tax – the gift will therefore be a net transfer and must be grossed up by the amount of the tax paid by George to give the gross amount by which the estate is depleted:

	Gross	Tax	Net
Value of transfer	160,000		
Less: AE 1994/95	3,000		
AE 1993/94	3,000		
(£150,000 @ Nil			154,000
4,000 @ 20/(100 − 20) = 1,000)		1,000	
Due 31 October 1995	155,000		

If George dies within seven years of the gift, the IHT on the gross transfer (£155,000) will be recalculated using the rates applicable at the date of death:

Assume rates at death = 1994/95
  £150,000 @ Nil
    5,000 @ 40%   £2,000
  Less: taper relief if death 3 – 7
        years after date of gift   (?)
        (20/80% × 2,000)
  Less: tax already paid   (1,000)
  Tax payable   ?

If this figure is negative, no refund of any IHT already paid can be made.

The gift of shares into a discretionary trust is also a chargeable disposal of chargeable assets. It will be a transfer to a connected person (a person is connected to the trustees of a trust of which he is settlor) and as such will be deemed to take place at market value. It is assumed that the capital gain of £35,000 on disposal of the shares takes this and the indexation allowance into account. Holdover relief will be available for the gift as an inheritance tax liability arises on the transfer – George's gain will be deducted from the trustees' acquisition value for capital gains purposes, that is, their base cost will be £125,000 (160,000 – 35,000). There will be no capital gains liability at the date of the gift.

b) George's income tax 1994/95

	£		Tax paid
Schedule E	65,000		
Less: profit related pay – max	(4,000)		
		61,000	19,708
Schedule F 24,000 × 100/80		30,000	6,000
			25,708
Statutory total income		95,000	
Basic allowance		(3,445)	
Taxable income	Dividend 30,000	91,555	
	other 61,555		

Tax due:
On non-dividend income:

£3,000 × 20% =		600
£20,700 × 25% =		5,175
£37,855 × 40% =		15,142
61,555		20,917

On dividend income:

£30,000 × 40% =		12,000
		32,917
Less APA relief (1,720 × 20%)		(344)
		32,573
Less tax paid		(25,708)
Tax payable		6,865

The mortgage interest paid has been excluded from the computation as it receives relief at source through the MIRAS scheme.

George should also retain basic rate income tax from rent paid to his non-resident landlord (400 × 4 × 25% = £400) and account for this to the Inland Revenue – this payment does not count as a charge.

c) With no further occupation of the house, the capital gains computation is as follows:

31 March 82

Sale proceeds	550,000
Less: 31 Mar 82/cost	(280,000)
	270,000
Less: indexation allowance	
$\frac{144.4 - 79.4}{79.4}$ (0.819) × 280,000	(229,320)
	40,680
Less: principal private residence exemption 102/153 (workings)	(27,120)
Chargeable gain	13,560

If George reoccupies the house, the principal private residence exemption would be 100% and there would be no chargeable gain.

George should therefore reoccupy his house.

	Deemed occupation (months)	Absence (months)
1/4/82 – 30/6/82 (occupied)	3	
1/7/82 – 31/12/84 (overseas duties)	30	
1/1/85 – 30/9/87 (occupied)	33	
1/10/87 – 31/12/91 (absent)*		51
1/1/92 – 31/12/94 (last 3 years)	36	
Total 141 months	102	51

* Absent for duties in the UK but not followed by a period of occupation – Extra-statutory Concession D4 allows this rule to be relaxed if he is prevented from reoccupation due to his duties of employment – his duties would not have prevented him from reoccupying the house.

8 a) i) Chargeable gain – Andrew gifts.

Pool A. ABC Ltd

	Nos.	Cost £	£
April 87. purchase	4,000	12,000	
Operative event. 1 Jan 89			
$\frac{111.0 - 101.8}{101.8} \times 12,000$		1,084	
		13,084	
Rights issue 1 for 1	4,000	16,000	
	8,000	29,084	
Operative event 1 Jan 95			
$\frac{144.7 - 111.0}{111.0} \times 29,084$		8,830	
		37,914	
Disposal 1 Jan 95	(8,000)	(37,914)	
Market value (8,000 at £7)			56,000
Indexed cost			(37,914)
Chargeable gain			£18,086

Pool B. ABC Ltd

	Nos	Jan 80 Cost £	Mar 82 £	Jan 89
1 Jan 80 subscribed	6,000	6,000		
March 82 value £2			12,000	
1 Jan 89 rights 1 for 1	6,000			24,000
	12,000	6,000	12,000	24,000
Disposal 1 Jan 95	(2,000)	(1,000)	(2,000)	(4,000)
Carried forward	10,000	5,000	10,000	20,000

	March 82 value £	Cost £
Market value (2,000 at £7)	14,000	14,000
Cost Jan 80		(1,000)
March 82 value	(2,000)	
Cost Jan 89	(4,000)	(4,000)
	8,000	9,000
Indexation allowance		
$\frac{144.7 - 79.4}{79.4} = 0.822 \times £2,000$	(1,644)	(1,644)
$\frac{144.7 - 111.0}{111.0} = 0.304 \times £4,000$	(1,216)	(1,216)
	5,140	6,140
Chargeable gain is		5,140
Total chargeable gain on gift by Andrew		23,226

ii) Chargeable gain – Betty gifts

Pool A. ABC Ltd

	Nos	Cost £	£
June 88	10,000	35,000	
Operative event 1 Jan 89			
$\frac{111.0 - 106.6}{106.6} \times 35,000$		1,445	
		36,445	
Proceeds – sale of rights <5%		(1,000)	
(of MV 10,000 @ £4)			
		35,445	
Operative event 1 Jan 95			
$\frac{144.7 - 111.0}{111.0} \times 35,445$		10,761	
		46,206	
Disposal 1 Jan 95	(10,000)	(46,206)	
Market value (10,000 @ £7)			70,000
Indexed cost			(46,206)
Chargeable gain on gift by Betty			23,794

b) i) **Inheritance tax. Gift by Andrew** (death before 31 Jan 98)

Related property valuation of gift

	Before			**After**		
			£			£
Andrew	20,000	@ £10	200,000	10,000	@ £7	70,000
Betty	10,000	@ £7	70,000	10,000	@ £7	70,000
	30,000	@ £21	£630,000	20,000	@ £10	£200,000

Value of gift, greater of:
i) unrelated gift value (200,000 – 70,000)   130,000
or
ii) $\left(\dfrac{20,000}{30,000} \times 630,000\right) - \left(\dfrac{10,000}{20,000} \times 20,000\right)$ 320,000

	£
Value transferred	£320,000
Business property relief 100%	(320,000)
	Nil

IHT liability assuming daughter owns shares at date of death   Nil

b) ii) **Inheritance tax – Gift by Betty** (death before 31 Jan 98)

Related property valuation rules may apply

	Before			**After**		
Betty	10,000	@ £7	70,000			Nil
Andrew	20,000	@ £10	200,000	20,000	@ £10	200,000
	30,000	@ £21	630,000	20,000	@ £10	200,000

Value of gift, greater of:

	£
i) unrelated gift value	70,000

or
ii) $\left(\dfrac{20,000}{30,000} \times 630,000\right) - \text{Nil}$ 21,000

ie Value transferred	210,000
Business property relief 100%	(210,000)
(shareholding, including related property > 25%)	Nil
Assuming the daugher still owns shares at date of death	
IHT liability (nil rate band)	Nil

CHAPTER 15 *Self test questions*

1. Subject matter, period of ownership, frequency, supplementary work, motive, circumstances of realisation.

2. £1,640 is an allowable deduction in Schedule D Case I computation each year for ten years.
[20,000 – 2% (20,000 × (10 – 1))] × 1/10.

3. £3,600 $\left[\dfrac{12,000 + 1/2 (15,000 - 12,000)}{15,000} \times 4000\right]$

4. i) 12 months long.
   ii) Only accounting period ending in fiscal year.
   iii) Immediately follows a previous valid accounting period.

5. Six years after the end of the third fiscal year of assessment.

6. 1 January 1993 to 5 April 1994.

7. 1 May 1992 to 5 April 1994.

8 Butterfield – Adjusted profit computation for the sixteen months ended 30 April 1993.

	£	£
Net profit per accounts		17,344
Add: Own consumption of food (£100 × 16)	1,600	
Personal use of items charged:		
Heating oil (1570 × 1/20)	78	
Water rates (130 × 1/6)	22	
Telephone (654 × 1/6)	109	
Gas (125 × 1/10)	12	
Electricity (1,037 × 1/20)	52	
Motor vehicle expenses:		
Loss on sale of car	400	
Depreciation	1,832	
HP interest (450 × 1/3)	150	
Petrol (1,131 × 1/3)	377	
Servicing and repairs (519 × 1/3)	173	
Licences (240 × 1/3)	80	
Insurance (320 × 1/3)	107	
Legal fees:		
Purchase of Ingledene	2,144	
Depreciation – building	763	
– furniture and fittings	2,441	
		10,340
Adjusted Schedule D Case I profit		27,684

Schedule D Case I assessments

1991/92	Actual profits (1 January 1992–5 April 1992)	5,191
	3/16 × 27,684	
1992/93	First 12 months (1 January 1992–31 December 1992)	£20,763
	12/16 × 27,68	
1993/94	No 12-month accounting period ending in preceding fiscal year –	
	as above	£20,763
1994/95	No valid accounting period ending in preceding fiscal year –	
	usually the Inland Revenue will use the 12 months	
	ending on permanent accounting date	£20,763

The taxpayer has the option to elect for actual basis of assessment in the second and third fiscal years (ICTA 1988,s.62).

1992/93	6 April 1992–5 April 1993 12/16 27,684	£20,763
1993/94	6 April 1993–5 April 1994	Not known

It is not possible to say whether an election would have been made except that if the profits showed a rising trend an election would not have been worthwhile and if the profits showed a falling trend, it would be worthwhile.

Assume no election made for actual basis of assessment in years two and three.

9 a) The choice of accounting date is important because it determines the interval between earning the profits and paying tax on the profits. For example, the year to 31 March 1993 – due date for first instalment of tax 1 January 1994 – interval nine months; the year to 30 April 1993 – due date for first instalment of tax 1 January 1995 – interval 20 months.

The choice of accounting date also affects the degree of overlap between basis periods on commencement and the length of gap which arises between basis periods on cessation.

b) The first step is to compute the profits on the basis that accounts are made up to either 31 March or 30 April.
i) Accounts to 31 March

	£
3 months to 31 March 1993 (3/12 × 10,440)	2,610
12 months to 31 March 1994 (9/12 × 10,440 + 3/12 × 16,200)	11,880
12 months to 31 March 1995 (9/12 × 16,200 + 3/12 × 13,200)	15,450

Assessments	£
1992/93 Actual (1 January 1993–5 April 1993)	2,610
1993/94 First 12 months (1 January 1993–31 December 1993)	
(2,610 + 9/12 × 11,880)	11,520
1994/95 Preceding year (y/e 31 March 1994)	11,880
1995/96 Preceding year (y/e 31 March 1995)	15,450
	41,460

An election under s.62 for actual is not considered since there is a rising trend of profits.

ii) Accounts to 30 April

	£
4 months to 30 April 1993 (4/12 × 10,440)	3,840
12 months to 30 April 1994 (8/12 × 10,440 + 4/12 × 16,200)	12,360
12 months to 30 April 1995 (8/12 × 16,200 + 4/12 × 13,200)	15,200

Assessments	£
1992/93 Actual (1 January 1993–5 April 1993	
(3/4 × 3,480)	2,610
1993/94 First 12 months (1 January 1993–31 December 1993)	
(3,480 + 8/12 × 12,360)	11,720
1994/95 As for year 2	11,720
1995/96 Preceding year (y/e 30 Apr 94)	12,360
	38,410

An election under s.62 for actual is not considered since there is a rising trend of profits.

From the above results, it would appear that his permanent accounting date should be 30 April. In this particular case, it gives lower assessable profits, a longer interval to pay any tax arising and, if he should cease to trade, he will have a longer gap on cessation.

10 **Cessation at 31 March 1994**

		£	£	£
Final assessment 1993/94	(6 April 1993 – 31 March 1994) (9/12 × 48,000 + 6,000)			42,000
Penultimate year 1992/93	y/e 31 December 1991	24,000		
	or 6 April 1992 – 5 April 1993			
	(9/12 × 36,000		27,000	
	3/12 × 48,000)		12,000	
				39,000
Ante-penultimate year 1991/92	y/e 31 December 1990	8,000		
	or 6 April 1991 – 5 April 1992			
	(9/12 × 24,000		18,000	
	3/12 × 36,000		9,000	
				27,000
		32,000	66,000	

The Inland Revenue would use s.63 to assess on an actual basis.

Cessation at 30 April 1994

		£	£	£
Final assessment 1994/95	(6 April 1994 – 30 April 1994) 1/4 × 7,000			1,750
Penultimate year 1993/94	y/e 31 December 1992	36,000		
	or 6 April 1993 – 5 April 1994			
	(9/12 × 48,000 + 3/4 7,000)		41,250	
				41,250
Ante-penultimate year 1992/93	y/e 31 December 1991	24,000		
	or 6 April 1992 – 5 April 1993			
	(9/12 × 36,000		27,000	
	3/12 × 48,000)		12,000	
				39,000
		60,000	80,250	

The Inland Revenue would use s.63 to assess on an actual basis.

1991/92	Year ended 31 December 1990	8,000
		90,000

G should be advised not to dispose of his business until 30 April 1994.

CHAPTER 16 *Self test questions*

1 To the capital allowance computation for the earliest fiscal year into which the basis period falls.

2 25%, writing down allowance × proportion of fiscal year during which the trade was carried on. First-year allowances, if appropriate.

3 Cars of a private type costing £12,000 or less, and used in the trade.

4   The writing down allowance is restricted to £3,000 per annum.

5   In general, to those short-life assets which would otherwise form part of the main pool.

6   None.

7   i)   Qualifying industrial buildings.
    ii) Buildings for the welfare of employees of i) above + sports stadia.
    iii) Qualifying hotels.
    iv) Commercial buildings in an enterprise zone.

8   For buildings in use for a qualifying purpose on the last day of the basis period (temporary disuse ignored).

9   The cost of the office extension, £20,000, exceeds 25% of the total construction cost £30,000 (£10,000 + £20,000) and does not therefore qualify as part of an industrial building. Allowances available are as follows:

		£	£
Qualifying cost			10,000
1967/68	Initial allowance 15% of £10,000	1,500	
	writing down allowance 4% fo £10,000	400	
1968/69–1992/93, 24 years			
	writing down allowance 4% of £10,000 max	8,100	
			10,000
Residue of expenditure 1993/94			£Nil
1993/94	writing down allowance		£Nil
1994/95	writing down allowance		£Nil

10 S – capital allowance computations

	Pool £	FA 80 pool £	Short life assets £	Car £	Allowances £
Plant and machinery					
1992/93					
(Basis period y/e 30 September 1991)					
Brought forward	24,000				
Additions	7,000		2,000		
Disposal proceeds	–		–		
	31,000		2,000		
WDA 25%	(7,750)		(500)		8,250
Carry forward	23,250		1,500		
1993/94					
(Basis period y/e 30 September 1992)					
Additions	127,000				
Sale proceeds	(1,400)				
	148,850		1,500		
WDA 25%	(37,213)		(375)		37,588
Carry forward	111,637		1,125		
1994/95					
(Basis period y/e 30 September 1993)					
Additions				18,000	
Sale proceeds					
	111,637		1,125	18,000	
WDA 25%	(27,909)		(281)		28,190
				(3,000)	2,400
Carry forward	83,728		844	15,000	30,590
Industrial building					
Factory – qualifying cost		200,000			
WDA 4% 1993/94 and 1994/95					£8,000
Patents:					
Cost			10,000		
WDA 1993/94 25%			(2,500)		2,500
			7,500		
WDA 1994/95 25%			(1,875)		1,875
Carry forward			5,625		

TAX PLANNING

	1992/93	1993/94	1994/95
	£	£	£
Plant and machinery	8,250	37,588	30,590
Industrial building		8,000	8,000
Patents		2,500	1,875
	8,250	48,088	40,465

11 a)

Factory	1	2	3	4
	£	£	£	£
Residue after sale (lower of price paid and original cost)	100,000	80,000	150,000	120,000
Remaining tax life (that is, out of 25 years)	1 year	Nil	21 years	15 years
IBA available per annum (residue/remaining life)	100,000	–	7,143	8,000
Basis Periods for which IBA available	y/e 31 March 1995	–	y/e 31 March 1995 to 31 March 2015	y/e 31 March 1995 to 31 March 2009

It would be in the interests of the CCD Trading Co. to purchase Factory 1 giving immediate capital allowances of £100,000. Depending on the level of profits made by the business, the allowance will reduce current year's taxable profits or will create a loss which can be set off against the partners' statutory total incomes for 1994/95 and/or 1995/96 with immediate cash flow benefits (see Chapter 18 – Trade Losses).

The allowances available on Factories 3 and 4 are greater in total but are spread over a much longer period.

b) i) Display lighting in a showroom will only be eligible as plant and machinery if it can be shown that its function is to create a special atmosphere (*IRC* v. *Scottish and Newcastle Breweries Ltd*). If this is not done, it will be regarded as part of the setting in which the business is conducted and disallowed (*Cole Bros* v. *Phillips*).

ii) Thermal insulation qualifies for relief as plant and machinery, by statute (that is, writing down allowance at 25% per annum on the reducing balance).

iii) The cost of constructing the canteen will be qualifying expenditure for industrial buildings allowances as part of the factory. A writing down allowance of 4% of cost per annum will be given.

CHAPTER 17 *Self test questions*

1 Actual basis applies to the first four years of assessment of the new partnership; year 5 onwards will be on a preceding year basis unless the taxpayer makes an election for years 5 and 6 also to be on an actual basis.

2 Within two years of the date of the change.

3 1:1:1

4 Preceding year basis of assessment continues to apply.

5 a) Yes.
  b) No.

6 Profit-sharing ratio (ignoring salaries and interest on capital) of fiscal year.

7 Tax implications.

  a) **Marriage 1 June 1992**
  In 1992/93, John will be entitled to a proportion of the married couple's allowance in addition to his personal allowance. Kate's tax computation should not change.

  b) **Partnership commencing 1 December 1993**
  When Kate is admitted as a partner, the business is treated as ceasing immediately prior to that date and a new business, carried on by the partnership, is treated as commencing. Note that the normal commencement rules apply and not the special partnership commencement rules. Kate and John may elect for the trade to be treated as continuing (within two years of the date of change) in which case there will be no cessation/commencement and assessments will continue to be raised on a preceding year basis.
  The relevant calculations (ignoring any adjustment to the projected profits for Kate's salary not being deductible) are as follows:

i) No continuation election
   Cessation 30 November 1993

		£	£	£
1993/94	Final year – actual profits (6 April 1993 – 30 November 1993)			36,000
1992/93	y/e 31 July 1991	27,360		
	Actual for fiscal year		43,167	43,167
1991/92	y/e 31 July 1990	21,750		
	Actual for fiscal year		31,453	31,453
	IR will elect for s.63	49,110	74,620	

Commencement 1 December 1993

		£	£	£
1993/94	First year – actual profits (1 December 1993 – 5 April 1994)			20,000
1994/95	1st 12 months	61,667		61,667
	Actual for fiscal year		63,333	
1995/96	As for year 2	61,667		61,667
	Actual for fiscal year		68,333	
	John not elect s.62	123,334	131,666	
				253,954

ii) Election for continuation

				£
1991/92	y/e 31 July 1990			21,750
1992/93	y/e 31 July 1991		27,360	
1993/94	y/e 31 July 1992	to 1 December 1993 8/12	22,333	
		post 1 December 1993 4/12	11,167	
1994/95	y/e 31 July 1993			48,000
1995/96	y/e 31 July 1994			60,000
				190,610

It would be beneficial to claim that a continuation basis of assessment should apply. Kate would be assessable on 50% of £11,167 in 1993/94 and in 1994/95 she would be assessable on 50% of £48,000 (less any capital allowances – see below).

c) **Car for Kate**
Once Kate becomes a partner in the business 15% of the running costs of the car will be disallowed in the Schedule D Case I computation (private use). A writing down allowance of 25% (maximum £3,000) on the cost of the car (reducing balance) will be given, restricted to 85% to take account of private use.

d) **Other capital expenditure**
The tax implications on the other capital expenditure depend on whether or not a continuation election is made when Kate becomes a partner.

If a continuation election is made, the basis period in which this expenditure is incurred is the year ended 31 July 1994 – assessable 1995/96.

If a continuation election is not made, the ovens acquired in the final period of trading and the other fixed assets will be deemed to be disposed of at open market value and balancing adjustments will be calculated. The partnership will be deemed to acquire the fixed assets at open market value and, together with the mixer acquired in the first period of trading will be eligible for a writing down allowance (25% × 4/12) for that fiscal year.

Alternatively a continuation election may be made for capital allowances (plant and machinery) only. In this case, the basis period for 1993/94 will be the year ended 31 July 1992 plus the period to 30 November 1993 and a writing down allowance will be given to the business of 25% × 8/12. The tax written down value will be taken over by the new partnership and together with the mixer acquired after the change will get a writing down allowance of 25% × 4/12.

8 Peter and Paul estimated income tax computations 1994/95

	£	Peter £	Paul £
Schedule D Case I	128,000		
Less: capital allowances	(36,520)		
	91,480		
Add: balancing charge	23,200		
Shared 40:60	114,680	45,872	68,808
Personal pension (Note 2)		(9,174)	(9,600)
Personal allowances		(3,445)	(3,445)
Taxable income		33,253	55,763

	Peter	Paul
	£	£
£3,000 × 20%	600	600
£20,700 × 25%	5,175	5,175
Balance 40%	3,821	12,825
	9,596	18,600
Less MCA relief £1,720 × 20%	–	(344)
	9,596	18,256

The mortgage interest has been omitted from the calculation as relief is given through the MIRAS scheme.

Capital allowancs computations – 1994/95

Plant and machinery	Pool £	Allowances £	£
Brought forward at 5 April 1994	18,400		
Additions	20,000		
	38,400		
Writing down allowance 25%	(9,600)		9,600
Carried forward	28,800		

Scientific research allowance	£		
Laboratory	18,000		
Allowance 100%	(18,000)		18,000

Industrial Buildings Allowances

	London £	Norway (Note 1) £	
Costs	90,000	25,000	
		130,000	
		2,000	
		40,000	
	90,000	197,000	
Less: cost of land	(9,000)	(25,000)	
grant		(30,000)	
Qualifying cost	81,000	142,000	
Writing down allowance 4%	3,240	5,680	8,920
			36,520

	Scottish £
Qualifying cost	40,000
Initial allowance 50% 1986/87	(20,000)
Less: WDA 4% 1986/87, 1987/88	(3,200)
1988/89, 1989/90, 1990/91, 1991/92, 1992/93 and	
1993/94 notional	(9,600)
Residue before sale	7,200
Sale proceeds (max cost)	(40,000)
Balancing charge restricted to	(32,800)
allowances given	23,200

Notes

1. An industrial building need not be located in the UK.
2.

	Peter	Paul
	£	£
Relevant income for personal pension	45,872	68,808
Maximum 20% (Age 45)	9,174	13,762
Premium paid 12 × 800	9,600	9,600
Allowable	9,174	9,600

CHAPTER 18 *Self test questions*

1. Within two years of the end of the fiscal year for which the loss relief is claimed

2. a) Added to the loss for purposes of a ss. 380/385 claim; or
   b) Not added to the loss for purposes of a s. 380 claim and carried forward under s.385.

3. The loss is treated as arising in the fiscal year in which the loss-making accounting period ends.

4   Losses incurred in any of the first four fiscal years of assessment of a new trade may each be carried back and deducted from the STI of the three preceding years (earliest year first).

5   Within 2 years of the end of the fiscal year in which the loss is incurred.

6   The last twelve months of trading is split into two parts by the intervening 5 April. The terminal loss is made up of, for each part:
    i)   trading loss not otherwise used
    ii) capital allowances not otherwise used
    iii) trade charges not otherwise relieved.

7   If the consideration is wholly or mainly in shares, the vendor may carry forward the losses (not capital allowances) for deduction against his or her future personal income from the company (firstly earned income and then dividends).

8   A loss on the disposal of shares (calculated under the CGT rules) is treated as a trading loss of the year in which the disposal was made. Relief is given as for s. 380 but it is given in priority to s. 380 loss relief.

9   a) i) *1994/95 – Partnership profit allocation*
            Year ended 31 October 1993 – £28,000

	Total £	Boris £	Steffi £	Ivan £
6/4/94 – 30/6/94				
3/12 × 28,000 = 7,000				
Salary 3/12	500			500
Profit share 3:3:1	6,500	2,786	2,786	928
1/7/94 – 5/4/95				
9/12 × 28,00 = 21,000				
Salary 9/12	7,500			7,500
Profit share	13,500	6,000	4,500	3,000
Assessable 1994/95	28,000	8,786	7,286	11,928
Assessable 1995/96	Nil	Nil	Nil	Nil
Assessable 1996/97	105,000	30,000	35,000	40,000

    ii *Year ended 31 October 1994 – £(30,000) – Partnership loss allocation*
        If all partners were to make a claim for relief under s. 380, the loss would be divided between them in accordance with the profit sharing arrangements which persisted during 1994/95.

	Total £	Boris £	Steffi £	Ivan £
6/4/94 – 30/6/94				
3/12 × (30,000) = (7,500)				
Salary 3/12	500			500
Loss share 3:3:1	(8,000)	(3,428)	(3,428)	(1,144)
	(7,500)	(3,428)	3,428	(644)

	Total £	Boris £	Steffi £	Ivan £
1/7/94 – 5/4/95				
9/12 × (30,000) = (22,500)				
Salary 9/12	7,500			7,500
Loss share 4:3:2	(30,000)	(13,333)	(10,000)	(6,667)
	(22,500)	(13,333)	(10,000)	833
Less: notional profit				(833)
apportion 4:3		476	357	
		(12,857)	(9,643)	
Total	(30,000)	(16,285)	(13,071)	(644)

    If all partners were to make a claim for relief under s. 385, the loss would be divided between them in accordance with the profit-sharing arrangements which persisted during the loss-making period.

	Total £	Boris £	Steffi £	Ivan £
1/11/93 – 30/6/94				
8/12 × (30,000) = 20,000				
Salary 8/12	1,333			1,333
Loss share 3:3:1	(21,333)	(9,143)	(9,143)	(3,047)
	(20,000)	(9,143)	(9,143)	(1,714)

TAX PLANNING

	Total £	Boris £	Steffi £	Ivan £
1/7/94 – 31/10/94				
4/12 × (30,000) = 10,000				
Salary 4/12	3,333			3,333
Loss share 4:3:2	(13,333)	(5,926)	(4,444)	(2,963)
	(10,000)	(5,926)	(4,444)	370
Less: notional profit apportion 4:3		211	159	(370)
		(5,715)	(4,285)	
Total	(30,000)	(14,858)	(13,428)	(1,714)

Each partner may individually decide to claim under either s. 380 or under s. 385. The apportionment in the accounting period forms the upper limit for each partner's loss relief where s. 380 amount is less than the s. 385 amount but if the s. 380 amount is greater this may be claimed.

iii) Advice to Ivan

Ivan may claim:

a) £644 under s. 380 and a further £1,070 under s. 385 (total £1,714).

£644 would be deducted from his 1994/95 assessment of £11,928 saving income tax at 25% (£161) and NIC at 7.3% (£47) on payments due 1/1/95 and 1/7/95.

£1,070 would be carried forward to 1996/97 assessment of £40,000 saving income tax at 40% (£428) but with no NIC saving on the payments due 1/1/97 and 1/7/97.

Total saving £636.

b) He may claim to carry forward under s. 385 the whole £1,714.

£1,714 would be carried forward to 1996/97 and deducted from his 1996/97 assessment of £40,000 saving income tax at 40% (£685) but with no NIC saving on the payments due 1/1/97 and 1/7/97.

Total saving £685

Based on purely financial considerations, he would be advised to choose option b).

b) *Boris – income tax computation 1994/95*

	Unearned and Earned £	Tax paid
Schedule D Case I	£8,786	
Less: capital allowances		
Schedule D Case III		
(assume PY basis applies) 200 – 70	130	
Building society interest		
10,740 × 100/75	14,320	3,580
	23,236	3,580
Less: 50% NIC (Note 1)	Nil	
Statutory total income	23,236	
Less: s. 380 loss relief	(16,285)	
Less: personal allowance	(3,445)	
	3,506	

Income tax liability	£
£3,000 × 20% =	600.00
£506 × 25% =	126.50
	726.50
MCA relief (1,720 × 20%)	(344.00)
	382.50
Tax deducted at source	(3,580.00)
Repayment	(3,197.50)

Note

1. NIC Class 4 payable pre loss relief claim: 7.3% × (8,786 − 6,490) = £167.60

   NIC Class 4 payable post loss relief claim: £Nil

   Note that the loss is offset initially against earned income, thus reducing the profits on which NIC is calculated.

c) *Boris – relief for personal pension contributions*

		£	£	£
1993/94 –	Unused relief brought forward £9,643 × 17.5%			1,688
1994/95 –	Schedule D Case I		8,786	
	loss relief	16,285		
	deducted trading profit	(8,786)	(8,786)	
	c/f	7,499		
	Net relevant earnings		–	
	Relief			–
1995/96 –	Schedule D Case I		Nil	
	loss relief bf and cf	7,499		
	Net relevant earnings		–	
	Relief			–
1996/97 –	Schedule D Case I		30,000	
	loss relief b/f		(7,499)	
	Net relevant earnings		22,501	
	Relief £22,501 × 17.5%			3,938
Maximum relief available				5,626

CHAPTER 19 *Self test questions*

1

			£	£
1994/95	£12,000 × 8/12 =			8,000
1995/96	A/cs to 31/7/95			12,000
1996/97	A/cs to 31/7/96			11,000
1997/98	15,000 +9,000		24,000	
	Overlap relief		(8,000)	16,000

2 The twelve months to 31 March 1999.

3 Capital allowances under the new rules are calculated in respect of accounting periods rather than basis periods. Thus any writing down allowance due will need to be proportionately increased/decreased if the accounting period is more/less than twelve months long. The allowances are deducted in computing the Schedule DI profits.

4 Relief under the existing rules is given in respect of the year of the loss and/or the following year. Relief under the new rules is given in the year of the loss and/or the preceding year.

5 i) Each individual partner will receive an assessment rather than the partnership as a whole.
ii) The partnership's profits/losses will be allocated by reference to the period of account rather than the year of assessment.
iii) A change in the members of a partnership, where there is at least one partner common to both the old and the new partnerships, will no longer be regarded as a cessation for tax purposes.

CHAPTER 20 *Self test questions*

1 Nil. Stock is not a chargeable asset. Plant (assuming not fixed plant) is a wasting chattel used for business purposes to which chattel relief applies – it is not a chargeable asset.

2 There will be no allowable loss as the net cost of the building (20,000 – 2,000) equates to the disposal proceeds. Indexation cannot create an allowable loss.

3 No.

4 Within the period 12 months before the disposal to 36 months after the disposal or such longer time as IR may allow.

5 None. The gain is fully chargeable, being lower than the proceeds not re-invested (£10,000).

6 *Disposal: November 1987*

	£
Sale proceeds	50,000
Cost (capital allowances ignored as sold at profit).	(30,000)
	20,000
Indexation allowance $\dfrac{103.4 - 81.9}{81.9} = 0.263 \times 30,000$	(7,890)
	12,110

a) Re-investment in freehold land and buildings is eligible for rollover relief – unrestricted as total sale proceeds are re-invested. No chargeable gain would be assessed in 1987/88.

Disposal January 1995

		£
Sale proceeds		120,000
Cost (January 1987)	75,000	
Less: gain rolled over	(12,110)	
		(62,890)
		57,110
Indexation allowance $\dfrac{144.7 - 100.0}{100.0} = 0.447 \times 62,890$		(28,112)
Assessable 1994/5 unless proceeds again re-invested		28,998

b) Re-investment in long leasehold property is eligible for rollover relief (the lease is longer than 60 years) but relief is restricted as only £40,000 of £50,000 sale proceeds are re-invested.

	£
Gain brought forward November 1987	12,110
Proceeds not re-invested	(10,000)
Rolled over gain	£2,110
Chargeable gain assessable 1987/88	10,000

Disposal January 1995

	£	£
Sale proceeds		50,000
Cost (January 1987)	40,000	
Less: rolled over gain	(2,110)	
		(37,890)
		12,110
Indexation $0.447 \times 37,890 = 16,937$		(12,110)
		–

Indexation loss £4,827

c) Re-investment in fixed plant and machinery is eligible for hold-over relief (depreciating asset) restricted to £2,110 as above (only £40,000 of £50,000 sale proceeds re-invested).

	£
Chargeable gain assessable 1987/88	10,000

Disposal January 1995

	£	£
Sale proceeds		25,000
Cost (December 1987	40,000	
Less: deemed capital allowances (40,000 – 25,000)	(15,000)	
		(25,000)
		Nil
Held over gain crystallised 1994/95		2,110

CHAPTER 21 *Self test questions*

1. No claim necessary, given automatically.

2. The same property throughout the two years prior to transfer or an earlier business property plus the current business property for at least two out of previous five years.

3. The same property for the purpose of agriculture throughout two years prior to the transfer or, if the current property replaced earlier property, for two out of the last five years.

4. Yes. A has more than 5% personally.

5. Yes. Yes. Note retirement relief has priority to gift relief.

6. Jeremy Thompson

Leashold holiday flat		**31 March 1982 value** £	Old rules cost £	Gain/ (Loss) £
Sale proceeds (January 1995)		78,000	78,000	
Less: incidental costs disposal		(2,200)	(2,200)	
		75,800	75,800	
Less: costs of acquisition				
price	38,000			
stamp duty	200			
legal fees	400			
	£38,600			
Restricted to % 18.5 years 69.744				
% 42.0 years 96.593			(27,871)	
		75,800	47,929	
March 1982 value £78,000				
Restricted to %18.5 years 69.744				
%31.3 years 88.699		(61,331)		
Unindexed gain		14,469	47,929	
Indexation allowance on 31 March 1982 value				
$\frac{144.7 - 79.4}{79.4} = 0.822 \times 61,331$		(14,469)	(47,929)	
Chargeable gain/allowable loss		–	–	

The indexation allowance (£50,414) has been restricted as it can no longer create an allowable loss. There will be an indexation loss of £2,485 (50,414 – 47,929).

8,000 share in Westbank – 4,000 Pool A
– 4,000 Pool B

Pool A	Nos of shares	Value £
15 May 1983	1,000	5,200
Indexed rise to 5 April 1985		
$\frac{94.8 - 84.6}{84.6} \times 5,200$		627
Value of holding at 6 April 1985	1,000	5,827
Operative event 1 December 1986		
Indexation $5,827 \times \frac{99.6 - 94.8}{94.8}$		295
Acquisition 1 December 1986	2,000	10,200
	3,000	16,322
Operative event 9 February 1988		
Indexation $16,322 \times \frac{103.7 - 99.6}{99.6}$		672
Acquisition 9 February 1988	1,000	5,000
	4,000	21,994

Pool A (contd)	Nos of shares	Value £	
Operative event April 1995			
Indexation $21,994 \times \dfrac{145.2 - 103.7}{103.7}$		$\dfrac{8,802}{30,796}$	{ Cost 20,400; Indexation 10,396
Disposal (mid-April 1995)	(4,000)	(30,796)	
Estimated sales proceeds (@ £4)	16,000		
Less: indexed cost (restricted)	(20,400)		
Allowable loss			(4,400)

Indexation loss £10,396

Pool B	Nos of shares	Value £
7 June 1971	2,000	11,680
21 October 1980	7,000	39,760
31 March 1982	3,000	16,200
	12,000	67,640
Disposal (mid-April 1995)	(4,000)	(22,547)
Balance carried forward	8,000	45,093

	31 March 1982 value £	Old rules cost £
Estimated sale proceeds (@ £4)	16,000	16,000
Less: 31 March 1982 value (£5.40)/cost	(21,600)	(22,547)
Unindexed loss	(5,600)	(6,547)
Indexation allowance		
$\dfrac{145.2 - 79.4}{79.4} = 0.829$		
$22,547 \times 0.829 = £18,691$	(5,600)	(6,547)
Allowable loss	–	–

Indexation loss £12,144

b/f				(4,400)

4,000 shares in Thompson Engineering Ltd.

	31 March 1982 Value £	Old rules Cost £
Estimated sale proceeds (£5)	20,000	20,000
Less: 31 March 1982 value/cost	(16,000)	(4,000)
Unindexed gain	4,000	16,000
Less: indexation allowance on 31 March 1982 value		
$16,000 \times 0.829$	(4,000)	(13,264)
No gain/no loss	–	2,736

(Sale mid-April – no retirement relief available as he was not 55 until 28 May 1995. In this case it is not applicable, but in other cases he would have been advised to delay the sale until after this date).   Nil

Antique chair – non-wasting chattel
Both cost and sale proceeds are below £6,000 – exempt   Nil
National Savings Certificates – exempt   Nil
Total chargeable gains   Nil

Allowable losses   4,400
Indexation losses   25,025   { Restricted £10,000

CHAPTER 22 *Self test questions*

1 Provided he makes taxable supplies in UK or supplies that would be taxable if made in UK, he is entitled to register (whatever the level).

2. When the goods are delivered or made available to the customer or earlier, if an invoice is issued earlier or payment is made earlier. It determines the rate of VAT and the accounting quarter for VAT.

3.
   a) Repayments due (monthly returns)
   b) Small business – annual estimate/10 – with a return at the end of the year.
   c) First and last period of registration + any change of return period.
   d) Large VAT payers (over £2 million per annum) – quarterly returns – monthly payments on account.

4. Six years.

5. If charged – VAT must be included in charge, and treated as output.
   If free or charged at less than cost – scale charge (output) or no scale charge (no output) but no input tax on any fuel reclaimed.

6.
   a) goods/services not for business
   b) motor cars (except dealer, taxi-driver, self-drive hire firms, driving schools and businesses leasing cars to such firms)
   c) goods/services for business entertaining (not staff entertaining).

7. Small businesses with turnover excluding VAT ≤ £350,000 which have a clean VAT record and are up to date with VAT returns + VAT outstanding < £5,000

8. Both the default surcharge and the persistent misdeclaration penalty require notices to be issued.

9. Dear Roger,

   You have been persistently late in the submission of your VAT returns and have incurred a penalty known as a default surcharge. This is incurred where a return is sent in late and results in the Customs and Excise automatically issuing a 'notice of liability'. This is valid for 12 months from the quarter of default (in your case, quarter 1 of 1994). If any further returns are submitted late the surcharge period will be extended to cover the four quarters following the latest default. It is only possible to terminate the surcharge period by submitting four consecutive quarterly returns on time – in your case this would mean submitting on time the returns for the fourth quarter of 1995 and the first and second quarters of 1996.

   The first delay during a surcharge period causes a surcharge to be made of 2% of the VAT due for the quarter. The next delay during the same (or extended) surcharge period increases the surcharge to 5% with subsequent steps of 5% for each late payment up to a maximum of 15% of the VAT due (minimum charge in each case £30 but Customs and Excise will not assess amounts less than £200, except if the rate of charge is 10% or more).

   If there is reasonable excuse for the lateness in submitting the returns, the delay will be disregarded but unfortunately, this will not apply in your case. It would seem to be advisable for you to engage another book-keeper without delay.

   I attach a schedule of the penalties you have incurred to date for your information.

   Yours sincerely,

   Schedule of penalties

   1994 1 No surcharge – Notice of liability issued
         2 1st default – Surcharge period commences, minimum charge £30 (2% × £1,100 = £22)
         3 2nd default £400 × 5% = £20, minimum charge £30
         4 No default
   1995 1 No default
         2 3rd default in surcharge period – £800 × 10% = £80
         3 No default

   Surcharge period will run for four quarters from 1995 2, that is, until 1996 2.

CHAPTER 23 *Self test questions*

1. By 5 April 1996 as income arises 1994/5.

2. Amount of tax.

3. 30 days, or, if reasonable excuse can be shown, such longer time as inspector may allow.

4. 1 December following end of year assessment.

5. The date from which interest on overdue tax is charged.

6. Assessments may be made for previous 20 years.

7. Interest is charged on overdue inheritance tax from the due date to the date the tax is paid.

8 a) If Bob later finds an error or omission resulting in:
Overstatement of profit – he can claim relief under the 'error or mistake' provisions. It does not matter if the error is one of fact or law although, if it is an error of law which reflected normal practice at that time, no relief will be given. The claim must be made in writing within six years following the end of the fiscal year in which the assessment was made. The relief may be refused if, in the Inland Revenue's opinion, it gives an inequitable result – in this case the taxpayer may appeal to the Special Commissioners and then the courts (if on a point of law).
Understatement of profit (see below).

b) If the inspector finds tax understated – 'discovers' – he may issue a further assessment. The discovery may result from a change of opinion or the realisation that an error has been made (including an arithmetical error) or from the receipt of new information. The further assessment must usually be made within six years after the end of the fiscal year to which the assessment relates unless the taxpayer is guilty of fraudulent or negligent conduct when the time limit is 20 years. In all cases the limit is three years after the end of the year of assessment in which the taxpayers dies.

9 a) Where a return has been issued to Paul, he must complete the return including details of his capital gains. Technically it must be submitted to the inspector within 30 days – the prescribed time limit – although in practice this is not enforced. The maximum penalty for failure to submit on time is £300 plus an amount equal to the amount of the tax to be assessed if the delay continues beyond the end of the year of assessment following that in which the return was issued – alternatively, the inspector may bring the delay before the Commissioners when the penalty becomes £60 per day for each day the delay continues.

Where a return is not issued to Paul, he is obliged to submit a return of his chargeable gain to the inspector within 12 months of the end of the year of assessment in which the gain arises (that is, by 5 April 1996). Failure to do so will give rise to a maximum penalty equal to the capital gains tax not assessed by virtue of the default – this will not apply where the assessment is raised before 5 April 1996 as a result of information from other sources.

b) Where Hugh receives a return, he too is obliged to complete and submit it as above. However, the chargeable gain may be omitted as the gain is below the exempt amount (£5,800) and the disposal proceeds are below £11,600.

If Hugh does not receive a tax return, he is not obliged to notify the Inland Revenue of the chargeable gain as it is below the limit and is not liable to capital gains tax.

QUESTION BANK – *Personal business taxation*

1 a) The sale of the assets of the business to Sadcake Ltd on 31 December 1994 constitutes a cessation of trade for Mr. Simple for income tax purposes. The final year of assessment will be 1994/95. Assessments will be as follows:

			Normal	s.63	Assess
1994/95	6 April 94 – 31 Dec 94				Nil
	(3/12 × 5,000 + (40,000))				
1993/94	y/e 30/6/92		11,000		11,000
	6/4/93 – 5/4/94			5,750	
1992/93	y/e 30/6/91		15,000		15,000
	6/4/92 – 5/4/93			8,750	
			26,000	14,500	
	IR will not make s.63 election				
1991/92	y/e 30/6/90				14,000
1990/91	y/e 30/6/89				12,000

Capital allowance basis periods will be adjusted as follows:

Capital allowance computations

1990/91	**Pool**	**Car**	**Private use**	**Allowances**
(y/e 30/6/89)				
brought forward	34,667	14,000		
WDA 25%	(8,667)	(2,000)	500	10,167
	26,000	12,000		
1991/92				
(y/e 30/6/90)				
WDA 25%	(6,500)	(2,000)	500	8,000
	19,500	10,000		
1992/93				
(y/e 30/6/91)				
WDA 25%	(4,875)	(2,000)	500	6,375
	14,625	8,000		

	Pool	Car	Private use	Allowances
1993/94 (y/e 30/6/92 + 5/4/94)				
Addition	1,000			
	15,625			
WDA 25%	(3,906)	(2,000)	500	5,406
	11,719	6,000		
1994/95 (6/4/94 – 31/12/94)				
Sale proceeds	(6,000)	(9,000)		
	5,719	(3,000)		
Bal (all)/chge	(5,719)	3,000	750	5,719 BA
				(2,250) BC

Trading losses in 1994/95 can be relieved under s. 380 (set off against STI of 1994/95 but not 1995/96) but as there is little other income (Schedule D Case VI £2,700) this would only result in wastage of personal allowances in those years.

The most appropriate claim therefore is terminal loss relief which carries back any unrelieved losses incurred in the last 12 months of trading for set-off against trading income of the same trade in the previous three fiscal years. Any remaining loss may be relieved under s. 386 against future remuneration from the company or income from shares in the company while ownership of the shares is retained.

Mr Simple – total income

	1990/91	1991/92	1992/93	1993/94	1994/95
DI	12,000	14,000	15,000	11,000	–
CA	(10,167)	(8,000)	(6,375)	(5,406)	
	1,833	6,000	8,625	5,594	–
TLR (Note 1)		(6,000)	(8,625)	(5,594)	
	1,833	–	–	–	
D VI	2,700	2,700	2,700	2,700	2,700
E	–	–	–	–	3,000
less s. 386					(3,000)
Total income	4,533	2,700	2,700	2,700	2,700

Terminal loss

Unrelieved losses in final 12 months

1994/95	(6/4/94 – 30/6/94) 3/12 × 5,000 =	1,250	
	(1/7/94 – 31/12/94)	(40,000)	
	Balancing charge	2,250	
			36,500
	Unrelieved capital allowances		5,719
	Unrelieved trade charges		–
1993/94	(1/1/94 – 5/4/94) 3/12 × 5,000 (profit)		–
	Unrelieved capital allowances		–
	Unrelieved trade charges		–
	c/f		42,219
s. 388 relief	1993/94		(5,594)
	1992/93		(8,625)
	1991/92		(6,000)
			22,000
s. 386 relief	1994/95 – remuneration from company in 1994/5 (4/12 × 9,000)		(3,000)
Carry forward against future income from company			19,000

b) A company may acquire a business for cash, debentures (loan) and/or shares in theory. A newly formed company will not usually have the cashflow to acquire for cash. If the business is acquired by creating a loan then funds can easily be withdrawn at a future date (for example, in three to four years) – this would also be cheaper than paying him remuneration at a future date which would require NIC (employee and employer) and PAYE. If the business is acquired for shares the funds are locked into the company although funds may be removed by the payment of a dividend – this also avoids payment of NIC and the tax liability of the company (@ 25%) would be passed on in part (20%) by way of tax credit on the dividend (it is assumed ACT would be fully recoverable). It would appear therefore that the payment of dividends would be as tax efficient as the repayment of a loan account – a minimal disadvantage would be the cashflow effect of the payment of ACT.

Remuneration could be in the form of benefits which would avoid the NIC charge and would nevertheless be eligible to fund approved pension contributions (unlike dividends).

The base cost of the shares, if a loan account was used in part, would be smaller which would in the longer term create a greater potential capital gain. This, however, will be avoided if the shares are retained until he dies or until he is eligible for sufficient retirement relief to cancel out any gains arising.

Capital gains roll-over relief is available if the business is sold wholly or mainly for shares. This would apply to the gain on goodwill (£10,724 see below) which would be deducted from the base cost of the shares and would be permanently postponed until he disposes of the shares. As indicated above this is unlikely to have any practical disadvantage. If it is desired to pay no capital gains tax but still have part of the consideration in the form of a loan then enough shares should be issued to leave chargeable only £5,800 which would be covered by Mr Simple's annual exemption.

	£
Gain on goodwill	
Sale proceeds	18,000
March 1982 value	(4,000)
Indexation	
$\dfrac{144.4 - 79.4}{79.4} = 0.819 \times £4,000$	(3,276)
Gain	10,724
Value of net assets – per balance sheet	23,000
goodwill	18,000
Value of consideration for business	41,000
Maximum loan to avoid capital gains tax	
$\dfrac{5,800 \times 41,000}{10,724}$	22,175
that is, 54% of consideration	

This size of loan is, however, much too high a proportion of the total consideration if s. 386 relief is to be available on Mr Simple's unrelieved Schedule D Case I losses (see above). For s. 386 relief to be available, the transfer must be wholly or mainly in exchange for shares in the company. Wholly or mainly is interpreted as being 80% or more of the shares following incorporation and the relief is the total of unrelieved trading losses at the date of incorporation (exclusive of capital allowances). As shown above, the amount available after terminal loss relief is £22,000 (this assumes that capital allowances were used first in the terminal loss claim). The maximum size of loan account which should be created is therefore 20% of £41,000 (£8,200) leading to a capital gain of £2,145 (8,200/41,000 × 10,724). The remaining gain (£8,579) would be rolled over against the base cost of the shares.

2 Jennifer

a) Capital gains tax

	£
Shares in Cardigan plc 45,000 @ £2.50	112,500
Cash	337,500
Consideration treated as part disposal and part, share-for-share exchange.	450,000

The 31 March 1982 value of the shares has been computed as 90% of the total net assets at the appropriate date, that is £216,000.

	31 March 1982 value £	Old rules costs £
Sale price	337,500	337,500
March 1982 $\dfrac{337,500}{450,000} \times 216,000$	162,000	
Cost $\dfrac{337,500}{450,000} \times 9,000$		6,750
Unindexed gain	175,500	330,750
Less: indexation allowances on 31 March 1982 value		
$\dfrac{145.0 - 79.4}{79.4} = 0.826$		
162,000 × 0.826	(133,812)	(133,812)
	41,688	196,938

Chargeable gain will be £41,688 (based on 31 March 1982 value as this is lower than the gains arising under the old rules).

Full retirement relief is then available as Jennifer has held the shares for a qualifying period of ten years and is aged over 55 years.

The amount of the gain eligible for relief is that given by the formula:

$$\dfrac{\text{Chargeable business assets}}{\text{Chargeable assets}}$$

Stocks, net debtors, bank and cash are not chargeable assets. The items of equipment are not chargeable assets as they are all less than £6,000 and exempt. The investment in Supplier Ltd is not regarded as a chargeable business asset.

$$41,688 \times \frac{100,000 + 255,000}{100,000 + 255,000 + 85,000} = 33,635$$

The amount of retirement relief available is £250,000 plus half of any gains between £250,000 and £1,000,000.

Retirement relief is therefore £33,635.

Gift of 30,000 shares in Cardigan plc to son – 1 April 1995 ie 2/3 of the remaining shares

	31 March 1982 value £	Old rules cost £
Disposal value 30,000 @ £2.50	75,000	75,000
March 1982 $\frac{112,500}{450,000} \times 216,000 \times 2/3$	(36,000)	
Cost $\frac{112,500}{450,000} \times 9,000 \times 2/3$		(1,500)
Unindexed gain	39,000	73,500
Less: indexation allowances on 31 March 1982 value $36,000 \times 0.826$	(29,736)	(29,736)
	9,264	43,764

	£
Chargeable gain (as above) Cardigan plc	9,264
Chargeable gains Woolway Ltd (41,688 – 33,635)	8,053
Annual exemption	(5,800)
Chargeable at Jennifer's marginal rate of income tax	11,517

A gift of quoted shares does not qualify for gift relief, while if the shares in Woolway Ltd had been gifted (shares in an unquoted family trading company) these would have qualified.

b) Inheritance tax

31 March 1995	Gifts of shares to son		75,000	
	Less: annual exemptions	1994/95	(3,000)	
		1993/94	(3,000)	
	PET		69,000	
1 April 1995	Cash to Helen		10,000	
	Less: marriage exemption		(2,500)	
	PET		7,500	
1 April 1995	Cash to NSPCC – charity – exempt			
1 April 1995	Cash to discretionary trust			200,000(net)
	Tax 150,000 @ Nil %	Nil		
	50,000 @ 20/(100 – 20)	152,00		12,500
	Gross transfer			212,500
1 April 1995	Loan to grandson – no inheritance tax implications			

3 a) This is an isolated transaction but whether the profit is assessable to income tax depends on whether the transaction is an adventure in the nature of a trade assessable under Schedule D Case I – it is not likely to be treated as an annual profit or gain falling to be taxed under Schedule D Case VI.

The Inland Revenue applies the badges of trade to identify whether a trade exists. The following facts all suggest that the transaction could be one of a trading nature:
i) the steps taken to acquire the car
ii) the work carried out to the car subsequent to the purchase
iii) the actual period of ownership – a 'short time'
iv) the likeness between the work carried out on the car and his employment occupation.

However, other factors suggest that the transaction is more likely not to be deemed to be of a trading nature:
i) there was no profit motive
ii) the asset itself is of a type often acquired for personal enjoyment
iii) there was only one such transaction
iv) finance was in the form of a personal loan presumably repayable out of future income from employment

v) the realisation of the asset was necessitated by it becoming unsuitable for the purpose for which it was acquired – the personal enjoyment of Bruce and Madeline.

Since it is not regarded as an annual profit arising from a trade, the profit will not be charged to income tax. It will, however, be regarded as a profit arising from the disposal of an investment – an investment for tax purposes is an asset held for personal enjoyment or to generate income – and as such will be within the capital gains tax legislation. Under capital gains tax a motor car is not a chargeable asset and the profit will therefore be free of capital gains tax.

b) The factors listed at a) above which implied that there was not a trade, would be reassessed and this time are likely to point to a trade existing.

In particular there is now a profit motive which in itself, if admitted, points to a trade being carried on. There are a number of transactions of a similar type, and the circumstances of realisation – and advertising – no longer cast doubt over the commercial nature of the activity.

Where a profit is chargeable to income tax it cannot also be chargeable to capital gains tax. Income tax takes priority.

c) i) Registration for VAT is required where taxable supplies (i.e. sales – excluding disposals of fixed assets) exceed or are expected to exceed certain limits. The limits are specified per 12 months (currently £45,000).

If you can identify in advance that you expect to exceed the limit (£45,000) in the next 12 months, you should notify the Customs and Excise and registration will then be effective from the date the grounds for the belief arose.

Where the historical limit is exceeded you should notify the Customs and Excise within 30 days and registration will take effect from the end of the month following the month in which the limit was exceeded.

Where the limit has been exceeded and it can be shown that the cumulative taxable supplies for the next twelve months will not exceed £43,000 registration will not be necessary.

ii) Failure to notify liability to register to the Customs and Excise will result in the registration being backdated to the date when registration should have taken place. You will become liable to pay to the Customs and Excise VAT for the period commencing with this date although none will have been collected by you. In addition there will be a penalty of 10% of the tax for delays of nine months or less, 20% for delays between nine and 18 months, and 30% for delays over 18 months –- the minimum penalty will be £50.

iii) The sale of second-hand cars by a registered person is a taxable supply and VAT at the current rate of 17.5% (or 7/47 × VAT-inclusive price) must be charged.

iv) The VAT scheme applicable to second-hand cars allows car dealers to account for VAT on only 7/47 of the amount by which the selling price exceeds the purchase price of each car. Where a car is sold for less than its purchase price, no VAT need be accounted for. This is advantageous to a trader who is registered for VAT when competing with dealers who are not registered as the VAT element of the sale proceeds is reduced and therefore he retains more of the profit.

v) VAT will be charged on the importation of a second-hand car and cannot be reclaimed. The VAT on importation is calculated on the total of the purchase price of the car plus any freight, insurance etc, plus any customs duty. The total plus the VAT is the purchase price of the car for the purposes of the retail scheme.

No VAT will be charged to you on cars you purchase from private individuals and none therefore can be charged as input tax.

VAT will be charged for the purchase of spares, accessories etc or for repair work done and may be reclaimed as input tax subject to the normal rules, but the cost must not be added to the purchase price of the car for purposes of the retail scheme.

d) SSAP 5, Accounting for Value Added Tax, recommends that where a trader is registered for VAT:
– turnover in the profit and loss account should exclude VAT
– any irrecoverable VAT should be added to the expenditure to which it relates
– amounts of VAT due to or from Customs and Excise should not normally be shown separately but should be included in debtors and creditors.

4 a) Assuming Jack's turnover stays below the VAT registration threshold, currently £45,000, the effect of registration, since most of his clients are members of the public and not themselves registered for VAT, would be either:
i) to increase the cost of the work performed by Jack (the price that his clients would pay), by the amount of the VAT (17.5 per cent)
ii) if the prices to his clients were left unaltered, for Jack's profit to be reduced by 17.5/117.5 (7/47)s of his fee income, the amount which would need to be paid to Customs and Excise.

The above would be offset by the recovery of VAT on inputs but as these are only small in value (£2,000), it is unlikely to be beneficial for Jack to register.

b) i) For income tax purposes, the assessments on Jack and Howard would be determined as if their businesses ceased trading on the date of the merger, 1 May 1994.

1994/95 – The final year of assessment would be assessed on an actual basis, that is from 6 April 1994 to 30 April 1994.

For 1993/94 and 1992/93 the normal preceding year basis of assessment would apply. Jack would be assessed on the profits for his accounts years ended 30 April 1991 and 30 April

1992. Howard would be assessed on the profits for his accounts years ended 30 June l991 and 30 June 1992. The Inland Revenue would have the option in each case to elect, under s63, for the assessments for both years to be amended to the actual basis if this would result in increased assessments.

The new partnership would be treated as a new business commencing on l May 1994. It would thus be subject to the new current year basis of assessment:

1994/95 – the profits to be assessed will be those from 1 May 1994 to 5 April 1995.

1995/96 – the assessment will be based on the accounts for the twelve months to 30 April 1995.

For 1996/97 et seq, the assessment will be based on the profits of the accounting year ending in the year of assessment.

Overlap relief will be available in respect of the profits arising between 1 May 1994 and 5 April 1995, as these have been assessed twice. This relief will be given either when the business ceases, or in any earlier year for which the basis period is longer than twelve months.

Alternatively, Jack and Howard could make an election for continuation under ICTA 1988, s. 113. The election must be made in writing and signed by both Jack and Howard. Jack would then continue on a preceding year basis of assessment (accounts to 30 April) without the cessation and commencement provisions outlined above. Howard would also continue on a preceding year basis but the Inland Revenue's practice on a change of accounting date would apply (accounts originally to 30 June now to 30 April). Making the continuation election would avoid the imposition of the new current year basis of assessment.

ii) Any unrelieved losses of Howard would be set against his first available assessable income under Schedule D Case I (ICTA 1988, s. 385) providing no change in the nature of the business has taken place. It appears that the relief would be available even if the cessation and commencement provisions applied (if no election was made for continuation). It is possible that terminal loss relief would be available to Howard if no election were made for continuation since a partnership did not previously exist but, under the circumstances, this is unlikely to be beneficial.

iii) The combined gross income of the new partnership may exceed the VAT registration threshold so that registration will become necessary. The result would be the additional costs to clients or reduced profit to the business as outlined above. There would also be the additional compliance costs in complying with the VAT requirements.

5   Dear Client,

Following our recent discussion, I am writing to advise you on the points raised.

The following kinds of information could have caused the Inspector to begin an investigation into your affairs:

a) As a businesswoman, your accounts may have been selected for detailed examination. The gross profit margin over the years may have varied inexplicably or it may be lower than that for other similar businesses in the area. The accounts may be inconsistent with other general information available, such as your lifestyle, the extent of advertising placed by you, contracts you have won, and your expansion to larger premises.

A qualified audit report may itself be sufficient to make the Inspector suspicious.

b) Your personal tax return may have been inconsistent with other information received by the Inspector.

The most common source of information giving rise to a discrepancy of this nature is a report from a bank or similar body. Banks are required to make annual returns of all persons to whom interest in excess of £150 is paid.

Information is also passed from one tax district to another, for example, on an interest-bearing loan or a gift of a chargeable asset from or to another taxpayer, from another branch of the Inland Revenue or from Customs & Excise (it is particularly important that VAT returns are consistent with your accounts).

The Inland Revenue also receive much anonymous information from neighbours, acquaintances, relatives, disgruntled employees and business contacts, giving details of suspected tax evasion.

c) The Inland Revenue also read local newspapers very carefully as this can be a productive source of information. Such information ranges from reports of burglaries which can be checked with your files for consistency, to the small advertisements revealing a business for which the Inspector has no records. Planning applications can be followed through to check on architects and building firms. Inspectors often live locally and hear a certain amount of local gossip which they may follow up.

I have set out below some of the matters which the Inland Revenue may take into account after completing the investigation and agreeing the amount of tax to be recovered, in deciding the sort of comment they will accept in respect of interest and penalties.

i) The gravity of the offence.

They will consider whether the omission was innocent or whether you were negligent or fraudulent in the records you kept and submitted.

The size of the underpayment and the number of years involved will be considered. If years which are now out of time limit are involved, this may make them unwilling to agree a significant reduction for the remaining years.

ii) The assistance given during the investigation.
They will consider whether there was any continued attempt to cover up or delay following their initial enquiries.

iii) Your personal circumstances.
Factors such as age, health, your assets and your ability to pay will be taken into account. Your level of education will be considered in determining whether you knew or ought to have known what you were doing. Mitigating factors such as domestic problems, business pressures and lack of clerical assistance are also taken into account.

I hope that this covers your questions fully.
Yours sincerely,

6 a) The provision of supplies as part of a catering business is standard-rated. The sales figure is regarded as VAT-inclusive so output tax of £1,415 (£9,500 × 7/47) will be due. The purchases are zero-rated so there is no recovery of input tax. The goods taken for Stephen's own use are subject to output tax based on their market value. The output tax due is therefore £611 (£4,100 × 7/47). Stephen's additional VAT liability will therefore be £2,026 (£1,415 + £611).

Stephen will need to pay income tax on the undisclosed cafeteria profit. The sales from this source will be net of VAT, so the profit will be: (9,500 − 1,415) − 4,600 = £3,485.

Stephen will also be liable to income tax on the selling price of the goods taken for his own consumption. The selling price will again be net of VAT: (4,100 − 611) = 3,489.

Stephen's revised income tax liability for 1994/95 is:

	£	£
Schedule D (per accounts)		52,000
Cafeteria profits		3,485
Own consumption		3,489
		58,974
Class 4 NIC relief (as before)	580	
Personal allowance	3,445	(4,025)
		54,949
Income tax due:		
£3,000 at 20%		600
£20,700 at 25%		5,175
£31,249 at 40%		12,500
		18,275
Original income tax liability		(16,685)
Additional income tax liability		1,590

There is no additional class 4 NIC due as Stephen has already paid the maximum.

b) i) Penalty interest under s88 TMA 1970 is charged when an assessment is raised for making good tax lost through:
– failure to give notice, make a return or provide a document or other information, or
– an error in any information or return supplied.

In order to impose penalty interest, the Inland Revenue must issue a notice of determination. Penalty interest runs from the normal due date of payment (as opposed to the alternative later date of 30 days after the issue of an assessment). Where penalty interest is charged, interest on overdue tax is not charged.

As there was an error in the information supplied by Stephen, he is strictly liable to penalty interest. However, the amount of additional interest involved is not material, so the Revenue will probably settle for interest on overdue tax instead.

ii) If penalty interest is not charged, the Revenue will instead charge interest on overdue tax in respect of the additional income tax liability of £1,590. The interest will run from the table date of 1 July 1995 until 28 October 1995 (the date of payment). The interest is therefore £51.84 (£1,590 × 10% × 119/365).

iii) Stephen has fraudulently or negligently submitted an incorrect return. He could therefore be charged a penalty up to 100% of the amount of income tax underpaid, that is £1,590. This penalty could be mitigated by the Revenue depending on Stephen's co-operation in the investigation. The Revenue would also take into account whether he voluntarily disclosed information and to what extent his actions were fraudulent.

c) A payment equivalent to the difference between the revised and original Schedule D assessments, namely £3,974 (58,974 − 55,000), would eliminate Stephen's additional income tax liability. As no tax would then have been lost, the Revenue could not impose either interest or penalties. Such a payment is well within Stephen's maximum of £10,320 (58,974 × 17.5%). The premium must be paid by 5 April 1996 and an election to relate it back to 1994/95 must be made by 5 July 1996.

7 a) As Andrew's business is commencing after 5 April 1994, he will be subject to the new current year basis of assessment. His capital allowances will be calculated in respect of his accounting periods and will be treated as trading expenses. They are thus deductible in computing his Schedule DI profits.

A depooling election should be made in respect of the equipment on 1 January 1996. The capital allowances due will therefore be:

	General pool £	Depooled £	Total £
A/cs to 30/4/95			
Additions	25,000		
WDA 10/12	(5,208)		5,208
	19,792		
A/cs to 30/4/96			
Additions	15,000	8,000	
Disposals	(14,000)	–	
	20,796	8,000	
WDA	(5,198)	(2,000)	7,198
	15,594	6,000	
A/cs to 30/4/97			
WDA	(3,899)	(1,500)	5,399
WDV c/f	11,695	4,500	

Andrew's profits for Schedule DI purposes will therefore be:

		£
Period to 30/4/95	(33,000 – 5,208)	27,792
Year ended 30/4/96	(48,000 – 7,198)	40,802
Year ended 30/4/97	(36,000 – 5,399)	30,601

His Schedule DI assessments under the new current year basis of assessment will therefore be:

		£
1994/95	£27,792 × 9/10	25,013
1995/96	£27,792 + (40,802 × 2/12)	34,592
1996/97	A/cs to 30/4/96	40,802
1997/98	A/cs to 30/4/97	30,601

Overlap relief will be available in respect of the profits of £25,013 assessed in both 1994/95 and 1995/96 and also in respect of the profits of £6,800 assessed in both 1995/96 and 1996/97. This will be given either when the business comes to an end or in any earlier year of assessment for which the basis period is longer than twelve months.

b) If Hilda is an employee for the first accounting period, any salary paid to her (plus employers' NIC at 10.2%) will be deductible in computing the business's Schedule DI profits. The operation of the commencement rules will enable the business to obtain relief almost twice for the one year's salary paid to Hilda. However, this benefit is only temporary as it will reduce the profits eligible for overlap relief.

As an employee, Hilda will be liable under Schedule E. Income tax and class 1 NIC will be deducted under the PAYE scheme. The Inspector will need to be satisfied that any salary is justifiable in relation to the work undertaken.

If Hilda is taken on as an equal partner from 1 July 1995, the assessable profits computed above will simply be divided equally between her and Andrew. However, Hilda will be treated as commencing to trade as at this date, and this will give rise to further overlap profits. Income tax and class 4 NIC will be payable in two equal instalments: 1 January in the year of assessment and 1 July in the following year. As an equal partner, Hilda's income from the partnership will not need to be justified to the Inspector.

Overall, the new commencement rules result in little, if any, benefit compared to the alternative of bringing Hilda into partnership from the commencement of trading on 1 July 1994.

Each partner will own a fractional share of the partnership's assets. This should result in a reduction in the CGT charged on any disposals as each partner has an annual exemption. As a partner, Hilda will be able to claim retirement relief on the eventual disposal of the business. This should result in the maximum possible relief as each partner will be 55 and will have been in business for ten years.

For IHT purposes, Andrew and Hilda each have annual exemptions which can be used to reduce the value of the business when it is eventually transferred to their son. This is of little benefit if the business qualifies for 100% business property relief, but would be useful if there were non-qualifying assets.

c) If the strategy in b) is followed, the couple will each have Schedule D Case 1 income of up to £22,500 per annum (45,000/2). Both Andrew and Hilda will have personal allowances of £3,445 p.a., together with a lower/basic rate tax band of £23,700 per annum. This will mean that they can each receive income of £27,145 per annum (3,445 + 23,700) before the 40% rate of tax is applicable. 50% of Class 4 NIC for each of them will also be deductible. It would therefore be beneficial to put the building society account and the unfurnished property into their joint names, so that the income therefrom is assessed on them equally. This would result in a tax saving of at least £696.75 per annum (27,145 – 22,500 × 15%).

The transfer of the building society account and the unfurnished property into the couple's joint names will also be beneficial in respect of both CGT and IHT. When the unfurnished property is sold, both Andrew and Hilda will be entitled to the CGT annual exemption of £5,800. They would also benefit if any of their 25% tax band was unused for the year of sale, although this would seem unlikely. For the purposes of IHT, assets of £107,500 ((125,000 + 90,000)/2) would be passed to Hilda, allowing her to utilise her annual exemption of £3,000, and to make use of her nil rate band of £150,000 both during lifetime and on death.

They could, to mimimise overall tax liabilities, transfer funds in the building society into tax-exempt investments – TESSA or PEP for example – although this would result in some loss of liquidity. They should each consider taking out personal pensions.

CHAPTER 24 *Self test questions*

1. 12 months to 30 November 1994.
   4 months to 31 March 1995.

2. 1 August 1992 – 31 October 1992.
   1 November 1992 – 31 October 1993.
   1 November 1993 – 31 December 1993.
   1 January 1994 – 30 April 1994.
   1 May 1994 – 31 May 1994.
   1 June 1994 – 12 months maximum.

3. a) New and existing companies incorporated in UK are resident in UK.
   b) Companies not incorporated in UK are resident in UK if their central management and control is in UK.
   c) A company is not treated as resident in the UK if it is regarded as resident in another country for the purposes of a double taxation agreement.

4. The country in which board meetings are held unless Inland Revenue can show that this is not where control is exercised.

5. FY 1993 three months.
   FY 1994 nine months.

6. 3,000 × 9/12 (nine months accounting period) = £2,250

7. $\dfrac{30,000 - 2\% (20-1) \times 30,000}{20}$ = £930 per annum deductible DI. 5 months to 31 December 1994, $5/12 \times £930 = £387$

8. $\dfrac{12,000 + 1/2 (15,000 - 12,000)}{15,000} \times 7,000 = £6,300$

9. Distribution received from a UK company plus the associated tax credit.

10. 30 June 1996.

11. i) Set-off against total profits of current accounting period.
    ii) Set-off against total profits of previous 36 months (provided claim for (i) made).
    iii) Carry forward and deduct from future profits of the same trade.

12 Scotia Circuits Ltd corporation tax computation – 12 months to 30 September 1994.

Schedule D Case I – adjusted profit computation

	£	£
Net profit per accounts		311,000
Add: Depreciation	27,800	
Hiring charges – car (Note 1)	2,400	
Property expenses re Schedule A 4,200		
4,600		
	8,800	
Legal expenses (Note 2)	6,898	
		45,898
		356,898
Less: UK company dividends	12,600	
Rental income	16,400	
Insurance recovery – capital part	21,800	
Profit on shares	16,000	
		(66,800)
		290,098
Less: Capital allowances (see below)		(51,100)
Schedule D Case I		238,998
Schedule A (see below)		10,000
Chargeable gains (see below)		1,520
Profits chargeable to corporation tax		250,518

Capital allowance computation 12 months to 30 September 1994

	Main pool £	Car pool £	Allowances £
Brought foward 1 October 1993	17,800	8,400	
Additions	24,000		
Disposal proceeds (fire)	(1,800)		
	40,000	8,400	
Writing down allowance 25%	(10,000)	(2,100)	12,100
Carried forward 30 Sept 94	30,000	6,300	
Industrial building allowance			
Qualifying cost of building	35,000		
Add: legal expenses	4,000		
	39,000		
Initial allowance – 100%	(39,000)		39,000
Carried forward	Nil		
Total allowances			51,100

Schedule A computation 12 months to 30 September 1994

	£	£
Rental income receivable (4 × £4,100)		16,400
Less expenses paid: rates, insurance	4,600	
estimated repair cost	1,800	
		(6,400)
		10,000

Outlay equal to estimated cost of repairs is deductible under Schedule A – Extra-statutory concession B4.

Chargeable gains computation 12 months to 30 September 1994

Shares – Pool A	Nos of shares	Value £
Acquired 6 September 1988	4,000	8,000
Indexation to 14 January 1994		
$\frac{142.0 - 108.4}{108.4} \times 8,000$	–	2,480
	4,000	10,480
Disposal 14 January 1993	(4,000)	(10,480)
Disposal proceeds (4,000/16,000 × 48,000)		12,000
Indexed cost		(10,480)
Chargeable gain		1,520

TAX PLANNING

Shares – Pool B	Nos of shares	Value £
Acquired 10 February 1982	12,000	24,000
Disposal 14 January 1994	(12,000)	(24,000)

	Old rules (cost) £	March 1982 Value £
Disposal proceeds (12,000/16,000 × 48,000)	36,000	36,000
Cost – Pool B/March 1982 Value	(24,000)	(21,000)
	12,000	15,000
Indexation allowance $\frac{142.0 - 79.4}{79.4} = 0.788 \times 24,000$	(12,000)	(15,000)
	–	–

The indexation allowance has been restricted as it cannot create an allowable loss.

It has been assumed that the insurance proceeds for the damaged showroom have been used in its repair and that any chargeable gain arising has been held over.

Notes

1 Hire of car – cost > £12,000 – restricted to:
   $\frac{12,000 + 1/2 (30,000 - 12,000)}{30,000} \times 8,000 = £5,600$ adjust £2,400

2 Legal expenses
      – insurance claim – capital part
        21,800/36,800 × 1,600   948
      – purchase of let property (capital)   1,500
      – purchase of Liverpool (Speke) building (capital)   4,000
      – expenses of debenture (stamp duty)   450
                            6,898

13 Barrel Ltd

	12 months to 31 December 1991 £	3 months to 31 March 1992 £	Year to 31 March 1993 £	Year to 31 March 1994 £	Year to 31 March 1995 £
Schedule D Case I	32,000	8,000	30,000	25,000	–
Less: loss relief s. 393 (I)	–	–	–	Nil	–
	32,000	8,000	30,000	25,000	–
Schedule D Case III	2,000	500	1,000	4,000	500
Net chargeable gains	–	–	2,000	10,000	–
Total Profits	34,000	8,500	33,000	39,000	500
Less: loss relief s. 393A(I)(a)		Nil	Nil	Nil	(500)
Less: loss relief s. 393 A(1)(b)	(19,000)	(8,500)	(28,000)	(34,000)	–
Less: charges – non-trade	(500)	–	(500)	(500)	(500)
Less: charges – trade	(5,000)	–	(5,000)	(5,000)	(5,000)
Profits chargeable to CT	9,500	Nil	Nil	Nil	Nil
Unrelieved trade charges					5,000

Unrelieved trade charges (see loss memo)

Loss memo
31 March 1995
            £

	£
Loss for year	90,000
Less: s. 393A(1)(a) y/e 31 March 1995	(500)
	89,500
Less: s. 393A(1)(b) 12 months to 31 March 1994	(34,000)
12 months to 31 March 1993	(28,000)
3 months to 31 March 1992	(8,500)
9 months to 31 December 1991*	(19,000)
Add: excess trade charges y/e March 1995	5,000
Carry forward	5,000

* lower of: remaining loss that is, £19,000
                Total profits 34,000 × 9/12 that is, 25,500
                (provided trade charges can be deducted from remaining profits).
                or (34,000 – 5,000) × 9/12 = 21,750

CHAPTER 25 *Self test questions*

1. $(M - P) \times \dfrac{I}{P} \times \text{TRF}$

2. I = 206,000; P = 230,000; lower limit 300,000 × 9/12 = 225,000
   upper limit 1.5 million × 9/12 = 1,125,000
   Taper relief applies
   $(1{,}125{,}000 - 230{,}000) \times \dfrac{206{,}000}{230{,}000} \times 1/50 = £16{,}032$

3. Profits chargeable to CT.

4. Profits chargeable to CT + FII (excluding group FII).

5. Year ended 31 March 1989
   First accounting period beginning six years prior to current account period; current account period began 1 October 1993; six years previous give 1 October 1987; next accounting period to commence on 1 April 1988.

6. Quarterly accounting on CT 61; cumulative over accounting period; at each quarter end (FP – FII) @ ACT rate gives ACT due for the year to date. By deducting ACT paid in the year to date the amount payable for the quarter is found.

7. Surplus FII is the amount by which FII is greater than FP in the accounting period. Yes, to the extent that it can give a future cash flow advantage. It is not an asset.

8. Trading loss can be set off against surplus FII of the current accounting period or previous accounting periods for which a s. 393(1)(b) claim has been made if appropriate (that is, up to 36 months prior to the current accounting period). The FII is deemed to be taxable profit and allows offset of the trading loss.

9. A FID is a Foreign Income Dividend, that is a dividend paid out of foreign source profits. It differs from a normal dividend in two ways:
   (i) surplus ACT in respect of the FID is recoverable
   (ii) a shareholder who is a non-taxpayer cannot reclaim any tax as the FID does not carry a tax credit as such.

10. An IHC is an International Headquarters Company which is a company with none of its shareholders owning less than 5% of its share capital and at least 80% of its shares being held by non-UK residents. An IHC is not required to pay ACT on its foreign income dividends at all.

11. a) MA Ltd corporation tax computation.

		Year ended 30 September 1993 £
Schedule D Case I		180,000
Schedule A		4,000
Schedule D Case III		5,000
Chargeable gains (loss to be carried forward)		–
		189,000
Less: charges paid – debenture interest	8,000	
– covenant charity	1,000	
		(9,000)
		–
Profits chargeable to CT (I)		180,000
Franked investment income (3,100 × 100/80)		3,875
(P)		183,875

	Total £	FY 1992 (6) £	FY 1993 (6) £
I	180,000	90,000	90,000
P	183,875	91,937	91,937
Lower limit		125,000	125,000
Upper limit		625,000	625,000

In FY 1992, small companies rate applies and in FY 1993 small companies rate applies.

Corporation tax liability		
FY 1992 I (90,000) @ 25%		22,500
FY 1993 I (90,000) @ 25%		22,500
		45,000
FP 17,980 × 100/77.5	23,200	
FII 3,100 × 100/77.5	4,000	
Paid @ 22.5%	19,200	(4,320)
Mainstream corporation tax payable		40,680

b)

	Year ended 30 September 1994	Loss memo
	£	£
Schedule D Case I	Nil	120,000
Schedule A	2,000	
Schedule D Case III	4,000	
Chargeable gains	12,000	
Less: loss b/f	(6,000)	
		6,000
Total profit	12,000	
Less: loss relief s. 393A	(12,000)	(12,000)
Profits chargeable to CT	Nil	108,000

Surplus ACT		
FP 14,600 × 100/80	18,250	
FII 6,400 × 100/80	8,000	
	10,250	
@ 20%		2,050

Year ended 30 September 1993	£	£
Total profit as above	189,000	
Less: loss relief s. 393A	(108,000)	(108,000)
	81,000	
Less: charges as above	(9,000)	
Profits chargeable to CT (I)	72,000	
Franked investment income	3,875	
(P)	75,875	
Small companies rate applies		£
FY 1992 I (1/2 × 72,000) @ 25%		9,000
FY 1993 I (1/2 × 72,000) @ 25%		9,000
		18,000
Less: ACT as above (Max £18,000)	4,320	
surplus ACT carried back	2,050	
		(6,370)
Revised MCT		11,630
Repayment due (40,680 – 11,630)	**£29,050**	

c) The trade charge of £4,000 debenture interest unrelieved in the year ended 30 September 1994 may be carried forward and deducted from the first available trading profit of MA Ltd. The non-trade charge, the deed of covenant to charity, cannot be carried forward.

CHAPTER 26 *Self test questions*

1 Unit trusts, investment trusts.

2 Assets used in earning profits may be eligible for capital allowances to be deducted from income of that source. Capital allowances on plant and machinery in general use are available to be deducted from 'business income' if an election is made.

3 The following are also treated as distributions:
   i) benefits in kind to participator or associate who is not an employee.
   ii) loans to participators and their associates.

4 Notional ACT is payable (not entered on quarterly returns – not a distribution) and is only repayable when the loan is repaid. If it is written off, it becomes income of the participator (gross). There may also be a benefit in kind treated as a distribution if the loan is at a beneficial interest rate.

5 Isla Mill Co. Ltd.
   Although J. Thompson and L. Bishop control Interface Systems (Mercia) Ltd, they do not control the Isla Mill Co Ltd and therefore the two companies are not associated companies for corporation tax purposes.

D. Knight is a participator but is not a director or a higher-paid employee and therefore the car benefit (not assessable under Schedule E) is a qualifying distribution with ACT payable through the quarterly accounting system. It is assumed that Schedule D Case I disallowance of motoring expenses has been made in arriving at the DI profits.

G. Bishop is an associate of a participator, and an amount equal to ACT £1,750 (7,000 x 20/80) is payable as a result of the loan to him. This amount is not ACT and is not available for offset against the company's corporation tax liability.

Corporation tax computation for the accounting period 12 months to 30 September 1994

		£
Schedule D Case I		260,000
Chargeable gain (Note 1)		–
Profits chargeable to corporation tax	(I)	260,000
	(P)	260,000

FY 1993 P (260,000/2) > 250,000/2 and < 1.25 million/2. Therefore I taxable at standard rate CT less taper relief.

FY 1994 P (260,000/2) < 300,000/2 and < 1.5 million/2. Therefore I taxable at small companies rate CT.

CT liability:

	£
FY 1993 I (260,000/2) @ 33%	42,900
FY 1994 I (260,000/2) @ 25%	32,500
Less: taper relief	
FY93 $\left[\dfrac{1.25 \text{ million}}{2} - \dfrac{260,000}{2}\right] \times \dfrac{260,000}{260,000} \times \dfrac{1}{50}$	(9,900)
	65,500
Less: ACT (Maximum) $\dfrac{260,000}{2} \times 22.5\%$ = 29,250	
$\dfrac{260,000}{2} \times 20\%$ = 26,000	
55,250	
ACT paid (Note 2)	(3,169)
Mainstream corporation tax	62,331

Notes

1

	31 March 1982 value	Old rules cost	Gain/ (Loss)
	£	£	£
Sale proceeds	130,000	130,000	
Less: 31 March 1982 value/cost	(80,000)	(50,000)	
Unindexed gain	50,000	80,000	
Less: indexation allowance on 31 March 1982 value			
$\dfrac{142.0 - 79.4}{79.4} = 0.788$			
80,000 × 0.788 (restricted)	(50,000)	(63,040)	
Gain/(Loss)	–	16,960	Nil

2   Dividends paid:

			£
December 1993	40,000 × 12.5p =		5,000
April 1994	40,000 × 7.5p =		3,000
Benefits to D. Knight:			
1993/94	Car £12,000 × 35% × 6/12 =	2,100	
	Less 1/3 for over 2,500 miles	(700)	1,400
1994/95	Car as above		1,400
1993/94	Fuel 760 × 6/12		380
1994/95	Fuel 810 × 6/12		405

Distributed to 5/4/94 (5,000 + 1,400 + 380) 6,780 × 22.5/77.5 =   1,968
Distributed post 5/4/94 (3,000 + 1,400 + 405) 4,805 × 20/80 =   1,201
                                                                 3,169

CHAPTER 27 *Self test questions*

1 Section 393A(1)(a); non-trade charges; trade charges; group relief; s. 393A(1)(b).

2 51% of ordinary share capital/distributable profits/assets on a winding up throughout the accounting period of both surrender and claim.

3 Dividends can be paid up to parent without accounting for ACT.

4 Group surrendered; paid in year; brought forward; carried back.

5 All or part, to one or more subsidiaries.

6 75% of ordinary share capital/distributable profits/assets on a winding up for corresponding accounting periods only.

7 Within two years of the end of the accounting period in which it arose. The claimant makes the claim but the company must agree to surrender.

8 Group relief; group income and charges elections.

9 One must be controlled by the other or they must both be controlled by the same person.

10 90 days before it is required to take effect.

11 H holds 75% of S which holds 75% of SS, and so on. H must have more than 50% interest in the profits and assets on winding up of all members of a capital gains group.

12 Assets may be transferred at no gain, no loss; rollover relief; joint elections for March 1982 values.

13 H Ltd

	12 months to 31 December 1993 £	9 months to 30 September 1994 £	Loss memo £
Schedule D Case I	25,000	–	45,000
Schedule A	3,000	4,000	
	28,000	4,000	
Less: charges paid	(2,000)	(2,000)	
Basic profit (also P)	26,000	2,000	

CT liability
at small companies rate:

FY 1992 3/12 × 26,000 × 25%	1,625	FY1993 3/9 × 2,000 × 25%	167
FY 1993 9/12 × 26,000 × 25%	4,875	FY1994 6/9 × 2,000 × 25%	333
	£6,500		£500

S Ltd

	12 months to 31 March 1994 £	12 months to 31 March 1995 £	Loss memo (H) £
b/f			45,000
Schedule D Case I	52,000	250,000	
Schedule D Case III	8,000	10,000	
	60,000	260,000	
Less: charges paid	(5,000)	(5,000)	
group relief	(13,750)	(30,000)	(43,750)
Basic profit (also P)	41,250	225,000	
		Carry forward	£1,250

CT liability
FY 1993 @ SCR 41,250 @ 25% 10,312

	£
FY 1994 @ standard rate 225,000 @ 33%	74,250
Less: taper relief (750,000 – 225,000) × 1/50	(10,500)
	63,750

Notes

1 Loss relief for corresponding accounting periods: loss for nine months to 30 September 1994 divides up into:

a) 3 months to 31 March 1994
   Loss of H Ltd 3/9 × 45,000 = 15,000   Group relief
   Profit of S Ltd 3/12 × 55,000 = 13,750   13,750

b) 6 months to 30 September 1994
   Loss of H Ltd 6/9 × 45,000 = 30,000   Group relief
   Profit of S Ltd 6/12 × 255,000 = 127,500 30,000

2 Initially H Ltd would not make a claim for loss relief under s. 393A(1)(a) as small companies rate applies, while S Ltd, in the corresponding accounting period (or part) is liable at 35%. A claim for the balance of £1,250 could be made for the period ended 30 September 1994, or the loss could be carried forward; this would depend on the level of profits expected by H Ltd in the future.

14 a) H Ltd – S Ltd

12 months to 31 March 1995

	H Ltd £	S Ltd £
Schedule D Case I	36,000	133,000
Schedule D Case III	4,500	15,000
Unfranked investment income	6,000	7,500
Chargeable gains	4,500	13,500
Total profits	51,000	169,000
Less: Loan interest	(7,500)	(6,000)
Charitable convenant	(1,500)	(1,500)
Profit chargeable to CT (I)	42,000	161,500
Franked investment income	18,000	28,500
(P)	60,000	190,000

H and S are associated companies.
FY 1994 lower limit 300,000/2 = 150,000

Upper limit 1.5 million/2 = 750,000

H therefore pays small companies rate and S will pay standard rate corporation tax less taper relief.

CT liabilities		H Ltd £		S Ltd £
I	@ 25%	10,500	@ 33%	53,295

Less: taper relief

$$(750{,}000 - 190{,}000) \times \frac{161{,}500}{190{,}000} \times \frac{1}{50}$$

				(9,520)
				43,775
Less: ACT – Maximum 20%	8,400		32,300	
(Note 1) Paid	10,112		Nil	
Set off	(8,400)	(8,400)		
	1,712			
Surrender				
S Ltd	(1,712)		1,712	(1,712)
MCT		2,100		42,063

Notes

1 H Ltd FP (43,900 + 10,950) × $\frac{100}{80}$ = 68,562

FII	(18,000)
FP – FII	50,562
ACT @ 20%	10,112
S Ltd FP	–
FII	28,500
Surplus FII	28,500

b) If S Ltd paid a dividend to H Ltd (without making a group income election not to account for ACT), the franked payment would be set against the surplus FII in S Ltd: no ACT would be payable by S Ltd and H Ltd would receive FII which would reduce the amount of ACT payable by it. Therefore a cash flow benefit would result.

c) If H Ltd had acquired the assets and liabilities of S Ltd and not the share capital, H Ltd's profit chargeable to corporation tax (I) for the year would be £203,500 and P would be £250,000. There would be no associated companies and so the small companies rate would apply to the whole of I.

	£
CT liability in S Ltd as above	43,775
S Ltd – I (161,500) @ 25%	(40,375)
Tax saving	3,400

The cash flow benefit referred to in (b) above will be automatic as the FII of S Ltd will become that of H Ltd and will be set off against FP of H Ltd.

These benefits could also be expected to arise in subsequent years. However, substantial costs would be incurred in winding up S Ltd.

15 a) 75% Group – A Ltd, B Ltd and D Ltd form a 75% group.
D Ltd and E Ltd form another 75% group.

The most efficient way of using the losses may only be determined by comparing the amount of tax savings arising from the various alternatives. This is done by looking at the marginal rate of tax of each company.

There are five associated companies and therefore the lower limit (FY 1994) is £60,000 (300,000/5) while the upper limit is £300,000 (1.5m/5) in each case. The highest marginal rate of tax occurs when P falls between the lower and the upper limit.

	A Ltd £	B Ltd £	C Ltd £	D Ltd £	E Ltd £
Schedule D Case I	76,000	–	90,000	65,000	–
Schedule D Case III	–	3,000	15,000	–	–
Total profit	76,000	3,000	105,000	65,000	–
Less: Charges	(3,000)	(1,000)	(4,000)	(2,000)	–
	73,000	2,000	101,000	63,000	–

A Ltd will be chargeable at the marginal rate of tax on the top £13,000 of its income.
B Ltd will be chargeable at small companies rate.
C Ltd has the greatest amount of profits taxable at this marginal rate but is not eligible for group relief.
D Ltd will be chargeable at the marginal rate of tax on £3,000.

Group relief should therefore be targetted at A Ltd and D Ltd up to £13,000 and £3,000 respectively. There are losses of £12,000 in E Ltd which can only be used by D Ltd. There are losses in B Ltd of £24,000 of which at least £13,000 should be surrendered to A Ltd – it is assumed here that the remainder is also surrendered to A Ltd.

	A Ltd £	B Ltd £	C Ltd £	D Ltd £	E Ltd £
Continued from above	73,000	2,000	101,000	65,000	–
Group relief	(24,000)	–	–	(12,000)	–
Chargeable to CT	49,000	2,000	101,000	53,000	–
CT liability:					
@ 25%	12,250	500		13,250	–
@ 33%			33,330		
Less: Taper relief			(3,980)		
(300,000 – 101,000)/50			29,350		

b) A group income election is normally made to aid the group cash flow by reducing the ACT payable by a subsidiary. The ACT would otherwise be offset at a later date, as FII, against FP of the holding company and the holding company's ACT would be reduced at that time.

Where the subsidiary has FII of its own which would not otherwise be used, the group income election should be set aside to the extent that FII exists. In this way the dividend is franked by the subsidiary without cost in terms of ACT and the parent company receives FII allowing it to 'save' on ACT.

16 a) Report on the VAT implications of acquiring subsidiaries and export activities.

Acquisition of subsidiaries

The acquisition of a subsidiary has in itself no direct VAT consequences.

If the acquiring company is VAT registered and the acquired company is VAT registered, then group registration for VAT ought to be considered. This would mean that the existing VAT registration numbers would be cancelled and a group registration number would be substituted. Group registration treats all the business carried on by members of the group as being carried on by the representative member – this has the effect that intra-group transactions are ignored for VAT purposes since they are self-cancelling.

It is not necessary for all group companies (companies under common control or one of which controls the other) to be brought within the group registration. It is necessary to plan tax-efficient VAT groups and the impact of group registration on the overall VAT burden must be carefully considered.

The group registration is held in the name of one of the companies – the representative member – which is responsible for the submission of VAT returns and for payment of the VAT on behalf of the group. All members of the group are jointly and severally liable for the tax due by the representative member. It is possible subsequently to add additional companies to the group registration or remove companies from it.

Export activities

Exported supplies are zero-rated. This means that they are supplies (at a nil rate) and VAT registration is still required where the turnover of total taxable supplied exceeds the thresholds. Input tax on supplies of goods and services attributable to zero-rate supplies is recoverable and often an exporter will be in a VAT repayment situation (and will be able to submit monthly repayment claims).

If it is intended that the export activities will be concentrated in one of the group companies (see above), then that company would probably do better to be excluded from the group registration. The benefits of not accounting for VAT on intra-group transactions would need to be weighed up against the disadvantages if it would otherwise be able to claim monthly repayments.

The terms import and export no longer apply to transactions with EC countries. From 1 January 1993 the EC represents a Single Market. Supplies to registered traders in EC countries may be zero-rated but supplies to non-registered persons will be taxed at the standard rate.

CHAPTER 28 *Self test questions*

1   £25,000, however, B can only absorb £20,000.

2   Nil, not a group member throughout accounting period.

3   The asset is deemed to be sold at market value and immediately reacquired at the date of the original transfer (if acquired on a 'no gain, no loss' basis within six years).

4   This allows the taxpayer to check that a reorganisation will work as planned before it is undertaken.

5   i)   Unquoted trading company.
    ii) Purposes must be for the benefit of the trade.
    iii) Vendor must be UK resident and have owned the shares for a minimum of five years.
    iv) Vendors' interest in company must be reduced by at least 25% to 30% or less.

6   Purchase of own shares.
    The three tests which determine whether a shareholding has been substantially reduced are as follows:
    i)   The shareholding of the vendor (together with his associates) after the purchase must not be more than 75% of the shareholding of the vendor (together with associates) before the purchase.
    ii) The share of the distributable profits available to the vendor (together with his associates) after the purchase must not be more than 75% of the share of the distributable profits of the vendor (together with his associates) before the purchase.
    iii) After the purchase, the vendor must not be connected with the company or any company within the same 51 per cent group. This means that the vendor (together with his associates) must not own more than 30% of the issued share capital.

7   Rosefield Ltd.
    i)   Harry's shareholding of total issued share capital before the purchase was:
    $$\frac{4{,}000 + 800}{4{,}800 + 3{,}200} = 60\%$$
    After the purchase, it becomes:
    $$\frac{750 + 800}{1{,}550 + 3{,}200} = 33\%$$
    Test passed.

    ii) Harry's share of distributable profit.

	Before £	After £
Reserves £8,000	6,667	
£1,500 (8,000 − 3,250 @ £2)		725
Preference dividend (12% × 3,200)	96	96
	6,763	821

    Reduced by more than 25% – test passed.

    iii) Harry owns 750 out of 1,550 ordinary shares which is more than 30%. He is therefore still connected with the company – test failed.
        The purchase will not be exempted from being treated as a distribution.

CHAPTER 29 *Self test questions*

1   Commencement rules (for business commencing pre 6 April 1994) result in overlapping basis periods; the smaller the profits the better; any revenue expenditure incurred before trading commences (up to seven years) creates a pre-trading loss for which relief is only given once. Trading should commence as early as can be justified.

2   Jean – inheritance tax considerations. Potentially exempt transfer provided that Jean survives seven years. If not, will the annual exemptions for current year and previous year be available for set-off? Size of estate and level of cumulative transfers to date.
    Mother – income tax considerations. Age allowance entitlement but as her only income is the state

retirement pension this means surplus allowances at present. Investment in a building society is a suitable plan as repayment of tax at source can be obtained – alternatively complete a gross interest declaration.

3 Any comparison of suitable properties must take into account both the industrial buildings allowances which would be obtained from each and over what period; that is, the residue after sale of each divided by the number of years of remaining life.

4 With an employee there is a Class I NIC liability (maximum 10% cost to employee up to a threshold + 10.2% cost to employer without limit). A self-employed trader has a Class 2 liability (flat rate) + a Class 4 liability (7.3% profits within certain limits).

5 Employer contributions are tax deductible and without limit to the extent they are used to secure approved benefits. They are flexible in that contributions may fluctuate from year to year and the fund may re-invest back in company. It is not a benefit in kind. The pension fund itself is exempt.

6 Loss relief is not locked into the business as with a company but available as deduction from STI under ICTA 1988, s. 380/s.381. (Under s. 381 it can be carried back for three years prior to the commencement of the business.)

7 Tax avoidance is the minimisation of tax liabilities within the law; tax evasion is the reduction of a tax liability through omission of income or false claim to allowances or reliefs.

8 Furniss v. Dawson; Ramsay v. CIR.

9 No.

10 Transactions (or parts thereof) undertaken for purely tax avoidance motives can be ignored or even overturned.

11 **Mr Slowman**

Inheritance tax
Where there is an alteration in any rights attaching to unquoted shares in a close company, the alteration is treated as having been made by a disposition by the participators who own the shares. The disposition so made is not a potentially exempt transfer and is therefore fully chargeable at the time of alteration of the rights. In this case, 100% entitlement to dividend is passed to Mrs Speedy but only 20% of the voting rights. Control of the dividend paid is still with Mr Slowman who can use this control to manipulate the capital value of his shares. Additionally Mr Slowman or his wife could at some later date reverse the resolution. The gift may therefore be treated as a gift with reservation.

12 **Mr Greaves**

Income tax
Income resulting from parental dispositions (including trusts set up otherwise than on death of a parent) to a minor child will be treated as income of the parent. His wife is among the potential beneficiaries. Any income from a trust to the settlor's spouse will be treated as the settlor's.

Inheritance tax
A transfer into a discretionary trust is a chargeable lifetime transfer. A discretionary trust in which the settlor's wife and children are beneficiaries may be regarded as a gift with reservation since the property could potentially revert to the settlor if the beneficiaries predeceased him. It would depend whether there were other beneficiaries, or whether the trust made alternative provisions for such an eventuality (not involving the settlor).

Capital gains tax
The settlor is connected with the trustees of the settlement and therefore any transfer of assets to a discretionary trust will be deemed to take place at market value. Any losses resulting from the computation will only be available for offset against future gains on transfers to the same trust.

Any gain arising will be able to be deferred if both parties elect for gift relief.

13 The classical interpretations by the courts in cases involving tax avoidance schemes were that the taxpayer was entitled to do whatever he could, within the letter of the law, to minimise his tax liability. In general, tax cases at this time involved the tax consequences of a single transaction. Since then tax avoidance has become more sophisticated and more artificial.

Since Ramsay v. CIR and Furniss v. Dawson the application of this principle has been limited. A series of transactions, circular in nature, finished with the financial position of the parties relatively unchanged in Ramsay v. CIR and it was held that when a preordained series of transactions is undertaken to avoid tax, the individual transactions and their fiscal consequences need not be considered in isolation.

In Furniss v. Dawson, it was held that the Ramsay principle above should not be confined to transactions circular in nature and that any transaction which is part of a preordained series of transactions, although in itself genuine, could be ignored if it served no commercial purpose and was entered into solely for fiscal reasons – for the avoidance, deferral or saving of tax. This was held to be the case even if the series of transactions overall had a legitimate commercial purpose.

The principle was later modified in Craven v. White which stated that for the Ramsay principle to apply, the preordained series of transactions has to be preordained with so much certainty that there was no practical probability that the transactions would not take place.

The implications of these cases for tax planning are as yet unclear. The business purpose test still prevails and only transactions which have no other purpose than the avoidance of tax will be caught – there are, however, areas like estate planning where this test is difficult to apply. No proper guidance has been issued by the Inland Revenue as to when the Ramsay principle will or will not be applied although a statement has been issued which gives help in a limited number of transactions. It appears that it is not mandatory to apply the Ramsay principle.

QUESTION BANK – *corporate taxation*

1 Stacker Ltd

Schedule D Case I – adjusted profit computation

	Year ended 30 Sept 92 £	Year ended 30 Sep 93 £	Year ended 30 Sep 94 £
Net profit per accounts	18,150	5,725	88,875
Adjustments:			
Depreciation	5,200	6,900	28,200
Debenture interest	6,750	9,000	9,000
Legal costs (Note 1)	800		1,200
Deed of covenant	200	200	200
Installation costs (Note 2)		900	
Investment income	(11,500)	(15,250)	(5,875)
Capital allowances:			
plant and machinery	(8,250)	(37,813)	(32,053)
industrial buildings		(8,000)	(8,000)
patents		(2,500)	(1,875)
Schedule D Case I	11,350	(40,838)	79,672

Corporation tax computation

	£	£	£
Schedule D Case I	11,350	Nil	79,672
losses brought forward (see loss memo)			(34,988)
Unfranked investment income	4,000	4,000	4,000
Total profits	15,350	4,000	48,684
Less: losses s. 393A(1)(a) (see loss memo)		(4,000)	
s. 393A(1)(b) (see loss memo)	(10,850)		
	4,500	Nil	48,684
Less: charges:			
Non-trade – lost	(200)	(200)	
Non-trade			(200)
Trade – c/f (Note 5)		(9,000)	
s. 242	Nil		
used	(4,500)		(9,000)
Profits chargeable to CT	Nil	Nil	39,484

	£	£	£
Corporation tax liability	Nil	Nil	
Repayments of tax credits			
under s. 242 claim		3,187	
I + FII < 250,000 (FY93) < 300,000 (FY94)			
Small companies rate applies			
FY 93 6/12 × 39,484 @ 25%			
FY 94 6/12 × 39,484 @ 25%			9,871
Less: ACT set-off (MAX 39,484 × 6/12 @ 22.5%			4,442
39,484 × 6/12 @ 20%			3,948
			8,390
ACT paid in year			(3,007)
Surplus ACT brought forward y/e Sep 92			(3,867)
			2,997
Less: Income tax – charges exceeded UFII			Nil
Mainstream corporation tax			2,997

The due date for payment is 9 months after the year end. Corporation tax for y/e September 1994 will be 1 July 1995.

Capital allowance computation

Plant and machinery

	Main pool £	Short life asset £	Car £	Allowances £
Brought forward Oct 1991	24,000			
Heating	7,000	2,000		
	31,000	2,000		
WDA 25%	(7,750)	(500)		8,250
Carried forward 30 Sept 1992	23,250	1,500		
Office equipment	19,000			
Plant	108,000			
Installation costs	900			
Sale proceeds	(1,400)			
	149,750	1,500		
WDA 25%	(37,438)	(375)		37,813
Carried foward 30 Sept 1993	112,312	1,125		
Car (Note 4)			18,000	
Sale proceeds		(150)		
	112,312	975	18,000	
Balancing allowance		(975)		975
WDA 25%	(28,078)		(3,000)	31,078
Carried forward 30 Sept 1994	84,234	–	15,000	
				32,053

Industrial buildings
Factory cost (exluding land) £200,000 WDA 4% pa £8,000
assuming brought into use
before year end

Patents

	Pool £
Cost	10,000
WDA 25% year ended September 1993	(2,500)
	7,500
WDA 25% year ended 30 September 1994	(1,875)
Carried forward 30 September 1994	5,625

Loss memo   Year ended September 1992

	£
Per Schedule D Case I	40,838
Set off other profit same year s. 393A(1)(a)	(4,000)
total profit previous year s. 393A(1)(b)	(10,850)
s. 242 y/e 30 September 1993	(14,687)
	11,301
Add: excess trade charges y/e 30 September 1993	9,000
Available to carry forward to y/e 30 September 1994	20,301
Add: s. 242 losses reinstated (see below)	14,687
	34,988
Relieved year ended 30 September 1994	(34,988)

ACT

Year ended Sept 1992 – Franked payments		27,467
(20,600 × 100/75)		
Franked investment income		(12,000)
(7,750 × 10/80) + b/f 2,000		15,467
Act @ 25%		3,867

Surplus ACT carry forward (use year ended 30 Sept 1994)

Year ended 30 Sept 1993 – Franked payments		Nil
Franked investment income		
(3,750 × 100/75)		(5,000)
7,500 × 100/75 (note 6)		(9,687)
Surplus FII		(14,687)
s. 242 claim using trade losses of year		14,687
Repayment 5,000 @ 25%	1,250	c/f Nil
9,687 @ 20%	1,937	
	3,187	

Year ended Sept 1994 – Franked payments

	(26,710 × 100/80)	33,387
	Franked investment income	
	(1,935 × 100/80)	(2,419)
		30,968
	ACT payable @ 20%	6,194
Set off against CT of year restricted by s. 242		
repayments already received:		
	Year ended Sept 1993	(3,187)
		3,007

The whole s. 242 claim is now reversed; all trading losses are reinstated £14,687 – see loss memo

Notes

1. The legal expenses associated with the debenture issue have been disallowed as it has been assumed that these are stamp duties and so on. If they were merely incidental costs of raising long-term loan finance, they would be allowable. Similarly legal costs of a share issue are capital and are not deductible.
2. Installation costs of plant are incidental costs associated with capital expenditure and as such are treated as capital.
3. Costs of registering patents are specifically allowed by statute.
4. No private adjustment is required for the managing director's car as it is owned by the company and the managing director is an employee.
5. In the year ended 30 September 1992, the debenture interest charged in the accounts is £6,750 (9 months since issue) but only £4,500 was actually paid in the accounting period.
6. For the purpose of the s. 242 claim the surplus FII for the year to 31 March 1994 has to be recalculated using a grossing fraction of 20/80 because the credit the company actually received was at the rate of ¼ of the dividend, and that is the amount they are entitled to recover on a s. 242 claim. For the purpose of calculating ACT the normal fraction of 22.5/77.5 is used.

2 a) i) **CT implications to Maura Ltd – Maura Ltd acquires the property**

The property is an office and is therefore not eligible for any industrial buildings allowances (assuming it is not situated in an enterprise zone). There would no longer be a rental deduction under Schedule D Case I and therefore trading profits would be higher. The bank interest on the loan to acquire it would, however, be tax deductible either under Schedule D Case I or as an annual charge, being yearly interest payable to a UK bank.

ii) **CT implications to Maura Ltd – Mr McIntyre acquires the property**

Rent would be payable to Mr McIntyre instead of to the existing landlord. The Schedule D Case I deduction may be more or less than previously.

b) i) **IT and NIC implications to Mr McIntyre – Maura Ltd acquires the property**

The use of the flat by Mr McIntyre's relatives rent free would constitute a benefit in kind to Mr McIntyre under Schedule E. This would be based on the gross rateable value of the flat. As yet neither the employer nor the employee is required to pay national insurance on benefits in kind.

ii) **IT and NIC implications to Mr McIntyre – Mr McIntyre acquires the property**

Mr McIntyre would be taxable under Schedule A on the rent receivable in the fiscal year from Maura Ltd less expenses actually paid associated with the office. The expenses associated with the flat are only deductible from rent receivable on the flat and if this is £nil, a loss will be shown. The loss cannot be offset against the office rent nor against his income from employment – nominal lease losses can only be carried forward and deducted from future profits on the same lease on the same property and in this case there is no lease so there will be no relief for the losses.

Interest on the loan excluding any related to the flat would be deductible as a charge from his total income up to a maximum of the net rental income received. Any additional interest could be carried forward and deducted from net rental income of future years.

Rental income is not trading income and there would be no NIC liability.

c) **Additional remuneration**

	£
Net cash inflow required by Mr McIntyre	3,500
Associated costs – NIC – already at maximum	–
– PAYE – gross at 40%	2,333
Additional remuneration required	5,833
Cost to company – additional salary	5,833
NIC: 10.2%	595
Reduction in trading profit	6,428
Save corporation tax (profits > £300,000)	
(marginal rate FY 94: 35%)	(2,250)
Cost to company	4,178

	£
Dividend	
Net cash inflow required	3,500
Higher rate tax liability: 20/60	1,167
Dividend required	4,667
Cost to company – Dividend	4,667
ACT 20/80	1,167
Recovery of ACT against CT	(1,167)
Cost to company	4,667

In this particular case, it would be better for him to finance the shortfall by taking additional remuneration than to pay a dividend as this will cost the company less – this is due to the marginal rate of corporation tax being suffered in FY94.

d) If Mr McIntyre acquires the property personally and leases it to Maura Ltd then he has an appreciating asset on which a capital gains tax liability is certain to arise. In seven years time, he will be 61 years of age and eligible for retirement relief. As he is a director of the company and the asset (65/70 thereof) has been used in the business for seven years then retirement relief will be available to mitigate the chargeable gain. Retirement relief will be lost to the extent that Maura Ltd pays a commercial rent for occupying the property.

If he sells the shares in the company at the same time, then retirement relief will also be available to mitigate this gain – he is a full-time working director of the company and controls > 5% of the votes and will have done so throughout a qualifying period of ten years.

Retirement relief after a qualifying period of ten years or more is currently as follows:
- The first £250,000 of gains are exempt
- The next £1,000,000 of gains are 50% exempt

e) The due date for tax under Schedule A is 1 January in the fiscal year. As an accurate amount of income will not necessarily be known at that date, the assessment is estimated and adjusted once the taxpayer has submitted the tax return.

Income tax benefits in kind may initially be assessed under Schedule E. In this case tax will be due within 30 days of the assessment. Subsequently an estimated benefit will normally be coded in. There should be no amounts due for NIC.

3

a) **Income tax**

If Mr Snow incorporates, his existing business will be deemed to cease at the date of incorporation (30 June 1994) and the Schedule D case I cessation provisions will apply. The value of the stock taken over by the limited company (£8,000) will be a trading receipt of the final period of trading – increasing the adjusted trading profits, as estimated, from £38,000 to £43,000 (£8,000 less stock cost £3,000).

The effect of this will be assessments as follows:

	£
1994/95 Final year – 6 Apr 94 to 30 June 94	
(3/12 × 43,000)	10,750

The assessments for 1993/94 and 1992/93 have already been made based on the accounts ending in the preceding fiscal year (£29,000 and £22,000 respectively). This leaves the profits earned in the period from 1 July 1993 to 5 April 1994 unassessed (33,000 + 9/12 × 43,000). However, as profits over the final years of trading were rising, this benefit will be partly offset as the Inland Revenue will exercise their option to amend the assessments for these years to an actual basis.

	£
1993/94 (9/12 × 43,000 + 3/12 × 33,000)	40,500
1992/93 (9/12 × 33,000 + 9/12 × 29,000)	32,000

The plant and machinery continuing to be used in the trade, for purposes of capital allowances, may be treated as transferred to the limited company at tax written down value if Mr Snow so elects within two years of the date of incorporation (Mr Snow and the limited company are connected persons). This avoids any additional tax liabilities which would otherwise result to Mr Snow from their disposal at open market value.

The capital allowance computation will be as follows:

	Main pool	Allowances
1991/92	£	£
(Basis period y/e 30 Jun 90)		
b/f	3,000	
writing down allowance	(750)	750
1992/93	2,250	
(Basis period 1 Jul 90 to 5 Apr 93)		
Additions	1,500	
	3,750	
writing down allowance	(938)	938
1993/94	2,812	
(Basis period 6 Apr 93 to 5 Apr 94)		
writing down allowances	(703)	703
1994/95	2,109	
(Basis period 6 Apr 94 to 30 Jun 94)		
writing down allowance × 3/12	(132)	132
Tax written down value transferred	1,977	

Under Schedule D Case I, tax has been due on the whole of the profits as follows: half on the 1 January in the year of assessment and half on 1 July following the end of the year of assessment – an interval of 18/24 months following the accounting year end. Corporation tax will be payable by Snow Limited nine months after the year end on the profits after deducting your salary.

You will be assessed under Schedule E on your salary and tax will be payable under PAYE whenever it is credited to you. You will also be assessable under Schedule E on any benefits in kind you receive from the company.

You will also be assessed on the amount of any dividend you receive from Snow Limited plus the associated tax credit (in 94/95, 20/80 of the dividend paid). The tax credit is equal to lower rate income tax on the dividend and will be set against your income tax liability for the year. Additional tax of 20% (40% – 20%) will be payable on any dividend received if you are liable to higher rate income tax in the year: this is likely as your income requirements stand at £24,000 after tax and higher rates become payable on taxable income in excess of £23,700.

Capital gains tax

A liability to capital gains tax will arise on the incorporation of a business to the extent that the business assets transferred are chargeable assets.

Stocks and other current assets are not chargeable assets and will not give rise to chargeable gains. Small items of plant used in the business (chattels, whether wasting assets or not, where both sale proceeds and allowable deductions are less than £6,000) are exempt assets and no chargeable gain or allowable loss can arise. This will apply to Mr Snow's plant and machinery.

The remaining assets, premises and goodwill, are chargeable assets and the chargeable gains on disposal must be computed separately as follows (assuming disposal at estimated values at 30 June 1994):

		31 March 82 value £	Old rules cost £	Gain/ (loss) £
i)	Goodwill			
	Disposal value	100,000	100,000	
	Less: 31 Mar 82 value/cost	Nil	Nil	
	Unindexed gain	100,000	100,000	
	Less: indexation allowance	Nil	Nil	
		100,000	100,000	
Chargeable gain				100,000
ii)	Premises	**31 March 82 value £**	**Old rules cost £**	
	Disposal value	65,000	65,000	
	Less: 31 Mar 82 value/cost	60,000	52,000	
	Unindexed gain	5,000	13,000	
	Less: indexation allowance on 31 Mar 82 value			
	60,000 × 0.801 (restricted)	(5,000)	(13,000)	
		–	–	
Net chargeable gains estimated 1994/95				100,000

$$\frac{143.0 - 79.4}{79.4} = 0.801$$

If the consideration for the sale of the business is wholly shares then all of the net gains would be deferred. Mr Snow wants to take as much as possible of the consideration in loan form but without incurring additional tax liabilities.

If he does this, a proportion of the net chargeable gains, equal to the proportion that the loan bears to the total consideration, will remain chargeable in 1994/95. In order not to incur additional tax liabilities this must not exceed the amount of the losses brought forward and Mr Snow's annual exemption for the year, that is, £20,800 (£15,000 + £5,800).

		£
Total consideration –	Goodwill	100,000
	Premises	65,000
	Plant	8,000
	Stock	8,000
	Debtors	1,500
	Cash/bank	2,400
		184,900
	Less: creditors	(4,400)
	bank loan	(25,000)
		155,500

$$\frac{\text{Loan}}{\text{Total consideration (155,500)}} \times 100,000 = 20,800$$

The maximum loan is therefore £32,344

The balance of the consideration (£123,156) must be in shares and the remaining chargeable gain (£79,200) will be deferred, being deducted from the acquisition value of the shares (they will therefore have a base cost for capital gains tax of £43,956 (£123,156 – £79,200)).

Value added tax

The incorporation of a business comes under the heading of a transfer of a business as a going concern. Provided that the assets will be used by Snow Limited in carrying on the same kind of business as Mr Snow carried on, that there is no significant break in the business and that Snow Limited immediately becomes a taxable person for VAT purposes following the transfer, the transfer of the business is not itself a taxable supply and VAT must not be charged.

The existing business will cease to exist and must de-register while Snow Limited must register as a taxable person unless they apply for the registration number of Mr Snow to be taken over by Snow Limited. The VAT records in any case must be transferred to Snow Limited and kept for six years.

b) Optimum dividend strategy

The payment of remuneration reduces the profit chargeable to corporation tax but increases the costs to the company by the amount of employer's national insurance contributions. The amount received by the director is also reduced by Class 1 national insurance contributions. However, in exchange for this, the director becomes entitled to social security benefits, a factor which is not to be ignored.

The payment of dividends does not reduce the profits chargeable to corporation tax but saves in national insurance contributions. Advance corporation tax is payable 14 days after the end of the quarter in which the dividend is paid but can be offset against the corporation tax liability within limits. The amount of the dividend paid should be restricted to the profits chargeable to corporation tax and its timing should be such that it is paid in the last quarter of the year. This minimises the interval between payment of the ACT and set-off against corporation tax.

A combination of remuneration and dividend usually gives the best result.

4 a) Adjusted profited and corporation tax computations for:

Year ended	30/9/92	30/9/93	30/9/94
	£	£	£
Unadjusted result	10,000	3,000	4,000
Debenture interest	2,500	2,500	2,500
Depreciation	5,000	5,000	5,000
Bank interest			(400)
	17,500	10,500	11,100
Capital allowances (note 1)	(5,274)	(3,955)	(2,966)
	12,226	6,545	8,134
Schedule D Case I	12,226	6,545	8,134
Schedule D Case III			400
	12,226	6,545	8,534
Less: charges (trade)	(2,500)	(2,500)	(2,500)
Basic profit (I)	9,726	4,045	6,034
Corporation tax			
FY 91/92/93 25%	1,216	506	754
FY 92/93/94 25%	1,216	506	754
	2,432	1,012	1,508

Adjusted profit and corporation tax computation for 6 months to 31/3/95

Projected unadjusted loss	(11,750)	
Debenture interest	1,250	
Depreciation	2,500	
Bank interest	(50)	
Sale of stock – loss	(5,000)	
	(13,050)	
Capital allowances	(6,899)	
	(19,949)	Loss memo
Schedule D Case I	Nil	19,949
Schedule D Case III	50	
Capital gains (note 2)	150	
Total profit	200	
Loss relief s. 393A(1)(a)	(200)	(200)
Trade charges	–	1,250
Basic profit	Nil	c/f 20,999

The above corporation tax computations would be those initially submitted to the Inland Revenue for each of the years concerned. When the computation for the period ended 31 March 1995 is submitted a loss claim under s. 393 A (1)(b) will also be submitted.

Final corporation tax computations year ended 30/9/94

	£		Loss memo £
Total profit	8,534		b/f 20,999
s. 393A(1)(b) restricted	(6,034)		(6,034)
Trade charges	(2,500)		
Revised basic profit	Nil	Unrelieved loss	14,965
s. 393A(1)(b) claims			
12 months to 30 Sept 1993	6,545		
Less: trade charges not set off	(2,500)		(4,045)
12 months to 30 Sept 1992	12,226		10,920
Less: trade charges not set off	(2,500)		(9,726)
Balance of loss unrelieved			1,194

Notes

1 Capital allowance

Assume £Nil balance in pool when plant and machinery acquired April 1989.

	£
Cost year ended 30 Sept 1989	50,000
WDA 25%	(12,500)
	37,500
Year ended 30 Sept 1990 WDA 25%	(9,375)
	28,125
Year ended 30 Sept 1991 WDA 25%	(7,031)
	21,094
Year ended 30 Sept 1992 WDA 25%	(5,274)
	15,820
Year ended 30 Sept 1993 WDA 25%	(3,955)
	11,865
Year ended 30 Sept 1994 WDA 25%	(2,966)
	8,899
6 months 31 March 1995 Sale proceeds	(2,000)
Balancing allowance	6,899

2 Capital gains

Held-over gain relating to asset held pre 31 March 1982 (£300) crystallises on disposal of plant and machinery. A claim would be submitted for the held-over gain to be reduced, that is, by 50 per cent, ie £150.

No chargeable gain arises on the disposal of the office.

b) The above claims would reduce the corporation tax liabilities for each of the above periods to £Nil. The mainstream corporation tax liability for the year ended 30 September 1994 is not due until 30 June 1995 and therefore the loss claims will merely cancel the liability and not result in a repayment. Repayments would be received of:

Year ended 30 September 1992	2,432
Year ended 30 September 1993	1,012
	3,444

c) Cash available for distribution

	£
Sale proceeds	131,000
Cash on hand	500
	131,500
Liabilities: current (4,000 – 1,508)	(2,492)
debentures	(25,000)
	104,008

Mr Ludd: Income tax computations:

	1994/95 £	1995/96 £
Total income	30,000	10,000
Personal allowances	(3,445)	(3,445)
Taxable	26,555	6,555
Marginal rate income tax	40%	25%

Total gain from capital distribution	£
Distributions (99.9% of £104,008)	103,904
Acquisition value at March 1982	(50,000)
	53,904
Indexation $\frac{145.0 - 79.4}{79.4}$ (not rounded)	(41,310)
	12,594

The only benefit in taking part of the cash in 1994/95 would be to use the annual exemption (£5,800) for that year. The bulk of the gain should fall into 1995/96 because his marginal rate of income tax in that year is only 25% and because this would give a cashflow advantage, delaying payment of the liability until 1 December 1996. However, if only a small proportion of the distribution was made in 1994/95, it is likely that the Inland Revenue would treat it as a small capital distribution to be deducted from the acquisition value and if a larger distribution was made, the total remaining distribution would be estimated and the whole would be deemed to fall into 1994/95. Ideally a distribution of approximately £47,852 (5,800/12,594 × £103,904) in 1994/95 with the balance in 1995/96 would be most tax efficient but it may be wise to make the distribution immediately following 6 April 1995.

5

Lincoln, Fields & Co.,
Certified Accountants,
London.

I. Davis, Esq,
Hackney Way,
London.

Dear Mr Davis,

Thank you for your letter of 4 June 1994. I have considered below the tax aspects of your proposals:

a) Your redundancy payment will be taxable in part and as a result will not be sufficient, when added to your bank loan of £148,000, to cover the £200,000 required to purchase the snooker tables.

The first £30,000 of any termination payment made is exempt from tax. The statutory redundancy payment of £7,000 is also exempt from tax but when paid in conjunction with any other termination payment it counts as part of the £30,000 exemption. Therefore a total of £30,000 is tax free leaving £22,000 fully taxable. It will be added to your other taxable income for 1994/95 of which £23,700 will be taxed at 20/25% and the balance at 40%.

b) The expenditure and income of the business is arrived at according to normal accounting principles but for tax purposes, only expenditure which is incurred wholly and exclusively for the purpose of the trade is deductible. Depreciation is not deductible but capital allowances will be available in its place (see c) below).

If you run the business as a sole trader, the profits will be assessable to income tax on you personally at a rate of 20/25% rising to 40% depending on the level of profits and your other income. If you commence on 1 September 1994, the first year of assessment will be 1994/95 in which you will be assessable on £11,667 (the actual profits earned in that period, that is, the seven months from 1 September 1994 to 5 April 1995 – 7/12 × £20,000) before relief for capital expenditure. In the second year, 1995/96, you will be assessed on the profits of the accounting period ending in the 1995/96 fiscal year (or the profits of the first twelve months of trading, if the aforementioned accounts do not cover a period of twelve months). In future years you will be assessed on the profits of the accounting period ending in the current fiscal year. As some of your profits will be assessed in both the first and second years of assessment, they will be eligible for overlap relief. This is given on the earlier of the year in which the business comes to an end or in any earlier year of assessment for which the basis period is longer than twelve months. Tax arising on these profits will be payable in two instalments: half on 1st January in the year of assessment and half on the following 31st July.

If on the other hand you form a company to run the business, your salary as a director will be deductible and the balance of profits will be assessed to corporation tax on the company at a rate of 25% (up to a limit of £300,000). All assessments will be on the actual profits of the accounting period and the tax will be due nine months after the end of the accounting period. Your salary as a director will be subject to PAYE and national insurance when paid.

c) Tax relief for the capital expenditure will be given under the heading Capital Allowances. Snooker tables are classed as plant and machinery for this purpose and a writing down allowance of 25% on the reducing balance will be given annually.

If you run the business as a sole trader, the WDA is calculated in respect of your period of account and is deducted in computing your Schedule DI profits. The WDA due for your first accounting year is £50,000 (£200,000 × 25%). This amount exceeds the assessment referred to in (b) above. The excess can be deducted from any other income which you have in that year or it may be deducted from your statutory total income of the three preceding tax years taking the earliest year first. This will give a repayment of tax which may in part at least offset the tax payable on the redundancy payment. For the second year an allowance of £37,500 (25% × (200,000 − 50,000) is available. Again this can be carried back and deducted from your statutory total income as above. Any amounts unrelieved in this way can be carried forward and relieved against future profits.

If the business is run through the company, the capital allowances are given with respect to the accounting period. Allowances of £50,000 (£200,000 × 25%) will be deductible from the profits of, say, £10,000 (after making allowance for your salary) assessable for that period, giving a loss of £40,000. This loss can be deducted from other income of the company but, if unrelieved in this way, it must be carried forward to be deducted from the trading profits of a future accounting period. It cannot be deducted from your personal income.

d) If you run the business as a sole trader, you will be assessed on the profits of the business personally under Schedule D Case I. Any personal expenditure will be deductible provided that it is incurred wholly, and exclusively for the purposes of the trade. The timing of the tax payments was referred to in (b) above.

If you run the business through a company you will be assessed under Schedule E on all remuneration, including benefits in kind which you receive as director and on the amount of any dividends you receive plus the related tax credits. In the latter case the tax credits are deemed to be lower rate income tax (currently 20%), and therefore you will only pay additional tax on the difference between 20% and 40% if the 40% rate is appropriate to you. Any expenditure you incur will be deductible under Schedule E only, provided that it is wholly, exclusively and necessarily incurred in the performance of your duties as director. You however, will be able to decide how much should be paid to you and therefore how much will be assessable on you – whatever the results of the business.

e) Increases in the value of the business or in the shares of the company will only be assessable to capital gains tax on sale. In computing the amount of the capital gain an allowance is given for inflation which has incurred during ownership – this may or may not equal the actual gain which has occurred during ownership.

If the business is sold and replaced by another business the capital gain will be 'rolled over' against the cost of the replacement business. Such a deferment is not available on capital gains tax arising on the disposal of shares unless you reinvest in an unquoted trading company.

If the business is continued until retirement (age 55), retirement relief will be available to exempt or reduce the gain arising on the disposal of either the business or shares in the business.

Yours sincerely
A. Lincoln
Certified Accountant

6 a) Corporation tax computations year ended 31 December 1994

	Xerxes £	Bella £	Donna £
Net profit per accounts	(71,000)	349,000	317,000
Interest not in accounts	22,500	(22,500)	
Corrected accounts	(48,500)	326,500	317,000
Expenditure not allowable DI:			
Interest	(22,500)	22,500	
Depreciation (note 1)	542	–	–
Capital allowances (note 2)	(2,372)		
Adjusted profits/losses	(72,830)	349,000	317,000
Schedule D Case I	Nil	349,000	317,000
UFII	22,500	–	–
Capital gains (note 3)	–	–	–
Less: charges	–	(22,500)	–
Less: group relief (note 5)	–	(72,830)	–
Profit chargeable to CT (I)	22,500	253,670	317,000

I = P in each case as group FII is excluded

		Lower	Upper
FY 93	£250,000 × 3/12 ÷ 3	20,833	
	£1,250,000 × 3/12 ÷ 3		104,167
FY 94	£300,000 × 9/12 ÷ 3	75,000	
	£1,500,000 × 9/12 ÷ 3		375,000

Corporation tax:	Xerxes £	Bella £	Donna £
FY93 3/12	25%	33%	33%
	5,625	83,711	104,610
FY94 9/12	25%	33%	33%
Taper relief (note 4)		(4,510)	(3,243)
ACT (note 6)	(4,641)	(12,778)	(65,381)
Income tax (UFII @ 25%)			
MCT	(984)	66,423	35,986

Notes

1 Depreciation on factory £542 ((90,000 − 25,000)/50 × 5/12)

2 Capital allowances on factory

Nugent Ltd	Qualifying cost May 1984	£35,000
	Selling price (90 − 25)	£65,000
Xerxes Ltd	Qualifying cost Aug 1994	£35,000
	Remaining life (25 − 10.25)	14.75 yrs
	Writing down allowance	£2,372

3 **Sale of office building**

	Value 31/3/82	Cost
Disposal value	72,000	72,000
Less: incidental costs of disposal	(3,000)	(3,000)
Less: allowable deductions:		
Mar 81 $\dfrac{72}{72 + 33} \times 22,000$		(15,085)
Mar 82 $\dfrac{72}{72 + 33} \times 40,000$	(27,429)	
May 84	(9,000)	(9,000)
Unindexed gain	32,571	44,915
Indexation allowance:		
$\dfrac{143.7 - 79.4}{79.4}$ (0.810) × 27,429	(22,217)	(22,217)
$\dfrac{143.7 - 89.0}{89.0}$ (0.615) × 9,000	(5,535)	(5,535)
Indexed gain	4,819	17,163
Rollover claim against cost of factory to Xerxes (part of the same 75% group)	(4,819)	
Chargeable	Nil	

4 **Taper relief – Bella**

FY93	(104,167 − 63,417) × 1/50	815	
FY94	(375,000 − 190,252) × 1/50	3,695	4,510

Taper relief – Donna

FY93	(104,167 − 79,250) × 1/50	498	
FY94	(375,000 − 237,750) × 1/50	2,745	3,243

5 **Group relief**

Xerxes could claim to set part of its loss off against its total profits for year under s. 393A(1) (a) but this would only save tax at an effective small companies rate (25%). Similarly it could make a s. 242 claim setting part of its loss off against surplus FII but this would only save tax at 20% Xerxes could claim to carry its loss forward under s. 393(1) against future trading profits. Future results are not known but there would be a cashflow disadvantage at the very least. Xerxes could surrender part or all of its loss to Donna but this would result in creating surplus ACT in Donna and only giving an effective tax saving of approximately 10%. By surrendering the whole of its loss to Bella, tax is saved at 35% with no ACT set-off problems arising.

6 **ACT – Xerxes**

	FP	FII	Net FP	ACT due 22.5%	ACT paid	ACT payable
Qtr 1.	361,290	283,871	77,419	17,419	–	17,419
Qtr 3	–	18,750	–	20%	–	–

ACT paid			
Used by Xerxes (max):		17,419	
(22,500 @ 22.5% × 3/12)	1,266		
(22,500 @ 20% × 9/12)	3,375	(4,641)	
Surrendered to Bella		12,778	

ACT Donna		ACT paid			
Franked payments (220,000 × 100/77.5)	283,871	63,871			
(15,000 × 100/80)	18,750	3,750			
		67,621			
Used by Donna (Maximum)		(65,381)	Surplus ACT to carry forward	2,240	
(Max 317,000 @ 22.5% × 3/12 17,831)					
317,000 @ 20% × 9/12 47,550)	65,381				

Note: 5 April is treated as if it were a year-end when ACT rate changes. Therefore Xerxes has surplus FII of £18,750 to carry forward.

Xerxes could elect to carry forward its surplus ACT or surrender it to Donna but either of these options would increase the immediate MCT liabilities leaving surplus ACT to carry forward – cash flow disadvantage.

Donna can only carry forward its surplus ACT. Donna should elect to pay (with Xerxes) its dividends without ACT, as this situation is disadvantageous from a cashflow viewpoint.

b) Services rendered in return for a management charge will be liable to VAT at the standard rate and therefore Xerxes will have to charge VAT at 17.5% on the market research (£1,750) and account for this as output VAT to Customs & Excise. The £1,750 will represent input tax to Bella. Since Bella's activities are partly standard rated and partly exempt, the input tax may not be recoverable. If the market research relates purely to exempt activities then none of the input tax will be recoverable. If the market research does not relate specifically to either the exempt or the taxable activities, the input tax will be apportioned between them under either the 'standard' method or the 'alternative' method and the input tax apportioned to the exempt activities will not be recoverable. There is insufficient information to calculate the loss under the standard method but under the alternative method the loss will be £525 (30% of £1,750). It is unlikely that the de minimus limits could apply to Bella's exempt input tax given the size of the profits. The £525 will be deductible under Schedule DI and therefore the actual tax loss to the group will be £341 (approximately 65% of £525).

7 a) i) Tax consequences Bloom Ltd – Ulysses buys net assets
On a sale of the assets, there is both a capital allowance and a capital gains consequence to Bloom Ltd.

Factory – capital gain computation

	31/3/82 £	Cost £	Gain (loss)
Sale proceeds	900,000	900,000	
31/3/82 value/cost	(350,000)	(40,000)	
Unindexed gain	550,000	860,000	
Less: indexation			
$\frac{143.8 - 79.4}{79.4}$ (0.811)	(283,850)	(283,850)	
Chargeable gain	266,150	576,150	266,150

Plant – capital gain computation

Sale proceeds are less than cost which implies that there are no chargeable gains. As no information is given, assume that chattel relief applies (all items less than £6,000).	–
Stock and so on adjusted in DI computation	–
Net chargeable gains	266,150

Industrial buildings allowance – factory (y/e 31/3/95)

	£	£
Tax written down value		5,000
Sale proceeds (maximum) original cost excl. land		(30,000)
		(25,000)
Balancing charge		25,000

Capital allowance computation – y/e 31/3/95

	£
Balance brought forward – pool	45,000
Disposal proceeds Max original cost	(10,000)
	(35,000)
Balancing allowance	35,000

Corporation tax computation – y/e 31/3/95

	£	£
Schedule D Case I insignificant		
Sale of stock	100,000	
Less: capital allowances	(35,000)	
Balancing charge	25,000	
		90,000
Chargeable gains		266,150
Profits chargeable to CT	I = P	356,150
CT liability		
FY 94 356,150 @ 33%		117,529
Taper relief (750,000 – 356,150 × 1/50)		(7,877)
(6 month period)		109,652
Less: ACT b/f	150,000	
max set-off (356,150 @ 20%)		
	(71,230)	(71,230)
Surplus	78,770	
MCT		38,422

Shareholders of Bloom Ltd
Distribution on liquidation

	£	£
Current values	1,440,000	
MCT	(38,422)	
	1,401,578	
Less: base cost of shares	(25,000)	
Gain @ 40%	1,376,578	550,631
Cash in hand – shareholders, ignoring costs of liquidation		850,947

Surplus ACT would be wasted unless Bloom Ltd continued in existence and invested its cash in a taxable source.

The transfer of a business as above may be regarded for VAT purposes as a going concern transfer which has special status for VAT purposes: it is not treated as a taxable supply provided that certain conditions are met (the purchaser must be registered; he or she must intend to use the assets for the same kind of business). The conditions would appear to be satisfied in this case but the clearance procedure should be followed as a precaution since the penalties are severe if the transaction is treated as qualifying when it does not. All VAT records would require to be transferred with the business. Bloom Ltd would subsequently need to deregister.

ii) **Tax consequences Bloom Ltd – Ulysses buys shares**

	Cost	Gain/(loss)
	£	£
Sale proceeds for shares	1,440,000	
Base cost of shares	(25,000)	
Gain @ 40%	1,415,000	566,000
Cash in hand – shareholders	874,000	

There would be no VAT consequences on the sale of shares. Bloom Ltd would continue in existence, claiming capital allowance, with no factory disposal and no uplift of stock value.

b) i) **Tax consequences Ulysses Ltd – buys net assets of Bloom**

Ulysses would acquire a second-hand factory for £800,000 on which industrial buildings allowances would be available as follows:

	£
Residue of expenditure to vendor	5,000
Balancing charge	25,000
Qualifying cost	30,000
Remaining life	10 years
Writing down allowance	3,000 per annum

(The base cost for capital gains purposes will be £900,000.)

The plant, acquired for £10,000, would be eligible for capital allowances. Stock will be brought in at cost, that is, £500,000.

No VAT input would arise on the acquisition if it was treated as a 'going concern' transfer. Ulysses Ltd's VAT position may change: previously it would almost certainly have been in a VAT repayment situation as 70% of its sales were exports; on the transfer of the business, the proportion of zero-rated supplies may not be so large and therefore there may be a cashflow disadvantage (monthly repayment claims may no longer be available').

ii) **Tax consequences Ulysses Ltd – buys shares of Bloom**

Bloom Ltd would be a wholly owned subsidiary of Ulysses Ltd and would therefore count as an associated company (thresholds for upper and lower limit SCR and taper relief would be shared between them); they would be able to make a group income election and group charges election; ACT could be surrendered by Ulysses to Bloom; group relief would be available; and they would form a capital gains tax group.

Surplus ACT of Bloom Ltd is unlikely to be recoverable as there will be a charge in ownership and either the trade of Bloom Ltd has become small or negligible and will revive or there may be a major change in the nature or conduct of the trade over the next three-year period.

Bloom Ltd and Ulysses Ltd could form a VAT group. This may not be efficient if monthly repayments were lost thereby. All latent liabilities of Bloom Ltd, tax and other, are transferred to Ulysses Ltd.

8 a) 1 The company must be an unquoted trading company or member of a trading group (unquoted means not listed and not a 51 per cent subsidiary of a listed company).
2 The purpose must be wholly or mainly for the benefit of the trade (not as part of a scheme of tax avoidance) or to allow the vendor to meet inheritance tax liabilities which would otherwise cause undue hardship (in which case no further provisions need to be satisfied).
3 The vendor must be resident and ordinarily resident in the UK when the shares are purchased.
4 The vendor or his spouse must in most cases have owned the shares throughout the period of five years preceding the date of purchase.
5 As a result of the purchase of the shares by the company, the vendor's interest (together with his associates') must be substantially reduced (vendor's interest constitutes both his percentage of the share capital and his percentage share of the distributable profits and substantial means by at least 25%).
6 After the purchase of the shares by the company, the vendor must cease to be connected with the company or any company in the same 51 per cent group (connected means generally owning with associates more than 30% of the issued share capital).

The final condition to be met is that the purchase of the shares must be wholly or mainly for the benefit of the trade. The Inland Revenue has indicated four circumstances which satisfy this test.
- A dissident shareholder is having an adverse effect on the running of the company's trade
- The majority shareholder is retiring to make way for new management
- An outside shareholder is withdrawing his investment
- The personal representatives of a shareholder who has died do not wish to keep the shares.

Conditions 1 to 6 above appear to be satisfied by Sally. But, while circumstance 2 would also appear to be satisfied in principle, the Inland Revenue is known to require almost the entire holding to be given up. Sally is keeping a substantial holding (27.5%) and perhaps may fail on this.

Zen may apply for clearance in advance.

b) i) **Sally: taxable income 1994/95**

	£	£
Schedule E		
Directors' remuneration	18,000	
Bonus	5,700	
Ex gratia payment	40,000	
Pension	2,850	
	66,550	
Less: PA	3,445	
Taxable income	63,105	

Relief for APA and WBA is given as a tax credit as relief for these allowances is now restricted to 20%.

TAX PLANNING

Annual bonuses to directors are assessed on the earlier of:
1) time of receipt
2) year end if bonus is determined at that date (y/e 31 March 1995.)

The ex gratia payment will be assessible in full as a result of Inland Revenue change in practice – deemed to be a lump sum for pension purposes. However, only lump sums up to 1.5 times salary are tax free for pension purposes and the £40,000 is therefore too large to qualify. Under previous practice the first £30,000 would have been tax free with only the balance of £10,000 assessable.

ii) **Capital gains tax liability 1994/95**

	£	£
Capital gain		200,000
Retirement relief		
250,000 × 7/10	175,000	
(200,000 – 175,000) @ 50%	12,500	
		(187,500)
Chargeable gain		12,500
Annual exemption		(5,800)
		6,700
Capital gains tax @ 40%		2,680

c) The following (corporation tax) deductions will be available:
  i) Directors' remuneration (18,000) plus Class 1 NIC employers (18,000 @ 10.2%: £1,836)
  ii) Bonus payment (£5,700) + Class1 NIC (5,700 @ 10.2% = £581.40)
  iii) Ex gratia payments are not necessarily regarded as wholly and exclusively for the purpose of the trade – resulting from a voluntary retirement. NIC is only payable on contractual payments.
  iv) No deduction will be allowed re purchase of shares. If conditions in a) satisfied, there will be no ACT payable.

CHAPTER 30 *Self test questions*

1 i) If he comes to UK to work for 2 + years.
   ii) If he comes to UK on a permanent basis (+ evidence).
   iii) R or OR person returning to UK after full-time employment.

2 Yes.

3 Under schedule D Case V and if paid to a UK-domiciled and resident individual, are allowed a 10% deduction.

4 a) Not to be more than 62 continuous days.
   b) Aggregate UK days should not exceed 1/6 of qualifying period to date.
   (Seafarers receive a more generous allowance in the UK.)

5 No.

6 Visit must be 60 days or more; they must be borne/reimbursed by the employer; no more than two outward and two return journeys per person per fiscal year.

7 In the country in which it is managed and controlled.

8 A will be treated as ceasing to be resident and ordinarily resident from the date he leaves the UK to take up employment in America (1 December 1994) following the principle set out in extra-statutory concession AII – an individual who is resident and ordinarily resident leaving the UK to take up full-time employment abroad the duties of which are wholly outside the UK. He will be treated as resident and ordinarily resident again from the date of his return.

The fiscal year of departure (1994/95) will therefore be split into the period prior to departure and the period thereafter. The salary earned prior to departure will be liable to UK tax but he will be entitled to full personal allowances for 1994/95. No UK tax will be charged on his American salary for 1994/95 and subsequent years.

The fiscal year of his return (1999/2000) will also be split into the period prior to his return and the period following his return. As before no UK tax will be charged on his American salary but the salary earned in the UK following his return will be liable to UK tax (he will be entitled to full personal allowances).

He must ensure that his visits to the UK do not exceed six months in any fiscal year and do not average three months or more per annum, otherwise he will be regarded as resident. If the latter condition was failed due to circumstances beyond his control, an exception might be made under SP 2/91.

Any rents received from the letting of his house (less expenses paid including mortgage interest, if any) will be liable to UK income tax as UK source income of a non-resident.

The capital gains tax exemption for principal private residence should not be affected by his absence for full-time employment abroad.

9

	Days abroad	Days in UK
12 April 1994–15 May 1994	33	
15 May 1994–9 June 1994		25
9 June 1994–29 September 1994	110	
19 September 1994–29 October 1994		32
29 October 1994–28 March 1995	150	

The period from 12 April 1994 to 29 September 1994 is 168 days of which 25 days are in the UK (less than 62 days and less than 1/6 of the total) and therefore qualifies.

The period from 12 April 1994 to 28 March 1995 is 350 days of which 57 days are in the UK (each less than 62 days and less than 1/6 of the total) and therefore qualifies but is less than 365 days in length. No 100% deduction is therefore available yet, it will depend on whether she satisfies the same criteria during the remainder of the contract.

If she returns to Brazil on 1 May, she will have been in the UK for 34 days and assuming she makes no further visits to the UK before she finally returns on 7 September 1995 she will have been in the UK a total of 91 days out of a total period of 513 days. This is more than 1/6 and there will not, therefore, be a 365-day qualifying period.

The maximum total days she can have in the UK during a period of 513 days is 85 (513/6). She has already had 57 days and therefore her current visit should be limited to 28 days maximum if the whole 513 days are to qualify for the 100% deduction. Dr Footloose should therefore be advised to return to Brazil if possible on 25 April 1995.

10 a) An American is a non-UK-domiciled individual and the Paris-based company is a non-UK-resident employer. If none of the duties of the Paris-based directorship are performed in the UK, the emoluments (being foreign emoluments) would be assessable in the UK only to the extent that they were remitted to the UK (under Schedule E Case III).

If the duties of the employment were performed partly in the UK and partly outside the UK the emoluments would have to be apportioned to the respective duties. Those in respect of the UK duties by a UK resident (not OR) would be assessable under Schedule E Case II while those in respect of the non-UK duties would be assessable under Schedule E Case III to the extent that they are remitted.

b) As the individual has worked in Rome for many years it is assumed that she is not resident or ordinarily resident in the UK before being sent to work in London. Her domicile is irrelevant.

If here on a 2-year contract she is likely to be treated as resident and not ordinarily resident from the date of arrival in London. She will be assessed under Schedule E Case II re her emoluments for her UK duties and under Schedule E Case III to the extent that her emoluments re her overseas duties are remitted to the UK.

CHAPTER 31 *Self test questions*

1 Companies incorporated in UK and companies, not incorporated in UK, whose central management and control is in the UK., unless treated as resident in another country for the purpose of a double taxation agreement.

2 Relevance to companies not incorporated in the UK. Main factor – who makes policy and strategy decisions and where?

3 State intention and date and give statement of all tax estimated to that date and arrangements to pay: all assets deemed disposal/re-acquisition at market value (exit charge) and no roll-over.

4 Re: any assets which are foreign assets (situated outside UK and used in trade outside UK) if company is a 75% subsidiary of a UK company and both companies elect.

5 If transactions are 'not at market value' between a UK company and a non-UK company, one country must be losing tax revenue on profits to the other country. The UK, with traditionally high taxation, is concerned about loss of revenue.

CHAPTER 32 *Self test questions*

1 i) Trade losses cannot be surrendered by/to that subsidiary.
   ii) Assets cannot be transferred to it on a no gain, no loss basis;
   iii) Group income/charges elections do not apply to that company.

2 By deduction from total CT liability before ACT deducted.

3 Tax suffered relating to the profits out of which the divident is paid.

4 $\text{Dividend + withholding tax} \times \dfrac{\text{Overseas tax paid}}{\text{Distributable profits (accounts)}}$

5 i) Not resident in UK.
   ii) Controlled by UK residents.
   iii) Subject to a lower level of taxation in country of residence (that is, < 75% of UK rate).

6   Apportionment provisions may apply to the chargeable profits of CFC (exclusive of chargeable gains).

7   The tax implications of transferring the residence of Q (USA) Inc.

The proposal to change the residence of Q (USA) Inc to a country with a low rate of taxation appears attractive but is likely to be affected by legislation in the UK regarding 'controlled foreign companies'.

A controlled foreign company is one which is resident in a country with a level of taxation less than three-quarters that which would apply in the UK and which is controlled by UK-resident persons and at least 10% of its shares are held by a UK company. This definition would appear to apply to Q (USA) Inc if it changed its residence to the Far East.

Where there is a controlled foreign company, the UK tax legislation may apportion its chargeable profits plus the creditable tax to UK corporate shareholders. P Ltd would therefore be liable for corporation tax on the apportioned profits at the rate applicable to its own profits in the accounting period in which the accounting period of Q (USA) Inc ends subject to relief for double taxation (dividends subsequently paid by Q out of the apportioned profits will be treated as already having been subjected to UK tax and relief will be available). Therefore if the only reason for the change in residence is to reduce the group's tax liabilities, it will not work.

The apportionment provisions are not mandatory and will only be applied if the Inland Revenue so direct. The intention is that bona fide commercial investments in tax havens will not be affected. In addition, the Inland Revenue have stated that there would be no apportionment in any of the following circumstances:

i) If Q (USA) Inc's profits are substantially remitted to P Ltd in the UK as dividends (50% is usually acceptable for a trading company).
ii) If the company trades in the country through a permanent establishment and is not merely managed there (and if the trade is not simply dealing in goods for delivery to and from the UK).
iii) If the profits are less than £20,000 per annum.

The interpretation of residence for this purpose (according to the UK tax authorities), is the place where effective control is exercised, taken to be the place where the board of directors usually meets. P Ltd may have problems in avoiding UK residence in these circumstances.

8   a) MN Ltd forms a 75% group for group relief purposes with C Ltd and D Ltd. O Ltd cannot be included as it is not UK resident.

D Ltd and E Ltd form a separate 75% group for group relief purposes. (E Ltd cannot belong to the same group as MN Ltd because 80% of 90% is less than 75% and the indirect holding through O Ltd cannot be included as O Ltd is not UK resident).

A Ltd and MN Ltd together form a consortium controlling B Ltd and therefore consortium relief is available.

The company to start with is D Ltd as it has the highest profits at the high marginal rate of tax (lower limit £300,000/6 companies – O Ltd is included for this purpose but A Ltd is not included).

i) E Ltd can surrender its loss of £5,000 up to D Ltd.
ii) C Ltd can surrender its loss of £10,000 across to D Ltd.
iii) B Ltd can receive A Ltd's loss up to a maximum of 12% of £70,000.
iv) The remaining losses of A Ltd must be carried forward in A Ltd.
v) The losses of O Ltd may only be carried forward for offset against future profits of O Ltd.

	£	£		Chargeable
A Ltd	(60,000)	6,000	(iii)	Nil
B Ltd	70,000	(8,400)	(iii)	61,600
C Ltd	(10,000)	10,000	(ii)	Nil
D Ltd	105,000	(5,000)	(i) (10,000) (ii)	90,000

	£	£		Chargeable
E Ltd	(5,000)	5,000	(i)	Nil
MN Ltd	22,000			22,000
O Ltd	(10,000)			Nil

CT liabilities   £

B Ltd   61,600 @ 33%   20,328
   Less: taper relief
   $\left(\dfrac{1.5\text{ million}}{6} - 44,000\right) \times \dfrac{1}{50}$ (3,768)
                                                                          ──────
                                                                          16,560

D Ltd   90,000 @ 33%   29,700
   Less: taper relief
   $\left(\dfrac{1.5\text{ million}}{6} - 90,000\right) \times \dfrac{1}{50}$ (3,200)
                                                                          ──────
                                                                          26,500

MN Ltd   22,000 @ 25%   5,500

b) Where a 75% group exists for capital gains, assets may be transferred between the group companies on a 'no gain, no loss' basis.

MN Ltd, C Ltd, D Ltd and E Ltd in the above example would belong to a capital gains tax group.

9   Bristol Adventurers Ltd Corpoation tax computation for the accounting period to 31 March 1995.

		£	£
Schedule D Case I			46,000
Schedule D Case V		92,000	
Add: underlying tax $92,000 \times \frac{40}{60}$		61,333	153,333
Profit chargeable to CT (I =P)			199,333
CT liability			
FY 1994 @ 33%			65,780
Less: taper relief			
FY1994 $(\frac{1.5 \text{ million}}{2} - 199,333) \times \frac{1}{50}$			(11,013)
			54,767
Less: double tax relief	Max $\frac{153,333}{199,333} \times 54,767$		
	= 42,128		
	Paid 153,333 − 78,200		
	=75,133		(42,128)
			12,639
Less: ACT	Max 46,000 @ 20% =	9,200	
	Paid 105 × 20/80	26,250	
		(9,200)	(9,200)
Surplus ACT		17,050	
MCT			3,439

CHAPTER 33 *Self test questions*

1   Trading in the UK through a branch or agency.

2   A branch or agency is deemed in UK tax legislation to exist whenever a non-UK company trades 'within' the UK – it may be a permanent establishment or merely a visiting employee.

3   Corporation tax is assessed as if it were a UK-resident company, on the chargeable profits which are determined according to normal principles, which include trading profits, non-trading income and chargeable gains. SCR may be available subject to associated company rules.

4   Double tax agreement takes priority over internal tax legislation; for example, under most agreements, a branch or agency will only exist if it is a 'permanent establishment'.

5   'Permanent establishment' in a double tax agreement is defined as:
   i) a place of management
   ii) a branch
   iii) an office
   iv) a factory
   v) a workshop
   vi) a mine, quarry, and similar extraction sites
   vii) a long-term construction site.

It is important because it means that where a double tax agreement is in force a trade cannot be deemed to be being carried on in the UK unless there is an establishment of one of the above types in existence. Otherwise, trading may be deemed to exist where sales are made through independent agents and by visiting employees.

6   The Warren Iron Company Inc is not a UK-resident company and, therefore, if it holds the investments in Gwent Metals Ltd and Denny Trading Co Ltd itself – even though the holdings are greater than 75% – the three companies will not be a 75% group for group relief purposes. The losses of Denny Trading Co Ltd will not be able to be relieved against the other companies.

If a UK holding company is formed to own the shareholdings in both Gwent Metals Ltd and Denny Trading Company Ltd then the holding company and these two companies now form a 75 per cent group for group relief purposes. (The Warren Iron Company now only holds shares in the UK holding company). Group relief will be available for the corresponding accounting periods as follows:

In 1995 corresponding accounting periods will run from 1 January 1995 to 31 March 1995.

Gwent Metals Ltd 3/12 × £152,000	38,000
Denny Trading 3/12 × £(54,000)	(13,500)

A claim for group relief of £13,500 may therefore be made. The remaining losses of Denny before it joined the group – £90,000 plus £36,000 – may be carried forward for deduction from future trading profits of Denny Trading Co Ltd. If profits are not expected in the near future, it may be wise to reduce the losses arising as far as possible in the year to 30 April 1995 by not claiming writing down allowances so that the group relief provisions may be better utilised in the future. Group relief will be available for April 1995 and subsequent corresponding accounting periods.

QUESTION BANK – *overseas activities*

1 JPW Income tax computation – 1994/95

	£
Schedule E	31,350
Personal allowance	(3,445)
Taxable income	27,905
Income tax liability:	
£3,000 × 20%	600
£20,700 × 25%	5,175
£4,205 × 40%	1,682
	7,457
Less MCA relief: 1,720 × 20%	(344)
	7,113

The mortgage interest receives relief at source
The amount payable would be this amount less whatever was paid under PAYE

Notes

		£
1 Schedule E – JPW Textiles 7/12 × 25,000		14,583
Western Tweeds 2/12 × 25,000		4,167
Industrial Fabrics 2 × 800		1,600
1 × 1,000		1,000
		21,350
Termination payment		40,000
Exempt		(30,000)
		10,000
Medical insurance – overseas trip – benefit		Nil
Wife's travel expenses – 60 + day trip – benefit		Nil
Total Schedule E		31,350

2 On the basis of the facts available Mr Poirot is domiciled by origin in France. He is UK resident from 1 March 1994 but is probably not ordinarily resident (visited UK > 6 months for substantial period but no expressed intention of establishing residence). He is therefore entitled to personal allowances. He will not be taxable on any income not arising or remitted to the UK.

Mr Poirot – Income tax computation 1994/95

	£
Schedule E (Case II)	45,000
Gross amount of bank interest (722 × 100/75)	963
Statutory total income	45,963
Less: personal allowance	(3,445)
Taxable income	42,518
Income tax liability:	
£3,000 × 20%	600.00
£20,700 × 25%	5,175.00
£18,818 × 40%	7,527.20
	13,302.20
MCA relief: 1,720 × 20%	(344.00)
	12,958.20

Visits by the family of a non-UK domiciled individual to the UK paid for by his employer (provided the employee has not been resident in the UK in any of the 5 years preceding) are not taxable benefits.

3 a) **Residence**

There is no statutory definition of residence. Residence is a question of fact and is determined principally according to a person's physical presence and case law, irrespective of the person's intention. A set of rules have evolved which may be used as a guide:

i) If the person is present in the UK for 183 days or more, excluding days of arrival or departure, he will be treated as resident. This is the only statutory provision.
ii) If he visits the UK on a regular annual basis for a substantial period of time in each case he will be regarded as resident – substantial has been regarded as 90 or more days on average per year, while regular has been regarded as meaning per year for four years.
iii) If a person is ordinarily resident in the UK and is temporarily abroad (more than six months but less than a full tax year) he or she is generally regarded as resident.

It is evident from the above that a person may be resident in more than one country at the same time.

Residence is normally determined for a fiscal year as a whole, although, by extra-statutory concession, residence may on occasion be determined from the date of arrival or departure.

Ordinary residence

No statutory definition of ordinary residence exists either. The term implies habitual residence and thus more permanence or continuity – a person's normal country of residence.

A period of three years would normally be taken to establish that residence had become ordinary residence. Similarly, on leaving the UK, three years would be taken to establish that a person was no longer ordinarily resident. However, in both cases, if evidence of intention can be established (for example, a full-time contract of employment abroad for more than a complete tax year) a person may lose ordinary residence (or acquire ordinary residence) from the day of departure (day of arrival).

Domicile

Domicile follows the common law rules. It is normally the country where a person has his or her permanent home – the country to which, if absent, he or she will eventually return to for retirement and to die. Every person has a country of domicile and may have only one.

A person acquires a domicile of origin at birth (from father or person on whom he is dependent) but, from age 16 may change it to his or her domicile of choice provided clear evidence is established by his conduct – if later actions indicate that the domicile of choice has been abandoned, domicile of origin will automatically be re-acquired.

A married woman no longer automatically assumes her husband's domicile and may establish her domicile according to the same factor as above. In practice, if they intend to live together, this is likely to be difficult.

b) William is likely to be treated as not resident or ordinarily resident in the UK from his date of departure. He will, however, be regarded as domiciled in the UK throughout.

Income tax

Being non-resident and not ordinarily resident, William will not be liable to UK income tax on income arising abroad, but he may be liable on income arising within the UK.

Interest arising on many UK Government securities held by non-residents is exempt from UK tax and dividends from UK companies will be treated as having suffered tax at lower rate. The rental income from UK properties collected by UK agents less any property expenses, mortgage interest and agent's commission will suffer deduction of basic rate tax at source by the agents and only the net rent after tax will be paid to William.

As a British subject, William is entitled in 1994/95 to claim the full personal allowances to which he would be entitled as a UK resident.

Although he is non-resident, William may still be liable to higher-rate income tax if his income exceeds the basic rate band but collection by the Inland Revenue is impracticable unless he has substantial income from a single source as William will not be required to complete a UK income tax return.

Capital gains tax

While William is non-resident and not ordinarily resident in the UK, he will not be liable to capital gains tax on any assets including those situated in the UK (as none are business assets).

William should therefore delay the realisation of any of his UK assets until after his departure. The rules giving non-resident status immediately following departure are not statutory and it may be prudent to delay the sale until he has received confirmation of such status. On the other hand, if any of his UK assets are showing a loss they should be realised while he is still UK resident.

Any assets disposed of following his return to the UK, whether situated in or outside the UK, will be liable to capital gains tax.

The purchase of a house overseas as a principal private residence will prevent his house in the UK from being regarded as his principal private residence for the period and this will have capital gains tax implications should he ever wish to sell it.

Inheritance tax

Inheritance tax liability is determined by a person's domicile and not his or her residence and therefore, as William is UK domiciled throughout, all his assets both in the UK and abroad will be liable to inheritance tax if gifted by him during his lifetime or if transferred on death.

4 Alpha Ltd

a) Adjusted profits computation year ended 30 November 1994

	£	£
Net profit per accounts		250,000
Add: Entertaining suppliers	8,000	
Entertaining UK agent	5,000	
Gift of food hampers	7,000	20,000
Schedule D Case I		270,000

Capital gains computation

	Cost	31 March 82 Value	Gain/(loss)
	£	£	£
Land Sale proceeds	277,000	277,000	
Cost/31 Mar 1982	(100,000)	(121,000)	
	177,000	156,000	

Indexation allowance

$$\frac{142.0 - 79.4}{79.4} = 0.788$$

121,000 × 0.788	(95,348)	(95,348)	
	81,652	60,652	60,652
Car: Exempt			–
Gilt-edged securities: Exempt			–
			60,652

Corporation tax computation – year ended 30 November 1994

Schedule D Case I	270,000
Schedule D Case V (10,200 × 100/85) Note 1	12,000
Chargeable gains	60,652
Profits chargeable to CT (I)	342,652
FII (24,500 × 100/80)	30,625
P	373,277

	£
CT liability: £342,652 × 33%	113,075
Less taper relief	
FY 93	
4/12 × (1,250,000 – 373,277) × $\frac{342,652}{373,277}$ × 1/50	(5,365)
FY94	
8/12 × (1,500,000 – 373,277) × $\frac{342,652}{373,277}$ × 1/50	(13,790)
	93,920
Less double tax relief: £12,000 × 15%	(1,800)
	92,120
Less ACT (see below)	(53,863)
MCT	38,257

The ACT of £53,863 has been computed as follows:

ACT on dividends paid	£133,000 × 22.5/77.5 =	38,613
	£73,500 × 20/80 =	18,375
		56,988
ACT on dividends received £24,500 × 20/80 =		(6,125)
Surplus ACT b/f		3,000
		53,863

Notes

1 The underlying tax is not taken into account as the shareholding is less than 10%.
2 The maximum set off of ACT is £70,375 computed as follows:

	UK income	Overseas income	Total
	£	£	£
	330,652	12,000	342,652
UK tax pro rata	90,631	3,289	93,920
Foreign tax – DTR		(1,800)	
		1,489	
ACT restriction Max (22.5/20%)	68,886	1,489	
i.e. 70,375			

b) Profit and loss account – year ended 30 November 1994

	£
Dividends receivable	30,625
UK Corporation tax based on profits of year	92,120
Tax credits on franked investment income	6,125
Irrecoverable ACT (Note 1)	–
Overseas taxation (Note 2)	–
Tax on ordinary activities	98,245

Dividends paid/payable

Interim dividend	73,500
Proposed final dividend	161,000

Balance sheet as at 30 November 1994

Creditors amount falling due within one year

Corporation tax on profits y/e 30 November 1994	38,257
Proposed dividend	161,000
ACT on proposed dividend	40,250

Current assets – Debtors

ACT on proposed dividend – not recoverable for 12 months	40,250

Notes

1   ACT proposed dividend (161,000 × 20/80)   40,250
    Tax credit FII (7,000 × 20/80)   (1,750)
                                                       38,500
    Set off against CT liability 30 Nov 95
       maximum (200,000 × 20%)   (38,500)
    Estimated irrecoverable   –

2   There is no overseas taxation suffered as it is wholly recoverable against the UK tax liability (93,920 – 1,800 = 92,120).

5   Domo Ltd

a) Corporation tax computation – year ended 31 March 1995

	£
Schedule D Case I	150,000
Schedule D Case V – Fjord Norland (11,900 × 100/85 × 100/70 Note 1))	20,000
Schedule D Case V – Valley Norland (10,200 × 100/85)	12,000
Schedule D Case IV – Lake Norland (12,000 × 100/80)	15,000
Chargeable gain (Note 2)	7,960
	204,960
Less: charges gross (10,650 × 100/75)	(14,200)
Profits chargeable CT (I)	190,760
FII (7,100 × 100/80)	8,875
P	199,635

CT liability   £
FY 94 I @ SCR
190,760 @ 25%   47,690
Less: double tax relief (Note 3)   (19,290)
Less: ACT Max 23,110 (Note 3)

	Paid in year:	£	
	FP (113,600 × 100/80)	142,000	
	FII	(8,875)	
		133,125	
	@ 20% ie	26,625	
	Set-off	(23,110)	(23,110)
	Surplus cf	3,515	
MCT			5,290

Notes

1   Underlying tax suffered overseas is only taken into account if the UK company holds at least 10% of the ordinary share capital of an overseas company.

2   Chargeable gain:

	£
Sale price	36,000
Cost	(20,000)
Unindexed gain	16,000
Indexation allowance	
$\dfrac{142.9 - 101.9}{101.9} = 0.402 \times 20{,}000$	(8,040)
	7,960

3   Double tax relief and maximum ACT set off

	DI UK £	O'seas £	D IV £	D Fiord £	D Case V Valley £	Gain £
Liable CT	120,000	30,000	15,000	20,000	12,000	7,960
Charges	(14,200)					
	105,800	30,000	15,000	20,000	12,000	7,960
UK tax (47,865)	26,450	7,500	3,750	5,000	3,000	1,990
Foreign tax	–	9,000	3,000	8,100	1,800	4,800
DTR	–	7,500	3,000	5,000	1,800	1,990
Max ACT	21,160	–	750	–	1,200	–

4   The problem of surplus ACT could have been avoided if Domo Ltd had elected to treat its dividend as a foreign income dividend. Such an election must be made prior to the payment of the dividend. The election enables the recovery of any ACT paid in respect of the FID, which would otherwise be irrecoverable.

b) Controlled foreign companies (CFC)

A controlled foreign company is a company which is:
i)   resident outside the UK
ii) controlled by persons resident in the UK
iii) subject to a lower level of taxation in the country in which it is resident than it would be in the UK.

If the company that is acquired is a controlled foreign company and Domo Ltd (together with any associates) acquires an interest of 10% or more in that company then the following consequences may apply:

a) The chargeable profits plus the creditable tax will be apportioned (according to the interest acquired) to Domo Ltd and brought into charge to UK corporation tax in the accounting period in which the CFC's accounting period ends (subject to relief for double taxation).
b) Dividends subsequently paid by the CFC out of apportioned profits will be treated as already having been subjected to UK tax and relief will be available.

The consequences are not mandatory and will only be applied if the Inland Revenue so direct. The intention is that bona fide commercial investments in tax havens will not be affected (that is, where the reduction of a tax liability was not the primary motive). There are also four circumstances when the Inland Revenue have said that there will be no apportionment:
i)   The profits of the CFC are less than £20,000
ii) The CFC has an acceptable distribution policy
iii) The activities of the CFC are exempt
iv) The CFC has a public quotation.

6   a) A controlled foreign company is a non-UK resident company, controlled by persons resident in the UK and subject to a lower level of taxation in the country in which it is resident than it would be if UK resident. A lower level of taxation is defined as less than three-quarters of the corresponding UK tax rate.

The profits of a controlled foreign company are apportioned to their corporate shareholders resident in the UK which have at least a 10% interest in the CFC and UK tax is levied on the apportioned income.

No apportionment may be directed by the Inland Revenue in specific excluded circumstances:
i)   the profits of the CFC are less than £20,000 per 12 month accounting period
ii) the activities of the CFC are exempt, that is, the CFC has a genuine business establishment in the country of its residence and it is effectively managed and controlled in that country. The activities must satisfy detailed conditions as to the nature of the business (broadly the business activities must be trading in nature and not investment)
iii) the CFC has a public quotation that is, not less than 35% of the equity voting power is held by the public and has been dealt in on a recognised Stock Exchange throughout the accounting period

iv) the motive for setting up the CFC and undertaking the transactions was commercial and not tax evasion.

If Haven Ltd does not pay a dividend then all of its profits (as calculated for UK tax purposes) will be apportioned to Multinat plc, credit being given for foreign tax suffered.

Multinat plc Extract from corporation tax computation (assuming no dividend paid) year ended 31 December 1994

Apportioned income (D Case V)	£160,000
CT liability	£
160,000 @ 33%	52,800
Less: double tax relief – lower of:	
a) foreign tax 165,000 @ 5% £8,250	
b) UK tax on foreign income £52,800	
	(8,250)
MCT	44,550

If Haven Ltd pays a dividend equal to 50% of its distributable profits on 1 April 1995, then this would constitute an acceptable distribution policy and no apportionment would be made.

Multinat plc Extract from corporation tax computation (assuming dividend paid) year ended 31 December 1994

Schedule D Case V (Note 1)		75,000
CT liability		£
75,000 @ 33%		24,750
Less: double tax relief – lower of:		
a) foreign tax	£4,125	
b) UK tax on foreign iincome	£24,750	
		(4,125)
MCT		20,625

Notes

1.
Haven Ltd pre-tax accounting profits	150,000
Ruritanian tax (165,000 @ 5%)	(8,250)
	141,750
Dividend payable	(70,875)
Retained profit	70,875

Gross dividend received by Multinat plc (no witholding tax but underlying tax as Multinat plc owns more than 10% of the voting power in Haven Ltd.):

	£
Dividend	70,875
Underlaying tax $\left(\dfrac{£70,875}{141,750}\right) \times 8,250$	4,125
Schedule D Case V	75,000

b) **Mrs Noble** – stays in Ruritania for 14 months.

The stay in this case will be from 8 December 1994 to 7 February 1996 and she will therefore not be absent from the UK for a full fiscal year. She will therefore remain resident and ordinarily resident in the UK throughout.

Overseas earnings in these circumstances will be liable to UK income tax under Schedule E Case I. She may be eligible for a 100% deduction for a 365-day qualifying period abroad. This deduction is available to UK-resident individuals who work abroad and whose interim visits to the UK satisfy certain criteria. A qualifying period consists of periods of actual absence from the UK plus the intervening period spent in the UK provided it does not exceed 62 days or one-sixth of the number of days from the beginning of the qualifying period to the end of the period of absence from the UK. This test is applied cumulatively to each intervening visit to the UK until the total days reach 365 or more; this then constitutes a 365-day qualifying period and entitles the individual to a 100% deduction for overseas earnings during that period. Mrs Noble's intended visits to the UK over the period – 2 weeks out of 13 weeks – satisfy these criteria but note that if she extends her visits beyond this on average, she would probably lose the relief.

The cost of travel to and from an overseas employment (however frequent), together with the cost of travel between overseas employments is an allowable expense if included in assessable emoluments. Even if the 100% relief above is lost, these should be tax free.

Mrs Noble – stays in Ruritania for 18 months.

The stay in this case will be from 8 December 1994 to 7 June 1995 and she will therefore be absent from the UK for a full fiscal year. It is normal Inland Revenue practice in these circumstances to regard her as non-resident and not ordinarily resident in the UK from the date of her departure to the date of her return.

As all her duties will be outside the UK, she will be outside the scope of Schedule E during this period. However, she will lose the benefit of non-resident status if her interim visits to the UK exceed three months on average per 12 months. Visits two weeks out of 13 weeks should not cause a problem but if they were extended to more than three weeks, her non-resident status may be affected.

Her reimbursed travel expenses should be exempt irrespective of her residence status above.

Multinat plc – tax deduction for salary and expenses

These costs are not wholly and exclusively incurred for the purpose of Multinat's trade and are therefore unlikely to be allowable (they should perhaps be recharged to Haven Ltd since they are for the purpose of Haven's trade). Exceptionally, Multinat may be able to show that its own trade will benefit from Mrs Noble's activities and in this case they would be allowable (Robinson v. Scott Bader and Co Ltd).

Rates of Tax and Allowances 1994/95

Income tax

		%
Lower rate	£1–£3,000	20
Basic rate	£3,001–£23,700	25
Higher rate	£23,701 and above	40

Personal allowances

	£
Personal allowance	3,445
Personal allowance: 65–74	4,200
Personal allowance: 75 and over	4,370
Married couple's allowance	1,720*
Married couple's allowance: 65–74	2,665*
Married couple's allowance: 75 and over	2,705*
Income limit for age-related allowances	14,200
Additional personal allowance	1,720*
Widow's bereavement allowance	1,720*
Blind person's allowance	1,200

* Allowances where relief is restricted to 20% in 1994/95.

Company car benefit

35% of list price (maximum list price £80,000). Reduce by one-third for cars four years old or over at end of tax year

Car fuel benefit table

	Petrol £	Diesel £
Cars with a cylinder capacity of		
Up to 1,400 cc	640	580
1,401 cc to 2,000 cc	810	580
2,001 cc or more	1,200	750

Company vans

Cash equivalent of benefit	£500

Mobile telephones

Cash equivalent of benefit	£200

TAX PLANNING

Personal pension contribution limits

Age	Maximum percentage %
Up to 35	17.5
36–45	20
46–50	25
51–55	30
56–60	35
61 or more	40

Corporation tax

Financial year	Full rate %	Small companies rate %	Taper relief fraction	ACT fraction	Upper limit £	Lower limit £
1989	35	25	1/40	25/75	750,000	150,000
1990	34	25	9/400	25/75	1,000,000	200,000
1991	33	25	1/50	25/75	1,250,000	250,000
1992	33	25	1/50	25/75	1,250,000	250,000
1993	33	25	1/50	22.5/77.5	1,250,000	250,000
1994	33	25	1/50	20/80	1,500,000	300,000

Marginal relief

$(M - P) \times I/P \times$ Tapering relief fraction

Inheritance tax

	%
After 10 March 1992	
£0–£150,000	0
Above £150,000	40
After 5 April 1991	
£0–£140,000	0
Above £140,000	40
After 5 April 1990	
£0–£128,000	0
Above £128,000	40

Rates of interest

'Official rate' of interest: 10% (assumed)
Rate of interest on underpaid/overpaid tax: 10% (assumed)

Capital gains tax

Retail price index

	1982	1983	1984	1985	1986	1987	1988	1989	1990	1991	1992	1993	1994	1995
Jan		82.6	86.8	91.2	96.2	100.0	103.3	111.0	119.5	130.2	135.6	137.9	142.0	144.7
Feb		83.0	87.2	91.9	96.6	100.4	103.7	111.8	120.2	130.9	136.3	138.8	142.2	144.9
Mar	79.4	83.1	87.5	92.8	96.7	100.6	104.1	112.3	121.4	131.4	136.7	139.3	142.5	145.0
Apr	81.0	84.3	88.6	94.8	97.7	101.8	105.8	114.3	125.1	133.1	138.8	140.6	142.6	145.2
May	81.6	84.6	89.0	95.2	97.8	101.9	106.2	115.0	126.2	133.5	139.3	141.1	142.9	
Jun	81.9	84.8	89.2	95.4	97.8	101.9	106.6	115.4	126.7	134.1	139.3	141.0	143.0	
Jul	81.8	85.3	89.1	95.2	97.5	101.8	106.7	115.5	126.8	133.8	138.8	140.7	143.3	
Aug	81.9	85.7	89.9	95.5	97.8	102.1	107.9	115.8	128.1	134.1	138.9	141.3	143.7	
Sep	81.9	86.1	90.1	95.4	98.3	102.4	108.4	116.6	129.3	134.6	139.4	141.9	143.8	
Oct	82.3	86.4	90.7	95.6	98.5	102.9	109.5	117.5	130.3	135.1	139.9	141.8	143.9	
Nov	82.7	86.7	91.0	95.9	99.3	103.4	110.0	118.3	130.0	135.6	139.7	141.6	144.2	
Dec	82.5	86.9	90.9	96.0	99.6	103.3	110.3	118.8	129.9	135.7	139.2	141.9	144.4	

Capital Gains Tax

Lease depreciation table

Years	%	Years	%	Years	%
50	100	34	91.156	18	68.697
49	99.657	33	90.280	17	66.470
48	99.289	32	89.354	16	64.116
47	98.902	31	88.371	15	61.617
46	98.490	30	87.330	14	58.971
45	98.059	29	86.226	13	56.167
44	97.595	28	85.053	12	53.191
43	97.107	27	83.816	11	50.038
42	96.593	26	82.496	10	46.695
41	96.041	25	81.100	9	43.154
40	95.457	24	79.622	8	39.399
39	94.842	23	78.055	7	35.414
38	94.189	22	76.399	6	31.195
37	93.497	21	74.635	5	26.722
36	92.761	20	72.770	4	21.983
35	91.981	19	70.791	3	16.959
				2	11.629
				1	5.983

Annual exemption

Individuals £5,800

National Insurance (not contracted out rates)

		Rate	Lower limit £	Upper limit £
Class 1	Employee	10.0%[1]	57 p.w.	430 p.w.
	Employer	10.2%[2]	57 p.w.	–
Class 2		£5.65 per week		
Class 4		7.3%	6,490 p.a.	22,360 p.a.

Notes:

1 Earnings below £57 p.w. are exempt; where earnings exceed this limit the first £57 per week is taxable at a reduced rate of 2%.

2 Reduced rates apply in respect of low earnings, as follows:

Band £ £	%
57–99.99	3.6
100–144.99	5.6
145–199.99	7.6

Industrial Buildings Allowance

Initial allowance	%	**Expenditure incurred**
Industrial buildings and sports pavilion	50	before 11 March 1981
	75	11 March 1981–13 March 1984
	50	14 March 1984–31 March 1985
	25	1 April 1985–31 March 1986
Qualifying hotels	20	11 April 1978–31 March 1986
Qualifying hotels and commercial buildings in enterprise zones	100	after 27 March 1980
Industrial buildings	20	1 November 1992–31 October 1993 (contract) + use by 31 December 1994

Writing down allowance	%	**Expenditure incurred**
Industrial buildings	4	after 5 November 1962
Qualifying hotels	4	after 11 April 1978
Qualifying hotels and commercial buildings in enterprise zones (if initial allowance not fully claimed)	25	after 27 March 1980

Industrial Buildings Allowance (contd)

Plant and Machinery | % | **Expenditure incurred**
Initial allowance | 40 | 1 November 1992 – 31 October 1993
Writing down allowance | 25 |

Agricultural Buildings Allowance | % | **Expenditure incurred**
Initial allowance | 20 | 1 November 1992 – 31 October 1993
Writing down allowance | 4 |

Glossary

Accumulation and maintenance trust
A privileged form of discretionary trust whereby the income is to be accumulated for one or more minors or used for their maintenance at the discretion of the trustees. Property in the trust must vest in the beneficiaries on or before they attain the age of 25.

Annual charges
See *charges on income*.

Associated companies
For tax purposes these are companies which at that time, or within one year previous, are under the control of the same person or persons, or one of which has control of the other.

Basis of assessment
Each of the income tax Schedules and Cases defines both the source of income it charges to tax and, for any fiscal year, which income is deemed to arise in that year (for example, the normal basis of assessment under Schedule D Case III is the income arising in the preceding year and therefore the income chargeable to tax in 1994/95 will be the income arising in 1993/94).

Chargeable transfer of value
A term used in inheritance tax to describe a transfer of value of chargeable property made by a chargeable person which is not an exempt transfer and which has been allowed all available exemptions.

Charges on income
These are not easily defined but are both transfers of income from one taxpayer to another and annually recurring liabilities to pay which tax law permits as a deduction from the payer's total income.

Chattels
Tangible movable property.

Clearance procedures
Procedures whereby a taxpayer who is in doubt whether transactions he or she is about to undertake will fall within specified provisions of the Taxes Acts, may approach the Inland Revenue in advance of undertaking the transactions to establish whether they will be treated as qualifying transactions or not.

Close company
A company under the control of five or fewer participators, or any number of participators who are directors, unless specifically excepted. For tax purposes, a close company is subject to corporation tax in the normal way but there are additional provisions which apply only to close companies. The primary purpose of the close company legislation is anti-avoidance.

Close investment-holding company (CIC)
A category of close company, introduced by the Finance Act 1989, which is not a trading company or a member of a trading group and whose business does not consist mainly of trading.

Company
Any body corporate or unincorporated association.

Consortium company
A UK-resident company of which at least 75% of the ordinary share capital is owned beneficially by other UK-resident companies (each owning at least 5% and not as much as 75% of the ordinary share capital).

Controlled foreign company (CFC)
A company, resident outside the UK, which is controlled by persons resident in the UK and which is subject to a lower level of taxation in

the country in which it is resident than it would be if resident in the UK.

Covenant
A promise to pay, and when it is for £ nil consideration, must be in the form of a deed to be legal. A charitable deed of covenant, to be effective for tax purposes, must be capable of exceeding three years.

Depreciating assets
Assets which are wasting assets or which will become wasting assets within ten years (that is an asset which has a life of 60 years or less).

Discretionary trust
A trust with no interest in possession and which includes accumulation and maintenance trusts and trusts for the disabled.

Dispensation
This may be given to an employer, on application to the Inland Revenue, if his or her system for reimbursing out of pocket expenses of employees is such that only those expenses are reimbursed which, when claimed by the employee, would be an allowable Schedule E deduction. If granted, it means that such expenses need not be shown on form P11D.

Enterprise Investment Scheme (EIS)
Provides income tax relief at 20% on new equity investment up to £100,000 per fiscal year in unquoted trading companies.

Exit charge
This is the corporation tax liability on the chargeable gain which arises on the deemed disposal of all assets as a result of a company becoming non-resident.

Financial year
Runs from 1 April to the following 31 March. The financial year 1994 is the year from 1 April 1994 to 31 March 1995. Corporation tax rates are fixed for a financial year.

Fiscal year
Runs from 6 April to the following 5 April. The fiscal year 1994/95 runs from 6 April 1994 to 5 April 1995. It may also be referred to as the income tax year or the year of assessment. Income tax rates are fixed for a fiscal year and both income tax and capital gains tax are chargeable on a fiscal year basis. Inheritance tax is not chargeable on a fiscal year basis but the annual exemption is given by reference to the fiscal year.

Foreign Income Dividend Scheme (FIDS)
Enables companies to obtain a repayment of surplus ACT when they pay dividends out of foreign source profits.

Franked investment income (FII)
The term used in corporation tax for a dividend or other distribution received from a UK company together with the related tax credit.

Franked payment (FP)
The term applied to the total of the qualifying distribution and the ACT of a UK company.

Free estate
The property that a deceased person actually owned and was free to dispose of at the date of death.

Fungible assets
One asset is identical to another (such as shares of the same class in the same company).

Heritage property
This is property designated as such by the Board of Inland Revenue: it includes items of national, scientific, historic or artistic interest; land of outstanding scenic, historic or scientific interest; buildings to be preserved for their historic or architectural interest together with any associated land for their protection and related objects.

Incentive scheme
A form of employee remuneration which encourages employees to be productive and to identify with the employers' interests. The government has given its backing to a number of such schemes by allowing tax privileges to approved schemes – profit-related pay, profit-sharing schemes, share option schemes.

Income tax year
See *fiscal year*.

International Headquarters Company (IHC)
An IHC is a company with none of

its shareholders owning less than 5% of its share capital, and at least 80% of its shares being held by non-UK residents.

Inter vivos transfers
A capital transfer tax term describing transfers of property made during a person's lifetime.

Investment company
A company whose business consists wholly or mainly of the making of investments and the principal part of whose income is derived therefrom.

Know-how
Any industrial information and techniques likely to assist in the production process. It is not protected under law but is often treated commercially in the same way as patents.

Lease premium
A lump sum paid for the granting of a lease (usually property). It is usually in addition to the rent payable under the lease and in the past (when the premium was treated as a capital receipt) the premium was increased at the expense of the annual rental.

Life tenant
See *trust with interest in possession*.

Link company
A UK-resident company which is both a member of a 75% group and a member of a consortium.

Market maker
A person recognised by the Stock Exchange as being willing to buy and sell securities at a price specified by him or her.

Minor child
An umarried child under the age of 18.

Option
The right to buy from or sell an asset to the grantor of the option within a specified time period at a specified price. An option is usually granted for a consideration and would be treated as a chargeable disposal for capital gains tax purposes (for which there is no allowable deduction). Most options are wasting assets but traded and financial options and futures are specifically excluded from being wasting assets.

Paper for paper takeovers
This occurs where one company takes over another company and a shareholder in the company taken over receives new shares and/or debentures (in the acquiring company) in exchange for his original holding.

Patent
The exclusive right, granted usually by the government of a country, to an inventor or his or her assignee in connection with the exploitation of that invention or technical innovation. The patent normally has a limited life but during that time, it may be retained by the patentee for his or her own use, or it may be sold or transferred, or a licence may be granted in respect of it.

Pay and File
A new system for paying corporation tax and filing corporation tax returns introduced from 1 October 1993 and effective for all accounting periods ending on or after 1 October 1993.

Personal Equity Plan (PEP)
A tax free form of investing in the stockmarket. The plan is managed by a plan manager. There is an upper limit to annual investment.

Permanent establishment
A term used in double tax agreements. It is defined as being: a place of management; a branch; an office; a factory; a workshop; a mine, quarry and similar sites for extraction activities; a long-term construction site. It is therefore a fixed place of business.

Qualifying distribution
This is any payment by a company to its members, other than a repayment of capital. The most common example of a qualifying distribution is the payment of a dividend. Whenever a company makes a qualifying distribution, it must account for ACT.

Remainderman
See *reversionary interest*.

Reversionary interest
The current value of property which will remain, once any existing rights in the property (such as a lease, or life interest) expire. The person entitled to

a reversionary interest in a trust is often referred to as the remainderman.

Statutory total income
An income tax term describing total income less charges on income and certain other specified amounts.

TESSA
This term stands for 'tax exempt special savings account' and was introduced in FA 90. The scheme is limited to one per taxpayer and there is an upper limit on investment.

Transaction at arm's length
A commercial (non-gratuitous) transaction between unconnected persons.

Trust
A trust exists whenever property is transferred in such a way that it is held by a third party (trustee(s)) for the benefit of a succession of person, or for the benefit of any person upon the happening of a specified contingency, or for accumulation and payment (of income or capital) at his or her discretion.

Trust with an interest in possession
A trust where one or more persons are entitled to the income arising from the trust property, generally for life. The person entitled to the income arising for the duration of his life is called the life tenant or is said to have an interest in possession.

Unfranked investment income (UFII)
The term used for the gross amount of income received net of basic rate income tax by a company.

Unfranked payment (UFP)
The term used in corporation tax for the gross amount of any annual charge paid subject to deduction of income tax at source.

Wasting assets
Assets with a predictable life of 50 years or less. Freehold property is never a wasting asset. Plant and machinery is always a wasting asset.

Year of assessment
See *fiscal year*.

Index

accommodation, job-related 39–40, 122–3
accounting periods
  75% groups 462
  ACT 425–6
  corporation tax 394–5
  VAT 352–3
accrued income scheme 75
accumulation and maintenance trusts 221–22, 229
ACT *see* advance corporation tax
additional personal allowance (APA) 12
additional voluntary contributions (AVCs) 77–8
advance corporation tax (ACT) 71, 419, 422–42
  51% groups 452–6, 472
  accounting periods 425–6
  anti-avoidance 434–5
  distributions 422–3
  imputation system 393
  rate changes 426–8, 431–32
  rates 423
  returns 425
  set-off limits 430
  surplus payments 432–5
  trade losses carried back 435
age allowance 13
aggregation relief 309
agricultural buildings
  capital allowances
    corporation tax 400
    Schedule D Case I 280–1
agricultural property, IHT reliefs 170–72
annual percentage rate (APR) 200–202
annuitants, trusts 219
annuities, retirement 78
anti-avoidance legislation 486–8
  ACT 434–5
  artificial price trading 514–15
  corporation tax 409
  non-statutory provisions 486–8
  parental settlements 222
  payment in assets 54
  statutory provisions 488
appeals
  by agreement 375
  by commissioners 375–6
  higher courts 376

postponement of tax 374–5
artificial price trading 514–15
assessments
  corporation tax 397–8, 420–21
  income tax 18–19, 249–55, 374
  partnerships 287–93
  property income 58–9
  self-employment 319–23
assets
  capital gains groups 456–8
  CGT 89–90, 97–100
  chattels 112, 114–24
  costs 99
  IHT 143–6
  market value 96
  negligible value 111
  revaluation 335
  sale after death 176–8
  short life 269–71
  situation of 90, 144
  tangible movable property 325
  trusts 223–5
  valuation at death 172
  wasting 112, 118–20, 325
associated companies, definition 451
associates, close companies 445

bad debt relief, VAT 361
badges of trade 238–9
balancing allowances
  agricultural buildings 280–1
  industrial buildings 277–8
  plant and machinery 267
banks, interest 71, 199
benefits in kind
  accommodation 39–40, 122–3
  cash vouchers 39
  company cars 43–4
  company vans 44–5
  credit cards 39
  directors 41–2
  gifts 41–2
  loans 45–6
  mobile telephones 45
  non-cash vouchers 38
  P9D employees 36–7, 40
  P11D employees 36–7, 41–2
  Schedule E 36–46
blind person's allowance 13
bonds
  accrued income scheme 75
  local authority 70

premium bonds 70, 191
bondwashing 75
bonus issues 131–33
building societies, interest 71, 199
business assets
  CGT, capital allowances interaction 325–6
  depreciating assets 330
  disposals 324–33
  gift relief 331–32
  goodwill 324
  inheritance tax 328, 332
  non trade use 330
  partnership disposals 326–8, 331
  re-basing 103–5, 331
  replacement 328–31
  roll-over relief 328–31, 344
  tangible movable property 325
  trading stock 324
business disposal
  between husband and wife 343
  between partners 334–6
    asset revaluation 335
    inheritance tax 336
    roll-over relief 336
  commercial transaction 337
  gift 343–5
  planning 338–9
  re-investment relief 344–5
  retirement 334–47
  transfer to limited company 313, 337–9
business property, IHT relief 168–70

capital
  expenditure 260–62
  losses 409–10
  movement in European Community 514
  reduction 475–6
capital allowances
  agricultural buildings 280–1
  CGT interaction 325–6
  corporation tax 398–400
  Finance Act 1994 321
  fiscal years 261–62
  industrial buildings 273–80, 399
  know how 282

mineral extraction 283
partnerships 293–5
patents 281–82, 400
planning considerations 272
plant and machinery 263–73, 325, 399
Schedule D Case I 260–85
Schedule E 35
scientific research 282
trading loss 300, 305
unincorporated businesses 260–85
VAT interaction 370
capital gains groups
  definition 456
  depreciatory transactions 458
  intra group transfer of assets 456–8
  roll-over relief 458
capital gains tax 88–114
  administration 373–80
  allowable deductions 98–9, 104
  assessments 91–2
  assets 89–90, 97–100
    depreciating 330
    negligible value 111
    short-life 269–71
    wasting 118–20
  basis of assessment 91–2
  capital allowances interaction 325–6
  capital cost 99
  capital reduction 475–6
  chargeable assets 89–90
  chargeable gains 88
  chargeable persons 90–1
  chattels 112
  collection 95–6
  compensation payments 108–9
  computation 96–100
  connected persons 97
  disposals 89, 96–102, 104–7
  exempt persons 91
  exemptions 112
    assets 90
    chattels 115–17
    disposals 89
    PPR 121–23
  gifts 107–8
    business assets 331–32
  hold-over relief 107–11
  indexation allowance 93, 102–4
  insurance receipts 109–11
  IT interaction 324
  legislation 88
  limited v unincorporated business 484
  loss relief 92–4, 301
  married couples 94
  no gain no loss disposals 106–7
  non-UK residents 505–6

  overseas income 506
  part disposals 100–2, 104
  payment by instalments 95–6
  piecemeal disposals 101–2
  PPR 121–23
  rates 91–2
  re-basing 105–6, 107, 111
  relief
    chattels 116
    EIS 83
  returns 92, 373
  roll-over relief 328–31, 336
  scope 88–91
  shares and securities 96–7
  trusts 223–5
  VAT interaction 370
  capital losses 409–10
joining/leaving a group 474
case law
  Ayshire Pullman Motor Services v CIR (1929) 486
  Ball v Johnson 32
  Ben-Odeco Ltd v Powlson 265
  Brown v Bullock (1961) 34
  Campbell Connelly & Co Ltd v Barnett (1992) 458
  Cape Brandy Syndicate v CIR (1921) 239
  CIR v Duke of Westminster (1935) 486–7
  CIR v Scott Adamson 309
  Cole Brothers v Phillips (1982) 263–4
  Cooke v Beach Station Caravans Ltd (1974) 263
  Cooper v Blakiston 32
  Craven v White (1988) 488
  Dixon v Fitch's Garages Ltd (1975) 263
  Elwood v Utitz 34
  Fall v Hitchen 35
  Floor v Davis 89
  Furniss v Dawson (1984) 486, 487
  Griffiths v Jackson 65
  Hall v Lorimer 35
  Hillyer v Leeke 34
  Hochstrasser v Mayes 32
  Humbles v Brooks (1962) 34
  Jarrold v John Good & Sons Ltd 264
  Law Shipping Co Ltd v CIR 241
  Market Investigations Ltd v Minister of Social Security (1969) 35
  Marsden v CIR (1965) 33
  Munby v Furlong (1977) 263
  Odeon Associated Theatres v Jones 241
  O'Grady v Bullcroft Main Collieries (1932) 242
  Pickford v Quirke (1927) 239
  Pook v Owen 3
  Ramsay v CIR (1981) 486, 487

  Ricketts v Colquhoun (1925) 33
  Roberts v Granada TV Rental Ltd 268
  Rutledge v CIR (1929) 239
  St John's School v Ward 264
  Shilton v Wilmshurst (1991) 47
  Tennant v Smith (1892) 32
  Van Arkadie v Sterling Coated Metals Ltd 265
  Wisdom v Chamberlain (1969) 239
  Yarmouth v France (1887) 263
cash accounting, VAT 364
certificates
  of full disclosure 384
  of tax deposit 379
cessation of business 252–4
  set-off against income 311
  terminal loss relief 311–13, 408–9
CFCs see controlled foreign companies
CGT see capital gains tax
charges on income
  corporation tax 401–403
  IT 7–11
charity donations, relief 10, 402
Chartered Association of Certified Accountants (ACCA) 205–6
chattels 115–19
  CGT 112
Child Support Agency (CSA) 27
children
  APA 12
  employment 28
  IT 27–8
  maintenance 27
  parental disposition 27
  parental settlements 222
CICs *see* close investment-holding companies
close companies 444–9
  annual payments 447
  associates 445
  benefits 446–7
  definition 445–6
  distributions 446–8
  inheritance tax 448
  participators 445
  principal members 446
close investment-holding companies (CICs) 448
clubs and associations 443
commencement of business 250, 254
  aggregation relief 309
  loss relief 309–11
  partnerships 292–3
  start-up relief 309–11
Commissioners, Inland Revenue 375–6

commorientes 185
companies
  capital gains tax 91, 98
  control 511–12
  disincorporation 476–8
  distributions 422–3
  liquidation 476–8
  own share purchase 475–6
  residence implications 511–16
connected persons
  CGT 97–8
  VAT 360
consortia 450–69
  51% groups 451–56
  associated companies 451
  benefits 450
  definition 462–3
  link companies 464
  reliefs 463–4
Consumer Credit Act (CCA) 1974
contract of services 35
contract for services 35
control
  definition 445
  residence 511–12
controlled foreign companies (CFCs) 523–4
corporation tax 393–413
  51% groups 451–56
  75% groups 458–62, 470–72
  accounting periods 394–5
  ACT 71, 393, 419, 422–42, 452–6
  anti-avoidance legislation 409
  assessments 397–8, 420–21
  associated companies 451
  capital allowances 398–400
    agricultural buildings 400
    industrial buildings 399
    patents 400
    plant and machinery 399
  capital gains groups 456–8
  capital losses 409–10
  chargeable gains 401
  charges on income 401–403
  charity donations 10, 402
  close companies 444–9
  computation 396–400, 415–42
  consortia 462–4
  deep-discount securities 402–3
  distributions 422–3
  double tax relief 429
  due dates 420
  examination, format 407–8, 410
  excess trade charges 406–7
  financial years 395–6
  franked investment income 401, 423–6, 427
  group companies 450–69
  interest 421
  investment companies 443–4
  IT comparison 396–7
  legislation 397
  losses 421
  mainstream 419, 429–41
  marginal relief 417–19
  partnership disposals 328
  pay and file 419–22
  penalties 421–22
  planning 410–1, 440
  rates 396, 415–16
    changes 431–32
    small companies (SCR) 416
  relief, 51% groups 452–6
  residence rules 394
  returns (CT200) 420–22
  Schedule A losses 410
  Schedule D Case I trading profits 397–400
  Schedule D Case III interest 400
  Schedule D Case V trade loss outside UK 410
  Schedule D Case VI transaction loss 410
  scope and principles 394–7
  shares 401
  taper relief 417–19
  terminal loss relief 408–9
  trading losses 403–9
  unfranked investment income 400–1
credit cards, benefits in kind 39
CSA see Child Support Agency
Customs and Excise
  organisation and powers 386–7
  VAT 348–71

death
  CGT 94
  estate at 151–52, 172–8, 428, 436
deeds of covenant 8
deeds of family arrangement 186
deminimus rule, VAT 365–6
Department of Social Security, pensions contributions 79
discretionary trusts 221–22
  exit charge 228
  inheritance tax 227–9
  principal charge 227–8
disposals see assets; capital gains tax; chattels
dividends
  income tax 14–15
  limited/unlimited comparison 481
domicile, definition 500
double tax relief (DTR)
  corporation tax, set off 429
  IHT 506–7
  overseas investments 518–22
double tax treaties 518
due dates
  corporation tax 420
  IHT 188, 385–6
  income tax 19, 376–7
  limited/unlimited comparison 483
  Schedule A 60
  Schedule D, Case I/II 254–5

EC (EEC) see European Community
EIS, 201; Enterprise Investment Scheme
employee share ownership plans (ESOPS) 53
employees
  incentive schemes 48–53
  NIC 54–5
  P9D 36–7, 40
  P11D 36–7, 41–2
  pensions 79
employment
  scope of Schedule E 32–58
  self-employment comparison 35
  United Kingdom 32–58
Enterprise Allowance Scheme 203
Enterprise Investment Scheme (EIS) 82–4, 198
ESOPs see employee share ownership plans
estate duty see inheritance tax
European Community (EC) 515
  single market 363–4
  VAT 348, 352, 363–4
examination format
  corporation tax 407–8, 410, 436–7
  tax planning 534–54
expenses
  deductable 33–4
  foreign income relief 521–22
  Schedule D Case I/II 241–43
  travel 33–4
exports, VAT 362

farming, averaging 255–6
FIDS see Foreign Income Dividend Scheme
FII see franked investment income
FIMBRA see Financial Intermediaries Managers and Brokers Association
finance
  APR 200–202
  business 202–3
  personal 205–10
    planning 232–7
    types of loan 201–202
Finance Act 1982, own share purchase 475
Finance Act 1984, share option schemes 52–3
Finance Act 1986, IHT 141
Finance Act 1988
  independant taxation 23
  maintenance payments 27

re-basing 105–6, 107, 111, 331
residence 394
Finance Act 1990, roll-over relief 458
Finance Act 1994
    capital allowances 321
    current year basis 319–23
    losses 321–22
    mortgage interest 8
    partnerships 322
    payment in assets 54
    Schedule D Case I 319–23
    tax-payer companies 473
Financial Intermediaries Managers and Brokers Association (FIMBRA) 205–6
Financial Services Act 1986 205–7, 211
financial years 395–6
fiscal year
    definition 2
    IT 261–62
fixed profit car scheme (FPCS) 33–4
foreign income *see* overseas income
Foreign Income Dividend Scheme (FIDS) 15, 432
foreign investments, in UK 527–30
FP *see* franked payments
FPCS *see* fixed profit car scheme
franked investment income (FII) 401, 423–6, 427
    set-off 437–40
franked payments (FP) 423, 425–6, 427
fraud, income tax 380
free standing additional voluntary contribution scheme (FSAVC) 77
FSA see Financial Services Act
FSAVC see free standing additional voluntary contribution scheme

gambling
    investment 191
    profit 240
gift relief, retirement relief interaction 343–4
gifts
    associatied operations, IHT 183
    benefits in kind 41–2
    business assets, relief 331–32
    businesses 343–5
    in consideration of marriage, IHT 157
    hold-over relief 106–8
    IHT, planning 186–7
    married couples 24
    with reservation, IHT 181–83
    small, IHT 157

goodwill 324
government securities 70
group companies
    51% groups
        ACT 451–56, 472
        definition 447
        group income election 452–4
        pay and file 455–6
        relief 452–6
        surrendered ACT 454–6
    75% groups
        corresponding accounting periods 462
        definition 458–9
        group relief 460–62
        no gain-no loss transfers 472–3
        trade losses 460–1
    associated companies 451
    capital gains groups 456–8
    capital reduction 475–6
    consortia 462–9
    corporation tax 450–69
    own share purchase 475–6
    reorganisations 470–78
    VAT 465–6
group relief
    75% groups 460–62
    joining/leaving a group 471–74
    liquidation 477
    s402 448 460–62

heritage property, IHT 184
hold-over relief
    CGT 107–11
    compensation 108–9
    insurance receipts 108–9
    part consideration 108–9
holiday lettings 67–8

ICTA see Income and Corporation Taxes Act (1988)
IHC see international headquarters company
IHT see inheritance tax
imports, VAT 362
IMRO see Investment Managers Regulatory Organisation
incentive schemes
    profit-related pay 48–9
    profit-sharing schemes 49–51
    share option schemes 51–3
income
    charges on 7–11
    definition 2–5
    earned 4
    investments 4, 69–71
    planning 232–7
    property 59–68
        assessable income 59
        deductions 60–1
        loss relief 61–3

void periods 61
Schedule E 32–3
trading 238–59
Income and Corporation Taxes Act (ICTA) (1988)
    s18(3) profits 238
    s62 taxpayers option 251–52, 289, 309, 311
    s63 Inland Revenue option 253, 289
    s113(2) partnerships continuation election 290–95
    s148 termination of employment 46
    s188 termination of employment 46
    s198 travelling expenses 33
    s242 set-off 437–40
    s350 charges 10–11, 308
    s356 mortgage interest 9
    s380
        closing years 311
        current year basis 321–22
        loss relief 299–300, 301–307, 309–11
        partnership losses 314–17
    s381 start-up relief 309–11
    s385 loss relief 299–300, 304, 308, 309–11, 315–17
    s386 transfer to limited company 313
    s388 terminal loss relief 311–13
    s391A(1)(b) loss relief 437
    s393(1) trading losses carried forward 403, 409
    s393A(1)(a) set offs 404, 406
    s393A(1)(b) excess trade charges 406–7
    s393A(7) terminal loss relief 408
    s393A 421
    s402 group relief 450, 460–62
    s765-766 anti-avoidance 514
    s768 anti-avoidance 409
income tax
    see also Schedules
    actual due date (ADD) 376–7
    administration 372–80
    appeals 374–6
    assessments 18–19, 249–55, 374
    certificates of tax deposit 379
    CGT interaction 324
    charges on income 7–11
    children 27–8
    collection 18–19
    computation 5–19
    corporation tax comparison 396–7
    CT61Z form 428, 436
    deeds of covenant 8
    dividends 14–5
    due dates 19, 376–7

earned income 4
examination by Inland
 Revenue 249
exempt income 4–5
exempt persons 2
farmers special relief,
 averaging 255–6
fiscal year 2, 261–62
fraud 380
incentive schemes 48–53
income, definition 2–5
investment income 4
liability 1–22
loans 9–10
loss relief 301
married couples 23–7
mistakes 376
mortgage interest relief 8–9
negligence 380
normal due date (NDD) 376–7
overdue tax 377–8
penalties 380, 384
personal allowances 11–14
reckonable date 377–8
relief
 EIS 82–4
 pensions 77
 PEPs 81–2
repayment supplements 379
returns 373, 428, 436
schedules 2–3
self-assessment 249
statutory total income 7–10
taxable persons 2
taxation at source 3–4
total income calculation 6–7
trusts 219–22
UFII 428–9, 435–6, 443–4
indexation allowance
 CGT 102–4
 losses 93
industrial buildings 273–80
 balancing allowances 277–8
 corporation tax 400
 definition 273–4
 initial allowances 275
 non-industrial use 278–9
 writing down allowances
  first user 275–7
  second and subsequent
   user 279–80
inheritance tax 140–63
 administration 384–6
 agricultural property, reliefs
  170–72
 appeals 385
 assets 143–6
  sale after death 176–8
  valuation at death 172
 basis 146–8
 business assets 328, 332
 business medium comparison
  484
 business property, reliefs
  168–70

capital transfer tax (1975-
 1986) 140–1
chargeable lifetime transfers
 148–50
chargeable persons 144–6
 trusts 145–6
commorientes 185
companies 145
computation 151–61
discretionary trusts 227–9
 exit charge 228
 principal charge 227–8
disposition, definition 143
due dates 188, 385–6
duty to report 384–5
estate at death
 computation 173–4
 definition 151–52
 valuation 172–8
estate duty 140
exemptions 156–9
 conditional 184–5
Finance Act 1986 141
gifts
 associated operations 183
 in consideration of
  marriage 157
 with reservation 181–83
grossing up 148
heritage property 184
instalment option 385–6
interest 386
land, sale after death 176–7
land and buildings, valuation
 165
liabilities at death, valuation
 172–3
life assurance policies,
 valuation 165–6
loss of value relief 175
overseas property 166, 506–7
partnerships 144, 328, 336
penalties 386
pension rights, valuation 166
planning 186–7
potentially exempt transfers
 146
property 143–4
quick succession relief 155
quoted investments, sale after
 death 176
rates 148
related property
 sale after death 177–8
 valuation 166–7
returns 187
scope 141–46
shares and securities,
 valuation 165
taper relief 152–5
tranferor, to pay 149–50
transfer of value 141–42
transferee, to pay 149
transferees, exemptions 156
transferors, exemptions 157–8

trusts 225–9
unit trusts, valuation 165
valuation principles 164–80
valuation reliefs 156, 168–72
wills, variations 185–6
woodland relief 185
Inland Revenue
 appeals 374–6
 capital statements 382
 certificates of disclosure 384
 Commissioners 375–6
 confidentiality of information
  354
 examination of accounts
  381–82
 foreign tax authorities 384
 IHT 157–8
 income tax
  assessments 18–19
  computation method
   15–18
 investigations 381–84
 organisation 372–3
 powers 382–4
 production of documents 383
 reorganisations, clearance 474,
  476
 search and seizure 383–4
 tax districts 373
interest see also mortgage
 interest
interest
 acquisition of new source
  72–3
 APR 200–202
 banks and building societies
  71, 199
 disposal of source 73
 loans relief 9–10
 overdue tax 377–8, 386, 421
international headquarters
 companies (IHC) 432
investment business 205–13
 regulation 205–7
investment companies 443–4
Investment Managers Regulatory
 Organisation (IMRO) 205–6
investments 190–204
 bank and building societies 71
 cash 198–200
 collectibles 200
 definition 190
 direct 193, 528
 diversification 193
 dividends 71
 EIS 198
 equities 194
 fixed income 192
 flexibility 215–18
 foreign, in UK 528–9
 gambling 191
 government securities 70
 growth 215–18
 income 4, 69–84
 indirect 193

investor identification 211–13
land and property 198
life annuity 71
life assurance 196–7
liquidity 214–18
local authority bonds 70
National Saving Bank 69
National Savings Certificates 69
nil income 193
not taxed at source 72
overseas 517–30
pensions 197
PEPs 194
planning 232–7
premium bonds 70
risk factors 213–14
Save As You Earn 69–70
savings 190
shares 191
speculation 191
tax free 69–71
taxation at source 70–2
TESSAs 70, 200
trusts 71–2, 194–5
types 191–94
unit trusts 195
variable income 192

know-how, capital allowances 282

land
  CGT, part disposals 99
  leases 112
  short leases 118–20
land and buildings
  business rates 60–1
  council tax 61
  IHT 143–6, 165
  income 59–68
  inheritance tax 164–80
  investments 198
landlord repairing lease 61
LAUTRO see Life Assurance and Unit Trust Regulatory Organisation
leases
  CGT 112
  full rent 61–3
  land 118–21
  landlord repairing 61
  nominal rent 62
  premiums 63–5
  tenant repairing 61
lettings
  furnished 65–8
    holiday lettings 67–8
    rent a room income 67
  loss relief 61–3
  owner-occupation 66
  unfurnished 58–65
  void periods 61
life annuity 71
life assurance

IHT 165–6
relief 80–1
types 196–7
Life Assurance and Unit Trust Regulatory Organisation (LAUTRO) 205–6
life tenants, trusts 219
limited companies, VAT 369
limited/unlimited comparison
  chargeable gains 484
  inheritance tax 484
  loans 484
  source of finance 484–5
link companies, groups and consortia 464
loans see also mortgage interest
loans
  benefits in kind 45–6
  close companies 447
  relief 9–10
  types 201–202
local authority bonds 70
loss relief 299–317
  75% groups 460–71
  aggregation relief 309
  capital allowances 300, 305
  CGT 92–4, 301–3
  closing years 311–13
  commencement of business 309–11
  concessionary basis 301–303
  corporation tax 403–9
  limited/unlimited comparison 483
  losses carried forward 299–301
  partnerships 314–16
    division of loss 314
    limited liability partners 316
  pre-trading expenditure 313
  s380 299–307, 309–11
  s385 299–300, 304, 308–11, 315–17
  s391(1)(b) 437
  s393(1) 403, 409
  s393A7 408
  statutory basis 303–4
  trade charges 308
  transfer to limited company 313
  unquoted companies 313–14
loss of value relief, IHT 175
losses
see also trading losses
  CGT 92–4
  Finance Act (1994) 321–22
LRL see Landlord repairing Lease

mainstream corporation tax (MCT) 419, 429–41
see also corporation tax
pay and file, due dates 420
maintenance payments, relief 10, 27
management expenses, investment companies 443–4
marginal relief, corporation tax 417–19
market value 96
married couples
  CGT 95
  gifts 24
  independant taxation 23–6
  investments 211–12
  joint property 23–4
  maintenance payments 27
  mortgage relief 24
  planning 187
  transfer of allowances 24–5
  transfer of business 343
  year of marriage 26
  year of separation 26–7
married couple's allowance 11–12
MCT see mainstream corporation tax
medical insurance, relief 10
mineral extraction, capital allowances 283
MIRAS see mortgage interest relief at source
mobile telephones 45
mortgage interest relief at source (MIRAS) 8–9
  interest on other loans 9–10
mortgage relief 8–9
  married couples 24
motor vehicles
  capital allowances 267–9
  cheap car pool (FA80) 267
  company cars 43–4
  company vans 44–5
  definition 268
  FPCS 33–4
  fuel 44
  pooled cars 43
  VAT 360, 362

National Insurance Contributions
  Class 2 256–7
  Class 4 10, 256–7, 295
  employees 54–5
  employers 55
  limited/unlimited comparison 480–1
  rates 54
National Savings
  Bank 69, 199
  Certificates 69
  Pensioner's Guaranteed Income Bonds 70
  products 199
negligence, income tax 380
NIC see National Insurance Contributions
non-UK residents

CGT 505–6
employment 507–8
income 507–8
personal allowances 508
trade 507–8

overseas income
  CGT 506
  double tax relief 504–6, 518–22
  employment 500–1
    travelling expenses 503
  expense relief 521–22
  remittance basis 503
  residence 497–500
  trade 531–33
  UK residents 500–1
    365-day rule 501
  unilateral relief 505
  withholding tax 519–20
overseas property, IHT 166, 506–7

participators, close companies 446
partnerships 286–98
  asessments 287–93
  assets
    disposals 326–8, 331
    individual 293–4
    partnership 293
    revaluation 335
  business disposal 334–6
  capital allowances 293–5
  CGT 91, 98
  charges 295
  commencement rules 292–3
  companies 296
  continuation election 290–93, 294–5
  Finance Act 1994
  IHT 144, 328, 336
  losses 287–9, 314–16
    claim for relief 314–16
    division of loss 314
    limited liability 316
    notional 288–9
  members change 92–3, 289–93
  NIC Class 4 295
  non trading income 296
  profit-sharing arrangements 287–8
  roll-over relief 331, 336
  s385 loss relief 315–17
  tax planning 295–6
  tax status 286
  valued added tax 368
  WDA 295
patents
  capital allowances 281–82
  corporation tax 400
pay and file system 419–22
  51% groups 455–6
penalties
  corporation tax 421–22

IHT 386
IT 380, 384
VAT 367–8
pensions 76–80
  AVCs 77–8
  contributions 77–9
  employees 79
  FSAVC 77
  IHT 166
  investments 197
  limited/unlimited comparison 482
  occupational pension schemes 76–8
  personal pension schemes 78
  retirement annuity policies 78
  self-employment 79–80
  unused relief 80
PEPs see personal equity plans
personal allowances
  IT 11–14
  married couples 23–7
personal equity plans (PEPS)
  definition 81–2
  investment 194
  relief 81–2
PETs see potentially exempt transfers
plant and machinery 263–73
  allowable losses 325
  ancillary expenditure 265–6
  balancing allowances 267
  corporation tax 399
  definition 263–5
  disposal value 266–7
  hire purchase/leasing 271
  motor vehicles 267–9
  planning 272
  short life assets 269–71
  successions to trade 272
  WDA 265–6
potentially exempt transfers (PETS) 146, 186–7
PPR see principal private residence
pre-trading expenditure 313
premium bonds 70, 191
principal members, close companies 446
principal private residence (PPR)
  CGT 112, 121–23
  deemed occupation 121–22
  dependant relatives 123
  multi residence 123
  residential let 123
profit-related pay 48–9
profit-sharing schemes 49–51
profits
  gambling 240
  trade 238–59
profits from trade/professions and vocations 238–59
PRP see profit-related pay

quick succession relief, IHT 155

re-basing 105–6, 107, 331
re-investment relief 344–5
reckonable dates 377–8
remittance basis, overseas income 503
remuneration, limited/unlimited comparison 480
rent-a-room scheme 67
reorganisations
  bonus issues 131–33
  capital distributions 134–5
  disincorporation 476–8
  group companies 470–78
  joining/leaving a group 471–74
  liquidation 476–8
  no gain no loss transfers 472–3
  rights issues 133–4
  share-for-share amalgamations 474–5
residence
  CGT 394
  companies 511–16
  definition 497–500
  extra-statutory concession 498
  leaving UK 499–500
  trusts 222, 225
  visiting UK 498–9
  visits in exceptional cicumstances 498
residents, non-UK 507–9
retailers, VAT 352, 365
retirement, business disposal 334–47
retirement relief 339–43
  gains qualification 340
  gift relief interaction 343–4
  qualifying period 340
  re-investment relief interaction 344–5
  share and securities 341–42
  succesive disposals 342–3
rights issues 133–4
roll-over relief 328–31, 344
  capital gains groups 458
  CGT 328–31, 336
  partnerships 336

save as you earn scheme (SAYE) 51–2, 69–70
SAYE see save as you earn
Schedule A
  corporation tax losses 410
  deductions 60–1
  due dates 60
  income from property 59–65
  loss relief 61–3
Schedule D
  Case I
    adjusted losses 299
    capital allowances 260–85
    current year basis 319–23
    furnished letting income 65

partnerships 287–93
trading profits 397–400
Case I/II 239
   adjusted profits 246–8
   allowable deductions 241, 244–6
   due dates 254–5
   short lease premiums 65
   VAT interaction 369–70
Case III
   corporation tax, interest 400
   investment companies 443
   investment income 69, 72–3
Case IV, foreign security income 503
Case V
   foreign possessions income 503
      foreign pension 504
      overseas trade 504
   losses 410
Case VI 239
   assessable income 74–5
   furnished letting income 65–8
   losses 410
Schedule E
   benefits in kind 36–46
   capital allowances 35
   chargeable income 32–3
   deductible expenses 33–4
   employer returns 37–8
   fees, bonuses and commissions 36
   incentive schemes 48–54
   overseas employment income 500–1
   payments on termination of office 46–7
   VAT interaction 370
schedules, income tax 2–3
scientific research, capital allowances 282
SCR see small company rate
securities
   see also shares
   CGT 96–7, 112
   coupon stripping 74
   deep discount 73–4, 402–3
   definition 75
   quoted, IHT 164–5
Securities and Futures Authority (SFA) 205–6
self-employment
   current year basis 319–23
   employment comparison 35
   NIC 10, 256
   pensions 79–80
   Schedule D 35
SERPS see State Earnings Related Pension Scheme
settlors 219
SFA see Securities and Futures Authority
share option schemes 51–3
share-for-share amalgamations 474–5
shares
   bonus issues 131–33
   capital distribution 134–5
   CGT 96–7, 112
   companies, own share purchase 475–6
   ESOPS 53
   fractions sale of 134
   gilt edged 136
   IHT 164–5
   investment 191
   matching rules 125–7
   nine day rule 127
   paper for paper 135–6
   Pool A rule 127–9
   Pool B rule 129–31
   profit-sharing schemes 49–51
   qualifying corporate bonds 136
   reorganisations 131–36
   retirement relief 341–42
   rights issues 133–4
   same day rule 127
small company rate (SCR), corporation tax 416
social security benefits, IT 4–5
start-up relief 309–11
State Earnings Related Pension Scheme (SERPS) 76
STI see statutory total income under income tax
superannuation funds 76–8

taper relief
   corporation tax 417–19
   IHT 152–5
tax evasion 380–84
   VAT 367
Tax Exempt Special Savings Accounts (TESSAs) 70, 200
tax management 372–88
tax planning 479–89
   anti-avoidance legislation 486–8
   business disposal 338–9
   capital allowances 272
   choice of business medium 479–85
   corporation tax 410–1, 440
   examination format 534–54
   executive reward 55–6
   finance 232–7
   gifts 186–7
   income 232–7
   investments 232–7
   partnerships 295–6
   trading losses 308
tax point, VAT 352
tax rates
   ACT 423, 426–8, 431–32
   CGT 91–2
   trusts 224
   corporation tax 396, 415–16, 431–32
   IHT 148
   limited/unlimited comparison 483
   SCR 416
   VAT 354–9
tax returns
   ACT 425
   CGT 92
   corporation tax 420–22
   IT 373
   mistake claims 376
   VAT 352–3
tenant repairing leases 61
terminal loss relief 311–13, 408–9
TESSA see Tax Exempt Special Savings Account
trade
   badges of 238–9
   definition 238–40
   profits 238–59
trading income 238–59
   annual trade profits/gains 240–1
   basis of assessment 249–55
   cessation of business 252–4
   commencement of business 250
   commencement/cessation interaction 254
   expenses 241–43
   gambling 240
   grants 241
   non schedule D income 248
   non-recurrent receipts 240
   stock, own use 241
trading losses
   75% groups 460–71
   ACT 435
   capital allowances 300–305
   closing years 311–13
   commencent of business 309–11
   corporation tax 403–9, 421
   planning 308
   s393(1) 403, 409
trading stock 324
travel expenses 33–4
   overseas employment 503
TRL see Tenant Repairing Lease
trusts
   accumulation and maintenance 221–22, 229
   assets 223–5
   CGT 91, 98, 223–5
   discretionary 221–22, 227–9
   income tax 219–22
   inheritance tax 225–9
   interest in possession 219–21, 225–7
   investments 71–2, 194–5
   residence 222, 225

settlors 219
tax planning 230

UFII *see* unfranked investment income
UFP *see* unfranked payments
underlying taxes 517–18
unfranked investment income (UFII) 400–1, 428–9, 436, 443–4
unfranked payments (UFP) 428–9, 436
unilateral relief 505, 518–19
unincorporated bodies 260–85, 443
unit trusts 71–2, 165, 195
United Kingdom
  leaving, tax status 499–500
  non-residents
    applications 512–13
    UK income 507–8
  overseas investment 517–30
  residents
    365-day rule 501
    double taxation relief 504–6
    foreign pension 504
    unilateral relief 505
  visiting, tax status 498–9

value added tax 348–71
  accounting periods 352–3
  administration 351–54
  appeals 366
  bad debt relief 361
  business definition 349
  capital allowances interaction 370
  cars
    business use 360, 362
    private use 360, 362
  cash accounting 364
  CGT interaction 370
  computer records 354
  connected persons 360
  deminimus rule 365–6
  destination system, EC 363
  enforcement 366–8
  European Community 363–4
  exports 362
  fraction 359
  group companies 465–6
  imports 362
  information confidentiality 354
  input tax, special circumstances 362–3
  interest payable 368
  invoices 351–52
  limited companies 369
  origin system, EC 363
  partial exemption 365–6
  partnerships 368
  penalties 367–8
  rates 354–9
  records 352–4
  registration
    compulsory 349–50
    divisional 369
    planning considerations 351
    voluntary 350–1
  reorganisations, group companies 466
  repayment supplement 368
  retailers 352, 365
  returns 352–3, 366
  Schedule D, Case I/II interaction 369–70
  Schedule E interaction 370
  scope 348–51
  second hand schemes 364–5
  self assessment 387
  self billing 352
  self supply 361
  supply
    definition 348–9
    EC to UK 363–4
    taxable 348–9
    types 357
    UK to EC 363
    valuation 359–61
  tax points 352
  taxable person 349
  zero rated supplies 357
value shifting 89

wasting assets 118–20, 325
WDA *see* writing down allowance
widow's bereavement allowance (WBA) 12
wills 185–7
withholding tax 519–20
woodland relief 185
writing down allowance (WDA) 399–400
  agricultural buildings 280
  industrial buildings 275–7, 279–80
  mineral extraction 283
  partnerships 295
  patents 281
  plant and machinery 265–6

Evaluation form – Textbooks 1995 edition

We are interested in knowing what you think of our products and would appreciate it if you could spend a few minutes completing the following questionnaire.

Please tick the appropriate box where necessary

Paper No. _____   **Paper title** _____

Are you a
Student ☐   **Lecturer** ☐

Have you purchased other CAEP products
Textbooks ☐   **Revision Texts** ☐   **Open Learning Packages** ☐

What do you think are the best features of this textbook?

_____
_____
_____
_____

What improvements need to be made?

_____
_____
_____
_____

How does the textbook compare with other textbooks or manuals you have used on your course?

_____
_____
_____

Did you find any errors? If so, we apologise and would greatly appreciate it if you could list them below with the relevant page number or attach a photocopy.

_____
_____
_____

If you would like to receive more information on CAEP's products please supply your name and address.

_____
_____
_____

Please return your completed questionnaire to the address overleaf.

Thank you for your help